The Nl

The NFL in the 1970s

*Pro Football's Most
Important Decade*

Joe Zagorski

Foreword by Rocky Bleier

McFarland & Company, Inc., Publishers
Jefferson, North Carolina

3064514684466

LIBRARY OF CONGRESS CATALOGUING-IN-PUBLICATION DATA

Names: Zagorski, Joe, author.
Title: The NFL in the 1970s : pro football's most important decade /
Joe Zagorski ; foreword by Rocky Bleier.
Description: Jefferson, North Carolina : McFarland & Company, Inc.,
Publishers, 2016. | Includes bibliographical references and index.
Identifiers: LCCN 2016021558 | ISBN 9780786497904
(softcover : acid free paper) ∞
Subjects: LCSH: National Football League—History. |
Football—United States—History.
Classification: LCC GV955.5.N35 Z34 2016 | DDC 796.332/6409047—dc23
LC record available at https://lccn.loc.gov/2016021558

BRITISH LIBRARY CATALOGUING DATA ARE AVAILABLE

ISBN (print) 978-0-7864-9790-4
ISBN (ebook) 978-1-4766-2534-8

Front cover: Pittsburgh Steelers running back Rocky Bleier
carries the ball against the Dallas Cowboys in Super Bowl X
at the Miami Orange Bowl on January 18, 1976
(Associated Press/Vernon Biever)

Printed in the United States of America

McFarland & Company, Inc., Publishers
Box 611, Jefferson, North Carolina 28640
www.mcfarlandpub.com

For my parents and for Frankie,
who were with me through it all

Table of Contents

Acknowledgments

Many people have helped me with this book project, and I will undoubtedly leave some out in these acknowledgments; any oversights are unintentional. All of the following in one way or another were important to the completion of *The NFL in the 1970s*.

There are several people at NFL Films, both past and present, who must be recognized, starting with the late Ed Sabol. He founded NFL Films right around the time I was born, and with his son, the late Steve Sabol, gave me one of my earliest reasons for falling in love with pro football. Decades later, I still thank these two men who made my autumn Sundays so much fun and still do through their company. NFL Films historian Chris Willis was always willing to provide me with the information I needed to make it easier to get the key details this book required. He also gave me advice on publications, as he himself has written a few books on various people and teams in pro football history. Todd Schmidt, like the rest of the NFL Films family, carries the torch in the finest of traditions established by the Sabols.

The Pro Football Hall of Fame in Canton, Ohio, is much more than just a museum. It houses a spectacular research library, and the folks there are very accommodating. Research historian Jon Kendle helped me during my many visits to look up obscure newspaper files, gamebook files, and a plethora of play-by-play documents. This book would never have been written without him. When I began conducting research at the Hall of Fame in the mid–1980s, I got a chance to meet and work with Beau Riffenburgh, who at the time worked for NFL Properties in both their Los Angeles and New York City offices. Beau treated me as one of his equals in pro football research (which I most certainly was not). A big thank you to Beau for all of his help and advice. The Hall of Fame's vice president of media relations, Joe Horrigan, was also supportive. His first advice to me way back in the 1980s is still the best I ever received in the field of pro football research and writing: "Carve your own niche." It is just as important to me today as it was then. People like Jon, Beau and Joe have been very inspirational, and I treasure their assistance and friendship.

I learned a lot about sportswriting at the *Coatesville Daily Record* and the *Evening Phoenix* newspapers. Fellow sportswriters and editors Tom DiCamillo, Ara Grigorian, Jim Knaub, Bob Orr, Barry Sankey, Randy Shantz and Todd Sherman are just some of the people who helped my writing efforts when I was younger. Thanks to some of the greatest pro football writers over the past half century and to some of the best public relations people in the NFL, including Kerry Byrne, Ray Didinger, Michael MacCambridge, Bob Swick, Cliff Christl of the Green Bay Packers, Rich Dalrymple of the Dallas Cowboys, and Bob Markowitz of the Cleveland Browns. Thanks to Vito Stellino of the *Pittsburgh Post-Gazette*, whose memorable stories and pro football knowledge are a large part of Pennsylvania sports history. Thanks to my professors at Kutztown University of Pennsylvania: Dr. John Delaney, Dr. Patricia Derr, Dr. Michael Gabriel, Dr. Gordon Goldberg, the late Dr. Al Leonzi and Dr. John McAndrew, each of whom not only taught me a lot about history and education but also a lot about writing. Dr. Gabriel also helped to proofread this book, for which I am very thankful.

I would be remiss if I did not recognize the former pro football players, coaches, and team owners who gave me their time and answered my questions. I am very fortunate to have met and conversed with many of these men, including Herb Adderley, Rocky Bleier, John Bunting, Jim Carter, Ben Davidson, Joe DeLamielleure, Herman Edwards, Weeb Ewbank, Sid Gillman, Donnie Green, Jim Houston, Lamar Hunt, Bruce Jarvis, Ron Jaworski, Rich Kotite, Earl Morrall, Tom Nowatzke, Vince Papale, Dave Robinson, Johnny Robinson, Dick Schafrath, Bart Starr, and Dan Sullivan, among others. I hope I've done them all justice.

I joined the Pro Football Researchers Association (PFRA) in the mid–1980s, and it has grown tremendously over the years. The patriarch of the PFRA, the late Bob Carroll of western Pennsylvania, gave me a lot of advice and published my earliest articles. Thanks also to other PFRA members, board members, and officeholders, including George Bozeka, Denis M. Crawford, Ken Crippen, Lee Elder, Mark L. Ford, Bob Gill, John Grasso, John Hogrogian, Todd Maher, John Maxymuk, Rupert Patrick, Andy Piascik, Ivan Urena, and Chris Willis, among many others. Some have written outstanding books and articles, while others have contributed stellar research. I've benefitted from their expert knowledge and advice, and I am very grateful for their friendship.

Last but certainly not least I would like to thank my late parents, Stephen and Natalie Zagorski, for the love and inspiration they gave me to follow my dreams all my life. I love and miss them both very much. Also gone but not forgotten is my childhood buddy Frank Sassaman, who loved football as much as I did, and who experienced the wonderful decade of the 1970s with me. Special thanks to him and to all fans of pro football in the 1970s.

Foreword by Rocky Bleier

Who knew the impact the 1970s would have in the evolution of the National Football League? Certainly not the players. We were just kids trying to fulfill a dream of playing professional football and getting a decent paycheck, along with bragging rights back home. In hindsight it was a decade of change, innovation and sometimes desperation, but it was also a decade of opportunities, miracles, and creating lifetime memories.

The Pittsburgh Steelers gave an undersized, banged-up Vietnam veteran an opportunity, and I am living proof miracles can happen. You make the most of it, and ultimately I became a member of four Super Bowl championship teams, in one of the greatest decades in NFL history.

Joe Zagorski's book on the 1970s in the NFL captures the memories that made the decade special, not just for me, but for millions of pro football fans across America. His book describes each year with sharp details, vivid descriptions of crucial plays, and fun personal anecdotes which make the book enjoyable to read.

The 1970s changed the NFL in many different ways. There were two player strikes. "No freedom, no football," was the chant, and the decade was also the beginning of free agency. Competition from the World Football League only furthered the continuity of the brand in the NFL. *Monday Night Football* became the league's center stage. What once was a regional showcase now was becoming a national pastime, and the networks became the league's financial partners. Eventually pro football needed to be more exciting, so the league altered the rules to help the offenses score more points—a direct result of the defensive dominance in the NFL. We like to think the Steelers played a big part in those changes.

Other changes involved strategy, like the use of the Shotgun offense, or desperation, like the 3–4 defense or the 53 Defense in Miami. This all had a direct result on the pressure to win, forcing many coaches to spend countless hours watching game film, searching for one or two critical plays to gain an advantage over their upcoming opponent.

Naturally, my fondest memories about the decade involve the relationships I made over the years with teammates and opponents alike. Guys like Terry Bradshaw, Franco Harris, Joe Greene, and so many others who are all featured in this book. And what about those special plays are memorable too? Plays like Franco Harris' "Immaculate Reception," Oakland's "Sea of Hands" game, and the "Hail Mary Pass."

How do I know all of this? Because I was there, I lived through those times, and now so can you! If you love pro football and NFL history, then this book needs to be in your collection. I hope you enjoy reliving the NFL in the 1970s.

Rocky Bleier was a Pittsburgh Steelers halfback in 1968 and 1971–1980. He played in the first four Steelers Super Bowl victories and caught the touchdown pass from Terry Bradshaw that gave Pittsburgh a lead it never relinquished in Super Bowl XIII. Bleier retired after the 1980 season with 3,865 rushing yards, 136 receptions for 1,294 yards, and 25 touchdowns. At the time of his retirement, he was the Steelers' fourth all-time leading rusher.

Preface

The decade known by many pro football historians and fans as the "Super Seventies" truly lived up to its name. The game experienced tremendous growth during those ten years. A merger in 1970 between the American Football League and the National Football League brought the ten AFL teams into a combined NFL. Franchise expansion also occurred in 1976, when two new cities (Tampa Bay and Seattle) joined the league. Major television contracts were signed with the three national networks (ABC, CBS, and NBC), and *Monday Night Football* became a viewing staple. Overall attendance at regular season and postseason games increased in many of the league's cities each year, and the Super Bowl became an undeclared national holiday. The 1970s thus added annual building blocks of excitement and dramatic history to the game. The spectacle the NFL became during the following decades had one of its biggest growth spurts as a result of events that occurred in that ten-year span.

The NFL took some major formative, innovative, and appealing new steps in the 1970s. I tried to include as many of these as possible in each chapter, with the hope that fans would observe the growth of the sport annually from 1970 to 1979. There were many different aspects of the pro game that made this decade special, from the teams' colorful uniforms, to the new stadiums opening seemingly every year, to the growing and competitive action every Sunday afternoon and Monday night. After all my research, however, I was still left with one major question: Can anyone—including me—undeniably claim that the 1970s was greater than all other decades in pro football history? The debate is sure to come up. This book is my attempt to provide evidence to support my belief that the 1970s should be regarded as pro football's greatest decade. At least some answers to prove my point are in the following. Trying to determine and gauge the criteria to answer the greatest decade question turned out to be a mix of objective and subjective factors.

All I had to go on were my memories, game film, newspaper and magazine articles, and anecdotes from the players and coaches themselves. I compiled them and came up with an underlying belief: the 1970s saw so many special events and firsts in league history, so many superstar players (who are still regarded by many fans as household names), and so many other noteworthy occurrences that changed the game, that all other decades simply pale in comparison. All these combined to ignite the public's interest in the NFL like never before. I felt I needed write a chronological, week-by-week account (for the most part) of the games and the divisional races. I wanted to make this book a way to re-live the decade, and it appeared based on my research that taking the reader from the start of each year to the end of each year, and devoting one chapter to each, was the best and most natural way to do it. Every year in the decade saw several important events and examples which added to pro football's greatness. I tried my best to mention and examine as many as possible, where the growth of football's excitement and popularity can be traced. This book may not persuade disbelievers to admit this is the most exciting of decades, but I hope it does. Baseball had always been known as the "national pastime." During the 1970s, pro football's popularity definitely closed the gap on baseball's lead. Former Oakland Raiders and Pro Football Hall of Fame defensive lineman Howie Long stated in his Hall of Fame induction speech in 2000 that pro football's nickname was fast becoming the "national passion." It could be successfully argued that such a passion for the game for both the players and the fans alike began in the 1970s.

The decade ushered in new heroes and new personalities. With the growth of the league's popularity in both the print media and on television, players such as O.J. Simpson, Roger Staubach, Fran Tarkenton, Joe Namath, and Terry Bradshaw became famous, and were regarded by thousands of fans as larger than life. The suit-and-tie wizards on Madison Avenue wisely selected pro football players to endorse a wide variety of products, and the commercials that were produced during the 1970s are still highly regarded by advertising executives as some of the most creative and memorable of all time. Be it Buffalo Bills running back O.J. Simpson sprinting through airports promoting the Hertz Rent-A-Car company, or New York Jets quarterback Joe Namath eating popcorn from his Hamilton Beach popcorn popper, or Pittsburgh Steelers defensive tackle Joe Greene showing his not-so-mean side by trading his jersey to a young fan for a Coca-Cola, NFL players were more than willing to promote the benefits to consumers of buying all kinds of merchandise. In so doing, they added to their fame on the football field, became highly popular pitchmen through the many new avenues of endorsement advertising, and sometimes earned cameo roles in television shows and movies. Many advertisers were more than happy to pay top dollar to promote their products during Sunday afternoons and Monday nights, knowing full well most of the nation was watching the games and would be tempted to buy what they were selling. The millions of dollars the league made thanks to the television contracts also turned on a financial spigot, and money for the owners started pouring in. Player salaries in contrast increased slowly over the course of the 1970s, but they did increase.

Also responsible for the NFL's notoriety during the 1970s was the growth of a company called NFL Films. Led by founder Ed Sabol and his son Steve, NFL Films documented each game with 16mm highlights, stirring music, and even more stirring narration from baritone John Facenda, a famous Philadelphia television news anchor from the 1960s and 1970s. Kids who grew up in the 1970s (I was one of them) readily recall staying up late on school nights to watch *This Week in Pro Football* or *NFL Game of the Week*, the backbone of NFL Films' television schedule. Today, NFL Films is the main vehicle by which the game has become as popular as it is.

New and increasingly modern stadiums also dotted the NFL landscape. The multi-purpose stadium serviced both football and baseball teams in 17 cities. Many people derided those shared stadiums as all too common, with no outstanding features. But despite their detractors, these new stadiums mirrored the growth of the pro game. All were large, some cavernous. Most had escalators and luxury boxes, which were virtually unheard of in most stadiums of the 1950s and 1960s. Domed stadiums were also growing in number. There were fans even then who absolutely despised dome stadiums, but I felt it was good for a few teams to have them, if for no other reason than to provide a sense of contrast in locations and settings. For fans of the 1970s, the sight of the Houston Oilers playing their home games in any stadium other than the Astrodome would be ridiculous.

As you read this book, you will notice a multitude of very exciting and memorable games (in both the regular season and the postseason) in NFL history were played each year during the 1970s. Competition was key, as underdog and unexpected teams fought hard to win, with thrilling moments the common result. From 1970 to 1979, there was at least one major upset in the NFL playoffs each year. Playoff money may have been the cause for the harder hits that were delivered more frequently in the postseason than in the regular season. The vast majority of the players from the 1970s naturally did not make the kind of money pro football players make today. For each player whose team made it to the playoffs, a boost in his salary was the welcome upshot, and worth giving that extra effort in postseason games. Today's playoff money is far greater than most average player salaries were then. The roster sizes were also smaller than now, meaning that a player would undoubtedly see more overall game action and be expected to play with injuries more often than today's players in their era of specialization.

Pro football's growth also ran parallel to what was happening in American society. The 1970s became known as the "me" decade. The turbulent 1960s—with all of its war, assassinations, anger and protests—were over. Dawning was a new decade with its own identity. Many of the young people labeled "hippies" in the 1960s cut their hair and donned business and leisure suits in the 1970s, and went to work in the corporate world. Recreational activities also underwent a transformation. While family picnics and drive-in movies were still in vogue, newer pleasures were competing for the free time of many citizens. The extravagant nightclub Studio 54 opened in New York City in 1977, as the rich and famous ushered in the disco era. With more nightclubs opening came greater use of illegal drugs, a problem which has increased over the last half century. Drugs over time made their way into the NFL. To be sure, the desire to experiment with drugs pervaded American society and professional sports. The NFL is replete with the names of fallen stars who have succumbed to the lure of illegal drugs.

On a happier note, new gadgets were also on the market and usually affordable. Citizens Band radios were installed in many vehicles, giving motorists a new distraction while driving their cars and trucks. More women entered the workforce for the first time in their lives, and more women also began watching pro football. And even kids were catching football fever, as the Tudor and Mattel toy companies, among others, produced electric football games and football strategy board games. A noticeable decrease in the amount of free time people as a whole had to spend on recreational activities continued. The competition for available time away from work to some degree defined the hobbies and pleasures of many citizens, and it still does. The NFL leadership knew this, and they did their utmost to make pro football as marketable and consumer-friendly as possible. The 1970s was undeniably the first decade to receive this sort of league-wide financial and planning attention, coming from each team and from NFL headquarters in New York City.

All Americans wanted to achieve success, both personally and professionally, and it was necessary for members of the younger generation to develop their own personalities. NFL players were no different. Cincinnati Bengals All-Pro defensive tackle Mike Reid was a concert pianist when he wasn't sacking quarterbacks. Minnesota Vikings defensive end Jim Marshall experimented with sled dog racing and skydiving in the off-season. The long list of pro players in the 1970s who had roles in feature movies included Joe Kapp, Alex Karras, Ray Nitschke, Carl Eller, Joe Namath, O.J. Simpson, and Mike Lucci, among many others. The players were indeed becoming more worldly.

The decade experienced its share of national events, which in reality made what was happening in the NFL look small in comparison. The Vietnam War ended for American soldiers and sailors in 1973. That traumatic conflict had taken its toll with thousands of lives lost, and millions of people across the nation were eager to turn a new page and look to the future. But more problems were on the horizon. An oil crisis in 1973 and an energy crisis in 1979 both resulted in high gasoline prices and rationing. Long lines of impatient and upset motorists at gas pumps, honking their horns, waiting for hours to refill their automobiles, wondering what they did to deserve this, was a familiar scene. Also in 1979, a near disaster at the Three Mile Island nuclear plant in south-central Pennsylvania frightened the populace and led to the end of nuclear plant construction in the U.S. for several decades. President Gerald Ford dodged two assassination attempts in 1975, and cult leader Jim Jones somehow convinced hundreds of people in 1978 to commit suicide in the South American country of Guyana by drinking Kool-Aid tainted with cyanide. In 1979, a total of 52 Americans were taken hostage in Iran, preceding decades of strife with that nation. Pro football became a brief but welcome respite from the bad news the U.S. endured in the 1970s.

Mirrors to the decade and its people could be seen on television, where new half-hour sitcoms like *All in the Family*, *The Jeffersons*, *M*A*S*H*, *Happy Days*, and others were required weekly viewing. Americans watched television more than ever before, and discussing those popular shows was a common activity during a break from work each day. Televisions themselves improved greatly, as brand names like Panasonic, Sony, RCA and Sylvania each came out with newer and improved screens and remote controls. Similarly, more and more Americans nestled into their living rooms on Sunday afternoons and Monday evenings during the autumns and winters to follow their favorite football teams, and the happenings in the NFL. Pro football by 1979 had grown into a significant diversion for the masses, an action-packed aid to help Americans take a break from their working lives. Pro football was an invitation for the public to experience the highs and lows of an exciting and growing sport. The NFL showcased plenty of action, hard hits, touchdown passes, exhilarating victories, and crushing defeats. The game was never dull, at least to most fans, and the league's competition committee made annual changes to the rules to keep the game from ever showing any visible signs of dullness. More and more rabid aficionados each succeeding season figuratively lived and died with the fortunes of their favorite teams. Pro football was quickly growing in popularity, and it was changing and growing every year.

NFL players took note of the changes, and they themselves changed too. Individualism flourished in society and in a game that was only winnable through teamwork. Most of the players were more than happy to be quoted by reporters. They sought out television cameras on the sidelines during games to say "Hi" to their moms. Television and NFL Films cameras appeared along the sidelines, in bench areas, and in locker rooms in greater numbers, attempting to instigate and capture the individual expressions of the players. Plenty of those athletes were willing to say anything to the national audiences when the cameras went live. Many younger players also came up with end zone dances to put an exclamation point on their touchdowns. This would seem to produce only jealousy or discord among the older players, but for many teams, that was not the case. Pro football, at its core, is a game of an emotional connection between the men on a team, and their desire to succeed. That will never change, and it was obvious and exciting for all to see.

Take, for example, the 1977 Dallas Cowboys. They had a rookie Heisman Trophy–winning tailback in Tony Dorsett, who easily became a darling of the press. Out-doing Dorsett on the Cowboys was outside linebacker Thomas "Hollywood" Henderson, who went out of his way to say outlandish things. Both men—in his own way—offered a challenge to the rigid discipline of head coach Tom Landry, who was thought of by most observers as one of the greatest coaches in league history. No coach had a more strategic background than Landry, and few coaches shunned the rah-rah emotional pep talks more than Landry. But the 1977 Cowboys flourished in moments of emotion, leadership, ability, and athleticism. They melded their dissimilar personalities and finished the year successfully as Super Bowl XII champions. Perhaps former Oakland Raiders head coach John Madden said it best when he regarded his players as "artists," and refused to deprive them of their moments of individual expression, as evidenced by their unique hair styles, their unusual pregame rituals, and even their words to the press. Madden fastened only a few rules to his players, because he wanted their artistry to shine on the football field, and so it did. "With the Raiders we don't have to put up with any Mickey Mouse stuff," said Oakland All-Pro tight end Dave Casper. "We don't have rules about keeping our chinstraps buckled on the sidelines. We don't have coaches encouraging a lot of false chatter on the practice field. The phony stuff is for losers. We're treated like intelligent human beings. We don't live by a lot of degrading rules.

Our coaches don't harass us because they know we're winners." The Raiders compiled one of the best winning percentages.

Coaches like Landry and Madden were scrutinized like never before, but so were all coaches. The influence and success of immortal Green Bay Packers head coach Vince Lombardi during the 1960s caused many coaches to imitate his caustic, tough, and demanding style. Conflicting and confronting this was the player of the 1970s, the player who craved attention and who yearned for the chance to become famous by making a game-winning play. The friction between this new style of player and the old style of coach was still apparent, but it was on the slow decline. It would require a lot of give and take between the coaches and the players to soothe and overcome this conflict and to develop winning teams. As always, winning resolved many problems. The term "player's coach" came about as an alternative to the abrupt nature of tough coaches in Lombardi's image. Coaches like Denver's John Ralston, Houston's O.A. "Bum" Phillips, or Cleveland's Sam Rutigliano were labeled as "player coaches" for their easygoing, relaxed, and motivational natures. None of these men ever won a Super Bowl, but their players remained intensely loyal to them, and were more than willing to play while injured as a viable trade-off to secure success for their coach. Baltimore Colts defensive end Bubba Smith once claimed rookie head coach John McCafferty "was such a nice guy, that you didn't want to play bad and disappoint him, to a point where he could possibly lose his job." McCafferty and his 1970 Colts ended that memorable year with a world championship. It is, however, important to note the Packers of the 1960s were also more than happy to play hard and play with numerous injuries for head coach Vince Lombardi. There has to be an exception to every rule, and there were plenty of exceptions floating around.

The 1970s was also a decade of revelry. The American Bicentennial celebration was held throughout 1976, and the NFL added to the excitement. Commissioner Pete Rozelle, himself directly responsible for much of the success of the league in the 1970s, took steps to make the product of pro football one of the most popular in American entertainment. Halftime performances were sponsored by each team for each game, as marching bands from local high schools and colleges performed on playing fields each weekend. Many pro teams also had their own cheerleader squads, some of which grew by leaps and bounds in popularity. Rozelle promoted a variety of forms of celebration, with the game always remaining the central focus. Pre- and post-game Super Bowl parties were given his blessing, as was fan tailgating at stadiums. The sport was actively growing. Rozelle knew it, supported it, and did whatever he could to elevate the game in tasteful measures. He was aware football could one day become over-saturated and possibly too big, and, in some way, he was at least partly responsible for that fate. But thanks to his efforts, pro football managed to surpass baseball as the most watched sport in the country, both live in stadiums and on television.

The 1970s was also a decade of innovation. In music, more unique genres were heard than ever before. Disco and punk rock were the offspring of rock and roll. In the NFL, the revival of an innovation of strategy made the mid- to late 1970s special. The "shotgun" offense was revived by Dallas head coach Tom Landry in 1975 (he called it the "spread formation"), and it helped to open up the passing game by positioning the quarterback several yards behind his center. Once he caught the snap from center, the quarterback would have more time to read the opposing defenses and more time to throw the ball. Landry realized the pro game by the end of the decade was leaning more to a wide-open style of play, where throwing the ball was becoming increasingly prevalent. Most teams today employ some version or another of the shotgun, a testament to Landry's vision. The NFL Rules Committee also grew. It consisted of several coaches, referees, and front office people who raised concerns, promoted ideas, and changed the rules of the game on an annual basis to make play better and more competitive. The status quo was for the stagnant. The NFL was geared to move forward, and to embrace the future.

All in all, there was a sense of curiosity as the new decade dawned. How would the AFL-NFL merger affect pro football? How would player free agency affect the game? Would a new dynasty or two surface, or would teams have trouble staying on top? Would a potential new league a few years in the future damage the NFL? Would the former AFL players excel when playing against the original NFL teams? Would higher player salaries hurt the financial dynamics of the game? Would rule changes affect the game for the better, or for the worse? All of these questions were on the minds of players, coaches, and fans alike as 26 teams lined up to kick off the 1970 season … and a brand new decade.

1970

A New Birth of Competition

An overcast and blustery sky hovered over venerable Tulane Stadium in New Orleans on January 11, 1970. A drizzling rain early in the morning ended prior to the pregame festivities of a world championship professional football game. The field had been resplendently painted in team colors in the end zones, and team helmets facing a painting of the championship trophy at midfield. By day's end, however, the playing surface would be trudged upon by the players' gouging cleats, by marching bands, and by a halftime re-enactment of the Battle of New Orleans, complete with horses and cannons. The result was a wet and muddy field that resembled a cow pasture by the final gun. Clumps of turf were strewn all over the place. Field crew members spread straw along the sidelines and bench areas in a feeble attempt to dry up the mud. Purists in decades since would agree that this scene was truly emblematic of the identity of pro football's past, where grass and mud and bad weather were the common elements of all late season games prior to dome stadiums and artificial turf fields. Traditionalists felt that this was how the game should be displayed and remembered, in legend and for all times. Two teams in physical and strategical combat on a soggy field, with a world title at stake. The 81,562 people who ventured into the old Sugar Bowl stadium to view the spectacle on this day would not just see colorful pageantry and gladiators on the gridiron, however. They would also see a glimpse of pro football's future. Super Bowl IV heralded the beginning of the greatest decade in the history of the sport.

The Kansas City Chiefs of the fledgling American Football League were set to meet the Minnesota Vikings of the historic National Football League in what was the final title game before the merger between the two leagues. Talk of a merger actually began several years prior to 1970, and it was the natural result of skyrocketing salaries in the owners' battle to sign the best players coming out of college. The discussions regarding the merger were both pro and con, but the majority of players in both leagues approved of it. St. Louis Cardinals linebacker Larry Stallings felt that "the club owners were going to kill themselves if they kept paying out money." Jack Kemp of the Buffalo Bills felt that the merger "will stop some of the ridiculous bonuses and no-cut contracts that were being handed out. Merged together, the one league and the sport will grow, and become more solvent."

Kemp was correct in his beliefs. The merger helped everyone in a variety of ways. A common draft was instituted, and this stifled the rampant collegiate player raiding that had occurred throughout the 1960s between teams of both leagues. Compromise formed the core of the merger, and in a short amount of time, the rift between the AFL and NFL began to disappear.

"I think that the merger was good for the game," said Kansas City safety Johnny Robinson in a 2012 interview. "By the time we drafted cornerback Jim Marsalis in 1969, the conflict between the two leagues was over. New guys like Marsalis didn't know anything about the conflict."

Agreements between the team owners resulted in overall pro football prosperity. Television networks split their coverages of the regular season and postseason games between the two new conferences, and an annual trade-off was instituted to televise the Super Bowl game. The new NFL would comprise a collection of the best players in the game. According to Kansas City quarterback Len Dawson, "this [the merger] is the best thing that could happen. Now we can return to the purpose of pro football—to entertain and, at the same time, prove who really plays it best."

While the Chiefs were going through their pregame warm-ups prior to kicking off Super Bowl IV, it was a bittersweet moment for the loyal followers of the AFL. Memories of ten years of being regarded as minor leaguers and perennial underdogs by the stubborn supporters, players, and team owners of the established NFL, were only hours away from changing forever. It was not just an appropriate moment to reminisce about the unique past of the AFL, however. It was also a time and an opportunity to view the promise of the future. Chiefs head coach Hank Stram called his offense "the Offense of the Seventies." Stram was a strategist of the highest caliber, forever frustrating opposing defensive coaches with new formations and designs. His multiple shifting movements on offense caused much confusion and indecision to his AFL foes throughout the 1960s. Under Stram's tutelage, the Chiefs displayed moving pass pockets, backs and receivers in motion several times prior to the snap of the ball, and situational substitutions on every down. Such strategies would be imitated by many teams in pro football throughout the 1970s.

"We feel that if we can complicate the recognition responsibility for the other team," Stram said, "then we have created an area of doubt and indecision and as a result they are more apt to make mistakes."

The Vikings were the ones forcing their opponents into mistakes for the better part of the 1969 season. Minnesota's defense was one of the best units in the history of the game, permitting only 133 points in the regular season (a pro record at that time for a 14-game season). Defensive ends Carl Eller and Jim Marshall teamed up with defensive tackles Gary Larsen and Alan Page to form the foundation of the "Purple People Eaters" (one of several team monikers). Three of the four—Eller, Marshall and Page—were named to the All-Pro team. The defense intercepted 30 passes in 1969, and had limited the powerful Cleveland Browns to one meager touchdown in the fourth quarter of the NFL championship game, which the Vikings won easily the week prior to Super Bowl IV, 27–7.

Fiery quarterback Joe Kapp led the Minnesota offense in 1969, and under his leadership, the team compiled an impressive 12–2 regular season record. Their basic nuts and bolts, ball control attack was bolstered by power runners like Dave Osborn, Oscar Reed and Bill Brown. Receivers such as Gene Washington and John Henderson were both explosive and reliable, and added a quality aerial mix to the Vikings offense. On paper, Minnesota had too much power and looked like a team that was destined to claim the world championship. The Chiefs were tabbed as 13-point underdogs by the oddsmakers going into Super Bowl IV. Most sportswriters across the nation agreed with those oddsmakers and felt that the Vikings would easily reclaim the dignity that the NFL had lost in the previous year, when Joe Namath's Jets shocked the heavily-favored Baltimore Colts in Super Bowl III.

Such was not the case, however. Stram's offense befuddled the Vikings' vaunted defense on the muddy field to claim a 23–7 victory. The Chiefs dominated the first half and executed some big plays throughout the game, including a 46-yard catch and run in the third quarter by wide receiver Otis Taylor for the contest's decisive touchdown. Several reverses to speedy flanker Frank Pitts combined with timely draw and trap runs by Mike Garrett, Robert Holmes, Warren McVea and Wendell Hayes to keep the Purple Gang off balance for most of the afternoon. Chiefs quarterback Len Dawson, later named the game's Most Valuable Player, directed the offense with quick hitch throws to his outside flankers and receivers, and finished the afternoon completing 12 of 17 passes. Kansas City's special teams also contributed three field goals by Jan Stenerud and a timely fumble recovery on a kickoff, which led to a second quarter touchdown by Garrett. Although Stram's offense grabbed most of the headlines, his defense also earned a tip of the hat for the way they bottled up the Vikings offense.

The Chiefs' defensive line, known by many as "the Redwood Forest," dominated Minnesota's offensive line throughout the game. Comprising the Kansas City line was Buck Buchanan, a 6'7" man-mountain in the trenches; Curley Culp, an immovable 265-pound defensive tackle; Jerry Mays, one of the most versatile and solid linemen in the game; and Aaron Brown, a huge, aggressive, and lightning-quick pass rusher. These men controlled the line of scrimmage, limiting the Vikings to a paltry 67 yards rushing. The Vikings were unaccustomed to throwing the ball from desperation in the second half, and were forced to play from behind throughout the game. Helping to stifle the Minnesota offense was a strategy that Stram employed with his linebackers. Known as a "stack," the Chiefs' linebackers would often lineup directly behind a defensive lineman, almost daring the opposition to run into a visible hole in the line. The stacked linebackers at the snap of the ball would then quickly fill into whichever hole they were needed, and the huge Kansas City linemen in turn would keep any potential blockers away from the linebackers. The strategy worked to perfection, shutting down the Minnesota runners and producing three interceptions in the fourth quarter, which denied the Norsemen any chance at victory. Minnesota's Kapp later remarked to a bunch of reporters in the cramped postgame locker room, "Those guys [the Chiefs

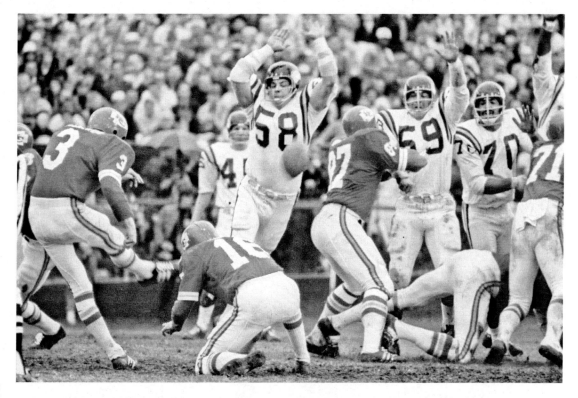

Kansas City Chiefs placekicker Jan Stenerud kicks one of his three field goals in Super Bowl IV, January 11, 1970, at Tulane Stadium in New Orleans, Louisiana. The Chiefs upset the heavily-favored Minnesota Vikings, 23–7 (AP Photo/NFL Photos).

defense] were all very active. They took the running game away from us. We went into the game wanting to run the ball, and they were able to take it all away with great defensive play." The Chiefs were stunning victors as the Louisiana sky darkened over the lights of Tulane Stadium, and a new era in pro football had begun.

The journey through pro football in the 1970s received a green flag with Super Bowl IV. Upsets like that one would not be uncommon during the decade, and the already established NFL with its increased number of teams would steadily see gains in popularity and excitement. The merger gave the sport a whole new look. Two new conferences, the American Football Conference (AFC) and the National Football Conference (NFC), comprised the new NFL. Innovations such as the players' names being displayed on the back of their jerseys (a staple in the old AFL) were now required for all teams. The same ball, manufactured by the Wilson Sporting Goods Company, would be used in all games. Prior to the merger, the AFL used a leaner ball from the Spalding Sporting Goods Company. The scoreboard clock would record the official time in each game, which took unnecessary pressure off of the game officials. A four-year settlement between the league and the players union regarding revenues and profits was reached prior to the start of the 1970 season. Finally, NFL Commissioner Pete Rozelle presided over the merger and named Lamar Hunt, the primary founder of the old AFL and the owner of the Chiefs, to be president of the new AFC. George Halas, the founder of the Chicago Bears and a pioneer of the early pro game, would serve as the president of the new NFC.

Curiosity was the common feeling among fans to the new NFL. How would the former AFL teams fare against the old guard of the NFL? The results of the previous two Super Bowls did much to dispel the myth that the old AFL teams were inferior. Would the new playoff format add to the excitement of the game? It certainly did. Beginning in 1970, the top team in each of the three divisions in both conferences would make the playoffs. The team with the best remaining record in each conference, known as the wild card team, would also make the playoffs, allowing for a total of eight teams to reach the postseason. This gave the playoffs a more solid structure, and it sparked increased interest in the journey to the Super Bowl. How would teams adapt to a new regular season scheduling format? Home and away contests for teams were now instituted for divisional games; three or five games were slated for teams in their own conference; and three or four interconference games were also scheduled, depending upon which division a particular team was situated. The scheduling formula—for the most part—worked quite well.

What fans observed in 1970 was easily the most competitive season that pro football had seen up to that point. The division champion in five of the six divisions was not settled until the final week of the regular season. New rivalries sprouted up throughout the league, some of the regional or cross-state variety (i.e., Cleveland versus Cincinnati, St. Louis versus Kansas City, and San Diego versus Los Angeles, among others), and others based on divisional foes fighting for a playoff spot (i.e., Baltimore versus Miami, Minnesota versus Detroit, and Dallas versus the New York Giants). Nineteen seventy was a breakthrough year for many strong rivalries in the NFL to flourish.

The new season would receive an unexpected roadblock just as summer training camps opened, however. A players strike was issued over disagreements with the team owners. The players wanted a better pension plan in the neighborhood of $26 million distributed to veterans who played for at least four years. The owners did not want to venture into that neighborhood, however, preferring instead to offer only $18 million to those same veterans. The strike would fortunately last only five days, as cooler heads prevailed. A compromise on pension plans, disability payments, widows benefits, and dental benefits was reached. Cost of living and per diem increases were also obtained by the players. The team owners as a final concession agreed to a $12.1 million pension increase over four years. It was a relief that no preseason games were cancelled. At that time, each team played at least six preseason games each year.

"If we lost the exhibition game[s]," said New York Giants President Wellington Mara, "we would have lost $1 million [per game]."

The 1970 season finally began in earnest, with a chance for redemption for the Minnesota Vikings. The schedule makers saw the value of revenge games to the viewing public when they sent the defending world champion Kansas City club to visit the Vikings on opening day. Unlike their performance in the previous Super Bowl, however, the Purple Gang performed admirably in the rematch, limiting the Chiefs to just one touchdown in a 27–10 win. A major contribution to the Minnesota victory was a spectacular 38-yard fumble recovery for a touchdown. On that play, Vikings defensive end Jim Marshall scooped up a Mike Garrett fumble after Garrett lost his grasp of the pigskin when he stumbled into his planned hole in the line. Chiefs quarterback Len Dawson quickly latched onto Marshall's jersey, but Marshall spun around and lateraled the ball back to trailing outside linebacker Roy Winston, who completed the play in the end zone. Minnesota's victory sent a message that they had strong hopes of returning to the Super Bowl. Suddenly, some of the coaches who planned on imitating Hank Stram's "Offense of the Seventies" were now doubting their decisions. Kansas City's loss in the season opener offered its first example that 1970 would be a tough year for supposedly dominant teams to stay on top.

Providing ample evidence of Minnesota's desire for revenge was their offensive line. Head coach Bud Grant instructed his linemen to fire out with straight man-on-man blocking against the Chiefs' stacked defense. The stacked defense once again made it more difficult to block linebackers on running plays. The Vikings, however, were able to control the ball long enough to gain 17 first downs and keep Kansas City's offense on the bench for much of the game. Such power running by Dave Osborn and Clint Jones would set a trend that produced 12 victories f or the Vikings in 1970. Detroit Lions linebacker Wayne Walker later attested to the strength of Minnesota's offensive line when he stated, "Those guys come and ram their heads right into you."

Vikings head coach Bud Grant reasoned further when he stated, "We don't have the people who can do things on the outside. What we have are strong straight ahead runners, athletes who can block as well as run. Right now, the quickest way to get up field is straight ahead. Get in there fast with power."

Minnesota's most powerful win was a 54–13 pasting of the eventual NFC champion Dallas Cowboys in the fifth week of the season. The Vikings dominated on both sides of the line of scrimmage, forcing Dallas into numerous errors. Minnesota cornerback Ed Sharockman intercepted two passes, returning one for a touchdown. Sharockman also returned a blocked punt for a touchdown against the Cowboys. As 1970 wore on, the Minnesota defense was regarded by most experts as the best in the game. They permitted a league-low 143 points (including two shutouts), and produced a league-leading 28 interceptions. Sturdy linebackers such as Roy Winston, Wally Hilgenberg, and Lonnie Warwick teamed up with an opportunistic secondary and their ever-intimidating front four to become the most feared defense in the NFL. By the final gun of their opening game triumph over Kansas City, any belief that Minnesota's defense would not be as tough as the previous season proved to be erroneous. It was the Minnesota offense, however, which displayed several vulnerabilities. Quarterback Joe Kapp had been traded to the Boston Patriots prior to opening day due to a contract dispute. Gary Cuozzo was his replacement, but his performance did not equal Kapp's from the previous season. Cuozzo's completion percentage in 1970 was only 49.8 percent, and he could muster only seven touchdown passes against 10 interceptions. No quarterback of any other playoff team in 1970 had worse statistics. The Vikings would thus have to deal with excellence on one side of the ball (defense), and futility on the other (offense) from opening day to their last play of the 1970 season.

Many other key contests which gave fans an idea as to how this season might go occurred on opening day as well. The Baltimore Colts outlasted the San Diego Chargers with a last-second field goal by rookie placekicker Jim O'Brien, 16–14. The fashion in which the Colts won this game would be repeated at the end of the year in a most dramatic style. The Cincinnati Bengals upended the formidable Oakland Raiders, 31–21, and the Detroit Lions trounced the Green Bay Packers, 40–0, in two more important opening games.

The Colts were led by their legendary quarterback, Johnny Unitas, and were infused by two explosive young receivers, Eddie Hinton and Roy Jefferson. Optimism was not at a high level for the Colts, however, as starting halfback Tom Matte sustained a season-ending knee injury early in the third quarter at San Diego. Baltimore was forced to rely on rookie runner Norm Bulaich, who at times resembled a steam locomotive rumbling down a hill, and at other times a darting gazelle with ample speed in the open field.

"Bulaich was a conditional type of runner," remembered veteran Colts offensive lineman Dan Sullivan. "He had a natural flow when he ran. He got his timing down pretty good in training camp. One thing that made him special was that he was a very accommodating guy. He always had great communication and talked all the time with our line. He was always asking us if he needed to adjust anything in order to make us more successful."

Bulaich would serve as a primary key for the Colts throughout 1970. Baltimore won six games by a touchdown or less during the regular season, and their running game, featuring Bulaich, Jerry Hill, and Tom Nowatzke, kept opposing defenses from devoting full pressure on Unitas. The Colts put together two strong winning streaks and recorded an 11–2–1 record, good enough to capture the American Football Conference's Eastern Division title.

The Bengals christened brand new Riverfront Stadium in grand fashion with their victory over the Raiders on opening day. Cincinnati's new stadium was typical of the "cookie cutter" stadiums that seemed to be sprouting up all across the league during the early part of the decade. The venue was termed a "multi-sports facility," meaning that both the Bengals and the city's baseball team (the Reds) were the stadium's occupants. Lower level seats could be transported on a set of large metal rollers to suit both sports. The stadium had a circular shape with several tiers of seats, a large scoreboard, updated press box facilities, improved and enlarged team locker rooms, and the most recent trend in the NFL … artificial turf. By opening day in 1970, no less than eight teams would have an artificial turf field. That number would increase to 14 by the end of the decade.

The bright green synthetic grass might have been considered by some conspiracy theorists as a possible reason why Cincinnati defeated the Raiders. Oakland's Alameda County Coliseum sported real grass, and teams that played their home games on real grass sometimes had difficulty in the early years of the decade adjusting to artificial surfaces. But a better reason for Cincinnati's victory might have been due to their young and aggressive defense, which limited Oakland's running game to a paltry 48 yards on 22 carries. Bengals running back Jess Phillips also turned in a strong outing, gaining 130 yards on 15 carries. This was only the beginning for the Bengals, one of the youngest teams in the league. Cincinnati would end up surprising the rest of the NFL by claiming a division title in 1970. "I didn't know we could do this well," said legendary head coach and team president Paul Brown at the end of the regular season.

Detroit's romp over Green Bay served as a statement game for the Lions. Detroit controlled the contest with a strong and consistent running attack. Mel Farr ran for two scores, and the Lions as a team accumulated a whopping 266 rushing yards. The Detroit defense also showed no mercy to the Packers. Green Bay could muster only 114 total yards and five first downs, the first of which did not come until midway through the third quarter. The Packers still had quite a few players on their roster who were members of their 1967 world championship team, but even those players were showing their age in this embarrassing defeat. The great swagger and confidence under former head coach Vince Lombardi was gone, and a changing of the guard was taking place. Teams like the Lions, the San Francisco 49ers, and the Miami Dolphins were representative of the up and coming teams who would revive their hopes to earn winning records in 1970.

Undoubtedly the most unique game of the initial week of the 1970 season was played under the lights at Cleveland's Municipal Stadium. The New York Jets faced the Cleveland Browns in the first weekly televised *Monday Night Football* game in NFL history. This "novelty" of a prime-time game on a week night was popular right from the start. Promoted and produced by Roone Arledge of the American Broadcasting Company, it would soon become a staple of television viewing by masses of national audiences for many decades to follow. Part of the lure of *Monday Night Football* was a three-man broadcasting team in the booth that quickly became the most entertaining and controversial of any broadcasting lineup, before or since. Keith Jackson was the play-by-play announcer during the Monday night games in 1970, but he was replaced the following year by former New York Giant great Frank Gifford. Another former athlete, Don Meredith (who had just retired from the Dallas Cowboys), served as the folksy color analyst and amateur country and western crooner. But undoubtedly the most notorious member of the threesome was noted New York City reporter Howard Cosell, who deftly utilized his Ivy League vocabulary and his dramatic voice and diction to "enhance" the game. Cosell was never afraid to criticize the players,

A new television phenomenon known as *Monday Night Football* debuted on ABC stations across the country in 1970. Since then, the spectacle of *Monday Night Football* has become the most anticipated three hours of television viewing each week in the fall. Pictured (from left to right) are the three most popular broadcasters in *Monday Night Football* history: "Dandy" Don Meredith, Howard Cosell, and Frank Gifford (Bettmann/Corbis/AP Images).

coaches, or even his co-workers in the booth. It all made for highly entertaining television, and it popularized the league like nothing else before.

"To Middle America, Howard was a representative of the East, liberalism, New York, and all they thought those things stood for," said Arledge in an interview with Larry Felser of the *Buffalo Evening News*. "Meredith became a favorite of those people because he played off Howard. His needling delighted the audience, particularly that part of it that reacted negatively to Cosell. We wanted [the play by play man] to be a glorified public address announcer. We wanted him to set the scene, tell where the ball was, the down, all the other pertinent information. The comment was to be left to Cosell and Meredith."

The first Monday night game featured two good teams, a marquee quarterback in Joe Namath, and a mixture of exciting plays, including a 94-yard kickoff return by Cleveland's Homer Jones, a 33-yard scoring toss from Namath to George Sauer, and a 25-yard interception return for the clinching touchdown by Browns linebacker Billy Andrews. The 31–21 Cleveland victory was an exciting start to the *Monday Night Football* series.

Most of the divisions in the NFL in 1970 were unique because of the alignment of the teams. The merger required many discussions and compromises among the team owners and the league front office before equitable solutions could be achieved. It was determined that the Eastern divisions in both conferences would sport five teams each, while the other four divisions in the league would each number four teams. The AFC East Division in 1970 included the Baltimore Colts, Miami Dolphins, New York Jets, Buffalo Bills, and the Boston Patriots. The AFC Central had the Cincinnati Bengals, Cleveland Browns, Pittsburgh Steelers, and the Houston Oilers. Rounding out the AFC was the Western Division, comprised of the Oakland Raiders, Kansas City Chiefs, San Diego Chargers, and the Denver Broncos. How did the old AFL and the old NFL solve the unequal number of teams in the merger? Baltimore, Cleveland and Pittsburgh reluctantly joined the former AFL teams in the new American Football Conference, but soon they would help to make it the league's toughest conference. The AFC would win 214 games against teams of the NFC by the end of the decade. The NFC would win 180 against the AFC in the same time span, and there would be six tie contests. The AFC teams would also capture eight of ten world championships during the 1970s.

The NFC realignment was a little more tricky to obtain than that of the AFC. A lottery had to be used to determine the makeup of this conference. The Dallas Cowboys and St. Louis Cardinals were placed in the NFC East along with the New York Giants, Washington Redskins, and the Philadelphia Eagles. Although the Cowboys and the Cardinals would be a better regional fit for the Central division, the decision to place them in the Eastern division was not unique. The Atlanta Falcons and the New Orleans Saints, teams which would also be a natural fit for the Central Division, were placed in the NFC Western division. Indeed, questions about regional alignment would haunt the league for many decades. Nevertheless, the alignment agreed to by the NFC teams in 1970 would last—for better or worse—for the next 32 years.

The NFC's Central Division was soon to be known as the "Black and Blue Division." It got its name for the relentless hard hitting and the resulting bruises that the Minnesota Vikings, Green Bay Packers, Detroit Lions, and Chicago Bears inflicted on each other, regardless of their records. Stalwart defenders like Chicago's Dick Butkus, Green Bay's Ray Nitschke, Detroit's Alex Karras, and Minnesota's Alan Page and Carl Eller, were wreaking havoc upon their opponents on a weekly basis. Their exploits were typical of the style of play that was common in the NFC Central, and their feats are legendary, even to this day. Pittsburgh defensive icon Joe Greene, himself a monster on the line of scrimmage, admiringly praised Dick Butkus. "Films don't do Butkus justice," Greene said. "He's greater than great." Pittsburgh head coach Chuck Noll was more succinct when describing Butkus with one word: "Maniacal." Author Paul Zimmerman once described Nitschke as "bald, toothless, and mean as a landlord" and a "physical destroyer." Redskin guard John Wilbur described Alex Karras' method of attack. "His specialty is the karate chop," said Wilbur. "It can numb you for a second if you don't know how to get out of the way of it." Dallas offensive tackle Ralph Neely called Carl Eller "one of the best defensive ends that I've ever faced." No less an authority on Alan Page was Miami head coach Don Shula, who called Page "the best defensive tackle in the game." Watching players being carried off the field on stretchers each week was almost common in Chicago, Detroit, Green Bay and Minnesota. Clearly, the Black and Blue Division was aptly named.

Completing the NFC was the Western Division, which featured the San Francisco 49ers, Los Angeles Rams, Atlanta Falcons, and New Orleans Saints. The alignment of the 26 teams that came about with the merger in 1970 was about as fair a solution as could be obtained in the midst of various compromises. The strong competition exhibited in the league in 1970 was visible proof of its success.

It did not take long for several teams to put together winning streaks as autumn turned to winter. The Lions, Dolphins and 49ers—among others—began to make positive strides towards the playoffs. The Lions were led by a formidable defense which gave up only 202 points, which tied for second-best in the entire NFL. Detroit defensive back Dick LeBeau led the NFC in interceptions with nine, while teammate Lem Barney tied for second in the conference with seven steals. The Lions defense achieved two shutouts (both against Green Bay) and gave up only 61 rushing first downs, which was tops in the league.

The Detroit offense was equally as tough, averaging 25 points per game and accumulating 243 first downs, which ranked third in the NFC. Reserve quarterback Greg Landry filled in for the injured Bill Munson during the second half of he season and performed admirably. Landry was one of the new breed of running quarterbacks, and he used his 6'4", 210-pound frame to break many tackles. Landry's most impressive showing came on Detroit's traditional Thanksgiving Day game against the always tough Oakland Raiders. The Lions decided to ignore tradition on that day, donning their white away jerseys instead of their usual home "Honolulu" blue jerseys. Such a choice gave the Detroit fans attending that Thanksgiving game a unique visual treat ... the Lions have never worn white jerseys at home since. The Raiders took command in the first quarter, as two Daryle Lamonica touchdown passes to Fred Biletnikoff on identical corner patterns gave them a quick 14–0 lead. Landry came back with three scoring passes of his own, however, including two to acrobatic tight end Charlie Sanders, which lifted Detroit to an impressive 28–14 triumph. "I saw the ball and said 'I don't have a chance [on one of his extraordinary diving catches],'" recalled Sanders. "Then I said, 'What the hell, I'll dive for it like I was taught in high school.' It hit and stuck." Sanders' catches spurred his teammates to excel in the win, as Landry completed 10 of his 15 pass attempts, and ran for 77 yards on seven rushes.

"We wanted to match our speed with theirs," said Landry. "We wanted to go deep. When we did, it took everybody deep—even their linebackers—and left nobody to stop me running." The Detroit offense also converted 10 of 13 third down situations versus the Raiders. Thanks in large part to Landry's efforts, the Lions gained some welcomed momentum on Turkey Day. Detroit struck for five straight victories to close out the regular season and captured the wild card playoff spot in the NFC.

Like the Lions had to face the rival Vikings for dominance in the NFC Central Division, so too did the San Francisco 49ers have to contend with the Los Angeles Rams in the NFC West. The competition brought out the best in both teams, as they split their home and away games with each other. The rosters of both clubs were filled with quality veterans and talented younger players. Strong quarterbacks were the premier reason why the Rams and 49ers were so formidable throughout 1970. Los Angeles signal caller Roman Gabriel presented the physique more of a linebacker than that of a quarterback. Gabriel stood 6'5", weighed 220 pounds, and was one of the toughest quarterbacks in the league for tacklers to bring down. Simple arm tackling was fruitless against Gabriel, as the burly quarterback would shrug off defenders like a minor inconvenience. As a result of his physicality, many teams would blitz the Rams in an attempt to fluster Gabriel and make him rush his throws. Gabriel seemed to thrive on such pressure. His passing, running and play calling contributed to the Rams scoring 325 points in 1970, the fourth-highest output in the league.

Gabriel's passing targets included wide receiver Jack Snow, who led the team with 51 receptions for 859 yards and seven touchdowns. Tight ends Bob Klein and Billy Truax were also reliable pass catchers and blockers for Gabriel. Both tight ends stood 6'5" and weighed 235 and 240 pounds, respectively. Gabriel had no trouble finding them or his top halfback downfield. Les Josephson led the Rams with 640 yards rushing and caught 44 passes for 427 yards. The 9–4–1 record that Los Angeles posted was strong evidence of their competitiveness. They barely missed the playoffs on the last week of the regular season.

San Francisco field general John Brodie did Gabriel one better by registering his best season in the pros. Brodie was named the league's Most Valuable Player, throwing for 2,941 yards and 24 touchdown passes in 1970. Equally impressive was Brodie's league-low 2.6 percent interception average. The San Francisco offensive line, which consisted of tackles Len Rohde and Cas Banaszek, center Forrest Blue, and guards Randy Beisler and Woody Peoples, permitted a meager eight sacks (a league record at the time), which gave the 35-year-old quarterback plenty of time to find his talented receivers. Gene Washington emerged as the 49ers' most explosive receiving threat, grabbing 53 balls for 1,100 yards and 12 touchdowns. Brodie was also adept at working the short game, connecting with tight end Bob Windsor and fullback Ken Willard for 31 receptions apiece. San Francisco scored a league-high 352 points, was ranked at the top in total team offense, and edged out the Rams by one game, winning the NFC West with a 10–3–1 record.

Two more elements helped San Francisco surge to the postseason. The 49ers defense showcased a strong pass rush, with stalwart defensive ends Cedrick Hardman and Tommy Hart, and sturdy defensive tackles Charlie Krueger and Roland Lakes. Backing up the front line were linebackers Dave Wilcox, Skip Vanderbundt, and Frank Nunley, who was irreverently nicknamed "Fudge Hammer" for his portly appearance and hard hits. But perhaps the most impressive players in the 49ers defense were found in their secondary. Cornerbacks Jimmy Johnson and sensational Rookie of the Year Bruce Taylor teamed up with safeties Rosey Taylor and Mel Phillips to account for 11 of the team's 22 interceptions. Few teams had better athletes in the defensive secondary than San Francisco. Bruce Taylor's athleticism proved even more beneficial for the 49ers when he was called on to return punts. He darted through oncoming tacklers for 516 yards on 43 punt returns (a 12-yard average).

The 49ers won the NFC West in an unorthodox fashion, however, as they struggled against teams in their own division. The Rams and Falcons each defeated San Francisco once, and New Orleans managed a 20–20 tie against Brodie's team in October. Head Coach Dick Nolan's squad defeated all four AFC teams that they faced, however, and they were primed to establish themselves as a strong contender for a possible Super Bowl berth.

"We're a very young team," said Brodie toward the end of the regular season. "Our young team hung in and beat teams with a lot more experience. But the thing is, once I saw these guys perform early in the year, I wasn't surprised later on."

Almost identical to the competition in the NFC West was the struggle between popular rivals in the AFC West. The Raiders and Chiefs had been involved in a hostile hitting fest for most of the past decade, and both teams carried this gridiron enmity with each other into 1970. The Chiefs entered the new season in a new position as defending world champions. They had defeated the Raiders, 17–7, in the final AFL championship game a week before Super Bowl IV. Similarly, the Raiders were also no stranger to success. They had won an AFL title in 1967, and had vanquished the Chiefs in seven of their last nine meetings entering the 1970 season. Because both were members of the new AFC West Division, both would play each other twice, just like they did when both were in the old AFL.

The Chiefs, however, succumbed to a problem that many defending champions have— namely, repeating as champions. Running back Mike Garrett was traded at mid-season to San Diego because of a contract dispute. Extraordinary defensive end Aaron Brown suffered an injury and was lost at mid-season. A lack of hunger for another title may have led some to believe that the team was becoming complaisant. This was not an uncommon occurrence, as only two teams during the 1970s managed to successfully defend a world championship. Those teams were the Miami Dolphins in 1972 and 1973, and the Pittsburgh Steelers in 1974 and 1975, and again in 1978 and 1979. Naturally, as reigning champions, the Chiefs had to contend with the best efforts from every team on their schedule. Two teams—the Raiders and the Cardinals—managed to record tie results against Kansas City. The last chance for head coach Hank Stram's team to reach the playoffs came during the final game of the season. The Chiefs were still breathing faintly with an outside shot at the wild card position in the AFC, but they failed to clinch it when they lost to the Mike Garrett–led Chargers. Kansas City also needed Miami to lose their final game against Buffalo, but the Dolphins destroyed the Bills, 45–7. After the season, Stram was philosophical about the past year. "We were proud to be champions in 1969," Stram said, "but football is a game of now. And now our only goal is to be champions again."

The Raiders in contrast had one of the most dramatic seasons in their storied history in 1970. Oakland had a roster filled with quality players. Quarterback Daryl Lamonica, known to many as "The Mad Bomber," was considered by many to be one of the best passers in the game. The Raiders were not timid when it came to throwing the ball deep down the field. Lamonica led the AFC in passing yardage (2,516), attempts (356), and completions (179) in 1970. He also tied for first in the AFC in touchdowns with San Diego's John Hadl (22). Lamonica's targets included the reliable and sticky-fingered Fred Biletnikoff, who was extremely adept at running precise short and mid-range patterns. Biletnikoff led the Raiders with 45 catches and contributed seven touchdowns. Speedy Warren Wells was the main deep threat for the Raiders. He caught 43 balls for 935 yards and 11 touchdowns. Rookie tight end Raymond Chester, who was later named the league's Rookie of the Year, caught 42 passes for 556 yards and seven touchdowns.

The Oakland running game consisted mainly of setback Hewritt Dixon, a big and rugged runner who pounded out 861 yards in 1970, which was good enough for third in the conference. Marv Hubbard was used less often, but was still a tough, hard-nosed runner. The Raiders offense relied on one of the best offensive lines in pro football. Tackle Art Shell and guard Gene Upshaw were, despite their young age (both were in their mid–20s), two of the best linemen in the game. Center Jim Otto was possibly the most dependable and savvy snapper in the league.

Unfortunately for the Raiders, their defense did not measure up to the performance of their offense. Oakland did possess a quality cornerback in Willie Brown, a strong and fast safety in George Atkinson, and two impressive defensive linemen in Tom Keating and Ben Davidson. The main flaw with head coach John Madden's defense, however, involved stopping the run. Oakland gave up 2,027 yards rushing, and this statistic more than any other kept the team from posting a better record in 1970.

The Chiefs-Raiders rivalry added an exciting new chapter in 1970. The Chiefs were 3–3 and the Raiders were 2–3–1 going into their first showdown of the season on November 1 in Kansas City. Like most of the games in this rivalry, both teams were more than happy to deliver their share of hard hits to each other. Both teams were also no strangers to controversy. Several months before in the final AFL title game in the Oakland Coliseum, Kansas City wide receiver Otis Taylor bobbled and then clutched onto a deep sideline pass thrown by quarterback Len Dawson from his own end zone. Replays showed conclusively that Taylor did not have possession of the ball as he stepped out of bounds, but the trailing field judge Bob Baur saw it differently and ruled a completion. Amidst strong and colorful vocal protests from the Raiders and their fans, Dawson took his team the rest of the way to the go-ahead touchdown that would pave the way to the championship.

In their first meeting since that epic contest, both teams would once again renew their animosity for each other. And just as in the previous AFL championship game, controversy would once again visit this rivalry. The Chiefs possessed the ball and a 17–14 lead with 1:08 to play in the fourth quarter. On third down and 11 yards to go, Dawson faked a handoff to halfback Ed Podolak and spun around his right tackle on what was a textbook naked bootleg play. The entire Raider defense followed the fake to Podolak, and Dawson was free to run. The rest of the Raider defense finally caught up to Dawson 19 yards downfield before he tripped on the legs of one of his blockers. As soon as Dawson fell to the ground with a game-clinching first down, however, Oakland defensive end Ben Davidson dove at him on the ground and speared the quarterback in the back with his helmet. "Maybe it wasn't a nice thing to do," said Davidson, "but I honestly wasn't sure if Dawson was touched down or not."

Cheap shots have been a part of the game of pro football since the 1890s, when the flying wedge formation resulted in extreme carnage and multiple injuries. Davidson's cheap shot was nothing new for him, as he had been guilty before of delivering his share of extra-curricular hits. His spearing of Dawson resulted in an immediate fight. Otis Taylor of the Chiefs instantly defended his quarterback by grabbing Davidson and throwing him to the ground. No less than a half dozen members of each team began to rapidly tackle and punch each other while the shrill whistles from every referee pierced the early evening air. According to author Bob Oates, Jr., "There were some people who knew whom they wanted to hit." A few well-placed kicks to lower anatomical areas, namely in the delicate nether regions, were also distributed by members of both teams. Yellow penalty flags from the referees promptly flew all over the field. It was definitely not a glowing example that the NFL wanted to use to promote the popularity of the game.

In 1970, crucial penalties could really affect the outcomes of games. A total of eight minutes elapsed before the referees could restore a semblance of order on the field and separate the combatants, but it sure seemed longer. More minutes passed before the officials could make a decision on the number of penalties and the resulting yardage accumulated by the Chiefs and the Raiders. Confusing the situation even more was the fact that the down and yardage markers had already been mistakenly moved from their original positions before the play began. According to referee Art Holst, game official Bob Finley asked his fellow zebras if they could determine the placement of the down and yardage markers, and if they had any other information regarding the penalties to Davidson and Taylor. The other referees displayed a collective blank look on their faces. Finley then cast a pleading look at the press box for any available data from the television or public address system announcers. They pretended to look the other way. The referees on the field were now on their own. Holst then began shouting at Finley: "Bob," Holst beckoned his lead official, "we've been standing out here for 20 minutes!" Finley shot right back at Holst. "So? I don't care if we have to stand here for an *hour* and 20 minutes! We're gonna' get it right!"

Although the ruling on the field was offsetting unnecessary roughness fouls and continuing action fouls on both teams for their fistfight, an obscure sentence in the rule book decided the issue. Davidson's hit was a live ball foul, whereas Taylor's was a dead ball foul. In such an instance, the teams would replay the down at the previous spot. The officials thus did not penalize Davidson's late hit. As a result, the Chiefs' first down was nullified, and they were required to replay third down (a statistician sent down word to the referees to spot the ball on the 50-yard line). Unable to pick up the first down that they had gained from the previous play, the Chiefs punted, and the Raiders quickly moved to midfield. George Blanda's 48-yard field goal barely cleared the crossbar with only seconds left, lifting Oakland to a 17–17 tie, and putting them in first place in the AFC West.

Prior to the final gun, several Chiefs players voiced their displeasure to Finley in the most colorful and uncomplimentary ways. Several 15-yard penalties were thus handed out to the Chiefs. Oakland ended up kicking off to their opponent from the Kansas City 30-yard line! The game ended amidst a chorus of boos and a race for the Raiders and the referees to the safety of the locker rooms. The referees made good time when running for their lives, especially on that day. As the refs were sprinting to the dugout of Kansas City's Municipal Stadium, a member of the also-endangered chain gang asked Holst if *he* could have the pistol that Holst used to fire the shot that traditionally marked the end of the game. An irate fan caught up with Holst and tackled him. Two nearby policemen pulled the man—who happened to be a Kansas City bank president—off of Holst.

"When I got to the dressing room," Holst remembered, "it was a madhouse! People were pounding on the door, demanding our scalps. I even thought I heard someone call for a rope! The police, who believed that scalping and lynching football officials would not give Kansas City a good image, remained with us in our dressing room to give us protection."

Kansas City head coach Hank Stram spent the time in his dressing room in a state of utter confusion. "What was the call?" asked an incredulous Stram to the reporters about Davidson's hit on Dawson after the game. "Nobody would explain it [to me]. I went over to the officials off the field and tried to find out what happened. I didn't find out."

This was the first of five "miracles" that the 43-year-old Blanda would have a say in during the regular season. Blanda, a placekicker and a substitute quarterback, became a folk hero, not just to Oakland fans but to followers of pro football all across the nation. After the Kansas City game, the Raiders managed to defeat the visiting Cleveland Browns in last-second fashion, with Blanda being the catalyst for victory. Oakland trailed the Browns 20–13 with four minutes remaining in the fourth quarter when Blanda was called upon to replace an injured Lamonica. Blanda's major deep threat, Warren Wells, managed to cut in front of Cleveland defensive back Walt Sumner, then dive to catch Blanda's dart just one yard inside the end zone. Following a timely interception by Oakland's Kent McCloughan, Blanda drilled a 52-yard field goal which won the game, 23–20. "There's a lot left in that leg of his," Lamonica said of his veteran teammate.

The next week, Blanda would once again figure in the outcome of a tight contest at Denver. Lamonica visited the bench after sustaining another injury in the second half, and Blanda promptly replaced him and tossed the game-winning touchdown pass to wide receiver Fred Biletnikoff on a corner pattern in front of defensive back Dick Daniels. Back at home on November 22, the Raiders edged the Chargers, 20–17, on another last-second field goal by Blanda. Warren Wells cashed in on another late miracle finish against the Jets at New York's Shea Stadium on December 6. Wells was triple covered, but still managed to make a diving catch from a Lamonica pass in the end zone after a deflection by Jets defensive back Earlie Thomas. Wells' 33-yard score and a Blanda conversion gave Oakland a 14–13 win and left them one game away from the division title. Thanks in large part to Blanda, the Raiders were looking like a team of destiny.

George Blanda was winning the battle for the hearts of elderly America. Despite his 21 years of experience, Blanda was enjoying one of his most memorable seasons. He was resurrecting the Raiders, helping them win key games, and inspiring them in their drive to the playoffs. According to columnist Ron Fimrite of the *San Francisco Chronicle*, "[Blanda] has given many of his contemporaries heart. We are all beginning to look at our bodies, swollen as they may be by years of disuse, a hard second look. Perhaps, there's a little more life in the old corpse after all."

The old man himself professed that the game had not passed him by. Blanda was still healthy enough to play at a competitive level. There was also something more to keep him buckling up his chin strap, however. "I think most athletes quit simply because they lose their love for the game," Blanda said. "I still enjoy it as much as ever."

Blanda and the Raiders would go on to play the Chiefs on the second-to-last Sunday of the regular season. Spirited by winning five of their past six games, Oakland easily defeated Kansas City, 20–6, thereby clinching the AFC West title. The Silver and Black offense controlled the ball virtually all game long, and their defense effectively shut down the Kansas City offense, limiting them to 121 total yards and only seven first downs.

While the Oakland-Kansas City rivalry was one of the most fierce in the league, the rivalry between Cleveland and Cincinnati was one of the most regionally bitter throughout the decade. Both teams were not only in the same division, but both were located only 250 miles from each other in Ohio. Fans in each city would annually make the trip to their rival's stadium and create a palpable sense of boisterous tension in the stands. The contention between the two cities, however, was meager in comparison to the distaste that Bengals president and head coach Paul Brown harbored with his former boss, Browns owner Art Modell. Brown was one of the game's greatest strategists and innovators, and he had overseen the development of the Browns from their humble birth in the fledgling All-American Football Conference in 1946, to winning three NFL championships during the 1950s. The enormous clash of egos between the two proud men, however, led to Modell's firing of Brown in 1963 and replacing him with Blanton Collier. No team seriously sought Brown's services after he was fired, with many football front office types believing that the game had passed him by. Brown had seven years remaining on his contract at the time of his departure, and ever since that day he longed for a chance to repay his former owner on the field. In 1970, he would make good on that goal.

An expansion AFL franchise in Cincinnati was awarded to Brown in 1967. The determined coach, hungry for redemption, would provide his new team with experience and direction. An allocation draft the following year gave the Bengals 40 players, many of them youngsters, and many of them mere castoffs from the rest of the league. Brown's squad was one of the youngest in the league in 1970. Visible progress was being made, however, and Brown never let the bitterness he fostered against his former boss to become extinguished. Brown was driven by that bitterness to one day defeat his old Cleveland team, and by his desire to build a winning unit from the ground up.

It certainly looked like Modell would get the better of Brown early in the 1970 season, however. Cleveland defeated Cincinnati, 30–27, in their first meeting at Cleveland's immense Municipal Stadium, a venue which held over 79,000 raucous fans. Leroy Kelly scored twice for the Browns in that game, and quarterback Bill Nelsen tossed two touchdown passes to boost Cleveland's record to 3–1. Most observers felt that even though the Bengals had shown some measure of improvement, they would still be a few years away from serious contention in the AFC Central Division. Paul Brown's club shook off their loss to Cleveland, however, and showed impressive resilience to stiff competition during the second half of the 1970 season. The Bengals took a woeful 1–6 record into Buffalo's War Memorial Stadium on November 8. Within a few hours, the Bengals scored five touchdowns en route to a 43–14 pasting of the Bills. Leading the scoring barrage for Cincinnati on this day was their special teams. Horst Muhlmann kicked four field goals, and speedy Lemar Parrish returned a second quarter kickoff 95 yards for a touchdown. Parrish was not finished, however. He would later return a blocked field goal attempt 83 yards down the sideline for the game's final tally. The great Cincinnati comeback had begun.

"I made up my mind that I was going to be tough," said Parrish of his scoring jaunts. "I just saw a couple of big holes and took off."

The next contest would be against none other than the Browns, this time at Cincinnati's Riverfront Stadium. By November 15, Cleveland's record had dropped to 4–4. Like their first meeting, both teams played a tough, physical game, and both had comparable statistics. This time, however, the Bengals were able to capitalize on enough of their opportunities to post a 14–10 victory. Halfback Paul Robinson's 1-yard burst in the third quarter proved to be the winning touchdown.

"We just happened to get that second touchdown and hung on for dear life," said a vindicated Paul Brown after the game. "This is my best victory. I wanted this so badly. This victory somehow makes coming back [to the NFL] worthwhile."

There would be more victories for Brown's team. Successive wins against Pittsburgh, New Orleans, San Diego, Houston, and finally Boston gave Cincinnati the AFC Central title. The Bengals' 45–7 thrashing of the Patriots included three more touchdowns by Paul Robinson, and concluded with their patriarch head coach being carried off the field in victory by his young squad. Paul Brown had his revenge and a Coach of the Year award to boot. The Bengals were going to the playoffs for the first time in their young history, thanks to their seven-game winning streak to end the regular season. The Browns would have to wait until next year for a chance at postseason play. "Personally, this was a dream come true," Brown said of his team's ascension to the division title. "This has been the most interesting and most gratifying season I have ever known."

While the Bengals were achieving their first taste of success, the youthful Dolphins of Miami were also experiencing a winning season. The similarities between the Bengals and the Dolphins were many. The Dolphins were another AFL expansion team, and they too benefitted from an allocation draft and a quality head coach. Don Shula's trip to a new team in some ways mirrored that of Paul Brown's. Shula played for Brown in Cleveland in 1951 and 1952. As head coach of the Baltimore Colts, Shula was blamed by Colts owner Carroll Rosenbloom for his team's loss to the New York Jets in Super Bowl III in 1968. By 1970, Shula was wooed by Dolphins owner Joe Robbie to leave the Colts and join his team. A controversy over Shula's contract and his availability to coach another team led to NFL Commissioner Pete Rozelle granting the Colts a first round draft pick in 1971 in exchange for Shula. The stage was set in 1970 for a new rivalry between the Colts and the Dolphins.

It did not take long for Shula to develop a young Miami team and build the foundation for an eventual champion. Bob Griese was a young quarterback from Purdue who was noted for his scrambling ability, but little else. Griese would develop poise and patience in the passing pocket under Shula's tutelage. In a short amount of time and training, Griese would become an accurate passer and an outstanding field general. Fullback Larry Csonka quickly earned recognition as the toughest runner in the league within Shula's ball-control offense. Only a few defensive players in the NFL could tackle Csonka all by themselves, and the sight of several defenders holding onto Csonka while he churned downfield was not uncommon. Shula then traded for quality wide receiver Paul Warfield, who was one of the most fluid and graceful route runners in league history. Shula also signed several offensive linemen who would come together to be regarded as one of the best blocking units in the game. Perhaps the most noteworthy group on the Dolphins roster was their defense, however. Coined in 1971 the "No-Name Defense" by Dallas head coach Tom Landry, the Miami defense was unheralded and somewhat underrated for many years. They became more effective than any other defense in the league during the early 1970s, however.

According to author Jack Clary, Miami's defensive philosophy was focused simply on preventing cheap touchdowns by the opposition. "We try to take away what our opponent likes," explained Shula in Clary's book *The Gamemakers*. "On the run, we want to contain the sweep or attack the inside play. On the pass, we want to force the quarterback to throw to areas where we can react and attack the receiver when the ball is in the area. The ultimate objective is to create long yardage situations and thus dictate the choice of plays the offense will be restricted to."

Shula's club—like Paul Brown's Bengals—also went on a long winning streak at the end of the regular season. The Dolphins won six straight, including victories against divisional foes Baltimore, Boston, the New York Jets and Buffalo, to finish second in the AFC East and gain the conference's wild card spot. In their November 22 rematch against visiting Baltimore, Griese threw for two touchdowns and ran for a third in a 34–17 victory. Almost 80,000 fans in the Orange Bowl Stadium that day and millions across the nation now knew for sure that Shula had turned the franchise around. Miami was on the winning track for the first time in their existence.

The Baltimore Colts were seemingly always on a winning track. They began 1970, however, donning the appearance of an also-ran. They had a wealth of experience on their roster, but they were not really intimidating the rest of the NFL. Following their opening day win over San Diego, the Colts were humiliated by Kansas City at home in front of a Monday night audience, 44–24. The Chiefs built a 31–0 lead before halftime, and the race for the fans to exit Memorial Stadium was on. But the Colts shook off their embarrassment and won a series of tough contests at midseason which helped them return to the top of the divisional standings. Baltimore had a healthy John Unitas back in the starting lineup as they visited the Astrodome in the fourth week of the season. Unitas once again displayed an example of his legendary leadership as he threw the winning touchdown pass to Roy Jefferson in the game's final moments. The Colts came from behind to edge the Oilers, 24–20. Unitas' confidence in his younger teammates was growing, and that confidence helped to produce victory. "It is something Roy and I worked out earlier," Unitas said of his winning touchdown pass against the Oilers. "We were trying to work Roy on a one-on-one coverage on the wide side of the field and we got our wish. He made a great curl on his man and then broke out. All I had to do was get the ball there."

The Colts also achieved a measure of revenge for their Super Bowl III debacle against the Jets in the fifth week of the season by defeating Joe Namath at New York's Shea Stadium, 29–22. Safety Jerry Logan and reserve linebacker Bob Grant each stole a Namath pass and returned it for a score. The Colts then went on to crush the Dolphins at home on November 1, 35–0. This victory brought enormous joy to Carroll Rosenbloom, who was still smarting over losing Shula to Miami owner Joe Robbie. The Colts endured a driving snowstorm at Buffalo's War Memorial Stadium on December 13, as they clinched the AFC East with a 11–2–1 record. Baltimore's gutty 20–14 victory over the Bills was highlighted by Charlie Stukes' interception late in the game, halting Buffalo's final drive. "The game was typical of the Colts all season," said Baltimore head coach Don McCafferty. "It scared the hell out of me."

The Colts' conquest of the AFC East was one of only two divisions in the NFL which were won by more than one game (Minnesota's 12–2 record in the NFC Central was the other). It seemed as if a new trend was developing in 1970. Division winners needed to go on a late-season winning streak in order to make the playoffs. The Dallas Cowboys followed that trend. They managed to defeat their last five opponents to claim the NFC East title. Dallas was one of the best teams in the league. Their roster sported a wealth of quality athletes, strong and able veterans, and energetic youngsters. Perhaps the most important weapon in the Cowboy arsenal was their head coach, Tom Landry, who was one of the game's most knowledgeable strategists. Dallas lost twice during the regular season to divisional foe St. Louis, but still managed to defeat quality teams such as Kansas City and Cleveland. On the final week of the season, Dallas romped over in-state rival Houston, 52–10, while their closest competition—the New York Giants—fell to the Rams, 31–3.

The Dallas offense was similar to that of the Chiefs, as they utilized formation shifts and man-in-motion strategies to confuse opposing defenses. Landry's team also benefitted from the services of three young and rugged running backs. Calvin Hill, Walt Garrison, and NFL Rookie of the Year Duane Thomas led Dallas to a league-high 2,300 yards rushing. Thomas led the league in rushing average with an astounding 5.3 yards per attempt. By season's end, the Dallas running game accumulated 119 first downs, and was ranked by most defensive coordinators as the most feared in the NFL.

The Dallas passing game on the other hand featured an Olympic gold medal champion known as "the World's Fastest Human." Bob Hayes only caught 34 passes in 1970, but "Bullet Bob" (as he was also known) managed to record an outstanding 26.1 yards per reception. Hayes in addition visited the end zone 10 times during the regular season. Despite Hayes' productivity, Dallas experienced a mid-season slump. Landry addressed his team's lack of scoring with his decision to call plays for his quarterback, Craig Morton. Landry's shuttle system in 1970 utilized his tight ends, Mike Ditka and Pettis Norman, sending one or the other in on alternating plays. The system worked well enough for Dallas, as Landry's offense scored 153 points in their final five games.

The most visible catalyst for the Cowboys' surge to the playoffs was their defense, however. The Dallas defense permitted their opponents a meager total of six points in the final four games, thus justifying their title as the "Doomsday Defense." They earned this nickname from a sportswriter in the late 1960s who declared that opponents supposedly would not score on them until "doomsday." Key contributors to this stinginess included linemen Bob Lilly, George Andrie, Jethro Pugh, and Larry Cole; linebackers Lee Roy Jordan, Dave Edwards, and All-Pro Chuck Howley; and defensive backs Herb Adderley, Cornell Green, Mel Renfro, and rookie Charlie Waters. The Cowboys defense did not rack up a lot of individual statistics, but that did not matter. When their backs were up against the wall during the mid-season, they strengthened their resolve and began shutting down opposing offenses.

"Landry realized that everyone was pushing too hard," remembered Bob Lilly in a discussion on the mid-season slump, "so he relaxed everything. For the only time in my career with the Cowboys, I heard him tell everyone to just have fun."

Dallas' foes down the stretch certainly did not have much fun going up against the Doomsday Defense. The Cowboys and Landry knew the truth of the old adage "Defense wins championships," but it took them until virtually the final month of the regular season to achieve the success that they needed to become a contender. Dallas' most formidable foe in the NFC East was the New York Giants, a team with a quality offense. The Giants failed to make the playoffs with an impressive 9–5 record, but they gave many NFC teams—including the Cowboys—a tough challenge during the regular season. New York was led by scrambling quarterback Fran Tarkenton, who helped the Giants record an NFC-high 257 first downs in 1970. Tarkenton's fame would come from his ability to avoid the defensive pass rush by running all around the passing pocket. His main methods of attack, however, were to dominate the time of possession statistics, make minimal mistakes, and move the yard markers. According to New York's star halfback Ron Johnson, Tarkenton provided the impetus to success for the offense.

"Fran is a tremendously smart quarterback," Johnson said. "He's the type that can see what it is the defense is giving him, and he can find a way to take it. It's the mark of a good quarterback not to force anything, and Tarkenton never forces. He uses all the weapons he has. On a team like ours, that's just what we need."

Johnson finished second in the league in rushing (behind Washington's Larry Brown) with 1,027 yards. Johnson benefitted from the timely blocking of his fullback, Tucker Frederickson. Tarkenton threw successfully to targets such as wide out Clifton McNeil (50 catches for 764 yards) and tight end Bob Tucker (40 catches for 571 yards). The Giants swept division rival St. Louis, an astounding feat when considering that the Cardinals shut out three straight opponents in mid-season. Tarkenton connected on 15 of 18 attempts in the Giants' first contest against the Cardinals. Five of those tosses went for touchdowns in a 35–17 romp. In the rematch on December 13, Tarkenton threw for three scores and ran for another in a 34–17 triumph. The Giants were making the most of their ball-control philosophy, and would have made the playoffs were it not for their meltdown against the Rams in the final week of the season.

The Cardinals were the team that was really unlucky by the end of the 1970 season. As previously mentioned, their defense registered three straight shutouts (44–0 versus Houston; 31–0 versus Boston; and 38–0 versus Dallas). In their next game at Kansas City, their defense gave up only two field goals in a 6–6 tie. So in the span of four straight games, St. Louis gave up only six points! They owned an 8–2–1 record and seemed to be a shoo-in for the postseason, yet they lost their final three games and missed out on the playoffs entirely. St. Louis quarterback Jim Hart threw for an impressive 2,575 yards in the NFL in 1970, which was the third-highest mark in the league. But in the end, Hart's statistics were not enough to beat a team like their rivals in the NFC East, the New York Giants. The Giants' Tarkenton was a better scrambler than Hart (indeed he was a better scrambler than virtually *every* other quarterback in the NFL), but Tarkenton also accounted for 2,777 passing yards, a mark that was good enough for second best in the league.

Defenses throughout the 1970 season had their hands full dealing with savvy quarterbacks like Tarkenton. Most defenses around the league did not receive many headlines, but nevertheless they were the dominating force on most game days in 1970. There were several reasons why. First (in random order), was the play of the cornerbacks around the league. The man-to-man defense was the most common defense that was being played, with many cornerbacks playing close and tight to opposing receivers. The Oakland Raiders utilized the bump and run defense to the extreme. The theory behind the bump and run was that cornerbacks would enhance their chances of success if they could knock a receiver off of his intended pattern. Oakland cornerbacks Willie Brown and Nemiah Wilson were two defenders who utilized the bump and run defense successfully on a regular basis. Brown and Wilson would line up just inches off of the line of scrimmage. As soon as the ball was snapped, both Brown and Wilson would hit the receivers they were covering as they came off the line. The cornerbacks would then run as tightly to the receivers as possible and cover them like a blanket until the ball was thrown. The ultimate goal of the bump and run defense was to deter the receivers from finishing their pass routes. The strategy was successful throughout the 1960s, but by the end of the 1970s, the bump and run would become a tactic that only a few teams with star cornerbacks could use against opposing offenses. This was thanks in part to the second reason why defenses dominated in the early part of the decade.

The popularity of zone defenses, which were being perfected as the 1970s approached, was that second reason. Receivers were becoming too successful against straight man-to-man defenses, and the addition of zone defenses answered that deficiency and helped to sway the pendulum back in favor of the defense. Coaches throughout the league were notorious for copying successful strategies, and the zone defense was no exception. Nowhere was the zone employed more successfully than in Baltimore, where linebackers Mike Curtis, Ted Hendricks, and Ray May dropped back deep into the secondary to help prevent long passes. The Colts' strong defensive line permitted such a move, thanks to their strong pass rush, which accounted for 41 quarterback sacks in 1970. In the zone, linebackers and defensive backs would not cover any one particular receiver. Instead, they would cover a particular area, or "zone," then converge on the area where the ball was being thrown. Teams like Miami, Dallas, Detroit, and San Francisco all played variations of zones similar to Baltimore's. Most of the playoff teams in 1970 became adept at utilizing zone defenses.

"We're seeing so many more zone defenses these days," said veteran Green Bay receiver Carroll Dale. "And speed doesn't help you against a zone. I don't need it as much. What I do need against these zones are the things Lombardi harped on—making sharp turns and coming back for the ball. As soon as I read a zone now, I head for the edge of it and then move back toward the quarterback. Football's a new game today."

The third factor in why defenses were taking over the game involved the play on the defensive line. Stalwart defensive linemen such as David "Deacon" Jones of the Rams perfected the "head slap," a calculated strike to disorient his opponent on the line of scrimmage. Jones would wind up and whack his blocker on the side of his helmet. This move allowed Jones an extra second to drive past the blocker and rush the quarterback while the blocker attempted to recover. No concrete statistics are available, but the common belief is that Jones was a major reason given by dozens of offensive linemen for their premature retirements.

Finally, offensive linemen were a victim of the rules which hindered their success. Back in 1970, offensive linemen were not allowed to extend their arms when blocking. They were also not allowed to grasp the jerseys of defensive linemen. The penalty for offensive holding was a severe 15 yards. Most offenses could not recover from holding penalties. A holding call on a third-and-10 play resulted in a difficult third-and-25 situation. All of these factors resulted in many low-scoring games throughout much of the decade.

Despite the offensive woes and injuries to big-name players like running backs Gale Sayers of Chicago, Matt Snell of the New York Jets, and quarterback Joe Namath of the Jets, pro football still showcased some remarkable individual achievements in 1970. Perhaps the most extraordinary accomplishment by a player occurred on November 8, when Tom Dempsey of New Orleans kicked a then–league record 63-yard field goal as time expired to defeat playoff-bound Detroit, 19–17. The drama was increased by Dempsey's physical handicaps. Dempsey was born without a right hand, and he wore a special shoe for his stump of a kicking foot. Nevertheless, Dempsey kicked his way into the record book.

"I knew I could kick it 63 yards," Dempsey said after the game, "but I wasn't sure that I could kick it straight. I got a good snap and a perfect hold. But all I was thinking about was kicking it as hard as I could. I couldn't follow it that far, but I did see the [officials'] arms go up and everybody start yelling and I knew it was good. It's quite a thrill."

Strategy was also involved in Dempsey's kick. Holder Joe Scarpati knelt down a yard deeper than usual, giving Dempsey an extra moment to kick the ball. Scarpati also told the Saints offensive linemen to "hold them [the Lions] just a little longer than usual." After the game, some of the Lions defensive players commented that they heard Dempsey's foot "explode" into the ball, and that the sound of that impact was "extremely loud." It was indeed a special moment for the history of the game. Today, the kicking shoe that Dempsey wore on that historic day is prominently displayed in the Pro Football Hall of Fame.

Pittsburgh Steelers running back John "Frenchy" Fuqua was also involved in another spectacular one-game performance in 1970. Fuqua set a team yardage record (which has since been broken by Willie Parker in 2006) as he ran for 218 yards on 20 carries against the Eagles on

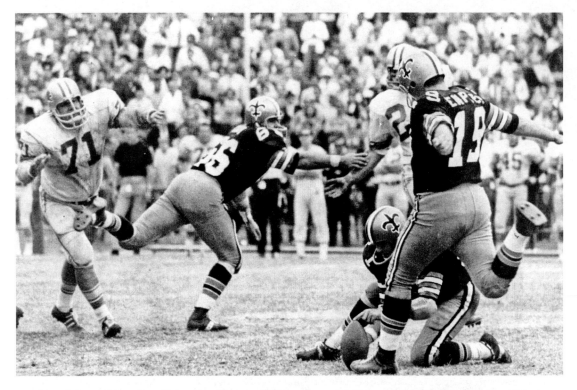

New Orleans Saints placekicker Tom Dempsey (19) moves up to kick a 63-yard field goal in New Orleans, November 8, 1970. The record-setting kick, with two seconds left in the game, gave the Saints a 19–17 upset win over the Detroit Lions. Detroit defensive lineman Alex Karras (71) rushes the kicker, and Saints Bill Cody (66) blocks while Joe Scarpati (21) is the holder on the historic kick (AP Photo/files).

December 20 at Philadelphia's Franklin Field. Included in his statistics were two long touchdown runs. In the first quarter, Fuqua broke tackles from Eagles defensive backs Al Nelson and Bill Bradley and sprinted for a 72-yard score. In the second quarter, the Eagles defense crowded the line of scrimmage. Fuqua blasted through a hole which opened in a split second in the line and ran untouched 85 yards for the longest touchdown run of the 1970 NFL season. "Fuqua ... played extremely well," said an understated Pittsburgh head coach Chuck Noll after his team's losing effort in Philadelphia.

Another running back in Washington, D.C., also made a name for himself. Larry Brown of the Redskins led the league in rushing in 1970, gaining 1,125 yards, and averaging 86.5 yards per game. Brown eclipsed the 100-yard plateau in six games, and he had one of the longest runs of the season against San Francisco on September 20. Brown's 75-yard jaunt to the end zone began as he took a pitchout from quarterback Sonny Jurgensen, swept right, broke two arm tackles, and sprinted down the sideline to score.

"There's no question that the Redskins' Larry Brown is the premier runner in pro football," claimed Tommy Nobis, the outstanding middle linebacker from the Atlanta Falcons. Veteran Washington safety Richie Petitbon took one look at Brown and said, "We've got some great young talent around here."

Perhaps the most unpredictable performance of 1970 came from Chicago Bears wide receiver Dick Gordon. The Michigan State alum caught only 36 passes in 1969, but he more than made up for that the following year. Gordon grabbed a league-high 71 passes in 1970. His 13 receiving touchdowns also led the league. Gordon's teammate Cecil Turner also added to the Bears highlights when he returned four kickoffs for touchdowns in 1970. Despite these standout perform-ances, Chicago could only register a mediocre 6–8 record.

One man who could never be described as "mediocre" was NFL Commissioner Pete Rozelle. The popularity and growth of the game during the 1970s was a direct result of Rozelle's vision and hard work. Rozelle had an opinion on everything that involved the game, from television coverage to ticket sales to player relations to the quality of paper used in printing the game pro-grams. Rozelle, who broke into the world of sports as a public relations man, was able to see the potential for the growth of pro football, especially during the early years prior to the merger between the AFL and the NFL. Rozelle's plans for the success of the league were visible for all to see as the 1970s wore on, and his ability to work with so many different people with differing per-sonalities almost guaranteed the success of his commissionership.

Rozelle described his beliefs at the beginning of 1970 in a statement that was sent out to all teams and hundreds of media outlets. In that statement, the Commissioner addressed the possi-bility for the game's overexposure, the importance of televised games (particularly on Monday night, which by the end of the regular season had seen a large increase in television ratings), and the intended growth of the game.

"We felt that reaching [a] broader market on Monday night gave us a chance to make new fans on television," said Rozelle, "fans who eventually will want to come out to our games." Rozelle knew that more people watched television during the evening hours than they did during the day. By televising games on Monday night, Rozelle believed that the game would attract new fans, many of whom never saw an NFL game.

"By reaching this broad market," Rozelle said, "we created a still broader market for television sponsors. And this, in turn, would help to insure that pro football on television would continue

Undoubtedly the greatest commissioner in pro football history was Pete Rozelle, a man who guided the game to remarkable heights from 1960 to 1989. He negotiated the first league-wide television contract in 1962, and the most important merger in pro football history in 1970. Rozelle is regarded today by many experts as perhaps the greatest commissioner in the history of American sports, and the popularity that the NFL enjoys today is thanks in large part to his vision and efforts (AP Photo).

as it had in the past. Our early ratings have indicated that we are, in fact, reaching a broader market than we normally do. By going to Monday night, we hoped to reduce the danger of overexposure on the simple premise that it is hard to overexpose an audience that includes many who have never been exposed at all."

Pete Rozelle's determination and vision produced a league that through the years has far exceeded even his dreams. Thanks to Rozelle, millions of new fans fell in love with the game during the 1970s. The NFL honored his contributions to the game with his induction into the Pro Football Hall of Fame in 1985. He is considered by most experts as the greatest professional sports commissioner of all time.

The final few weeks of the regular season helped to focus the sphere of which teams would make the playoffs and which would fail. San Francisco needed to win their final three games in order to clinch the NFC Western Division title. They managed to do just that by defeating Atlanta, New Orleans and Oakland to claim a playoff spot. Their final game across the bridge at Oakland on December 20 was played on a water-logged field at rainy Oakland County Coliseum. The 49ers completely destroyed the Raiders, 38–7, behind three touchdown passes by quarterback John Brodie. "They [the team] did what they had to do," said 49ers head coach Dick Nolan of his team's 1970 season. "The coaches did a great job. Also, John [Brodie] executed real well." Brodie's performance stemmed from being sacked only eight times all year, a league record at the time. "He doesn't wait," said Raiders defensive tackle Tom Keating of Brodie's time with the ball in the pocket. "He gets rid of that ball right now."

The Miami Dolphins and the Detroit Lions secured the wild card spots in their respective conferences with late-season victories. The Dolphins won their final six games, while the Lions claimed wins in their final five games to make the postseason. Of Detroit's key conquests down the stretch were triumphs against San Francisco and Los Angeles. "I said when we were 5–4 we could do it," said Detroit middle linebacker Mike Lucci of his team's late-season winning streak. "Sure I thought we could make it," admitted Detroit owner William Ford. "But they [the players] knew they were good and they just took each game as it came. Looking back, it's more impressive because we had to win five in a row against some pretty touch clubs."

The Minnesota Vikings stayed on top of the NFC Central Division with wins in their final three games against Chicago, Boston, and Atlanta. The Norsemen had to keep winning, because Detroit kept breathing down their necks all season long. Minnesota finished with a league-best 12–2 record, while Detroit finished with a 10–4 mark. "Yes, I felt some pressure," said Minnesota quarterback Gary Cuozzo on producing for his club during the final weeks of the season. "However, the only pressure was in stepping into a position where the only different person on the starting team is you. Now we just need three more [wins]."

The fans who enjoyed a great 1970 regular season would ultimately be treated to a highly-competitive postseason. Four divisional playoff games would produce four teams who would play for their conference's championship. The AFC divisional playoffs featured the youthful Central Champion Cincinnati Bengals visiting the East Champion Baltimore Colts, and the equally youthful wild card Miami Dolphins traveling to Oakland to play the West Champion Raiders. Both games were victories for experience.

It was a sunny and windy day in Baltimore's Memorial Stadium, where 30-mile-per-hour gusts swirled the dirt surface, and where the Colts defense stymied the inexperienced Bengals offense all game long. Virgil Carter, Cincinnati's young quarterback, led his team to an impressive seven-game winning streak as they headed into the playoffs. Against the Colts and their formidable zone defense, however, he could only manage 76 yards passing. His running game did not help him either, as Jess Phillips and Essex Johnson could only muster 63 yards against a dominating

Baltimore front defensive line. The Bengals never got past their opponent's 42-yard line and fell to the Colts, 17–0.

"The Colts made absolutely no turnovers," lamented Carter after the game. "If we were going to put any points on the board, we'd have to do it from 80 yards out. We planned to work on the zone, but it just wasn't there to go against that often. We tried to flood a zone by having me roll at a zone with three receivers already there. It worked a couple of times but we couldn't run it often enough."

Baltimore's offense came into this playoff contest with a tried and tested game plan. The Colts established their running game, took an early lead, and then dominated the time of possession en route to their victory. The star of the running game was rookie Norm Bulaich, who ran for 116 yards on 25 carries. The Colts employed a power sweep that rode on Bulaich's determination. Bulaich either carried a Bengal defender or two around the end, or he bounced off of them. His performance was needed, because the Colts passing game was not up to its usual high standard. Colts quarterback Johnny Unitas had to work against the same windy conditions that Carter did. Unitas completed only six of 17 passes, but two of his completions went for touchdowns. In the first quarter, Unitas lofted a high arching pass to wide receiver Roy Jefferson, a tall and strong pass catcher. Jefferson grabbed the ball at the Bengal 12-yard line, then carried Cincinnati defensive back Fletcher Smith on his back as he crossed the goal line. A 44-yard field goal into the wind by rookie placekicker Jim O'Brien gave the Colts a 10–0 lead at halftime.

There was no scoring in the third quarter, but in the fourth quarter, Unitas put the game away with a 53-yard scoring pass to speedy wide out Eddie Hinton. Unitas threw under the zone coverage to Hinton over the middle, and once he caught the ball at the 35-yard line, he ran behind a clearing block by Bulaich and past three other Cincinnati defenders into the end zone. The Colts were headed to the AFC title game. "I was really ready," said Bulaich after the game. "Everybody was fired up." Colts head coach Don McCafferty may not have been "fired up," but he was content with his team's overall effort. "It was a fantastic job," said McCafferty.

The Colts' opponents in the conference championship game would be determined by the winner of the Miami-Oakland divisional playoff contest. The game was played at Oakland, where the field surface was well below sea level and had been the victim of a full day of rain prior to the game. The Raiders avenged their loss to Miami on October 3 by earning a hard-fought 21–14 victory on the wet and muddy field. This was a bitter game for the Dolphins. They dominated for much of the first half, and out-gained their opponents in first downs (16 to 12), rushing yardage (118 to 114), and total plays (63 to 52) by game's end. Nevertheless, Oakland made a couple of big plays that proved to be the difference.

In the third quarter with the game tied 7–7, Oakland corner back Willie Brown stepped in front of a Bob Griese pass at midfield and scored. "We were in a zone defense and I dropped back and read the quarterback," Brown said. "I had no idea who was in back of me or to my left. And when I saw the ball coming directly at me, I intercepted it."

Oakland quarterback Daryle Lamonica added to Brown's tally in the fourth quarter. Lamonica settled in at his own 18-yard line, and with sturdy blocking he overcame a Miami blitz with a deep pass down the near sideline. Raider wide receiver Rod Sherman caught it on the fly over Dolphin cornerback Curtis Johnson, who was covering in tight and was not prepared for a long bomb. Sherman completed the 82-yard scoring play, with Johnson in fast pursuit. His sprint to the end zone gave the Raiders a 21–7 cushion. "I thought we would be going for just the first down, so I felt I was the secondary receiver," Sherman said of his touchdown. "But then I looked over my shoulder and saw that Daryle had chosen me. I was in a good position with my eye on the ball all the way while Johnson was turned around with his back to the ball and had to play catch up."

To their credit, the Dolphins did not give up. Griese led his team to one more touchdown, hitting Willie Richardson for a 7-yard score. The Dolphins were behind 21–14 when they had one last chance. Unfortunately for Griese and his teammates, they had to travel 87 yards on their final possession in order to force a tie. The Raiders defense did not allow them to come close, as Griese's final desperate passes fell incomplete.

"We never even considered losing," Griese said from the postgame locker room deep in the bowels of the Oakland Coliseum. "You're thinking about going on and on. Then, when we didn't get the first down that we had to have with 1:48 left, it hit me. It's all over. All gone."

Griese's lament would be repeated by the members of every team that loses a playoff game to the present day. Miami would return to the playoffs in the future, but Oakland was moving forward to play for the AFC championship.

The drama of the NFC divisional playoffs was also exciting. Detroit went to the Cotton Bowl to play Dallas in a game that many felt would be dominated by two outstanding defenses. In fact, no playoff contest throughout the decade featured as much stalwart defense as what was exhibited in this game. Dallas prevailed, 5–0, but the verdict was not determined until the game's final minute. Detroit wide receiver Earl McCullouch ran a mid-range post pattern as the last few seconds ticked off the clock. He was able to get open for a brief moment, and it appeared as if the Lions were going to produce a miracle touchdown. Detroit quarterback Bill Munson's desperation pass was too high, however, and McCullouch leaped for the ball and tipped it. Dallas safety Mel Renfro tipped the ball also, but managed to grab hold of it on the Cowboys' 15-yard line to preserve the victory. "If the ball had been a little bit lower to McCullouch we would have been in there," said depressed Detroit head coach Joe Schmidt.

Dallas kicker Mike Clark booted a 36-yard field goal in the first quarter. Both defenses took over from that point on. The Lions fumbled the ball twice in Cowboy territory, thwarting two promising drives. "Our defense played as well as they could have played it," admitted Coach Schmidt. "Of course, that's because we have a little more age on our defense. Our offense is inexperienced."

The Dallas offense finally started clicking in the fourth quarter, but also failed to score. Their 15-play, 77-yard drive ended unsuccessfully when, on fourth down from the 1-foot line, the Lions tackled Cowboy halfback Duane Thomas just inches short of paydirt. Thomas was upset by this missed opportunity, but he still managed to be the game's leading rusher with 135 yards on 30 carries. Fortunately for Dallas, their defense did not fret about their offense's struggles. They stayed focused on their mission. "We didn't worry at all when the offense didn't get a touchdown," said All-Pro defensive tackle Bob Lilly. "That just made the rest of the game a gamble. That's all right. We like it that way. Life's a gamble."

The Detroit offense was forced to gamble on their play selections in the fourth quarter. They were backed up against their goal line, and they tried desperately to move the ball via the pass. Quarterback Greg Landry was in the game for Munson at this point, but he failed to find an open receiver. Dallas defensive end George Andrie and defensive tackle Jethro Pugh teamed up to sack Landry in the end zone for the game-clinching safety. The victory was extremely satisfying to the Cowboys despite the low score. Dallas head coach Tom Landry reflected on what his defense just achieved from the postgame locker room. "This was the kind of game that it was a shame either club had to lose," said Landry. "You win playoff games with defense, and you saw the zero on the scoreboard today. In a game like this, the momentum can turn either way."

Momentum was a factor that both the San Francisco 49ers and the Minnesota Vikings had in abundance heading into their divisional playoff game the following day. Both teams had won their final three regular season games heading into the playoffs. Minnesota finished with an NFL-best 12–2 record, and the 49ers won their division with a 10–3–1 mark.

The game was played in eight-degree weather at Metropolitan Stadium in Bloomington, Minnesota. The grounds crew employed propane torches and large tarpaulins to keep the field from freezing before the opening kickoff. San Francisco quarterback John Brodie was not daunted by the frigid temperature, however. At least that's the way it looked to his teammates, and even to some of his opponents. San Francisco's equipment manager failed to pack Brodie's cold-weather gear with the rest of his uniform. Brodie accepted his situation as a simple case of mind over matter. Instead of the Vikings' players trying to unnerve their opponents by pretending that the frigid cold did not affect them, it was the 49er quarterback who gave the Vikings a taste of their own medicine. Brodie spent the whole contest wearing only his short-sleeved jersey, and proved to Minnesota that his MVP award was no fluke.

The biggest contrast in this game involved the ranking of the offenses and defenses of both teams. San Francisco came into the game with the league's best offense. Their 2,923 net yards gained was the most in the NFL in 1970. Minnesota came into the game with the league's best defense. The Vikings allowed less than nine points per game in 1970. Something would have to give. This would turn out to be a game of field position. Both teams struggled to maintain possession of the ball as the game progressed, and both made only rare visits inside their opponents' 20-yard line. San Francisco fumbled the ball five times, losing three. Minnesota fumbled three times, losing two. Minnesota quarterback Gary Cuozzo also threw two interceptions. The 49ers converted only six of 15 third downs, but the Vikings faired even worse, converting only two of 12 third downs.

The Purple Gang made an early statement when free safety Paul Krause returned a Ken Willard fumble 22 yards for a 7–0 Minnesota lead in the first quarter. Krause meandered through a maze of blockers and would-be tacklers to reach the end zone untouched. "We were especially unhappy to miss [tackling] Paul Krause [on that play]," said reserve 49ers special teams player Al Randolph.

Brodie was not deterred by this setback, however. He was determined to stick to his game plan. The veteran quarterback got rid of the ball quickly on flare passes to his running backs and short-range patterns to his wide receivers. As a result, he was sacked only once all day. He also helped Willard to get over his early fumble by handing the ball to him often, even when Minnesota's linemen plugged up all the running gaps. Willard would finish the game as the overall leading rusher with 85 yards on 27 carries. Brodie would strike for a score later in the first quarter. He found flanker Dick Witcher all alone on a post pattern for a 24-yard touchdown which tied the game.

"It was an out play," said Brodie. "We ran that two or three times before but I think [Vikings cornerback Ed] Sharockman got caught on the ice and couldn't get turned around."

San Francisco's lead grew in the second quarter. Minnesota halfback Clint Jones committed a costly fumble which resulted in a 40-yard Dick Gossett field goal. Both defenses took over from that point until late in the game. The hard hitting and dedicated stubborn play from both defenses resulted in continual changes of possession all throughout the third quarter. The 49ers would have to wait until the fourth quarter to increase their lead. Rookie 49ers cornerback Bruce Taylor had been playing tight coverage on Vikings receivers all game long, and managed to intercept a Cuozzo pass in the third quarter. It was in the area of special teams, however, where Taylor made his biggest plays. In the first quarter, Taylor's 30-yard punt return set up San Francisco's first score. In the fourth quarter, his 23-yard return of Tom McNeill's short punt set up the game-winning touchdown. John Brodie plunged into the end zone from the 1-yard line on a quarterback sneak to give the 49ers a commanding 17–7 lead with less than two minutes remaining.

Cuozzo frantically tried to close the gap, and he did so with a 24-yard scoring lob to wide receiver Gene Washington. Unfortunately for the Vikings, Washington's score came with but one second remaining on the clock. Bob Hoskins of the 49ers cradled Minnesota's ensuing onside kick, and the game was over. Credit for San Francisco's 17–14 victory went to the 49ers defense and special teams as much as to their offense. A key sack by linemen Cedrick Hardman and Tommy Hart caused Vikings kicker Fred Cox to come up two yards short on a field goal which would have tied the game early in the fourth quarter.

The 49ers offense did what it needed to do, however, to secure the win. Brodie's plan of ball control resulted in 71 offensive plays from scrimmage. The San Francisco offense overcame two early fumbles to retake the lead before halftime. Finally, Brodie's 16 completions resulted in 193 net passing yards and kept key drives alive in the second and fourth quarters. "The one thing that you can't do against Minnesota is to get second and third down with more than 10 yards to go," Brodie said as he thawed out in the postgame locker room. "Their pass rush is exceptional. But we managed to avoid this pretty well."

The new NFL in 1970 would now showcase the first AFC and NFC championship games. The Raiders would play the Colts in Baltimore in the AFC title game, and the Cowboys would play the 49ers in San Francisco in the NFC title game. All four teams had a firm desire to make amends for past failures. Both the Raiders and the Colts lost a previous Super Bowl game, and both desperately wanted another chance at the world championship. Coming up short in the play-offs was becoming a hallmark for the Cowboys, who lost to Green Bay in two consecutive NFL title games in 1966 and 1967, and who most recently lost in two consecutive divisional playoff games to Cleveland in 1968 and 1969. The 49ers had been in existence since 1946, but had yet to claim a championship. One of these four teams would realize their ultimate dream in 1970.

The AFC title game began with the time-honored tradition of the Baltimore Colts Marching Band, heralding the arrival of their team with their melodious theme song, "Let's Go You Baltimore Colts." This would eventually become one of the great days in Colts history, and the color and the pageantry of the afternoon would be vividly remembered for future decades by players and fans alike in Memorial Stadium.

Critics of the Baltimore club remembered that the Colts enjoyed a fairly easy schedule to reach the AFC championship. There was some merit to their assertions. The Colts played only two teams (Kansas City and Miami) who finished with winning records in 1970. Nevertheless, first-year head coach Don McCafferty knew that his team was playing better as the season neared its end. John Madden's team lost the final AFL title game the year before to the Chiefs, and thanks to a bevy of miracles in the 1970 regular season, were now poised to redeem themselves. The Raiders were led by quarterback Daryle Lamonica, the AFC's leading passer. Lamonica was the leader of the NFL's best offense, but neither he nor his passing targets had faced a defense as tough as Baltimore's. The Colts' defense had given up only 234 points in 1970, which was the second-best mark in the conference. Their defensive line, which featured the mammoth 6'7" end Bubba Smith, was getting stronger each week. It was that line which put constant pressure on Lamonica early in the championship game. Lamonica completed only one pass in the first quarter for a meager six yards.

In contrast, Colts quarterback Johnny Unitas did not seem to be intimidated by the pass rush of the Oakland defensive line. Unitas mixed his runs and passes well in the first half. A 16-yard field goal by Jim O'Brien gave the Colts a 3–0 lead. George Atkinson of the Raiders then fumbled an arching punt by David Lee early in the second quarter. Unitas wasted no time from there. He found flanker Eddie Hinton open on a deep crossing pattern, and hit him for a big gain down to the 2-yard line. Rookie halfback Norm Bulaich ran right behind fullback Tom Nowatzke on the following play, and scored as he burrowed in between tackle Sam Ball and guard Cornelius Johnson.

Now behind 10–0, the Raiders saw their situation go from bad to worse. The crowd at Memorial Stadium began yelling out their favorite warlike slogan, "Kill Bubba Kill! Kill Bubba Kill!" with bloodthirsty zeal. It reverberated from the upper deck down to the lower level, and it certainly fired up Bubba Smith and the Colts defense. The chant grew increasingly louder each time Oakland had the ball. Smith eventually satisfied the crowd by blasting into the Oakland backfield and driving his helmet into Lamonica's sternum. Lamonica hit the ground hard and suffered a bruised thigh muscle. The result of his injury meant that the best quarterback in the AFC would have to watch the rest of the game from the bench. The boisterous and overzealous Colts fans had accomplished their mission.

George Blanda was undaunted, however. He stepped in for Lamonica like he had done so many times before during the regular season. The 43-year-old Blanda was appearing in his eighth championship game, and it did not take him long to change the complexion of the game. Blanda kicked a 48-yard field goal just before halftime to get the Raiders on the scoreboard. The grey-haired signal caller then connected on several key passes early in the third quarter to tight end Raymond Chester, setback Hewritt Dixon, and wide receivers Warren Wells and Fred Biletnikoff. Blanda culminated the drive by beating a weak side blitz and hitting Biletnikoff for a 39-yard touchdown. The game was now tied, 10–10.

Unitas immediately answered Blanda's success with a scoring drive of his own. A go-ahead touchdown pass went right through the hands of receiver Roy Jefferson. Undaunted, the Colts settled for another O'Brien field goal, but Unitas was just warming up. The Colts offense continued to throw the ball against Oakland's bump-and-run defense. The offensive line gave Unitas extra time in the pocket, and he found both Hinton and Jefferson for big gains on successive third downs. Head coach Don McCafferty then decided to call for the old "Statue of Liberty" play from the Oakland 11-yard line. The play worked to perfection. Unitas dropped back as if to pass, then handed the pigskin off to Bulaich, who had reversed around behind the quarterback. Key blocks by center Bill Curry, fullback Tom Nowatzke, and Hinton gave Bulaich a wide alley to paydirt. Bulaich careened around the end, headed for the end zone flag, and scored. Baltimore now owned a more comfortable 20–10 lead.

The Raiders entered the fourth quarter with their backs to the wall, but that predicament was nothing new to them, having faced similar situations often during the regular season. Blanda came out throwing successfully against the Colts in the fourth quarter, but he was also aided by a 22-yard run on a draw play by halfback Charlie Smith. From the Baltimore 15-yard line, Blanda threw a dart to Wells, who caught it and was immediately hit by Colts defensive backs Rick Volk and Jim Duncan. Wells fumbled the ball, but the ball popped out of his grasp after he had already crossed the goal line. The Raiders had pulled back to within three points at 20–17.

Baltimore's defense would never let Oakland get any closer, however. They managed to intercept Blanda three times in the fourth quarter to end key Raider drives. Unitas put the icing on the cake when from his own 32-yard line, he lofted a third down pass to reserve flanker Ray Perkins, who beat cornerback Nemiah Wilson on a deep corner pattern. Perkins, who was playing with a broken toe, caught the ball at the Raiders' 45-yard line and outran Wilson down the sideline to the end zone. The Colts were 27–17 victors, and were headed to the Super Bowl.

Both Unitas and Blanda played well, but Unitas kept many Colt drives alive. He converted eight of 18 third down opportunities. His offense accounted for 70 plays from scrimmage to Oakland's 52. Unitas also passed for 237 net yards against a tough Oakland defense. Perhaps the most important statistic, however, was interceptions. Blanda had three. Unitas had none. "When their receivers turned around, Unitas had the ball there," said Raiders All-Pro cornerback Willie Brown. "He's just too good. You can mix defenses on him, but it doesn't help. He knows what you're doing. He just knows." Blanda echoed his teammates' remarks when discussing the Baltimore signal caller. "Statistics don't mean a thing," said Blanda. "It's the final score that counts. Unitas is still the best quarterback in football."

Across the tunnel in Baltimore's joyful locker room, Coach McCafferty knew his team was excelling at just the right time. "This was our best performance of the year," McCafferty said. "But I don't think we've reached our peak. Our best football is still ahead of us."

The Dallas Cowboys also knew that they had one of their best chances in years to make it to the Super Bowl. They matched up well with the San Francisco 49ers, easily outnumbering them in players with playoff experience. The Cowboys, however, did not take that advantage for granted. They were expected to claim a championship in each of the past two seasons but failed. This year would be different. They had put together a strong latter part of the season heading into the 1970 NFC title game. Head coach Tom Landry shrank his play book down to its basic elements after a 38–0 loss to St. Louis at mid-season. The change worked wonders, and the victories added up.

Following their upset win over Minnesota the week before, the San Francisco 49ers were not strangers to the Cowboys. The 49ers head coach Dick Nolan had spent several years as a Dallas assistant coach under Landry. Nolan employed a similar defense to that of the Cowboys (some would say an identical defense to that used by the Cowboys), and he had a sound knowledge of his opponent's strengths and weaknesses. The Dallas offense going into the game was not as prolific as the 49ers' offense, but the Dallas defense was playing better than ever. Adding to the excitement of this championship tilt was the fact that this would be the final game played in San Francisco's old Kezar Stadium. The 'Niners would be moving into the modern Candlestick Park in 1971. So sentimentality, familiarity, and a chance for a championship were all on the line in the first NFC title game.

San Francisco drew first blood with a 16-yard Bruce Gossett field goal. Gossett's kick was set up by a 42-yard bomb to wide receiver Gene Washington, who beat Dallas cornerback Herb Adderley deep down the sideline. Washington could not stay on his feet as he made the catch, however. Had he done so, he probably would have scored a touchdown.

A trend in Dallas strategy was becoming evident for all to see by the middle of the second quarter. The Cowboys running game was starting to have success on sweeps and trap runs against the 49ers defense. Particularly effective were delayed draw plays, where the Dallas offensive linemen drifted backwards and allowed the 49ers defensive line to rush forward and take themselves out of the running lanes. The Cowboys offensive line would then aid 49er linemen like Cedrick Hardman and Tommy Hart by shoving them forward and away from the ball carrier. Cowboys rookie halfback Duane Thomas provided the major rushing surge with the delayed draws, gaining 78 of his 143 yards in the first half on these plays. Other Dallas runners such as Claxton Welch and Walt Garrison also found success on the ground against the 49ers. Dallas placekicker Mike Clark tied the game at 3–3 just before halftime with a 21-yard field goal.

The contest was won by Dallas in the third quarter. Two key interceptions thrown by San Francisco quarterback John Brodie told the tale. On the first, Brodie hurried his pass in the face of an intensive rush by Dallas defensive end Larry Cole. Dallas middle linebacker Lee Roy Jordan intercepted the low pass and fell forward to the 49ers' 13-yard line. "I was trying to dump the ball," Brodie said. "I threw it toward the ground and Lee Roy Jordan make a heck of a play to pick it up."

Duane Thomas scored on the next play, taking quarterback Craig Morton's handoff, breaking two tackles from linebacker Skip Vanderbundt and cornerback Jimmie Johnson, and swept to the left corner of the end zone.

On the second Brodie miscue, again facing a strong Dallas rush, he lofted a long pass down the sideline which was intercepted by Cowboys cornerback Mel Renfro. The theft by Renfro was quite amazing due to the blinding sun that shone in his eyes at that end of the field. Dallas immediately went on a eight-play, 62-yard drive to what turned out to be the winning score. From the 49ers' 5-yard line, Thomas picked up a blitz by linebacker Frank Nunley, and Morton found fullback Walt Garrison alone in the corner of the end zone for a touchdown.

San Francisco pulled to within seven points with 2:18 left in the third quarter with a 26-yard scoring pass from Brodie to flanker Dick Witcher, who beat Adderley in the corner of the end zone. That was as close as the 49ers would get, however. Dallas shut down Nolan's offense the rest of the game, blitzing more than usual to make passing more difficult for Brodie. Dallas' impressive 17–10 win highlighted their desire to run the ball and shut down their opponents' running game. The Cowboys' running game racked up a total of 229 net yards, while the Dallas defense permitted only 61 yards on the ground. Tom Landry's team had finally won a title game and was headed for the Super Bowl.

"Lee Roy Jordan's interception was the real key play," admitted Landry from the cramped but victorious Dallas postgame locker room. "But the key to the game was our ability to run the football."

Super Bowl V on January 17, 1971, would match the Cowboys and the Colts, two teams with outstanding defenses and average offenses. The game on paper looked as if it would be a low-scoring affair. No one, however, could imagine beforehand that the game would turn out the way it did. The game featured several new factors which made it special, or at least, unique. First, the victor's trophy was renamed the Vince Lombardi Trophy following Lombardi's untimely death from cancer on September 3, 1970. Lombardi had become famous as the head coach of the legendary Green Bay Packers of the 1960s, winning five league titles in seven years, including the first two Super Bowls. The world championship trophy thus became a legacy of Lombardi's greatness and a tribute to the man that has lasted to this day. Next, this would be the first Super Bowl that would be played on artificial turf. The Poly-Turf field at Miami's Orange Bowl would be blamed—justly or not—for numerous slips, fumbles, and blunders throughout the game. Third, this would mark the first Super Bowl that went down to the wire, with a winner not determined until the game's final seconds. Finally, this would be the first and only Super Bowl where the Most Valuable Player would come from the losing team.

Another new element of sorts occurred in the pregame Dallas locker room. The Cowboys usually wore white jerseys at home, and by the yearly agreement between the two conferences, it was the Cowboys' turn to be designated as the home team in Super Bowl V. But the NFL in 1970 required that the home team of the title game wear dark jerseys. So the Cowboys wore their dark royal blue jerseys when they took on the white jersey-clad Colts on Super Sunday. Ironically, it was the Cowboys of 1978 who found a way through the rigidness of the league office to buck this trend/agreement when they wore their home white jerseys in Super Bowl XIII.

It did not take long for both the Cowboys and the Colts to begin making mistakes in Super Bowl V. In the first quarter, Baltimore quarterback Johnny Unitas attempted to connect with halfback Norm Bulaich, who was circling out of the backfield. Dallas linebacker Chuck Howley lunged for the ball, tipped it, then caught it as he fell to the turf. Howley quickly sprang up and returned the ball 22 yards to the Colts' 46-yard line. "That pass was an error in judgment on my part," Unitas said after the game. "There were two linebackers out there and I tried to force it between them. I should have lobbed it over the top."

Dallas could not move the ball from there, but they quickly got the ball back when Baltimore return specialist Ron Gardin fumbled Ron Widby's punt at the Colts' 9-yard line, and Dallas defensive back Cliff Harris made the recovery. Cowboys quarterback Craig Morton could not spur his offense to reach the end zone, however. Dallas had to settle for a 9-yard Mike Clark field goal.

Dallas head coach Tom Landry stubbornly stuck with his game plan of having Morton mix short passes with basic running plays. Morton did manage to register some success against the Colts defense with this plan late in the first quarter. All the same, the Dallas quarterback was still not shy about throwing the ball deep on occasion. An eight-play drive, highlighted by a 41-yard bomb to wide receiver Bob Hayes, placed the Dallas offense in close scoring range again. The Baltimore defense stiffened up once again, however, and the Cowboys were forced to settle for another Clark field goal—this one from 30 yards out—and a 6–0 lead as the second quarter began.

The Dallas defense had no problems with Unitas and the Colts offense throughout the first quarter. The Colts were unable to gain a single first down, and it seemed that everything they tried was unsuccessful. That would all change with one freak play in the second quarter. Unitas dropped back to pass from his own 25-yard line and threw down the middle for flanker Eddie Hinton. The pass was too high for Hinton, but he managed to tip the ball. Dallas cornerback Mel Renfro also leaped for the ball, but like Hinton, he too could only get a fingertip on it. Baltimore tight end John Mackey had been running behind Hinton in an attempt to clear the Dallas defensive backs away from the pass. Mackey could not believe his luck when the ball settled perfectly in his grasp. He turned around and found no one in front of him, and the nearest Cowboy more than 10 yards behind him. Mackey strode into the end zone to complete the 75-yard play. Up to that time, it was the longest touchdown pass in Super Bowl history.

There was some controversy regarding the touchdown. In 1970, no two offensive players could legally touch the ball consecutively. A defensive player would have to intervene between the two offensive players and make contact with the ball for it to be a legal play. Several Dallas players refused to believe that Renfro touched the ball, and they jumped up and down and verbally protested the resulting score to the referees. "I didn't think I touched it," Renfro said. "But then I saw the films on television. The ball did change direction so I must have touched it although I didn't realize it at the time." Close scrutiny of the postgame film proved that Renfro did, in fact, touch the ball, making the score legal. "Renfro's contact with the ball was minute," said Landry, "but it was contact. It couldn't have been closer."

The score tied the game, but rookie placekicker Jim O'Brien's extra point attempt was blocked. Reserve Dallas cornerback Mark Washington stormed in from the corner and dove into the flight of the ball as it left O'Brien's foot.

The fluke touchdown upset the Dallas defense, and they quickly took out their frustration on Unitas. The Baltimore quarterback was forced from his passing pocket midway through the second quarter, and scrambled to avoid the fierce pass rush. Cowboys linebacker Lee Roy Jordan met Unitas with a bone-jarring hit, dislodging the ball. Dallas defensive tackle Jethro Pugh fell on the loose pigskin at the Baltimore 28-yard line. Morton then immediately took the Cowboys offense in for their only touchdown of the game. A short run by Thomas and a quick swing pass to reserve running back Dan Reeves placed the ball at the Colts' 7-yard line. From there, Morton beat a Baltimore blitz and hit Thomas out in the flat (an open area between the tight end and the wide receiver). Thomas caught the pass and scored, giving Dallas a 13–6 lead.

Unitas tossed another interception on his next series, this one caught by Renfro. Dallas defensive end George Andrie steamrolled into Unitas on the play, drilling him in his rib cage. One of the greatest quarterbacks in NFL history was through for the day with a torn rib cartilage. Earl Morrall came in to replace Unitas, and he quickly found success throwing the ball. He hit

Eddie Hinton for a 26-yard gain on a crossing pattern over the middle against the Dallas prevent zone defense. He then found wide receiver Roy Jefferson all alone for a 21-yard gain. The Colts were now deep in Dallas territory as the first half was nearing its end. Three straight running attempts by Norm Bulaich from the Cowboys' 2-yard line gained absolutely nothing, however. McCafferty eschewed a field goal attempt on fourth down and instead decided to take one more shot at a touchdown. Morrall tried to cross up the Dallas defense with a pass to Colts tight end Tom Mitchell. The pass drifted over Mitchell's fingertips, however, and the first half ended with Dallas in the lead.

"You look back over your career," Morrall said in a 2012 interview, "and you remember certain plays that you would like to have over. That was one that I would like to have over. Tom [Mitchell] stepped on a linebacker's foot and lost his balance and stumbled all through his route. I tried to hold the ball as long as I could and lob it to him. He got close to the ball but he couldn't pull it in. You think about a play like that and wish that you had done better."

Dallas looked like they were going to have a better second half as the third quarter kickoff produced yet another Colts turnover. Baltimore returner Jim Duncan was plastered by Cliff Harris and Claxton Welch, fumbled the ball, and Richmond Flowers of the Cowboys recovered. Morton moved his offense all the way down to the Colts' 2-yard line. Baltimore's luck, however, changed again in a big way on second and goal. Thomas took a handoff from Morton, cutback against the grain, dove for the goal line, and fumbled. Another controversy now came in to play. Baltimore defensive lineman Billy Ray Smith immediately started yelling, "Colts ball! Colts ball!" The back judge, Ed Marion, ran to the rear of the pileup and immediately signaled that the Colts had recovered. As Marion was pointing in the Colts' direction, Dallas center Dave Manders arose with the ball in his hands. Marion ignored Manders, and his call stood. The Cowboys were livid.

"If one of their guys recovered the fumble," Landry questioned, "then why didn't he get up with the ball? Our center, Dave Manders, is the man who stood up with it." Ironically, two Colts players—Billy Ray Smith and Jim Duncan—insisted that they each recovered the ball. Neither of those two players was within two yards of Manders when he came up with the ball. Standing and watching the play from the sideline, Dallas defensive tackle Bob Lilly lamented afterward how much the fumble hurt his team. "That was the big play," Lilly said. "We'd have been ahead by two touchdowns and I know the Colts weren't going to score two touchdowns on us."

Earl Morrall used the turnover to ignite his offense. He led the Colts to their most time-consuming drive of the game, taking up 11 plays and over six minutes. Unfortunately for the Colts, the Dallas defense finally held. Jim O'Brien's 52-yard field goal attempt fell short, and another Baltimore scoring opportunity was gone.

It did not take long for Morrall to move the Colts to within scoring range again, however. Morrall hit fullback Tom Nowatzke with a 45-yard pass to the Cowboys' 15-yard line. Nowatzke circled out of the backfield unnoticed and was all alone down the middle of the field. Dallas cornerback Herb Adderley chased Nowatzke from clear across the other side of the field to make the tackle. "I threw it high and I was a little off-balance when I threw it," Morrall said. "I hung it up there a little bit and led Tom. If I had thrown it a little further he might have caught it further downfield and scored."

Morrall's success did not last for long, however. On the first play of the fourth quarter, he lofted a pass in the end zone for Bulaich, but Howley drifted in front of the intended target and made his second interception of the game. Howley tried to be modest after the game, but upon reflecting on his afternoon's performance, he admitted something which many onlookers agreed with. "I don't believe that I made a mistake in the game," Howley said.

The Colts experienced another mistake on their next offensive series, this one being one of the most memorable in Super Bowl history. Morrall had brought his team to the Dallas 30-yard line when a decision was made to try a flea-flicker play. Morrall turned and handed the ball off to reserve halfback Sam Havrilak, who was supposed to throw the ball back to Morrall. Unfortunately for Havrilak, Dallas defensive tackle Jethro Pugh got in between he and Morrall, thereby blocking Havrilak's passing lane. Undaunted, Havrilak eluded Pugh for a moment and fired the ball down-field. Both Mackey and Hinton were in the same area, and both could have caught the pass. Hinton grabbed the ball and just barely missed bumping into Mackey. Hinton then started to race toward the goal line when Dallas safety Cornell Green dove for him and stripped the ball from his grasp. No less than six different players scrambled for the bouncing pigskin, but to no avail. The ball rolled out of the end zone for a Dallas touchback.

"I was thinking six, six, six," said Hinton, believing that in a moment he would have a touch-down. "Then I felt something from behind, and it wasn't a tackle. All of a sudden the ball wasn't there anymore. I was down [and] crawling, then I couldn't crawl anymore. Renfro had hold of me."

The wacky play left Dallas in a firm hold of their 13–6 lead as the fourth quarter neared its midway point. The Baltimore defense realized that it would have to make some big plays if the Colts were going to have any chance at victory. They did just that when Morton, being pressured by Baltimore defensive end Roy Hilton, threw a pass in the flat to Walt Garrison, who was unable to jump high enough to catch it. Garrison tipped the ball, however, and Colts safety Rick Volk intercepted it, returning it 30 yards to the Dallas 3-yard line. "Roy Hilton did most of the work," Volk said. "He got a good rush, and he had his hands up, so Morton had to throw the ball higher

Baltimore Colts safety Rick Volk prepares to hit Dallas Cowboys halfback Duane Thomas in Super Bowl V, January 17, 1971, in Miami's Orange Bowl Stadium. The hard hitting among both teams in this game resulted in a total of 11 combined turnovers. The Colts defeated the Cowboys, 16–13, on a last-second 32-yard field goal by rookie Baltimore placekicker Jim O'Brien (AP Photo).

than he wanted. It bounced off Walt Garrison's fingers and fell right to me. All I had to do is run with it. I ran for my life."

Tom Nowatzke cashed in for the Colts a couple of plays later with a 2-yard touchdown blast. The scoring play was a typical off-tackle run, but Nowatzke made a key adjustment that made the play work. "All through the first half I was blocking for Norm [Bulaich] on strong-side runs," Nowatzke said, referring to runs on the side where the Colts' tight end lined up. "When we got the ball after Volk's interception, we decided to have Norm block for me on the short side. The first time we tried it I was too tight inside and ran into [tight end] Tom [Mitchell] and didn't gain anything. We then went back into the huddle and I told Earl to call the same play again. This time I ran it correctly and we scored."

Nowatzke's touchdown and O'Brien's ensuing extra point tied the game at 13–13. The last 7:35 of the game featured savage hitting from both teams. Both defenses were not letting up, and both offenses were not finding any measure of success. It would take another costly error with less than two minutes remaining to give one team a golden opportunity to claim victory. Morton rolled to his right on a third-and-25 play and threw for running back Dan Reeves. Just as Garrison earlier tipped one pass into the hands of a Colts defender, so too did Reeves. Baltimore middle linebacker Mike Curtis caught the tipped pass and wove his way to the Dallas 27-yard line. "I had a deep drop to help out the safety on the deep pattern," Curtis said. "When [safety] Jerry Logan hit Dan Reeves as he was catching the pass, the ball popped up, and I caught it. I almost squeezed the air out of [the ball]. My only thought was: Don't fumble."

A couple of quick runs placed the ball where Morrall wanted it for his kicker, Jim O'Brien. The rookie placekicker came through with the biggest kick of his life, a 32-yard boot with five seconds left, which won Super Bowl V for the Colts, 16–13. "I just told him to kick it like normal," Morrall said. "There was no wind. He hit it perfectly. He would have made it if he was 10 or 15 yards further back." Several years later, O'Brien recalled, "I never concentrated so hard in my life as I did those last few seconds in Miami. It was like there was no one in the stands, nobody watching at all. Everything ceased to exist except the football. It was the ultimate for me in concentration. I guess the situation must have created it."

Baltimore lineman Dan Sullivan concentrated also, as he lined up on the game-winning kick and fully expected a strong Dallas surge. To his surprise, however, the Cowboys had lined up most of their defenders on his opposite side where they thought the path of the kicked ball would go. "Dallas overloaded one side, and I had no one to block," Sullivan said. "I turned around to see if there was anyone I could block, but there wasn't. Years later my late father-in-law looked at a photo that I have of O'Brien's kick and asked me 'What the heck were you doing?' I told him that 'the Cowboys were afraid of me.'"

Jim O'Brien's game-winning kick and his subsequent leap for joy ended one of the most unique games in pro football history. *Sports Illustrated* columnist Tex Maule derided the game as "The Blunder Bowl" because of all of the mistakes, fumbles and interceptions. The *Washington Post* agreed and labeled the game "The Embarrassment Bowl." And author Bert Gambini described the game as "upsetting, and ultimately unsettling." True, there were 11 turnovers in the game (still a Super Bowl record), but many of them were caused by the hard hitting from both teams. Both defenses were two of the toughest that have ever played in a Super Bowl, and that toughness managed to shut down many sound offensive units throughout the year. Both the Colts offense and the Cowboys offense prided themselves by their ability to control the ball for long stretches of time, but the respective defenses virtually eliminated any long drives from occurring in Super Bowl V. Linebacker Chuck Howley of the Cowboys accepted the Most Valuable Player award for his outstanding play, but he easily would have traded that for a victory. The Colts had vindicated themselves from their loss in Super Bowl III. The Cowboys, however, would hear still more clamoring from the press that they "couldn't win the big one."

The Cowboys' frustration was epitomized by defensive tackle Bob Lilly, who after O'Brien's winning kick, flung his helmet 40 yards downfield. Players from both teams stopped what they were doing and watched Lilly's helmet fly through the air and bounce off the Poly-Turf. Lilly, in a state of failure and embarrassment, sheepishly jogged across the turf to reclaim his headgear.

Lilly's bitter feelings were not shared by the majority of pro football followers across the nation, however. Even though Super Bowl V was chock-filled with miscues, the fans had witnessed a truly great and competitive season. The sport had survived a merger and had increased immensely in popularity. Super Bowl V had proved that the pro game was reaching new levels of excitement, as the television revenues from the game were the highest in sports history up to that time. The 1970 season would be declared by hundreds of sports reporters as the benchmark of the NFL's modern era, thanks mostly to the merger between the AFL and the NFL. In actuality, the league's "modern era" was regarded by most pro football experts and historians as beginning in 1950, when three teams from the All-America Football Conference joined the NFL, thus increasing the amount of teams in the NFL to 13. Regardless of which opinion you believe, the 79,204 fans who streamed out of the Orange Bowl on the late afternoon of Super Bowl V may not have cared about the league's past. They had seen great football in 1970 to begin the decade, and they witnessed a Super Bowl with plenty of excitement, two great defenses, and a dramatic ending. Those fans, however, must also have had one big question left on their minds as they walked down the ramps of the Orange Bowl and onto the parking lots: What would 1971 do for an encore?

1971

The National Game

Pro football was increasingly becoming a beloved national game by 1971. Total combined paid attendance during the regular season topped 10 million for the first time in league history. The merger from the previous year had given the teams in smaller media markets in mid–America the chance to grow and prosper through the collective bargaining agreement, where all teams would share equally in television revenues. Television coverage from the three major networks resulted in high ratings on a regular basis among viewers from both coasts and all in between. A total of 761,713 spectators entered NFL stadiums during the third week of the 1971 season to set a new league record. Fans across the nation were recognizing and cheering for popular players on every team and avidly following their exploits every week. *Football Digest* magazine began its publication history, offering the American populace monthly stories on players and coaches on each of the league's 26 teams. Ed Sabol and his cinematically-artistic son Steve were promoting the game in Hollywood fashion with their NFL Films corporation. The Sabols presented the highlights of all the games in new and theatrical ways, including dramatic music, close-up sidelines shots, on-field microphones, and stirring narration from the likes of John Facenda, Jack Whitaker, and William Woodson (among others). Facenda's voice-overs sounded so dramatic, that combined with the stimulating music and the visual football action from the films, one might think that the future of the earth was in jeopardy. Concerted with the creativity element of NFL Films, was the down-to-basics football knowledge that Mr. Sabol's editors possessed. "I don't think anybody knows as much about football as my people," said Ed Sabol in the early 1970s. "We see more than anyone in the world. A coach or player may see one game a week, but we see fourteen professional games every week."

Pro football was now taking larger steps in 1971 toward overtaking pro baseball in spectator popularity. The NFL was stepping out into a promising future.

The stages upon which the game was played were also becoming more futuristically modern. It was an era of a new colossus, as five teams moved into new stadiums in 1971. Those teams were the Chicago Bears, the Philadelphia Eagles, the San Francisco 49ers, the New England Patriots, and the defending NFC champion Dallas Cowboys. Artificial turf was the chosen surface for each of these new venues, and each of the new stadiums had unique architecture and special features. Additional seating capacities in the new arenas benefitted the teams in financial ways by producing higher revenue from the increased numbers of ticket sales.

The Bears' new stadium was actually an old stadium. Soldier Field was built in the 1920s (at that time it was known as Municipal Grant Park Stadium) and held its first event in 1924. The Bears of decades past even played there from time to time, but for many years played their home games at Wrigley Field (until the end of the 1970 season). Soldier Field was designed to be a memorial to Chicago's sons who died in World War I. The people of the city would in later years dedicate the stadium to be a memorial for all of Chicago's soldiers and sailors in all subsequent wars. Many hundreds of events were held at Soldier Field since the 1920s, including military band concerts, pageants, processions, track and field events, bicycle races, horse shows, and perhaps the most popular, the College All-Star Game.

Soldier Field's Classic Revival architecture was striking. Horseshoe-shaped stands encircled the field, with a large, opened end. That end was filled in 1971 with a set of bleachers which could be moved forward or backward to allow for higher attendance and better sight-lines for the fans. The most impressive features of the stadium, however, were the concrete Doric colonnades above the east and west seats. Each consisted of two rows of 32 columns, towering just over 32 feet high. The colonnades at Soldier Field resembled the long row of colonnades of the Parthenon in Rome, and were commemorative of the Roman Empire's spectacle of the gladiators who fought in the ancient Coliseum, within the shadows of those columns.

The Dallas Cowboys were primed to build their own football empire by 1971, and they wanted to build a stadium worthy of that status. They had to wait until it was finished being built before they could move into it at mid-season. It was called Texas Stadium, and nothing like it had ever been seen before in pro football. Texas Stadium featured a Tartan Turf playing surface and a partial dome which had a rectangular hole in it over the playing field. Any rain that fell would thus only descend on the players, not on the fans. The stadium was a football-only stadium, meaning that it could not be used for baseball like all of the multi-purpose stadiums seen across the league. It had a giant scoreboard above the lower tier of seats at one end zone, and a large club facility across the field looking down at the other end zone. The Stadium Club—as it was called— was used for banquet dining and meetings, special club events, and even for future cheerleader tryouts. Texas Stadium represented one of the first and finest of the league's luxury stadiums. It had modern and futuristic private boxes for wealthy fans who wanted to enjoy the games in comfort. Common amenities of those boxes included leather upholstered and cushioned seats, plush carpeting, Sony television sets so they could watch instant replays, and ritzy food choices like prime rib and filet mignon.

The reason why the Cowboys decided to leave a hole in the roof was a matter of opinion. Reserve Dallas linebacker D.D. Lewis coined the popular explanation for the hole, "so that God could watch his favorite team play on Sundays." Another reason might have been due to the Dallas front office's time-honored tradition of saving money. Filling in the hole and covering the whole field would have required massive air conditioning costs. Dallas owner Clint Murchison reasoned, "We could easily have closed up the hole in our roof, but I don't like watching football in the Astrodome. Our fans are protected but can still see the sky."

One of the Cowboys' rivals in the NFC East was the Philadelphia Eagles. Their new stadium, called Veterans Stadium or "The Vet" for short, was built to honor all American veterans. The Eagles shared their new multi-purpose stadium with the Philadelphia Phillies baseball team. Like all "cookie-cutter" stadiums, the Vet was a bowl-like structure which had two large seating levels. The Vet, however, would become famous—or infamous—for its playing surface. Players across the league throughout the decade would have plenty of reasons to hate Veterans Stadium's Astro-Turf field. Numerous lumps and creases in the surface would be blamed for dozens of injuries. "Veterans Stadium aroused vile passions almost from the day it opened," said ESPN NFL analyst Sal Paolantonio. "You could twist an ankle or a knee too easily on that horrid turf."

Veterans Stadium was not the only venue which had issues with its playing surface. Schaefer Stadium did also, but for different reasons. Schaefer Stadium was built specifically for the Patriots, who changed their name from the Boston Patriots to the New England Patriots in 1971 to better reflect the location of their new stadium and the loyalties of their fans all across the New England states. Schaefer Stadium was located in Foxboro, Massachusetts, and it was probably one of the most basic pre-fabricated stadiums ever built, with aluminum benches in many of the less-expensive sections. Schaefer Stadium was named after the beer that was sold in the stands, and those stands ran parallel to the sidelines and included two smaller sections skirting the end zones. The sidelines represented the most unique aspect of this stadium. The field's Poly-Turf surface was flanked along the length of its edges by a small section of natural grass. The Patriots were under severe time restrictions to complete the new stadium before the start of the 1971 season. They also had to adhere to a strict $7 million budget. To save funds, the management decided to keep costs low by laying Poly-Turf only on the playing field, and keeping natural grass on the sidelines and behind the end zones. This decision required extra work to take care of the grass, however, and by 1977, the entire field was finally covered completely in artificial turf.

The San Francisco 49ers moved into Candlestick Park in 1971, another multi-sports stadium that they shared with the San Francisco Giants baseball team. The stadium was an oval shape ... sort of. It looked like the architect wanted it at first to have a rectangular shape, but then either changed his mind or just felt that a more circular shape at opposite ends would best suit the overall visibility of the field for the fans. One factor that definitely did not suit the teams was the playing surface. Like Veterans Stadium, Candlestick Park had one of the hardest and slickest artificial surfaces in the NFL. It was not uncommon to see many players lose their footing as they tried to run or make sharp cuts downfield. A study of football stadiums in the mid–1970s by *Football Digest* magazine listed Candlestick Park as one of the two worst venues in the league (along with New York's Shea Stadium).

"Shea is a hard place to play," said New York Jets center Wayne Mulligan, "but Candlestick Park is worse. Not only do you get those winds, which are the worst in the league, but the field is made of AstroTurf. Everybody thinks that artificial surfaces look so nice and that everybody should love them. Well, maybe everybody does who isn't a player. But most of the guys on our team, and I'm sure most of the guys in the league, would much rather play on grass any day of the week instead of AstroTurf or any other artificial surface."

San Francisco quarterback John Brodie concurred with Mulligan. "I hated that stuff at Candlestick," Brodie admitted after his playing days were over. "It wasn't suitable to play on and all the players felt that way."

But playing on any surface in any stadium was the goal of rookies and younger players, many of whom dotted team rosters in 1971. The winds of change were evident as a few previously also-ran teams were suddenly winning games and challenging for the playoffs, thanks in large part to the performances of those younger players. Various individual records were broken and set by young performers in 1971, and they were quickly becoming standouts on their teams. Many head coaches put key rookies in starting positions, which had rarely been the norm prior to the 1970s. Those rookies would soon become household names in the NFL.

John Brockington was one such rookie. He came out of Ohio State University and immediately gave the Green Bay Packers a strong running game. Brockington ran for 1,105 yards in 1971, enough for the top rushing mark in the NFC. He was the first rookie to eclipse the 1,000-yard mark in NFL history, and he commenced a display of his speed and power in the second week of the season against the Denver Broncos. On one play in the second quarter, the burly runner burst through the line of scrimmage untouched and outran the Denver defensive secondary for a 52-yard touchdown in a 34–13 Packers victory. He totaled four games of over 100 yards rushing in 1971, and his 5.1 yards per game average was the highest mark in the NFC among running backs with at least 100 carries. Brockington's first season in the pros was good enough for him to be named All-Pro and win the Rookie of the Year award in the NFC. He was also good enough to earn the praise of his blockers.

"To tackle John a defensive lineman has to have complete control of his body," said Packers center Ken Bowman. "We just have to occupy the linemen because John is going to bust any arm tackles." Green Bay offensive tackle Dick Himes added, "Brock runs harder than any back I've ever blocked for." Fellow offensive guard Bill Leuck called Brockington "as hard a running back as I've seen. An arm tackle won't slow him down, and the speed he has at his size is amazing."

"Coming through the line, I try to accelerate as quickly as possible," said the bullish Brockington, whose running style, despite his modesty, often resembled a charging rhinoceros. "The holes close very fast in this league. I'm not looking to run over people unless I have to. You can't last long in this league if you play like that. I never dreamed something like this [gaining 1,000 yards in his rookie season] would happen. It was really a beautiful feeling."

Another young running back in Los Angeles had his greatest season ever. Willie Ellison ran for 1,000 yards in 1971, which was almost 700 yards better than his rushing total from the year before. Included in his best year was a single-game league record of 247 yards rushing against New Orleans on December 5. Ellison began his epic afternoon in the sun-splattered Los Angeles Memorial Coliseum by taking a first quarter pitchout on a halfback sweep from his 20-yard line. The Rams offensive line blew open a big hole, and Ellison was off to the races. Saints defensive back Hugo Hollas had the angle on Ellison at the New Orleans 25-yard line, but he overran Ellison and failed to bring him down. Ellison jaunted into the end zone for his only touchdown of the game, but he continued to run the pitchout play to perfection throughout the day. His second-longest run was a 48-yard race to his left off of a similar pitchout in the second quarter. Ellison set the new record on 26 carries as the Rams won, 45–28.

"Just about everybody told me at halftime that I would get the record," Ellison said. "The line did a tremendous job of blocking and Gabriel did a great job of selecting plays against the New Orleans defense. Everything was working for us. We were gaining inside, outside, on quick hitters and sweeps. It seemed like I just kept on running, that I wasn't going down."

Two more running backs in Miami—Larry Csonka and Jim Kiick—became roommates on the road and folk heroes in the public eye. Csonka and Kiick donned western garb like Paul Newman and Robert Redford did in the movies, rode a couple of horses down a boulevard in town, and posed for the cameras as the NFL's version of Butch Cassidy and the Sundance Kid. Their play on the football field did nothing to tarnish their colorful adaptations of those cinematic icons. The Dolphins relied on the running game as their main weapon, and both Csonka and Kiick turned in splendid performances in 1971. Csonka was the prototypical power runner, big and bruising with his legs pumping through the line of scrimmage like iron pistons. "My role is to make the power running game work," explained Csonka. "A lot of plays I run are momentum plays. They are not designed for long gains. If you make four or five yards, everyone is happy."

Kiick was happy showing off a different game than Csonka, and earned accolades with his multi-purpose abilities. Dolphins head coach Don Shula used Kiick on short-yardage situations, third-down passing situations, and as a blocker for Csonka. By season's end, Csonka would run for 1,051 yards, and Kiick would tally 738 more. Miami led the league in overall team rushing in 1971.

"Larry and I complement each other," said Kiick after the season. "I know where Larry is going to be and how I should block for him." The yardage gained and the teamwork exhibited by Butch and Sundance were a couple of tangible results, stemming from the camaraderie on the team, as the Dolphins surged to the playoffs. "We made an agreement in our rookie year that we'd block for each other," Csonka recalled. "We could see that one's accomplishment is the other's gain. We started doing this even before we became good friends."

It did not take long for Heisman Trophy winner Jim Plunkett to make friends in New England. The first round draft pick brought respectability to a Patriots club which had won only twice in 1970. Plunkett threw for 2,158 yards and 19 touchdowns in 1971, and spurred his young team to impressive upset victories over Oakland, Miami, and defending Super Bowl champion Baltimore. In 1971, Plunkett would also become the first quarterback in the modern era of pro football to play every down of every offensive series for his team. He was justly named the AFC Rookie of the Year for his exploits.

"Jim Plunkett ... has what it takes to be an NFL star," said John Ralston, Plunkett's head coach at Stanford University, "and he has the will. I don't think Jim Plunkett knows how good he is. You've got to keep reminding him."

To remind the public of all of the headline-makers of 1971, however, one also has to look at the other side of the ball. Pro football's defenses did not sit idly by as the offenses produced stand-out players. Many exemplary defensive players were also being praised by the media for their ability to squelch opposing passing attacks. Defensive coaches around the league were perfecting their zone coverages, and many of these short and deep coverages were reducing their opponent's passing statistics. Zone coverages were being used for linebackers, one or both safeties, or a combination of both on passing plays. Given the common name of "packages," these coverages relied on coordination among all defensive players on the field. Some zone coverages worked in coordination with blitzes by linebackers. Others used some defenders to stay in man-to-man coverage while the rest in the defensive backfield stayed in a zone coverage. A coverage like "five short, two deep" would refer to the two safeties dropping back deep, while three linebackers and two cornerbacks would maintain areas closer to the line of scrimmage. Another coverage referred to as "zone strong, man weak," would call for a zone coverage on the strong side of the field (where the tight end would line up) and a man-for-man coverage on the weak side of the field. The tendency for many offenses was to run or throw to their strong side, and thus the increased number of defenders would be needed to go to that area and stop the play. Perhaps the most widely used zone coverage was the rotating zone, a strategy where safeties and cornerbacks would flow or "rotate" toward a specific area of the field, all the while maintaining their vision on the offense's point of attack. By alternating the different zones and man-to-man coverages, and weak side and strong side coverages on every down, opposing offenses were finding it increasingly difficult to throw the football. It is important to note that zone defenses did not originate in the 1970s, but they were perfected to a large degree during the decade. As it was with all other successful strategies, coaches all around the league would intentionally copy the strategical breakthroughs of their contemporaries.

"The zones have made it tougher," said Detroit wide receiver Ron Jessie. "You can put a thousand moves on a guy and if you're not a threat to his zone, he won't pay any attention to you. The zone has put a real crimp in passing attacks."

Baltimore's zone defense was one of the best in modern NFL history in 1971. They permitted only nine touchdown passes in the regular season. They also gave up only 140 points, which ranked as tops among AFC defenses. Colts defensive end Bubba Smith, outside linebacker Ted Hendricks, and safety Rick Volk each made the All-Pro team in 1971, and safety Jerry Logan made the All-Conference team. Smith and Logan each made the Pro Bowl. The Baltimore zone defense relied on each player to make adjustments to the direction of the offense as the play developed. One of the best at doing this was Hendricks, one of the most lanky and aggressive outside linebackers in the business.

"I treat the zone more like a man-to-man," said Hendricks. "I get upset at someone who just sits in the middle of his zone and waits for something to happen. When I get back there, I try to look around and see where the action is. A lot of times, if you move with the quarterback's eyes, you'll see what's coming. When I see where the receiver is, I get over to him. What's the use of waiting until he makes the catch?"

Perhaps no other middle linebacker in the league was a better fit for his defense than Mike Curtis was for the Colts. Curtis was a defensive hero in Baltimore's drive toward Super Bowl V the previous year, and his ferocious and free-ranging style of play was obvious to any offense which opposed him. "We've got to destroy people," said a passionate Curtis after a 24–0 win over Buffalo late in the season. "We've got to intimidate them, [and] make them respect us."

Ample proof of defensive intimidation and dominance in 1971 came from a zone defense's ability to shut down the long bomb. Former New York Giant great Frank Gifford asked a *Monday Night Football* audience at mid-season, "How often do you see the long bomb anymore, with a receiver working individually against a cornerback? Not very often," was his own reply. The lack of long bombs was undeniable proof that defenses were controlling many of the games. Overall team statistics and points given up in 1971 were also unmistakable outcomes, as many offenses struggled to crack their opponent's end zones. There were 14 shutout games during the regular season in 1971, and both Baltimore and Minnesota each accounted for three of them. The four best defensive teams in the NFC (Dallas, Washington, Minnesota and San Francisco) and the three best defensive teams in the AFC (Miami, Baltimore and Kansas City) all made the playoffs. Miami, Baltimore, Washington and Minnesota each gave up less than 200 points, which kept their teams competitive throughout the season. The Vikings defense created 45 turnovers in 1971, caused primarily by their penchant for hard hitting and their practice of surrounding the ball carrier in the event of a fumble. Minnesota gave up a league-low 139 points. Washington's pass defense intercepted a league-high 29 passes, and five different Redskin defenders each returned one of those interceptions for scores.

Several exemplary individual efforts on the defensive side of the line of scrimmage were exhibited throughout the year. Ken Houston, a defensive back for the Houston Oilers, established a league record in 1971 by scoring five touchdowns, four of which came on interceptions. In the final game of the regular season against the visiting San Diego Chargers, Houston returned two John Hadl passes for touchdowns, which tied another league record. "I wanted the record that day," Houston later recalled. "I went after it in that game. And because we used a zone defense for the first time on an Oiler team, I was up on the line of scrimmage for both passes. As a safety-man, I wouldn't have been there in a man-for-man defense, and might not have had either touchdown."

Bill Bradley, a safety with the Philadelphia Eagles, was also skillful in intercepting passes. Bradley led the league in thefts with 11. He also earned All-Pro and Pro Bowl status, and was equally as dangerous as a punt returner and as a spare punter. What makes Bradley's interception total so impressive, however, was the fact that the Eagles did not possess a very good pass rush. "Super Bill" as he was known, had to rely on his own instinct, quickness, and coverage abilities to gauge where opposing quarterbacks were targeting their throws. "It's gratifying personally," said Bradley about being named All-Pro near the end of the season, "but our team is still gonna finish below .500. I'm not too happy about that. I don't do anything special. I'm just me. I do what comes naturally."

Undoubtedly the most impressive defensive performance of 1971, however, was turned in by Alan Page of the Minnesota Vikings. Page, a five-year defensive tackle from Notre Dame, became the first defensive lineman ever to be named the league's Most Valuable Player. Page was a constant target for double teams, but his quickness off the snap of the ball helped him to brush past many would-be blockers. Page was credited with 109 solo tackles, including 10 quarterback sacks. Page's best game occurred against the visiting Detroit Lions on December 11. In that game, Page was called for unnecessary roughness and roughing the passer on consecutive plays in the second quarter. He took out his frustration on Lions quarterback Greg Landry, and sacked him on the third play for a 9-yard loss. Two plays later, Page tackled Detroit running back Altie Taylor for a 4-yard loss. Later in the game, Page blocked a Herman Weaver punt which resulted in a safety. The Vikings triumphed over the Lions for the eighth straight time, 29–10.

"Alan was just showing some of his potential," said Vikings head coach Bud Grant of Page's efforts. "It shows you what he's capable of. Sometimes his power is frightening. He has remarkable reaction at the snap. He gets into the blocker before the man can set up properly. He's the personification of a great football player who sees the opportunity to make a big play, then has the ability to carry through and make it."

While new players were making headlines, the league also saw many new head coaches on the sidelines. Ed Khayat of Philadelphia, Nick Skorich of Cleveland, Dan Devine of Green Bay, Tommy Prothro of Los Angeles, Bob Hollway of St. Louis, George Allen of Washington, and Harland Svare of San Diego all became pro head coaches in 1971. Most of the new coaches experienced only moderate success in their initial campaigns. Prothro's Rams enjoyed a winning season, however, accumulating an 8–5–1 record. Prothro's hiring was an obvious example of the changes that were fomenting in the NFL among the team owners. Several owners who were mired in failure over a stretch of years were willing to break from the norm in order to turn their fortunes around. Prothro made his mark as a college coach at UCLA, and in 1971, most new head coaches did not come from the college ranks. Once hired, he immediately breathed new life into the Rams by applying a more wide open style of offense to create excitement. Prothro was willing to try any new strategy to advance the ball. The Rams utilized flanker reverses and flea-flickers with uncommon regularity, as a variety of ball carriers got their chance to make big plays. Prothro even flip-flopped his offensive guards and tackles from one side to another depending upon the Rams' position on the field and the play to be run. This move helped to create confusion for his opponents, and it opened the way for some big yardage gains throughout the season. The growing excitement in the City of Angels resulted in a full (or mostly full) Los Angeles Memorial Coliseum, with fans that ranged from the curious to the loyal diehards. The two most successful new coaches in 1971, however, were George Allen and Nick Skorich. Allen's club rebounded from a miserable 1970 season and made the playoffs as a wild card team in 1971. Skorich's team also bettered their record from the previous season and also found themselves in the 1971 postseason.

Allen's philosophy "The future is now" translated into his penchant for making numerous trades for older, experienced players to improve his team. Allen gave up many of his draft picks for those trades. This was considered by many in the front office and coaching ranks to be suicidal. But his decision to do so produced immediate positive results, igniting the team to their first playoff berth in 26 years. No less than six former Rams donned Redskin jerseys in 1971, including linebackers Jack Pardee and Myron Pottios, defensive back Richie Petitbon, and defensive tackle Diron Talbert. Allen also brought in wide receiver Roy Jefferson from the Colts, and quarterbacks Billy Kilmer from the Saints and Sam Wyche from the Bengals. Allen described Kilmer as a leader who had "a burning desire to win." The experience and hunger of Coach Allen's players helped Washington to a 9–4–1 record. Included in the Redskins' victory ledger were key wins over each of their NFC East rivals, as well as a big 38–24 triumph over the familiar Los Angeles Rams in the second-to-last week of the regular season. A banner at one end of the Los Angeles Memorial Coliseum mockingly read, "The Redskins Have Arthritis." Allen's team sure didn't play like it, though, with two touchdown bombs coming from Kilmer against the Rams' fierce pass rush.

"This is a great, great victory," said Allen after the Rams game. "It's the best win of our lives.

It's so rewarding." Allen's players were more than happy to yell out a cheer after each triumph, and to cheer on their head coach. "George is the most complete coach I've ever seen," said Billy Kilmer. "He always knows what the offense is doing. He's always thinking about football. He doesn't do anything else. He's in command of all the little details and he's always one step in front of you."

The Browns regained the one step that they needed to redeem themselves from a dismal 1970 season, earning a 9–5 record in 1971. Cleveland's mark was good enough to win the AFC Central title. Included in their victory total were big wins over Baltimore and Washington, and a two-game sweep of their arch-rivals, the Cincinnati Bengals. Nick Skorich's club won its final five regular season games to destroy their divisional competition. Skorich was a no-nonsense type of leader who did not mince words. His hardened approach to the game stiffened the resolve of his team as the season wore on. Perhaps the biggest reason for Cleveland's success, however, was their ability to fight through numerous injuries, particularly on the offensive side of the ball. Quarterback Bill Nelsen had one of his best seasons despite his nagging shoulder and his surgically-repaired knees. Nelsen threw for 2,319 yards. Halfback Leroy Kelly scored 10 touchdowns, even though he was the common target for many bone-jarring hits. In the end, Skorich's team won their division by three games over the next closest competition, the Pittsburgh Steelers.

The Detroit Lions endured a 1971 season that was very similar to the season before. They were a competitive team, and they even managed to lead the NFC in overall rushing with 2,376 yards. But unfortunately for the team from Motown, they were stuck in the same division as the dominant Minnesota Vikings. Detroit did have two outstanding performers on offense though. One was quarterback Greg Landry, who established the NFL rushing record for quarterbacks in 1971 with 530 yards. The other was Heisman Trophy–winning running back Steve Owens, who earned his only 1,000-yard rushing season in 1971 with 1,035 yards on 246 carries (a 4.2 yard average). Owens' longest run of the season was only for 23 yards, a testament to his bullish style of up-the-gut running. The Lions relied on Owens' performance throughout the season, as they were forced to deal with an unexpected tragedy on October 24 in a game against the visiting Chicago Bears. Detroit wide receiver Chuck Hughes collapsed on the field and died that day of a heart attack. The Lions would wear a black armband on their jerseys for the remainder of the season in honor of their fallen teammate, but his death left a pall on the team that never seemed far from their minds. Detroit lost their final three games and finished the 1971 season with a mediocre 7–6–1 record. "We were strong for a while," said Detroit head coach Joe Schmidt," but we just couldn't keep surging after losing Chuck. We gave it our best though."

As defending world champions, the Baltimore Colts knew that they would be the recipient of the best efforts from their opponents in 1971. Head coach Don McCafferty kept his team from becoming complacent, however, and the leadership on the field kept the team hungry for another shot at the Super Bowl. Quarterback Johnny Unitas split time with Earl Morrall for much of the season. Neither of these two signal callers had outstanding seasons, but the Colts did not rely on throwing the ball that much anyway. Running backs Tom Matte and Norm Bulaich were both healthy through most of 1971, and they teamed up with rookies Don Nottingham and Don McCauley (among others) to contribute to a team total of 2,149 yards on the ground. The Baltimore defense lost defensive tackle Billy Ray Smith to retirement, but the rest of the defense was better than ever. Don McCafferty's team appeared to be shoo-ins for repeating as AFC East champions.

The Colts' biggest problem in 1971 may have been that the Dolphins were also in their division. Miami head coach Don Shula was not satisfied by just making the playoffs in 1970. He wanted more, and so did his team. Shula ran what many experts considered to be the toughest summer training camp in the NFL. The sweltering heat and humidity of a south Florida summer took its best shot at the Dolphins, but their conditioning and strength improved. The rigors of training camp gave Miami the impetus to win several games in the fourth quarter, when the toughness of a player's mind and the will of his body often separates winners from losers. Quarterback Bob Griese took advantage of the experience that he had accumulated in 1970 by turning in an even more impressive season in 1971. Griese led the AFC in passing, throwing for 2,089 yards and 19 touchdowns. The young quarterback only threw nine interceptions, a mark that proved his increased maturity in a strong offensive system. Catching Griese's passes were the same set of exceptional players as the season before. Paul Warfield was once again the superstar wide receiver, catching 43 balls for 996 yards and 11 touchdowns. His 23.2 yards-per-catch average was the highest mark among starting receivers in the AFC. Jim Kiick caught 40 passes circling out of the backfield, and flanker Howard Twilley grabbed 23 more. Powered by their dynamic rushing attack, the Dolphins offense was quickly becoming one of the most formidable in the league. They would split their home and away regular season series with the Colts, but they would eventually meet them again in the postseason.

Just as the Baltimore-Miami rivalry was heating up, so too were a couple of rivalries in the NFC. The San Francisco 49ers surprised many teams in 1970 with their rise to a division title, and they figured that the Los Angeles Rams were in no condition to make a comeback in 1971. The Rams lost a lot of experienced players in the George Allen purging, and their new coach, Tommy Prothro, was new to the pro game. But the Rams were in no mood to place a crown on the 49ers just yet. Prothro's team defeated San Francisco twice in 1971, and were inspired by Willie Ellison's superb season and by the strong play from quarterback Roman Gabriel. The Rams scored 313 points, the third-highest mark in the NFC, and 13 points more than the 49ers.

The Rams' victories over the 49ers should never have happened. San Francisco was in control in both games, but made key mistakes which allowed the Rams to win both contests. Prothro's boys won the first game in San Francisco on October 10 by a score of 20–13. Several big plays gave the Rams the lead and ultimately, the victory. Defensive back Gene Howard intercepted one pass near his own goal line to thwart a promising San Francisco drive, and later returned a fumble four yards for a touchdown and a 10–3 advantage in the third quarter. Rams halfback Larry Smith then ran 64 yards on an off-tackle play for the game-winning score in the fourth quarter. "No gimmicks on that one," said Prothro. "It was a blackboard play." Fellow running back Les Josephson also contributed a 57-yard run to put Los Angeles in scoring position. The Rams' 219 yards rushing went unnoticed, however, because their passing attack reached dismal and noteworthy lows. Quarterbacks Jerry Rhome and Roman Gabriel could combine for only two completions in 12 attempts for a pitiful 13 total yards. San Francisco's pass defense was one of the best in the league, and Prothro knew that if his team was to challenge for the division title, they would have to improve their passing game. Fortunately for Prothro and his team, the 49ers committed various crucial turnovers and penalties, which paved the way for the Rams' victory.

The second game between the two teams on November 21 in Los Angeles featured more throwing on the part of both teams. Gabriel did not split time with Rhome in this game, and threw for 69 yards and a 13-yard touchdown to receiver Jack Snow on an out pattern in the corner of the end zone. San Francisco's John Brodie passed for 297 yards, but his success was tempered, however, by his four interceptions. Once again, Rams defensive back Gene Howard did his share of damage, snaring three of Brodie's passes. The most costly Brodie interception, however, occurred in the second quarter. Rams cornerback Jim Nettles stepped in front of 49ers wide receiver Dick Witcher, picked off Brodie's pass, and raced down the sideline to the end zone with a 29-yard score to propel Los Angeles to victory, 17–6.

"I had no business throwing that pass," said Brodie. "I couldn't even see Dick [Witcher] on the pattern, because of the rush but I couldn't hold it back."

John Brodie was not deterred by those losses, however. The San Francisco quarterback did not repeat his MVP performance from the previous year, but he did throw for 2,642 yards and 18 scores. Brodie also relied on one of the strongest running games in the NFL. Ken Willard and Vic Washington each ran for over 800 yards, and Washington also added 317 more yards as a pass receiver. The 49ers' main strength, however, was their defense, a unit which gave up only 216 points during the regular season. San Francisco's defense had few weaknesses, and four of their players made the Pro Bowl. Defensive end Cedrick Hardman ranked as one of the best young players at his position in the league. Hardman would use his speed to become one of the great unheralded pass rushers in NFL history.

"You can't out-run him," said 49ers assistant coach Paul Wiggin of Hardman. "Great pass rushers are born, not made. Their speed and talent is God-given. In our concept of defense, there is no place for a one-man show. This puts a restriction on guys who want to blow in on every play. But Cedrick has taken to our concept very well. Every man has a responsibility, and he must fulfill that responsibility."

The responsibility to repeat as conference champions fell for the first time to the Dallas Cowboys, a team whose dominance was growing in recent years. A new rivalry, however, was just heating up in the NFC East, and it would become one of the most famous in NFL history. The Dallas Cowboys and the Washington Redskins formed an intense hatred for each other in the early 1970s. The bitterness between those two teams would last far beyond the 1971 season, however. If one were to look at the genesis of the enmity that each of those teams had for each other, one would have to look no further than the day that George Allen came to Washington. Allen challenged his squad to interrupt the Cowboys' ownership of the NFC East. His brash tone and verbosity struck a bitter chord with Dallas head coach Tom Landry, a man whose silent demeanor and humble personality camouflaged an intense desire to win. "When I'm on the sidelines," explained Landry of his approach to coaching, "I must be completely absorbed in the game. I must be thinking two or three plays ahead all the time as to what's coming. Therefore, I'm not even conscious of crowd response or great plays being made by either team. You can't do that and really concentrate. That's our system, and [it] ... has really made me appear very cold on the sidelines." The two teams would thus become mirror images of their coaches, with Allen's squad voicing a loud and strident spirit, and Landry's players personifying the dedicated poise and cool confidence of their mentor.

The first game between the two teams on October 3 in a driving rainstorm in Dallas ignited the war of words between the two coaches. The Redskins surprised the Cowboys, 20–16, behind a steady and dependable running attack. Charlie Harraway swept to a 57-yard touchdown over left tackle, and the Redskins accumulated 200 overall rushing yards against the Doomsday Defense on the rain-soaked Cotton Bowl turf. The Dallas offense was in the throes of indecision, as quarterbacks Craig Morton and Roger Staubach both saw playing time. Landry had not yet selected a proven starter behind center, so he continued to play both men. Both Morton and Staubach led the team to one touchdown drive apiece, but the Redskins defense held on in the fourth quarter for the win. The postgame comments between the two head coaches added a caustic exclamation point to the action on the field.

"I can't remember when I've ever lost to a Landry team," boasted Allen. The game was fairly even in a statistical sense. The Redskins out-gained the Cowboys only slightly, 285 yards to 267. Landry responded to Allen's comments by verbalizing a rare moment of contempt. "They're a guessing defense and today they guessed right," Landry scoffed. "The league's young, and Washington won't be hard to catch. They're not going to play good football every week themselves."

While the Cowboys and Redskins were enacting their own version of a holy war in the NFC East, the Minnesota Vikings experienced no real competition in the NFC Central. Page, Eller, Marshall and Company gave up yardage and points grudgingly in 1971. The Purple Gang shut out three opponents, and were directly responsible for the team's 11–3 record and their division title. Their closest competition in the "Black and Blue Division" came from the Detroit Lions, who only managed to win seven games. Gary Cuozzo was once again the Vikings' starting quarterback, but his injuries forced head coach Bud Grant to use youngster Bob Lee and veteran Norm Snead for much of the year. For the second straight season, the Minnesota offense could not measure up to the stellar performance of their defense.

Nineteen seventy-one was also another year for a long-standing rivalry in the AFC West. The Kansas City Chiefs and the Oakland Raiders had spent the previous eight years in ferocious competition with each other, and both teams were eager to continue their bellicose struggles with the other. The Chiefs' All-Pro left tackle Jim Tyrer might well have been thinking about the Raiders when he once asked a reporter, "Where can you find a job where you get paid so well to beat the hell out of someone?" Later in the season, the Atlanta Falcons beat the Oakland Raiders, 24–13. The following Monday night, the Chiefs defeated Atlanta's divisional rival, San Francisco, 26–17. After that game, Kansas City defensive end Aaron Brown commented, "We owed Atlanta the professional courtesy of a victory for beating Oakland." Not to be outdone, Oakland fullback Marv Hubbard was more direct in his targeted opinion of the Chiefs. "I don't like the Chiefs and I hope they hear what I'm saying," Hubbard said. "I have an intense hatred for them."

The Chiefs and the Raiders did not know it at the time, but their famous contentions of the past would diminish little-by-little after 1971, when the Chiefs would start to become a mere shadow of their former selves, and the Raiders would increase their dominance in the conference. There would still be selected moments of heated competition between the two clubs throughout the decade, but the rivalry that helped to make the AFL popular in the 1960s would rarely reach the same feverous level in the following decade. The 1971 season, however, would become one of the Chiefs' most exciting seasons ever. First round draft choice Elmo Wright added 26 receptions and a 20.2 yards-per-catch average from his flanker position. He also contributed animation and artistry in the end zone. Wright invented his own dance and spike of the ball after scoring his first touchdown against San Diego on October 10. The dance began with Wright's rapid legs pumping like pistons up and down, and his arms tucked in horizontally as if in a blocker's stance. He then completed the dance with a windmill spike of the pigskin. The hometown crowd in Kansas City simply loved it.

The Chiefs and the Raiders fought to a 20–20 tie in Oakland in their first meeting on October 31. That contest was about as even as the score indicated. The Raiders accumulated 252 total yards, while the Chiefs had 248. Kansas City halfback Ed Podolak scored twice from short yardage, giving his team a 17–10 lead heading into the final quarter. Oakland's penchant for coming back in the clutch was already well established by 1971, and there was no exception to that trend on this day. George Blanda came into the game once again, and threw a 24-yard touchdown pass to Fred Biletnikoff late in the game.

"George Blanda is a rare individual," said Oakland head coach John Madden. "The amazing thing is that he's throwing and kicking better than he did four years ago. Don't ask me why. He doesn't have any secret formula that I know about."

The rematch was held in Kansas City on December 12. This time the tables were turned. It was Kansas City who won this—the final regular season game in old Municipal Stadium—with a last-minute scoring drive. Jan Stenerud's field goal and Jim Kearney's interception of a George Blanda desperation throw gave the Chiefs a division-clinching 16–14 victory. The win kept the

Raiders from making the playoffs for the first time in five years. "We realized what we had to do today," said Kansas City All-Conference offensive tackle Jim Tyrer. "It was a pressure situation. We have the people who excel under pressure."

The chance to make the playoffs, although still a long way in the future, was on the minds of many contending teams as the 1971 season began. The aforementioned rivalries notwithstanding, all teams wanted to get off to a good start, regardless of who they were playing. The excitement of the first week of the regular season included a high-scoring contest in Green Bay, a couple of rookie quarterbacks making memorable debuts in New Orleans and in New England, and a scoring assault in Buffalo.

The New York Giants met the Green Bay Packers in a Wisconsin rainstorm on opening day. The Giants also met new Packer head coach Dan Devine on the sidelines, as two New York defenders dove into the coach while chasing a Packer ball carrier. Devine was carried off the field on a stretcher with a broken leg. The accident seemed to be a harbinger of what would happen to his team, as two costly Green Bay fumbles by Dave Hampton led to two easy New York touchdowns in a 42–40 Giants victory. Hampton's first fumble on his 1-yard line was recovered in the end zone by Ralph Heck of the Giants for a quick score. On the following kickoff, Hampton misplayed the ball, picked it up and incredibly fumbled it again, this time *in* his own end zone. New York's Joe Green recovered it for another score. The Green Bay miscues, however, overshadowed an offensive shootout. New York quarterback Fran Tarkenton threw for four touchdowns, including three to wide receiver Rich Houston. Green Bay's offensive output included scoring passes from both Scott Hunter and Zeke Bratkowski. The Packers also scored on Ken Ellis' 100-yard return of a missed New York field goal. Green Bay's five turnovers were a bitter taste for them to swallow, however, and the main reason why they lost their opening game. "We sure were in great position to do it [win]," said Packers defensive back Doug Hart after the game, "but that just wasn't very good fundamental football."

Archie Manning, the much-heralded rookie quarterback from the University of Mississippi, started his first game for the New Orleans Saints against the visiting Los Angeles Rams. Manning marshaled his team to a surprise 24–20 upset over their division rival. After throwing for one score to wide receiver Dave Parks, Manning ran for the game-winning touchdown with just three seconds left on the clock. Manning's touchdown was not without its share of controversy, however. From the 1-yard line, Manning swept to the left, followed his blockers, and was tackled by Rams defensive backs Dave Elmendorf and Gene Howard. Television and film replays showed that while his helmet and shoulders crossed the goal line, the ball did not. Head linesman Cal LePore was standing alongside of the goal line, and he signaled a touchdown just the same. Umpire Lou Palazzi was also standing alongside of the goal line, but several players separated him from the area where Manning was tackled. Palazzi immediately waved the play dead at the 1-yard line. He then looked over at LePore, who adamantly continued to signal a touchdown. Palazzi relented within a couple of seconds and also signaled a touchdown. Emotional dissent on behalf of the Rams was vivid and raged with nose-to-nose protestations with both of the aforementioned officials. Cornerback Jim Nettles slammed his helmet to the brand new Poly-Turf field in anger. The official call stood as a touchdown, however, and suddenly an also-ran defeated a contender.

"Those guys really stung me," said Manning of the Ram defenders. "My head was spinning but I do remember getting into the end zone. I saw [Dave] Parks wide open in the end zone, but I already committed myself on the run. I was high-lowed at the goal by two Rams. I knew I had possession of the ball at the plane of the goal, and that's all that's necessary to score a touchdown. The crowd went nuts, obviously, because we had won, and the Rams went nuts because they felt they had stopped me. Their players threw their helmets down in the end zone and really protested, and rightly so because the play was THAT close. [Rams coach] Tommy Prothro ... really bad-mouthed the officials."

Jim Plunkett, another rookie quarterback with high expectations, duplicated Manning's performance with an upset victory of his own. The New England Patriots shocked the visiting Oakland Raiders on opening day, 20–6. Plunkett tossed two touchdown passes in the game, and the inspired Patriot defense kept the Raiders out of the end zone in the second half. "Jim Plunkett showed a lot of poise," said Oakland head coach John Madden after the contest. "I was impressed with him before the game and I still am. He ran the team well." One of Plunkett's scoring tosses was a 34-yard strike to wide receiver Ron Sellers, and the other was a perfectly placed lob to tight end Roland Moss, who high-stepped into the end zone to complete a 20-yard play.

Visiting the end zone was something that both the Dallas Cowboys and the Buffalo Bills did often in their first week encounter in Buffalo's War Memorial Stadium. Dallas tailback Calvin Hill scored a career-high four touchdowns, and Cowboys quarterback Craig Morton threw for two more scores. One of them was a beautiful 76-yard bomb to wide receiver Bob Hayes, who used his speed to outrace the Buffalo secondary. Bills quarterback Dennis Shaw threw for four touchdowns of his own, including a 75-yard strike to Marlin Briscoe and a 73-yard bomb to Haven Moses. In a season where defense ruled, it was both offenses in Buffalo which had no trouble accumulating yardage and points. The 401 total yards given up by Dallas on this day would rank as the most that they would give up all year, but the Cowboys prevailed, 49–37.

"Shaw is a very unusual second-year quarterback," said Dallas head coach Tom Landry. "He's very poised and works well under pressure."

As the season progressed, certain trends developed. Teams like the Dolphins and 49ers were continuing the success that they enjoyed the previous season. Other teams like the Browns and the Redskins were showing vast improvement from the 1970 campaign. The Dolphins started fairly slow, but by Week 7, were claiming first place in the AFC Eastern division all to themselves. The key game which established Miami as a team to be reckoned with came in the Los Angeles Memorial Coliseum against the Rams on October 31. The key play in that game occurred in the first quarter when Bob Griese was forced out of his pocket by a strong Rams pass rush. Griese ran to his left and spotted Paul Warfield streaking down the sideline. Griese hit the fluid Warfield with a 74-yard score. Teams that spent much of their preparation time trying to find ways to stop the Dolphins' rushing attack were now forced to find ways to stop Paul Warfield. The No-Name Defense kept improving too, and squelched a furious Rams rally in the second half to give Miami a 17–14 victory.

"I felt this was a key game for us," said Miami head coach Don Shula. "We were playing a team that is on the way up. We did a great job defensively. We hit hard early. I think we're on our way."

The San Francisco 49ers were on their way to an unimpressive 2–2 record to start the 1971 season. They then went on a four-game winning streak to reclaim the lead in the NFC West. The 49ers' most important mid-season victory came at Minnesota. San Francisco held on for a hard-fought 13–9 win over the Vikings when wide receiver Gene Washington caught a tipped John Brodie pass in the end zone. Dick Nolan's team still had some challenges to face, however. They were upset the following week by the visiting New Orleans Saints, 26–20. Later in the year they were upended at home by the Kansas City Chiefs on *Monday Night Football*, 26–17. Clearly gaining a divisional lead and keeping it were two separate challenges for the 49ers.

The Atlanta Falcons drafted some very talented rookies prior to the start of the 1971 season, and those rookies helped to make the team competitive. The most notable first year Falcons were wide receiver Ken Burrow and cornerback Tom Hayes. Burrow caught 33 passes for 741 yards and six touchdowns. Burrow also averaged 22.5 yards a reception, his longest going for 84 yards. Hayes scored three touchdowns, two on fumble recoveries and one after he returned a blocked punt for a score against Detroit. The 1971 Atlanta draftees called themselves the "Brand X" rookies, and taped a small white "X" on the back of their helmets to proudly identify themselves. Thanks to the abilities and youthful exuberance from the "Brand X" players, the Falcons finished the year with their best record ever at 7–6–1, and upset strong teams like San Francisco, Cleveland, Cincinnati and Oakland.

The Cleveland Browns enjoyed one of their best starts ever by winning four of their first five games, including a 14–13 win over the defending Super Bowl champion Colts in rain-drenched Baltimore Memorial Stadium. Cleveland's defense intercepted five Baltimore passes in the victory, and limited Earl Morrall and Johnny Unitas to a combined three completions in 19 attempts for a paltry 41 passing yards. Cleveland continued to show marked improvement when they traveled to Cincinnati's Riverfront Stadium and beat the Bengals, 27–24, on October 17. It certainly did not appear that the Browns stood much of a chance late in the game, as Cincinnati built a 24–13 lead with but ten minutes remaining. Cleveland fullback Bo Scott then went on a scoring spree. Scott scored all three of Cleveland's touchdowns, the last of which coming in the game's final minute. Two Don Cockcroft field goals provided the margin of victory.

"If [Bo] Scott utilizes his ability," said former Cleveland head coach Blanton Collier, "it will give [Cleveland] one of the better backfield combinations in the league."

Nick Skorich's Browns were not without their share of problems, however. They would have to deal with a four-game losing streak at mid-season, the likes of which would probably have eliminated lesser teams. Unexpected losses to Denver, Atlanta and Pittsburgh, and a predictable loss to Kansas City, brought the Browns down to a lackluster 4–5 record. The veteran Cleveland squad managed to regroup, however. Skorich wisely shuffled his starting offensive lineup, replacing three positions on the front line with younger players. He also inserted newly-acquired Frank Pitts for veteran Gary Collins at the wide receiver position, a move which increased the Browns' point production during the second half of the season. Cleveland's five-game winning streak late in the year propelled them to the playoffs. Included in that flurry of victories was their second win over the Bengals and a strong triumph over the Redskins on the season's final Sunday.

Their 31–27 win over the Bengals at Cleveland's Municipal Stadium on December 5 featured two rushing touchdowns from halfback Leroy Kelly and two scoring passes from veteran quarterback Bill Nelsen. Their 20–13 victory over Washington on December 19 was highlighted by two more touchdown passes by Nelsen, the final one coming late in the fourth quarter on a 4-yard pass to tight end Chip Glass. Undoubtedly the biggest play of the game, however, occurred when the Redskins were driving for a go-ahead score in the second half. Cleveland defensive back Mike Howell intercepted a Billy Kilmer pass and wove his way 68 yards down the sideline, breaking two tackles en route. The play inspired the Browns to their winning touchdown.

"I read the pass all the way," said Howell, "and Kilmer more or less threw it right to me. He rolled out to the left and apparently was off balance when he threw it. When I'm playing free safety I can read the quarterback. He can fake all he wants, but he has to look to get the ball where he wants. And I can see him and make my move." Cleveland made its move by enduring a challenging season with a new coach and a bevy of injuries to rightly claim a division title.

Key games like the Browns' victories over Cincinnati served as a valid indicator of Cleveland's success. An important game in New York's Shea Stadium on November 28 featured the San Francisco 49ers taking on the Jets, and would serve as a visual indicator of one superstar's physical health. Two critical factors made this an important contest. One involved the 49ers, who were 6–4 at the time and in the midst of a tight NFC West division race. They could ill-afford to lose this game against an old AFL team that they never played before. The other factor involved the return to action of beloved New York quarterback Joe Namath, who had spent the entire 1971 regular season up to that point on the bench due to an injury he sustained in the preseason. Namath, as only he could do, enthralled the home crowd with 258 passing yards and three touchdowns against San Francisco in a little more than three quarters of action. The Jets eventually lost to the 49ers, 24–21, but Namath's return sparked his team to make a strong comeback in the fourth quarter as he excited the home town fans. Their star quarterback was finally healthy, and they were grateful, giving him several standing ovations during and after the contest. "I don't feel I played well," admitted Namath afterward. San Francisco safety Johnny Fuller, who intercepted Namath's final pass of the game, disagreed. "Namath really puts a lot of pressure on you," he said.

Another major interconference game took place earlier in the season between the undefeated Washington Redskins and the 4–1 Kansas City Chiefs. It occurred on October 24 at Kansas City's Municipal Stadium, and it was also a pressure-filled game. The Redskins dominated the first half, taking a 17–6 lead going into the third quarter. The Redskins suffered a major loss late in the first half, however, when wide receiver Charley Taylor was tackled by Chiefs defensive back Emmitt Thomas. Taylor limped off the field with a fractured ankle, and would not see action again in 1971. The Chiefs turned the tables on the Redskins in the second half, as Kansas City quarterback Len Dawson threw for three touchdowns. One of them went to Elmo Wright, who delighted the capacity crowd with another dance and spike in the end zone. Two more of Dawson's scoring passes went to Otis Taylor, the final one coming late in the fourth quarter on a spectacular one-handed catch by the All-Pro receiver.

"I practice that one-handed stuff a lot," said Taylor in an calm tone to a throng of reporters in the Kansas City locker room after the game. "Some receivers have great speed, great moves," said Dawson. "Otis has all that plus size and strength, too … he's a complete player. He can catch it in a lot of people." Kansas City's 27–20 victory over Washington knocked the Redskins from the ranks of the undefeated, and spurred the Chiefs' drive to the playoffs.

Another important mid-season game served as a low point for the Dallas Cowboys. Tom Landry's club fell to the Chicago Bears, 23–19, on October 31. In that game, Landry substituted his quarterbacks on almost every play. The idea was a hopeful experiment more than a devised strategy. Landry wanted to keep the Bears defense from keying on both Craig Morton and Roger Staubach. Dallas gained 481 yards compared to Chicago's 194 yards, but far too many illegal procedure penalties kept the Cowboys from developing any sense of momentum. A 28-yard pass in the fourth quarter from Bears quarterback Bobby Douglass to wide receiver Dick Gordon provided Chicago with the winning points. The upsetting loss forced Landry to take a good hard look at his plan. The next day, Landry announced that—for better or worse—Staubach would be his starter for the remainder of the season. His decision would have dramatic results as the year wore on.

As the regular season neared its end, several teams were feeling the effects of unexpected injuries and upsetting losses. New York Jets quarterback Joe Namath sustained his second straight year of injuries, and his team could only manage six wins as a result. Other key quarterbacks such as Johnny Unitas of the Colts and Daryle Lamonica of the Raiders spent time on the bench due to nagging aches and pains. Archie Manning of the Saints showed much early promise, only to sustain an assortment of injuries. The Saints limped to a 4–8–2 mark in 1971. The Bengals took a step backward when their quarterback, Virgil Carter, was unable to lead his team to wins in several tough contests. The Bengals lost six games by four points or less, and could only muster a depressing 4–10 season.

Only a smattering of teams like the Cowboys, Chiefs, Vikings, Browns and Dolphins were able to put together substantial winning streaks during the latter part of 1971. Once again, one or two key games for each of these teams ignited their playoff runs. The Dolphins lost two successive contests to the Patriots and Colts in December, and those losses forced Don Shula's players to refocus their efforts. Miami finished the regular season by romping over the visiting Green Bay Packers, 27–6. In that game, Larry Csonka teamed up with his buddy Jim Kiick to rush for 155 total yards and two touchdowns. Csonka also eclipsed the 1,000-yard mark in this game, and quarterback Bob Griese completed an efficient 13 passes in 21 attempts. The Dolphins had thus regained some measure of momentum heading into the playoffs.

"I would love to return to the Super Bowl," said Shula, who coached the Baltimore Colts in their Super Bowl III defeat at the hands of the New York Jets. "I'm proud of my football team and glad to be heading into the playoffs as divisional champions."

One unique and original aspect to Miami's season occurred in the ninth week, when the Dolphins hosted the Colts in their first grudge match of the season. Dolphins radio announcer Rick Weaver observed that many Dolphins fans in the Orange Bowl listened to the game via their transistor radios in the stands. Weaver wanted to capture the emotions and excitement of the fans, especially when the Dolphins scored a touchdown. He instructed those fans over the airwaves during the week prior to the game with the Colts to bring white handkerchiefs to the game, then wave them on his signal while they listened to the game. The phenomenon of tens of thousands of white hankies waving would inspire both the players and fans. Miami came from behind to beat the Colts, 17–14. White hankies have been waved at every Dolphins home game since.

"What I get out of this," Weaver said, "is the satisfaction of knowing that my broadcasts have produced the first and probably the only tradition the Dolphin fans have ever had."

Another NFL tradition, the annual Thanksgiving Day game, was once again held at Tiger Stadium in Detroit. The Chiefs lost the 1971 version of this annual holiday contest to the Lions, 32–21, but then won their final three games to capture the AFC West crown. Head coach Hank Stram's "Offense of the Seventies" scored 302 points in 1971 against tough competition. Kansas City lost only one game against their divisional foes, and their strong defense gave up an average of only 14.8 points per game. Linebackers Bobby Bell and Willie Lanier once again made the All-Pro squad, as did cornerback Emmitt Thomas, and defensive tackle Curley Culp. On the offensive side of the ball, tackle Jim Tyrer and wide receiver Otis Taylor also made the All-Pro squad. Several other Chiefs made the All-Conference team. Kansas City's chances of achieving success in the 1971 playoffs appeared to be as promising as those of any good team. Stram's players accounted for 10 victories despite numerous retirements prior to the start of the season. Stalwart veterans like defensive lineman Jerry Mays, tight end Fred Arbanas, and center E.J. Holub all called it quits after the 1970 campaign. The Chiefs had quality replacements for those retirees, but their leadership would never be duplicated.

"Do I allow myself to be sentimental?" Stram asked a reporter when questioned about the loss of those three players. "Yes," was his immediate reply. "It's tough not to. It's always tough when people who have played such a prominent role in your success leave you." Head coaches throughout the decade were ultimately faced with the dilemma of keeping older players over promising young athletes. Showing loyalty to older players by keeping them on the roster past their prime would be the downfall of some pro coaches as the decade wore on. The most successful coaches knew that a quality balance between older and younger players was needed in order to keep a team on the winning track. The same practice is still required for today's winning teams.

The Baltimore Colts were just such a winning team in 1971, and were fulfilling their role as defending world champions by crushing the host Oakland Raiders on November 28, 37–14. Baltimore's solid running game served as the catalyst for this impressive victory, as Norm Bulaich,

Tom Matte, and Don Nottingham bulled through the Raiders defense for 210 yards and four touchdowns. The Colts defense also contributed six pass interceptions and held Oakland head coach John Madden's offense scoreless until the fourth quarter. On December 11, the Colts avenged their earlier loss to the Dolphins by beating them at Memorial Stadium, 14–3. This time it was Baltimore's passing game which controlled the ball and the time of possession. Johnny Unitas completed 16 of 19 passes for the Colts in building a 14–0 halftime lead. The Baltimore defense took care of matters in the second half, permitting yards but not points. Head coach Don McCafferty's team had thus vindicated themselves, and were looking like they were destined to return to the Super Bowl.

The Baltimore defense was keeping the team in close games throughout the 1971 season. According to Buffalo quarterbacks coach Tom Flores, the Colts zone coverages were the key reason why. "It's not that Baltimore does it that much differently from anyone else in the zone," Flores said in the latter part of the season, "but they disguise their coverages so well. The quarterback never has much time to read what kind of coverage they're in. They give you the same look on every play."

All the Colts had to do in their final game in order to win the AFC East was to beat the young Patriots at home. New England quarterback Jim Plunkett spoiled Baltimore's plans, however. Plunkett tossed two scoring passes to Randy Vataha to post a 21–17 upset. One of those touchdowns was a bomb of 88 yards over the shocked Colts zone defense in the fourth quarter. "It was one of the biggest plays of my life," said Vataha. "All I could think of as I ran toward the goal line was that if I scored we probably would win the game." They did, and by virtue of Miami's win over Green Bay on the same day, the Colts would have to settle for the AFC wild card spot in the playoffs. The Dolphins' winning streak in the middle of the season had proved good enough to win their first division title in team history.

But undoubtedly the most impressive winning streak in 1971 belonged to the Dallas Cowboys. Tom Landry's team rode a see-saw during the first half of the season, earning a less than stellar 4–3 record. Following their loss to the Bears, the Cowboys knew that they were at the crossroads. It was at this time that the Dallas players relied on what was regarded by everyone as the consensual cure-all for all that ails a supposed contender … the team meeting. A "players only" team meeting in Dallas after the Bears game forced every man to assess his own performance. The players that emerged from that foregathering was a much-regrouped unit, one with a strong desire to win one game at a time. The result would be greater than even Landry expected. The Cowboys' seven-game winning streak to end the regular season displayed weekly building blocks of individual and team successes. "We're a pretty good football team," said an understated Landry late in the season.

A rematch with the hated Redskins on November 21 highlighted their string of victories. An overcast day and a crowd of overzealous Redskin fans greeted the Dallas players as they jogged onto the grass at RFK Stadium. Roger Staubach's 29-yard run served as the game's only touchdown. The Doomsday Defense registered their only shutout of the season, as Dallas prevailed, 13–0. The game displayed how badly the Cowboys desired to make amends for their earlier loss to the Redskins. Dallas wanted to send a message to all of their upcoming opponents: They would be tougher to beat than ever, hungrier for victory than ever, and finally operating at peak condition for the stretch drive to the playoffs.

"This was a big win, but I'm not personally satisfied," Staubach admitted after beating the Redskins. "The championship is what I want. These games are forgotten if you don't win the championship."

In a year known for stalwart defensive play, the Cowboys' Doomsday Defense was a principal element in their winning streak. Longtime defenders like Bob Lilly, Jethro Pugh, Chuck Howley, Lee Roy Jordan, George Andrie, Mel Renfro, Herb Adderley, Cornell Green, etc., were more determined than ever to return to the Super Bowl. Tom Landry's defense did not accumulate a bunch of jaw-dropping statistics. Good teams were able to move the ball against them. Scoring on the Doomsday Defense was another matter entirely, however. The Cowboys' defense gave up only two touchdowns in their final three regular season games, and would give up only one touchdown in three postseason games. The success of Landry's defense was the result of unselfish play and coordination to fill holes along the line of scrimmage.

"If the ball carrier is going inside," said Dallas defensive line coach Ernie Stautner, "it isn't easy for a lineman to learn to go outside. They've got to learn that Tom's [Landry's] way is the right way. Once they become accustomed to it, they'll find it's the easiest way to play the game."

The Cowboys won their not-so-easy Thanksgiving Day game against the Los Angeles Rams at Texas Stadium with a couple of big plays. Reserve return specialist and defensive back Isaac Thomas brought back the opening kickoff 89 yards for a touchdown. Thomas burned right up the middle of the field, with forlorn defenders in futile pursuit. Another Dallas speedster, Bob Hayes, scored when he caught a 51-yard bomb from Roger Staubach. Cowboys halfback Duane Thomas swept left and scored the winning touchdown in the fourth quarter on a 5-yard run. The Cowboys prevailed, 28–21, their fourth straight victory.

Duane Thomas was an interesting story ... unless you were a sportswriter covering the Cowboys in 1971. That was because Thomas was determined not to talk to the press—or anyone else for that matter—as a sign of protest against the Dallas front office for not renegotiating his contract. His teammates and coaches struggled to ignore his sullen and bitter attitude, which exhibited itself most often during practices and team meetings. The press simply could not ignore him, however, mainly because he was leading the team in rushing and was busy scoring more rushing touchdowns than anyone else in the NFL (11). His silence just increased the interest of his story among the public. Dallas head coach Tom Landry was stuck in an unenviable situation, trying his best to deal with Thomas without hurting the psyche of his team.

"He [Landry] made exceptions for Duane," remembered quarterback Roger Staubach. "Landry slackened his rules. It became a double-standard situation. Duane got away with talking back to coaches, not answering roll call, not wearing a tie on road trips. Duane became an introvert. He withdrew from everyone. What the players saw, however, was that he was being handled as a separate case."

The Thomas predicament did not hurt the team on Sundays, however. The Dallas offense began to increase its point production as the season wound down. The Cowboys scored 125 points in their final three regular season games, an average of 42 points per game. Dallas crushed the visiting New York Jets on December 4, scoring an incredible 28 points in the first quarter. The 52–10 romp over the Jets began in grand fashion once again with Isaac Thomas, who returned the opening kickoff for a touchdown, this one coming from 101 yards out. Roger Staubach threw for three touchdowns, halfback Calvin Hill scored three touchdowns, and backup quarterback Craig Morton was inserted in the game by Coach Landry as a token of mercy for the Jets. Morton promptly threw a 20-yard scoring strike to flanker Lance Alworth. The Cowboys racked up 439 yards and permitted only 149, most of which came in the second half when Dallas substitutes were on the field. "I can't remember when our first unit looked as good as it did in that first quarter," Landry said after the massacre.

The following week Dallas traveled to Yankee Stadium and stomped all over the New York Giants, 42–14. Staubach once again threw for three touchdowns, including two to wide receiver Bob Hayes. Perhaps the most beautiful throw of the season was a high-arching bomb from

Staubach, who ducked a heavy pass rush, then completed the 85-yard score to the streaking Hayes, who left two defenders in the dust. Duane Thomas and Calvin Hill each scored twice, and the Cowboys recorded another 439 total yards on offense. The Dallas defense gave up only 64 yards rushing, and once again gave its substitute players plenty of game experience in the second half.

"We are more hungry than we were early in the year," Staubach admitted. "When we go into the playoffs, we are going to play the best football we know how. One way or another, we're going to win."

Staubach's prophetic prediction came just before Dallas closed out the regular season at home against the St. Louis Cardinals, the team that they beat in Week 8 with a last-minute field goal, 16–13. That victory began their current winning streak. This time, the Cowboys had no trouble defeating the Cardinals, crushing them 31–12. Duane Thomas was the star of this game, scoring a career-best four touchdowns. The Cowboys had successfully defended their NFC East title, and in so doing so had earned the recognition as the top-ranked offense in the NFL.

"The Cowboys work very, very hard," said All-Pro cornerback Mel Renfro after the game. "The coaching staff, the administration, and the players, spend a lot of time on football, on the field and off. Probably much more than most other teams. Most of the pressure comes from Tom Landry, and there's a lot of it. He just demands winning. He wants no less than the best out of everybody at all times."

Landry got the best from his tight ends during the season, adeptly utilizing them to run in the plays to the offensive huddle. Both Mike Ditka and Billy Truax were nearly identical in size. Truax was 6'5" and weighed 240 pounds. Ditka stood 6'3" and weighed 213 pounds. Truax was a better pass receiver than Ditka, but Ditka was the better blocker of the two. Ditka caught twice as many passes as Truax (30 to 15), but both men were quality options downfield for quarterback Roger Staubach. The Dallas offensive line was blocking better than ever during the last half of the season. Tackles Rayfield Wright and Tony Liscio, guards Blaine Nye and John Niland, and center Dave Manders were giving Staubach time to find his receivers, and were learning how to maintain their blocks while Staubach scrambled out of the pocket. Staubach's impromptu runs resulted in an 8.4-yard rushing average for the ex–Navy star. Despite Landry's disapproval, "Roger the Dodger" moved the chains on a regular basis and contributed mightily to the Cowboys' 2,249 rushing yards during the regular season.

"He really doesn't say a great deal," Staubach said in 1971 of Landry's feelings on a running quarterback. "Sometimes he says something like 'Well, you'll learn.' He knows when I've run it's helped. It hasn't been a hindrance to the team. With more experience, I'll be able to stay in the pocket even more. But running is still going to be an asset if used properly—it'll help the team."

The Dallas offense, indeed the whole Dallas team, was invigorated with each Staubach run and with each win down the stretch. Several weeks prior they were at the crossroads, but they persevered. Their determination to return to the Super Bowl was something that every man on the squad was more than willing to sacrifice for.

The polish and success of the teamwork exhibited by the Cowboys was not always visible on other teams around the league. Nevertheless, individual efforts and achievements could still be seen throughout the NFL. The league's offenses tried various approaches to defeat the zone defenses. The two most common strategies were running the ball, and then throwing the ball on short patterns to tight ends and running backs coming out of the backfield. Bob Tucker, a tight end for the New York Giants, led the NFC in pass receptions with 59 catches for 791 yards. The Denver Broncos had no air threats to speak of, so they rarely threw the ball. Instead, their star halfback Floyd Little was given the responsibility to run the ball as much as possible. Little finished 1971 as the league's leading rusher, gaining 1,133 yards on a league-high 283 carries. Little's statistics were impressive when one considers his compact size (he stood only 5'10"). His determined heart and desire to play pro football were the impressive ingredients which produced his success.

"When I came up to the pros," Little said in an interview after the 1971 season, "everybody said I was too small. They still say it. Every time I go on the field, I've got to prove myself again. In my case, I'd say speed is my strong point. Some are faster, but I can run as fast sideways as I can straight ahead, which few can. I'm small, but that helps me to hide. I mean it. I'm hard to spot behind big linemen. I may not be big, but I don't back off from anybody who puts on shoulder pads same as me. He may be bigger than me, but his heart works the same way. He can go down."

Most defensive philosophies in 1971 dictated that you focus on stopping running backs like Floyd Little first and foremost. Limiting an opponent's passing game was usually a secondary goal, especially if your opponent ran the ball more than they threw it (which most teams certainly did in the early years of the decade). The eight playoff teams prided themselves in their ability to put a halt to opposing rushing attacks and to display a strong pass defense as well. Zone coverages throughout the year were so strong that only one receiver—Kansas City's Otis Taylor—managed to gain over 1,000 yards on pass receptions. Only one quarterback—San Diego's John Hadl—threw for over 3,000 yards. Hadl made the most of the weapons that he had, namely wide receivers Gary Garrison and Billy Parks, both of whom possessed incredibly reliable hands with which to catch the ball. Hadl also threw often to tailback Mike Garrett, who was traded from the Chiefs to the Chargers in the middle of the 1970 season. Garrison, Parks and Garrett were outstanding at gaining extra yardage after they caught the ball, which aided Hadl's yardage totals. Unfortunately for San Diego, the excitement that their offense produced did not lead to a winning record. The Chargers earned a mediocre 6–8 record, which was only good enough for third place in the AFC West.

Teams vying for a chance at the playoffs during the final stages of the regular season would predictably fight hard going down the stretch in order to extend their seasons. The AFC East title would go down to the final Sunday. Baltimore, by virtue of their 21–17 home loss to the New England Patriots, lost any chance to defend their division title. Miami's 27–6 victory over visiting Green Bay lifted the Dolphins to their first ever AFC East title. The NFC West endured a similar situation. It took a clutch 31–27 San Francisco victory over visiting Detroit in the final game of the regular season for the 49ers to outlast the Los Angeles Rams in the standings. In contrast, both Minnesota in the NFC and Cleveland in the AFC won their respective Central Division titles with barely a modicum of competition. The Vikings' 11 wins was four more than their next closest competition (Detroit with seven wins), while the Browns' nine victories were three better than Pittsburgh's six wins. Minnesota's defense was the key to their success. "Their people-eating front four of Carl Eller, Gary Larsen, Alan Page and Jim Marshall has been the best defensive line in the game for several years," said former great New York Giants quarterback Charley Connerly.

The 1971 season also saw some team disappointments. The Oakland Raiders, who were becoming accustomed to winning division championships, hit an injury-filled roadblock in 1971. Oakland managed to earn plenty of stellar statistics, and their substitute players did an excellent job replacing the likes of injured stars like running backs Charlie Smith and Hewritt Dixon. Nevertheless, they finished with a lackluster 8–4–2 record, good enough for a seat in their living rooms to watch the playoffs. A fellow California team, the Rams, also found themselves out of the playoffs for the second straight year. Los Angeles' 8–5–1 mark was a game worse than their 1970 record. The two Pennsylvania teams, the Eagles and the Steelers, each won six games and showed some improvement, however, and each looked forward to the day when they both could earn titles. But for Pittsburgh head coach Chuck Noll, having a "respectable" record was not going to be good enough. "Who wants to be respectable?" Noll asked reporters after the season. "That's spoken like a true loser. Forget that respectable stuff. We're aiming for a championship now. We're not aiming for respectability or any other such words. The only true respectability in this game is winning the championship."

Noll's Steelers would not have too long to wait for that ultimate show of respect, but for the 1971 regular season, each playoff team knew that their level of play would have to be increased if they were to continue their success. Oddsmakers made their picks, but doubt was still evident among most onlookers as to which teams would advance into the conference championship round. One thing was certain, however. The game's fans across the nation were heartily enjoying the product that pro football had become in 1971.

Nationalistically-speaking, America once again got its savory taste of NFL excitement and competition down the stretch. Games like the 49ers' last-minute triumph over the Lions on the final Sunday of the regular season evoked pandemonium among the masses. Indeed, the fans at Candlestick Park on that special Sunday went wild as the final gun signaled another playoff berth for their team. Where sports like baseball and basketball were stop and go (mostly stop), pro football had become solid minute-by-minute action, where virtually any team could put together a string of wins and earn a title when the pressure to perform was at its greatest. The 49ers did just that by beating the Lions. Had they lost, the Rams would have been the NFC Western Division champions, not San Francisco. "We came up with the big plays when we needed them," assessed San Francisco linebacker Frank Nunley.

The emphasis for the teams who remained alive in the postseason would focus on defense, where championships were usually won. The teams with the best defenses were deemed by most observers as probable favorites to win. The playoffs would confirm that fact for the most part, but they would also end up taking the fervor of the regular season to an even higher level. The 1971 divisional playoff round would provide the decade with one of the greatest games in pro football history.

First off, however, came the playoff game in Cleveland, where the AFC Central Division Champion Cleveland Browns played host to the defending world champion Baltimore Colts. This game would turn out to be a test of team roster depth. Neither squad was totally healthy going into the contest. Cleveland quarterback Bill Nelsen was still not playing at 100 percent, but at least he was in the lineup. Baltimore's best runner, Norm Bulaich, would not suit up for this game, having ruptured his groin against Miami two weeks prior to the playoffs. Bulaich's injury in front of a national television audience was quite graphic. Collective moans and gasps echoed in unison throughout Baltimore's Memorial Stadium when Bulaich was twisted like a pretzel by Miami linebacker Doug Swift. The Colts, in the wake of the absence of "Big Boo," would still rely on their remaining ground weapons, however. The most notable of Baltimore's ground gainers was rookie running back Don Nottingham, who was described in the media as "the human bowling ball," due to his roly-poly body type.

It was Nottingham who did the yeoman's work of solid running against the Cleveland defense in their playoff tilt, particularly in the first half. Nottingham rushed for 92 yards on the wet and muddy field of Cleveland's Municipal Stadium. He also scored two second quarter touchdowns. The first one climaxed a 17-play, 92-yard drive, as he bulled in from the 1-yard line. The second score came as Nottingham faked a move to his left, then ran off right tackle from the seven and tumbled into the end zone. The 14–0 Colt lead at halftime forced the Browns to throw the ball for much of the second half. "We got a great job from Nottingham here," said Baltimore head coach Don McCafferty, "especially when you consider he is a rookie."

Not surprisingly, the Baltimore zone defense squelched any potential Cleveland comeback by intercepting three Bill Nelsen passes, and limited the Browns to 11 first downs. Two costly Cleveland fumbles insured the end of the Browns' five-game winning streak. Colts placekicker Jim O'Brien booted two second half field goals, and huge defensive end Bubba Smith blocked two Cleveland field goal attempts. McCafferty's squad cruised to a 20–3 triumph, earning a ticket to the AFC championship game.

"We had great coverage in the secondary," said Baltimore defensive tackle Fred Miller from a victorious Colts locker room, "but it was a good all-around defensive effort that won for us. It took us awhile to get our pass rush started, but with coverage like that in the secondary we had to get something started sometime."

Later that same day, the NFC Western Division Champion San Francisco 49ers also started out slow when they played host to the NFC wild card Washington Redskins in their divisional playoff game. Both of these teams were similar in that they both possessed strong defenses. They also both had key veteran leadership throughout their lineups. The game was played on a cloudy day with intermittent drizzling rain in San Francisco's new stadium, Candlestick Park. The stadium's upper deck would still not be completed until the following year, and viewing films of that game, it is somewhat strange to watch a pro football game from an unfinished location. The 49ers really wanted to leave Kezar Stadium badly, however, and were quite content in playing in the half-finished Candlestick Park throughout 1971. Head coach Dick Nolan's offense appeared to be incomplete as well, as they struggled throughout the first half against the Redskins defense. San Francisco could muster only one field goal during the first two quarters. The 49ers' special teams performed no better in the first half. Washington's John Jaqua blocked a Steve Spurrier punt in the first quarter, thereby setting up the Redskins' first touchdown. Redskins quarterback Billy Kilmer found his tight end Jerry Smith alone in the 49ers' end zone for a 7–0 lead.

Nolan's special teams let him down again late in the second quarter, giving up a 47-yard punt return by Washington's Ted Vactor. The 49ers defense stiffened, however, as linebacker Frank Nunley blocked a Curt Knight field goal attempt. The Redskins then looked like they would add to their 10–3 halftime lead when return specialist Speedy Duncan brought back the second half kickoff 66 yards. If Nolan ever needed his defense to put a stop to the Washington offense, now was the time. Nolan got his wish on fourth down from deep inside 49ers territory. Redskins running back Larry Brown was stopped short of a first down by Nunley and fellow linebacker Skip Vanderbundt. "Earl Edwards and Charlie Krueger stopped his steps and I just went in and grabbed him," said Nunley.

That fourth down stop ignited the struggling 49ers' offense. Quarterback John Brodie quickly connected on a 78-yard bomb to wide receiver Gene Washington which tied the score at 10–10. Redskin free safety Pat Fischer made a leaping dive for Brodie's pass, but came up short, and watched helplessly from his position on the ground as Washington streaked all alone into the end zone. "I called an audible," said Brodie of Washington's touchdown, "and went for it. It looked like something that might work. And we were going nowhere before that."

The complexion of the game changed abruptly with Washington's score. San Francisco's defense wasted no time in building on the new momentum. Defensive back Rosie Taylor was in the right place at the right time to intercept a Kilmer pass during the following series. Taylor's interception and 17-yard run back set up Brodie for another touchdown pass, this one going to reserve tight end Bob Windsor, who caught the ball on a fade pattern over Redskins linebacker Harold McLinton for a 17–10 San Francisco advantage.

Washington did not despair from the sudden loss of their lead, however. Speedy Duncan once again showed his prowess by returning the ensuing kickoff 67 yards. Curt Knight came through a few moments later with a 36-yard field goal which shortened San Francisco's lead to

17–13. Nolan's special teams finally redeemed themselves midway through the fourth quarter. Reserve 49ers linebacker Bob Hoskins recovered a poor center snap in the Washington end zone for what turned out to be the winning touchdown. The low snap caused the ball to skid along the artificial turf and through the legs of Redskins punter Mike Bragg. Hoskins dove for the pigskin and wrestled it away from Bragg for the score. "We made too many mistakes," said Redskins head coach George Allen, "and they [the 49ers] didn't make any."

The Redskins fought back late in the fourth quarter when Kilmer tossed a 16-yard pass to Larry Brown for a touchdown. The 49ers would give up no more points, however, and prevailed, 24–20. Nolan's team answered the call to their playoff challenge when their backs were against the wall. His offense revived itself from its first half slump and had accumulated a total of 285 yards, 173 of which came through the air. San Francisco's defense proved itself also, shutting down Kilmer's passing game to 93 yards. Star Redskin runner Larry Brown was held to 84 yards on 27 carries (a 3.1-yard average). Nolan could not be totally satisfied, however. His own running game could muster only 112 total rushing yards against the Redskins. Nolan knew that if his team was to achieve success in the upcoming NFC championship game, his own runners would have to gain more yardage, particularly when going up against another tough defense. But he also knew that his quarterback, John Brodie, was a quality signal-caller capable of producing victories in tough contests.

"John has a great deal of ability and confidence in himself," said Nolan. "The players believe in him and what he does. He's not a holler guy—he does things positively."

The previous day in Minnesota's Metropolitan Stadium, two of the best defenses in the NFL would square off in their divisional playoff game. Both the Cowboys' Doomsday Defense and the Vikings' Purple Gang had no problems stopping opposing runners in 1971. Both teams ranked at the top in the NFC in giving up the least amount of overall rushing yards. Both defenses became famous for forcing turnovers and changing momentum in games. Both head coaches, Bud Grant of Minnesota and Tom Landry of Dallas, were uniquely similar in their approach to strategy. Both preferred to play a safe and conservative brand of football. The similarities ended there, however. The two major distinctions between these two teams were seen on the offensive side of the ball. The Vikings offense had struggled during 1971, scoring only 245 points, and accruing only 1,655 passing yards (the lowest mark of any playoff team). In contrast, the Cowboys' offense accumulated a league-leading 5,035 total yards. Most prognosticators and football analysts believed if the Dallas offense would remain patient in this game, they should be able to take advantage of the breaks that their defense was bound to give them. Those prognosticators and analysts could not have been more correct. Turnovers told the tale in this playoff game, as Minnesota committed five turnovers, while Dallas committed none. The first half was dominated by both defenses, as was predicted. Mike Clark kicked two field goals for the Cowboys, while Fred Cox kicked one for the Vikings.

The game's biggest play, however, occurred early in the third quarter. Minnesota quarterback Bob Lee lofted a floating second and one pass which Dallas safety Cliff Harris intercepted. Harris' effort on the play was extraordinary. He drifted into the zone and broke on the ball as soon as Lee released it. Lee's pass was intended for his flanker, Bob Grim, but Harris picked the ball off just inches in front of Grim. Harris' momentum forced him to tumble to the grass upon making the interception, but he quickly bounced up and ran the ball back to the Vikings' 13-yard line. Grim was also well-covered on the play by Dallas cornerback Mel Renfro. So much so, in fact, that even if Harris was nowhere near the ball, Renfro would have easily picked it off. "It was the big play," said Landry. "It gave us momentum in the second half."

Dallas halfback Duane Thomas scored on the ensuing play. The call was a typical draw play, and the execution was flawless. The Cowboys' offensive line slanted their blocks to the strong side, and did such a fine job of it that when Thomas took his first step, a giant hole opened up right up the middle. Thomas sped through the hole, broke a diving attempt at a tackle from Minnesota defensive back Bobby Bryant, and pranced into the end zone with a 13–3 Dallas lead.

Later in the third quarter, Staubach hit flanker Lance Alworth for 29 yards on a third and 14 play along the sideline. Alworth was embarrassingly open on the play, easily beating Minnesota cornerback Ed Sharockman, and his effort put the Cowboys in prime position for another score. "Sharockman hates the turn-in-and-go," said Alworth after the game. "He's scared to death of it because he doesn't have a lot of speed. I ran a turn-in in front of him, faked upfield, then turned and stopped again. Roger laid it right there."

Staubach then escaped a rush by Minnesota defensive end Jim Marshall out of his passing pocket, ran to his left, and spotted wide receiver Bob Hayes in the far corner of the end zone. Hayes' catch of Staubach's bullet boosted the Dallas lead to 20–3. "You have to watch Roger and move to him," Hayes said. "I beat Sharockman to the inside, but when I saw Roger running I switched directions."

The entire fourth quarter belonged to the Vikings defense. They did not permit another Dallas first down, and premier defensive tackle and 1971 NFL Most Valuable Player Alan Page even sacked Staubach in the end zone for a safety. Dallas guard John Niland was given the unenviable task of blocking Page throughout the day, but he survived, as did his team. "Alan is the best I've ever played [against]," said Niland. "Alan is so fast, so quick. I knew I couldn't run over him, so I just got in the way. I thought I had a pretty good game."

Bud Grant then replaced Lee with Gary Cuozzo in the hopes that a change in quarterbacks would bring about a change in momentum for the Vikings offense. Unfortunately for Grant, Cuozzo could only achieve marginal success against the Doomsday Defense. Cuozzo did manage to throw a 6-yard touchdown pass to tight end Stu Voigt, but he also threw two interceptions, the final one on a desperation pass which Cowboys cornerback Herb Adderley intercepted. Dallas had prevailed, 20–12, and were once again headed to the NFC championship game.

"There would be no point in talking about things that went wrong," said Minnesota running back Clint Jones, "because it would detract from the way Dallas played, and they played very well." Coach Landry added, "We've got a better blend of offense and defense than last year. In recent games the offense has come into its own and taken considerable pressure off the defense."

The Dallas victory was an obvious example of how well the Cowboys managed to take advantage of the breaks. Minnesota out-gained the Cowboys in total yardage, 311–183. Minnesota had 17 first downs, compared to Dallas' 10. The Vikings' defense permitted only 85 net passing yards, and effectively shut down the Cowboy runners. The Dallas defense intercepted four passes, however, and placed their offense in outstanding field position for several scoring opportunities. Staubach and Company were able to make several key plays, and were satisfied to run as much time off of the game clock as possible in the fourth quarter to preserve the win.

The game clock would get an incredible workout later that Christmas Day in Kansas City. A national television audience received a holiday treat when the AFC Eastern Division Champion Miami Dolphins faced the AFC Western Division Champion Kansas City Chiefs in one of the greatest divisional playoff games in NFL history. Both teams entered the game with identical 10–3–1 records. Both had outstanding coaches in Don Shula (Miami) and Hank Stram (Kansas City). The Chiefs had more overall experience, but both teams had quality superstars on offense and equally strong defenses. The game would become an offensive shootout, would see both teams exchange the lead and momentum with virtually every exchange of the ball, and would produce incredible individual and team efforts for the record books. The game was decided by a field goal in the *sixth* quarter, and would last an incredible 82 minutes and 40 seconds.

In what would be the final game ever in old Municipal Stadium, the hometown Chiefs started the contest with two strong offensive drives which resulted in a 10–0 lead. On their first drive, quarterback Len Dawson threw several short passes to halfback Ed Podolak, eventually producing a 24-yard field goal from placekicker Jan Stenerud. The Chiefs' second drive began when middle linebacker Willie Lanier intercepted a Bob Griese pass and returned it to the Dolphins' 35-yard line. Culminating this drive was Podolak, who caught a 7-yard swing pass from Dawson and streaked into the end zone between two perfect downfield blocks for the 10-point Kansas City advantage.

Miami came right back. Griese kept hitting his talented wide receiver, Paul Warfield, who would finish this contest with seven catches for 140 yards. Dolphins tight end Marv Fleming would also be on the receiving end of several Griese passes, particularly when his quarterback was chased out of the pocket. Griese was known for his mobility in the pocket, and it was on just such a play early in the second quarter that the Dolphins made their first deep penetration into Chiefs territory. Griese escaped a fierce rush from Kansas City defensive end Marvin Upshaw, ran to his right, and found Fleming in the open at the Chiefs' 4-yard line. Dolphins fullback Larry Csonka completed the drive with a 1-yard dive up the middle. The pattern for this game was thus established: Kansas City would forge ahead, then Miami would respond with a score of their own.

It was the Kansas City mistakes which helped to keep Miami in the game, however. The Chiefs committed two costly fumbles, and Len Dawson was also guilty of throwing two interceptions. Perhaps the most glaring of Kansas City's failures belonged to the usually sure-footed Stenerud, however, who missed an incredible two of his four field goal attempts, and had another one blocked. In retrospect, if any one of his three failed attempts would have been successful, Kansas City would have won the game.

Griese threw two interceptions as well, but he also made some key plays throughout the

Kansas City Chiefs setback Ed Podolak scores the first touchdown in a 1971 AFC divisional playoff game on Christmas Day, 1971, against the Miami Dolphins. Podolak set an NFL playoff yardage record this day. Despite his efforts, the Chiefs fell to the Dolphins in the longest game in NFL history, 27–24 (AP Photo).

game which led to important Miami points. Late in the first half, Miami took advantage of a Podolak fumble when Stenerud's adversary—Miami's Garo Yepremian—booted a 14-yard field goal which tied the game at halftime, 10–10. On that scoring drive, Kansas City's All-Conference safety Johnny Robinson suffered a groin injury which knocked him out of the game. "They [the trainers] injected me with Novocain at halftime," Robinson recalled, "but I couldn't move around like I needed to, so they kept me out of the game."

The loss of Robinson would be deeply felt by the Chiefs' defense in the second half, as Griese would take advantage of the lack of savvy leadership in the middle of Kansas City's secondary. Many of Griese's passes were directed towards his second and third downfield options, particularly while he scrambled around to find more time. Both offenses expanded their passing games in the second half, and both defenses were forced to make strategical adjustments. The Dolphins focused their efforts on stopping All-Pro Chiefs wide receiver Otis Taylor, holding him to just three catches for a minimal 12 yards. Conversely, Miami's defense failed to pay enough attention to halfback Ed Podolak, who was busy shredding the No-Name defenders. Kansas City's defense keyed on Miami fullback Larry Csonka, holding him to 86 yards on 24 carries (a 3.6-yard average). This choice opened the way for Dolphins receiver Paul Warfield to have one of his best playoff games ever.

As darkness descended on Municipal Stadium, Kansas City's offensive unit started the third quarter by reasserting itself and moving the ball downfield. Ed Podolak once again shined for the Chiefs. According to author Frank Ross, Dawson used Podolak's running and receiving abilities "like an adding machine throughout the game." Podolak would account for a playoff record 350 total yards, a mark which still stands today. Podolak rushed for 85 yards, caught eight passes for 110 yards, and returned kickoffs and punts for another 155 yards. As extraordinary as Podolak's performance was, Dawson still had other weapons to use. Miami's defense continued to shut down Otis Taylor, so Dawson handed the ball off to Wendell Hayes, who led all rushers with 100 yards on 22 carries. Dawson also took advantage of reserve fullback Jim Otis, who capped Kansas City's first drive of the second half with a 1-yard touchdown dive.

Miami once again responded quickly. Griese hit flanker Howard Twilley on an out pattern for 24 yards. He then connected with Warfield on a down-and-in route for another 24 yards. Jim Kiick completed the drive when he powered in from the 1-yard line to tie the score at 17–17.

Both teams had promising offensive drives in the fourth quarter. Dawson decided to throw deep the next time Kansas City got the ball. Knowing that Taylor would be double-covered, Dawson instead threw a high-arching bomb to Elmo Wright, who caught the ball over his shoulder and was tripped up at the 3-yard line by Miami safety Jake Scott. Wright's 63-yard reception also included his trademark dance and spike in the end zone, even though it was only one play premature. Ed Podolak took a pitchout from Dawson on the next play and crashed into the end zone for a 24–17 Chiefs lead.

Podolak's second touchdown came with just seven minutes left in the game, but everyone in the stadium and millions more on television had a distinct feeling that somehow this game would include still more drama. The Chiefs were displaying their championship pedigree, converting drives and taking the lead. The Dolphins were doing their utmost to earn one, summoning up their youthful strength and coming back to tie the score once more. Warfield caught two key passes on the ensuing Miami drive. The first one was down the middle for 18 yards, and the second one was just beyond the reach of Kansas City cornerback Emmitt Thomas down the sideline for 28 yards. Griese was soon faced with a second down at the Chiefs' 5-yard line. He rolled right to avoid another heavy Chiefs rush, and found tight end Marv Fleming deep in the end zone for the tying score.

The ledger was now knotted at 24–24 with just a little over a minute of regulation time left. Ed Podolak was not finished, however. He took Miami's succeeding kickoff up the middle, broke to his left, and was off to the races. Curtis Johnson pushed Podolak out of bounds 78 yards later, as the partisan crowd went into a screaming frenzy. All Kansas City had to do was kick a short field goal, and they would advance to the conference championship game. "I took it at the goal line," Podolak recalled when describing the kickoff, "and a wedge of blockers immediately began forming in front of me. I had a pretty clear path upfield, but as I got around the fifty-yard line, Yepremian got in my way. He didn't really hit me, but he forced me to cut to the sideline. Still, for a second, I thought I'd go all the way. But unbeknownst to me, Curtis Johnson of the Dolphins was coming over from the other side of the field. Johnson had the perfect angle. He wanted to simply knock me out of bounds, and I had no chance of outrunning him. As far as preventing the touchdown, he made the play, so you have to give him the credit."

Kansas City's Jan Stenerud was about as accurate a placekicker as the NFL produced during the 1970s. On this fateful day, however, Stenerud followed up Podolak's kickoff return by missing a 22-yard chip shot to the right which would have won the game in regulation. The Miami bench breathed a collective sign of relief. They had been granted an enormous reprieve.

"There was no question in my mind that I was going to make it," Stenerud said in a 1974 interview. "I still don't know to this day how I missed it. I hit the ball perfectly. I hit the ball firm and well. There was hardly any wind at all. The turf, especially at that spot, was pretty good."

The game had advanced to sudden death overtime. The first team to score would be the winner. No scoring would occur in the fifth period, however, as tension ratcheted up. Stenerud had a chance to redeem himself, but Dolphins middle linebacker Nick Buoniconti blocked his 35-yard attempt. Not to be outdone in the field goal failure column, Miami's Garo Yepremian missed a 52-yard field goal which fell just a few feet short. Dawson once again got his offense moving, but he threw an untimely interception to end the threat. The contest went into the sixth period.

The Kansas City defense had kept star Miami runner Larry Csonka in check all afternoon. One misdirection run by Csonka, however, would lead to the winning score. Csonka bulled through a gaping hole on a trap play over his weakside left tackle, as Miami's offensive line shifted their blocks to the strongside. "It was a roll-right trap," said Csonka after the game. "Kiick and Griese start towards the strongside and I go the other way. The two guards cut with me and then it's up to me. It was a great call by Griese. He's the kind of quarterback who is aware of the running game. You can have the best running backs in the world but if the quarterback doesn't realize it, it doesn't do any good." Csonka would later recall that he would lose so much weight in the prolonged struggle that his "pants were loose by the end of the game, and I constantly had to re-tighten my belt."

Csonka's 29-yard run put the Dolphins in range of another field goal attempt, and this time, Yepremian's kick was true from the 37. The Dolphins had somehow outlasted the Chiefs, 27–24, in the longest game in NFL history.

"I thought when we were driving I could make anything under 50 yards," said Yepremian. "After I kicked the ball, I looked up at the sky and thanked God for giving me the chance to kick it. As soon as I kicked it, I knew that it was good." Miami head coach Don Shula was elated with the way his team responded to the Chiefs' challenge: "We've never had a bigger one," said Shula of the playoff game. "We had guts and determination and our guys refused to be beaten. We had the big blocks on the plays which set up the field goal. Garo has all the confidence in the world."

As the Dolphins bench erupted in jubilation, the Chiefs trudged off the field in forlorn anguish. They did not know it at the time, but they would never reach the playoffs again during the 1970s. Their epic loss to the Dolphins on that Christmas Day still leaves a bitter taste for the members of Hank Stram's team. "That game is memorialized in my memory," said Johnny Robinson many years later. "We shouldn't have lost that game. Jan never missed a short field goal attempt, but that one he did. It was my toughest defeat in pro football." Podolak would be forever remembered for his total yardage record that day, but the heartbreaking loss has somewhat vanquished that, at least in his mind. "We didn't reach our ultimate goal," said Podolak, "I've tried to forget that day, because it is still one of the biggest disappointments I've ever experienced in football."

Stenerud himself, in a more contemplative mood, described that day's events by surmising, "If you look at it from an unselfish point of view, it was a fantastic game. But in my mind, it will stick out as a personal disaster." Coach Stram echoed his kicker's torment in his postgame remarks. "It was unbelievable ... unbelievable," said Stram. "It's a shame to play that hard, play that well and not win. [But] you've got to give them [Miami] a lot of credit, coming back the way they did, playing the way they did. They're a hell of a team."

The conference championship games the following week featured none of the excitement that the Miami-Kansas City playoff game exhibited. They did, however, showcase some unique individual and team performances by the four teams still in contention for the Vince Lombardi Trophy. Both the Dallas Cowboys and the San Francisco 49ers were participating against each other for the second straight year for the NFC title. Both teams brought outstanding defenses to the game, and it was the defenses which dominated. A capacity crowd in Texas Stadium witnessed two very good offenses struggle. San Francisco's running game accumulated a whopping 2,144 yards in 1971, but on this day against the Doomsday Defense, they could muster only 61 rushing yards. The Cowboys offense scored a league-high 406 points during the regular season (an average of 29 points per game), but against the 49ers, they could put up only 14. Those 14 points would be enough, however, for the Cowboys to secure victory.

Undoubtedly the game's biggest play occurred in the second quarter, when 49ers quarterback John Brodie attempted a screen pass deep in his own territory. Drifting out to his right was veteran Dallas defensive end George Andrie, who was hidden from Brodie's view. Brodie's target was fullback Ken Willard, but Andrie stepped in front of Willard and intercepted the pass at the 49ers' 9-yard line. Andrie lumbered to the 2-yard line before he was tripped up by 49ers' offensive tackle Len Rohde, giving the Cowboys a first and goal situation. Dallas fullback Calvin Hill dove into the end zone two plays later. "Obviously, I didn't see him," Brodie muttered when asked about Andrie. "Give 'em [the Dallas defense] credit."

The Cowboys took their 7–0 lead into the third quarter, when the 49ers offense finally started to show signs of life. Key receptions by wide receiver Gene Washington and tight end Ted Kwalick got the 49ers close enough for a field goal from placekicker Bruce Gossett. Dallas now had a 7–3 lead going into the fourth quarter, and at this point, the game was still up for grabs.

Dallas quarterback Roger Staubach proved to be the most important factor in reacquiring the momentum for the Cowboys. Staubach left his passing pocket eight times in the contest, and gained a team-high 55 yards rushing. On one of his runs, Staubach journeyed to his left and eluded San Francisco defensive tackle Earl Edwards, then turned and sprinted to his right, evading the 49ers' defensive end Tommy Hart, then passed the ball to reserve halfback Dan Reeves for a 17-yard gain and a first down. The scrambling from the former Midshipman from Navy was vital to the Cowboys' success in the fourth quarter, mainly because San Francisco's pass defense was continuing to perform at peak level, limiting Dallas to just 103 total passing yards.

"Roger's scrambling was the difference," said San Francisco head coach Dick Nolan. "We couldn't contain him. The Cowboys didn't move the ball that well except for his scrambling."

Midway through the fourth quarter, Staubach connected on key passes to his tight ends Billy

Truax and Mike Ditka, which set up the final Dallas touchdown. From the San Francisco 2-yard line, Staubach keenly observed a weakness along the edge in the 49ers' defensive lineup. He motioned to halfback Duane Thomas to switch his stance from the strongside to the weakside, believing that Thomas could outrun any 49ers defender to the corner of the end zone. Thomas did exactly that, taking a quick pitch from his quarterback and sprinting to his left untouched into the end zone for a 14–3 Dallas lead. A key block on the play came from flanker Lance Alworth, who managed to get in the way of two 49ers linebackers.

"That drive used up seven and a half minutes," said Dallas middle linebacker Lee Roy Jordan after the game, "and it had to take it out of them [the 49ers]. From then on, they had to throw."

The 49ers were desperate to move the ball via the air as time was running out on their championship dream. Two key interceptions late in the game, one by Jordan, and the other by safety Cliff Harris, ended San Francisco's season at the same mile marker as the year before, as they watched the Cowboys advance once again.

"It wasn't very exciting, was it?" asked Landry from the victors locker room. "It was just a step toward the Super Bowl. We felt it was the big step but it was still just a step."

The AFC championship game later that same day would pit two more familiar adversaries ready to take that same step, the Baltimore Colts and the Miami Dolphins. Both teams split their regular season series. Both teams were buoyed by two very strong defenses. Both teams had quality quarterbacks in John Unitas for the Colts and Bob Griese for the Dolphins. The one prominent difference between the two squads, however, involved the health factor. Miami entered the title game in pretty good shape, with all of their team leaders in the lineup. Baltimore did not. Both of Baltimore's leading rushers—Norm Bulaich and Tom Matte—were unable to play due to their respective injuries.

A humid south Florida rain fell just prior to the game, and as a result, a solid rainbow streamed across the north end of the jam-packed Orange Bowl. The Dolphins would claim the pot of gold at the end of that rainbow and find in it not gold, but instead a ticket to Super Bowl VI.

The Colts had defeated the Dolphins just three weeks prior to this championship game by dominating the first half with two time-consuming drives. Miami head coach Don Shula was determined to force the Colts into a different strategy in this game. On their second series from their own 25-yard line, the Dolphins tried a deep sideline pass to their premier wide receiver, Paul Warfield. Bob Griese faked a handoff to Larry Csonka, then threw a perfect pass that Warfield caught over his shoulder. Warfield immediately spun upfield and raced down the sideline and into the end zone, beating Baltimore safety Rick Volk, who was in hot but futile pursuit. The Colts would now be forced to play from behind on the scoreboard, and Shula's strategy of striking quickly provided the spark of confidence that his young team needed.

The Baltimore running game, minus Bulaich and Matte, could register only 89 yards on this day. The Colts actually out-gained the Dolphins (302 total yards to 286 total yards), however, and they also controlled the ball (68 plays to Miami's 45). Shula's defense, however, was geared to keep opponents out of the end zone. A big play had given Miami the early lead. An even bigger play in the third quarter would provide the Dolphins with timely insurance to claim their first conference championship.

Johnny Unitas tried to throw a bomb to wide receiver Eddie Hinton, but both Hinton and Miami cornerback Curtis Johnson jumped for it at the same time, and both deflected the ball at the same instant. Miami strong safety Dick Anderson was trailing the play and easily caught the deflected ball. Anderson turned upfield and discovered that most of his defensive teammates immediately began throwing key blocks. Providing a convoy for Anderson were Jake Scott, Bob Heinz, Mike Kolen, Bill Stanfill, Tim Foley and Doug Swift—the core of the No-Name Defense.

Anderson ran across the field toward the Miami bench, then he sprinted down the sideline, then he cut across the field behind his blocks to reach paydirt. The 62-yard play devastated the Colts and gave the Dolphins a commanding 14–0 lead.

"It was just fantastic the way our people pulled out," said Anderson after the game. "I found a wall set up like on a punt return. I knew I was still a long way from the end zone, but by then I could see some running room. I've never seen so many people [Colts] landing on their heads, just upended, like that before."

Don Shula was equally gleeful. "I was more proud of that than any play I've seen in football," beamed Shula. "I thought that Anderson was going to get four or five yards at the most. You could see the blocks form from the sideline. That's what real football is all about."

As the fourth quarter began, Baltimore abandoned its weakened running game in favor of more Unitas passing. He experienced only modest success against the Miami defense, however. The Dolphin defenders limited Unitas' receivers to short and inconsequential receptions. It was one more long pass from Griese to Warfield, however, which covered 50 yards and led to the final touchdown of the game. On that play midway in the fourth quarter, Griese was faced with a third and short yardage situation. The Dolphins could afford to take a calculated risk at this point of the game, as their 14–0 lead and the play of their defense had given them enormous confidence as the second half wore on. Griese faked once again to Csonka and threw the ball over the middle. Warfield caught Griese's pass at the Baltimore 25-yard line. He then stopped on a dime with his back to the end zone, faked a move to his left, then turned once more and ran to his right toward the sideline, evading a couple of would-be Colt tacklers. Warfield was eventually run out of bounds by Baltimore middle linebacker Mike Curtis at the Colt 5-yard line. Csonka crashed in to score on the next play. Amid a capacity crowd of hanky-waving fans, the Dolphins had built an insurmountable lead, and in a few short minutes prevailed over their arch-rivals, 21–0. Thus Baltimore's reign as world champions ended. One of the league's youngest teams in both age of franchise (the Dolphins were only in their sixth pro season in 1971) and age of players (the team's average age per man was 25) was suddenly headed to the Super Bowl.

"Coach Shula is a football genius," said a dejected Baltimore outside linebacker Ted Hendricks as he stood in front of his postgame locker. "He's absolutely brilliant. He knows weaknesses and strengths. He can look over a team and tell you in a split second what will work against a certain defense and what will stop that team's attack." Johnny Unitas added that Miami was a team that "didn't make many mistakes."

Super Bowl VI marked the second time that the big game would be held in New Orleans. As the Super Bowl became more and more popular in the early 1970s, the hoopla prior to the world championship game grew with each passing year. New Orleans is a city that was built for holiday parties and colorful extravaganzas. The throngs of media that converged on both teams prior to the big game had increased by 1971, and with them came the predictable but anxious excitement in the days before kickoff. The NFL decreed that two weeks would separate the conference championship games and the Super Bowl, and that left plenty of time for distractions. Some of those distractions included interview requests, autograph sessions, the search for available tickets, and the evening nightclub scene along the French Quarter in downtown New Orleans. All of these amusements added to the impending sense of nervousness which both teams were forced to address. The belief during the early 1970s was that most young teams making their first visit to the Super Bowl would be so overwhelmed with the numerous distractions that they would inevitably become too nervous and play poorly.

The NFC champion Cowboys were making their second straight trip to the Super Bowl, and most experts were favoring them to defeat the young and inexperienced Dolphins. The Cowboys themselves were eager to erase the belief that they "could not win the big one," a belief which was based on fact. Dallas was making its sixth straight appearance in the postseason tournament, and none of their previous attempts ended in the ultimate success of a world championship. Their appearance in Super Bowl VI caused them once again to reflect on the feelings of coming up short in a championship game. The Cowboys desperately wanted to put those feelings to rest once and for all.

The AFC champion Dolphins had exceeded all expectations by making it this far in such a short amount of time. Miami was an AFL expansion team which obtained the perfect coach to make them a winner. Don Shula was, in his own words, "about as subtle as a punch in the face." Shula's direct approach to coaching spared few players from his bombastic yelling and simmering gaze whenever they made a mistake in practice or in a game. The young Dolphins responded as much out of fear for their coach as they did from any other impetus. The resulting 12 victories and an AFC title in 1971 was ample proof that Shula's hardened methods were working. The only question that remained would be how well his team would respond to the determined Cowboys.

A brilliant sunshine and a cloudless sky covered Tulane Stadium and its new artificial surface on Super Sunday. Several dozen American flags flapped in the chilly wind during the pregame ceremonies, symbolically ending a super season with colorful pride and patriotism. NFL Commissioner Pete Rozelle liked to showcase the championship game as more than just a football game. Rozelle intended the Super Bowl to be a vibrant display of color and pageantry, and a fitting and exciting culmination to each spectacular season. The history of New Orleans jazz music provided the major theme of the entertainment at Super Bowl VI. That entertainment included a tribute to the late New Orleans musical legend Louis "Satchmo" Armstrong. Singers and celebrities like Ella Fitzgerald, Carol Channing, and the famous jazz musician Al Hirt, were all there to entertain the 80,591 in attendance. The Super Bowl would eventually grow into a new type of national holiday, and the sixth version of this game increased its popularity. NFL Films released a special film about the 1971 season entitled *A Glorious Game*. The final words in the film seemed to capture the growing spirit and excitement of the NFL in a very popular season: "For the player, victory makes the game glorious. For the fan, the glory *is* the game." The glory of the annual Super Bowl game did much to help the "National Game" of pro football quickly become entrenched in the midst of favored American traditions.

The Miami Dolphins recent tradition was to establish their powerful running attack. Things looked promising for them on their second series, as the Dolphins drove to the Dallas 46-yard line. Fullback Larry Csonka then inexplicably mishandled a handoff from quarterback Bob Griese. "I was reading the hole and had my eyes too high," Csonka said.

Csonka's first fumble in 238 carries (and his first this season) was recovered by Dallas linebacker Chuck Howley. Now the Cowboys had a chance to establish their running attack. Dallas runners such as Duane Thomas, Walt Garrison, and Calvin Hill, each took turns carrying the ball and gaining yardage. A whole lot of yardage. By game's end, the Cowboys would set a then–Super Bowl record with 252 overall rushing yards.

"There's only one thing that won this game," Staubach said afterward. "When the Cowboys run the football, everything else works." Calvin Hill added, "There were such big holes that anybody could have gotten through."

The strategy that Dallas head coach Tom Landry used against a quick pursuing team like the Dolphins involved cutback running. The Dallas runners took a step in the same direction as their blockers, then took a handoff from quarterback Roger Staubach, and then abruptly changed directions and ran against the flow and momentum of the play. The strategy worked to near perfection, as the gaping holes mentioned by Hill were found often in the Dolphins front line. A major tenet of Dallas' cutback running strategy also involved blocking Miami middle linebacker Nick Buoniconti. The Dallas linemen, tight ends, and blocking backs were instructed to block or shield Buoniconti on virtually every running play. "Buoniconti was very quick," said Cowboys All-Pro guard John Niland, "and we wanted to make his quickness run him out of the play." Dallas center Dave Manders was more blunt in his pregame prediction. "Buoniconti is going to spend Sunday afternoon on his ass," Manders said.

Dallas drove to the Miami 2-yard line with this strategy when the No-Name Defense finally held. Mike Clark's short field goal late in the first quarter gave the Cowboys a 3–0 lead.

The Cowboys' dominance on the line of scrimmage was not just limited to their offense, however. Dallas' Doomsday Defense was also starting to contain and frustrate Griese. On the final play of the first quarter, Dallas pass rushers Bob Lilly and Larry Cole chased down Griese as he frantically tried to locate an open receiver. Lilly finally trapped the exasperated and back-pedaling quarterback for a 29-yard loss, the biggest quarterback sack in Super Bowl history.

Lilly's performance on this day was the highlight of his outstanding career. In describing his epic sack of Griese, Lilly claimed, "I looped outside of George Andrie, our left end, and Larry Cole beat his man on the right side. Griese kept giving ground, turning little loops. He was trying to buy time, clear a receiver, make something happen. Cole and me just kept herding him back. It was like how riders hem up a cow they want to take. I think Griese was okay until he realized how much ground he'd given. He might have gotten a little nervous then."

The Dallas running attack was showing no signs of nervousness, however, as Garrison's bullish thrusts into the Dolphins line accumulated big chunks of yardage. And to Landry's pleasure, his offense received an added boost late in the second quarter when flanker Lance Alworth caught a key third-down pass for 21 yards across the middle. Staubach threw the ball perfectly over a leaping Miami linebacker Doug Swift's reach and into Alworth's nestling arms. From there, three straight runs by Calvin Hill brought the Cowboys to the Miami 7-yard line. Staubach then rifled a pass to Alworth in the corner of the end zone for the first touchdown of the game. Staubach would later admit, "I never threw a pass any harder." Alworth just barely got his feet down inside the end zone flag, beating Dolphins cornerback Curtis Johnson.

Shula quickly decided to focus his attention on his passing attack. The week prior to the game, Shula had received a telephone call from America's #1 football fan, President Richard M. Nixon. The Commander-in-Chief suggested that Griese should try a quick down-and-in pass to wide receiver Paul Warfield. Shula attempted the President's suggestion twice in the first half. It failed both times. Dallas cornerback Mel Renfro and safety Cornell Green effectively double-teamed Warfield throughout the game, limiting him to only four receptions for a meager 39 yards. After batting down a pass intended for Warfield on one particular play in the first quarter, Dallas safety Cliff Harris quipped to Renfro, "Nixon is a great strategist, isn't he?" Renfro did yeoman's work in defending Warfield, an effort indicative of his desire to succeed against one of the game's best receivers. "Warfield's like a jackrabbit," described Renfro. "He jumps and skips with his feet moving fast. Some receivers have speed and moves but can't catch the ball. Paul can do everything.

"I can't worry about the down-and-in or he'll beat me on something else. I'd rather give him five yards in front of me than 50 behind me. I knew I had a job to do. It would make or break me."

With less than two minutes remaining in the first half, however, Warfield did manage to break free of Renfro's containment, and Griese found him for a key 23-yard pass, which set up Miami's only points of the game, a 31-yard field goal by placekicker Garo Yepremian.

Dallas received the second half kickoff and immediately drove to a championship. An eight-play, 71-yard drive was culminated by Duane Thomas, who took a pitchout from Staubach and swept left. Thomas broke an arm tackle from a diving Buoniconti and waltzed into the end zone to give Dallas a 17–3 lead. Thomas carried four times on the drive, gaining 37 of his game-high 95 yards. "Duane Thomas was a really good back [today]," said Dallas tight end Mike Ditka in the crowded and joyous locker room after the game. "And the thing he did best was cut back. He'd get in a hole quick, he would clear it, and then he'd look, right away, to cut back across the pursuit grain."

The quick offensive surge was the result of some key halftime adjustments by Landry, who figured that the Miami defensive line would try to seal up the middle by moving their tackles closer together. Once they did, the Cowboys utilized quick pitches and sweeps to the outside. A 16-yard run by wide receiver Bob Hayes on a reverse was also effective in limiting Dolphin pursuit.

Later in the fourth quarter, Chuck Howley intercepted a Griese pass that was intended for halfback Jim Kiick, and returned it 41 yards to the Miami 9-yard line. Howley fell down on the play, attempting to knock Dolphin flanker Howard Twilley off of his route. He jumped up quickly, however, and found himself directly in Griese's passing lane. Three plays later, Staubach, who would be named the game's Most Valuable Player, connected with Ditka in the corner of the end zone for a 24–3 cushion. Ditka had beaten Miami safety Dick Anderson on the play, who was lured to the inside when Alworth ran across the middle.

Miami had one more final drive, but a Griese fumble on a poor center-quarterback snap resulted in another Dallas recovery. The Cowboys ran out all but the last few seconds of the clock.

Dallas Cowboys fullback Walt Garrison gains yardage against the Miami Dolphins' No-Name Defense in Super Bowl VI, January 16, 1972. The Cowboys won their first world championship with a 24–3 triumph over the Dolphins (AP Photo/NFL Photos).

The Cowboys finally won the big one by a dominating score of 24–3, and had achieved the ultimate vindication. Their defensive effort in Super Bowl VI retains a record to this day. The Doomsday Defense on January 16, 1972, has been the only defense which has held an opponent to zero touchdowns and the least points allowed in the history of the Super Bowl. Tom Landry would receive a victory ride on the shoulders of his joyful players as the final gun sounded. In the triumphant and crowded Cowboys locker room after the game, the Vince Lombardi Trophy was gleefully passed around to hold and treasure by all of the Dallas players and coaches. "I think the dominant feeling in the dressing room afterward was one of relief," said Howley. "We had won the big one people said we couldn't win. The tension was gone. We no longer had to prove ourselves."

Staubach affirmed Howley's sentiments. "I remember a feeling of complete satisfaction," he said after the game. Smiles were on many faces, and even Duane Thomas came out of his shell for a moment when being interviewed by Tom Brookshier of CBS. When asked by Brookshier if he was as fast as it seemed on this day, Thomas gave a one-word answer: "Evidently." The room erupted in cheers. Across Tulane Stadium in the Miami dressing room, Dolphins coach Don Shula later commented that Dallas played "a near-perfect game."

The following year, the word "perfect" would be mentioned again.

1972

Perfection and Miraculous Memories

Pro football historians could easily argue with success that 1972 was the most notable, the most exciting, and the most legendary year in the history of the game. The 1972 season produced the first undefeated and untied team in NFL annals, as well as the most improbable finishes ever to a couple of remarkable and celebrated playoff games. The season also yielded the most 1,000-yard rushers in league history up to that point. A total of ten running backs eclipsed the 1,000-yard mark, and several others came within 100 yards of joining them. One of those running backs actually reached the 1,000-yard mark, then lost it while being tackled for a loss on his final carry of the season. The 1972 season also saw the longest pass play in NFL history that *did not* result in a touchdown. When total yardage is being discussed, an aerial assault in the second week of the season accounted for the most combined passing yards in one game in league history up to that year. The two teams involved in that scoring fest were two of the most famous adversaries in league history. By season's end, a new individual pass receiving record was established, and a new rushing record for quarterbacks was achieved. These were just two of many new standards that were set in this special season. All in all, 1972 was one heck of a year, and one well worth remembering.

The harvest of 1,000-yard runners was the product of a change to every football field just prior to the beginning of the season. The league decided to move the hashmarks (or inbounds lines) closer to the middle of the field. The new placement of the hashmarks would now be equal to the distance between the uprights of the goal posts (18 feet, 6 inches). The change enlarged the open areas between the sidelines and the hashmarks to 23 yards, 1 foot, 9 inches, which permitted many a runner some extra space to find daylight. The main hope for the change among the league owners was to increase scoring and to nullify to some extent the success of the zone defenses. Both of those hopes were realized, but the additional yardage totals by the running backs was the most noticeable result of the change. The more ground yardage was gained, the more the number of ground touchdowns were scored, from 333 in 1971 to 364 in 1972. Another rushing statistic of note involved the popular benchmark for all runners, the 100-yard game. In 1971, the 100-yard rushing effort was achieved 48 times. In 1972, that figure was surpassed in the season's ninth week.

The league owners also approved of a change which determined won-lost percentages in the standings. Up until 1972, tie games were not counted in the standings. From 1972 on, however, tie games would count as a half-game won and a half-game lost. Improved winning percentages among teams with tie games were the result.

A change in ownership for several teams also occurred in 1972. Robert Irsay became the new owner of the Baltimore Colts, and Carroll Rosenbloom went west, taking ownership of the

Los Angeles Rams. A long-time owner, Art Rooney, saw his beloved Pittsburgh Steelers experience their best season ever, making the playoffs for the first time in their 40-year history. Rooney's team finally experienced a popular doctrine in the NFL: A winning team will attract fan support. The fans in the Steel City grew to capacity in Three Rivers Stadium, developed vocal fan clubs for many Steeler players, and reveled in each of Pittsburgh's 11 regular season victories in 1972.

Many of those fan clubs were highly visible and loud enough to rattle opposing signal callers. Undoubtedly the most popular was "Franco's Italian Army," named after star rookie halfback Franco Harris, and based on Harris' part–Italian heritage. "Gerela's Gorillas" was another noteworthy fan club, being named after placekicker Roy Gerela. "Franco's Italian Army" consisted of a bunch of Italian-American Steeler fans donning army uniforms and waving the national flag of Italy. Several members of Franco's followers also parked old Army jeeps in the corners of the end zones at Three Rivers Stadium. "Gerela's Gorillas" saw several "normal" people dressed in gorilla outfits and eating bananas in the stands. The fun and excitement provided by such fan clubs coincided with the fact that the Steelers were starting to see positive results from the NFL draft. Many quality Pittsburgh draft selections from the past few years like defensive tackle Joe Greene and quarterback Terry Bradshaw were beginning to bring prestige to the Black and Gold.

One of the NFL's perennial quality teams, the Dallas Cowboys, entered the 1972 season as defending world champions. The Cowboys underwent several changes in their lineup before the season began, however. Disgruntled halfback Duane Thomas was sent packing to San Diego, quarterback Roger Staubach sustained a shoulder separation during the preseason and was sidelined for much of the regular season, and new receivers Billy Parks and Ron Sellers took playing time away from longtime veterans Bob Hayes and Lance Alworth. Rookie Robert Newhouse was a small but bullish running back who helped to make up for the loss of Thomas in the backfield, and Craig Morton filled in admirably for Staubach. The result of all of these changes led to a more conservative offense, but one that was still one of the league's most formidable. Dallas accumulated 256 first downs in 1972, the second-best mark in the NFC. The Dallas roster was filled with experience and determination, but the determination to unseat them as champions came from all over the league.

One of the teams that desperately wanted to knock the Cowboys off of their perch was their division rivals, the Washington Redskins. George Allen's team had more veteran leadership than most teams could ever hope for, and having had a taste of the playoffs in 1971, the Redskins were poised to go further this season. Allen was driven by the love of winning, and he described that love in life lessons that he told to his team. "Every time you win, you're reborn," said Allen. Conversely, losing to Allen was figuratively gut-wrenching. "Every time you lose you die a little," he admitted. "Not all of your organs, a portion of you; maybe just your liver." Allen was a perfectionist who prided himself on instilling pride and excellence in every phase of his lineup. Most coaches and experts around the league would rate Allen's special teams as some of the best in league history. The Redskins worked very hard on punt and kickoff coverage units, and their punt and placekick-blocking squads were extremely feared throughout the NFL. Washington's older players bought in to his fervor for winning and the unabashed enthusiasm that Allen displayed on a daily basis, and were fondly referred to as the "Over the Hill Gang." They would prove to be not so "over the hill" by season's end.

The Green Bay Packers had experienced many great seasons during the previous decade, but had failed to make the playoffs during the past four years. A quick turnabout in 1972 was not expected for the Pack, but that is exactly what they got. Head coach Dan Devine drafted several talented rookies and made a few important trades to boost his roster. The Packers' new offense included fullback MacArthur Lane, who was acquired from St. Louis, and guard Malcolm Snider, who came in from Atlanta. Their defensive secondary improved greatly with the addition of stand-out rookie cornerback Willie Buchanon, and by Devine's willingness to move several players to better-suited positions. Cornerback Al Matthews moved over to the strong safety position, and Ken Ellis switched to the right cornerback spot. Veteran Jimmy Hill was brought in from San Diego and was inserted in the free safety position. Those changes proved quite successful, as Green Bay's defense gave up only 226 points, 72 fewer than the previous season. The defensive secondary gave up a meager seven touchdown passes throughout the 14-game regular season, the best mark in the league in that category.

"The first day Willie [Buchanon] got to camp, we got out on the field," recalled Jimmy Hill. "The first thing the kid says to me, before he even said hello, was 'Where's my help coming from?' Right then and there, I knew he was gonna be good, and I knew we were gonna be good."

The Packers also benefitted from the likes of rookie placekicker Chester Marcol, who led all kickers with 33 field goals and who led the league in scoring with 128 points. "We knew that we had to improve our kicking game," said Devine, "if we were going to have a chance at coming back. Chester was the answer to that problem." The Packers were poised for a comeback.

Another team that desperately wanted to redeem themselves in 1972 was the Oakland Raiders. The Raiders failed to make the playoffs in 1971 for the first time in five seasons. Oakland head coach John Madden was faced with the all-too-common chore of many pro coaches—rebuilding his team. He brought in several new players who made an immediate impact in the Raiders lineup. Oakland's new defensive line featured a youth movement in players like Horace Jones, Otis Sistrunk, Art Thoms and Tony Kline. Each one of these linemen performed better than expected, as did two new linebackers, Gerald Irons and Phil Villapiano. The Oakland offense also upgraded itself when Cliff Branch, a world-class sprinter from the University of Colorado, joined the receiving corps. The new additions would prove to be extremely successful, and the Raiders would continue their time-honored tradition of winning by claiming another division title in 1972.

Across the San Francisco Bay, the 49ers were also striving to improve. Head coach Dick Nolan's squad had seen their past two seasons end just one step from the Super Bowl, and they were eager to see if the third time would be the charm. The 49ers struggled early, however. Quarterback John Brodie was forced to deal with nagging injuries during the first half of the year, but Steve Spurrier filled in admirably for him. San Francisco's great duo of running back Vic Washington and wide receiver Gene Washington continued to produce for the team. The 49ers ranked first among NFC teams in total offense in 1972, and surged to win key games down the stretch. Dick Nolan's team would end up being crowned NFC West champions for the third straight year.

Several teams which did not win divisions in 1972 were nevertheless competitive throughout the season. The Cincinnati Bengals recovered well from the previous season, going from 4–10 in 1971 to 8–6 in 1972. Leading the Bengals attack in 1972 was young quarterback Ken Anderson, who would eventually become one of the decade's most accurate passers. Anderson started all 14 games and completed 56.8 percent of his passes. Cincinnati did not have a strong receiving corps, but Anderson made the most of his weapons. The Bengals finished fourth in the AFC in 1972 in passing offense. Head coach Paul Brown's team improved enough to win three of their final four games of the season.

The expectations going into the 1972 season were high for the Kansas City Chiefs, and by mid-season, it looked like head coach Hank Stram's team would fulfill those expectations. Unfortunately for the Chiefs, three straight losses in November gave their arch-rivals, the Oakland Raiders, the AFC Western crown. The Chiefs' balanced attack was missing receiver Elmo Wright through much of the season to injuries. Moreover, young replacements at several key positions led to critical mistakes. Kansas City regrouped, however, and won their final three games to post an 8–6 record, finishing just two games out of first place. Veteran quarterback Len Dawson threw for 1,835 yards and 13 touchdowns to pace the Kansas City attack.

Speaking of touchdowns, the Detroit Lions scored 40 of them in 1972. The Lions ranked second in the NFC in total offense, totaling 339 points. Included in their statistics was over 2,000 yards in both rushing and passing. Quarterback Greg Landry was just as dangerous carrying the ball as he was throwing the ball. Landry ran for 524 yards and threw for 2,066 yards as the Lions roared to a 8–5–1 record. Two other Detroit ball carriers—Altie Taylor and Steve Owens—each ran for more than 500 yards. The Lions would undoubtedly have gained more receiving yards had not All-Pro tight end Charlie Sanders been kept out of five games with an injury. Detroit scored more than 30 points in five of their contests, and like the Chiefs, missed the playoffs by just two games.

The Minnesota Vikings missed the playoffs for the first time in five seasons in 1972. The Vikings brought back prodigal son Fran Tarkenton from the New York Giants to be their quarterback, and they also traded to obtain speedy and elusive wide receiver John Gilliam from St. Louis. Both of these key additions were in their prime. However, both did little to produce enough victories to defend their division title. Minnesota struggled through a disheartening 7–7 season. Their defense did not pack its usual strong punch, giving up 252 points in 1972. With Tarkenton throwing the ball, the Vikings offense showed improvement, but five of their seven losses were by three or less points. Head coach Bud Grant's team surprised the league by not staying competitive down the stretch.

Competition around the NFL was expected by many of the league's perennial playoff contenders, however. Surprises were in store for the first week on the 1972 season, though, as some teams made key statements, and some teams suffered startling upsets. The schedule makers were once again at the top of their game, pitting a rematch on opening day of the NFL's longest game from last year's AFC divisional playoff between the Miami Dolphins and the Kansas City Chiefs. Fans across the nation were expecting a primal battle from these two teams, which would set the tone for the remainder of the season. The game would be held on a new stage, however. Kansas City's sparkling new Arrowhead Stadium seated 78,907 people and was quite simply one of the most beautiful and modern stadiums to ever be showcased on the NFL landscape. Chicago Bears owner and NFL patriarch George Halas commented that Arrowhead was "the most revolutionary, futuristic, sports complex that I have ever seen." Arrowhead featured a Tartan Turf playing surface, two large end zone scoreboards, outstanding sight lines for the fans, and over a dozen luxury boxes.

The 91-degree game time temperature was certainly not luxurious for either team, however. The temperature on the artificial surface was even hotter, hovering at a simmering 102 degrees. A thermometer would later record the field temperature at 120 degrees. Those hot and humid summers at Don Shula's training camp/oven proved their worth on this day, as Miami outlasted the Chiefs, 20–10. Spoiling the debut of the Chiefs at Arrowhead Stadium was Miami's No-Name Defense, a unit which took control of the game when it mattered most. Kansas City quarterback Len Dawson was able to move his offense up and down the field, but as soon as they neared the Dolphins end zone, the Chiefs were unable to cash in on their opportunities. Miami's defense erected a concrete wall near the goal line, intercepting two of Dawson's passes and recovering two Kansas City fumbles. Kansas City scored their only touchdown with but seconds remaining in the game. The Dolphins had taken their first step in what would become their most remarkable season ever.

"We were able to capitalize on some errors and later got into ball control," said Shula. Kansas

City head coach Hank Stram aptly described the results of those errors. "They [Miami] didn't have to drive more than half the field the whole game," said a dejected Stram following the game. "You just can't play a good team and not make them use the whole field. It goes to show you that when you make mistakes against a good team you're going to lose, and that's what happened to us. Turnovers, penalties, and fumbles were our big mistakes. We can't blame anybody but ourselves for those."

The Pittsburgh Steelers also made a statement in their first game of the season as they defeated the visiting Oakland Raiders, 34–28. Big plays were the main catalyst for Pittsburgh's surprise victory. Reserve linebacker Henry Davis returned a blocked punt five yards for the Steelers' initial score. Quarterback Terry Bradshaw scored two more Steeler touchdowns, as his team built a 27–7 cushion going into the fourth quarter. One of Bradshaw's scores came from 20 yards out as he rumbled right up the middle of the Oakland defense. Pittsburgh's defense limited Oakland to 97 rushing yards on 30 carries and forced five turnovers for the win.

"I wouldn't say we're the best necessarily," said a satisfied defensive end Dwight White after the game. "But we can play with the best."

The Washington Redskins also proved competitive when they made a Monday night visit to Metropolitan Stadium in Minnesota to wrap up the first weekend of the 1972 season. George Allen's club upended the Vikings in a thrilling contest, 24–21. Reserve Redskins wide receiver Bill Malinchak stormed into the Minnesota backfield in the first quarter, blocked a Mike Eischeid punt, recovered the ball, and sprinted into the end zone for a quick 7–0 lead. The Redskins offense then took advantage of two key Minnesota fumbles and scored two decisive fourth quarter touchdowns. Washington's quick strikes on runs by Larry Brown and Charlie Harraway must have come as a shock to the Minnesota defense, a unit which had been a fixture at the top of the league standings in shutting down opposing ground attacks for the past several years. The Vikings led the league in fewest points allowed from 1969 to 1971. Not so in 1972. Minnesota permitted 113 more points than they did the previous year. Such a statistic was glaring proof that the "typical" Vikings defense was missing in action.

The following week in Baltimore's Memorial Stadium, no sight of any defense could be found as the Jets played the Colts. The game was billed as a matchup between two great quarterbacks and a rematch of Super Bowl III. Joe Namath of the Jets would be going up against the man he idolized as a youngster, the veteran and legendary signal caller of the Colts, Johnny Unitas. Namath's legs were not in the best of shape after two consecutive injury-plagued seasons in 1970 and 1971, but his arm was just fine on this day. He threw for a robust 496 yards as he seared the famed Baltimore zone defense. Six of Namath's 15 completions went for touchdowns.

Namath's stellar performance inspired columnist J. Suter Kegg to comment, "No team has ever had so many receivers open so many times against the fabled Colt zone as the Jets." Namath himself downplayed his achievement by stating, "I don't think I was at my best today. Several of my passes were short, several were too long, and I hung a couple." The fact is this game—along with Super Bowl III—were the two most memorable in cementing Namath's status as one of the most famous quarterbacks in the history of the game and a member of Pro Football's Hall of Fame.

Johnny Unitas—who also has a handsome bust in Canton—turned in one of his best performances as well, connecting on 26 of 45 throws for 376 yards and two scores. One of Unitas' passes came on the same flea-flicker play that had failed against the Jets in Super Bowl III. This time, however, it was Unitas—and not his former teammate Earl Morrall—who found flanker Sam Havrilak alone in the end zone for a 40-yard score. The 872 combined aerial yards between the two future Hall of Famers set an NFL passing record which lasted until 1982.

New York's 44–34 victory over the Colts was sewn up in the fourth quarter, when two of Namath's passes were caught by Rich Caster. The first one went for 79 yards. The second one went for 80 yards. Caster described his final score in detail as part of a successful strategy, part innate athletic talent, and part being the beneficiary of having a superstar quarterback with a tremendous throwing arm. "I split out as the only receiver on one side," Caster recalled. "I ran a corner route, got behind the guy covering me, and made the catch on the run at around their 45-yard line and I had myself another … touchdown. Joe [Namath] hit me right on the money. It was unbelievable."

All tolled, Caster had his best day as a pro, catching six passes for 204 yards and three touchdowns. "It was the wildest game I ever played in," Caster admitted. New York's Eddie Bell also brought in seven of Namath's passes for another 197 yards, including a 65-yard touchdown. The various big plays from both teams occurred on seemingly every exchange of the ball, making this one of the most memorable games of the decade. Unitas told reporters prior to the game, "You can't throw long against the zone [defense]." Namath took that as a legitimate challenge, and with his quick release and solid protection, he bombarded the Baltimore zone defense. "You have to try to design pass patterns that are flexible enough to get somebody open no matter what defense they are playing," said Namath. "You can't go after the strength of a pass defense. You try to hit it where it is weak."

The Oakland Raiders' defensive secondary was rarely—if ever—described as "weak" during the 1970s. A popular member of their group, free safety Jack Tatum, contributed another league record on the same afternoon of the Namath-Unitas passing fest. Tatum returned a fumble 104 yards for a touchdown in Oakland's 20–14 win at Green Bay. His score broke the 49-year-old mark of 98 yards held by NFL patriarch George Halas, who set the previous standard when he was still a player for the Chicago Bears during the NFL's infancy. "I was surprised all right," said Tatum upon seeing the loose ball dribble near him. "It was a good bounce. I just took off, I thought they [the Packers players] might have been closer than they were behind me."

By the early part of the 1972 season, it became readily apparent that this was a special year in the making. A trend was being established as each successive week brought with it an outstanding game or a unique and newsworthy happening in the league. The third week of the season was a case in point. The defending world champion Dallas Cowboys paid a visit to Milwaukee's County Stadium to play the up-and-coming Green Bay Packers. Head coach Dan Devine and his reconstructed Packers pulled off a major 16–13 upset of the Cowboys, benefitting from three timely interceptions and a potent rushing attack. The Green Bay defense forced five Dallas turnovers and Packer running back John Brockington gained 91 yards in the victory. The simple, brute, and constant power thrusts of Brockington and his running mate MacArthur Lane weakened the resolve of many a defense, particularly in the fourth quarter of several key games. The Packers were showing signs that they were for real early in 1972.

"We're such a young team," said Lane. "We have a heck of a line. If we get healthy again [Green Bay had sustained several key injuries in the first two weeks], there's no telling how far we can go."

There certainly was no doubt that the Miami Dolphins were for real. On the same day that the Packers defeated the Cowboys, the Dolphins posted their third straight win. Miami beat a tough Minnesota team and their scrambling quarterback Fran Tarkenton, 16–14, in Metropolitan Stadium. The victory left Miami as the only undefeated team remaining in the NFL. Dolphins tight end Jim Mandich caught Bob Griese's 3-yard touchdown pass with but seconds left in the fourth quarter to claim the victory. Mandich had snuck into the Minnesota end zone undetected and caught Griese's pass with no defender anywhere near him. The victory inspired the Dolphins, who were now convinced that they could defeat tough teams in desperate situations.

"This victory against the Vikings was ... gratifying," said Shula after the game. "You've got to feel that our defense was exceptional. We talked before the game about this being their toughest day [because of Tarkenton], that it would be chase and catch. Well, they chased and caught."

The Dolphins would be placed in their most difficult situation of the year a couple of weeks later. Quarterback Bob Griese suffered a broken ankle against the visiting San Diego Chargers. The sight of their reliable field general being carted off the Orange Bowl turf on a stretcher disheartened the Florida faithful. Fortunately for Don Shula's team, veteran reserve quarterback Earl Morrall was acquired prior to the start of the season, and his experience and leadership won over his new teammates. Morrall took over right where Griese left off, throwing for two touchdowns and producing a 24–10 victory over the Chargers. The Dolphins team rallied around Morrall, stuck with their tried and tested formula of basic running football, and just kept winning games. The defense did pretty well too, keeping their opponents' scores low each week.

"Bill Arnsparger was our defensive coordinator," said Morrall. "He really kept everyone on the defense working well together. It took teamwork to make our defense work, and we had the players on defense who could get to the point [of the play] and react from there. Everyone on that defense covered up for everyone else."

The Miami defense was also not above experimenting with certain personnel to achieve strategical advantages. Reserve linebacker Bob Matheson was a perfect example. Shula and Arnsparger came up with a special defensive alignment for Matheson, and used him as a pass rusher on the defensive line, as a blitzing linebacker, or as a pass-covering linebacker. They called it the "53 defense" because Matheson's number was 53, but what it really amounted to was a 3–4 defense (three down linemen and four linebackers) geared to frustrate the opposition's passing attack. Matheson (6'4", 235) was big enough in the 1970s to play on the defensive line. Yet he was also agile and quick enough to succeed at linebacker. Matheson had the ability to fill in wherever he was needed on any given play, and his versatility made the No-Name Defense one of the toughest to score on in the league. Thanks in part to the success achieved by Matheson's prowess, versions of Miami's 3–4 defense would be utilized by several teams as the decade wore on.

The Baltimore Colts had a pretty good defense too, but on the same day that Miami defeated San Diego, the Colts could not cover up their numerous deficiencies on offense against the visiting Dallas Cowboys. Baltimore turned the ball over three times and could manage only 175 total yards in their 21–0 loss to Dallas. This particular game stands out as important because of the action *off* the field. New Colts general manager Joe Thomas ordered head coach Don McCafferty to bench the legendary but ineffective Unitas. McCafferty did not have the heart to do so, and was fired immediately after the Dallas game. Assistant coach John Sandusky replaced McCafferty as head coach for the remainder of the season. Baltimore's championship year of glory in 1970 suddenly seemed like a very long time ago.

"I have been benched before," admitted the 17-year veteran Unitas, who had quality statistics in 1972 but who was having trouble putting points on the scoreboard. Trade talk soon visited the Colts' locker room. Players like Unitas, center Bill Curry, safety Jerry Logan, and wide receiver Eddie Hinton were rumored to be on the trading block by the end of the season. "I'm not going to be invited back next year to be a $125,000 reserve," said a regretful Unitas in the middle of the season.

While the Colts were having their share of problems, the Green Bay Packers were experiencing a revival of sorts. The fifth week of the 1972 season featured another telling contest which ignited a Packers drive to another division championship. Green Bay had fallen behind their NFC Central rivals, the Detroit Lions, by a 17–0 score before a Monday night television audience and a capacity crowd at Tiger Stadium. The situation changed in the second half, however. Young

Packers defensive back Ken Ellis caught a Herman Weaver punt late in the third quarter, broke to his left, and streaked down the sideline 80 yards for a touchdown. Ellis' score turned things around for the Packers, as their defense got stingy and their offense capitalized on two of Detroit quarterback Greg Landry's interceptions. Green Bay wide receiver Leland Glass caught a 15-yard Scott Hunter pass in the corner of the end zone late in the fourth quarter for the winning score. The Packers' impressive 24–23 comeback victory over the Lions left them on top of the NFC Central with a 4–1 record.

"A large majority of the players played … like I'd like them to play, as far as effort is concerned," said victorious Green Bay head coach Dan Devine. "In fact, I'm very proud of what our people did."

Several prideful performances were visible in key games in the following week. Drama occurred in Miami, where the Dolphins withstood a strong challenge from the Buffalo Bills, a team which was not expected to give Don Shula's team any real trouble. But Buffalo proved resolute, and exhibited strong play by both their offensive and defensive units in the Orange Bowl. Bills linebacker Ken Lee intercepted a pass and returned it for a touchdown, giving the Bills a halftime lead. Miami came back in the third quarter, however, when defensive tackle Manny Fernandez knifed through the line of scrimmage and stole a handoff intended for Buffalo fullback Jim Braxton. Miami fullback Larry Csonka converted Fernandez' great play into a touchdown. The Bills kept the contest close in the fourth quarter, but fell just short of victory. Miami's 24–23 win over a seemingly inferior team boosted their record to 6–0.

Two teams going in opposite directions met once again on Week 6. The New York Jets and the Baltimore Colts faced each other earlier in the season and caused the scoreboard to overheat. They would not score as many points this time around, but they would continue to deliver more drama to another chapter of their exciting rivalry. The scene was New York's Shea Stadium, and the hero for the second time around in 1972 was once again Joe Namath. The Jets quarterback completed only 5 of 16 passes, and three of his attempts went to Colt defenders. But Namath made the key throw late in the fourth quarter to win the game. His 83-yard bomb to Eddie Bell was deflected by Colt defensive back Charlie Stukes. Bell was in the right place at the right time, however. He caught the deflection on the run and sprinted untouched into the end zone to complete the winning play. "He [Namath] told me to run my tail off," said Bell, "and that's what I did." New York's dramatic 24–20 victory kept them in second place in the AFC East at 4–2, while the loss dropped the Colts to a dismal 1–5 record.

Two NFC teams met later that same day and added another chapter of excitement to their growing rivalry. The defending world champion Dallas Cowboys visited their arch-rivals, the Washington Redskins, in the first of what would be three meetings between the two clubs in 1972. Dallas quickly built a 10–0 first quarter lead, highlighted by a 39-yard scoring pass from quarterback Craig Morton to wide receiver Ron Sellers, who had easily beaten Redskins safety Les Duncan on a deep corner route to the end zone. Washington struck back in the second half, however. Redskins tailback Larry Brown scored his second touchdown on a 34-yard dash, and placekicker Curt Knight brought the Redskins to within three points with a field goal at 20–17. Charlie Harraway then secured the comeback win for Washington when he took a pitchout from reserve quarterback Sonny Jurgensen and scored on a 13-yard run late in the fourth quarter. George Allen's team had taken a big step towards taking control of the NFC East with their dramatic 24–20 win over Dallas.

"We started off exceptionally well," said Dallas head coach Tom Landry. "Morton made a big play to Sellers. But [running back Calvin] Hill dropped a touchdown pass. You hit that one and maybe they [the Redskins] don't come back. In the second half, we sat on our hands. We didn't have any staying power. It looked like we would win easy and we relaxed. That was our tendency."

The Cleveland Browns' tendency over the past few years was to start off strong and to stay ahead of their competitors in the AFC Central standings. But in 1972, the Browns had suffered through some embarrassing losses early in the season. A key reason for those defeats were a rash of injuries, several of which devastated their lineup. Running back Bo Scott, defensive end Ron Snidow, and offensive linemen Jim Copeland and Bob McKay were among those hampered by painful injuries for much of the season. Head coach Nick Skorich's team had battled back from misfortune before, however, and they would do so again in 1972. Skorich traded with Miami for standout center Bob DeMarco, a move which solidified the offensive line. The Browns then began a six-game winning streak on October 22 by coming from behind to defeat the Houston Oilers in the Astrodome, 23–17. Young Cleveland quarterback Mike Phipps scored the winning touchdown in the fourth quarter on a 1-yard plunge. The victory evened the Browns' record at 3–3. Cleveland's method of coming from behind to win would be repeated several more times throughout the season, as they gained strength and character with each passing week.

"To evaluate this club properly you have to throw out the first six games and look at the statistics in the last eight," said head coach Nick Skorich at the end of the regular season. "Because of injuries those first six games were not a true indication of the team, the one I thought we'd have by the opener. The injuries sidetracked us, but we've been coming along well."

Teams like the Browns succeeded by fighting back in the face of adversity. One team that had unusual difficulty in staying tough and winning close games during the season was the Minnesota Vikings. Head coach Bud Grant's team lost five games by three points or less, and blame for those losses could be spread around to all members of the squad. The defense still contained many great athletes, although a variety of injuries kept the Purple Gang from establishing their usual level of continuity. The offense, particularly the passing game, improved enough to score 56 more points in 1972 than it had scored in 1971. But the most glaring weakness on offense was the lack of a breakaway runner. The Vikings ranked 20th in the league in rushing, and their leading rusher, halfback Oscar Reed, could muster only 639 yards and two touchdowns.

Minnesota entered their game with the Green Bay Packers on October 29 with a disappointing 2–4 record. They knew that losing this contest would virtually eliminate them from any chance of playoff contention. The Purple Gang summoned up their strength, however, and returned to their accustomed form of dominance in the fourth quarter against the Packers. Safety Paul Krause intercepted a Scott Hunter pass along the sideline and returned it 32 yards for a touchdown. Minnesota outside linebacker Wally Hilgenberg then caught a tipped pass and also returned it for a score a few minutes later. Minnesota had survived for the moment by defeating Green Bay at Lambeau Field, 27–13. It appeared to some that the Vikings were finally going to right their ship.

"We are sure back in the race after losing four games by a total of 10 points," said Minnesota head coach Bud Grant after the victory. "Which really means we lost each game by one play a ball game. We would have won them all with just one more successful play."

Another mid-season contest at Texas Stadium between the Detroit Lions and the Dallas Cowboys offered more clues as to the struggles faced b y the defending world champions during the 1972 campaign. The Cowboys sported a 4–2 record as they entered their Monday night tilt with the Lions on October 30. Dallas struck quickly with two scoring passes from Craig Morton, who was filling in admirably for the injured Roger Staubach. Billy Parks caught the first of Morton's touchdown tosses on a straight fly pattern from 38 yards out, and Calvin Hill caught the second one down the middle of the field from 33 yards out. The remainder of the game, however, showed how far the Cowboys had dropped from the lofty heights of the championship mountain from the previous season. The formidable Doomsday Defense began giving up yards and points in the second half of several games, causing them to hang on for dear life in their efforts to preserve their leads. Dallas prevailed over Detroit, 28–24, and suffered through similar trauma the following week when they survived a second half surge by the San Diego Chargers. In that game, the visiting Cowboys built a seemingly insurmountable 31–0 lead, then looked on in disbelief as the Chargers responded with four unanswered second half touchdowns to make a game of it. Untimely letdowns when games were apparently in the bag were fast becoming a Dallas trademark this season, and one that they certainly were not proud of. The fortunate Cowboys, however, survived their struggle against the Chargers, 34–28, leaving them just a game behind the Redskins in the NFC East with a 6–2 record.

"We got far ahead," admitted Dallas head coach Tom Landry after the San Diego scare, "and started playing it too safe."

One team that knew no such struggles at the mid-season point of 1972 was the Miami Dolphins. Head coach Don Shula achieved a first for the league when he notched his 100th coaching victory in only ten years on the sidelines with a 52–0 beating of the New England Patriots on November 12. The victory boosted Miami to a 9–0 record. Every facet of the Dolphins attack was working to perfection. The stingy No-Name Defense had given up a league-low 103 points by the ninth week of the season. The offense was having no problems scoring points, even with the absence of their starting quarterback Bob Griese. Earl Morrall was a sagacious expert at reading defenses, and his performance throughout the season in Griese's stead was nothing short of spectacular.

The Miami rushing attack was also achieving much success week in and week out, and was considered by many defensive coordinators around the league as the most feared in the NFL. The 1970s was a decade which featured both fullbacks and tailbacks as legitimate rushing threats, and many teams like the Dolphins required all of their runners to be able to block as well as carry the pigskin. A typical fullback in the 1970s could expect to carry the ball at least ten times a game. Compare that to today, when fullbacks on average may see one or two carries per game. For some of today's pass-happy teams, that number of carries for fullbacks is even generous. Some teams today do not even have a fullback on their rosters, as some coaches consider the position to be obsolete. Miami's runners benefitted from the increased amount of carries that they got in 1972. Tailback Mercury Morris was one such beneficiary. Morris ran all over the Patriots in the Orange Bowl, scoring three times.

Many Dolphin backups saw valuable playing time in the New England massacre, and even their youngsters proved that they could succeed in putting points on the scoreboard. Third-string quarterback Jim Del Gaizo came into the game in the fourth quarter and connected on four of six passes for 145 yards and two touchdowns. The Dolphins were somehow getting stronger with each successive week.

"I'm proud to get 100 wins," said Shula after the trouncing of New England, "but it is only really meaningful if it happened in a year we get a world championship. I'm happy to have received the game ball, but the one I want is at the end of the year. All we've been doing every week is telling our people that if they look around they can see upsets happening every week. Upsets are what we want to read about, not have happen to us."

Miami's resolve to avoid any potential upset was tested in the season's tenth week by the visiting New York Jets. The Jets came into the Orange Bowl with a 6–3 record, and were always a tough opponent when Joe Namath was healthy enough to play. Namath would give the Dolphins quite a challenge on this day. He threw two touchdown passes and lifted the Jets to a three-point lead over the Dolphins as the final quarter commenced. Miami was determined to retake the lead, however, and they did so not surprisingly with the strength of their running attack. Halfback Mercury Morris had one of his best days of the season, rushing for 107 yards and scoring two touchdowns. Morris' second touchdown midway through the fourth quarter on an off-tackle burst from 14 yards out served as the winning tally. Miami's 28–24 triumph over New York improved their record to 10–0.

"We won by controlling the ball," recalled Griese many years later. "None of [our backs] except Kiick was a good receiver, so we ran. And we had [assistant coach] Monte Clark doing a hell of a job coaching the offensive line and drawing up running plays."

The Dolphins easily occupied the winning side of the won-loss scale in the NFL standings in 1972. Several other teams, however, earned their notoriety by how many games they lost. The Philadelphia Eagles and the Houston Oilers were the two most notable examples. Both of these teams lacked quality starters and quality depth. They both also had plenty of injuries and more than their share of bad luck. By the time that the Eagles met the Oilers in the Houston Astrodome on November 12, both teams were already out of contention for the playoffs. The game was billed at the "Johnny Rodgers Bowl," because the loser would have a leg up on the first selection in the college draft, who most experts believed would be Johnny Rodgers, the outstanding Heisman Trophy–winning flanker from the University of Nebraska. The Eagles managed to win the game, 18–17, and as a result would lose the chance to make the first pick in the upcoming draft. Scoring all of Philadelphia's points in this tight contest was placekicker Tom Dempsey, who kicked six field goals. The Eagles would finish the 1972 season with a woeful 2–11–1 record, while the Oilers managed to win only once.

While the Eagles-Oilers tilt was a glaring example of overall offensive futility, the Vikings-Rams game on November 19 was anything but. Both teams were known for their stellar defenses. But both teams were facing stiff competition throughout 1972, and both needed to win this game to stay in contention in their divisional standings as the regular season neared its end. The host Rams took a 20–10 lead into halftime. The Vikings, however, emerged from the intermission with renewed momentum, and were soon spurred on by two quick touchdowns in the third quarter. Los Angeles tailback Willie Ellison was hit hard by Minnesota defensive end Jim Marshall and fumbled the ball. Vikings free safety Paul Krause was in the right place at the right time, scooping up the pigskin and returning it 30 yards for a score. Fullback Bill Brown added the second post-halftime touchdown a few minutes later. Brown circled out of the backfield, caught a pass down the middle of the zone from quarterback Fran Tarkenton, bowled over Ram defenders Jim Nettles and Jim Purnell, then raced to the end zone to complete a 76-yard scoring play.

The Vikings were far from finished, however. After a Jim Bertelsen touchdown (his second of the game) for the Rams, Minnesota wide receiver John Henderson ran past Los Angeles defensive back Gene Howard on a deep post pattern and caught Tarkenton's pass in stride. Henderson's sprint to the end zone was the first of five touchdowns that would be scored in the fourth quarter. This see-saw game had a total of three lead changes in the second half, a total of 801 yards accumulated by both teams, and an amazing total of 11 touchdowns. All fans in attendance at the Los Angeles Memorial Coliseum on that day knew that they had gotten their money's worth as the final quarter wore down. Minnesota wide receiver John Gilliam's 66-yard reception for a score provided the margin of victory for Minnesota, 45–41. Gilliam's speed on the deep fly pattern was the key to the play, as he outraced the winded Rams coverage down the sideline.

"We haven't made the long bomb a part of the offense," said Minnesota head coach Bud Grant after the game, "but we always like to. It was just a matter that the balls were thrown well by Fran Tarkenton. He read the defenses well and he had plenty of time to throw. They [the Rams defense] forced us to go to the pass by shutting off our running game."

This type of contest was not normal for either team, with both preferring to control games with their stalwart defenses. But then again, several teams in 1972 were turning in similarly unpredictable performances. The Pittsburgh Steelers were just such a team. They were in the midst of their most productive and most successful season in their 40-year history. Head coach Chuck Noll's players had defeated seven teams before their grudge match against their division rivals, the Cleveland Browns, on the tenth week of the season. The Browns came into that game at 6–3, a game behind the 7-2 Steelers. The Steelers had failed to defeat the Browns in Cleveland's Municipal Stadium in each of their past eight attempts, a grim streak that they were eager to snap. This would turn out to be one of the most dramatic games of the season. An overcast sky lofted above the muddy field, where both rainfall and cold temperatures made their appearance. Sure footing would be almost nonexistent by the second quarter thanks to the elements. The Browns jumped in front and took a 20–3 lead just before halftime. Cleveland quarterback Mike Phipps was the catalyst for his team, running for one score and throwing for another to wide receiver Frank Pitts.

The Steelers came back strong in the second half, however. Sensational rookie runner Franco Harris ran a sweep to his left, and with his free right arm threw converging Browns defensive back Thom Darden out of the way. Darden flew from Franco's thrust as if he were spring-loaded. Harris then cut towards the hashmarks and sprinted untouched down the field to complete a 75-yard run for a touchdown. Harris' splendid effort gave Pittsburgh a 24–23 lead late in the game.

"Our running game has just gone so well that it's put our passing game out of balance," assessed Noll during the latter stages of the regular season. "We've been so successful with the run this season that we haven't had to play catchup football. When you're ahead you're not going to throw the football that often."

Phipps did not panic when forced to play catch-up, however. He had led the Browns to come-from-behind victories earlier in the year against Houston, Denver, and San Diego, and he would work his magic once again on this day. Phipps led a last-minute surge into Steeler territory with two critical passes. Both were down the middle deep into the Pittsburgh zone defense. The first one was caught by wide receiver Fair Hooker, and the second one was grabbed by fellow pass catcher Frank Pitts. Both receivers paid a price for their key receptions, as both were leveled by Steeler defensive backs as soon as they caught the pigskin. Those two passes set up Cleveland placekicker Don Cockcroft, who converted on a 26-yard field goal with but 13 seconds remaining on the clock to defeat the Steelers, 26–24. Both teams were now tied for first place in the AFC Central at 7–3, but both would see each other again two weeks later.

"I don't really feel that we've reached our potential yet," Noll said. "Offensively, we can be much more proficient. We still have a long way to go before we learn to use all the weapons we have." The loss hurt the Steelers, but it did not kill them. "Now we have something to prove," said a defiant Pittsburgh linebacker Andy Russell.

NFL fans in 1972 were getting used to seeing several standout individuals prove their worth each week, regardless of whether their teams were in contention for the playoffs or not. Men like Buffalo's O.J. Simpson displayed his Heisman Trophy pedigree by leading the league in rushing with 1,251 yards. This would mark the first of an incredible four times in the 1970s that Simpson would capture the NFL rushing crown. Philadelphia Eagles defensive safety Bill Bradley once again led the league in interceptions for the second consecutive year with nine. The venerable George Blanda of Oakland led the AFC with 44 extra points in 44 attempts after a touchdown, marking the seventh time that he led the AFL/NFL in that category. But for every extraordinary performance by a popular player came several incredible showings by relatively unknown or uncelebrated players, many of whom were eager to make their mark in the league.

One such player was Chicago quarterback Bobby Douglass. Most fans and observers considered Douglass unusual because he was a left-handed passer. The NFL had seen only a few lefty quarterbacks in its early history. What really made Douglass stand out, however, was his size (he stood 6'4" and weighed 225 pounds) and his running ability. Douglass rushed for an incredible 968 yards in 1972, the most ever by a quarterback up to that time. Douglass' record would stand until 2006, when Atlanta quarterback Michael Vick would eclipse it with 1,039 yards rushing. It is noteworthy to mention, however, that Douglass reached his mark during a 14-game regular season, while Vick benefitted from two extra games (a 16-game regular season) to set his record.

Many critics of Douglass claimed that he was nothing more than a misplaced running back. His passing statistics were never impressive. Rarely did he get into his second read in the passing pocket before he decided to escape the pass rush and run with the ball. His running style was formidable though. Douglass employed a strong straight-arm to ward off impending tacklers, all the while stretching forward and gaining every extra yard possible. Cut in the mold of quarterbacks like Roman Gabriel of Los Angeles and Greg Landry of Detroit, Douglass was never shy about lowering his shoulder and plowing into defenders. Douglass was even tougher to tackle when he got within sight of the goal line. Seldom did one lone defender bring him down, as two or three tacklers were usually needed. Nevertheless, Douglass had plenty of critics who derided his passing abilities and his play-calling.

"He's my quarterback," said Chicago rookie head coach Abe Gibron in a defensive tone, "[and] nothing else. If he's got the ability to throw it hard, he has the ability to throw it soft. Spend some time with the young man and see how intelligent he is. I'm satisfied with his play-calling."

The Bears did not finish with a winning record in 1972, but this was a rebuilding year for them. Abe Gibron did not have a lot of tools to work with. Their defense was led by ferocious but injury-plagued middle linebacker Dick Butkus, but they had little else. Their offense struggled throughout the year, but by using Douglass' running talents on bootlegs, options and scrambles, Gibron was able to see his Bears win one more game than the previous year. Douglass would register a league-leading 6.9 yards-per-attempt rushing average in 1972. He would also be responsible for filling up Soldier Field. According to Chicago Tribune sports columnist Robert Markus, Douglass kept the games exciting: "Is [Douglass] really the quarterback of the future?" pondered Markus. "[He] well could be. The professionals certainly don't want to do anything to tamper with the successful format that has thrilled the fans. The forward pass is an exciting part of pro football. But, then, so is Bobby Douglass."

Kansas City defensive back Jim Kearney was another unheralded but nonetheless exciting player who turned in another key performance in 1972. His four interceptions returned for touchdowns in one season tied a league record set the previous season by Ken Houston. Kearney took two of those four back for scores in one game at Denver, tying another league mark. The Chiefs fell just short of making the playoffs, but Kearney's efforts kept the team in contention for much of the year. His knack for intercepting the pigskin developed because of several important factors: "There's a combination of about three things," explained Kearney. "We're playing a little more zone this year than usual. In the past we played mostly man-for-man and I think other teams expect us to be in that. We try to disguise our zone so it'll look like man-to-man coverage. Then the rush has something to do with it. And last I guess you've got to say there's a little luck involved, of being in the right place at the right time."

Kearney was also realistic enough to know that the zone defenses were in the league to stay. His personal preferences, however, revealed his affinity for a different strategy. "I don't like the zone [because] it's hard to get involved in the game," Kearney described. "Football is an emotional game and when they give you one man to cover—when one guy is in a position to take the bread out of your mouth—it gives you an extra incentive. When all you have is a zone to cover, there's a tendency to relax. You lose the edge off your talents."

Norm Snead was a journeyman quarterback who made the most of his talents in 1972. He managed to lead the New York Giants to a winning record, something that they missed out on in the previous year. Snead also led the NFL in passing for the first time in his career, compiling the best league mark in percentage of completions (60.3). Catching Snead's accurate passes was tight end Bob Tucker, who followed up his outstanding 1971 season by coming in second in the NFC in receptions in 1972 with 55. Snead's longest pass of 94 yards went for a touchdown to wide receiver Rich Houston in the second week of the season in a 23–14 loss to Dallas.

But one pass in the NFL in 1972 went even further, and surprisingly it did not result in a touchdown. St. Louis quarterback Jim Hart was backed up on his own 1-yard line against the visiting Los Angeles Rams on December 10. Hart lofted a deep ball towards the sideline, which Bobby Moore—who in 1974 would change his name to Ahmad Rashad—caught by outleaping Rams cornerback Gene Howard. Moore then straddled the sideline, broke an attempted tackle by Rams defensive back Jim Nettles, and surged to the center of the field. Moore's race to the far corner of the end zone was halted at the 1-yard line by Rams defensive back Al Clark, who brought Moore down just one yard shy of paydirt. The 98-yard reception was the league's longest, and it helped the Cardinals to overcome the Rams, 24–14. "I was really tired," said Moore after his long-distance play. "That's the longest play that I've ever been in on. Jim [Hart] just put the ball in there."

Philadelphia's Harold Jackson also caught quite a few deep balls in 1972. He led the NFL in receptions with 62, in spite of his team winning only twice. Jackson's smallish frame (5 feet, 10 inches, 175) belied his elusiveness and speed. Jackson made each reception an adventure, as he spun and wove his way through a mix of defenders, many of whom could rarely get a good shot at him. Jackson also led the NFL in overall yardage gained receiving (1,048) in 1972.

"Harold's No. 1 asset is speed," said former NFL head and assistant coach Leeman Bennett. "He's fast enough to go deep and get open on anybody." Jackson confidently agreed with Bennett. "Nobody can cover me one-on-one," he stated at season's end.

Perhaps the league's most explosive offensive weapon was not a pass receiver like Jackson but a runner like Buffalo's O.J. Simpson. Gaining yardage on off-tackle runs and pitchouts was fast becoming Simpson's trademark. In a season dominated by 1,000 yard runners, Simpson's league-leading mark served as a portent of things to come. The former University of Southern California star benefitted from the offensive philosophy and play calling of new head coach Lou Saban. "Lou has all of our people blocking at Buffalo," Simpson said. "Two of our offensive linemen—Donnie Green and Reggie McKenzie—are going to be super players. And Saban put cages on the helmets of our wide receivers, Bobby Chandler and J.D. Hill, and told them to block—or else."

Several teams vying for potential playoff spots felt a similar ultimatum as the regular season winded down to the final weeks: win—or else. San Francisco visited Dallas on Thanksgiving as decided underdogs, sporting a lackluster 5–4–1 record. They emerged from Texas Stadium as 31–10 victors. The 49ers linebacker Skip Vanderbundt turned in the game of his life, recovering a Craig Morton fumble and returning it 73 yards for a score, and intercepting a Morton pass along the sideline and returning it for another touchdown from 21 yards out. Mixed in with Vanderbundt's heroics was a Ken Willard 1-yard touchdown plunge and a 12-yard scoring pass from Steve Spurrier to tight end Ted Kwalick. San Francisco's celebrated beat-down of the defending Super Bowl champions gave head coach Dick Nolan's team a small measure of revenge for losses to Dallas in the past two NFC title contests. It also gave them a half-game lead over Atlanta in the competitive NFC West. Dallas defensive back Mel Renfro dryly quipped following the game, "This really messed up our Thanksgiving."

The Detroit Lions also won on Thanksgiving, defeating the visiting New York Jets, 37–20. Detroit produced a strong 17-point effort in the fourth quarter to post their victory. Lions quarterback Greg Landry scored twice, and halfback Altie Taylor's 38-yard dash put the game out of reach. On that play, Taylor broke an attempted tackle by Jets defensive lineman Mark Lomas, then changed directions and raced past Jets safety W.K. Hicks to the corner of the end zone. The win boosted Detroit's record to 7–4, keeping them tied with Green Bay for the lead in the NFC Central Division.

At the same time, Miami kept building on its lead in the AFC East. They had already clinched the division by the tenth week of the season, and had coasted into their final games of 1972 with growing confidence. Victories over St. Louis, New England, and the New York Giants increased the Dolphins' record to 13–0. A 16–0 shutout victory over visiting division rival Baltimore completed an incredible regular season for Miami. They were the first pro team in the modern era to post a perfect 14–0 record heading into the playoffs. Many critics complained that the Dolphins were the beneficiaries of a soft schedule, with only a smattering of contending teams on their slate. Others preferred instead to sing the praises of the No-Name Defense, which had limited opponents to a grand total of 171 points during the regular season, the best mark in the league. Regardless of the opinions, Miami kept stringing together victories, a testament to their determination and desire. Those traits had their origin in the words and actions of their head coach.

"You set a goal to be the best," said Don Shula, "and then you work hard every hour of every day, striving to reach that goal. If you allow yourself to settle for anything less than number one then you are cheating yourself. You've got to have a burning desire to compete, and that's something that's in me. I believe you go out every day trying to win and every week trying to win."

The Pittsburgh Steelers were a young team like the Dolphins. By Week 11, they were embarking on their first playoff season ever. They proved their mettle by defeating a perennial winner, the Minnesota Vikings, by a score of 23–10 on November 26. The host Steelers held the Vikings to just three points until the fourth quarter, and Pittsburgh's offense contributed 206 rushing yards against the Purple Gang. A quarterback sneak by Terry Bradshaw and a 17-yard scoring pass from Bradshaw to flanker Frank Lewis provided the margin of victory. Lewis' score came when he caught a flare pass in the flat, then wove his way into the end zone behind key blocks by Steeler offensive linemen Jon Kolb and Jim Clack.

"I was apprehensive right down to the final gun," said Pittsburgh head coach Chuck Noll after his team's victory over Minnesota. "It was a defensive victory and the offense came up with the big plays."

The Minnesota game was a big one for the Steelers. The contest the following week against Cleveland would be even more crucial, however. Both teams were tied for the division lead, and the Browns had narrowly defeated the Steelers just two weeks prior to their rematch. Pittsburgh's Three Rivers Stadium would be the site for another one of those "statement" games in the NFL. The Steelers learned the lessons of their previous loss to the Browns, however, as their defense led the way to an impressive 30–0 butt-kicking victory. Pittsburgh's defense effectively shut down Cleveland's rushing attack, limiting the Browns to 99 ground yards. Even more impressive was Pittsburgh's pass defense, which held Cleveland quarterback Mike Phipps to only 59 passing yards.

Rookie Steeler halfback Franco Harris tied Hall of Famer Jim Brown's NFL record by rushing for his sixth straight 100-yard game. The excitement that Harris' 102 yards and two touchdowns gave the Steeler fans reverberated throughout Three Rivers Stadium. "The fans help you a lot here in Pittsburgh," said Harris after the game. Terry Bradshaw put an exclamation point on the

Steelers' dominance when he hit rookie tight end John McMakin for a 78-yard score. McMakin was not even the intended receiver on the play, but he caught Bradshaw's spiral at his 38-yard line, broke free from Cleveland's defensive backs, and rumbled 62 yards untouched into the end zone. The Steelers were now one full game ahead of the Browns and all alone in first place in the AFC Central with a 9–3 record.

The Baltimore Colts, however, were going in the opposite direction. Baltimore's most depressing season in years was in full bloom, with narrow losses mixing in with blowout defeats. The Colts had their share of injuries, and by the last few weeks of 1972, had changed their starting lineup over several times. The loyal Colts fans at Memorial Stadium on December 3 bid a memorable goodbye to their legendary quarterback, Johnny Unitas, who was going to be released by new general manager Joe Thomas after the season. Baltimore was shutting out the lowly Buffalo Bills, 28–0, when Unitas entered the game in the fourth quarter, replacing an injured Marty Domres. The man who was largely responsible for helping to popularize pro football in the late 1950s and throughout the 1960s was granted by the football gods one more moment of glory. Unitas threw a deep sideline pass to wide receiver Eddie Hinton, who had to come back for the ball. Hinton grabbed the pass at the Buffalo 46-yard line, fought off Bills defenders Robert James and Pete Richardson, then raced to the end zone to complete the 63-yard score. Johnny U. jogged off the field amidst the raucous screams of the crowd, many with tears in their eyes. History and memories had been made by Johnny Unitas ... one more time.

"Today was a storybook situation," said Domres, who went to the hospital for treatment for his injured back and pelvis. "I'm glad things worked out both for John and the fans."

The Dallas Cowboys were attempting to make history also. They were striving to be the first team to defend their Super Bowl championship since Green Bay did it in 1967. That goal was appearing to be difficult to achieve, however. Starting quarterback Roger Staubach was recovering from a separated shoulder injury that he sustained in the preseason. The Doomsday Defense was still smarting after their Thanksgiving Day loss to San Francisco. Finally, the rival Washington Redskins kept winning, and showed no signs of slowing down. Dallas visited frigid St. Louis on December 3, sporting an 8–3 record (a full two games behind Washington). The Cowboys started to improve their situation on many fronts in this contest, however. Dallas defeated the Cardinals, 27–6, behind three touchdowns by running back Walt Garrison. Staubach himself saw some much-needed action late in the win. The victory put Tom Landry's team in a good position to claim the wild card berth in the NFC. One more victory over either of their final two opponents would give Dallas a ticket to the playoffs.

The Cleveland Browns were also still alive for a playoff berth. They were seeking one more victory over their cross-state rivals, the Cincinnati Bengals, on December 9. Cleveland experienced no difficulty in defeating Cincinnati in the third week of the season, 27–6. The Browns knew that the Bengals would give them a tougher fight the second time around. The Bengals simply *had* to win in order to have even a slight chance at a playoff berth. This second meeting between the two foes at Cincinnati's Riverfront Stadium would be one of the most exciting of the season. The game's first touchdown exhibited the type of hitting that would be evident throughout the contest. Cleveland's Frank Pitts caught a Mike Phipps pass down the middle and ducked a big hit by Bengal defenders Neil Craig, Ken Avery and Lemar Parrish, all at the same moment of impact. Pitts spun away from the collision and outraced linebackers Bill Bergey and Al Beauchamp to the end zone to complete the 50-yard score. Craig, Avery, and Parrish each required several moments to get back on their feet following the effect of their hit on each other.

Both teams traded scores for the remainder of the game. Cleveland scored on a 5-yard touchdown run by halfback Leroy Kelly, and another touchdown pass from Phipps to flanker Fair

Hooker. Running backs Essex Johnson, Doug Dressler, and quarterback Virgil Carter each reached the end zone for Cincinnati. A 27-yard field goal late in the fourth quarter by Cleveland placekicker Don Cockroft gave Cleveland a 27–24 lead. Cincinnati stormed back, but Cleveland linebacker Billy Andrews intercepted a Virgil Carter pass at the goal line with less than a minute to play to win the game for the Browns. The loss eliminated the Bengals from playoff contention. The resilient Browns, however, were just now one win away from a wild card berth.

"We wanted to win to stay alive," said a relieved Cleveland head coach Nick Skorich after the game. "We had to keep Cincinnati out of that 'wild card' and keep ourselves in."

Perhaps the most resilient team in the NFL in 1972 was the Washington Redskins. George Allen viewed the advanced age of his numerous veterans as a strength, not a weakness. Men like Diron Talbert, Jack Pardee, Billy Kilmer, Pat Fischer, and Charley Taylor brought a wealth of experience to the team. According to veteran safety Richie Petitbon, experience was the most common and most valuable denominator on the team. "I'm lucky to be playing for a coach who believes you get better with age—especially on defense," said Petitbon in early 1972. "Look around and you'll see that your best defensive teams are ones with plenty of age and experience."

The Redskins strung together nine straight wins during the middle of the season, the longest streak of victories in the NFC in 1972. Washington's defense was the main reason for the streak, as they gave up the least amount of points (218) in the conference. The Redskins clinched the championship of the NFC East by the 12th week of the season with a 23–7 win at Veterans Stadium over Philadelphia. The positive attitude that the winning streak fostered permeated the team's roster. It proved to be highly contagious, even amongst the most hardened veterans. "Something beautiful is going to happen," said Redskin receiver Charley Taylor, who led the team in receptions in 1972 with 49. "I don't know when or where. But I do know it's going to be great."

Redskin running back Larry Brown achieved the label of greatness by leading the league in rushing in 1970. Brown led the NFC in rushing in 1972 with 1,216 yards, in spite of sitting out the final two games of the regular season. Had he played in those two games, he would have undoubtedly won the league rushing title. The yards that Brown did accumulate did not come easy. Brown withstood some of the hardest hits in the league, and it was not uncommon to see him limping back to the huddle by the second half of most games. Brown was a small back (5–11, 195), and his running style bordered on a reckless drive and desire, where he ignored the pain of countless tackles to gain that one extra yard.

"I don't mind the struggle," Brown said. "I don't mind the hitting. I work on being quick. Quickness is the salvation of a little back. I aim to get off with the ball every last time. There's no other way for a small runner to survive in the National Football League."

Brown's running style inspired much respect among his teammates. Quarterback Billy Kilmer commented, "Larry takes unreal spills. I cringe every time he goes down and wonder if he'll be able to get up." Fellow quarterback Sonny Jurgensen added, "Brown is so intense all the time. [He's] taking those spills time after time."

The greatness that Brown exhibited would be missing from the lineup as the Redskins marched into their Week 13 encounter with the Dallas Cowboys. The Redskins had already insured their spot in the playoffs, and it was obvious right from the beginning that they were treating this contest as little more than a scrimmage, with Brown resting on the sidelines. A Dallas win would give the Cowboys the conference wild card, and they played like they were hungry for victory. It did not take Dallas long to break out in front in the first quarter at Texas Stadium. Calvin Hill opened the game up with a 10-yard scoring run on a sweep to his right. He then added a 26-yard touchdown reception from Craig Morton, who managed to elude a vigorous Redskins pass rush on the play. Hill circled out of the backfield and beat Redskins linebacker Jack Pardee down the middle for his second score. Dallas fullback Walt Garrison ran a misdirection draw play 25 yards for another touchdown and a 21–0 lead. The Cowboys built a 31–10 lead going into the fourth quarter, but not all the news was great for Dallas. Washington scored on touchdown passes from quarterback Billy Kilmer to draw closer. The Cowboys then lost starting outside linebacker Chuck Howley with torn ligaments to his left knee. By that time, however, Dallas had built too much of a lead. Their 34–24 triumph opened the door to the playoffs, which the Cowboys were only too happy to surge through. The win also gave Dallas a small measure of revenge for their previous loss to the Redskins.

"The first half is as good a half as we played all year," said Dallas head coach Tom Landry. "Compared to last year's Super Bowl team, we had a little more power offensively. We have to play better defense in the playoffs."

The Green Bay Packers had previously lost to the Minnesota Vikings earlier in the 1972 season, but by Week 13, were one game ahead of the Norsemen in the NFC Central standings. A Green Bay victory at Minnesota with two weeks left in the regular season would give the Packers their first division title since 1967. The game on December 10 was held in sunny but frigid Metropolitan Stadium in Bloomington, Minnesota, a locale that usually gave the Vikings a tremendous home field advantage. The Packers, however, were also used to playing in freezing temperatures. The thermometer at kickoff read zero degrees, and another reading at halftime put it at two degrees, making it the sixth-coldest NFL game in history, and the coldest game of the decade. The wind chill factor of minus-18 degrees helped to confirm these records. But both squads played like they were oblivious to the cold weather. Minnesota took a 7–0 lead in the second quarter when tight end Stu Voigt ran an end-around for a 1-yard touchdown. Their lead held up until the third quarter, when the Packers offense started to move.

Momentum in a football game starts with one big play, and then builds on emotion and desire … and more big plays. A defensive play by Green Bay linebacker Fred Carr was a case in point. The Packers were trailing 7–3 in the third quarter when Carr picked up a Bill Brown fumble on a swing pass at the Green Bay 46-yard line, then rumbled down to the Minnesota 28. Several plays later, Green Bay quarterback Scott Hunter dove in from the 1-yard line to give the Packers a 10–7 lead. The momentum would continue for the Packers on the next series. Another Minnesota turnover was the cause, and the effect would be the same as before. Packer defensive back Willie Buchanon caught a tipped pass near midfield and ran it back 25 yards deep into Viking territory. Green Bay fullback MacArthur Lane blasted in off right tackle from three yards out for a 17–7 Packer lead. Buchanon would intercept one more pass later in the game, as would fellow Packers defensive back Ken Ellis. Two more Chester Marcol field goals gave Green Bay a 23–7 triumph and the NFC Central championship. The momentum that the Packers had built on in the second half of the game turned into an illustration of robust dominance. Green Bay defensive end Clarence Williams accounted for three of his team's four sacks of Minnesota quarterback Fran Tarkenton. Green Bay's defense limited Minnesota's offense to only four plays in the entire fourth quarter. The Packers offense would hold on to the ball for 13 of the fourth quarter's 15 minutes. The joyous scene of Green Bay's celebration as they ran off of the frigid field at Metropolitan Stadium included the sight of victorious Packers head coach Dan Devine, riding on the shoulders of his players. It was a lasting visual picture of a bona fide 1972 success story … the Pack was back.

"It's the first step out of the crib," said youthful Green Bay quarterback Scott Hunter after the game. "It is not a climax, but a start." Packers running back MacArthur Lane was beaming as he spoke from the victorious locker room. "I've never been in this spot before," said Lane of his first career trip to the NFL playoffs in his fifth year in the league. "This team has a lot of character; nothing but class."

Minnesota's final game of the 1972 season against the San Francisco 49ers would end in an even more depressing fashion than their loss to the Packers. The host 49ers needed to defeat the Vikings in order to claim the NFC West title. The 49ers succeeded by scoring two touchdowns late in the fourth quarter to achieve victory, 20–17. San Francisco quarterback John Brodie came off the bench to direct the two scoring drives, the first one ending with a 24-yard pass to wide receiver Gene Washington, who beat Minnesota defensive back Bobby Bryant on a post pattern down the middle. The second one won the game for the 49ers. Brodie rolled out to his right from the Minnesota 2-yard line and found flanker Dick Witcher alone in the end zone for the deciding score with but 25 seconds left on the clock. For the second straight week, the beaten Vikings watched their opponents celebrate a playoff berth at their expense.

The Pittsburgh Steelers were in a similar situation as the 49ers in their final regular season game against the host San Diego Chargers. A Steeler victory would give them the AFC Central title. Unlike the 49ers, however, Pittsburgh wasted no time in achieving their goal. Their stingy defense limited San Diego to 172 total yards. The Chargers tried to run the ball 30 times, and gained only 56 yards on the ground. The Chargers were also forced to commit seven turnovers, which greatly helped the Pittsburgh cause. Several key Steelers performers on offense were inactive due to injuries, but it did not matter. Pittsburgh won easily, 24–2. The division championship was bound for a new home in the Steel City, and a new chapter in Steeler history had begun. But the real inspiration to win the game was for their owner, the generous and lovable patriarch of the team, Art Rooney.

"When Mr. Rooney walked in [to the postgame locker room]," said linebacker Andy Russell, "all the guys went over to him and hugged him. We had gone out and won this championship for him. I was happier for Mr. Rooney than I was for myself. He's been living and dying with the Steelers since before I was born."

Neither the Atlanta Falcons nor the Kansas City Chiefs would make the playoffs in 1972, but their game on the final Sunday of the regular season was somewhat emblematic of the entire year in the NFL. Both teams would make big plays in the game. The exciting 17–14 Chiefs victory on a fourth down touchdown pass from Len Dawson to Ed Podolak represented just one of the league's many last-second wins, observed by millions of fans in this incredible year. There was something even more astounding that was developing in the Chiefs-Falcons game, however. Atlanta running back Dave Hampton needed 70 yards to reach the coveted 1,000-yard plateau for the first time in his career. Hampton had missed the equivalent of two whole games with injuries; nevertheless, he achieved this impressive goal late in the fourth quarter against the Chiefs. Hampton was taken out of the game to a standing ovation. But because Atlanta was striving for their second straight winning season, the talented runner was re-inserted in the game by head coach Norm Van Brocklin. The ball was spotted deep in Kansas City territory with only a few seconds remaining, when Hampton bobbled a quick pitch to his left and was run out of bounds after losing five yards. He never got another opportunity to make up those yards, and therefore lost his 1,000-yard season, finishing with 995 yards. Statisticians and historians alike went scurrying through the record books to see if a similar event had ever occurred before, but to no avail. Dave Hampton would become famous, not for his achievement, but for his almost achievement. Nineteen-seventy-two was that kind of year.

Don Maynard of the New York Jets would be luckier than Hampton in 1972. Maynard had been running pass routes in pro football for 15 seasons, and his final reception of the year in a Monday night game at Oakland gave him a league record 632 career pass receptions, one better than legendary Baltimore receiver Raymond Berry. Maynard thus became a shoo-in for the Hall of Fame. "I'm really honored to be put in the same class with Raymond Berry," Maynard said after his team's 24–16 loss to the Raiders.

None of the eight playoff teams wanted to experience Hampton's misfortune and take a step backwards. Most hoped to emulate Maynard's success. Teams which made it to the playoffs in 1971 and eventually lost put together game plans to vindicate their previous playoff results. The only exception to this was goal was the Dallas Cowboys, the incumbent world champions who wanted nothing more than a repeat of their 1971 playoff victories. The 1972 divisional playoffs would include three teams (Pittsburgh, Oakland, and Green Bay) which were absent from the postseason in 1971, adding some new spice and excitement to the upcoming tournament. The playoff games in 1972 would stand out as some of the most exciting in the decade.

The Cleveland Browns returned to the postseason by visiting the Orange Bowl in Miami to take on the Dolphins. This was a playoff game that, on paper, appeared to be an easy Miami win. But the Browns made it to this stage the season before in 1971 when they lost to the Colts in the divisional playoffs. Head coach Nick Skorich's team desperately wanted to make amends for that loss and upset the seemingly flawless Dolphins. Miami was on the precipice of history. They were attempting to become the first undefeated, untied team in modern NFL history. The law of averages proclaimed that the Dolphins were surely "due" for a defeat.

But even occurrences off the field were going in favor of the Dolphins in 1972. Miami halfback Eugene "Mercury" Morris received a holiday gift from NFL Commissioner Pete Rozelle just before the playoff game with the Browns. Rozelle viewed the films from a previous game against Buffalo where Morris was charged with a 9-yard loss. Rozelle claimed that the loss on a supposed lateral should have been credited as a fumble by quarterback Earl Morrall. The league added those nine yards back to Morris' rushing total, giving him exactly 1,000 yards for the season. This gave the Dolphins two 1,000-yard rushers in one season (Larry Csonka gained 1,117 yards), the first time in league history that one team had two such players reaching the 1,000-yard plateau. Miami as a team would accrue 2,960 rushing yards, an all-time league record, but one which would stand for only one short year.

Miami was not thinking about records, however, when they kicked off their playoff game with Cleveland on a sunny December 24 afternoon. The Dolphins surged to a 7–0 first quarter lead when rookie defensive back Charlie Babb stormed in and blocked a Don Cockcroft punt. Babb dove on the dribbling ball at the 8-yard line, and after discovering that no Cleveland player was pursuing him, strolled into the end zone amidst a convoy of teammates.

"I think our blockers got confused," said Skorich. "They missed their blocking assignments and that was disastrous. It was an easy seven points. You should not make that mistake in a playoff game." Babb admitted after the game that the play was accomplished without too much difficulty. "I didn't hit anybody going in," said Babb.

A Garo Yepremian field goal increased the Miami cushion to 10–0 by halftime. Things were going according to plan for the Dolphins. Establish an early lead, control the ball, and dominate on defense. This formula had won the past 14 regular season games for head coach Don Shula's Dolphins. But Shula had to be feeling some concern, however. Earl Morrall had managed to throw for only 12 yards in the first half. Miami's offense had only one first down through the air in the first half, and converted on only one third down in the entire game.

Cleveland added to Shula's concern by showing some resolve in the second half. Browns quarterback Mike Phipps had a tough day when throwing against the Miami zone defense, but he somehow managed to direct his team to a touchdown in the third quarter. Phipps rolled out to his right, and after discovering that Miami's defenders had all of his receivers covered, sprinted for the corner of the end zone. Phipps allowed Dolphins linebacker Mike Kolen to overrun him, then lunged for the flag while breaking an attempted tackle by Miami defensive end Vern Den Herder. Phipps' 5-yard scoring run gave Cleveland new life, and the whole team responded with inspired play. Cleveland's defense managed to hold Miami fullback Larry Csonka to a mere 32 yards on 12 carries, a key element in giving the Browns at least a chance to stay close to the Dolphins.

Midway through the fourth quarter, Cleveland's offense began another march toward the Miami goal. Browns wide receiver Fair Hooker ran a flag pattern and found himself alone as he ran to the sideline. Phipps withstood a strong Miami pass rush and just as he was hit, he lofted the ball to Hooker. The Cleveland pass catcher slowed down to cradle the ball, then skipped one yard inside the end zone flag for the touchdown. Hooker's score and the ensuing extra point gave the Browns a shocking 14–13 lead with just eight minutes remaining in the game. "I think they [the Dolphins defensive secondary] just guessed wrong," said Phipps when questioned later why Hooker was so wide open.

Miami did not achieve an undefeated record in 1972 by accident, however. They proved their determined mettle by conducting a seven-play, 80-yard drive to the winning score. The key man on this drive was wide receiver Paul Warfield, himself a former player for the Browns. Warfield caught two key passes on the drive, one in which he was leveled by Cleveland defensive backs Ben Davis and Thom Darden and still managed to hold on to the ball. A few plays later, Warfield drew a pass interference penalty from Cleveland linebacker Billy Andrews, which resulted in another Dolphins first down. Finally, Warfield's catch of a deep pass down the middle over Davis led directly to the winning score. Reserve halfback Jim Kiick culminated the clutch drive with a 8-yard touchdown run up the middle of the Cleveland defense. One final Browns surge ended when Miami linebacker Doug Swift intercepted his second pass of the game, and the fifth overall that the Dolphins picked off against Mike Phipps. Miami prevailed ... or rather, survived, 20–14, in one of the tightest contests that they had fought all year.

"I knew how tough the Browns would be," said Miami head coach Don Shula after the game. "This is a team that has been coming fast in recent weeks. You know I've been burned by the Browns a couple of times in the past. We knew it wouldn't be easy."

The Green Bay Packers had been burned by the Washington Redskins earlier in 1972, and like Shula had felt about the Browns, they too knew that winning a playoff game against George Allen's team would not be easy. The Packers had accumulated 2,127 yards rushing as a team, one of the best marks in the NFC. Running backs John Brockington and MacArthur Lane were both power runners, preferring to wear down opposing defenses with constant, brutal thrusts into the line. Many defenses crumbled under these Packer surges, particularly in the second half of most games. Green Bay's passing attack was nowhere near as strong as their rushing game, however, and the Redskins knew this. The Redskins employed a five-man defensive line to confound the Green Bay running attack.

Manny Sistrunk was the main man that Washington head coach George Allen used in this formation. Sistrunk positioned himself, usually right before the snap of the ball, right over the head of Packers center Ken Bowman. The Packers had dealt with this strategy before in their earlier game against the Redskins, and felt that they had mastered it. But Washington only used this strategy a few times in that previous game. In their playoff game, however, Sistrunk would be a permanent fixture in the middle of the line of scrimmage. The Redskins would successfully blunt the inside runs of the Packers runners and leave them with long distances to go on many third down situations. Brockington totaled a mere 13 yards in nine carries. Lane was also held below his average, rushing for 56 yards on 14 carries. In describing his efforts against Bowman, Sistrunk said after the game, "I told myself I was going to whip his butt and I whipped it." Green Bay altered its rushing strategy in the second half to run outside, but that strategy failed also. Veteran Redskins cornerback Pat Fischer made play after play on the outside, hitting Brockington and Lane below their waists and hanging on for dear life until help from his teammates arrived. Fischer stood only 5'9" and weighed only 170 pounds, so he had to rely on smarts and positioning to avoid the churning knees of the Packers rushers from blasting into his face mask while he attempted to tackle those human tanks in Green and Gold. Fischer's efforts helped pave the way to victory. "You leave a weakness when you take out a linebacker for a fifth lineman," said Packers head coach Dan Devine, "but we couldn't exploit that weakness."

The game was not as one-sided as the statistics would indicate, however. Washington quarterback Billy Kilmer sustained his share of hits in this game as well. Kilmer was leveled in the pocket both high and low in the first quarter by Packers defensive ends Clarence Williams and Alden Roche. On the play, Kilmer's cheekbone was bludgeoned by Williams' forearm. The veteran quarterback was helped to the sideline, but returned in the second quarter to throw a 32-yard touchdown pass down the middle to wide receiver Roy Jefferson, who had outraced seldom-beaten Green Bay defensive backs Al Matthews and Willie Buchanon.

"It was a play-action play," recalled Jefferson. "They [the Green Bay defensive secondary] were double-teaming on the weak side. I went back to the huddle and told Billy about it and he called the play. I just went inside and that was the touchdown."

Three field goals from the foot of Curt Knight added more insurance and lifted the Redskins to a 16–3 triumph. An overjoyed George Allen told his team after the defensive struggle, "We beat them [the Packers] at their own game."

The Dolphins and Redskins advanced to their conference championship games with victories that have become somewhat of an afterthought when discussing NFL history. This is because of what occurred a day before those two contests. The date of December 23, 1972, will forever go down in league lore as perhaps the most exciting date in the annals of the pro game. Only two divisional playoff games were played on that date, but those two games are still being talked about by fans, players, coaches, and football historians today. The Dallas Cowboys had beaten the San Francisco 49ers in each of the past two NFC championship games, and the 49ers were poised to reverse that trend in the 1972 playoffs. They had crushed Dallas at Texas Stadium on Thanksgiving, and even though they had just barely won their division with an 8–5–1 record, head coach Dick Nolan's squad felt confident that they could defeat Dallas one more time. The game would be played at San Francisco's Candlestick Park on a wet artificial surface. The morning rains subsided just before game time, however, and the beams of northern California sunshine lit up the skies for this colorful contest. The excitement produced in this tilt between familiar rivals would mark the first come-from-behind miracle victory of a legendary quarterback.

San Francisco 49ers halfback Vic Washington set the stage for the thrills to come by returning the opening kickoff 97 yards for a touchdown. Washington raced down the sideline, relying on his speed to outrun a host of Dallas defenders. The Cowboys responded with a field goal, but then fell victim to a series of turnovers which would lead to a seemingly insurmountable deficit. Dallas quarterback Craig Morton fumbled when he was hit by 49ers defensive back Windlan Hall. San Francisco recovered, then fullback Larry Schreiber cashed in on the turnover when he dove in from the 1-yard line six plays later for a 14–3 lead. Morton threw an interception to San Francisco linebacker Skip Vanderbundt on the following series, and just as before, Schreiber plowed into the end zone from one yard out to increase the 49ers' lead to 21–3. Dallas did what they could, however, to disrupt the San Francisco scoring surge by putting together a seven-play touchdown drive late in the second quarter. Morton found flanker Lance Alworth in the middle of the 49ers' zone. On the play, Alworth had benefitted from a slip on the wet turf by San Francisco cornerback Jimmy Johnson. Alworth caught Morton's bullet pass, regained his balance, and burrowed into the end zone amidst several would-be tacklers to score. Dallas now trailed their opponent, 21–13, at halftime.

The second half began with the 49ers missing a field goal and the Cowboys committing two more turnovers. Morton's second interception, again with Vanderbundt the culprit, was not detrimental to the Cowboys. Halfback Calvin Hill's fumble deep in Dallas territory was, however, and it lead to another San Francisco touchdown. Once again, Schreiber crashed in from the 1-yard line to boost the 49ers' lead to 28–13. Schreiber's three scores in a postseason game set a team record which stood for 21 years.

Setting records was the last thing on Dallas head coach Tom Landry's mind as the second half wore on. His team was foundering on offense, with Morton being sacked four times for losses, and his completion percentage hovering at a sub-par 38 percent. Landry was finally convinced with 1:48 remaining in the third quarter that Morton would be unable to ignite his team to victory, so he replaced him with Roger Staubach, the Most Valuable Player in Super Bowl VI. Staubach had been injured with a separated shoulder late in the preseason and had seen only limited action during the latter part of the regular season. Staubach's appearance did not result in immediate success, however, as his shoulder still showed signs of rust from inactivity. San Francisco's 15-point lead midway through the fourth quarter appeared safe. So much so that several 49ers players used those moments to verbalize their disdain for the Cowboys. San Francisco linebacker Dave Wilcox yelled across the line of scrimmage, "How do *you* guys feel about losing?" to the Dallas offense. San Francisco's bravado was premature, however. The barbs and insults put some fire into the Dallas offense. Staubach led his team on a seven-play drive midway through the fourth quarter which resulted in a 27-yard Toni Fritsch field goal. Several minutes later, Staubach connected with wide receiver Billy Parks on a post pattern touchdown which brought Dallas to within 28–23. Parks had told his quarterback in the huddle that he could "run the post." Staubach simply responded, "Great, do it." Parks broke free from 49ers cornerback Bruce Taylor and snared Staubach's missile at the goal line. The dinsome cheers of victory amongst the crowd at Candlestick Park started going silent, replaced instead with the unmistakable feelings and gasps of anxiety and nervousness.

"I mean we had them in a position and a situation where we knew they had to score some points in a hurry," remembered San Francisco linebacker Dave Wilcox. "In a situation like that, with that kind of lead, you should be able to stop the other fellows. But we didn't."

Parks' touchdown came with but 1:30 left in the game, but the Cowboys were far from finished. The momentum that was growing amongst the Dallas players reached an even higher level on the next play. An onside kick is seldom successful when the receiving team is expecting one to occur. Everyone knew that the Cowboys needed to try an onside kick. A San Francisco recovery would cement victory for the 49ers. A Dallas recovery meant one more chance to pull off one of the greatest comebacks in league playoff history. Naturally, 49ers head coach Dick Nolan loaded up his special teams squad with reliable ball handlers, anticipating the onside kick. But even that tactic did not matter. Dallas placekicker Toni Fritsch, a former soccer player in his native Austria, gently approached the ball. He then employed a trick from his soccer background. Fritsch's twisting, behind one leg kick gave a unique spin to the football. Upon hitting the artificial turf, the bouncing ball resembled a speeding rubber ball on ice. The ball skidded off of 49ers receiver Preston Riley's chest. Riley later recalled that the ball was both "twisting and turning." Dallas' Mel Renfro made a diving recovery, claiming, "All I saw was the football on the ground. I grabbed it and hung on for dear life." The Cowboys were still alive, and every Dallas player from that point on felt a surge of invincibility.

"The feeling came over me that we were going to win," remembered Staubach. "Everyone sensed it. There was electricity in the air. No one said anything to me when we came back on to the field after recovering the ball. We sort of had this quiet confidence." Dallas guard Blaine Nye agreed: "The odds of pulling that [the onside kick] off must be a thousand to one. But once we did, I knew there was no way we wouldn't score."

Staubach did his part to quiet the partisan San Francisco crowd on the very next play, running up the middle for 21 yards. "It was instinctive," said Staubach after the game. "As soon as I saw the hole I didn't even look [for a receiver] anymore. I just took off."

Billy Parks took off on the following play and faked a pattern similar to his earlier touchdown. But instead of cutting toward the post, Parks broke to the sideline. Staubach lofted a perfect pass, and Parks got both of his feet inbounds as he came down with the ball at the San Francisco 10-yard line. Fifty-six seconds remained on the clock. The expression of smiles and laughter on the 49ers' sideline and the defensive huddle were now completely gone. The Cowboys sideline in contrast could not have been more different, and they erupted on the next play. Staubach correctly read a San Francisco blitz and hit wide receiver Ron Sellers across the middle for the game-winning touchdown. On the play, Sellers cut in front of 49ers defensive back Windlan Hall right in front of the goal post.

"I know where I should have been, but I wasn't there," said Hall in an obviously dejected tone. "I should have been playing him [Sellers] inside more, but once he got inside of me it was too late."

Staubach's bullet pass nestled into Sellers' gut, setting off a riotous Cowboy celebration. The receiver was mobbed by his teammates in the end zone, and Dallas defensive end Larry Cole and flanker Lance Alworth rolled around in joy on the turf along the sideline by the Cowboys' bench. Even head coach Tom Landry was seen hugging several of his players. "I've never experienced anything this exciting," Landry said afterward. "You can be in that situation 100 times and probably win one of them." Dave Wilcox regrettably agreed with Landry. "For them it was a million-to-one shot and they pulled it off," he lamented.

Their gleeful reactions aside, the key plays down the stretch and the stalwart confidence of the Cowboys team would become legendary from this contest on throughout the decade of the 1970s. This playoff game served as the genesis of Staubach's famous reputation as a quarterback who could pull out a win in the most dire of situations. It also gave birth to his newest nickname … "Captain Comeback." Down by 15 points with less than half a quarter to play, the Cowboys had achieved a miracle victory. "It was unbelievable the way the players refused to give up," remembered Landry. "It was the best comeback I've ever seen by a Dallas team. Roger has this thing about him. He can turn things around." Author Frank Luksa in later years perhaps best described Staubach's performance in the clutch. "He was softspoken," said Luksa, "but on the field, he was a killer. He never thought he was out of a game."

Forever gracious in victory, many Dallas players could not help but feel sorry for the 49ers, a team which appeared to finally get the Dallas monkey off of their back, only to lose to them once more in the playoffs. "I felt so sorry for those guys when the game was over," said Nye. "I couldn't even look at them." San Francisco linebacker Dave Wilcox composed himself enough after the game to reflect on the main lesson for his—and all—teams. "For one thing, it [the loss to Dallas] taught us that you have to play for 60 minutes, not 58 or 59," said Wilcox.

Earlier that same day, another west coast team experienced a similar feeling of unbelief at the conclusion of their playoff contest. The Oakland Raiders visited the Pittsburgh Steelers on a grey and overcast afternoon at Three Rivers Stadium. The Steelers had defeated the Raiders 34–28 on opening day, but both teams had changed much since then. Both of their defenses were now playing at the peak of performance. Both of their offenses were putting up high numbers in points and yardage. Both teams overcame nagging injuries to key personnel. The Raiders had won their last six straight games heading into their playoff match with Pittsburgh. Among those key Oakland victories were wins against all three of their division foes (Denver, Kansas City, and San Diego), and a thrilling Monday night triumph over the visiting New York Jets. The Steelers won their last four regular season games to claim the AFC Central championship. The Raiders were no strangers to postseason play, having been a regular participant in the playoffs in four of the previous five seasons. In contrast, the Steelers were taking part in the first playoff game in their 40-year history.

This playoff contest would go down in the annals of league history as one of the greatest and most important of all time. It featured one of the most astounding and memorable plays of the decade ... a miraculous play which decided the outcome of the game. The game's legendary status was earned as much by the stories that surround the game as by the play of both teams on the field. The dramatic ending featured equal amounts of controversy, edge-of-your-seat excitement among the witnesses, and an incredulous disbelief concerning what actually happened on the winning play. Even today, the program and a ticket stub from that game are treasured mementos, and the claim "I was there" is a faithful badge of honor amongst fans in the Steel City.

None of those feelings or the cherished final moments could have been foreseen during the first half of the game, however. Both offenses struggled mightily against the opposing defenses. The Raiders could gain only 13 net passing yards in the first half, and the Steelers could attain only 22 net passing yards in the same span of time. Both teams put together modest drives during the first half, but both offenses were squelched by outstanding defensive play. The Raiders had more total yardage in the first two quarters than the Steelers, but they also had the edge in turnovers (two to zero).

It was not until the third quarter that one team started to assert itself. The Steelers received the second half kickoff and put together their second-longest drive of the game. Pittsburgh marched from their 22-yard line to the Oakland 11. Running back John "Frenchy" Fuqua dropped quarterback Terry Bradshaw's key third down pass, however, and the Steelers had to settle for a Roy Gerela field goal from 18 yards out for a 3–0 lead. A fumble by Raiders quarterback Ken Stabler midway through the fourth quarter led to another Gerela field goal from 29 yards out to give the Steelers a 6–0 cushion.

Pittsburgh's lead appeared safe. There was 3:42 remaining on the clock. Oakland needed a touchdown and a conversion to win, and they were 80 yards away from accomplishing that feat against a defense which had stifled them all day. Ken Stabler's nickname was "The Snake," however, and it proved to be an appropriate nickname for the former Alabama star. Stabler managed to put together the best Raider drive of the game when he needed it most. Key passes to tight end Raymond Chester, running back Pete Banaszak, and receivers Fred Biletnikoff and Mike Siani brought Oakland to the Pittsburgh 30-yard line. From there, Stabler was chased out of his pocket to his left, and much to his surprise, found no Steeler defender anywhere near him. He rambled the entire distance and dove into the end zone, setting off a wild celebration among his teammates, and thoroughly deflating the Pittsburgh partisans. George Blanda kicked the extra point to complete the 12-play drive, giving the Raiders a 7–6 lead with but 1:13 remaining to be played.

The Steelers' dream of a championship appeared over. Certainly the Raiders in their history had almost patented late-game heroics, and this would be just one more miracle finish for them. But the football gods had one more miracle in the works. Pittsburgh had moved the ball to their own 40-yard line, but were faced with a fourth and 10 situation with only 22 seconds remaining. Steelers head coach Chuck Noll called for a "66 pass," a medium-distance play which would target receivers on the left side of the field. Pittsburgh quarterback Terry Bradshaw quickly found his pocket under assault, however, with scrambling as his only immediate option after discovering that all of his receivers were adequately covered. Bradshaw ducked a potential sack from Raiders defensive lineman Tony Cline, rolled backwards to his right, and rifled the ball a medium distance down the middle of the field, where he thought he saw a black jersey without a Raider near it.

Bradshaw's pass was intended for Fuqua, who was in line to catch the ball at the Raiders' 34-yard line. Oakland safety Jack Tatum, known throughout the league as "The Assassin" for his jarring hits, saw the ball in flight at the last second. Tatum wasted no time in steaming towards his target. "I immediately broke for the ball," Tatum recalled. "When I saw I couldn't get it, I aimed for Fuqua to try to either jar the ball from him or at least make the tackle. I hit him and I thought the game was ours." Tatum, Fuqua, and the ball all met each other at the same exact moment. "Tatum darn near went through my shoulder," admitted Fuqua. The Steeler setback and the ball flew in separate directions after Tatum's blast of a hit. The NBC sideline television camera followed the action up to that point, and instead of following the ball, which had ricocheted backwards eight full yards, kept its focus on Fuqua and Tatum.

Steelers running back Franco Harris stayed in the backfield to block on the play, but once Bradshaw started to scramble, he broke free from the pocket and started running down the middle of the field. Raiders linebacker Phil Villapiano noticed Harris' escape, and ran with him downfield. A photograph taken from the sideline shows both Harris and Villapiano running stride for stride with each other. A second later, however, Villapiano slowed down for just a brief moment to survey the situation. Harris did not. The rookie runner from Penn State surged toward the ball, which was plummeting quickly towards the Tartan Turf. Harris caught the ball just inches before it hit the ground at the Oakland 42-yard line. Villapiano could not really be faulted for his brief moment of inaction. Indeed, many of the players on both teams stood still once Tatum made his hit and the play appeared to be just another incompletion. Raider defensive back Jimmy Warren even leaped in the air with his arms raised in jubilation after the collision. Harris immediately noticed the lack of pursuit among the Raiders as he ran to his left. Steeler tight end John McMakin peeled back and brush blocked Villapiano, which gave Harris that one extra step he needed to make it into the Raider secondary. Racing down the sideline and with over 50,000 Pittsburgh fans in full screaming mode, Harris eluded a diving grab at the Oakland 10-yard line by Warren (who had an epic "oh no!" moment after his brief celebration), the last defender with an actual chance at tackling him. Had Warren not made a premature celebratory gesture following Tatum's hit, he may have had a better angle with which to knock Harris out of bounds around the 5-yard line or so. Harris stayed inbounds however, and crossed the goal line with only five seconds left on the clock.

Throngs of Steeler fans stormed onto the field in joyous celebration. Bradshaw's 60-yard touchdown pass to Harris had saved the day ... or had it? The Raiders stood around dumbfounded, as did most of the referees. Did all this really just happen? What actually happened? The league rules in 1972 stipulated that no two offensive players could touch the ball in succession. Oakland players insisted to the referees that Tatum hit Fuqua, and that Fuqua was the last person to touch the ball before Harris made his catch, thereby making the play illegal.

"I never did touch the ball," said Tatum afterward. "I hit the man only. I was trying to knock the ball loose from him because we got to it at about the same time. There wasn't any way I could have made contact with that ball." Fuqua said later, "I saw stars because I really got hit by a good hit by Tatum."

Steeler players and the swelling number of Steeler fans on the field verbally (and colorfully) disagreed with Oakland's claim. The referees were now in quite a fix, so some of them decided to go into the dugout area of Three Rivers Stadium where they might have some sense of privacy and talk on the phone to Art McNally, the league official in charge of all referees. McNally was up in the press box, and even he could not absolutely confirm what had actually occurred on the critical play. But he was convinced enough to tell referee Fred Swearingen that, after looking closely at replays, he believed it was a "double touch," meaning that Fuqua touched the ball first, then Tatum, thereby making the play legal. Popular legend has it that Swearingen was told by McNally to signal a touchdown, instead of taking the unnecessary risk of being assaulted by the raucous Pittsburgh fans on the field. This was a far-fetched story that many Raiders players and coaches believe to this day.

Raiders head coach John Madden was one of those who vehemently protested the play, claiming that no ruling was made on the field at the conclusion of the play. Madden was incorrect, however. An NBC television replay from the end zone angle showed back judge Adrian Burk following the play down the sideline and clearly signaling touchdown as soon as Harris crossed the goal line. Unfortunately, that replay was also inconclusive as to who touched the ball when Tatum and Fuqua collided. Several zebras (referees) eventually emerged from the dugout. In 1972, referees did not have microphones to make any announcements for penalties or rulings on the stadium's public address system, so Swearingen's on-field signal would serve as the only method of communication which would declare the verdict to the fans and the television audience. As the yelling amidst the players and fans who were surrounding him continued, Swearingen raised his arms over his head to indicate a touchdown, and what was voted by a committee of pro football writers and broadcasters as the greatest game of the decade of the 1970s was finally over. Pittsburgh 13, Oakland 7.

Almost a decade after that fateful day, Swearingen would give an interview to reporter Bill Dwyre, in which at least some of the troubling questions concerning the game-winning play would finally be answered, or at least come into a sharper focus. Swearingen's role on the play was to stay behind the quarterback during the process of his throw, and to make sure that Bradshaw was not hit late after the ball was thrown. He recalled: "I saw him [Bradshaw] throw the ball downfield and by the time I looked up, Harris somehow had the ball and was going down the sidelines for a touchdown. Now, all I knew was that there were fans on the field, the people [police and security personnel] were out trying to clear the people away, my officiating crew was scattered all over because a pass play like that forced them to do so, and John Madden was screaming at me that whatever happened was illegal. I got downfield as fast as I could, through fans and players and even dogs, and got my crew together. Then I polled them, one by one, all five of them individually, to see what they saw. I ended up with four 'I don't knows,' including my own, and two 'I think the defensive man hit it.' Then I asked if anybody could say for sure if the defensive man [Tatum] hit it and nobody could. In the middle of all of this, a guy from Pittsburgh named Jimmy Boston who's always on the sidelines has a headset on [and] tells me McNally wants me on the phone. McNally was in the press box. There was a phone in the Pittsburgh dugout, and I asked this guy [Jimmy Boston] where that phone went to, and he said right to McNally. So I picked it up and talked to him and he said everything was okay and to just get the people off the field. But as soon as everybody in the press box saw me pick up the phone, the assumption was that I had asked for an instant replay. Jim Kensil [the number two man to Commissioner Pete Rozelle] was there with McNally and he told the press that I had called to clear up a confusing situation. That wasn't the truth at all. I had called because I thought they were calling me. That game finished me as a referee. Shortly after that, I went back to being a field judge again."

The play that won the game for Pittsburgh and hailed the beginning of a dynasty would forever be known as the Immaculate Reception. A fitting name for a play that required nothing less than a miracle for it to occur. The play, with Franco Harris snaring the pigskin just above his shoelaces and sprinting down the field, has been shown by NFL Films more than any other single football play in television history. In the years since, the play has been dissected so many times

Franco Harris of the Pittsburgh Steelers eludes the grasp of Oakland Raiders defensive back Jimmy Warren in a 1972 AFC divisional playoff game on December 23, 1972. Known to history as "The Immaculate Reception," Harris' controversial play served as the genesis of an NFL dynasty (AP Photo/Harry Cabluck).

from every possible angle that it has become the NFL's version of the Zapruder film (the film taken by Dallas dress manufacturer and amateur photographer Abraham Zapruder during the John F. Kennedy assassination in 1963). In the emotional Steelers locker room after the game, Harris was lauded by Pittsburgh head coach Chuck Noll, who stated, "Franco made that play because he never quit on the play. He kept hustling, [and] good things happen to those who hustle." John Fuqua refused to tell reporters after the contest whether he touched the ball or not. He still has not *officially* told reporters to this very day. He has on several occasions commented that he did touch the ball, and on several more occasions that he did not touch the ball. Fuqua claims that his surviving family members will release a letter upon his death disclosing his *official* story of the moment. Steeler owner Art Rooney urged Fuqua to keep his story to himself and to "keep the play immaculate."

Rooney himself had a unique story to tell about Franco's game-winning play. Rooney took the press box elevator down to the tunnel leading to the Pittsburgh locker room after Stabler's touchdown. He wanted to get down there and console his team and thank them for a great season. By the time he reached the locker room, however, the deafening roar of the crowd overwhelmed him. The Steelers had achieved the greatest victory in their history and had accomplished the greatest single play in their history, and their longtime owner was stuck in an elevator. Many years later, the stainless steel elevator panel was removed just prior to the implosion of Three Rivers Stadium. It now resides in the collection of the Pro Football Hall of Fame in Canton, Ohio.

No sooner had the Raiders and Steelers entered their postgame locker rooms, when some murmurings of doubt as to the reliability and infallibility of Swearingen's decision were heard. To the Raiders, the call on the field was inconsistent with what they saw. Could an instant replay system, similar to the kind that fans were watching on television, be used to aid officials in making the absolute right call to avoid any potential errors? More than a few players and fans across the country thought that it could. But the petition at that time was not taken too seriously by most team owners, however, as many of them believed that the human element of making calls on the field should not be infringed upon. Referees were humans, and humans make mistakes, and sometimes those mistakes were part and parcel of the unpredictability of the game. Indeed, it would be 14 more years and many more controversial calls later before instant replays were used in NFL games. Nevertheless, in the aftermath of the Immaculate Reception playoff contest on December 23, 1972, the cry amongst teams, fans, and a few owners for the inclusion of an instant replay system to help the referees was faintly heard across the nation for the very first time.

The AFC title contest a week later would not contain controversy, but it would provide fans with an intriguing matchup. The Miami Dolphins would be visiting Three Rivers Stadium to take on the Steelers. Back in 1972, sites for conference championship games alternated each year by division. It just so happened that the AFC Central representative, the Steelers (11–3 regular season record), would be the home team, and the AFC East representative, the Dolphins (14–0 regular season record), would be the visiting team. The NFL changed this practice in 1975, when the team with the best regular season record would be awarded home-team status in conference title games.

Pittsburgh's home-field advantage was certainly a factor to consider heading into the title game. The team was one win away from their first Super Bowl. They had just pulled out the most miraculous win in their history, and although the Dolphins were undefeated, most Steelers fans believed that Miami was overrated, and that 1972 was a truly magic year for their beloved Black and Gold. But the Steelers players themselves knew that Miami would provide an even tougher matchup for them than Oakland did the previous week. The Dolphins had come this far before, and even though many sportswriters derided them for their soft schedule, they knew how to win a game like this. It would be that knowledge which proved vital in defense of their AFC crown.

The setting at Three Rivers Stadium on December 31 was unusual, to say the least. A rather balmy 63-degree temperature and clear, calm skies greeted the players, many of whom were expecting a more frigid climate. Any notion that the Steelers would be intimidated by the mighty Dolphins on this day was laid to rest in rapid fashion. The stalwart Steelers defense picked off one of Miami quarterback Earl Morrall's first passes. Pittsburgh defensive back Glen Edwards awaited Morrall's overthrow and returned the interception 28 yards to the Miami 48-yard line. Pittsburgh quarterback Terry Bradshaw quickly drove his team down the field on ten plays for the game's first touchdown. From the Miami 3-yard line on third down, Bradshaw bootlegged around left end and dove for the end zone pylon. He was quickly upended, however, by Dolphins safety Jake Scott. The collision caused the ball to pop out of Bradshaw's grip and bounce into the end zone. Steeler offensive guard Gerry Mullins hustled after the play and dove for the ball, recovering it just before it rolled out of the end zone. The Steelers had scored, but the touchdown had a detrimental result. Bradshaw landed hard on the play and injured his throwing shoulder. He was taken out of the game after one more series and would not return until the fourth quarter.

Pittsburgh's defense was having their way with Morrall and the Miami offense for most of the first half. It was late in the second quarter, however, where Miami's experience helped to turn the game around. Head coach Don Shula's club was hitting hard, but was playing a conservative style of game, doing their best to avoid mistakes and stay close to the Steelers. But when the opportunity presented itself, the Dolphins executed a play of good fortune. Miami punter Larry Seiple was standing at his 36-yard line when he prepared to punt the ball back to the Steelers. He quickly noticed that only one opponent—Barry Pearson—attempted to rush him from the outside. All the other Pittsburgh players were peeling back and setting up for a return. Seiple took quick and decisive action. He sprinted past Pearson and headed downfield along the sideline. Pittsburgh players and coaches along the sideline were yelling, "Fake! Fake!" Their teammates on the field, however, were unresponsive until it was too late. Seiple was finally driven out of bounds 37 yards later at the Steelers' 12-yard line. The gamble paid off tremendously for Miami.

"I have complete confidence in Larry," said Shula after the game. "He's so intelligent that when he makes up his mind to do something like that, I never worry. If he decided to take the risk, there must have been a good reason for it."

Seiple's critical run set up Miami's first score. Fullback Larry Csonka caught a swing pass from Morrall from nine yards out and blasted through an attempted arm tackle by Steelers defensive back Mel Blount, who was trying to cover Miami receiver Paul Warfield. Csonka left Blount strewn on the turf and trotted into the end zone to tie the game just prior to halftime, 7–7. "I don't think I ran him [Blount] over in the true sense of the word," Csonka said afterward. "Rather, he was trying to recover from inching over on Warfield and wasn't in position."

The Steelers hung tough, however. Reserve quarterback Terry Hanratty had his best series of the game early in the third quarter, leading his team on a nine-play drive to produce a 14-yard Roy Gerela field goal. Key plays in the drive were passes from Hanratty to tight end John McMakin (for 22 yards and a first down) and receiver Ron Shanklin (for 24 yards and a first down). The Steelers had regained the lead and some much needed confidence.

Miami's Larry Seiple made a key decision earlier in the game which changed the momentum in favor of his team. Miami head coach Don Shula would make another wise decision in the third quarter which would do the same thing. Shula replaced Morrall with Bob Griese, who had spent much of the season recuperating from a fractured ankle. Shula felt that Griese would give his offense a spark. Three plays after coming in, Griese did exactly that. The ex–Purdue star quarterback sent Warfield on a quick slant pattern. The Steelers defense decided to blitz on the play, a move which they instantly regretted. Griese drilled Warfield with a bullet that was just past the diving reach of Pittsburgh outside linebacker Jack Ham. Warfield sprinted downfield with a 52-yard gain, setting up the Dolphins with great field position at the Pittsburgh 24. Reserve halfback Jim Kiick took a pitchout from Griese several plays later and dove into the end zone to score from two yards out. Miami now possessed their first lead of the game, 14–10. Shula's decision to insert Griese in at quarterback was ample proof of his coaching genius.

"We weren't getting sustained drives," Shula said later. "Griese had been working well in practices so I thought he might get our offense moving. He deserved the chance."

The Miami No-Name Defense then refused to allow the Steelers a chance to regain the momentum. They effectively shut down Hanratty for the remainder of the game, and blunted the Pittsburgh rushing attack, limiting the Steeler runners to 128 total yards on 26 carries. Miami's runners, in contrast, started to take over the game. Csonka's short but pounding thrusts wore down the Pittsburgh defenders, and tailback Mercury Morris contributed several key sweeps to keep the chains moving. Miami's first possession of the fourth quarter resulted in their third touchdown of the game. The Dolphins ran the ball ten times on an 11-play drive which culminated with Jim Kiick's second scoring run, this time following a Csonka block on a 3-yard surge up the middle.

The Steelers found themselves trailing 21–10 midway through the fourth quarter. Steelers head coach Chuck Noll happened to see Bradshaw warming up on the sideline and decided to reinsert him in the game. Bradshaw responded quickly, throwing four passes in just over two minutes which produced another score. The sore-shouldered quarterback hit rookie wide receiver Al

Young for a 12-yard touchdown to bring Pittsburgh to within four points of Miami at 21–17. Young made a fantastic catch on the touchdown, leaping over Dolphins safety Jake Scott, all the while concentrating on Bradshaw's incoming missile of a pass. Young grabbed the ball with one hand, kept it above Scott's reach, then spun into the end zone.

There were still just over five minutes remaining in the game. Visions of the Immaculate Reception from the previous week were dancing in the minds of the Steeler fans as their defense kept Miami from getting a first down on their next series. Pittsburgh's throng of vociferous supporters in Three Rivers Stadium knew that there was still enough time left on the clock to score one more touchdown. Those fans went from optimistic euphoria to hopeless dejection, however, during the next two sets of downs that their team had the ball. Miami linebackers Nick Buoniconti and Mike Kolen each intercepted a Bradshaw pass on succeeding drives, and the Dolphins' dream of a perfect season was still alive. Miami had successfully defended their AFC title by a 21–17 score over Pittsburgh, and were headed for Super Bowl VII.

"I never got the feeling we had turned it around," said a relieved Shula following the game. "Not until the game was over. I don't think you ever get that feeling against the Steelers. It was a helluva tough game." Miami center Jim Langer added, "We had to play our best game of the year to win."

The Steelers were feeling their first impression of a playoff defeat. "The difference in the game was the big plays," said veteran Steelers linebacker Andy Russell. "They made them, and we didn't." Pittsburgh's stalwart defensive tackle Joe Greene commented, "Miami's a better ball club than I thought. Films have a way of deceiving you. They didn't look as good [in films] as they were."

Awaiting the Dolphins in the Super Bowl would be the winner of the NFC title game. Both the Dallas Cowboys and the Washington Redskins had turned in excellent seasons in 1972, and both were looking good heading into their third meeting of the year at Robert F. Kennedy Stadium in Washington, D.C., on New Year's Eve. Both had split their regular season series, and the rivalry between the two had already reached noteworthy proportions. Few rivalries in the history of pro football delivered as much bulletin board material as the rivalry during the 1970s between the Cowboys and the Redskins. Some of the verbal assaults prior to the 1972 NFC title game came from a variety of sources. All-Pro Dallas offensive lineman John Niland voiced his anger for the Redskins when he commented to reporters in a bitter tone. "I hate the Redskins," Niland said. "I just like to knock them down and pound them."

Washington quarterback Billy Kilmer heard that Dallas head coach Tom Landry described the journeyman signal caller as "a good leader but not a great quarterback." Kilmer bitterly responded that Landry's statement "teed me off." Dallas middle linebacker Lee Roy Jordan labeled the Redskins as "probably the best mouthers in the league." As game time neared, however, all players on both teams knew that actions—and not words—would win this contest. Washington's Bill Brundige summed it up best when he said, "This is the way it should be, head to head. It'll be the shootout at the OK corral, and may the best team win."

The best team on game day was easily the Washington Redskins. They effectively and continually halted the Cowboys offense throughout the game. The Cowboys could not register a first down for the first 24 minutes of the game. It seemed that almost every time that the Dallas offense got the ball, they started their possessions deep inside their own territory. Landry decided to start Roger Staubach at quarterback in place of Craig Morton, who had filled in for Staubach during the regular season while Staubach was recuperating from his shoulder injury. Staubach's winning performance at the end of the previous week's playoff tilt at San Francisco, however, convinced Landry that Staubach was ready to take over the offense.

"Roger brought us to this game [the NFC championship game] and I felt he should have the chance," said Landry.

But Staubach was still a bit rusty, and the Redskins knew it. They limited his scrambling lanes throughout the game, thereby keeping him in the pocket. The success that Dallas achieved in the final minutes against the 49ers was something that the Redskins desperately wanted to prevent from occurring again. They knew that Staubach was capable of bringing his team back from large deficits, so they double-teamed his receivers throughout the game and kept one of the best quarterbacks in the league from hitting his secondary targets. Staubach completed only nine of 20 passes in the game for a meager 98 yards. Washington's Over the Hill Gang limited Dallas to only eight first downs, a total of 170 yards, and a mere three points. In the third quarter, the Redskins permitted Dallas to gain only 23 yards and no first downs.

"They were playing excellent football in every phase," said Landry of the Redskins. "We had our opportunities, but we missed them—and they didn't."

Washington's offense had very few problems with the Dallas defense. Kilmer conducted a nine-minute drive in the first quarter, focusing his throws in the direction of Dallas left cornerback Charlie Waters. Kilmer rotated his receivers—Charley Taylor and Roy Jefferson—to take full advantage of Waters' lack of closing speed. Kilmer sent Taylor on a deep fly pattern in the second quarter, and connected with him for a 51-yard gain. Several plays later, Taylor ran a quick post pattern and caught Kilmer's perfect pass for a 15-yard touchdown. "We wanted to pick on the weakest man," Kilmer said, "and that is nothing personal against Charlie Waters. We didn't want to go to the other side against [right cornerback] Mel Renfro because he can make the big play. I guess they thought I was going to throw more to Roy Jefferson and to Jerry Smith. So I went to Taylor."

Kilmer and Taylor made another big play in the fourth quarter. Taylor ran a similar fly route as he did before, but this time, it was against reserve Dallas cornerback Mark Washington, who replaced Waters after Waters suffered a broken arm earlier in the contest. Taylor beat Washington easily down the sideline for a 45-yard touchdown which boosted the Redskins' lead to 17–3. The young cornerback had misjudged Taylor's speed on the play, and it cost his team a touchdown.

While Washington's defense continued to frustrate Staubach and the Dallas offense, Kilmer kept putting his team in scoring position throughout the fourth quarter. Redskins placekicker Curt Knight made good on many of those possessions, as he set an NFL championship game record with four field goals, three of which came in the final quarter. Kilmer finished the day completing 14 passes in 18 attempts. The Redskins had triumphed over their dejected arch-rivals, 26–3, and were headed to their first Super Bowl.

Thousands of joyous Redskins fans immediately stormed the field at the final gun, making it difficult for players from both teams to reach the entrance to their locker rooms. George Allen was carried off the field by those fans as the fight song "Hail to the Redskins" reverberated throughout RFK Stadium. The Redskins were regarded by most experts as pro football's most emotional team during the first half of the decade, and that raw emotion was now highly visible in the throes of unabashed celebration for all to see. Allen had described his team's performance against Dallas as "very nearly perfect." In two weeks, he would meet the perfect team.

Super Bowl VII would be held in the Los Angeles Memorial Coliseum, the same stadium which hosted the first Super Bowl game in January of 1967. The Redskins had not won a league title in 30 years, and were riding a huge wave of emotion going into the game. That was their trademark, and it served them well throughout 1972. The Dolphins were more business-like, employing the demeanor of their head coach, Don Shula, who was making his third appearance as a head coach in a Super Bowl. Shula had failed in his previous two attempts to win the Lombardi Trophy, and he was intensely determined to avoid another losing effort in Super Bowl VII. Just the year before, Shula's Dolphins had suffered a demoralizing defeat at the hands of the Dallas Cowboys in Super Bowl VI. The memory of that disaster festered among the minds of his players, and they were also very eager to avenge that loss.

Oddsmakers still could not bring themselves to believe that any team could go undefeated during the course of an entire NFL season, and so they picked Washington as one-point favorites. The oddsmakers were not alone. Many fans throughout the country believed that the Dolphins had been more lucky than good in several of their games, and that they would have endured a few losses if they had played against tougher competition throughout the regular season. Redskins fans believed that their team was battle-tested and hardened enough to smite the mighty Dolphins on the nation's grandest stage. Regardless of the pregame point of view, Super Bowl VII would make history for one of these teams.

Super Bowl VII started under a sunny but smoggy Southern California sky. The game was a defensive stand-still until late in the first quarter when the Dolphins drew first blood. Miami quarterback Bob Griese culminated a six-play drive by sending his flanker, Howard Twilley, on an out pattern from the Washington 28-yard line. Griese's pass floated just over the reach of reserve Redskins linebacker Harold McLinton and into the waiting arms of Twilley at the 5-yard line. Waiting for Twilley was Washington defensive back Pat Fischer, who latched onto the 5'10", 185-pound Dolphins receiver. Twilley's momentum and desire helped him to drag the 5'9", 170-pound Fischer into the corner of the end zone for the first score of the game.

"I did a little three-step move inside," Twilley said, "and then broke to the outside. Fischer bit [on the inside move]."

Miami's No-Name Defense took over the remainder of the first half, dominating the Redskins at the line of scrimmage. Washington halfback Larry Brown was limited to just 72 yards on 22 carries against the Dolphins. Brown also endured a bevy of hard hits from several Dolphin defenders, each of whom were focused on stopping Washington's cutback running strategy by maintaining their gaps and lanes of attack. Miami safety Dick Anderson once hit Brown so hard in his midsection that Brown's helmet popped off. The Dolphin defensive line also helped to control the Redskins offense. Miami defensive tackle Manny Fernandez thoroughly dominated action along the line of scrimmage, making seven tackles, three of which went for a loss of yardage. "He [Fernandez] is a hell of a tackle," said Washington guard John Wilbur, who had the unenviable task of blocking Fernandez. "[He's] very quick and very fast laterally." Fernandez' performance was the result of preparation for Washington strategy. "We knew Washington tried to win with its running game," said Fernandez. "And we knew the key man was Brown. Everyone knew it. We watched him on film and we saw how he always tried to cut back. So that's what we concentrated on."

Miami safety Jake Scott also played a super game. Scott's first interception in the second quarter was a thing of beauty. Redskins quarterback Billy Kilmer intended his pass for wide receiver Charley Taylor, but Scott leaped in front of Taylor and tipped the ball. Almost immediately, Miami linebacker Bob Matheson accidentally knocked Scott down, but the crafty safety reached out with one hand and grabbed the ball just one foot above the turf.

Another Miami interception late in the second quarter led to an increase in the Miami lead. A blitz by Dolphins linebacker Doug Swift forced a hurried throw by Kilmer. Miami middle linebacker Nick Buoniconti caught the ball and chugged down the sideline for 32 yards, placing his team in prime scoring position. "He [Kilmer] didn't see either Buoniconti or Scott," explained Shula on the first two of his team's interceptions. A key 19-yard pass on third down from Griese to tight end Jim Mandich brought Miami to the Redskins' 2-yard line. Mandich made a splendid diving catch on this, his only reception of the game. Two plays later, reserve running back Jim Kiick plowed into the end zone from one yard out for a 14–0 Miami lead at halftime. "It was my specialty," Kiick said after the game. "The one-yard gallop."

Washington began the third quarter with a determined drive, aiming to get on the scoreboard and build some measure of momentum. They succeeded in the latter ... but only briefly. Kilmer came out throwing on his first series of the second half, utilizing his wide receivers on quick out patterns. Roy Jefferson and Charley Taylor caught several passes along the sidelines which moved the chains in the 11-play drive. Washington's offense was soon in scoring position, but unfortunately for the Redskins, the Miami defense woke up just in time. Fernandez broke through his blockers and sacked Kilmer on third down to force Washington to settle for a field goal attempt. Any thoughts that this would be Washington's day were quickly erased when Redskins placekicker Curt Knight missed from 32 yards out.

To their credit, however, the Redskins defense kept fighting. Dolphins fullback Larry Csonka broke through them for a 49-yard gain late in the third quarter. Csonka rumbled down the field on his pounding run, fighting off five tacklers before being brought down. But Washington defensive back Brig Owens shut down the Miami drive by pulling off a one-handed interception of a Griese pass in the end zone. Owens leaped over tight end Marv Fleming to secure the pass and give his team a touchback.

With time at a premium, Kilmer put together another offensive surge in the fourth quarter. Kilmer mixed quick passes with several runs, a scramble, and a tight end reverse on a 14-play drive to bring his team to the Miami 10-yard line. Once again, however, bad luck would intervene. Kilmer sent tight end Jerry Smith on a post pattern, and Smith managed to get open. The pass was right on target, but the ball never reached Smith's hands. Kilmer's pass bounced off of the crossbar of the goalpost. Kilmer tried a similar pass on the very next play, but Jake Scott, who would later be named the game's Most Valuable Player, showed up the crossbar by intercepting the ball. Scott could have stayed in the end zone for a touchback, but he decided to bring the ball out, despite the vehement advice to stay in the end zone by several of his defensive teammates. Scott's gamble paid off, though, as he sped down the sideline on a 55-yard return.

"Kilmer didn't see me cut over and the ball came to me," Scott said. "I stopped for just a second, thinking I would down the ball for a touchback. Then I saw a lane open up and I decided to run it out."

Scott's second theft gave his team good enough field position to have a chance at obtaining a symbolic irony. The Dolphins were lined up for a 42-yard field goal attempt late in the fourth quarter. A successful kick would boost Miami to a 17–0 lead, in a season where they achieved a 17-win, zero-loss record. Placekicker Garo Yepremian kicked the ball low, however, and Redskins defensive lineman Bill Brundige got the credit for blocking it. Replays showed, however, that the low trajectory of the ball caused it to thud against the back of Dolphins interior lineman Bob Heinz' helmet. Yepremian picked up the bouncing ball, ran to his right, and attempted to pass. The ball, however, was too big for the Cypriot kicker's small hands, and it slipped out as he cocked his arm. Yepremian then reached for the loose ball, and inadvertently popped it skyward. Redskins defensive back Mike Bass was trailing the play and was close enough to grab the ball as it descended. Bass bolted for the uncluttered sideline, and raced past a stunned Yepremian. Bass reached the end zone for a 49-yard score which gave the Redskins at least some small measure of hope.

"We knew we didn't need any more points," said Miami offensive guard Bob Kuechenberg years later. "Our defense was in control there. And then we come up for the field goal in the last

Miami Dolphin defenders Dick Anderson (40), Manny Fernandez (75), and Doug Swift (59) corral Washington Redskins running back Larry Brown in Super Bowl VII, January 14, 1973. The Dolphins completed the NFL's only perfect season with a 14–7 victory over Washington (AP Photo/NFL Photos).

couple of minutes. That would have made it 17–0, right? Gee, that would have been a nice final score, wouldn't it? Perfect score, in fact. Then Garo did his little thing."

Washington's final offensive drive was snuffed out, however, and Yepremian was off the hook. Kilmer was sacked deep in Redskin territory by Miami defensive ends Bill Stanfill and Vern Den Herder on the last play of the game. "I knew that was the ball game," Den Herder said later. "Stanfill just went crazy after the play, grabbing me, hugging me. Then I realized we were still on top of Kilmer."

Perfection was achieved by Miami by a score of 14–7, as Shula was carried off the field in ultimate triumph. A Super Bowl record 90,192 spectators in the Los Angeles Memorial Coliseum and millions more on television had watched the undefeated world champions accomplish what many thought was impossible ... a 17-win season with no blemishes in the loss column—only a zero. "This is the greatest team I've ever been associated with," said a gleeful Shula after the game.

The Miami Dolphins thus became a legendary team. They are forever etched in NFL history as the proud owners of the league's only perfect season, accomplished in what could be described as the league's most legendary season.

1973

The Odyssey Towards Stardom

The season of 1972 proved beyond a shadow of a doubt that anything was possible in the NFL during the 1970s. The season of 1973 would add further evidence to support that belief. A popular running back would make the leap to super-stardom during that epic year, breaking records and establishing a rushing mark for a season that only a few other men have eclipsed since. New names, new faces and new places were in vogue in the league through various trades, with all teams searching diligently for the right formula and personnel to obtain success. The annual player draft would once again bring about many rookies who quickly helped to turn their teams around, while several popular veterans made room for those first-year players by announcing their retirements. A total of 238 rookies made NFL rosters in 1973, and 48 of those men quickly became starters for their respective teams.

Several other important issues made the season of 1973 an intriguing one. Preseason prognosticators debated whether the Miami Dolphins could repeat as world champions, and whether or not any Cinderella teams might make a possible showing. Discussions and rulings on the game's television policies were common throughout the league during the off-season, furthering the growing business factors and revenue concerns of the sport. Rumors on talks of a new league flourished in the media, and rivalries between several teams in both conferences also reached high levels. The 1973 season was one in which the game continued to prosper in popularity, and served as a natural extension of the excitement and growth of the game that was firmly established by the incredible 1972 season.

The league's public relations department also continuously made strides to enhance the image of the NFL. A non-profit organization called NFL Charities was formed in 1973 with a dual purpose. NFL Charities would help communities in NFL cities with educational projects and various charitable needs. It would also lend support to former NFL players to help them with their medical expenses, post-career surgeries, and economical concerns. NFL Charities has granted millions of dollars for these goals since its inception. To fund NFL Charities, the league would—through NFL Properties—sell licensing league and club trademarks in the form of clothing and various catalog items to fans all across the country. Fans in all stadiums soon began wearing their favorite team jerseys, sweatshirts, hats, tee-shirts and jackets. To inspire the early years of NFL Charities, the league asked several popular players to star in United Way television commercials, which not only helped the United Way gain notoriety and donations to aid the needy, but it also put a sensitive and caring face on the league. It was soon apparent that fans who tuned into the games on television would be more than willing to donate their time and money to causes supported by NFL Charities, thanks in part to some of those commercials. The three major television networks would have to deal with more than commercials, however, when televising NFL games in 1973. All three networks—CBS, NBC, and ABC—would find themselves at the mercy of the United States Congress prior to the beginning of the season. Congress decreed that hometown television blackouts on games which were sold out at least 72 hours prior to kickoff were to be lifted. This meant that many fans who usually could not afford to attend their team's home games could now watch them on television, provided that someone—anyone—purchased all of the remaining available tickets by the Thursday afternoon prior to the game. Oftentimes it was the local television stations themselves who purchased the final hundred or so tickets in order to televise the game locally. This law by Congress resulted in the term "no-show," a label given to fans who decided to watch the game on television instead of sitting in a stadium on a cold day, perhaps watching two teams with losing records who were not going to make the playoffs. It was not uncommon to see stadiums late in December with many an empty seat, as thousands of fans preferred instead to watch the game from the comforts of their own home.

The blackout ban was supported by the Nixon Administration and the Federal Communications Commission, which further frustrated the networks. If a game was not sold out in the time allotted, the networks would just give that city's television market another game on the schedule to watch. That game usually featured a full stadium, and a team with a winning record or noteworthy players. Thus the unintended consequence of the "blackout rule" would involve the luring of fans in the greater New York area—where the Jets and the Giants were mired in mediocrity and thus not drawing huge crowds—into becoming fans of teams like the Dallas Cowboys and the Pittsburgh Steelers, who were drawing new fans from all over the country, thanks to television (and Congress). Other cities also experienced this effect throughout the decade. Naturally, many of the also-ran teams opposed the new rule, as did the league's owners, as they foresaw and some eventually experienced dropping sales in season tickets.

There were a few other important factors to consider with the blackout rule. According to *Washington Post* staff writer Dave Brady, "Today's 'no-show' is tomorrow's lost fan. Even the possibility of televised home games to the local viewing markets would give those fans an overriding reason to stay home, above and beyond the weather factors, or their team's performance, or the availability of two other attractive NFL games on TV in their homes.

"But 'no-shows' affect others too," continued Brady. "The taxpayers who have built public stadiums where parking and concession income has been projected to pay off civic debt. Each 'no-show' represents approximately $1.50 in parking and concession expenditures. The overall loss in such expenditures was more than one million dollars in 1972, according to the NFL survey showing 624,686 tickets purchased and not used."

Clearly, a fan's choice to attend the games or not was more complex than ever before. The 1973 schedule was fortunately chock-filled with great games to watch, in person or on television. This was evident right from the first week, and continued through much of the season. Perhaps no other season during the decade had so many foreshadowing games in the first week which predicted the fortunes of the teams involved. Seven interconference games began the season in fine fashion. The defending NFC champion Washington Redskins were visited by the San Diego Chargers, a team with a new face behind center. The legendary Johnny Unitas was signed for one year by the Chargers following his unceremonious release by the Colts. "I've always enjoyed playing," said the 38-year-old Unitas upon his arrival in San Diego. "As long as I can help and still give 110%, I'll continue to play. If I can't, I'll get out."

The 18-year veteran was little more than a drawing card, however, as his once-golden arm was way past its prime. Furthermore, the Chargers did not possess one of the league's better offensive lines. The Over the Hill Gang had no problems ravaging Unitas' pass pocket, limiting the Chargers to 75 total yards through the air, and picking off four San Diego passes. Washington romped over their under-talented foes, 38–0, and thus once again laid claim to the top spot in the NFC East. Unitas would retire at the end of the year, and would soon become a pro football color analyst for CBS television. The Chargers would struggle throughout the 1973 season, and would end up winning only two games.

The Los Angeles Rams entered the new season with a colorful new look, donning new uniforms with golden horns on their helmets (replacing the previous white ones) and gold pants mixed with gold trim on their jerseys. The new look was not totally new, as the Rams had worn golden horns once before in the 1950s, but it was purely "golden" in 1973 against the host Kansas City Chiefs on opening day. Los Angeles defeated the Chiefs 23–13, and benefitted from the likes of two new players who came to the team via trades and who would make the 1973 season one of the best in the team's history. Quarterback John Hadl came to the Rams thanks to a trade with the Chargers, and wide receiver Harold Jackson arrived from a trade with the Philadelphia Eagles. Both men would go on to make the All-Pro team in 1973, but both were hardly needed against the Chiefs. Los Angeles relied on a newly-found rushing attack which would make frequent visits into the Kansas City defensive secondary. Running backs Jim Bertelsen and Lawrence McCutcheon would rush for 143 and 120 yards, respectively. The Los Angeles defense also did yeomen work, limiting the Chiefs to just 40 yards on the ground. The Rams were definitely one team which appeared from the outset to be much improved from the previous season.

Another such team which exhibited improvement was the Minnesota Vikings. They took a big step forward in the NFC Central Division by defeating the Oakland Raiders in the first week of the season, 24–16. The Minnesota passing tandem of quarterback Fran Tarkenton and wide receiver John Gilliam linked up for a 43-yard touchdown in the first quarter against the Raiders. Oakland came back to take a 16–10 lead, thanks in large part to a dazzling 63-yard punt return by George Atkinson, who broke three attempted tackles on his twisting, darting, and frenetic run to the end zone. But Tarkenton proved resilient, hitting his newest weapon—rookie halfback Chuck Foreman—for a go-ahead touchdown on a 9-yard outlet pass in the third quarter. Tarkenton would soon rely on Foreman for many receptions, not only in 1973 but for several years to come. Foreman would become one of the finest pass catchers coming out of the backfield during the decade. Long-time veteran Bill Brown joined Foreman in the Minnesota backfield, and his 6-yard run up the middle early in the fourth quarter added the insurance in Minnesota's victory over Oakland. The Raiders would get over their loss to the Vikings on opening day, however. Both of these teams would eventually find themselves in their respective conference's championship games.

Minnesota's divisional rival—the Green Bay Packers—also had an interconference game to start their season. The Packers took on the New York Jets in Milwaukee's County Stadium in the first *Monday Night Football* game of the season. Green Bay's hammering rushing attack of John Brockington and MacArthur Lane continued where they left off in 1972, controlling the ball for 155 total ground yards. Brockington's 1-yard burst in the fourth quarter gave the Packers a commanding 23–0 lead en route to a 23–7 victory. New York's star quarterback, "Broadway" Joe Namath, constantly fired into the teeth of another Packer strength, their defensive secondary. Namath completed only 48 percent of his passes on opening night against the formidable Green Bay pass defense. New York's loss to the Packers foreshadowed their dismal 4–10 season.

Another divisional champion from the previous season—the Pittsburgh Steelers—found themselves in a similar position as the Packers in their home opener against Detroit. The Steelers started off on the right foot by dominating Detroit, 24–10. Pittsburgh relied on their strong rushing attack, particularly in the fourth quarter, to grind out a win. Steeler halfback John Fuqua, who was subbing for an injured Franco Harris, ran for 100 of his team's 241 total rushing yards.

Pittsburgh ran the ball an incredible 60 times against the overwhelmed Lions defense. Pittsburgh quarterback Terry Bradshaw iced the win with two scoring passes in the final quarter, one to tight end John McMakin and one to flanker Ron Shanklin. The Steelers did what all strong teams do— they won a game that they were expected to win against an inferior team.

The defending world champion Miami Dolphins were another team that was expected to win their season opener against the visiting San Francisco 49ers. The heat in the Orange Bowl was a blistering 110 degrees on the field, and that may have factored in the less-than-stellar performances of both teams. Miami was trailing the 49ers going into the fourth quarter, but their championship persona bailed them out. Paul Warfield caught a 10-yard scoring pass from Bob Griese, and Garo Yepremian added two field goals to lift the Dolphins to a 21–13 win. San Francisco quarterback John Brodie was one of many in this game who was adversely affected by the heat and humidity. "I got drained," he later said.

The Dallas Cowboys had a tough opener as well. Tom Landry's club visited Chicago and met a fired-up Bears squad which kept the outcome in doubt until late in the game. Dallas built a 17–3 halftime lead on the strength of two Roger Staubach touchdown passes. Staubach threw medium-range darts over the middle and hit wide receivers Otto Stowe on a 23-yard score, and Bob Hayes on a 18-yard touchdown. Stowe came to the Cowboys via a trade with the Dolphins, and became a valuable weapon in the Cowboy offense during the early part of the season. Chicago's Ike Hill awoke his team up in the third quarter, however, when he returned a Marv Bateman punt 59 yards for a touchdown. Chicago tailback Carl Garrett then tied the game in the fourth quarter on a 15-yard run. Late in the struggle and deep in their own territory, the Bears inexplicably decided to take an unadvised risk and fake a punt to obtain a needed first down. The attempt failed, as Dallas rookie tight end Billy Joe DuPree stormed into the Chicago backfield and leveled tight end Bob Parsons, who had taken the direct snap from center and tried to run up the gut for the needed yardage. Toni Fritsch's ensuing 11-yard field goal with 1:26 remaining claimed a 20–17 win for Dallas.

The Atlanta Falcons would endure no such challenges in their opener in New Orleans. Everything that Atlanta tried against the Saints worked to perfection. Atlanta registered an incredible eight touchdowns in their 62–7 thrashing of their divisional foes. It was the most impressive showing in Falcons history. Atlanta would go on to challenge for a playoff spot in the NFC, and this game certainly got them off to a great start. The Saints did not do much to help their cause in this mercy killing, as they committed eight turnovers and accumulated a meager 35 net passing yards against the visiting Falcons.

The Denver Broncos took a similar initial step toward respectability in the league with a definitive 28–10 triumph over a pretty tough squad, the visiting Cincinnati Bengals. The Broncos relied on three touchdowns from halfback Floyd Little, and the improving generalship of veteran quarterback Charley Johnson. Denver head coach John Ralston entered his second year at the helm in 1973, and his positive outlook on all aspects of the team permeated his roster. Ralston managed to get his players to perform better than most had ever done before, and those performances were evident on opening day. "I'm a self-improvement nut," said Ralston, a master in getting his players to become enthusiastic toward the team and the game itself. "I think people want to get better so I explore every avenue. You grow or you go." For his part, Ralston went where no modern head coach dared to go before. He joined his kickoff teams in their huddle out on the field prior to each kickoff, gave them a rah-rah pep talk, then ran to the sidelines prior to each kickoff. It was unusual, it was pure Ralston, and it was an unforgettable sign that the Broncos were serious about building a winning attitude.

The St. Louis Cardinals showed off how much they had grown up from previous years in their first game of the season at Philadelphia. New Cardinals head coach Don Coryell was built from the same mold as Ralston, coming to St. Louis with a positive attitude, which he developed during a stellar career as the head coach of San Diego State University. Coryell was different than many coaches, however, in that he was more than willing to ignore the age-old adage about using the running game to set up the forward pass. Coryell often had his quarterback Jim Hart throw the ball on first down, believing that many defenses would not be expecting it. Coryell put together and preached the utilization of an explosive offensive strategy, and in St. Louis, he had many of the tools that were needed to make that strategy successful. Rookie tailback Terry Metcalf displayed his elusiveness on opening day in both the rushing and receiving categories, accumulating 133 yards on the ground against the Eagles, and catching one pass for 25 yards. Veteran running mate Donny Anderson accounted for three touchdowns, and speedy wide receiver Mel Gray caught seven passes from Hart. St. Louis built a quick 21–0 cushion over Philadelphia en route to a 34–23 triumph. The Cardinals' first game was a hint to their future, as they would become a competitive team in the NFC in 1973.

All of the aforementioned games did much to set the stage for the competitive teams and their destinies this season. But the game of the week was held in New England, where O.J. Simpson and the Buffalo Bills broke away from the Patriots, 31–13. Simpson began an individual odyssey unlike that of any other before in NFL history when he rushed for 250 yards against New England, a new single-game league record. It would be just one of many impressive records that the former Heisman Trophy winner from the University of Southern California would set in 1973. Simpson had more natural talent than perhaps any other runner in the game's history up to that point. He clocked in a 9.4 time in the 100-yard dash, and combined that speed with elusive moves and underestimated acceleration and leg power. Most of O.J.'s runs into opposing secondaries resembled track meets. "Our offense is geared to get me into the secondary," Simpson explained. "I have very good peripheral vision ... and I know where everyone is supposed to be."

Simpson also benefitted from a young and strong offensive line which bulldozed many a defensive front wall. That line was comprised of tackles Donnie Green (6'7", 272 pounds) and Dave Foley (6'5", 255), guards Joe DeLamielleure (6'3", 254) and Reggie McKenzie (6'4", 255), and centers Mike Montler (6'5", 254) and Bruce Jarvis (6'7", 250). Tight end Paul Seymour (-6'5", 252) was an offensive tackle in college at the University of Michigan, but he was switched to tight end by Buffalo head coach Lou Saban, and he quickly became one of the best blockers in the league at that position. Buffalo's offensive line was given a nickname by the Bills public relations department to help promote Simpson's popularity, but it also helped to make those linemen household names as well. "The Electric Company" was the new moniker of the offensive line, given to them because they turned on the "Juice" (which was Simpson's nickname). The Electric Company was poised to deliver standout performances and become one of the best offensive lines in the league in 1973. Yet it almost did not happen. Saban decided on the final starting lineup of his line just after the Bills lost their sixth and final preseason game. Going with a couple of rookies and inserting different players in new positions, Saban's lineup was an experiment that eventually proved successful.

"Many of the guys on the offensive line were from Big-10 colleges," remembers guard and future Hall of Famer Joe DeLamielleure. "We knew how to block coming into the pro game, because running the ball was what a lot of Big-10 teams did."

The Bills did a lot of running against the Patriots on opening day ... a *lot* of running. Besides Simpson's 250 yards and two touchdowns, fullback Larry Watkins (6–2, 230) rumbled for 105 yards and two touchdowns of his own. But it was Simpson who naturally gathered most of the attention from the New England defense.

Early in the first quarter, the Bills attempted a run which would become a staple for them throughout the season. Simpson took a handoff from quarterback Joe Ferguson from the Buffalo 20-yard line and ran to his right on a fundamental sweep. Simpson followed blocks from pulling guard Reggie McKenzie and fullback Jim Braxton (6'1", 243), broke two attempted tackles from New England defensive tackle Dave Rowe and cornerback George Hoey, and was off to the races. Simpson's 80-yard touchdown run down the sideline ignited his record-breaking performance and set the stage for the greatest rushing year of the decade. The most common view that the Patriots would seemingly get of O.J. on this day would be that of the back of his jersey. According to Patriots rookie head coach Chuck Fairbanks, Simpson "looked like Grant going through Richmond. We were helpless and couldn't slow him down." New England linebacker Edgar Chandler further described why Simpson succeeded: "He [Simpson] has that deceptive speed," said Chandler. "You think you have the angle on him, then he's gone."

It was not just Simpson's abilities, however. The Buffalo offensive line was also achieving great success in gouging open holes in New England's defensive line. This is somewhat astounding considering that The Electric Company did not employ a myriad of movements or shifting of players. Moreover, they did not even utilize a large number of plays from the playbook.

"We only had five basic plays," remembered DeLamielleure. "It was a real simple type of system. Really a basic system with sweeps and traps. The goal on most of the plays was to give a double team at the point of attack. We always wanted an extra blocker to go to the point of attack. That extra blocker would help to drive the targeted defender back, and our fullback would kick out the other defensive player who would come up to the line of scrimmage to force the play."

Buffalo's rushing strategy had its origins in a legendary running team from the previous decade. Jim Ringo was the offensive line coach for the Bills. He was also a key component in the great offensive lines with the Green Bay Packers during the Vince Lombardi era. That line stressed the diligence of repeated perfection, strict attention to detail, and simple but profound desire. Ringo pushed those traits upon his charges at Buffalo, and his players responded favorably. The simplistic running game had Saban's blessing, as Ringo's line kept opening up holes for Simpson. By season's end, Simpson would eclipse the 100-yard mark in 11 of 14 games, a new league record.

"Jim Ringo put it all together," recalled tackle Donnie Green. "We had a lot of quick-hitting plays. The 28 sweep, the 48 sweep, and the 44 trap were some of my favorites. We also had fullback Jim Braxton, and he was like another offensive lineman in the backfield."

Somewhat surprisingly, Simpson's success in setting the single-game rushing record against the Patriots on opening day almost did not happen. Saban had decided to give his star runner a rest by taking him out of the game with but a few minutes remaining. Then word came down from the press box that Simpson needed only 15 more yards to set the record. Saban quickly sent Simpson back into the game, and he got the needed 15 yards. Incredibly, another carry-by-carry review from the press box indicated that one more miscalculation occurred, and that Willie Ellison's 1971 record of 247 yards was still the standard by a few yards. Into the action went Simpson again, and this time, his second-to-last off-tackle run broke Ellison's record. "That was a pretty nerve-wracking experience," Simpson said after the game.

Simpson and The Electric Company were wracking the nerves of many defenses in the early stages of the season. But one defense across the country delivered some inspiring play in the second week of the season to stop another vaunted rushing attack. The Oakland Raiders hosted the defending world champion Miami Dolphins at the University of California's Memorial Stadium. The reason for the change in venue was due to the scheduling conflict that the Raiders had with the Oakland Athletics baseball team, who were busy hosting a World Series game at the Oakland-Alameda County Coliseum. The Dolphins had won their past 18 games, but that streak was finally halted by the determined Raiders defense. Oakland crushed the Miami running game, allowing them only a total of 105 yards on the ground on 24 carries. The Oakland pass defense also experienced success on this day, limiting Miami quarterback Bob Griese to only 90 total yards through the air. Even though the Raiders could only muster four George Blanda field goals themselves, those points would be enough to secure a big victory. Oakland's 12–7 triumph over the Dolphins sent a firm message to the rest of the league that the Raiders were determined to repeat as AFC Western Division champions. To Miami head coach Don Shula, it just meant an unexpected early road block.

"It has been a long time since I've had to talk about losing," Shula dryly quipped after the game. "We were the champions going into the game," said Miami fullback Larry Csonka. "The Raiders looked like champions coming out of it."

Neither the Philadelphia Eagles nor the New York Giants were going to be compared to the likes of the Raiders or the Dolphins in 1973. A playoff berth would not be attained by either of those two squads, but they both would take part in a historic game during the second week of the 1973 season. The contest ended in a 23–23 tie, but what made the game memorable was the fact that it would be the final regular season pro football game ever played in Yankee Stadium. "The House That Ruth Built" was slated to undergo extensive renovations, and the Giants were forced to play the remainder of their home games at the Yale Bowl in New Haven, Connecticut. Yankee Stadium opened in 1923 and was the home of the NFL's Giants since 1956. The famous stadium hosted three league championship games during its history, including the 1958 NFL title game between the Giants and the Colts, regarded by many pro football historians as "The Greatest Game Ever Played."

The St. Louis Cardinals had not produced a whole lot of historic victories in Busch Memorial Stadium, but their 34–27 win in the season's second week against the Washington Redskins may have been one of their best ever. Cardinals head coach Don Coryell was building an offense that he hoped would outscore many of his highly-touted opponents. His hopes were realized against the defending NFC champions, as St. Louis put up the most points ever against a George Allen defense. The game was tied 7–7 at halftime until both teams opened up their attacks. St. Louis running back Donny Anderson scored his second and third touchdowns of the game in the second half, and reserve running back Don Shy returned a Washington kickoff 97 yards for a score. The Redskins answered with setback Charlie Harraway's 10-yard touchdown reception from quarterback Sonny Jurgensen. Redskins runner Herb Mul-Key also contributed a 97-yard kickoff return. Jim Bakken's second field goal iced the game for St. Louis, however, and the Cardinals were suddenly sitting in first place in the NFC East with a 2–0 mark.

Up-and-coming teams like the Cardinals were building fan support and adding to the yearly growth in the popularity of the pro game. Interest in developing a new league to take advantage of that popularity and compete against the NFL had happened many times since the 1920s. Most of those fledgling leagues enjoyed only modest and fleeting success. Undaunted by this fact, a group of eager and determined businessmen, led by American Basketball Association founder Gary Davidson, decided to try their luck and form another new league—the World Football League—in 1973. The WFL would eventually begin play in 1974, and would hopefully include cities outside of the continental United States. Honolulu, Tampa, Tokyo and Toronto were all included as potential charter members of the new league. Other cities mentioned for possible inclusion were Memphis, Norfolk, Charlotte, Birmingham, Houston and Boston. Not all of those cities would end up fielding teams, but the new league would become a reality in a short amount of time. Several players in the NFL and many rookies fresh out of college would—through the advent of the WFL—have an alternative to the NFL and more options to further their professional careers. Many player agents agreed that the new league would force the average NFL salary to double within a couple of years, in order for the NFL owners to keep their superstars playing under the NFL shield. The WFL was inspired by the ultimate success of the AFL in the 1960s, and the new league would provide fans with several distinctive differences that would separate it from the brand of football that the NFL exhibited.

One of those differences was called the Dicker Rod, a newfangled measuring stick which differed greatly in appearance from the common first down markers and chains used in the NFL. The Dicker Rod resembled a land surveyor's marking device which retracted several feet from its vertical post to distinguish down and distance. After the laughter from the NFL officials and team owners concluded, the Dicker Rod was never seriously considered for use in the NFL. Another difference between the two leagues involved scoring. A touchdown would be worth seven points in the WFL, and the extra point was not mandatory. If a team wished to try a conversion, they could do so by running or passing only, with the ball being placed at the opposing 3-yard line. But despite their novelty, these differences could not mask the fact that the WFL would be a risky venture for all concerned. The AFL in the 1960s succeeded because of its stockpiles of monetary capital (thanks mostly to multi-millionaire Kansas City Chiefs owner Lamar Hunt). The WFL would struggle greatly to obtain much lesser amounts of cash funding.

The potential future success of the WFL would be doubted by many in the face of the established NFL. It would take time for fans to become accustomed to the new league, and it would take an even longer time for rivalries to evolve. Those were details for future years, however. Several current rivalries in the NFL needed no extra boost to make them interesting. The Oakland Raiders may have overlooked the Kansas City Chiefs when they visited Arrowhead Stadium on the third Sunday of the 1973 season. The Chiefs were still smarting from losing the AFC West to the Raiders the previous season, and they badly wanted to get even. Head coach Hank Stram's team took a measured step in doing just that as they defeated the lackluster Raiders, 16–3. Stram's defense did a number on the Oakland offense, limiting them to 149 total yards, including just 77 yards rushing on 25 carries. Kansas City middle linebacker Willie Lanier was in the right place at the right time when a fourth quarter Ken Stabler pass bounced off the chest of Raiders running back Pete Banaszak. Lanier intercepted the ball and out-raced Oakland offensive tackle Art Shell 17 yards to the corner of the end zone for the game-clinching touchdown.

"It was a defensive game all the way," said Lanier, who was affectionately referred to as the "Honey Bear" by his teammates. "It wasn't a game where one big play won it. Our defensive line was coming all day, and they [Oakland] knew it."

The Raiders-Chiefs rivalry could be depended upon for its unpredictability. Another rivalry in California was feeling the effects of change as well. The San Francisco 49ers had won the NFC Western Division in each of the past three years. The Los Angeles Rams had come in second place twice during that same time span, but they were poised in 1973 to place a roadblock in the path of a fourth consecutive title for the 49ers. The Rams visited Candlestick Park on September 30 and upended the 49ers, 40–20. Los Angeles continued to have success running the ball, accumulating 223 yards on the ground against the 49ers. The outcome was never really in doubt. Cullen Bryant returned a kickoff 93 yards for a Rams touchdown in the first quarter, and the Los Angeles defense limited San Francisco to 99 total rushing yards. The Rams also intercepted 49ers quarterback John Brodie three times to spur their victory.

"I kept my balance," said Bryant about his kickoff return after the game. "That's why I went all the way. The kicker tried to catch me [but] I cut left and got away free."

Rams coach Chuck Knox was once again a gracious winner. "The 49ers are a heckuva good team," Knox admitted. "It [the game] wasn't easy. It never is."

A week later, two teams that did not have a popular rivalry met in Buffalo's brand new Rich Stadium. The winless Philadelphia Eagles came into Buffalo with a highly-regarded passing attack, but with a porous defense. They left Buffalo still winless. The Bills and in particular O.J. Simpson ran through the Eagles defense with ease. Simpson ran for 171 yards against Philadelphia, giving him 647 yards in four games. Simpson's desire was evident on one play in particular, where he caught a short pass from quarterback Joe Ferguson and broke six attempted tackles to put the Bills in scoring range. Yet despite all of O.J.'s brilliance, Buffalo would require a stroke of good luck in order for them to notch their third victory of the season. Philadelphia placekicker Tom Dempsey missed a chip-shot field goal with no time remaining, and Buffalo was suddenly in first place in the AFC East.

"I felt sorry for him [Dempsey]," said Buffalo placekicker John Leypoldt, who himself booted a 47-yard field goal late in the fourth quarter to provide the final margin of victory for the Bills, 27–26. "I don't wish ill fate on anybody, [but] I didn't want them [the Eagles] to win." Buffalo head coach Lou Saban added in a fortunate tone, "You need to win one like this once in a while."

Two teams that were battling for first place in the NFC East would meet each other on a memorable Monday night to close out the fourth week of the season. The action between the Dallas Cowboys and the Washington Redskins at Robert F. Kennedy Stadium was colorfully described in the 1973 Redskins highlight film as "uglier, bloodier, and only more civilized than a cockfight." The hitting was ferocious, and typical of the raw rivalry that had developed over the past few years between these two teams. On one play, Dallas running back Calvin Hill ran a sweep near the sideline when Washington defensive back Mike Bass torpedoed him. Bass' helmet hit Hill square in the jaw, and Hill's helmet immediately sprung from his head. Hill was left staggering along the sideline, trying to get up twice, but falling down twice in an obvious loss of equilibrium. The dazed Dallas runner needed help to walk off the field, but in fairness, several players on both teams required aid from the trainers and medical staffs to make it through this battle. The Over the Hill Gang and the Doomsday Defense were distributing bruises on virtually every play, and the score reflected it. The only points put up during the first three quarters came on a 15-yard toss from Dallas quarterback Roger Staubach to wide receiver Otto Stowe, who made a magnificent diving catch on his post pattern touchdown.

Momentum finally changed hands in the fourth quarter when the Redskins put together a short drive to score a game-tying touchdown. Washington quarterback Sonny Jurgensen threw to wide receiver Charley Taylor in the end zone, but Dallas defensive back Charlie Waters kept Taylor from catching the ball by interfering with him. The resulting penalty placed the ball at the Dallas 1-yard line. Jurgensen hit Taylor on the next play on a quick-out pattern in the corner of the end zone for a score. Taylor had once again victimized Waters just as he did in the previous year's NFC championship game.

Things would get worse for Dallas, however. The Redskins struck again when defensive back Brig Owens stepped in front of a Craig Morton pass and returned the ball 26 yards for a touchdown. Dallas head coach Tom Landry was seldom afraid to shuffle his lineup—including at the quarterback position—in order to produce some positive results. Landry inserted Morton behind center after watching Staubach endure his seventh sack of the night. Morton's interception had many questioning Landry's decision, but the coach stuck with Morton for the remainder of the game. The Redskins' seven-point lead appeared safe as the final quarter neared its end.

Morton managed to rally his team during the game's final minute, however. The Cowboys drove down to the Washington 4-yard line when a fourth down pass to Walt Garrison provided the setting for one of the greatest tackles in NFL history. Washington safety Ken Houston met Garrison at the 1-yard line just as Garrison was coming down with Morton's pass. Houston hung on to the bullish fullback for dear life. Garrison stretched with all of his might to reach the end zone, but Houston's desire to keep him out was greater. Houston managed to wrestle Garrison to the ground to save the game for the Redskins, 14–7. Garrison spent his off-seasons as a rodeo cowboy, but in this instance the tables were turned, and it was Garrison himself who was roped down. "That's the biggest tackle that I've ever made in my life," Houston said. "I was looking for that play, [and] they had been trying to hit that flare all night. As strong as he [Garrison] is, I thought he should have scored, but I managed to keep him out."

Ken Houston's famous tackle is still remembered and spoken of fondly by many fans today in the District of Columbia, as well as by many of his Redskin teammates. "I'll never forget it," said Washington's Brig Owens years later. "Garrison never crossed that final chalk stripe and even now I can see him thrashing and churning, his legs off the ground, desperately trying to get across the goal line."

Harold Jackson of the Los Angeles Rams had no trouble getting across the goal line during a 37–31 triumph over the visiting Cowboys in the fifth week of the season. The diminutive but speedy wide receiver caught four touchdown passes in the first half from quarterback John Hadl. Very few other players in league history have equaled that mark, and only three other men (up to this date) have caught more touchdown passes in a game. The Rams had planned well for the Cowboys, and had seen in the films how to take advantage of the weakest element in the Dallas defense, cornerback Charlie Waters. Jackson would have even better success against Waters than Charley Taylor of the Redskins did the week before. Jackson's first pattern—a deep fly route—gave ample indication of how the day was going to go for both Jackson and those covering him. Jackson beat Waters by a full seven yards and coasted into the end zone with a 63-yard touchdown. "I've caught quite a few long ones against zones," said Jackson. "You can still get deep, find open people, if you have the right personnel."

Dallas fumbled the ensuing kickoff, and Hadl and Jackson quickly took advantage of the gift. Jackson ran a quick slant route from the 12-yard line and caught Hadl's perfect pass for another first quarter score. The Cowboys did not have a solution to stop Jackson in the second quarter, either. Following Mel Renfro's touchdown on an interception return which brought Dallas to within 14–7, the Rams struck back quickly. Jackson ran a deep post pattern and caught Hadl's 67-yard pass in stride as he loped into the end zone. Waters was once again the victim on the play, as he and safety Cliff Harris would also be a few moments later. Jackson's fourth touchdown came on a 36-yard pass from Hadl as Los Angeles built a 34–14 halftime lead.

The Cowboys came back strong in the second half, however. Roger Staubach connected with wide receiver Otto Stowe on six passes, two of which went for touchdowns. The Doomsday Defense delivered a spirited effort in the second half, allowing the Rams only one field goal. But the hole that the Cowboys dug for themselves in the first half was too much of an abyss for them to overcome, and Los Angeles prevailed. Jackson finished the game with a career-best 238 yards receiving. The Rams remained undefeated at 5–0, while Dallas fell a game behind the Redskins in the standings.

"The game, without a doubt, is the one I remember the most," Jackson said several years later. "It was one of the most satisfying days in my nine seasons in the National Football League." Jackson would end up playing for five different teams in his extraordinary 16-year pro career.

The Cincinnati Bengals were likewise looking to make grand memories for themselves in 1973. A rivalry in the making in the AFC Central Division pitted them against the Pittsburgh Steelers. Both of these teams would offer spirited competition to each other throughout the decade. The Steelers appeared to have a strong edge in the division standings when they traveled to Cincinnati in the fifth week of the season, but the Bengals sent a statement to the rest of the league with a resounding 19–7 win. Head coach Paul Brown's team was so dominating that they permitted Pittsburgh only six first downs and 138 total yards. Cincinnati also unveiled to the league one of their noteworthy draft picks, 12th-round selection Boobie Clark, who from his half-back position dented the "Steel Curtain" with 112 rushing yards and one touchdown. Clark's score came on a power drive from three yards out as he plowed through two attempted tackles and strode into the end zone. The Bengals and the Steelers would meet again later in the season, and would make the race in the AFC Central one of the most competitive of the season.

The race for supremacy of the NFC East would not include the Philadelphia Eagles or the St. Louis Cardinals, but both of those teams would meet in Week 5 and contribute a competitive game with a very entertaining finish. Since their Week One encounter, the Cardinals had earned a 2–2 record, while the Eagles were still winless. Philadelphia's acquisition of quarterback Roman Gabriel from the Rams—in exchange for Harold Jackson—was starting to finally pay off, however. New Eagles head coach Mike McCormack's passing game was the main factor in keeping his team competitive in most games. Gabriel was the focal point of that passing game, and he would go on to lead the league in passing yardage with 3,219 yards. His use of quality receivers Harold Carmichael, Ben Hawkins, and rookie tight end Charlie Young would frustrate many defensive coaches during the season. Both Carmichael and Young would make the Pro Bowl and be named to the All-Pro squad in 1973. Carmichael would catch more balls than anyone else in the NFL (67) for more yards than anyone else in the NFL (1,116). Young caught 55 passes himself for 854 yards to lead all of the league's tight ends in those categories. Gabriel's prime targets got so good that they gave themselves a nickname … the "Fire High Gang."

Yet it was unheralded Eagles wide receiver Don Zimmerman who caught the winning touch-down pass from Gabriel to beat the Cardinals, 27–24, for Philadelphia's first victory. St. Louis had built an 11-point lead in the fourth quarter, but with less than two minutes remaining, Philadelphia had whittled that lead down to four points. The Eagles then recovered an onside kick and quickly drove down the field on Gabriel's arm. Zimmerman grabbed Gabriel's dart on the final play of the game and burrowed into the end zone amidst three Cardinals defenders to set off a delirious Eagles celebration.

"He [Zimmerman] came up with a great catch and tremendous extra effort," said a gleeful Gabriel from the victorious Eagles locker room. Zimmerman's score, however, was also the result of a helpful shove. "They [Cardinal defenders] grabbed my legs and I was trapped on the 2-yard line," Zimmerman described. "Then someone hit me from behind and knocked me in [the end zone]." Thanks to Zimmerman's heroics, the Cardinals had lost a game that they should have won, and would end up struggling for the rest of the season.

The Oakland Raiders were also predicted to defeat the Denver Broncos a week later on an eventful Monday evening in Denver. But the Raiders ran into a team that was tired of being the whipping boys of the AFC West. Denver delivered blow for blow with Oakland throughout the contest, and parlayed several draw plays to put themselves in field goal position with but seconds remaining in the game. Placekicker Jim Turner booted a 35-yard field goal with no time left on the clock to tie the Raiders, 23–23. The tie was a morale booster for the Broncos, for it proved that they could compete with a perennial powerhouse in their division. No coach in the league was more in tune with boosting his team's morale than Denver's John Ralston.

"The big thing is not to allow a positive attitude to become negative," explained Ralston. "It's an ongoing process that begins the moment a team begins preparing for a game until it is over. It is a necessary ingredient in all of our motivational processes."

The motivational levels of the Los Angeles Rams and the Green Bay Packers were moving in opposite directions by the time they both met at the Los Angeles Memorial Coliseum on October

21. The Rams had built an impressive 5–0 record going into their Week 6 encounter with the 2–1–2 Packers, who were mired in a rather unimpressive slump. Green Bay's passing game had been virtually invisible during the early part of the season, and with only their running game to rely upon, the Packers knew that they would face a concerted Rams run-stopping defensive effort. Green Bay's lack of success on offense continued against the Rams, as they managed to gain only 63 total yards. Symbolic of head coach Dan Devine's frustrations came in the fourth quarter when Los Angeles defensive end Fred Dryer stormed into the Green Bay backfield and sacked quarterback Scott Hunter in the end zone for a safety. A few minutes later, Dryer repeated the play with a sack of backup quarterback Jim Del Gaizo in the end zone for another two points and an individual NFL record for safeties in a game. The Rams went on to coast to a 24–7 win.

Green Bay's defense fared no better than their offense. Standout Packers cornerback Willie Buchanon broke his ankle in the game, and that loss would be felt throughout the remainder of the season. It soon became apparent that the Packers would have an uphill struggle in their effort to repeat as NFC Central champions.

The Atlanta Falcons were just beginning to excel as teams like the Packers were faltering. The Falcons put together one of their most impressive showings of the season on October 21 as they ventured into San Diego and shutout the Chargers, 41–0. Virtually everything that Atlanta tried met with success. Their rushing attack was the key to victory, producing 196 yards and five touchdowns. The Falcons evened their record to 3–3 with the win over San Diego, and it was readily evident that they were quickly reaching respectability in the league.

Two teams in the AFC met in a mid-season Monday night game to challenge for respectability and to get back on the winning track. Both the Kansas City Chiefs and the Buffalo Bills had lost their previous game, but both still sported winning records heading into their October 29 contest at Buffalo's Rich Stadium. The rainy evening did not affect the Buffalo rushing attack, as a couple of records dissolved before a national television audience. O.J. Simpson carried the ball an incredible 39 times, at that time a league record. Simpson also reached the 1,000-yard rushing plateau in just seven games, also an NFL record in the 1970s. Simpson's efforts did more than just boost his Bills to a 23–14 triumph over the Chiefs. It also opened the eyes of his teammates as to the future possibilities for making history. Buffalo guard Reggie McKenzie told his fellow lineman Donnie Green, "We could get O.J. 2,000 yards." Upon defeating Kansas City, "we knew that we had a real chance for 2,000," recalled Green.

Opportunities for competitive teams to surge to the top of the standings were manifested during the mid-season part of the schedule. Both the Los Angeles Rams and the Minnesota Vikings represented two teams in the NFC who had real legitimate chances to win their respective divisions. Both would meet each other on October 28 in Minnesota in a battle of 6–0 squads. The Rams were on everyone's radar by this point of the season, as they were dominating in many statistical categories. "How tough are the Rams?" asked Minnesota head coach Bud Grant. "Just look at their record. They've been able to score on everybody they've played, and their defense is sound, too."

The Vikings would emerge from the game as the league's only undefeated team following a tight 10–9 victory over the Rams, but it would not be easy. This was one of the toughest defensive struggles of the season. The Los Angeles rushing attack had been one of the most productive in pro football coming into the game, but they would be without the services of tailback Lawrence McCutcheon, who would sit out the game with an injury. The Purple Gang managed to hold the other Rams runners to an unusually low 89 combined yards on 30 carries. The Vikings defense was also effective in shutting down the Rams passing attack. Los Angeles quarterback John Hadl could throw for only a meager 87 total yards, and was intercepted twice in the game.

"I tried everything," said Hadl, "but they just out-executed us all day. No doubt about it, that's the best defensive team that we've played all year. It was just a battle all day long. We never got the momentum."

Minnesota's offense relied on the game-breaking abilities of their rookie running back Chuck Foreman, whose penchant for making big plays out of the backfield helped to win many big games for his team. On the 12th play of a second quarter drive against the Rams, Foremen snuck around the line of scrimmage on a circle route and caught quarterback Fran Tarkenton's pass at the goal line for the game's only touchdown. The inability to adequately cover Foreman on this one play was the only real mistake by the Rams defense, but it cost them the game.

The Dallas Cowboys made several mistakes at Philadelphia's Veterans Stadium in their Week 7 contest versus the inspired Eagles. Roman Gabriel threw two touchdown passes and ran for another score in Philadelphia's 30–16 upset victory over their division rivals. Dallas had no trouble moving the ball against the Eagles, accumulating 27 first downs and 362 total yards. But they also committed four key turnovers which greatly helped curtail their momentum throughout the game. Making matters worse for the Cowboys was the loss of wide receiver Otto Stowe, who broke his ankle after catching two touchdown passes from Roger Staubach. The loss dropped Dallas to 4–3 in the NFC East, a full game behind division-leading Washington. Philadelphia's win over Dallas boosted their record to 2–4–1. More importantly, a win over a perennial playoff team like Dallas helped Philly to build up some measure of respectability in the league.

The New Orleans Saints were of the same mind-set as the Eagles when the Washington Redskins visited them at Tulane Stadium on October 28. New Orleans also wanted to prove that it could compete with some of the best teams in the NFL. They had failed to accomplish that goal so far this season, but an unexpected 19–3 victory over the Redskins elevated the Saints' record to 3–4, and gave them a needed surge of momentum. The Saints had built an impressive 16–0 lead going into the fourth quarter before the Redskins could manage a field goal. The New Orleans runners gained a vigorous 203 yards against the Over the Hill Gang, and their offense as a whole avoided costly mistakes for one of the few times this season. Many in the Redskins camp felt that their team took New Orleans for granted going into the game. It would be common for some teams to overlook other inferior teams in the 1970s (and indeed even today) if they had a more difficult contest coming up in the following week. The possibility of defeat sometimes awaited those who neglected to focus their attention on those lesser teams.

The Steelers were one team which avoided that trap at all costs. They had division rival Cincinnati visiting them in a rematch on October 28. This time around, Pittsburgh gave the Bengals some of the same medicine that they received in their first encounter in Week 5 (a 19–7 Pittsburgh loss). The Steelers put together a strong effort in the third quarter of the rematch, as they produced 10 key points and gave up zero during that 15-minute span of time. Pittsburgh survived the loss of their starting quarterback Terry Bradshaw, who left the game in the first half with a broken collarbone. Terry Hanratty dutifully filled in for Bradshaw until he himself was injured. Before he left the game, however, Hanratty threw a 51-yard touchdown strike to wide receiver Ron Shanklin. Pittsburgh held on to win, 20–13. The victory gave the Steelers a two-game lead in the AFC Central with a 6–1 record.

Two division rivals in the NFC also saw a statement being made in San Francisco's Candlestick Park. The visiting Atlanta Falcons put together a solid offensive effort in their 17–3 win over the 49ers. Atlanta quarterback Bob Lee threw the ball only 13 times, but he connected on 11 of those tosses for 236 yards and two touchdowns. Wide receiver Ken Burrow scored both Atlanta touchdowns, and running back Dave Hampton contributed 100 rushing yards to the Falcon cause. Burrow's first touchdown came on a 51-yard bomb from Lee. His second score came when he just barely got both of his feet inside the end line of the end zone as he caught Lee's 22-yard pass. The win avenged an earlier defeat to the 49ers, and put the Falcons on firm footing in the NFC West with a 4–3 record at mid-season. Atlanta head coach Norm Van Brocklin was relieved to see his team finally achieve success, and even praised Lee a couple of weeks before the 49ers game by stating, "It looks like we've finally got ourselves a chucker."

A quick look at the standings going into the second half of the season revealed that most of those teams winning on opening day were still in first place in their respective divisions. Minnesota was still the league's only undefeated team, but teams like Miami and Pittsburgh were looking just as strong. Competitive teams like Buffalo and Washington were also making their division races interesting, as was Atlanta and Oakland. Some teams, however, were mired at the opposite end of the standings. The Houston Oilers were winless going into their Week 8 game at Baltimore. The Colts were also experiencing their own run of bad luck, injuries, and youthful mistakes. General manager Joe Thomas trimmed Baltimore's roster by dealing away 21 veterans (including 12 starters) from the previous season. The Colts had won only twice by the mid-season point of 1973, and this unaccustomed record must have been depressing for a team that only a few short years ago was one of the league's best. The Oilers had fired their head coach Bill Peterson just prior to mid-season, and had brought the legendary AFL coach Sid Gillman from his general manager seat down to the sidelines to take over the head coaching duties for the remainder of the season. The Colts were experiencing rebuilding at the hands of rookie head coach Howard Schnellenberger. Both of these teams would produce one of the most exciting games of the season to begin the second half of their schedules.

The contest was a see-saw affair with the Colts trailing 21–17 going into the fourth quarter. Then the Colts got hot and wrested control of the final stanza. Baltimore quarterback Marty Domres had brought his team back into the lead with less than two minutes remaining in the game, 27–24. It was at this point, however, that the Oilers pulled off what would be their best offensive drive of the season. Houston quarterback Lynn Dickey completed five passes on the drive, that last of which came on a screen pass to running back Fred Willis, who followed perfect downfield blocking into the end zone for the game's winning score. Houston's 31–27 triumph over Baltimore would be their only win this season, but it was enough for the team to retain Gillman for another year as head coach. After the game, Gillman was quoted as saying, "There's nothing like winning. It even beats sex."

Both Chuck Knox of the Los Angeles Rams and Norm Van Brocklin of the Atlanta Falcons were a couple of head coaches who were definitely not worried about their employment status going into their Week 8 rematch. Both of these men were encouraging their respective teams to the most success that each had enjoyed in recent years. The Rams shut out the Falcons in the second week of the season, 31–0, and had limited the Falcons to only two meager first downs in that game. Atlanta was much improved since that contest, however, and they would prove it this time around in front of their home crowd at Atlanta Stadium. Van Brocklin's boys did not score a touchdown in their 15–13 victory over the Rams, but they benefitted from the kicking prowess of rookie placekicker Nick Mike-Meyer, who booted five field goals to secure the win. His final three-pointer from the 16-yard line came with just 52 seconds remaining in the game. "So far, that has to be the biggest of my career," Mike-Meyer said of his winning field goal.

Atlanta's record thus improved to 5–3, just one game behind the Rams. A triumph like this did much to ignite the resolve of the Falcon team, whose players now knew that they could complete and win against a really good team. "We think we can catch the Rams now," declared Atlanta quarterback Bob Lee.

The Washington Redskins and the Pittsburgh Steelers were two more really good teams who met each other on a Monday night in Pittsburgh on November 5. The Steelers were suffering from injuries at the quarterback position, but nevertheless had managed to produce a 6–1 record going into their Week 8 tilt with the Redskins. Washington was still licking its wounds from the previous week when they were upset by the Saints. Against the Steelers, the Redskins were definitely not operating on all cylinders. The Pittsburgh Steel Curtain defense may have had something to do with that. Pittsburgh effectively shut down the Washington offense, limiting the Redskins to only 76 passing yards and 190 total yards. Pittsburgh's offense was not much better, however. The Steelers could muster only 102 passing yards, and their quarterbacks threw four interceptions. A key 46-yard completion by third-string Pittsburgh quarterback Joe Gilliam to wide receiver Barry Pearson produced the winning touchdown in a 21–16 Steelers victory. Pearson caught the ball at the 30-yard line and sprinted past several Washington defenders into the end zone on the play. Washington's loss and the subsequent 38–10 victory by the Cowboys over the Cincinnati Bengals on the previous day dropped the Redskins into a first place tie with Dallas in the NFC East.

Another team in the NFC East—the New York Giants—were not expected to give the host Oakland Raiders much of a challenge in their Week 8 contest. The experts who picked Oakland to win this game with no trouble could not have been more right, as the Raiders romped over the Giants, 42–0. Oakland accumulated 28 first downs to New York's 11, and ran for 211 yards while giving up only 57 yards on the ground to the Giants. The score probably would have been even more lopsided had the Raiders not committed four turnovers in the game. The win gave Oakland a temporary lead over Kansas City in the AFC West, while the loss dropped New York to a 1–6–1 record, easily the worst mark in the NFC.

Many so-called experts also predicted the New Orleans Saints to likewise fold up against the Buffalo Bills at Tulane Stadium on the same day that the Giants succumbed to Oakland. But the Saints proved to be a resilient bunch who came into the Buffalo game with a sound strategy to stop O.J. Simpson. The Saints defensive line did yeoman's work in tying up Buffalo's offensive linemen, which allowed the New Orleans linebackers to roam freely and make tackles. Simpson was held to his second-lowest rushing total of the year, gaining only 79 yards on 20 attempts, and Buffalo quarterback Joe Ferguson could muster only 87 passing yards. The New Orleans offense registered 13 points in the first half, then held on to win, 13–0. "They were on us that day," recalled Buffalo offensive tackle Donnie Green. "They were a tough bunch of cats. It was a tough game for me. New Orleans kind of had us outnumbered all day." It was definitely one of the most impressive wins of the season for New Orleans, and it was also a very detrimental and unexpected loss for the Bills. As it turned out by season's end, one more win would have given Buffalo a playoff spot in the AFC.

Buffalo's main rival in the AFC East—the Miami Dolphins—were under no such pressure to win. They were running away with their division, and when they met Baltimore in the Orange Bowl on November 11, they proved how much strength and depth they had on their roster. Miami routed the Colts 44–0. It was a mercy killing. Miami's rushing attack accumulated 315 yards against the porous Baltimore defense. Coach Don Shula began substituting his players at the beginning of the third quarter, but the Miami reserves continued lighting up the scoreboard. After tailback Mercury Morris scored from 48 yards out in the first quarter and 53 yards out in the second quarter, third-string tailback Charlie Leigh rushed for a 34-yard score in the fourth quarter. Miami's win was so impressive that even their special teams chipped in with two touchdowns. Defensive back Tim Foley broke through and blocked two David Lee punts and carried both of them in for Dolphin scores. This humiliating loss would not soon be forgotten by the Colts, however. They would meet the Dolphins again in Week 13.

Buffalo tried to shake off their humbling loss to the Saints the following week by taking on a contender in the AFC, the Cincinnati Bengals. Unfortunately for the Bills, they fought an uphill battle throughout the game, and lost with no time remaining. A 33-yard Horst Muhlmann field goal on the last play of the game defeated the Bills, 16–13. O.J. Simpson was held under 100 yards for the third and final time this season, but it was Buffalo's sub-par passing game which really hurt them against the Bengals. Dennis Shaw filled in for Joe Ferguson at quarterback after Ferguson was injured, and could muster only 50 passing yards on five completions. The Bills would have little time to regroup, however, for their next opponent was none other than their AFC East rivals, the Miami Dolphins.

The Pittsburgh Steelers–Oakland Raiders rivalry was also revving up, especially after their memorable divisional playoff meeting in 1972. Oakland was spoiling for some payback after losing to Pittsburgh in the Immaculate Reception game. In 1973, the two teams met each other in Oakland on November 11, but the hometown Raider fans would leave the Oakland Coliseum in a state of disbelief. The Steelers were thoroughly dominated in most statistical categories, but they still managed to defeat the Raiders, 17–9. A bevy of penalties and four interceptions did the Raiders in. Pittsburgh defensive end Dwight White intercepted two passes, but it was another Pittsburgh defensive lineman who, wittingly or unwittingly, added more fuel to the fire between the two teams. Tom Keating had played for the Raiders for six years before he was traded to the Steelers in 1973. Keating was an obvious target for reporters after the game, and he did not let them down. He embellished a story that the Raiders had written obscenities on the ball for the officials to see. He then confirmed that the Raiders would put grease on their shoulder pads to make it easier for their runners to slip tackles. Finally, after continuous pressure from a flock of football beat writers, he gave in and corroborated the false belief that the Raiders would deflate the balls prior to a game to harm the effectiveness of opposing placekickers. None of these things actually happened, but it made for interesting conversation in a rivalry which was reaching epic proportions.

"I couldn't imagine these guys [the reporters] were buying all of this," Keating recalled five years later. "But they did. All of it showed up the next day in the papers. Everyone got upset, especially the Raiders, and it nearly reached the point where charges were going to be made to the commissioner's office."

Pittsburgh's victory over Oakland gave them a commanding 8–1 record in the AFC Central, while the Raiders fell to 5–3–1 and a first-place tie with Kansas City in the AFC West. Things would not get any better for Oakland the following week, when Cleveland ventured into the Oakland Coliseum and left with a 7–3 win over the Raiders. Cleveland quarterback Mike Phipps connected with wide receiver Fair Hooker on a fade pattern in the end zone for the game's only touchdown. Hooker beat veteran Oakland cornerback Willie Brown on the scoring play. This was undeniably one of Oakland's worst games of the year. The league's number one offense was effectively plugged by Cleveland's staunch defense. Were it not for three Cleveland turnovers, the score would probably have been lopsided. But the Raiders would regroup from this loss, and they would not lose again for the rest of the regular season.

The Steelers, on the other hand, were just about to begin a string of games which would test their ability to stay on top of the AFC Central. The up-and-coming Denver Broncos visited Three Rivers Stadium on November 18 and delivered a stunning 23–13 upset of the Steelers. Pittsburgh's recent proclivity towards not taking full advantage of their opportunities finally caught up with them against Denver. The halftime score stood even at 6–6, but the Steelers would waste several prime opportunities to put more points on the board in the second half. Denver—in contrast—put together a solid final two quarters when halfback Floyd Little contributed some nifty runs, and quarterback Charley Johnson hit on some key passes. Little ran through the Steel Curtain defense on a draw play for a 10-yard touchdown, and Johnson hit tight end Riley Odoms on a 2-yard scoring toss to add to Denver's lead. Pittsburgh still had a chance to pull the game out, however, when quarterback Terry Hanratty threw a fourth quarter bullet to wide receiver Ron Shanklin from 42 yards out. Shanklin roamed just beyond the Denver deep zone coverage, caught Hanratty's perfect pass over the middle, then sprinted through the Broncos defensive backs to reach the corner of the end zone. Denver's defense stiffened up from there, though, and Pittsburgh suffered their first loss in a month. This was one of Denver's most inspirational wins of the season, and it lifted their record to a respectable 5–3–2 in the AFC West.

"This is the biggest moment of my pro career," said Little, who led all rushers in the game with 88 yards. "We've always been out of the race at this point, but this year is different. It's a great feeling."

Pittsburgh, however, would be denied any great moments when they traveled to Cleveland the following week and played in one of the toughest games of the season. This was another typical Steelers-Browns struggle at Cleveland's Municipal Stadium, where the outcome would be in doubt until the game's final seconds. The Browns on paper were inferior to the Steelers, but they had several things going for them in this contest. First, Pittsburgh's quarterback situation was shaky at best. Terry Bradshaw would not play due to an injury, and second-string quarterback Terry Hanratty managed to throw only one pass before he was knocked out of the game. That left untested second-year man Joe Gilliam under center. Cleveland's defensive line of Walter Johnson, Jerry Sherk, Nick Roman and Joe "Turkey" Jones would be licking their chops at the thought of sacking a raw youngster. Secondly, the Browns had some younger players who were starting to really play well. Chief among them was rookie tailback Greg Pruitt of Oklahoma, who ended his first season by rushing for a 6.0 yards-per-carry average. Pruitt would go on to play a pivotal role in this game. Finally, this was a must-win contest for Cleveland. A win and they would pull to within a half game of Pittsburgh in the AFC Central standings; a loss and they would for all intents and purposes lose out on any chance for a wild card spot.

Both teams scored a touchdown in the first quarter. Pittsburgh scored on a 9-yard pass from Gilliam to wide receiver Ron Shanklin. Cleveland answered on a 1-yard quarterback sneak by Mike Phipps. A few minutes later in the second quarter, Phipps hit Pruitt on a down-and-in pattern from the Pittsburgh 15-yard line. Steelers outside linebacker Andy Russell could not match Pruitt's speed, as the rookie runner sprinted past him into the end zone after catching the pass. Pittsburgh answered with three Roy Gerela field goals, however, to take a 16–14 lead late in the fourth quarter.

Phipps would go on to engineer one more vital scoring drive for Cleveland. On a key third down play with just over 2:00 remaining, Phipps escaped a fierce rush from Steelers defensive linemen Tom Keating, Dwight White, Joe Greene, and L.C. Greenwood. He then dodged blitzing Steelers defensive back Glen Edwards and threw long for Pruitt, who caught the ball at the Pittsburgh 35-yard line. Pruitt broke three tackles before he was corralled at the 19-yard line.

"I was not the primary receiver on the play," said Pruitt. "I was the decoy. When Mike [Phipps] got into trouble, I knew he would come to me, so I stayed where I was and he found me in the clear."

A few plays later, Pruitt ran a sweep left behind guard Gene Hickerson and reached the corner of the end zone with the winning touchdown. The Browns had successfully stayed alive in the AFC Central by beating the Steelers, 21–16. As the final gun sounded, the Cleveland fans stormed the field once again (as was their custom after a big victory). Pruitt might have evaded the Steelers defenders on this day, but he had more than his share of difficulty dodging the Cleveland faithful. "They were all around me," Pruitt said of the mob. "They had me everywhere. I thought I was going to the Cleveland dugout, but when I realized where I was, it was the Pittsburgh dugout. They tried to take my helmet, my uniform, and everything."

The Buffalo Bills were also trying to keep their wits about them in the AFC East, but they had a tough opponent standing in their way on November 18. The Bills had lost to the Miami Dolphins earlier in the season, and were eager to make amends for that defeat when Miami visited them in Rich Stadium. Buffalo finally got its running attack in gear against Miami on this day, rushing for an impressive 238 yards. Both O.J. Simpson and Jim Braxton rushed for over 100 yards apiece. Unfortunately for the Bills, the No-Name Defense kept quarterback Joe Ferguson in check all day, limiting him to 98 passing yards. True to their practice of bending but not breaking, the Dolphins defense allowed plenty of yardage, but protected their goal line with unmatched ferocity as they shut out the Bills, 17–0. Conversely, Miami's business-like offense did all of its scoring in the first half on a Larry Csonka 1-yard touchdown run, a 39-yard Garo Yepremian field goal, and a 17-yard pass from Bob Griese to Paul Warfield.

"I'm not elated over the win," confided Dolphins tailback Mercury Morris. "That's what we came here for." Miami wide receiver Paul Warfield added "There's not a lot of excitement. It was something we expected to do."

Miami's victory over Buffalo lifted their record to 9–1, good enough to clinch the AFC East title with four games still remaining on their schedule. Buffalo, on the other hand, had just lost their third straight game, and would need a strong finish in order to return to some form of competition for the playoffs.

At the same time that the Dolphins were winning their division, the Dallas Cowboys were keeping pace with their hated rivals, the Washington Redskins, in the NFC East. The Cowboys hosted Philadelphia on November 18 and gained a measure of revenge against the Eagles from their previous meeting. Dallas spotted Roman Gabriel and Philadelphia 10 points, then scored 31 of their own for a 31–10 win. Roger Staubach threw two touchdown passes, one to setback Walt Garrison, and one to wide receiver Bob Hayes to pace the Dallas offense. Garrison scored another touchdown on a 1-yard plunge, and placekicker Toni Fritsch added a 23-yard field goal to complete the Dallas scoring. The Cowboys and the Redskins entered the final four games with identical 7–3 records after Washington upended Baltimore, 22–14, on the same day that the Cowboys beat the Eagles. An exciting finish for both Dallas and Washington would be highly anticipated.

One team that did not have any late-season competition in their division was the Minnesota Vikings. They had won nine straight games before entering their Monday night contest at Atlanta to face the 6–3 Falcons. Atlanta head coach Norm Van Brocklin used to coach Minnesota quarterback Fran Tarkenton in the 1960s when both were members of the Vikings. Both left the team, but Tarkenton came back in 1972. On this night they would compete against each other, and Van Brocklin would find out just how good his team was. Former Viking Bob Lee was Van Brocklin's starting quarterback on this night, and he delivered a pretty good impersonation of Tarkenton in escaping the stalwart pass rush of the Purple Gang. Lee would throw for two touchdowns, both coming in the second quarter. On his first scoring toss, Lee hit halfback Dave Hampton coming out of the backfield on a 19-yard swing pass. On his second, Lee broke an attempted horse-collar tackle by Minnesota defensive end Carl Eller, ran towards the sidelines and evaded Vikings linemen Gary Larsen and Alan Page, then flung a deep pass to running back Eddie Ray, who had drifted unnoticed out of the backfield. Ray caught Lee's 39-yard pass at the goal line behind Vikings safety Paul Krause for a 17–7 Atlanta lead. "I saw he [Ray] was open but I didn't want to motion to him and attract attention," Lee said.

Minnesota would pull closer, but despite Tarkenton's 214 passing yards, the Falcons prevailed,

20–14. The loss did not affect the Vikings too much. They had already clinched their division title the previous week. The victory was a really important win for the Falcons, however. It allowed them to remain a game behind the division-leading Rams. It also sent a further message to the rest of the league that the Falcons were a legitimate contender who could upset anyone on any given day (or night). That's all any team could hope for as the final games toward the postseason arrived.

Following their win over Philadelphia, the Dallas Cowboys played in their annual Thanksgiving Day game and sustained a tough blow to their playoff hopes. The Miami Dolphins came into Texas Stadium and edged the Cowboys in a tight contest, 14–7. This was a defensive struggle from start to finish. The Dolphins began the game like they began most games … by taking an early lead. Fullback Larry Csonka scored on a 1-yard touchdown run, then flanker Paul Warfield caught a perfect pass from quarterback Bob Griese for a 45-yard score. The No-Name Defense then took over and thwarted the Dallas offense until late in the game. Dallas running back Walt Garrison scored the lone Cowboy touchdown on a 1-yard run in the fourth quarter.

The early game on Thanksgiving featured none other than the Washington Redskins, who traveled to Detroit's Tiger Stadium and shut out the Lions, 20–0. Before fans could complete their post-dinner pumpkin pie, the Redskins were once again on top of the NFC East by one game over Dallas. "We were a little more determined," said Washington head coach George Allen after his team's easy win. "We blocked better, ran harder, rushed better. We had to win."

The Denver Broncos had a similar opportunity later that weekend when they hosted the Kansas City Chiefs at Mile High Stadium. A Denver win would give the Broncos their first lead ever in the AFC West this late in the season. The Broncos scored two touchdowns in the second quarter on two Charley Johnson touchdown passes, both going to wide receiver Haven Moses. The first one went for 18 yards, and the second one went for 40 yards. The Broncos then held on for dear life. Kansas City gained the edge in first downs (17–12), but not in points. Denver's defense forced Kansas City tight end Gary Butler to fumble a key pass reception late in the game, thereby clinching a 14–10 upset victory over the Chiefs. An improbable dream of winning a division title for the very first time was now in sight for the Denver Broncos. "Our players have believed all along," said Denver head coach John Ralston, "and here we are, right in the thick of the battle."

The 12th week of the season brought on some key games which unfortunately helped to muddle the playoff picture in both conferences. The Buffalo Bills traveled to Atlanta after a key 24–17 win over Baltimore the previous week. Buffalo managed to produce a 17–6 win over the surging Falcons. Head coach Lou Saban's team once again ran the ball to harvest the key to victory. The Falcons defense could not slow down Buffalo's runners, as O.J. Simpson delivered another stellar effort with 137 yards gained, and fullback Jim Braxton contributed 80 more and busted through from short distances for both of Buffalo's touchdowns. The win gave the Bills a 7–5 record, which was still not good enough to secure a wild card spot. Nevertheless, if Buffalo would win their final two games and if a couple of teams in the AFC Central (either Pittsburgh, Cleveland or Cincinnati) faltered, the Bills just might make the playoffs. Atlanta's loss dropped them to 8–4. All they needed to do to make the playoffs was to win their final two games and hope that one team in the NFC East (either Washington or Dallas) lost at least one of their final two games.

The Los Angeles Rams had done so well in 1973 that by Week 12, all they needed to do was win one more game, and they would be crowned champions of the NFC Western Division. The Rams faced the 3-8 Chicago Bears at Soldier Field and proceeded to systematically dismantle their hosts, 26–0. The Rams continued to use their rushing game to perfection, accumulating 296 ground yards against the Bears. Pacing the Rams was halfback Lawrence McCutcheon, who failed to score a touchdown but who registered 152 yards on 24 carries. "It's the best game I've had in yards but I'm always disappointed when I don't score," said a chuckling McCutcheon after the game.

By season's end, the Rams would be ranked first in the entire league in offense, producing a league-high 294 first downs. The Los Angeles defense was also earning league-wide recognition, finishing as the NFL's top-ranked defense and allowing the Bears to gain only 100 total yards. The Rams had won their division in Chuck Knox's first year as head coach. He promised to make the team winners in his first year, and he kept that promise. "The execution was great," said Rams quarterback John Hadl. "The championship is a tribute to Chuck Knox and the coaching staff. They've done a tremendous job."

The Minnesota Vikings had shown plenty of promise throughout the season, being the first team in the league to clinch a playoff spot. The Vikings had claimed their division title before Thanksgiving, but on Week 12, they faced a competitive AFC team who was involved in a tight divisional battle. The Cincinnati Bengals entered their game with Minnesota as a third-place team in the AFC Central, but not by much. Cincinnati stood only one game behind division leader Pittsburgh and only a half game behind second place Cleveland. Head coach Paul Brown's squad knew that to keep pace with those clubs, his Bengals had to thwart the strong Minnesota offense. This his team did, to great efficiency. The Bengals destroyed the visiting Vikings at Riverfront Stadium, 27–0, in a game that showcased just how strong Cincinnati had become. The Bengals ran for 227 yards against the Purple People Eaters, and the Cincinnati defense shut down Minnesota's running backs, allowing them only 81 total ground yards on 26 carries. The Minnesota loss was shocking, but Vikings head coach Bud Grant was his old emotionless, analytical self in the postgame locker room.

"Our mistakes made us look bad," said Grant, "but even if we didn't make any mistakes Cincinnati was the better team on this day. You have to gain some benefits from something like this. A team can see what can happen if you are not ready every time." Grant's team would not lose again until Super Bowl VIII.

The Washington Redskins had not lost to the New York Giants since 1970, and had easily defeated them 21–3 in their first meeting in the fifth week of 1973. Their second meeting in Week 12 would be more competitive. New York struck early against the Redskins and built a 21–3 lead in the second quarter. But head coach George Allen's Redskins would hang tough and chip away at New York's lead. Washington quarterback Sonny Jurgensen replaced starter Billy Kilmer in the second half after Kilmer sustained an ankle injury. Jurgensen proceeded to connect on 11 straight passes on two long scoring drives. But the major catalyst for the Redskins comeback was none other than halfback Larry Brown, who contributed two rushing touchdowns and one receiving touchdown. It was Brown's 16-yard catch and run from Jurgensen with 3:45 remaining in the fourth quarter that lifted Washington to a 27–24 victory. Brown completed the winning score by bowling over Giants defensive back Spider Lockhart at the goal line. The Redskins had thus improved to 9–3 and kept their one-game lead in the NFC East standings over the hated Dallas Cowboys, with but two games remaining in the regular season.

The final game of Week 12 was a Monday night spectacular. Two of the best teams in the AFC tangled at the Orange Bowl in a contest which was really two separate games, and which produced one incredible individual performance. The Pittsburgh Steelers went into their game against Miami with banged-up quarterbacks and a two-game losing streak. The Steelers would start "Jefferson Street" Joe Gilliam at quarterback. Jefferson Street was a nickname that ABC commentator Howard Cosell used for Gilliam, but the origin of the moniker came from Gilliam's college teammates. Another Pittsburgh quarterback—Terry Bradshaw—was recovering from his earlier collarbone injury, but would be available should Pittsburgh head coach Chuck Noll need him. Unfortunately for Noll and the Steelers, the need for Bradshaw came quickly.

Miami safety Dick Anderson had perhaps the greatest first half of a game that any defensive back has ever had in league history. Anderson dove and intercepted Gilliam's second pass of the night and returned it for a 27-yard touchdown. "Once I had it there were just white stripes and green AstroTurf to the end zone and we were on the scoreboard," Anderson recalled.

Anderson would go on to intercept three more passes in the first half. He totaled 121 yards in interception returns for one game, and helped to boost the Dolphins to a 30–3 halftime cushion. His efforts also helped to reacquaint Joe Gilliam with the Pittsburgh bench in the second quarter. To be fair to Gilliam, the quarterback who replaced him (Bradshaw) also threw three interceptions in the game, and one of those was also returned by the ever-present Anderson for a score.

But Bradshaw and his team came back strong in the second half. The Pittsburgh defense got mad at their embarrassing first half deficit, and made amends for it in the second half by shutting out the Dolphins. Franco Harris led the Pittsburgh rushing attack with 105 yards and contributed a touchdown in the fourth quarter. Bradshaw hit setback Preston Pearson for a 5-yard touchdown in the third quarter and wide receiver Barry Pearson for a 17-yard score in the fourth quarter. Fortunately for the Dolphins, they had built enough of a lead to take an intentional safety late in the game to preserve their 30–26 victory. Even though their third straight loss hurt, the strong second half exhibited by Noll's team at Miami would be a harbinger for them for the remainder of the regular season. They would go on to destroy both the Houston Oilers (33–7) and the San Francisco 49ers (37–14) in the final two weeks to claim the AFC's wild card spot.

Those final two weeks of the 1973 regular season featured a struggle for survival. No less than eight teams were still fighting for one of the five available playoff spots during those weeks. The Dolphins, Vikings and Rams had already clinched their berths, but for teams like the Cowboys, Redskins, Bills, Steelers, Bengals, Raiders, Broncos, and Falcons, a loss in either of their last two games could be devastating to their playoff hopes.

The first big game in Week 13 featured the Redskins traveling to Dallas to take on the Cowboys in a rematch for what could decide the NFC East division. The Redskins had a 9–3 record coming into the game, and if they defeated Dallas in this game, the division title would be theirs. Dallas had an 8–4 record prior to the game, but they weren't focused on records too much when they lined up against their hated rivals. Dallas pounded Washington in every phase of the game, building up a 27–0 lead in the fourth quarter before the Redskins scored their lone touchdown on a blocked punt. The Dallas running game was the key to their 27–7 victory, as it produced 193 rushing yards and three touchdowns. The Doomsday Defense also did yeoman work, limiting Larry Brown and Company to just 59 rushing yards.

"They [Dallas] played a super game," said Washington head coach George Allen. "They played well offensively, defensively, and on their specialty teams. I thought they were outstanding." The Cowboys and Redskins now each held a 9–4 record going into the last game of the season.

Another big game in Week 13 took place in snowy Buffalo, where the Bills and Patriots faced each other for the second and final time this season. The field conditions were not helpful to most offenses, but you would not know that by observing how well the Bills moved the ball against the Patriots. Many of the Bills players regarded the snowfall and the slippery field as friendly alliances. "When it was bad weather," recalled Buffalo offensive tackle Donnie Green, "we were like kids in a candy store. The defenses that we played couldn't hardly do anything in the snow."

Buffalo's impressive 37–13 win kept their slim playoff hopes alive. It included a 90-yard kick-off return for a touchdown by Wallace Francis, and two scoring tosses from Joe Ferguson to wide receiver Bob Chandler. Buffalo's standout superstar runner also excelled on the snow-covered field. O.J. Simpson's dream of breaking Jim Brown's record of rushing yardage in a season came closer to reality when the Juice ran for 219 yards against the Patriots. Simpson thus needed only 61 yards in his final game to break Brown's record, an achievement that many before the season thought impossible. Even more incredible was the fact that Simpson was now within potential range of a 2,000-yard season, something that had never happened before in NFL history.

The Oakland Raiders defense did not experience the same difficulties that the New England defense had to contend with. The field was surprisingly dry and fast at the Oakland Coliseum as the Raiders squashed visiting Kansas City, 37–7, thus eliminating the Chiefs from playoff contention. Oakland's brutal defense allowed Kansas City only 24 rushing yards, and forced four crushing turnovers, each of which led to Raider points. The Denver Broncos kept pace with first place Oakland by outscoring San Diego, 42–28. Thus the Broncos would travel to Oakland in the season's final week to take on the Raiders in a game that would decide the champion of the AFC West.

Another rivalry in the AFC Central played out in Week 13 when the Cleveland Browns went into Cincinnati and got punched in the mouth. Cleveland's chances of making the playoffs were slim going into the game. The Bengals, in contrast, had won their previous four straight games, and were licking their chops at a chance to pay back the Browns for their earlier 17–10 loss to them in the fourth week of the season. Cincinnati benefitted from the exemplary performance of rookie wide receiver Isaac Curtis, who caught five passes for 117 yards and three touchdowns in the 34–17 Bengal victory.

Speaking of standout performances, St. Louis placekicker Jim Bakken accounted for six field goals in a 32–10 upset victory over host Atlanta. The loss did major damage to Atlanta's playoff hopes. The Falcons would now have to win their final game against New Orleans, and then hope that either Dallas or Washington would lose their final game in order for Norm Van Brocklin's team from Dixie to secure a spot in the postseason.

Hope was all that the Baltimore Colts would have going into their Week 13 game against the defending world champion Dolphins. The Colts were finishing out their worst season in 19 years, having only two wins to show for all of their injuries, hard work and misery. Baltimore was in the midst of getting their younger players some much-needed experience during this forlorn season, but they still had a few good veterans in uniform who refused to quit. They were not spoilers going into their game with Miami, but they were eager for redemption. The Dolphins had embarrassed the Colts 44–0 in their earlier contest in November, and payback was in order. True, the Dolphins were sitting out some key players due to nagging injuries, but the Colts refused to consider excuses on this day. Baltimore prevailed over Miami in Memorial Stadium, 16–3. Lydell Mitchell rushed for 104 yards against the No-Name Defense on 35 bone-jarring carries. The Dolphins out-gained the Colts, but three Miami turnovers secured the satisfying win for Baltimore.

"Whenever you beat a great team like the Dolphins, a lot of things have to go right for you," said Baltimore head coach Howard Schnellenberger. "They did for us today. This is the result of a team which committed to work hard despite all that has happened. It is a team which continued to believe in itself."

The always loyal Colts fans stormed the field after the sparkling win, just as many of them had done during the team's glory years of the 1950s and 1960s. The hero that they carried off the field on this day was defensive end Roy Hilton, who successfully pressured former Baltimore teammate and current reserve Miami quarterback Earl Morrall throughout the contest. It was easily Baltimore's sweetest win of the season, and it proved that even the greatest of teams could lose on any given Sunday.

Avoiding a loss in the final week of 1973 was the goal for several teams as the push for the playoffs finally reached its end. The winner of the Denver-Oakland rematch would be headed to the playoffs. The Broncos had never gotten this far before in their history, but despite all of their efforts, the Raiders were the better team at the wire and defeated Denver, 21–17. Oakland grabbed an early lead in the game, then held off a desperate second half surge by the Broncos to claim the win. The 9–4–1 Raiders thus were named AFC West Champions for the second straight year. The Broncos could take solace in their 7–5–2 record, however, which served as their first winning season ever. Denver led the AFC in passing yardage in 1973, and head coach John Ralston was named AFC Coach of the Year for his outstanding efforts.

"I told the team I was proud of them for what they'd accomplished over the entire season," said Ralston after the loss to Oakland. "They did all that we asked of them and more. We did a lot of good things this year, but it was just a beginning. We'll be back."

The Houston Oilers were in line to obtain the top draft choice when they hosted the Cincinnati Bengals on the final Sunday. But the Oilers delivered a dedicated performance as they almost lost the rights to that draft choice by producing a shocking near-upset. Cincinnati—like Oakland—built a big enough lead to barely hold off their foes, 27–24. Once again it was wide receiver Isaac Curtis who spearheaded the Bengals toward the AFC Central title. Curtis caught only two passes against Houston, but both went for spectacular touchdowns. The first Curtis score came in the second quarter from 77 yards out. Curtis caught quarterback Ken Anderson's bomb in stride and pranced untouched to the end zone. On the second Curtis touchdown, no less than five Oilers defenders had a shot at tackling the lanky receiver, but all failed as Curtis strode along the sideline to complete a 67-yard score. Now only two playoff spots remained in the NFL.

Both of the spots were claimed by teams in the NFC East. The Dallas Cowboys routed the host St. Louis Cardinals in frigid Busch Stadium, 30–3, and the Washington Redskins defeated the Philadelphia Eagles in snowy and muddy RFK Stadium, 38–20. The Cowboys won the division title based upon their superior point differential against Washington in head-to-head games. The Redskins would have to settle for the wild card position. "The defense has really played well," said Dallas head coach Tom Landry of his Doomsday defenders. "We have a blend of a lot of guys from our Super Bowl team [1971] and a lot of young guys doing a good job."

The Buffalo Bills almost claimed a wild card spot by finishing the 1973 season with a record of 9–5. The Bills defeated the New York Jets on the season's final Sunday, 34–14, in snowy and windy Shea Stadium. One more win would have landed Buffalo in the postseason for the first time since 1966. But despite their disappointment at missing the playoffs, the Bills still had something vital to play for. Superstar tailback O.J. Simpson was having a season to savor, and he was expected to break the great Jim Brown's single-season rushing record of 1,863 yards, set in 1963. Simpson broke Brown's record in the first quarter on an off-tackle run, then received the first of several standing ovations on the day as he delivered the game ball to the sidelines amidst the hugs and congratulations of his teammates. He then spent the rest of the game running for a mark of further greatness. Simpson trudged through the snow in carry after carry (34 in all) behind his stalwart and inspired offensive line, and darted and dashed through the Jets and the snow to eclipse the 2,000-yard mark, a plateau that no one associated with the game ever thought possible.

"Those guys up front [the Buffalo offensive line] wanted that record for themselves as much as I did," recalled Simpson. "They wanted to be the line that ground out the most yards rushing in a season. In the huddle they kept nudging me, saying, 'Let's go, Juice. Let's go, Juice. Let's get it. Let's get it.' On this day, they were as super as they ever were."

A somewhat ignored factor which helped Simpson greatly on this day was the standout play of the Buffalo defense. They stunted the New York offense, forcing numerous three-and-outs and seven punts. This kept the Bills on offense, thus keeping the Juice on the field. Buffalo's defense limited New York to a meager 39 rushing yards, a big factor in keeping the Jets in punting formation. Simpson kept breaking out of the I-formation during the second half and kept accumulating yardage towards the ultimate league rushing record.

Simpson made NFL history when he eclipsed the 2,000-yard mark with just under six minutes remaining in the game. Taking a pitchout and sweeping left, Simpson cut behind a kick-out block by fullback Jim Braxton, and followed his guard and good friend Reggie McKenzie into history on a 7-yard run. O.J. had completed his odyssey … 2,003 yards in one season. Simpson's effort of 200 yards against the Jets (his third 200-yard game of the season) also gave Buffalo a team rushing record for one season, as the Bills runners recorded 3,088 ground yards in 1973. Simpson's joyful teammates carried their larger-than-life star runner off the field in triumph, and Simpson returned the gesture in the postgame locker room, when he invited his entire offensive unit into the press area for media interviews. "Think of how we feel," said McKenzie after the game. "He takes us to a press conference that's for him. I feel ten feet tall."

Buffalo's win over the Jets will not be remembered as a great game. The Bills did not make the playoffs despite their efforts, and the Jets finished the year with a lackluster 4–10 mark. The game will, however, be remembered for the historic memories that were made on this day. O.J.

O.J. Simpson of the Buffalo Bills runs through the New York Jets defense at Shea Stadium on the final game of the 1973 regular season. Simpson ran for 200 yards in this game, and thus became the first man in NFL history to rush for more than 2,000 yards in one season (AP Photo).

Simpson earned heroic honors and Player of the Year awards from virtually every sports publication in the country for achieving a remarkable rushing record. Also on this day, Jets head coach Weeb Ewbank retired from pro coaching. Ewbank himself was a record holder, being the only head coach in pro football history to win championships in two leagues (in the NFL in 1958 and 1959 with the Baltimore Colts, and in the AFL with in 1968 with the Jets). Those fans who sat through the cold and blustery snow at Shea Stadium were thus witnesses to history. Ewbank would—like Simpson—be mobbed by a throng of reflective admirers as he left the field. Simpson's greatest moment in his greatest season is still thought of fondly by many of his teammates to this day.

"I could have played three or four more games that same day," remembered Buffalo offensive tackle Donnie Green. "We were really hyped up for that day. That's how inspired I felt. Just being on that team. That's an awesome feeling of accomplishment." Buffalo offensive guard Reggie McKenzie recalled, "The attitude of the offensive line was that we weren't going to be denied. There was no doubt in my mind that we'd do it [help Simpson break the 2,000-yard rushing barrier]. With the combination of our blocking and O.J.'s running, we couldn't miss."

The Miami Dolphins were on a quest to achieve a great team accomplishment also when they began the opening round of the playoffs. The Dolphins were trying to become only the second team in history to win back-to-back Super Bowls (the Green Bay Packers were the first team to accomplish the feat in 1966 and 1967). Miami would face the newly-crowned AFC Central Champion Cincinnati Bengals at the Orange Bowl in the first round of the 1973 playoffs. The Dolphins would rely on their time-honored strategy of ball control, solid defense, limited or no mistakes ... and for the heck of it, more ball control. Cincinnati's defense was fed a steady diet of Miami running plays, and both Larry Csonka and Mercury Morris crammed the ball down the Bengals' throats. Miami accumulated 241 rushing yards on 52 carries in the process of building a 21–3 lead midway through the second quarter.

But the Bengals stormed back late in the first half with a startling interception by cornerback Neil Craig, who stepped in front of an ill-advised sideline throw by Miami quarterback Bob Griese. Craig raced down the sideline untouched for a 45-yard score. Cincinnati then converted a six-play drive with a 46-yard field goal by placekicker Horst Muhlmann. On the ensuing kickoff, Miami returner Mercury Morris had trouble fielding the ball, which skipped and bounced along the Poly-Turf. Cincinnati's Jim LeClair emerged from the pile of Dolphins and Bengals with the slick pigskin, and Muhlmann added to Cincinnati's point total with another field goal on the final play of the first half.

Miami's once-comfortable lead had shrunk to 21–16. Dolphins head coach Don Shula would not permit his team to slack off any further, however. The No-Name Defense struck quickly in the third quarter when safety Dick Anderson intercepted a Ken Anderson pass and returned the ball to the Cincinnati 28-yard line. Griese hit tight end Jim Mandich with a 7-yard touchdown a few plays later, and the Dolphins never looked back. Two field goals by Miami placekicker Garo Yepremian increased the Dolphins lead, and the Miami defense limited Cincinnati's offense to only four first downs in the second half. Miami prevailed, 34–16.

"We went out in the second half with the idea the score was nothing-to-nothing and we had to win again," said a relieved Shula after the game. "Dick Anderson's interception and the fact we capitalized on it opened things up again."

Two other AFC teams continued their bitter rivalry in the first round of the playoffs. The Oakland Raiders were still smarting from their defeat at the hands of the Pittsburgh Steelers in the Immaculate Reception playoff game from the previous year. This year, the Raiders would face an injured Steelers team in the Oakland Coliseum. Pittsburgh had defeated Oakland in the same stadium in Week 9, 17–9. This time around, the Raiders were ready to redeem themselves in front of their home crowd. Oakland's offense performed with peak efficiency. Quarterback Ken Stabler was nearly flawless, hitting on 14 of 17 passes. The Raiders' rushing attack contributed 232 yards to the cause. Marv Hubbard ran for 91 yards and two touchdowns, and halfback Charlie Smith added 73 more. Pittsburgh's offense enjoyed far less success. Steeler runners could manage a total of only 65 yards, and quarterback Terry Bradshaw threw three costly interceptions.

The game, however, was tight until the second half, when the Raiders began to assert themselves. Oakland held a 16–7 lead late in the third quarter when Oakland cornerback Willie Brown broke in front of a Bradshaw pass intended for Barry Pearson, tipped the ball, then grasped it and sprinted 54 yards down the sideline for a touchdown. This key turnover allowed Oakland to play the ball control game for the remainder of the contest. It also forced the Steelers to abandon their running game and focus on throwing the ball downfield, which soon produced another interception. From there, Raider runners burrowed their way to another touchdown and a field goal. Oakland got its revenge, 33–14.

"It was a great team victory," said victorious Oakland head coach John Madden afterwards. "We just went out and played our best. I felt that we moved the ball well and that was the big thing." Pittsburgh head coach Chuck Noll contrasted Madden's point of view after the game. "They beat the hell out of us," lamented Noll. "It's as simple as that. Their line blew us out. And their backs ran through tackles. Not very much about the game was worth a damn as far as we're concerned. There are no high points for us."

The Dallas Cowboys were looking for another high point after seizing the NFC East from the clutches of the Washington Redskins. The Cowboys would get a chance to play the Los Angeles Rams once again. Their previous meeting earlier in the season in Los Angeles saw Dallas lose, 37–31. The Cowboys would be ready this time in Texas Stadium to exact some revenge on the Rams. The top priority for Dallas head coach Tom Landry was to find a way to keep Los Angeles wide receiver Harold Jackson from duplicating his Week 5 performance against the Cowboys. Jackson torched the Dallas secondary for four touchdowns in that game, and even though the Cowboys tried to make adjustments and give beleaguered cornerback Charlie Waters some help, Jackson was consistently getting open. The playoff rematch would exhibit different results.

The plan this time for the Dallas secondary was to mix their zone coverages with man to man coverages on virtually every play. Such a strategy was helpful, but it was only a part of what aided the Cowboys. An extremely strong and aggressive pass rush also forced Los Angeles quarterback John Hadl to get rid of the ball quicker than he had to in the previous game with Dallas. This meant that Jackson would not have the time to run deep routes, which helped out Waters greatly.

"We had a little different game plan," said Dallas safety Cliff Harris afterwards, "but definitely the difference [between the playoff game and the first game versus the Rams] was the mental attitude. We had a super rush. The cornerbacks did a great job. I didn't like what happened the last game and I felt like I had something to make up for."

Dallas bolted to a quick 14–0 lead in the first quarter thanks to two Rams turnovers in Los Angeles territory. The first turnover occurred when Hadl rolled right on the first play from scrimmage and threw an interception to Dallas middle linebacker Lee Roy Jordan, who had read Hadl's intentions all the way. Cowboys running back Calvin Hill converted Jordan's theft with a 3-yard touchdown run up the middle. A few minutes later, Dallas defensive back Mel Renfro recovered a fumble by Los Angeles runner Lawrence McCutcheon. The succeeding nine-play drive ended with another touchdown when Dallas quarterback Roger Staubach hit rookie wide receiver Drew Pearson on a quick out pattern for a 4-yard score before the first quarter was halfway through. A

39-yard field goal by placekicker Toni Fritsch boosted the Dallas lead to 17–0 early in the second quarter.

The Los Angeles defense gave up only 178 points during the regular season, the second-best mark in the conference. They relied on that defense to get back in the game. The Cowboys would earn only one first down in the span of the next two quarters, and would not score again until ten minutes remained in the fourth quarter. While the Rams defense were busy putting a halt to the Dallas surge, the Rams offense crept back to within one point at 17–16. Los Angeles placekicker David Ray connected on three field goals, and running back Tony Baker added a 5-yard touchdown run early in the fourth quarter. The Rams were prepared to take the lead when the Cowboys succeeded on one of the greatest deep passing plays of the decade.

Dallas was faced with a third-and-14 situation from their own 17-yard line. Staubach dropped back and threw long down the middle for Pearson, who was double covered by Rams cornerback Eddie McMillan and safety Steve Preece. Staubach's pass was right where it had to be for a completion to occur. Any other spot and the ball would have been incomplete or intercepted. "We had run the same play in the second quarter," recalled Staubach, "but I told Pearson to run a post pattern instead of a deep curl like he is supposed to. He came back and said he thought he was open. So in the fourth quarter when Coach Landry sent in the same play, I checked Preece and when he hesitated for just a split second I just fired the ball in there as hard as I could throw it."

Pearson leaped for the ball and split the coverage in an instant, coming down with the pass at the Los Angeles 48-yard line. Both McMillan and Preece also jumped for the ball, but both missed it and landed on the turf. Pearson sprinted the rest of the way for the game-breaking score. Dallas would add one more field goal and the Doomsday Defense would shut down the Rams the rest of the way to achieve redemption from their earlier defeat in Los Angeles. Dallas had prevailed, 27–16.

But things were not all fine and dandy for the Cowboys. Their star halfback Calvin Hill suffered a dislocated elbow in the fourth quarter against the Rams as he attempted to recover one of his own fumbles. The loss of Hill did not harm the Dallas cause against the Rams, but it would have dire consequences for them the following week in the NFC championship game.

The Washington Redskins were attempting to return to the NFC title game for the second straight year when they faced off against the Minnesota Vikings in Metropolitan Stadium. The Redskins endured a tough season with what was becoming an annual dilemma for them, that of injuries at the quarterback position. Both Billy Kilmer and Sonny Jurgensen had to cope with nagging aches and pains once again in 1973. Kilmer made it out of the hospital just before the final game of the regular season to help his team defeat the Eagles and earn the wild card spot in the NFC. He then returned to the hospital to deal with a stomach virus right after the Eagles game.

Kilmer showed his mettle in the first half against the Vikings. The gutsy quarterback led his team to a second quarter touchdown a couple of series after a Minnesota field goal. Washington special teams player Bob Brunet fell on a fumbled punt by Minnesota's Bobby Bryant at the Vikings' 21-yard line to ignite the scoring drive. A 17-yard pass from Kilmer to wide receiver Charley Taylor set up Redskins halfback Larry Brown, who surged into the end zone from three yards out to give Washington a 7–3 halftime advantage.

What happened at halftime was actually the most reported story of this game. Mammoth Minnesota defensive end Carl Eller frightened his teammates in the locker room by smashing a blackboard and angrily exploding into a verbal tirade. Eller's message could not have been misunderstood by anyone in the room. "Eller didn't write on the blackboard," said Minnesota running back Oscar Reed after the game. "He punched it, tossed it around, and kicked it. Man, he was really worked up. He told us to get off our dead behinds and start playing football."

"When a guy like Moose [Eller's nickname] stands up and says something like that, you listen," added Minnesota quarterback Fran Tarkenton. "When that blackboard crashed to the floor, I felt like crawling in my locker."

Eller's actions were uncommon for a guy generally thought of by his teammates as soft-spoken. But Eller was extremely tired of losing in the postseason. Minnesota had lost first round playoff games in 1970 and 1971, and they failed to make the playoffs in 1972. "I didn't say much," commented Eller. "I just wanted to express my feelings. I pointed out that we were four points behind and we had to go out and do the job. It's not good practice for a player to do it. It's the coach's place to talk in the locker room—nobody else. But there were things that needed to be said." What he said was geared to stimulate the Vikings tremendously in the second half. Eller told his teammates to "forget about X's and O's, [and] don't think about anything but hitting. If we hit, we win. Any of you who don't feel like hitting, just stay in here and let the rest of us go out and finish the game."

After listening to Eller's halftime diatribe, every Viking player was eager to get back on the field and do some hitting. A seven-play Minnesota drive started the third quarter and was highlighted by a spectacular 46-yard run by Reed, who twisted through a maze of would-be Washington tacklers until he was finally dropped at the 2-yard line by Redskins linebacker Chris Hanburger. Reed would finish the day with 95 yards rushing and 76 yards receiving. Bill Brown blasted in from there to score and put the Vikings ahead, 10–7.

The Redskins answered back on the following drive. Kilmer drove his team to the Minnesota 44-yard line, but could go no further. Erratic placekicker Curt Knight contributed his best kick of the year—from 52 yards out—to even the score. The third quarter ended with a 10–10 tie, and this struggle could go either way. Both teams would take more chances and risks on offense in the fourth quarter, and the key decisions behind those risks would pave the way for a Minnesota victory.

Curt Knight added another field goal to begin the final stanza, but the Vikings answered back quickly. Tarkenton used rollouts and play-action passes to lead his team on a 71-yard drive in eight plays for the go-ahead score. Tarkenton concluded the drive with a 28-yard touchdown pass to John Gilliam, who had sprinted down the sideline on a fly pattern. Gilliam beat Redskins cornerback Speedy Duncan on the play, and the Vikings had a 17–13 lead.

Tarkenton and Gilliam were not finished, however. Minnesota cornerback Nate Wright gave them another chance when he intercepted Kilmer's next passing attempt and returned the ball 26 yards to the Washington 8-yard line. Tarkenton scrambled around his pocket two plays later and found Gilliam all alone in the corner of the end zone for another touchdown. The two keys to this play involved both passer and receiver. Tarkenton avoided charging Washington defensive linemen Verlon Biggs and Bill Brundidge, and linebacker Dave Robinson, while Gilliam broke off his intended route and snuck around the Redskins' secondary until they lost coverage of him. The play gave Minnesota a lead which they would not lose.

The Redskins to their credit did not quit, however. A high snap to Minnesota punter Mike Eischeid led to a blocked punt by Ken Stone, which gave Washington great field position at the Vikings' 28-yard line. On the very next play, Kilmer hit wide receiver Roy Jefferson for a spectacular touchdown which pulled the Redskins to within four points at 24–20. Jefferson beat Nate Wright and made his catch while juggling the ball, then clutching it in between his knees, all the while staying in bounds in the rear of the end zone.

Minnesota took over with 5:18 remaining on the clock. Tarkenton had to use up as much time as possible, and he did just that. The scrambling Minnesota quarterback led his team on a nine-play drive which resulted in a 30-yard field goal by Fred Cox. Tarkenton relied on his runners on all but one play of the drive, which boosted the Vikings' lead to 27–20. Kilmer got the ball back with just 1:36 remaining in the game, but could only get to the Minnesota 42-yard line before his final pass on fourth down bounced in front of his intended receiver. The Vikings had prevailed in a hard-fought playoff game, and were headed to the NFC championship.

"We came out throwing at the start," said Tarkenton in a *calmer* postgame locker room, "and we were throwing at the finish. [Oscar] Reed really did the job for us. When a team that has a lot of stars, and we have them, the ability of a person like Reed is overlooked. He's given us as fine a job as you can ask. We gave him the game ball."

Game balls would be a prized possession the following week in the conference title games, but the biggest prize would be a ticket to Super Bowl VIII. The Oakland Raiders would visit the Orange Bowl to take on the Miami Dolphins in the AFC championship game. It would be a rematch for the two teams that met in the second week of the season in California. The Raiders prevailed in that contest, and the Dolphins were eager for a chance to even the score.

Miami's offense laid the groundwork for their revenge by running the ball down Oakland's throat to start the game. Fullback Larry Csonka and tailback Mercury Morris carried the ball three times apiece during the first Miami drive, which culminated with Csonka's 11-yard burst up the middle for the game's initial touchdown. This show of power football was somewhat surprising considering that Oakland had the second-best defense against the run in 1973.

"We knew we weren't going to finesse them," said Miami All-Conference offensive tackle Norm Evans, "so we just buckled it up and went right at them." Miami offensive guard Bob Kuechenberg claimed that what happened in the previous game against Oakland would serve as the inspiration for Miami's line play in the AFC title game. "Oakland talked a lot when they beat us in September," Kuechenberg recalled, "and the best way to shut up a talking defense is to beat them down physically."

The Dolphins offensive line continued to break open holes in the Raiders defensive line throughout the first half. Csonka successfully completed a 15-play drive late in the second quarter by plowing over All-Pro guard Larry Little's trap block from the Oakland 2-yard line for his second touchdown. Csonka contributed 50 yards rushing on the 63-yard drive. Miami now had a secure 14–0 lead at halftime. "I wasn't surprised by the success of our running game," said Miami head coach Don Shula. "We felt we had one [a good running game] and felt our job was to go out and establish it."

The Raiders knew that their offense had to establish some points, and they did just that on their first drive of the third quarter. Placekicker George Blanda culminated a 12-play drive with a 21-yard field goal. Blanda's counterpart across the field was Garo Yepremian, and he responded with a 42-yard field goal of his own a few minutes later. Oakland appeared to be treading water at this stage of the struggle, gaining some momentum but then losing it in a short amount of time. They needed some big plays and they needed to make a few visits into the Miami end zone. One big play that came Oakland's way occurred ironically with a rare Miami mistake. Oakland faced a key third-and-two situation when a pass interference penalty on Dolphins middle linebacker Nick Buoniconti gave the Raiders a much needed first down. Oakland capitalized on Buoniconti's mistake by scoring a touchdown four plays later. Oakland quarterback Ken Stabler spotted wide receiver Mike Siani all alone in the back of the end zone. Siani's 25-yard score was the result of a mix-up in the Miami secondary. Cornerback Lloyd Mumphord bumped into safety Dick Anderson, and Siani slipped in between them. Neither defender reacted toward Siani as he drifted toward the end zone. In fact, Anderson did not turn around to find Siani until the ball was already caught. Oakland was back in the game, 17–10.

Miami was not about to let the Raiders come any closer, however. The Dolphins responded with a 12-play drive which ended with another Yepremian field goal. A few minutes later, Oakland was faced with a fourth-and-one situation. Running back Marv Hubbard dove into the line, and was promptly met by diving Miami safety Dick Anderson. The resulting collision caused the ball to pop out of Hubbard's grasp. Stabler recovered it and ran desperately toward the first down marker, but was tackled just short of the needed yardage by Miami cornerback Curtis Johnson. The Dolphins took over from there, and never looked back.

A 10-play drive culminated with another Csonka touchdown plunge, and the issue was decided. Each play in their final scoring drive was fittingly a running play. Miami had amassed 266 yards on the ground in their 27–10 victory over the Raiders. The Dolphins were headed back to the Super Bowl for the third straight year. Miami's rushing attack was once again the backbone of their success, but their defense also delivered another stellar performance.

"After we scored our touchdown I thought the momentum had turned," said dejected Oakland head coach John Madden after the game. "In a game like this, it's field position, turnovers that determine the game. They [Miami] executed and didn't make mistakes. I tell you, they just pounded us. Their defense is very good."

That Miami defense played its best in the most crucial times of the game. Their style of play came by familiar design and steady teamwork. "The No-Name term is very appropriate," said Miami defensive back Tim Foley, "because the success of our defense is based on the fact that most of the stress isn't placed on any one individual. The responsibility is distributed throughout the players, and the reason we perform so well is because everyone contributes. There's no one person who really stands out."

Both the Minnesota Vikings and the Dallas Cowboys stood out in 1973 as two very competitive teams who had very strong seasons. On the same afternoon that Miami defeated Oakland, the Vikings and Cowboys would determine the NFC representative for Super Bowl VIII. The NFC title game was played in Texas Stadium, but Dallas' home field advantage was offset by the loss of their injured star tailback, Calvin Hill. Minnesota's running attack experienced no such dilemma, and they took a page from Miami's playbook to start the contest. The Vikings ran the ball nine times in an outstanding 18-play drive which took almost eight minutes off the first quarter clock. The drive culminated with a 44-yard Fred Cox field goal.

Minnesota's second drive, although only a *mere* 14 plays long, was even more successful. The Vikings ran the ball nine times on that drive, which concluded in the Dallas end zone. Minnesota rookie tailback Chuck Foreman took a handoff from quarterback Fran Tarkenton and swept right for five yards and a touchdown.

"We're not known as an outside running team," said Minnesota head coach Bud Grant, "so the Cowboys tried to stack us up in the middle. The wrinkle was Foreman going outside while a couple of our linemen blocked inside going the other way. They [Dallas] didn't think we would do much running outside."

Minnesota's 10–0 halftime lead that their rushing attack earned would not be safe, however. In fact, not much was safe in the second half of this game. An incredible 10 turnovers were committed during the final two quarters, many of which came one right after the other. Dallas got back into the game by ironically committing their first turnover. Quarterback Roger Staubach threw a deep pass on third down for wide receiver Drew Pearson, but Minnesota defensive back Bobby Bryant reacted quickly and intercepted the ball at his own 2-yard line. Bryant was promptly tackled right there, and would have been better off knocking the pass down and forcing a Dallas punt. The Doomsday Defense quickly forced a critical three plays and done situation, which resulted in Dallas' first score. Minnesota's Mike Eischeid boomed a 58-yard punt out of the back of his end zone. Golden Richards of Dallas drifted backwards to field the high and deep kick and began his return at his own 37-yard line. He ran to his left and wove his way through key blocks by teammates Dave Edwards, Billy Joe DuPree, and Charlie Waters. Richards completed his 63-yard jaunt as he coasted across the Minnesota goal line. The Cowboys were now securely back in the game, 10–7.

Minnesota answered the Dallas score with a big one of their own. Three plays after Richards' touchdown, Tarkenton threw the ball as long as he could deep down the middle of the field for his favorite wide receiver, John Gilliam, who was one stride ahead of Dallas defensive backs Mel Renfro and Cornell Green. Gilliam caught the perfect pass as he crossed the goal line, and Minnesota had suddenly regained the momentum and their 10-point lead, 17–7.

"I didn't see him catch it," said Tarkenton of Gilliam's touchdown, "but when he took off I knew he had the ball and we had a score." Bud Grant described the play as a "rainbow pattern." Gilliam relied on his speed and on the perfect execution of the play. "I just took off and Fran put it right on the money," Gilliam said after the game.

Dallas responded with a quick field goal to pull to within a touchdown, but the contest got very sloppy from that point on as the third quarter expired. Each team tried its hardest to give the game away to the other. Chuck Foreman fumbled, and on the very next play, Roger Staubach threw an interception. Tarkenton returned the generosity three plays later when he threw an interception. Staubach was hit by Minnesota defensive end Jim Marshall three plays later and promptly fumbled. Vikings defensive tackle Gary Larsen made the first of his two fumble recoveries on the play. Two plays later, Foreman fumbled again and Dallas recovered. Three plays after that, Staubach threw another interception that resulted in a Minnesota touchdown.

On that pivotal play, Minnesota defensive back Bobby Bryant followed Dallas wide receiver Bob Hayes as he went in motion. Bryant kept his eyes on Staubach and made his move as soon as the ex–Navy star looked to Hayes. Bryant flashed in front of Hayes, grabbed Staubach's pass along the sideline, and raced 63 yards untouched for a Vikings score. "I looked back at Staubach as he was getting ready to throw," Bryant confided. "I knew it was coming my way and I went straight for the ball. Once I caught it I didn't see Hayes until after the touchdown."

Staubach would throw one more interception which resulted in a Minnesota field goal. The Vikings and Cowboys would each fumble once more. Finally, Minnesota ran out the clock with a 13-play drive which ended the game and sent them to their second Super Bowl, 27–10.

"We had nothing going for us until Richards' punt return," lamented Dallas head coach Tom Landry. "Then everything was going for us. Then they turned around and hit Gilliam. We may have taken advantage of our later opportunities if he [Gilliam] hadn't taken the starch out. Minnesota did an excellent job against us."

The 1973 NFC championship game would not go down as a display of excellence. It would, however, go down as a game where one team overcame its multitude of errors and produced enough big plays to win. "The mistakes kind of destroyed the esthetics of the game," said a relieved Grant afterward. "But when you are in a fight and somebody hits you on the jaw, you can't stand around and ask somebody what happened. You have to keep going."

Breaking jaws, forearm shivers, and rugged trench warfare would be the most visible elements as the Minnesota Vikings met the Miami Dolphins in Super Bowl VIII. The game would be won or lost on the line of scrimmage, as is most football games. But before the two conference champions kicked things off on in Houston, Texas, on January 13, 1974, the news and notes of the two weeks prior to the game would be some of the most unique in Super Bowl history. The Vikings complained about their sub-standard locker room and practice facilities at the high school in Houston where they spent the week before the game. The Dolphins complained that the married players could bring their wives to the game at the expense of team owner Joe Robbie, but the single players could not extend the same invitation to their mothers.

Regardless of the inconveniences and imperfections for the teams, the exciting spectacle of the Super Bowl was growing by leaps and bounds, and it was visible for all to see. Parties celebrating the game and the season were held in record numbers everywhere across the country. Celebrities showed up all over Houston, where the world championship game would be held for the first time. Rice University Stadium was chosen as the site of the game instead of the nearby Astrodome. Many of the 68,142 spectators on Super Sunday would have to plant their posteriors on the wooden and aluminum benches at Rice Stadium instead of the cushioned seats inside the Astrodome, but most spectators agreed that would be a small concession to make. The fans who attended the game were excited to witness what they hoped would be a fitting conclusion to an exciting season.

Only the Dolphins fans exited Rice Stadium satisfied, however. A cloudy and fog-shrouded scene greeted the players and spectators on this day, but by game's end, the gloom that it produced would only symbolize the plight of the Vikings. The Dolphins were six-point favorites by oddsmakers going into the game, and they were determined to make those oddsmakers look like geniuses. They were also determined to employ their favorite strategy against the Vikings by running the ball and establishing ball control right from the outset. Miami won the opening coin toss and turned their first drive into a clinic for basic, no-frills, running football. The Dolphins offensive line mixed cross-blocking with power drive blocking to confuse the Minnesota defensive line. Miami's rushing calls included misdirection trap runs and draws, and the ever-present off tackle slant run to thoroughly frustrate the Purple Gang. The Miami style of play used up the clock and produced a 7–0 lead when fullback Larry Csonka plowed into the end zone from five yards out.

The next Miami drive had similar results. Csonka and halfback Mercury Morris kept moving the chains with their running attack, and reserve halfback Jim Kiick culminated the drive with a 1-yard plunge to boost Miami's lead to 14–0. Csonka's rumbling excursions into the Minnesota secondary were so overpowering that Vikings free safety Paul Krause had to make four unassisted tackles of the burly fullback in the first half. Not to be outdone by Csonka, Dolphins quarterback Bob Griese kept the Vikings defense puzzled on both early drives by completing short passes to tight end Jim Mandich and wide receiver Marlin Briscoe. Griese would end the day by throwing the ball only seven times, but he completed six of those throws. All but two of his completions went for first downs.

Miami struck again in the second quarter with an eight-play drive which resulted in a 28-yard Garo Yepremian field goal which gave the Dolphins a 17–0 lead. Minnesota's back was welded to the wall. They had to move the ball, but up to now they had been thwarted by the No-Name Defense. Miami's defenders were flying around on each play and were swarming and gang-tackling every Minnesota ball carrier. The Vikings had obtained only one first down with just a few minutes remaining in the first half. Minnesota quarterback Fran Tarkenton finally decided to throw caution to the wind and throw deep for wide receiver John Gilliam. His 30-yard completion to Gilliam was the first showing of life that the Vikings exhibited all day, and it put the Norsemen on the Miami 15-yard line.

Miami extinguished Minnesota's surge in quick order, however. One of the key plays in the game occurred when on fourth-and-one from the Miami 6-yard line. Miami middle linebacker Nick Buoniconti blasted Minnesota running back Oscar Reed as Reed attempted to break through the line. Reed abruptly fumbled the ball, which was recovered by Dolphins safety Jake Scott. The Vikings drive ended with zero points, and the Dolphins defense added yet another epic achievement to their legend. Their status as the toughest defense in the NFL to score upon was showcased in this Super Bowl.

"The word to describe our defense is efficient," said Miami defensive back Tim Foley. "I think that our coaches get the most out of the players and the individual abilities that they have, because they have the defensive scheme set up so well. And, if we're exceptional in any way it's in the discipline with which we all carry out our assignments."

Another major factor that hurt the Vikings in Super Bowl VIII was their lack of any semblance of good luck. It seemed that whenever a rare big play would occur for Minnesota, their lack of poise would result in a penalty that negated the big play. Such was the case at the opening of the second half, when John Gilliam returned Miami's kickoff 65 yards. Minnesota's Stu Voigt was called for clipping on the play, and the Vikings were forced to begin that drive at their own 10-yard line. Earlier in the game, a fumbled punt by Miami's Jake Scott was surrounded by three Vikings. Scott somehow made the recovery. Later in the contest, an onside kick by Minnesota was recovered by Terry Brown of the Vikings. Unfortunately for Minnesota, Ron Porter was offsides on the play, which eliminated that golden chance of stealing a possession.

Csonka increased the Miami lead in the third quarter when he finished off an eight-play drive with a 2-yard dive into the Minnesota end zone. Csonka blasted through the attempted

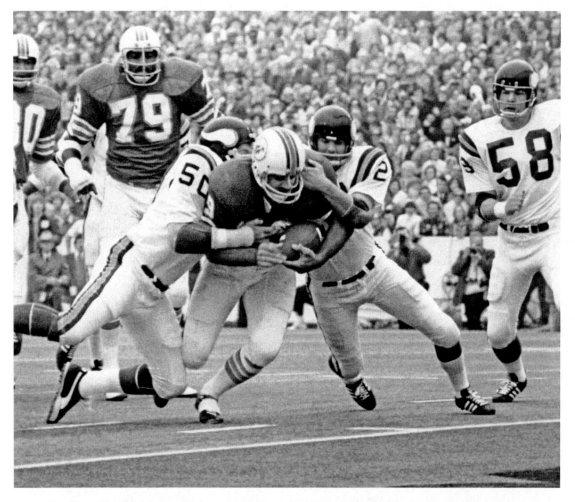

Larry Csonka was named the Most Valuable Player in Super Bowl VIII, January 13, 1974, by rushing for 145 yards and two touchdowns in Miami's 24–7 victory over Minnesota in Houston's Rice Stadium. Here Csonka drags Vikings linebacker Jeff Siemon and safety Paul Krause into the end zone for Miami's first score in the first quarter (AP Photo).

tackle of Minnesota linebacker Wally Hilgenberg on the play, and went on to become the Most Valuable Player of the game. Csonka would finish the day with a Super Bowl record 145 yards on 33 carries. His bruises, disfigured nose, and black eye (which he got courtesy of a Hilgenberg elbow) served as testament to Csonka's powerful running style. The Vikings could well attest to Csonka's dominance on this day. "It's not the collision that gets you," said Minnesota middle linebacker Jeff Siemon. "It's what happens after you tackle him. His legs are just so strong he keeps moving. He carries you."

The Vikings were down 24–0 early in the fourth quarter, and were destined to lose their second Super Bowl. But they had their pride, and they continued to fight in spite of their frustration. Vikings All-Pro defensive tackle Alan Page epitomized that frustration when he was penalized twice in the fourth quarter for unnecessary roughness. Tarkenton's failures in the fourth quarter included an interception which ended another potential scoring drive. Simply put, nothing went right for Minnesota all game long. Nevertheless, Tarkenton set a Super Bowl record for completed passes (18), and he salvaged at least a small portion of pride for his team by leading them on a ten-play scoring drive to avert a shutout. The scrambler ran a bootleg option around his right end and dove into the end zone for a 4-yard touchdown. "We wanted a shutout," said Miami defensive tackle Manny Fernandez, "but Tarkenton is no quitter."

Miami's 24–7 conquest of Minnesota secured history for the defending champions. The Dolphins had equaled the back-to-back Super Bowl championship seasons that Green Bay accomplished in 1966 and 1967. Miami stood out as the finest team in the NFL for the second straight season, and the other 25 teams could only stand in awe of them.

"The Dolphins are just a super, super team," declared the great Chicago Bears middle linebacker Dick Butkus. "They have the best defense in football and far and away the best offensive line. They are certainly the greatest team we're going to see for a long, long time."

Another AFC team would prove Butkus' prediction a little premature only one year later.

1974

A New Breed, a New Dynasty

A new breed of player spread across the NFL spectrum by the time the season of 1974 rolled around. Just as the decade of the 1970s in America was referred to as the "me" decade, so too was the "me" player reflected on many team rosters in pro football. Individuality among players had grown in stages during the latter years of the previous decade and in the early years of the 1970s. The trends of individuality included several outward signs. More and more players were donning longer hair, facial hair, and even a brave few were wearing earrings. Many younger players in the early 1970s experimented and perfected end zone dances upon scoring. The stoic and older players, coaches and owners, observed these changes and dealt with them in various ways. Coaches like Kansas City's Hank Stram, Detroit's Rick Forzano, and Cincinnati's Paul Brown required their players to be clean-shaven throughout the season. Several coaches reprimanded their players for showing off after scoring. Oakland head coach John Madden, in contrast, simply did not care what his players looked like or what they did when they crossed the goal line.

"I just had three simple rules," Madden stated. "Be on time for all meetings, pay attention in all meetings, and play like hell on Sunday."

But a more pressing problem than player grooming practices and touchdown celebrations was looming upon the NFL horizon during the months preceding the 1974 season, and it was a problem that was rooted in this new class of individuality. The National Football League Players Association (hereafter referred to as the NFLPA or the players union) was in the midst of trying to obtain a new contract with the team owners. The players were adamant about obtaining fairness with a new collective bargaining agreement. The owners believed that their position displayed plenty of fairness to the players in answering the terms of negotiable pay wages and various other player concerns. The labor dispute of 1974 would keep the summer preseason schedule in doubt, as talk of a players strike loomed ahead. The idea of going on strike was not new to NFL players. They had done so before in the summer of 1970, but that strike lasted only a few days and accomplished little in the way of substantial improvements in player wealth and free agency. The issues that the players brought forth in 1974 for the owners to address were numerous. Some, like the ability to request trades while under contract, were more serious than others. Most players were wise enough to realize that they would not get all of their demands. But the NFLPA was as strong as it had ever been by the time 1974 rolled around, and the players decided to test their union's strength against the owners. Players of bygone eras like the 1930s and 1940s would never have threatened to strike, because they knew that they would be out of a job. But the player of 1974 was bolder, more brash, and more confident in his individual worth to the game than his predecessors ever were. His coaches were also more confounded and perplexed when trying to identify with him.

"I know as a player I never had any voice in [player demands]," said Houston assistant coach

Richie Petitbon. "I don't know where some of these demands are coming from or who thinks them up. Some of the demands now are absolutely ridiculous."

The player demands were centered on what they called "freedom issues." Those issues included monetary items like more money for exhibition (preseason) games; safety issues like the eventual elimination of AstroTurf playing surfaces throughout the league; and contract issues that focused on more maneuverability for players in their potential and future free agent status. Perhaps the most noteworthy player demand involved "The Rozelle Rule," named after NFL Commissioner Pete Rozelle. The Rozelle Rule inhibited player movement from team to team. It stated that when a player chose to play out his option with one team, the new team that signs him must pay some level of compensation (namely money, another player or players, or draft choices) to his former team. Most new teams were unwilling to do this, hence many players were inevitably forced to renew their current contracts with the team that initially signed them. The majority of players wanted to see this rule obliterated or at the very least altered to make it easier for players to sign with new teams. According to NFLPA President and Houston center Bill Curry, "the Rozelle rule will have to be eliminated."

As the summer of 1974 wound down, it was still unclear as to whether the veteran players in the league would strike over their demands. Many members of the league's management council believed that cooler heads would prevail and that the players would refrain from striking. "We think a strike can and will be avoided," said John Thompson, the executive director of the NFL management council. "At this moment, there is optimism, if you will call it that."

Many of the players were not optimistic, however. Quite a few were getting picket signs printed and distributed. Players like Bill Curry did his utmost to keep union representatives on each team abreast as to the negotiations, but those talks were not going well. The players presented several key issues to the owners, including the reserve list, the waiver system, the option year, and the compensation rule. Each of these issues should be altered to help the players achieve a more balanced level of freedom to move from team to team, and fairness to obtain a wage that was comparable to the market value for professional athletes. The owners were not budging, however, and Ed Garvey, the Executive Director of the NFLPA, went so far as to accuse the owners of "bad faith negotiating," among other denunciations.

"We think they [the owners] are in violation of the law," Garvey told reporters just prior to the opening of summer training camp. "Their asking for a no-strike pledge is an insult. They are presuming there will be a strike. We say we want to reach a settlement and avoid a strike."

Bill Curry piled on top of Garvey's comments with some caustic statements of his own. "We were admonished and chastised [by the owners] for making proposals that would destroy a system that has worked for 54 years," Curry said. "We're saying the NFL can work without being an unregulated monopoly. The real argument is whether what we're talking about can lead to anarchy and the destruction of football. Nothing could be further from the truth."

"You would have thought that Attila the Hun had come to town, and I was there to rape, pillage and plunder," said All-Pro St. Louis offensive tackle Dan Dierdorf of his support of the strike. "It was beyond belief."

Many of the player demands from 1974 appear to us many years later as paltry and insignificant. But back then, the players were fighting for their very livelihoods. The players wanted increases in the minimum salaries to $20,000 for rookies and $25,000 for veterans. Many players who were not superstars would often have to work second jobs in order to make ends meet in the early 1970s. A higher wage scale for players would greatly help them and their families.

One thing that did not help them was ironically their own union. Garvey and a variety of player representatives increased their overall number of demands to 90. The owners were more put off by this decision as they decided to open up training camps to rookies (who were not yet members of the NFLPA). Slightly more than two months of practices and six preseason games per team were at stake if a strike was to occur. The owners decided to sign as many rookies and free agents as possible in order to fill roster spots in case of a strike. Atlanta Falcons board chairman Rankin Smith would open up his team's training camp to "rookies, veterans, friends and bartenders." This move really irritated the rank-and-file veterans, many of whom believed that most rookies would not dare to cross a picket line when confronted by several famous and popular players whom those rookies idolized just a few short years ago.

"I'm not so sure," conjectured Curry, "what they [the rookies] will do if, for example, they have to go by a [Rams defensive lineman] Merlin Olsen [on the picket line]."

No settlement would be reached as the training camps opened. Throngs of rookies crossed picket lines, eager for a chance to make their NFL dreams a reality. The striking veterans were not bashful about jeering the rookies as they walked by. Most veterans on the picket lines carried signs and wore t-shirts proclaiming "No Freedom, No Football." It was a scene not unlike that of any other labor strike in America, save for the fact that these men on strike were famous in the public eye. Curry said that there were only 20 or so veterans who reported to training camp, while over 1,200 held picket signs. The tension of the strike produced strong opinions on both sides. Perhaps those who felt the pressure the most were the rookies trying to make a team. Linebacker Frank LeMaster was one such rookie who tried to reason with the Philadelphia Eagles veterans as he crossed their picket line.

"I can see the Players' Association point of view and I agree with the things they are doing," LeMaster told reporters. "But they [the association] must understand that I must make the team as a rookie before I can be in the union. It's ridiculous to think that I can strike and still make the team. I wouldn't have a chance."

The team owners tried to be as fair in their negotiations as possible, but they were feeling the ill-effects of a tumultuous off-season. A few players on some teams were migrating to the new World Football League (WFL), causing a clamor with player agents and salary demands. The 1974 players strike just added to the palpable bitterness that was being played out in the media between the owners and the players. Most of the demands from both the owners and the players were involved in the open discussions. But there was one major aspect of the owners' position that they refused to give up in the meetings with the players union. "Everything is negotiable," said Philadelphia Eagles owner Leonard Tose, "but the prerogatives of management to run teams as they see fit. All money issues are negotiable."

The strike was unsettling to say the least. Within a few days, more brave veterans decided to cross the picket lines to honor their contracts. Baltimore middle linebacker Mike Curtis refused to strike back in 1970, and four years later, he suited up to play again amidst the stern looks from his teammates.

"You know me," Curtis said to the press. "I'm an establishment man, and I'm not in the players association. A lot of things the players are asking for are ridiculous. [But] a lot of the owners are complete jerks." Curtis also went on to accuse Ed Garvey, the head of the NFLPA, of being "a communist."

The preseason began as it always did before with the Pro Football Hall of Fame Game in Canton, Ohio, this year featuring the Buffalo Bills and the St. Louis Cardinals. That contest featured nothing but rookies and walk-ons trying to make an NFL team. Hardly any fans in attendance could recognize any of the players. This was actually good for the NFLPA, because, as Curry commented earlier, "if this game [the Hall of Fame Game] is played, and the public sees how bad those teams are. It's the fans who will get the short end."

A group of NFL players in Denver walk a picket line in the summer of 1974, as the NFL Players Union took part in the longest strike in pro football history (up to that time). This scene was repeated in NFL cities across America, as the slogan "No Freedom, No Football" was chanted by hundreds of veteran players. The strike lasted for eight weeks, but during that time, many rookies got a chance to earn roster spots (AP Photo).

A few days later, the annual College All-Star Game was scheduled to be played in Chicago. The NFLPA refused to sanction the contest, and as a result, it was cancelled. The strike was beginning to have a marked effect on the preseason schedule.

The players strike would last for a total of eight weeks. By mid–July, several teams started to see more and more veterans put down their picket signs and pick up their shoulder pads. The owners were counting on this to happen, and it eventually did. At least 13 Miami Dolphins veterans ignored the strike early and reported to camp. Increasing numbers of defectors crossed the picket lines around the league on a daily basis towards the end of July. Miami center Jim Langer spoke for many disgruntled but realistic veterans when he stated, "If you've got a job and you want some conditions changed, it's up to you to suggest it. I'm not against the association," Langer continued. "I've never missed a [dues] payment. I've worked under Blanton Collier [at Cleveland] and [Don] Shula [at Miami], and I've certainly been treated fairly."

Oakland center Jim Otto concurred with Langer's sentiments. "We're professionals," Otto said. "We're not union in the true sense. Nobody is going to get anywhere with 63 demands."

The players called off the strike on August 10, preferring to agree to a "cooling-off" period while continuing their battle with the owners through a mediator and the National Labor Relations Board. This decision would allow the players to return to their teams and start playing football. The standoff with the owners in the courts lasted until a settlement was finally agreed to in 1977. Bill Curry was one of several casualties of the 1974 players strike, as the Houston Oilers unceremoniously cut him from their roster. Curry was not alone in the purging. Oilers head coach Sid Gillman waived seven other striking veterans as soon as they returned to training camp. A predictable rancor between the players union and Gillman immediately ensued. "As long as Sid Gillman is in Houston," Ed Garvey declared, "I wouldn't believe anything that came out of that organization. He [Gillman] is the symbol of what we [the union] are fighting against." In fairness to Gillman, quite a few coaches around the league decided to cut key union players.

The 1974 NFL Players Strike produced no real winners. Yes, the players finally obtained a new collective bargaining agreement in 1977, and with that agreement they gained more money in salaries and a better pension plan. But they also lost a lot of trust with the fans. During the 1970s, the game of pro football became more of a business, and that fact was readily apparent by observing and studying the actions and decisions of both the players and the owners in the strike of 1974. Many fans who at one time elevated the players to a near god-like status were now acutely aware that they were people just like themselves, and susceptible to the rugged demands of living and paying bills in American society. The idolization of the players still occurred, but beneath it, lay a firm foundation of honesty and realism amongst the fans. The game was no less great on the field, but off the field, it was becoming more of a working occupation, and increasingly more people in America were beginning to understand that.

The players in the "me" decade would receive another option to exhibit their talents in 1974 when the World Football League began its inaugural season. The league name was a misnomer, as despite the league's original plans, none of the 12 teams were from any country other than the United States. The WFL was based on a failed concept of trying to lure big name NFL players away from the NFL, with a big signing bonus as the bait. The problem with that was that the league as a whole was insolvent, with very little money to go around. The WFL operated on a shoestring budget, and that fact was never far from the minds of anyone involved. Several coaches had to buy rudimentary supplies for their teams, and after the 1974 season ended, the WFL Champion Birmingham Americans were forced to watch the sheriff's department impound their uniforms to cover a portion of the team's debt. Even though the 1974 WFL regular season lasted 20 games long, very few team owners and players felt that the teams would even see a second season. The fan interest was almost non-existent, with virtually all of the teams padding their attendance totals with fictitious numbers. Most teams ended up giving away tickets to the games. The league was so unstable that two of the teams transferred to different cities before the 1974 season ended. Some of the NFL players who left to play in the WFL in 1974 included Jim Nance, Tommy Reamon, Virgil Carter, John Huarte (a former Heisman Trophy winner), Larry Willingham, George Mira, and Dennis Homan (among others). They joined a bunch of rookies who failed to make NFL rosters, and a smattering of former NFL players who were past their prime and who came out of retirement to play one more season. The WFL would somehow make it through the season, and would make its final headlines when the fledgling league folded in 1975.

When the current NFL players returned to work in August following their strike, they were greeted by a somewhat different game, at least as far as the rules were concerned. A bunch of new rules were instituted by the rules committee that were geared to give the game a boost, open up the offenses, and increase scoring and excitement. Many of the new rules involved the kicking game.

One of the new rules was more practical than anything else. The goal posts were moved back 10 yards to the end line. This move would eliminate the common occurrence of players accidentally running into this padded but unbending obstacle at the goal line. Placekickers, however, were definitely not fond of the new placement of the goal posts. Most kickers believed that it was tough enough to kick field goals without adding 10 more yards to each attempt. There were 309 fewer field goals attempted in 1974 than there were in 1973. "They are penalizing the field goal kickers for excellence by moving the goal posts to the end line," said CBS-TV commentator and former New York Giants kicker Pat Summerall.

Speaking of kicking, the art of kicking the ball off to start the game or after each score was also going to undergo a rule change. The spot where the ball would be positioned on the kicking tee was sent back five yards from the 40-yard line to the 35-yard line. This would allow speedy and elusive return artists a better chance to excite the crowd by returning the ball instead of taking a touchback in the end zone. The results were dramatic. The NFL saw a total of nine touchdowns from kickoff returns in 1974, compared to five in the previous year. There was also an ample increase of 2,420 total yards in kickoff returns from 1973.

The punting game was also the subject of a new rule in 1974. Only two outside men (known as gunners or bombers) would be allowed to run down the field at the snap of the ball to cover the punt. The rest of the players would have to wait until the ball was kicked before they headed downfield. Before this season, punt returners would have to endure a torrid rush of defenders breathing fire as they all stormed to meet him and knock him senseless. Now, punt returners had a fighting chance to catch the ball and follow his blocks. Punters, in contrast, would have to punt the ball deeper and increase their hang times in order to keep the dangerous return men from breaking free and accumulating yardage. The result was that punt return averages increased overall by almost five yards per return. "The new rule on punts may make a punt return the most important play in the game," said Miami head coach Don Shula. Many punters adjusted to the new rule by kicking the ball out of bounds to avoid any return at all. The "coffin corner" kick, as it was called, was used by punters to pin the opposition back as close to its goal line as possible.

The rule makers were still not finished with the kickers, however. A new rule stated that any missed field goal beyond the opponent's 20-yard line would be brought back to the line of scrimmage instead of being placed at the 20. This obviously aided the opposing offenses by giving them less yards to travel to score. Indeed, many coaches started to see the wisdom in eschewing a longer field goal attempt in place of a punt. Teams started to place a much higher level of importance in placekickers and punters who had strong legs. They also inadvertently took a much more determined look at the game's strategy. No longer were deep men expected to be back at the goal line to return a missed field goal, because the ball would automatically be returned to the line of scrimmage anyway. This meant that the deep man could now be placed on the line, rushing the kicker with 10 of his teammates in their efforts to block the field goal attempt. Teams that employed quality special teams players were suddenly the beneficiaries of many of the new kicking and punting rules.

Another new rule helped pass receivers. Defensive backs in 1974 were only permitted one hit or "chuck" of the receiver. This rule virtually spelled the death knell for the bump-and-run coverages which were so successful during the previous decade. The adjustments that the players and coaches had to make to the new rules were instantaneous. The quicker they could adapt, the better chance they had to take advantage of the new rules. One more rule which aided many offenses was the decreasing of holding penalty yardage. Offensive holding and illegal use of hands penalties in 1974 would call for a 10-yard walk-off, as opposed to the old 15-yard punishment. This change helped offenses to control the ball for longer periods of time.

But undoubtedly the rule change that has had the most long-lasting effect on the game involved sudden death overtime. The league decided to add a 15-minute overtime period for each preseason and regular season game which ended in a tie. Using the sudden death rules that were currently used in the playoffs (where the first team to score wins the game), the NFL would now employ somewhat the same rule for the preseason and regular season games. The difference was that if no team would score during the extra period, the game would end in a tie. In the playoffs, the teams would keep playing until a winner emerges. This extra period has lasted until this very day, and has eliminated many tie games from the NFL standings.

The large number of rules changes in 1974 were the most that the league had ever seen since its earliest years. The reasoning for the dramatic changes was obvious. More offensive production and scoring was needed to bring the pro game out of its low-scoring, defensive battles, and into some high-scoring, offensive shootouts. The league may have also wanted to put more fans in the stands, and more scoring in the games would hopefully accomplish that goal. The changes worked in at least one of those areas. A total of 31 more touchdowns were scored in 1974 than in the previous season, an achievement that made many offensive-minded fans happy. But the attendance in 1974 was slightly less than in 1973. This was possibly due to the lingering animosity among some of the fans toward the players and their summer strike. Indeed, a paltry 24,000 fans showed up in Cleveland for a December 1 game between the Browns and the San Francisco 49ers. Neither of those two teams would have winning seasons in 1974, and Cleveland's 7–0 victory in the snow and mud was ample evidence that at least some punch of scoring excitement was lacking in the league. Over 50,000 ticket holders also failed to show up in Atlanta for the Packers-Falcons game on the final week of the regular season.

"The clubs felt frustration," said NFL Commissioner Pete Rozelle following the 1973 season. "They [the team owners] wanted to see more offense."

More offense would be evident during the season of 1974 thanks to the new rules, but that was just a part of what made the pro game exciting. Some teams which were not expected to compete for the playoffs were suddenly becoming contenders, and thus were producing interest amongst their fans. One of those teams was the New England Patriots. Head coach Chuck Fairbanks led his team through an incredible first half of the season. The Patriots were undefeated in their first five games, easily their best start in their 15-year history. New England's offense was led by quarterback Jim Plunkett, a youthful signal caller who experienced the best start in his four-year career. Running backs Sam "Bam" Cunningham and diminutive Mack Herron joined Plunkett in the backfield, and this rushing combination was a key to the team's offensive success. Cunningham could bowl over defenders with his power, or he could run past them with his speed. Herron (5'5", 170) used his lack of size and elusiveness to surprise defenders. Herron hid behind his blockers often, then sprung through small holes for vital yardage. He was also a good pass catcher and a really good punt and kickoff returner. Herron accounted for 517 yards in punt returns in 1974, the second-best mark in the NFL. By season's end, Herron would eclipse the total combined yardage record (rushing, receiving and punt and kickoff returns) of former Chicago great Gale Sayers. Herron accounted for 2,444 total combined yards in 1974. Plunkett, Cunningham and Herron exhibited their abilities in the season opener against the defending world champion Miami Dolphins. The Patriots offense earned 175 rushing yards and scored four touchdowns against the No-Name Defense en route to a 34–24 upset win at Foxboro. "They're much improved," said Miami head coach Don Shula of the Patriots. "They have a lot of young kids on defense. They're not going to make the big mistakes they did last year."

The main reason for New England's impressive start to the 1974 season, however, was their defense. Fairbanks installed a 3–4 stack defense, and it proved very successful during the first half of the year. Fairbanks is recognized by football historians as the first head coach to use the 3–4 defense on a full-time basis for an entire season. Today, many teams employ the 3–4. New England's defense in 1974 permitted their opponents only 61 points during the first five games. Leading Fairbanks' defense were defensive linemen Ray "Sugarbear" Hamilton, Julius Adams, Mel Lunsford, Tony McGee, and a 15th-round draft selection, rookie linebacker Sam Hunt out of Stephen F. Austin State University. New England's defense improved vastly from 1973. In 1973, they were last against the run in the AFC. In 1974, they ranked tops in the AFC in that category.

The Pats had a reasonably tough schedule. They would play six of the previous eight playoff teams across the league, as well as division rivals Buffalo and Miami twice. The Pats would win three of those contests before the midpoint of the season. Perhaps the most telling New England victory during the early stretch of games came in the third week of the season against the visiting Los Angeles Rams. New England controlled the line of scrimmage throughout much of the game, and spirited by their defense (which allowed the Rams only 109 rushing yards), held on for a 20–14 victory. The Patriots definitely had a Cinderella look about them as the 1974 season revved up.

The Rams were one team that was unable to punch a Cinderella card in 1974. They would not be sneaking up on any team, but their success in 1973 would be repeated again the following year with few problems along the way. The Rams had a multi-faceted offense that could wear you down with a punishing running game, or it could drop bombs on your defensive secondary with little trouble. Running back Lawrence McCutcheon was the only NFC runner to top 1,000 rushing in 1974. The Rams' defense led the NFL against the run. The only notable change from the previous year occurred when General Manager Don Klosterman engineered a deal with Green Bay to trade their veteran starting quarterback, John Hadl, to the Packers for an incredible amount of five draft picks. Klosterman could make this deal thanks in large part to the abilities of young backup quarterbacks James Harris and Ron Jaworski. He also probably felt that Hadl, in his mid-30s, was probably not going to get any better with age. The game that sealed the deal came ironically against the Packers on October 13. Hadl failed to engineer any offense against a suspect Green Bay defense. The Rams were upset, 17–6, and Hadl had a new home in a matter of days.

Two other playoff teams from 1973 were unable to duplicate Los Angeles' feat of repeating as division champions. One of them was the Cincinnati Bengals, who won the tough AFC Central Division in 1973, but struggled through a difficult 1974 season. Key injuries to star running backs Essex Johnson and Boobie Clark derailed the Bengals' rushing attack. Moreover, the loss of key offensive linemen Vern Holland and Bob Johnson gave Cincinnati quarterback Ken Anderson only limited protection. Despite being under more pressure, Anderson's numbers improved enough for him to lead the league in the passer ratings with a 95.9 mark. He also threw a league-high 213 completions, and accumulated a league-best 2,667 yards passing. But Anderson proved to be the only real bright spot of the season for his team. Head coach Paul Brown's squad could not equal Anderson's superb performance, and Cincinnati finished a woeful 7–7. The Bengals watched the playoffs from their living rooms.

"You can't just play the big ones," Brown said during the latter part of the year. "You've got to discipline the emotions and be consistent. We've learned that now."

The Dallas Cowboys were definitely not expected to be inactive for the playoffs, but that's exactly what happened. Their failures, mostly during the early part of the season, helped them to miss the postseason for the first time in eight years. Dallas opened the season with a lackluster (if one could call it that) 24–0 win over host Atlanta. In Week 2, the bottom fell out. The Cowboys were leading the Eagles late in a Monday night divisional contest in Philadelphia. In the fourth quarter, reserve rookie running back Doug Dennison out of tiny Kutztown State College in Pennsylvania took a pitchout from quarterback Roger Staubach at the Eagles' 2-yard line. Philadelphia middle linebacker Bill Bergey drew a bead on Dennison and shattered his solar plexis with a helmet hit, dislodging the ball. Eagles cornerback Joe "Bird" Lavender picked up the bouncing pigskin and sprinted down the far sideline untouched for a go-ahead touchdown in a 13–10 victory. Dallas would lose their next three games to start the season with a depressing 1–4 record.

The Washington Redskins, who were stuck with the league's toughest schedule, appeared to be foundering during the early part of the 1974 season as well. But somehow, someway, they managed to string together some crucial victories to duplicate their 10–4 record from 1973. Head coach George Allen's team claimed six of eight divisional contests and two of three contests against AFC foes. One of those key wins came against defending Super Bowl champion Miami at RFK Stadium on October 13. The Dolphins held a narrow lead with less than a minute to play when Washington displayed some comeback magic. Reserve quarterback Sonny Jurgensen would make his first start in 1974 against the Dolphins, and he made it a memorable one. The portly Jurgensen piloted a 60-yard drive by connecting on six of seven passes, the last of which went to setback Larry Smith with 16 seconds remaining to corral victory, 20–17. Smith just barely made it across the goal line before being torpedoed by Dolphins middle linebacker Nick Buoniconti. It would not be the last big win for the Redskins as the season progressed.

"There was no doubt that we were going to win today," said Washington halfback Larry Brown from the victorious postgame locker room.

Big wins were a rarity in Buffalo for many years. In 1973, however, the Bills achieved nine victories and narrowly missed the playoffs. In 1974, head coach Lou Saban's squad would finally get into the playoffs as the AFC's wild card entry. Buffalo started the season by giving the Oakland Raiders their only loss on *Monday Night Football* during the 1970s with a dramatic 21–20 win at Rich Stadium. Oakland would incidentally finish the decade with a 13–1–1 record on *Monday Night Football*, easily the best mark in the league. O.J. Simpson suffered an ankle injury in the second quarter of the opening night game, and the situation seemed hopeless for the Bills. But standout performances by quarterback Joe Ferguson and newly-acquired wide receiver Ahmad Rashad (obtained in an off-season trade from St. Louis) helped to make this win the springboard for a super season. Rashad snatched two Ferguson touchdown strikes in a 90-second span of time in the fourth quarter to earn a 1–0 start to the season. It appeared as if the Raiders would put Buffalo away throughout the second half, but the Bills fought back each time. "I guess this should prove that the Bills' offense doesn't consist solely of O.J.," said Simpson after the game.

Several playoff teams in 1974 would naturally require the key performances of a number of their gamebreakers if they hoped to obtain success. The Minnesota Vikings, still smarting after their loss to Miami in Super Bowl VIII, would once again rely on quarterback Fran Tarkenton, running back Chuck Foreman, and receiver John Gilliam. Minnesota's goal of repeating as NFC Central champions would prove to be easily obtainable. The Vikings burst out of the starting gate with five wins, and remained at least two games ahead of their divisional challengers throughout much of the season. A big win in Week 4 against the host Dallas Cowboys highlighted head coach Bud Grant's offense. Foreman caught five of Tarkenton's passes on that day for 131 yards and two touchdowns. Foreman also ran for 72 yards, but it was his pass catching abilities coming out of the backfield which hurt Dallas the most, and which made him one of the biggest offensive threats in the league. It took placekicker Fred Cox to win the game, however. Cox booted a 27-yard field goal which just barely stayed inside the right upright with one second left on the clock to trim the Cowboys, 23–21. Minnesota's victory would not have happened, however, were it not for Tarkenton's savvy in keeping several scoring drives alive with his ability to escape the Cowboys' pass rush.

"Tarkenton is a gifted quarterback," said Dallas head coach Tom Landry following the game. "He's been playing this game 15 years and he has picked up a lot of knowledge."

The accumulated skill of veteran players like Tarkenton could not be exaggerated in 1974. With so many rookies dotting NFL rosters, veterans across the league had to provide and share their wisdom and skills to the younger players if a team was to have success. The New York Giants signed an incredible number of 21 rookies to their team in 1974. The rookies who became pros in the midst of the summer strike were relying on that mentoring, and many would excel in the early weeks of the season. Doug Kotar of the New York Giants, Roger Carr of Baltimore, Brian Sipe of Cleveland, Nat Moore of Miami, Carl Barzilauskas of the New York Jets, and J.V. Cain of St. Louis all had superlative first seasons. Other rookies like Ed "Too Tall" Jones of Dallas and Don Woods of San Diego each had incredible first seasons. Jones was the first pick of the entire draft, and he did not disappoint. The 6'8" Jones devastated pass pockets from his defensive end position. His huge size made it difficult for opposing quarterbacks to throw over him on out patterns toward the sidelines. Almost immediately, Jones drew double team blockers into his side, and thereby relieved pressure on fellow defensive line teammates like Harvey Martin, Larry Cole, Bill Gregory, and Jethro Pugh. Jones succeeded right from the start, accumulating two and a half sacks in his first pro game in 1974 at Atlanta, a 24–0 Cowboys victory. "We've got a good defensive nucleus for the future," said Dallas head coach Tom Landry following the win over the Falcons. "They [Jones, Martin, etc.] were moving off the ball and tackling well."

On the offensive side of the line of scrimmage, running back Don Woods was waived by Green Bay just prior to the start of the regular season. The Chargers obtained him for the $100 waiver price. Woods would go on to set a rookie rushing record with 1,162 yards and a 5.1 yards per carry average. His rushing totals were the highest in San Diego history at that time. In the third week of the season, Woods ran the power sweep several times against visiting Miami for a total of 157 yards and a touchdown in a 28–21 loss. The next week against the visiting Philadelphia Eagles, Woods rushed for 133 yards on 21 carries in a 13–7 loss. A third straight 100-yard game was earned by Woods in a narrow 14–10 loss to arch-rival Oakland the following week. Woods was now becoming a marked man. Defenses were ready to key on him, but San Diego's offensive line was good enough and healthy enough to keep opening holes for the rookie runner. By midseason, it became obvious that the Packers had made a big mistake in letting Woods go. Packers head coach Dan Devine said it bluntly by stating, "We goofed." The Chargers would only win five games in 1974, but Woods made first-year history in the NFL and was named the league's consensus Rookie of the Year.

No other team in NFL history, however, had a better class of rookies than the 1974 Pittsburgh Steelers. Of the 15 first-year players who made the Steeler squad, four would later be named to the Pro Football Hall of Fame. Receivers John Stallworth and Lynn Swann joined center Mike Webster and middle linebacker Jack Lambert to don a gold Hall of Fame jacket in future years. Incredibly, all four were selected in the first five rounds of the 1974 draft. Other Steeler rookies from that season like defensive back Donnie Shell, tight end Randy Grossman, and running back Reggie Harrison, would all one day become Pittsburgh Super Bowl heroes.

The Steelers also found themselves making league history in the second week of the 1974 season when they visited the Denver Broncos. The game marked the first time that the new league overtime rules came into play. It was part track meet, part boxing match, and all see-saw. The lead changed hands several times, and both defenses struggled throughout the day. A major standout performer for the Broncos was running back Otis Armstrong, who rushed for 131 yards and added another 86 yards receiving. Armstrong also posted two touchdown receptions against the Steel Curtain defense. Pittsburgh countered with the play of quarterback Joe Gilliam and fullback Steve Davis. Gilliam threw for one score and ran for another, and Davis tallied two short touchdown runs and one magnificent 61-yard touchdown reception on a screen pass from Gilliam. The game ended when Denver's Jim Turner missed a field goal near the end of the overtime period. Not to be outdone, Steelers kicker Roy Gerela had his previous game-winning field goal attempt blocked at the end of the fourth quarter. "This game was destined to be a tie," said Denver head coach John Ralston. "Both teams played their hearts out. We came on strong early and had good momentum, but Pittsburgh is that kind of team which will come back and just whittle away. We had our shot, and they had theirs. I don't think either team deserved to lose and neither did."

Another overtime game later in the season earned the distinction of becoming the first regular season overtime game where a winner was declared under the new overtime rules. The New York Jets visited the historic Yale Bowl on November 10 to play their cross-state rivals, the New York Giants. The Jets were mired in a six-game losing streak. Many of their fans had long since given up on them for the season, but the Jets were confident that they could at least beat the Giants (2–6), who had only won one more game than the Jets at that point of the season. Fortunately for the Jets, their star quarterback Joe Namath was healthy enough on this day to play. Namath had braces curtailing movement in both of his multi-injured knees. Yet there he was, calling signals over center. In order to tie the game and force an extra overtime period, however, the gimpy-legged Namath called what was perhaps the most surprising play of the decade. On third down from the Giants' 3-yard line, Namath called "34 wham," a straight-ahead dive play where the halfback follows lead blocks right into the line behind the right guard. But instead of handing the ball off to halfback Emerson Boozer, Namath faked the handoff and bootlegged around left end for the tying touchdown. The play was unique because no one on the Jets expected Namath to keep the ball. "Of course I didn't tell Boozer, I didn't tell anyone," Namath said later. "It works better that way." The teams were thus knotted at 20–20 and were headed for sudden death overtime.

Even more fortunate for the Jets was a controversial 42-yard missed field goal in the overtime period by Giants kicker Pete Gogolak, the league's first soccer-style kicker. "They [the referees] took it away from me," said Gogolak after the game. "It wasn't even close."

The Jets moved down the field after Gogolak's miss and put together the elements of a winning drive. Namath once again displayed his passing prowess and his strategical awareness. On one crucial play, he quickly noticed the Giants defense shift into a double-double coverage, where the cornerbacks and safeties double-teamed both wide receivers. Jets tight end Rich Caster noticed it too, and sprinted down the middle of the field like a startled deer in a wide grassy field. Namath hit him in stride for 42 yards. A few plays later with the ball at the 5-yard line, Namath threw a bullet pass in the corner of the end zone to Boozer, who snared it for the winning touchdown. The Jets had prevailed, 26–20, with 6 minutes and 53 seconds elapsed in the overtime period. The Jets had won the bragging rights for New York City, and they would not lose another game for the remainder of the season.

Speaking of losing, another team in 1974 who came into the year with a history of consecutive losing seasons was the Houston Oilers. Head coach Sid Gillman replaced Bill Peterson near the end of the previous year, and assumed the dual roles of head coach and general manager. Gillman was credited by many football historians with perfecting the modern pro passing game. His 1963 AFL Champion San Diego Chargers were legendary for their point-scoring abilities through the air. Oiler fans hoped that Gillman would bring some of that magic to Texas and resurrect a team that was 1–18 prior to his ascension to the head coaching position. Right from the very first game in 1974, Oiler fans could tell that their team was new and improved. Houston defeated the visiting Chargers on opening day, 21–14. The Oilers then lost five straight games, and the public began feeling let down again. During that time, however, Houston traded defensive end John Matuszak to the Kansas City Chiefs for nose guard Curley Culp. This one switch helped the Oiler defense immensely, and they began surrendering points grudgingly. The Oilers rebounded to win their next four games, with their defense giving up an average of only 14 points per game during that streak. At one point in an 18-quarter span late in the season, the Houston defense gave up only two touchdowns. Included in the winning binge were stunning victories in both divisional contests against defending AFC Central Champion Cincinnati. In the 12th week of the 1974 season, Houston traveled to Pittsburgh and in a steady and freezing rain they managed to upset the Steelers, 13–10. The Oiler defense limited the Pittsburgh offense to a lowly total of 84 yards, and by season's end, had accumulated 40 quarterback sacks, good enough for third best in the NFL. "We've been patsies, but I hope we'll not be patsies anymore," said Gillman after the game.

The Oilers went from one win in 1973 to achieving a 7–7 record in 1974, and Gillman could now add "miracle worker" to his resume. Gillman was ultimately named Coach of the Year in the AFC.

The Coach of the Year in the NFC had his own reclamation project in the works in 1974. Don Coryell left the San Diego State University head coaching job in 1973, and immediately began rebuilding the St. Louis Cardinals. Like Gillman, Coryell had gained a solid reputation as a teacher of the passing game. To quarterback his offense, Coryell settled on veteran Jim Hart, who was an on-again, off-again starter for the club since making the team's taxi squad in 1966. Coryell built a very strong offensive line to protect his quarterback. Included in that line was future Hall of Fame tackle Dan Dierdorf and notorious guard Conrad Dobler, who earned that notoriety from his style of play. Dobler was unanimously accepted by his peers as the dirtiest player in the league, and quite possibly the dirtiest player in NFL history. The stories of his exploits are voluminous, and very few questionable elements were off limits for Dobler. Be it eye gouging, leg whipping, spitting in the face of an opponent, head slapping (if defensive linemen could do it, so could Dobler), hitting an opponent after the whistle, offensive holding (yes, most offensive linemen were guilty of it on occasion, but Dobler could have been flagged for it on almost every play), and kicking an opponent, Dobler could do it all. Perhaps the worst place for an opponent of Dobler's to find himself was in a pileup, a place where Conrad exhibited his true talents. Screams and groans were often heard by players who were stuck in a melee of bodies with Dobler nearby.

According to many defensive linemen, Dobler's most artistic cheap shots came when he leg whipped an opponent. To pull this move off, Dobler would allow a defensive lineman to get a step past him while rushing the quarterback. He would then—from a crouched position—wheel his outside leg backwards in a lightning fast motion, with his heel striking the back of an opponent's leg, sending the unfortunate recipient to the turf. Many a linemen would spend countless hours in a whirlpool after a Sunday contending with Conrad Dobler. The most humorous aspect to all of this (if one could call any of Dobler's actions humorous) was the fact that Dobler would regularly insist on his innocence, as he complained constantly to the referees that his opponents were off-sides.

Dobler was also not above using foreign materials to help him get an edge in battle. He once played with an injured forearm, and had it wrapped in a plaster cast. Dobler was not the first nor the last lineman to utilize such "padding," but he used that weapon all day long in a game against Dallas. Lee Roy Jordan, the Cowboys' veteran middle linebacker, was accused of biting Dobler, an infraction that Dobler was accused of numerous times. "Yeah, I tried to bite him," Jordan admitted. "But I was on my back and he was trying to shove his cast through my facemask."

Other players in later years recalled their favorite memories of Dobler. In a game against the New York Giants toward the end of the season, Jim Pietrzak, a defensive tackle for the Giants, recalled, "I just went up to him [Dobler] and wished him good luck in the playoffs, and he turned around and punched me in the throat." For his part, Dobler always responded in a matter-of-fact style. "All I know is that I'd hate to play across from someone like me," he said. "My style is aggressive … robust … competitive." Dallas defensive tackle Jethro Pugh once described Dobler as "the holdingest mother in the league." According to authors Bruce Nash and Allan Zullo in the book *The Football Hall of Shame*, Dobler was becoming known around the league for biting opponents, a charge that Dobler denied, due to what he described as his "high regard for oral hygiene." Minnesota defensive end Doug Sutherland had to face Dobler in the 1974 divisional playoffs, and actually asked the team physician at halftime for a rabies shot because Dobler was biting him. "I never played a football game before where I had to worry about rabies," Sutherland recalled. Nash and Zullo also relate a story when Dobler decided to punch Oakland linebacker Phil Villapiano in the ribs because, as he later told Villapiano, "I knew your ribs were injured." A final example from Nash and Zullo spotlighting Dobler's competitive nature occurred during another game with Dallas. Dobler noticed that Cowboys safety Cliff Harris was groggy after a block from another player and was just getting back on his feet. "I was about 20 yards away," Dobler stated. "But I thought, 'Why not? What the hell!' I hit him [Harris] alongside the earlobe and his head bounced three or four times." Harris was carried off the field on a stretcher after this incident.

Dobler and the Cardinals quickly showed their competitive nature and surprised everyone in the league by building a 7–0 record to start the 1974 season. Included in those seven victories were wins against division rivals Philadelphia and Dallas, and a season sweep of arch-rival Washington. It was a big play offense that made St. Louis contenders. Halfback Terry Metcalf was nothing short of sensational, breaking a club record for total combined yardage (rushing, receiving, and returns) with 2,058 yards. Fleet wide receiver Mel Gray was a feared game breaker, catching 39 passes for 770 yards (a 19.7 yards per catch average) and six touchdowns. Fellow receiver Earl Thomas caught 34 more passes and five touchdowns, and tight end Jackie Smith grabbed 25 more passes for 413 yards. Quarterback Jim Hart was named NFC Player of the Year, leading the conference with 200 completions and 20 touchdown passes.

"We're so pleased with Jimmy and the way he's come into his own," said Coryell. "He's been a very good leader out there, very calm, very cool, and he doesn't seem to get rattled at all." Hart, who was emerging into the upper echelon of signal callers in 1974 as one of the better passers in the league, returned the complement by admitting that Coryell is "a very offensive-minded coach. His offense is very imaginative, innovative, and very exciting."

The Cards by season's end would succeed by producing big plays, and would lose the ball on fumbles only nine times. Hart contributed to controlling the pigskin by throwing only eight interceptions all year, and two of those bounced off his receivers' hands. The St. Louis defense was also vastly improved, giving up only 218 points in 1974 compared to 365 the year before.

"The best approach [for our team] was beating both Philadelphia and Washington in the first two games and giving them three and ten points," said Cardinals defensive coordinator Ray Willsey. "Our players could see that what we had been preaching to them could come to pass."

Despite the strategical approaches and changing trends in the game, a couple of seeming constants remained … well, constant. Both the Miami Dolphins and the Oakland Raiders continued their winning ways in 1974. The Dolphins entered the year in quest of a third straight world championship, something that had not been accomplished since the legendary Lombardi-led Packers of the late 1960s. The challenge would be difficult to put it lightly. No team had ever won three straight Super Bowls, and head coach Don Shula wanted desperately to make history by being the first team to earn that distinction. The Raiders were still smarting after their loss to Miami in the 1973 AFC championship game, and they were determined to make amends for that loss in 1974.

The Dolphins began the season by suffering a surprise 34–24 defeat at the hands of the New

England Patriots in Foxboro on opening day. Head coach Chuck Fairbanks' team surprised the No-Name Defense with a balanced offensive attack. Running backs Sam "Bam" Cunningham and Mack Herron combined for 175 yards rushing and one touchdown apiece. But it was Fairbanks' defense which determined the victor. The Patriot defense sacked Miami quarterback Bob Griese four times and continually pressured him throughout the game. The Dolphin rushing attack was limited to 89 yards in a losing effort. The Dolphins were not defending world champions by accident, however. They responded with eight victories in their next nine games.

"Letdowns are for losers," said Miami middle linebacker Nick Buoniconti. "Besides, how can you have a letdown the way that guy [Shula] keeps you working on an even keel."

The Raiders also lost their first game (to Buffalo), but they also responded by running off a string of victories. Oakland won their next nine games, and would lose only once more in the regular season. Included in the Raider winning streak were key wins over divisional foes Kansas City, San Diego, and Denver. Head coach John Madden's defense had given up only 200 points by the 12th week of the season, a mark which was third-best in the AFC. Oakland's offense was even better, scoring 355 points in 1974, the highest total in the NFL. Oakland's statistics were compiled by an unlikely group of men. Madden's players earned the reputation of renegades, men who wore out their welcomes at other teams and who were given one last chance to stay in the league with the Raiders. That may have been true to an extent, but Madden was always looking for something more than stop-gap measures when forming his roster.

"We look for players who can contribute to the organization over a long period of time," Madden said. "We look for long-range solidity, not for the momentary contribution." Such veteran leadership made it easy for Oakland to focus in on the playoffs.

The mid-season of 1974, however, brought into focus some of the divisional battles that would take place in this highly competitive season. Some teams that had a good start had already begun their decent into losing, while others were getting a first taste of defeat. Still other teams were able to make amends for their earlier mistakes and began putting together winning streaks. The Philadelphia Eagles began the season with optimistic 4–1 mark, but by mid-season were mired in the middle of a six-game losing streak. The New England Patriots would take their undefeated record into Buffalo and would have their hands full in dealing with a strong Bills team. The St. Louis Cardinals hit several stumbling blocks which brought them back to reality, and teams like the Los Angeles Rams, the Minnesota Vikings, and the Pittsburgh Steelers each eventually took control of their destinies and won some key games in their drives for division titles.

Head coach Mike McCormack's Eagles had a formidable passing attack, but little else. Tight end Charlie Young led the NFC in pass receptions with 63, and 6'8" wide receiver Harold Carmichael caught eight touchdown passes, tops in the conference. Venerable signal caller Roman Gabriel was often injured during 1974, however, and his statistics fell accordingly from the previous year. Still, Gabriel's abilities were a weapon worth having ... when he was on the field. Once defenses caught up to what Philadelphia was doing on offense, they shut down the air lanes and sent the Eagles back to earth. Philadelphia was shutout by cross-state rival Pittsburgh on November 3, 27–0. Two weeks later, they could manage only three points in a loss to division rival St. Louis. Their second loss to Washington on November 24 was a 26–7 thrashing. The Eagles' offense scored 68 fewer points in 1974 than what they scored in 1973, the direct result of their mid-season losing streak. McCormack decided late in the year to replace Gabriel with Mike Boryla, a rookie quarterback from Stanford. Philadelphia rallied behind Boryla to win their final three games of the season and finished with a 7–7 record, their best mark in eight years.

The New England Patriots visited Rich Stadium in Buffalo on October 20 with an undefeated record. The Bills had only lost once and were boasting a 4–1 mark entering the first of two important divisional games with the Pats. Both of New England's starting wide receivers—Darryl Stingley and Randy Vataha—would both miss this first game against Buffalo with injuries, and one of their other receivers—Reggie Rucker—played the game with a fractured wrist. New England's 3–4 defense, designed by head coach Chuck Fairbanks, was strong, however, and had not given up a touchdown in the previous nine quarters of play. Buffalo's defense was also tough, as it was ranked number one in the AFC. Yet it was the offenses which told the tale in this game. Right from the first play from scrimmage, you could tell that this was going to be a high-scoring affair. New England running back Sam "Bam" Cunningham broke off right tackle and was off to the races. His 75-yard touchdown jaunt gave the Patriots some early momentum, but Buffalo answered back with three touchdowns of their own—all in the first quarter. Buffalo quarterback Joe Ferguson had one of the most productive games of his career. He threw three touchdown passes against the Pats. One went to superstar runner O.J. Simpson, and two went to tight end Paul Seymour, who caught his first touchdown on a 10-yard pass over the middle, and his second on a 40-yard rollout pass deep down the sideline. Simpson's catch and carry for a score was pure Simpson. He juked to the middle of the field, slipped two attempted arm tackles, broke to the wide side of the field, and raced into the end zone to complete a 29-yard scoring play. Both defenses settled down in the second half, however. The Bills never lost the lead after the first quarter, and New England left with their first blemish of the season, 30–28.

In the second meeting at Foxboro between these two teams, both were 6–1 heading into the game. Both were also once again able to move the ball on each other. In fact, a total of over 700 yards was accumulated by both teams on offense. Mack Herron would end up catching two touchdown passes from Jim Plunkett, and scored once more on a short run late in the third quarter. It was evident that it would take some big plays to make the difference in this contest, and it was the Buffalo defense that made them. Buffalo linebacker Merv Krakau quelled a second quarter New England drive near the Bills' goal line with a key interception of an errant Jim Plunkett pass. Krakau toted his prize 37 yards, which set up a Buffalo scoring drive and a 1-yard Simpson touchdown dive just before halftime. Bills' outside linebacker Dave Washington then did teammate Krakau one better when he snagged a Plunkett pass in the third quarter and sprinted 72 yards down the sideline for a touchdown. Plunkett's pass down the middle was intended for Sam Cunningham, but the lanky 6–5 Washington stepped in front of Cunningham and was never touched as he ran into the end zone.

New England to its credit came back and retook the lead when Herron swept right for a 2-yard touchdown, giving the Patriots a 28–26 lead. Buffalo answered back with a 47-yard field goal by John Leypoldt, his third of the game. It gave the Bills a 29–28 lead. New England responded in the final two minutes with a drive down to the Buffalo 39-yard line. Patriots kicker John Smith attempted a 46-yard field goal attempt with but a few seconds left on the clock. Incredibly, Buffalo substitute defensive tackle Jeff Yeates burrowed into the line at the snap of the ball and managed to block Smith's attempt. The Bills had prevailed again over their divisional foes, 29–28. After the game, Yeates claimed that his blocked kick was "one of those things you practice 100 times, and it works once."

Like the Patriots had experienced with the Bills, the St. Louis Cardinals also ran into a buzzsaw at Busch Memorial Stadium on a Week 9 Monday night contest against the Minnesota Vikings. The Vikings had a reputation for pulling out tough games, but 1974 was a year that saw head coach Bud Grant's team lose its share of those close games as well. Minnesota was at home in Week 7 and took a 14–10 lead late in the fourth quarter against New England. Two key passes by Patriots quarterback Jim Plunkett made the difference. One of Plunkett's passes went to wide receiver Randy Vataha, who made a splendid over-the-shoulder catch on a deep fly pattern for 55 yards. The second one to tight end Bob Windsor won the game for the Pats, 17–14. Windsor caught the ball at the 2-yard line and wedged himself close to the end zone while stretching the ball over the goal line to complete the winning 10-yard reception with no time remaining. Windsor, unfortunately, broke his leg on the play and was out for the season.

Minnesota had a two-game lead in the NFC Central Division going into the St. Louis game, and the Cardinals were fresh from their first loss of the season, a 17–14 nerve-wracker in Dallas. The Vikings were behind at halftime against St. Louis, but this time, their comeback was secured with a 13-yard run on a misdirection trap play by halfback Chuck Foreman, and an 11-yard rollout score by quarterback Fran Tarkenton. Minnesota's defense also came through when it needed to most on St. Louis' final drive. A couple of Jim Hart's desperation passes were deflected by Minnesota defenders and fell incomplete. The Vikings prevailed, 28–24. St. Louis was its own worst enemy in this game. Two Cardinal fumbles led directly to two Minnesota touchdowns. "We just didn't have enough time at the end and the two early fumbles hurt us," said Cardinals head coach Don Coryell after the game. A bright spot for the Cards was the play of quarterback Hart, who completed 28 passes for 353 yards and two touchdowns against one of the best defenses in the NFL.

The mid-season was now past, and the real contenders for the playoffs were beginning to surface. Most of the divisions had at least two teams vying for control. The NFC East was a competitive division but also one that seemed to open up a bit by the end of the tenth week of the season. The Dallas Cowboys were just about in a must-win situation when they traveled to Washington to play the first of two games against their arch-rivals, the Redskins. It was a tale of two halves, as the Redskins dominated the first half, and the Cowboys did likewise in the second half. Washington's 28–0 halftime lead was highlighted by a spectacular punt return by Ken Houston, who leapt over one Cowboy and broke attempted tackles by two others en route to a 58-yard journey to the end zone. Dallas came back strong in the second half with power runs by halfback Calvin Hill, and some clutch catches by tight end Billy Joe DuPree. Late in the fourth quarter, DuPree dove for a Roger Staubach pass and snared it in the end zone with Ken Houston draped all over him. It was DuPree's second scoring catch of the game, and it tightened the score to 28–21. The Cowboys were only a seven yards away from a tie with seconds left in the game when Staubach's desperation fourth-down pass skidded off wide receiver Drew Pearson's shoulder pad and bounced to the turf. The Redskins prevailed, but barely.

"Staubach got too much time to throw," said Redskins defensive tackle Diron Talbert. "He's accurate when he gets time." Washington head coach George Allen was despondent at his team's failure to stay focused. "It seems like we have to do everything the hard way," Allen said. "I warned them at halftime but it's pretty difficult to get the point across when you're that far ahead." Talbert concluded, "We played hard when we had to play hard."

Another big game with two hard-playing teams in the tenth week of the season occurred in the AFC East, where the Buffalo Bills traveled down to the Orange Bowl to take on the Miami Dolphins. Both teams were 7–2 entering the contest, with New England hot on their backs at 6–3. Buffalo looked like they would shock Miami when safety Tony Greene intercepted a Bob Griese pass intended for Paul Warfield deep in the end zone. Greene broke several attempted tackles and raced down the sideline for an apparent 107-yard return for a touchdown. Buffalo was called for defensive holding, however, and on the next play, Miami running back Larry Csonka plowed through the middle of the line for a 2-yard touchdown. The Dolphins scored once more before the half when Griese hit Warfield for a 49-yard touchdown on a deep post pattern. The teams traded touchdowns in the third quarter, and they also traded injuries. Csonka went out for the Dolphins with an overturned ankle, and quarterback Joe Ferguson went out for the Bills with knee contusions. The fourth quarter saw an incredible five touchdowns scored between the two teams. Buffalo linebacker Dave Washington picked up a Mercury Morris fumble and sped to a 42-yard touchdown. When the Bills got the ball again, Ferguson's replacement, rookie Gary Marangi from Boston College, connected on his first ever pro pass for a score. On that play, Marangi launched the ball deep for wide receiver J.D. Hill, who make a spectacular diving catch as he crossed the goal line to give Buffalo a 21–21 tie. Vital to the outcome of that play was a spectacular block by fullback Jim Braxton, who leveled blitzing Miami linebacker Larry Ball.

An 11-yard touchdown run by Csonka's replacement, Don Nottingham, was answered with a late scoring drive by Marangi, who hit wide receiver Bob Chandler on a 5-yard rollout pass to tie the game at 28 apiece. With but seconds remaining, the Buffalo defense had nothing left in their tank, and permitted another long pass to Warfield down the sideline. Warfield finished the day with four catches for 139 yards and a touchdown. Nottingham finished the winning drive with a 23-yard trap run up the middle against a safety blitz for a score with 19 seconds left to play. The Dolphins had proved once again victorious over the Bills, 35–28. "We've got to beat these people one of these days," lamented Buffalo head coach Lou Saban, "but we haven't been able to do it."

A New York Jets squad had trouble beating the Dolphins too, but on the following Sunday, they managed to do just that at Shea Stadium. Joe Namath threw two touchdown passes to tight end Rich Caster, the second one a 45-yard beauty right down the middle of the field late in the fourth quarter. "We showed them [Miami's defensive secondary] a formation that they hadn't seen all day," said Caster. "They got mixed up and I got wide open behind them." New York running back John Riggins returned from a previous injury and contributed 93 yards rushing to the cause, and rookie cornerback Roscoe Word ended the drama by intercepting a last-minute Bob Griese pass to preserve a dramatic 17–14 win. The Jets had avenged an earlier loss to the Dolphins, and had quietly and suddenly put together a three-game winning streak.

Similar to the Jets win over the Dolphins was the Denver upset victory over Oakland on the same day. The Denver rushing attack had its best day of the year. Fullback Jon Keyworth gained 148 yards and halfback Otis Armstrong ran for 146 more on 29 carries. Both runners broke numerous attempted Raider arm-tackles throughout the game. The Broncos ended Oakland's nine-game winning streak with a 20–17 win.

The Rams also made a statement against the visiting Vikings on November 24. The Rams came from behind to beat Minnesota, 20–17, and improved their record to 8–3, thus becoming the first NFC team to clinch their division title. Behind 17–6 in the fourth quarter, Los Angeles quarterback James Harris led two clutch scoring drives against the Purple Gang. The first ended with a 1-yard dive by Harris, his second rushing touchdown of the game. The second ended with a Harris lob into the end zone that was snared by wide receiver Jack Snow over rookie Minnesota cornerback Jackie Wallace for a 8-yard touchdown with 1:14 to play. "The play was a quick go," said Snow after the game. "Wallace came up to bump me at the start. I made a little quick move and got passed him. James [Harris] laid it right out there." The victory gave Los Angeles the confidence it needed to know that they could come back and win a tough game over a playoff-caliber team.

The two traditional Thanksgiving games were important to the playoff picture. In the first game, both the Denver Broncos and the Detroit Lions were still mathematically in the fight for the postseason. Detroit had won six of its past seven games, while the Broncos could not afford to lose any more games with a 5–5–1 record. Earlier in the season, the Lions managed to beat nemesis Minnesota for the first time in 14 games. They still—with some luck down the stretch—could contend for the NFC wild card. The Lions took a 17–10 lead against Denver into halftime, but were crushed in the third quarter by a 21-point Bronco barrage. Denver regrouped amidst the snowflakes of Tiger Stadium with a key recovery of an onside kickoff by reserve running back Fran Lynch to begin the second half. "Myrel Moore suggested the onside kick at halftime," explained Denver head coach John Ralston, referring to one of his assistants. "That had to be the big play of the second half," admitted Detroit quarterback Greg Landry. Denver running back Jon Keyworth ran for his second 1-yard touchdown of the game in the third quarter, and halfback Otis Armstrong became the league's first 1,000-yard rusher of the season when he accumulated 144 yards against the strong Detroit defense. Denver held on for a 31–27 victory, and remained alive for a possible playoff berth.

The Dallas Cowboys were also trying to remain alive for the playoffs, but the going for them would be tough. The second Thanksgiving game of 1974 has been regarded by many fans and pro football historians alike as the most memorable Thanksgiving contest ever. A sportswriting panel at the end of the decade regarded the game as the fourth-most memorable regular season game of the decade. The Cowboys had to contend with the visiting arch-rival Washington Redskins, who were two full games ahead of Dallas in the NFC East standings. On the surface, this appeared to be just another typical Cowboys-Redskins bruise-a-thon, and by all accounts, it certainly was. But the game was much more than that. It showed a glimpse into the past in the elements of NFL strategy, and it also took a glance at the league's future. In the second half of this contest, the game's strategy was narrowed down to throwing the ball to the open man. It was also marked by the hope that all rookies in the league have, that they can come in off the bench and contribute to the welfare of their team by producing a game-winning effort or play in one way or another.

The Redskins and Cowboys began this rematch in Texas Stadium by being unable to penetrate each other's end zones. Washington's Mark Moseley kicked three field goals in the first half, while Dallas placekicker Efren Herrera managed to kick one for a 9–3 halftime deficit. The battle of field goals did little to indicate the amount of expected hard hits that were distributed by both defenses, however. The "Over The Hill Gang" did the most damage in the middle of the third quarter. Redskins linebacker Dave Robinson knocked out Dallas quarterback Roger Staubach by giving him a concussion to put an abrupt ending to one of his scrambles. Washington defensive tackle Diron Talbert planned for just such a benefit earlier in the week when he told reporters "If you knock Staubach out, they don't have anyone with any experience behind him. That's one of our goals."

Staubach's injury left Dallas head coach Tom Landry with a forlorn predicament. Landry only had a rookie to back Staubach up, and although no one knew it at the moment, Clint Longley (the rookie) would become the answer to a sports fan's trivia question for generations to come. Longley, from Abilene Christian, entered the game without so much as a warm-up toss on the sideline, and systematically picked the Washington pass defense apart. Longley hit on 11 of 20 passes for 203 yards and two touchdowns against one of the most experienced defenses in the NFL. Dallas defensive end Larry Cole described Longley's performance as "a victory for the uncluttered mind," meaning that the young quarterback did not have enough basic information to dissect the keys and tendencies in head coach Tom Landry's complicated offense. Longley simply threw the ball to whomever he saw open. Calling an audible at the line of scrimmage? No way. Just call the play that the coach sends in. Longley stuck to that strategy and drove the Cowboys downfield. He threw his first touchdown pass to tight end Billy Joe DuPree from 35 yards out, then led another drive which resulted in a Walt Garrison 1-yard scoring plunge.

Longley's efforts were needed, because the Redskins had earned a 16–3 lead, then later in the fourth quarter a 23–17 lead, thanks in large part to the rushing and receiving heroics of a prodigal son (of sorts). Duane Thomas had returned to Dallas wearing a Redskins uniform, the result

of his efforts to get back into the NFL following a career that was cut short by his own disillu-
sionment with the sport. Three years after contributing to the Cowboys' first world championship
in Super Bowl VI, Thomas on this Thanksgiving Day did everything he could to put an end to
his old team's playoff chances. Thomas caught one scoring pass when he circled out of the backfield
and made a great adjustment to the ball in the end zone on a 9-yard pass from quarterback Billy
Kilmer. He also ran to daylight in the fourth quarter when he saw the middle clogged up and
sprinted to the outside for a 19-yard score, outracing Dallas defensive backs Benny Barnes and
Cliff Harris to the end zone pylon.

The scene was now set for Longley's greatest pro football moment, and one that would be
remembered by Dallas fans everywhere and for all time. Saddled with a six-point deficit and facing
a third down situation at midfield with only seconds remaining, Longley dropped back and threw
deep down the sideline for wide receiver Drew Pearson. The Washington pass rush on the play
was good, but so was the Dallas pass protection. Pearson outraced reserve Redskins safety Ken
Stone, who inexplicably stopped running at the 15-yard line when he turned his head backward
to locate the arching football. Pearson did not stop running, however, and caught the ball in stride
as he crossed the goal line. Bedlam erupted in Texas Stadium, and the name Clint Longley went
into the history books. "Passing is the part of the game that's always intrigued me," said Longley
after the game. "It has the most shocking influence on the game. Things happen so much faster."
The Cowboys had shocked the Redskins, winning 24–23, and as a result had survived for one
more week. They were (thanks to Longley's miraculous effort) still in the hunt for a playoff berth.
"We really let Dallas off the hook today," lamented Washington safety Brig Owens. The Redskins
nevertheless remained a game ahead of Dallas with an 8–4 mark, but were still a game behind the
NFC East–leading St. Louis Cardinals.

Desperation was now setting in amidst teams which found themselves in must-win games.
Teams like New England, Houston, Denver, Cincinnati, Dallas, and Detroit were facing elimination
from the postseason if they could not put together a string of victories during the final three
games. Other teams, like the Buffalo Bills and the Washington Redskins, found themselves just
one or two wins away from clinching a playoff berth. It seemed as if the 1974 season had more
than its share of competitive games during the final month of the season, possibly more than any
other year in the decade.

The Bills faced the visiting Baltimore Colts at Rich Stadium on November 1, but they also
faced frigid temperatures and a wind that was whipping at 30 miles per hour. Both the Bills and
the Colts were unable to put together any strong offensive drives throughout the game. Young
and daring Baltimore quarterback Bert Jones somehow managed to pierce the biting winds for
170 yards passing. Unfortunately for Jones, the Buffalo defense was able to infiltrate his passing
pocket to the tune of eight sacks for 70 yards in losses. "We were stunting about fifty per cent of
the time," explained Buffalo defensive end Walt Patulski, "and they weren't picking us up." Buffalo
superstar running sensation O.J. Simpson gained 67 yards on the ground, good enough for him
to break the 1,000 yard rushing mark for the third straight season. But Buffalo tight end Paul Seymour felt some measure of misfortune when he dropped an easy touchdown pass in the second
half. Seymour was covered loosely in the end zone by Colts safety Rick Volk on the play, but he
(Seymour) was fully covering his hands. Seymour wore leather gloves for one of the rare times
in his career, and those gloves did not help him grasp a perfect pass from quarterback Joe Ferguson.
The Bills would have to settle for two wind-blown field goals by placekicker John Leypoldt. Fortunately for Buffalo, their defense delivered one of its best performances of the season, and shut
out the Colts. Key to the outcome of the game was a goal line stand by the Bills defense in the
fourth quarter. The 6–0 final score would be just enough for the Bills to clinch the AFC wild card.

Another important game in Week 12 was held in Pittsburgh's Three Rivers Stadium. The Steelers had been dealing with a hard-to-determine season, good one week, lackluster the next. Regardless of how well or how poorly they played, Pittsburgh nevertheless continued to win games. Quarterback Terry Bradshaw had won his job by default. Both Joe Gilliam and Terry Hanratty had started at quarterback for the Steelers in several weeks in 1974, but Bradshaw proved to be the best (and healthiest at this point of the season) of the three. Head coach Chuck Noll's team had won eight, lost two, and tied one heading into their contest with a surprising Houston Oilers team. The Oilers were in the midst of their best season in years, compiling five wins and beating teams that no one expected them to beat. Pittsburgh was one of those teams, but sub-par weather conditions such as a freezing rain combined with strong and blustery winds, was not enough to keep the Oilers from accomplishing their mission. Houston's Fred Willis caught a 6-yard second quarter flare pass from quarterback Dan Pastorini which gave the Oilers a 7–3 lead. Houston linebacker Gregg Bingham then intercepted a Terry Bradshaw pass which bounced off of wide receiver Ron Shanklin's chest late in the fourth quarter. Bingham ran it back 18 yards to the Pittsburgh 19-yard line, setting up the winning score. Oilers placekicker Skip Butler connected on a 34-yard field goal with 2:32 remaining to claim a 13–10 upset victory over their AFC Central foes. The win was Houston's sixth in the past seven games.

The New York Jets were—like Houston—experiencing a sudden string of wins. The Jets won their fourth straight game by defeating visiting San Diego on December 1, 27–14. Key to the New Yorkers' triumph was the play of quarterback Joe Namath, who in the midst of a torrential downpour, completed 17 of 27 for 254 yards and a touchdown. Jets running back John Riggins scored all three of New York's touchdowns. "We felt like we could throw on them," said Namath after the game. "Our running game was going good too, so we could mix it up pretty well." San Diego Rookie of the Year Don Woods—despite the loss—kept his marvelous season going strong with 142 rushing yards, his sixth 100-yard rushing effort of the year.

The Minnesota Vikings had lost two straight games prior to Week 12, but then the New Orleans Saints paid a visit to Metropolitan Stadium. Minnesota regained its winning ways with an easy 29–9 victory, highlighted by three Fran Tarkenton touchdown passes. "We put somebody in the Pro Bowl every week," dead-panned the disgusted Saints head coach John North. "This week it was Tarkenton." The win gave the Vikings another NFC Central Division title, their second in a row and their fourth in the past five years. "Now I can sleep better with the division race over," said relieved Minnesota head coach Bud Grant.

With two weeks left in the 1974 season, the playoff picture was finally getting clearer to see. Teams like the Miami Dolphins and the Pittsburgh Steelers would clinch division titles in Week 13. Other teams like the New England Patriots and the St. Louis Cardinals were mired in losing streaks which could be fatal to their postseason aspirations. The Cards, however, were the beneficiaries of weaker competition in the NFC. Late-season losses by Dallas, Detroit and Green Bay insured that St. Louis, by virtue of their better record, would at the very least obtain the NFC wild card slot in the playoffs. The knowledge of that fact may have caused the lackluster efforts from the Cardinals in losses to Kansas City and New Orleans. Still other teams like the Oakland Raiders and Los Angeles Rams were resting their starters en masse, with both having clinched their divisions a long time ago.

The defending champion Miami Dolphins ignored key injuries throughout the season to string together enough victories to earn the second-best record in the NFL. The Dolphins' 17–16 clutch victory over up-and-coming division rival Baltimore clinched the AFC East for Miami for the fourth straight year. The Dolphins took an early lead then held on for dear life as the Colts' comeback ended just short of victory. Head coach Don Shula's team won their final three games to post an impressive 11–3 mark. Miami had won eight of its past nine games, a typical streak for a Shula team to accomplish.

The Pittsburgh Steelers went into New England in Week 13 and won a tough game against the Patriots, 21–17. Like Miami discovered against the Colts, a team that is already eliminated from the postseason and therefore a team that has nothing to lose can often present huge problems for teams that are trying to clinch a playoff spot. The spoiler Patriots gave the Steelers a challenge with the offensive output of Mack Herron, who scored both New England touchdowns. Pittsburgh came back with their trademark rushing attack, led by Franco Harris, who accumulated 136 yards on the ground. "That Franco Harris is a load," said New England safety Jack Mildren. "He is the best running back that we played this year." Pittsburgh indeed had the best rushing attack in the AFC in 1974, gaining a total of 2,417 yards. A 7-yard Terry Bradshaw pass to diving wide receiver Lynn Swann, and a sack of Patriots quarterback Jim Plunkett in the end zone for a safety by defensive end L.C. Greenwood, cemented the victory for Pittsburgh. The win gave the Steelers their second division title ever and their third playoff appearance in the past three seasons. "This makes it three years in a row in the playoffs," said veteran Pittsburgh outside linebacker Andy Russell following the Patriots game. "Now we've got to do something—get into the big game, the Super Bowl." Pittsburgh's Steel Curtain defense would be a tough nut to crack in the playoffs. "We have a unique type of defense and it is honed around the kind of talent we have," admitted All-Pro Pittsburgh outside linebacker Jack Ham. Pittsburgh's defense was rated the best overall defensive unit in the AFC by year's end.

Sadly for the Patriots, they could not continue the blistering winning streak with which they had begun the 1974 season. Whereas the Jets turned their season completely around and started winning game after game during the second half of the season, the Patriots did the exact opposite. They started losing game after game, and with each loss, they watched their playoff chances get smaller and smaller. The bitter losses to Buffalo were a preview for embarrassing losses to teams like the Cleveland Browns and the New York Jets. Mack Herron would go on to set the all-purpose combined yardage record on the season's final Sunday, but even he felt that winning was more important. "Records is cool, but I'd rather have a win," Herron admitted after the Pats lost their last game of the season at Miami. The loss gave New England an unsatisfying 7–7 record for 1974. "I'm a competitor!" snapped New England head coach Chuck Fairbanks at a reporter after the Miami loss. "I don't like to lose no matter what the stakes are."

The stakes on winning were high for the St. Louis Cardinals, who also started out strong, but were hit with a couple of consecutive losses. On December 8, the Cardinals traveled to New Orleans and played down to below the level of their opponent. The Saints, behind third-string quarterback Larry Cipa, shut out the Cards, 14–0. The upset was triggered by Saints running back Alvin Maxson, who dashed for a 66-yard touchdown and who set a Saints team record by gaining 148 total ground yards. Maxson shrugged off five attempted tackles on the way to his touchdown. St. Louis shrugged off their lethargy and rebounded in the final week of the season by coming from behind to defeat the visiting new York Giants, 26–14. The Giants managed to take a 14–0 lead into halftime, something which undoubtedly had St. Louis worried. Cardinals head coach Don Coryell was expecting a comeback, however, and was quite impressed by his team's second half performance. "There were no inspiring words at halftime," recalled Coryell. "I knew my players were terribly embarrassed by the way the first half went. The second half was one of the finest comebacks of my football team I've ever been connected with."

St. Louis' key competitors in the NFC East were the Washington Redskins, who were busy with a tough contest in Los Angeles on *Monday Night Football*. The game with the Rams on December 9 in the Los Angeles Memorial Coliseum turned out to be a playoff preview, although no one knew it at the time. The Redskins scored 20 points in the second quarter en route to a 23–17 triumph. The win gave Washington a share of the NFC wild card heading into the final game of the season.

Buffalo had already earned the AFC wild card when they came to muddy and rainy Shea Stadium to take on the resurgent Jets. After a scoreless first half, Buffalo took a 7–0 lead when quarterback Joe Ferguson hit wide receiver J.D. Hill for a 41-yard catch and carry that culminated in the New York end zone. Hill came back for the ball on a hook pattern, wheeled around Jets cornerback Rich Sowells, and flashed his speed past Jets safety Phil Wise down the sideline for the score. The Jets responded by two touchdown passes from Joe Namath, one down the middle to tight end Rich Caster and one to wide receiver Jerome Barkum. Namath threw the ball high to Barkum, who out-jumped Buffalo defensive back Donnie Walker for the catch. Putting a final stamp of approval on the 20–10 Jets victory was veteran New York linebacker Ralph Baker, who caught a tipped Ferguson pass intended for O.J. Simpson and squashed 67 yards through the mud for the clinching touchdown.

The Dallas Cowboys did not have to contend with mud at Texas Stadium when they took on the Cleveland Browns, but they did have to deal with the specter of missing out on the playoffs for the first time in eight years. Dallas kept their slim playoff chances alive going into the final game of the year with a 41–17 thrashing of the Browns. Highlighting the Cowboys' scoring surge were three Roger Staubach touchdown passes, two of which went to wide receiver Golden Richards, and one to tight end Billy Joe DuPree. A week after Dallas' win over Cleveland, however, both the Redskins and the Cardinals won their respective games, thus giving the Cowboys a bitter taste of staying at home for the postseason.

The Oilers would be staying home for the postseason also, but they undoubtedly had a better feeling going into it than their North Texas neighbors. Houston and their head coach Sid Gillman outlasted visiting Cleveland 28–24 on the season's final Sunday, which earned for the Oilers a 7–7 record. Gillman had already decided by this time to turn over the head coaching reigns to one of his assistants, O.A. "Bum" Phillips. The Oilers could look back to 1974, however, as a season where they finally turned the corner and were done with the losing ways of the early part of the decade.

"I've been in this business a long time," said Gillman from a blaring postgame locker room following the victory over the Browns, "but this is the most satisfying season I've ever been through."

The Jets were also satisfied. They did some major league rebounding in 1974, dealing with the epic failure of a 1–7 start to finish 7–7 with a 45–38 win at Baltimore. The success of 1974 for New York hinged on gaining momentum from key upsets over division rivals Miami, New England, and Buffalo. Ironically, had the Jets defeated the Bills the first time that they played on September 29, they would be named the AFC's wild card team, not Buffalo. The Bills, however, were headed back to the playoffs for the first time since their old AFL days. The Steelers, Raiders, and Dolphins would join them in the AFC postseason, while St. Louis, Washington, Minnesota and Los Angeles would vie for supremacy in the NFC playoffs.

The 1974 season produced its share of important achievements, as well as its share of disappointing failures. Players like Baltimore's Lydell Mitchell and Denver's Otis Armstrong won individual honers. Mitchell from his halfback position led the league in pass receptions (72), a statistic that proved the opinion that many quarterbacks were dumping the ball off quicker instead of waiting in the pocket for a wide receiver to come clear in the confusing zone coverages in the defensive secondary. Armstrong led the league in rushing with 1,407 yards, almost 300 yards more than his next closest challenger. Armstrong's performance is even more astounding when one considers that the year before, he gained only a meager total of 90 yards rushing. Mack Herron of New England would go on to set the league's all-purpose yardage record, accumulating 2,444 yards rushing, pass receiving, and kick returning (punt and kickoff returns).

Several teams stood out in 1974, for both good and bad reasons. The Atlanta Falcons scored a league low of 111 points, the lowest number of points since the 14-game schedule was established in 1960. The Cleveland Browns ended the season with a record of 4–10, their first losing season since 1956. The Cincinnati Bengals won the AFC Central Division in 1973, but in 1974, they barely won seven games. Quarterback Ken Anderson won the NFL passing title, but head coach Paul Brown's squad suffered from losing both of their games with division foe Houston, and being upset by the likes of San Diego and Detroit. In their loss to Detroit, once the Bengals discovered that Pittsburgh had clinched the division with their win at New England, a majority of the Cincinnati defensive players suffered a letdown. Lions wide receiver Ron Jessie found himself all alone in the middle of the field and contributed a 45-yard catch and run which set up the winning touchdown. Speaking of Detroit, they had to contend with the unexpected death of their head coach (Don McCafferty) just prior to the start of the season. Yet under replacement head coach Rick Forzano, Detroit managed to improve their record to 7–7. All in all, the 1974 regular season offered opportunity to both young players (thanks to the early preseason players strike) and to the advantageous teams to achieve success.

The excitement produced in the 1974 regular season would be extended into the playoffs. The first postseason contest featured the NFC East Champion St. Louis Cardinals traveling to Minnesota to take on the NFC Central Champion Vikings. Both teams had played each other in the regular season, with the Vikings coming from behind in Busch Memorial Stadium to win a Monday Night contest over the Cardinals, 28–24. The day of the playoff game at Metropolitan Stadium was cold and overcast, which was perfect for winter football. An occasional gust of snow flurries filled the air, particularly in the second and third quarters. The Cardinals' big play passing offense was considered to be a formidable test for the Purple Gang. In the first quarter, the St. Louis offense was able to move the ball with the passing accuracy which marked their regular season success. The Vikings defense gave up yardage, but toughened up to stop Cardinal drives short of scoring. The same result was also true for St. Louis' defense. Minnesota surged into enemy territory, but could not register a score.

In the second quarter, the Cardinals benefitted from a couple of excellent deep punts by their punter, Hal Roberts. With the field position battle on their side for the moment, the Cards took over on the Minnesota 49 with 11:32 left in the second quarter. They put together a 10-play scoring drive, mixing an occasional run with a few accurate Jim Hart passes. The drive included a brief letdown on a 15-yard personal foul penalty by lineman Conrad Dobler (who else?), and was topped off by a 13-yard pass from Hart to wide receiver Earl Thomas for a touchdown. Thomas ran clear across the field, outran Minnesota middle linebacker Jeff Siemon and cornerback Jackie Wallace, caught Hart's pass in stride and was tackled by Wallace as he cross the goal line.

Minnesota's offense wasted no time in responding to the St. Louis touchdown. It took Minnesota quarterback Fran Tarkenton eight plays to direct a scoring drive. Tarkenton had 1:17 left in the second quarter when he rolled out to his right and hit wide receiver John Gilliam for a 16-yard touchdown in the corner of the end zone. The Cardinals drove down the field quickly following Gilliam's score, but placekicker Jim Bakken missed a 23-yard field goal attempt. The halftime score was knotted at 7–7. "They [the Cardinals] certainly had the edge in play during the first half," said Minnesota head coach Bud Grant.

The second half saw Minnesota defensive strategy produce positive results. The Vikings decided to find a way to get to Hart by lining up five defensive linemen to rush the St. Louis quarterback. At times, defensive lineman Bob Lurtsema would be the extra man. At other times, linebacker

Siemon took a down stance as a defensive tackle. The measure worked well in the final two quarters, as Hart by game's end was sacked twice and completed only 18 of 40 for 184 yards. One of Hart's passes at the beginning of the third quarter was intended for wide receiver Mel Gray. But Minnesota safety Jeff Wright made a diving interception. He quickly popped up and ran the ball back 18 yards. An ensuing Fred Cox field goal gave the Vikings a 10–7 lead.

Then came about the play that most witnesses agreed was the play that changed the outcome of the game. Cardinals tailback Terry Metcalf took a Hart pitchout and ran to his right. Minnesota defensive end Carl Eller penetrated into the backfield and interrupted the flow of the play. Eller reached Metcalf with his hand and pulled the runner's right arm away from the football. Metcalf tried to secure the ball with his left arm, but just as he did, Minnesota defensive tackle Alan Page wrapped his arms around the runner and dislodged the ball out of Metcalf's arm. Vikings cornerback Nate Wright saw the dribbling ball on the turf, quickly recovered it, and outraced Hart 20 yards to the pylon for a touchdown and a 17–7 Minnesota lead.

"He [Wright] is one of the best cornerbacks in the league," said appreciative Vikings teammate Chuck Foreman. "He hasn't been burned once all year, and I think that he's only been called once for interference."

The Vikings defense limited the Cardinals to three plays and a punt on their next offensive series. Tarkenton then threw three deep bombs with the intention of hitting Gilliam for another score. The first two bombs fell incomplete. The third did not. Gilliam rushed past Cardinals cornerback Norm Thompson and caught Tarkenton's 38-yard pass for a touchdown and a 23–7 Vikings lead. "I've played with some great ones," said Tarkenton after the game, "but Gillie is the best in football." Fred Cox missed the extra point, but by this time, Minnesota was in control of the game.

Both teams traded possessions for the remainder of the third quarter. Midway through the fourth quarter, the Vikings capitalized on a 12-minute, 10-play drive when halfback Chuck Foreman dove over left guard for a 4-yard score. St. Louis responded for a small measure of pride with a 11-play drive of their own. With 1:04 left in their season, Metcalf, who could only muster 55 yards rushing all day, ran a draw play down the middle for an 11-yard touchdown and the final points of the game. "He's a pretty durable player," said Grant of Metcalf, "but he takes a lot of shots and, as the game went on, I think he tired."

The Vikings prevailed, 30–14. "We are a veteran team, a patient team," said Tarkenton. "We received several Christmas presents early from the Cardinals," admitted Grant. Indeed, the Cardinals' turnovers resulted in 10 Vikings points to start the third quarter. St. Louis had nothing to be ashamed about though. They were at best an average team for the past several years. In 1974, they became a legitimate playoff team, claiming a division title in one of the toughest divisions in the NFL. "I thought we would be much better than last year's squad," admitted St. Louis head coach Don Coryell. "The most important thing was that we were much better prepared because we knew more about the players."

Two of the toughest teams in the NFL would play each other later that same day in an epic playoff contest that has since earned a nickname. The Sea of Hands game got its name from its heroic ending, but the drama and wealth of big plays throughout the game also contributed to make it one of the most memorable playoff contests in league history. In fact, a group of football writers in 1979 declared the Sea of Hands game to be the fifth most memorable game of the decade. The AFC Eastern Division Champion Miami Dolphins would attempt to defend their Super Bowl championships from the previous two seasons. The host AFC Western Division Champion Oakland Raiders were out to put an emphatic end to the Dolphin dynasty. The Raiders were still smarting from their loss to Miami in the 1973 AFC championship game, and they felt that, with the best record in the NFL at 12–2, they were finally strong enough and equipped enough to deliver some payback.

Oakland did not start the game with bravado and brilliance, however. On the opening kickoff, Miami rookie Nat Moore followed his blocking wedge up the middle, broke through a hole on the left, and sped down the sideline with an 89-yard kickoff return for a touchdown. It was just the first of many extraordinary plays which would see momentum sway with virtually every quarter. The first quarter, however, saw nothing but trading possessions. Neither team could manage to get into scoring range. Miami safety Dick Anderson managed to intercept a Ken Stabler pass (on his initial pass attempt of the game), but his return to midfield was wasted by a couple of short runs and a Bob Griese incompletion on third down.

The second quarter was different, however. On a third and five situation midway through the quarter, Stabler sent halfback Charlie Smith down the middle of the field on a deep fly route. Smith circled out of the backfield and outraced Miami middle linebacker Nick Buoniconti to the back of the end zone. Stabler's perfect pass lofted just above Buoniconti's outstretched fingers and into the waiting hands of Smith, who got both of his feet down before going out of the end zone. The game was tied, 7–7.

The Dolphins came right back on the next possession. Trading off runs by Larry Csonka, Jim Kiick and rookie Benny Malone, Miami completed an 11-play drive with a 33-yard Garo Yepremian field goal. The 10–7 Miami lead would be the halftime score, but the Dolphins should have had more points on their ledger. They spent most of the first half in Oakland territory, having moved the ball for longer drives than the Raiders by comparison. One statistic that the Dolphins wish they did not have more of was injuries, however. Miami defensive backs Jake Scott and Curtis Johnson were injured in the first half, and although Johnson would return in the second half, Scott with his knee wrapped in ice would not. Had Scott been on the field for Charlie Smith's touchdown reception, it is doubtful that the Raiders would have scored on the play. Scott usually played a deep centerfield style of safety, and he would have been able to cut off Smith deep.

Miami's loss of Scott would be Oakland's gain. On their second possession of the third quarter, Stabler led a nine-play drive that ended in the Miami end zone. Key plays in the drive were passes to wide receiver Fred Biletnikoff and tight end Bob Moore. Stabler hit Biletnikoff in the right corner of the Miami end zone for a spectacular 13-yard scoring pass that gave Oakland the lead for the first time at 14–10. On the play, Miami cornerback Tim Foley was draped all over Biletnikoff, yet the skinny Florida State product managed to tip the ball, then snare it with his left hand while Foley pinned his right hand to his body. Incredible clutch catches like this were becoming common for Biletnikoff, but he did have his detractors. Many of his critics claimed that he used the gooey substance called "stickum" more than any other receiver in the league. Stickum was a glue-like matter that when spread liberally on one's hands, would make holding on to things (like flying footballs) so much easier. Receivers and running backs throughout the league would use stickum, applying it to their socks, then rubbing it on their hands throughout the game. It wasn't until 1981 that the league outlawed its use. To be fair and to reiterate, Biletnikoff was certainly not the only user of stickum, but throughout the 1970s he was the most famous exploiter of the goo.

The Dolphins stuck it to the Raiders on their very next possession. Bob Griese took advantage of an interference penalty by Oakland linebacker Phil Villapiano, who held up Kiick from reaching for a pass down the sideline. On the very next play from the Oakland 16-yard line, Griese dropped back deep and watched wide receiver Paul Warfield come free down in the corner of the end zone. Griese hit him for the score that returned the lead back to Miami, 16–14. Warfield got wide open on the play because Oakland cornerback George Atkinson slipped and fell on the turf.

But the Raiders earned some solace on the drive when veteran defensive end Bubba Smith blocked Yepremian's extra point attempt.

It appeared as if Miami had taken control of the momentum at this point of the game. Oakland had accumulated far more net passing yards than Miami (124–27) at the end of the third quarter, but the Dolphins were converting on more of their opportunities. That fact was about to change, however. Csonka ran for 15 yards to close out the third quarter, and the first few plays of the fourth quarter saw the Dolphins drive down to the Oakland 28-yard line. One of the most important plays of this game occurred on a third and three situation. Paul Warfield was wide open for a first down on a hook pattern, and Griese hit him in the numbers. Warfield could not hold on to the ball, however, and Miami had to settle for a field goal and a 19–14 lead. Had Warfield held on to the pass, the Dolphins might have gone on to score a touchdown. At the very least, they would have used up one or two more minutes of ball possession, something that undoubtedly would have changed the outcome of the game.

Two possessions later with the ball on their own 17-yard line and with less than five minutes remaining in the final quarter, the Raiders displayed the comeback magic that had been a big part of their history in the 1960s, and in the 1970s as well. Stabler completed an 11-yard pass to Biletnikoff to give Oakland a first down at their own 28-yard line. On the next play, Stabler threw deep for wide receiver Cliff Branch, who was covered by Curtis Johnson's replacement at cornerback, Henry Stuckey. Stabler's pass deep down the sideline was underthrown, however, and Branch adjusted to the ball. Stuckey did not. Branch dove for the ball and fell as he caught it. He then got up before Stuckey could react to touch him down on the play. Branch spun past Stuckey and showed off his blazing speed down the sideline, completing a 72-yard score. "I knew in professional football you can get up and run again," Branch said. "I had been practicing that and that's what I did." Certainly Stuckey was to blame for Branch getting up and scoring, but the referees could also have been to blame for the completed reception. NFL Films camera angles appear to show (after the fact mind you) that Branch trapped the ball as he made the catch. Still in 1974, no instant replay rule was in effect, so the score counted. Oakland regained the lead, 21–19.

The Raiders' lead lasted for only four more plays. Griese hit wide receiver Nat Moore for 23 yards, then gave the ball to Csonka for the next two carries, accumulating 22 more yards. On first and ten from the Oakland 23-yard line, Griese handed the ball off to reserve halfback Benny Malone on a sweep right. Malone broke four tackles and scored standing up to give the lead back to the Dolphins, 26–21. Football experts have debated for years the wisdom in Miami scoring so quickly and not using up more of the clock. Of course, in retrospect, Miami would have been more fortunate to use up more time on their last scoring drive, but there was also no guarantee that had they used up more time, they would have scored a touchdown. There are no guarantees in football, and the Dolphins—and Benny Malone in particular—gave everything they had on the touchdown.

There was 2:01 left on the clock when Oakland got the ball back at their own 32-yard line and trailing 26–21. Stabler showed the poise of a winner on the final drive, and he would make a name for himself (besides "Snake") which would cement his status as a great two-minute quarterback. "When we are in the huddle," Stabler said, "I look my guys in the eye and tell them exactly what we are going to do. I don't try to con them or pump them up. They know what we have to do; I know what we have to do. So we do it." Stabler hit Moore for six yards, Biletnikoff for 18 yards on the right sideline and then again for 20 yards down the middle. Miami's No-Name Defense was playing a prevent strategy, with three down linemen and an extra defensive back. It did not matter. Stabler kept hitting the open man, and at least one man kept coming open on each play. "The thing I recall about that last drive was they [Miami's defense] never really put a heavy rush on me," Stabler recalled.

A completion to Branch for four yards and a completion on a slant pattern to little-used Frank Pitts for five more yards put the ball at the Miami 8-yard line with 35 seconds left in the game. Stabler dropped back on first down but found no one open. Forced out of his pocket by a determined and (by this time) desperate Miami rush, Stabler ran towards the goal. Miami defensive end Vern Den Herder dove for Stabler's legs and tripped him up as The Snake threw a floating pass to the end zone. Stabler's pass lofted into the air and gave running back Clarence Davis a chance to run under it. Davis fought for the ball with Miami linebacker Mike Kolen and defensive back Charlie Babb and pulled it away from both of them. Almost instantaneously, Miami defenders Larry Ball and Manny Fernandez tackled Davis, but by this time as he tumbled to the ground, the hero halfback had secured not just the ball, but also a treasured place in Oakland Raiders playoff history.

"It was just a dying duck going out there," said Stabler of his game-winning throw. "I was falling forward when I released the ball and it kind of floated. The ball was up for grabs, but somehow Clarence got his hands on the ball. Clarence made one super catch." Stabler finished the game by completing 20 of 30 passes for 294 yards against the No-Name Defense. Oakland's John Madden whittled it down to the basics. "He [Davis] made a super play." Davis recalled the catch of his life with an analytical, step-by-step description to reporters: "I just out-wrestled two guys," said Davis. "I didn't know I was that strong. [The catch was] just pure concentration. I knew we needed a touchdown and I pulled the ball out. All of a sudden, I saw a whole lot of people on the field. I've got scratches all over me from people who wanted that ball." The Miami-Oakland playoff game was thus determined by who wanted to grab the ball more, and when that happens in the NFL playoffs, the game boils down to its most individual aspects. For the Raiders, Clarence Davis was the right man at the right place at the right time.

The 28–26 Oakland victory reached its culmination a few moments later with a Phil Villapiano interception of a desperation Bob Griese pass, but it was Davis' touchdown catch that is remembered to this day. The Raiders had done it. They had put an end to the Dolphin dynasty. A throng of Raider fans stormed onto the field, and head coach John Madden took a victory ride on the shoulders of his victorious players. This playoff game marked not only one of the greatest moments in Raiders history, but in pro football history as well. The Sea of Hands game, as it was called for posterity, was "one of the all-time great classics of football," claimed Oakland defensive tackle Art Thoms. "They [Miami] are a hell of a team," said Stabler, "but we are too." All-Pro Miami guard Larry Little summed it up with his belief that "those were the two best teams in football." Little's teammate Paul Warfield lamented, "It's unfortunate you have to have a loser in a game like this."

The following day, Oakland's opponent for the upcoming AFC championship game was hoping to avoid losing a heartbreaker like Miami just did. The location was Pittsburgh's Three Rivers Stadium, where the AFC Central Division Champion Steelers would play host to the AFC wild card Buffalo Bills. The Steelers looked like the far better team—on paper at least. "I know that I felt like we would win the game," said Buffalo offensive tackle Donnie Green. "I think all of our guys felt that way." Buffalo certainly played like they were going to win, at least in the first quarter. The Bills spotted the Steelers a field goal, then charged down the field on this sunny day and scored a touchdown against the vaunted Steel Curtain defense. From the Pittsburgh 22-yard line, Buffalo quarterback Joe Ferguson rifled a pass through the outstretched hand of rookie Steelers linebacker Jack Lambert and into the arms of Bills tight end Paul Seymour, who with his 6'5", 243-pound frame, bowled over Pittsburgh safety Glen Edwards (6', 185 pounds) and dove into the end zone. The Bills had a 7–3 lead as the first quarter expired.

The Bills would not score any points in the second quarter, but the Steelers sure did. Pittsburgh

Oakland Raiders quarterback Kenny "The Snake" Stabler lobs a pass late in the fourth quarter of an AFC divisional playoff game on December 21, 1974, against the defending world champion Miami Dolphins. Stabler's pass was caught by Oakland setback Clarence Davis for a miracle touchdown which dethroned the Dolphins, 28–26. The game would forever be known as "The Sea of Hands Game," due to the number of players who tried to grab Stabler's desperation pass in the end zone (AP Photo/stf).

put up 29 points with three short Franco Harris scoring runs and a touchdown pass from quarterback Terry Bradshaw to fullback Rocky Bleier. On the scoring toss, Bleier circled out of the backfield, and Bradshaw had at least six seconds all alone in the pocket to aim his pass. Bleier caught it in stride at the goal line. The nearest player to him on the play was his own teammate, Franco Harris. Later in the game, Bleier grabbed a Bradshaw pass with one hand for a handsome gain, and wide receiver Lynn Swann made a diving catch for a 35-yard advance down the middle, both of which led to touchdowns.

The 29–7 halftime score epitomized the abilities of the Steelers offense when functioning with all of its independent parts in prime working order. Bradshaw was nearly perfect on all of the scoring drives, hitting key passes to Swann, tight end Larry Brown, and Bleier. Swann even ran a reverse for 25 yards, and Bradshaw himself ran for 12 yards and a first down. Along with his short touchdown runs, Harris accumulated 16 yards in the second quarter. "I never lost confidence in our offense," admitted Pittsburgh head coach Chuck Noll. "I'm impressed," said Buffalo's Ferguson. "They [the Steelers offense] never made any mistakes."

The Steelers defense took pride in forcing its opponents into making mistakes. They only allowed one more Buffalo touchdown in the game, a 3-yard rollout pass from Ferguson to setback O.J. Simpson in the third quarter. Pittsburgh virtually shut down the Bills, allowing only 15 first downs (compared to Pittsburgh's 29), and causing a key fumble by Buffalo fullback Jim Braxton in the second quarter that resulted in one of Harris' touchdowns. Simpson himself was limited to 49 yards rushing, one of his lowest totals of the year. Pittsburgh's runners totaled 235 yards on the ground by contrast. With just under nine minutes remaining in the game, the Steelers started substituting players, but still held the ball for 17 straight plays, virtually eliminating any possible Buffalo comeback. One more Roy Gerela field goal in the fourth quarter made the final score 32–14.

The standout player of the game, however, had to be Bradshaw, who completed 12 of 21 passes for 203 yards. "I've never seen Terry so calm and confident, calling plays cooly and quickly," said Pittsburgh offensive tackle Jon Kolb. "It was the best game I've ever had in the pros," Bradshaw surmised. The victory moved the Steelers back into the AFC championship game, a place where they had not been to in two years. They could be forgiven, however, for looking ahead to their next opponent. "Oakland is the team to beat," said Pittsburgh All-Pro defensive tackle "Mean" Joe Greene. "They've got the best record and they have the best all around performances."

The Los Angeles Rams wanted to take advantage of good performances also in the final game of the divisional playoff round. The NFC Western Division Champion Rams would play host to the Washington Redskins, the NFC's wild card team, in the Los Angeles Memorial Coliseum. No one was really sure what to expect from this game. The Redskins had defeated the Rams 23–17 in the Coliseum just a couple of weeks ago, so there was no doubt that they were capable of beating the Rams. Both teams had identical 10–4 regular season records, but Los Angeles was never seriously challenged in their division. For Washington, the whole season was a challenge. They lost the NFC East by mere percentage points, having lost the tie-breaker to St. Louis.

The first quarter of this playoff tilt featured strong defensive play from both teams. The hitting on both sides was savage. Washington middle linebacker Chris Hanburger leveled Los Angeles halfback Lawrence McCutcheon on a pass incompletion, and a few plays later, Redskins safety Ken Houston followed McCutcheon as he cut across the grain and rammed his forearm into his helmet, which abruptly flew off of McCutcheon's head. The ball was also separated from McCutcheon on this play, but the Rams recovered. The Rams' defense responded in kind, as their linebackers surrounded Redskins star running back Larry Brown and plowed him into the turf almost as soon as he took each handoff. Brown ended the game with a mere 39 yards on 18 carries (a 2.2 average per rush).

It was Los Angeles quarterback James Harris who first started putting a scoring drive together midway through the first quarter. Harris hit wide receiver Harold Jackson on passes of 13 and 22 yards. This led to the game's first touchdown, a 10-yard pass on third down from Harris to tight end Bob Klein, who found himself all alone in the corner of the end zone. The Redskins were so busy keying on McCutcheon that Klein was able to slip into the secondary and beat Washington safety Brig Owens on the play. "The touchdown that I caught was supposed to be to Harold Jackson," said Klein. "I just happened to be in the area which sometimes happens on a crossing pattern. Harris just laid it up there and I caught it."

Washington's offense responded on the next series with a 35-yard field goal by Mike Bragg. The Redskins knew that they could not trade field goals for touchdowns, however, so they went about trying to get the ball into the end zone. It all started when Harris tried to connect with Klein again, but to his dismay, Redskins cornerback Pat Fischer stepped in front of his pass and intercepted it at the Rams' 40-yard line. Fischer returned the pirated pass 17 yards to the Los Angeles 23-yard line. Washington quarterback Billy Kilmer took advantage of the outstanding field position with a few strong runs, a key pass to wide receiver Charley Taylor, and a Ram penalty. The drive concluded on third and goal from the 1-yard line when Redskins running back Moses Denson plowed off right tackle and into the end zone. The half ended with a 10–7 Washington lead.

The teams traded possession of the ball five times in the third quarter before another score was registered. Los Angeles put together a 13-play drive that culminated with a 37-yard field goal by Rams placekicker David Ray. A fumble by Washington's Doug Cunningham on the following kickoff and a recovery by Los Angeles' Cullen Bryant led to another Ray field goal from the 26-yard line. The Rams were now ahead 13–10 with a few minutes elapsed in the fourth quarter.

The play that won the game occurred on the next series. Washington head coach George Allen replaced Kilmer at quarterback with Sonny Jurgensen. Allen wanted to rejuvenate his offense, which in three quarters with Kilmer produced only 10 points. The move appeared wise, as Jurgensen hit Taylor for 27 yards on the first play of the drive. Unfortunately for the veteran Jurgensen, his next completion went to a Ram. Los Angeles linebacker Isiah Robertson stepped in front of a third down pass intended for Larry Brown, and immediately yelled "Fire!" which meant to his teammates to turn into blockers and head downfield. Robertson weaved his way across the field and 59 yards later was triumphantly trotting into the Washington end zone. "I got hit in the face and it took something off the ball," Jurgensen said. "Brown was wide open but Isiah cut in front of him and just made a good play."

The Rams now had a 19–10 lead, and would not allow the Redskins any more trips into scoring position. Jurgensen was intercepted twice more, once by Rams linebacker Jack "Hacksaw" Reynolds, and once by Rams safety Bill Simpson. Los Angeles could not revive their offense either, but it did not matter. The Rams had prevailed, 19–10. They had avenged their earlier defeat at the hands of the Redskins, and had punched their ticket to the NFC championship game. "This is the kind of game where our people rose to the occasions," said Rams head coach Chuck Knox. "We are happy to win and like most wins, it was not easy. Our people did one hell of a job today. The Redskins are one hell of a football team."

Neither conference championship game the following week was expected to be easy or one-sided either. The Los Angeles Rams traveled to warm (30 degrees) and sunny Minnesota to take on the Vikings, a team that they had barely defeated in Week 11, 20–17. The championship game would feature more mistakes than two games usually would. Minnesota committed three turnovers, while the Rams faired even worse with five more. The first quarter was a defensive standoff. A mixture of fumbles, interceptions and penalties resulted in a scoreless struggle until midway through the second quarter. An eight-play Vikings drive reached a successful conclusion when quarterback Fran Tarkenton lofted a 29-yard touchdown pass to wide receiver Jim Lash, who beat Rams cornerback Al Clark on the play.

Los Angeles got on the scoreboard just before halftime with a 27-yard field goal by placekicker David Ray. The Rams had several chances on this scoring drive from inside the Minnesota 10-yard line, but failed to get the ball into the end zone. The first half ended with a 7–3 Vikings advantage, but the second half would produce even more mistakes for both teams than what was exhibited in the first half.

The most incredible and most telling sequence of plays in the third quarter began with a punt. Minnesota punter Mike Eischeid booted a perfect coffin corner kick from the Rams' 38-yard line, which bounced out of bounds at the 1-yard line. The Rams had 99 yards to go for a touchdown. They would end up going 98. Los Angeles quarterback James Harris began this crucial drive in the shadow of his end zone with an unexpected quarterback sneak. The play gained eight yards, and gave the Rams some breathing room in which to eventually launch one of the biggest plays of the game. Several plays after his sneak, and with the ball resting on his 25-yard line, Harris dropped back to pass and was met face-to-face with a Vikings blitz. Minnesota rarely blitzed, thanks in large part to the outstanding pass rushing abilities of their front four. But on this rare instance they blitzed, and got burned. Harris eluded the grasp of linebacker Roy Winston, who came free up the middle and had a direct shot at the tall and muscular quarterback. Harris then broke tackles from defensive end Carl Eller and linebacker Jeff Siemon. The big and evasive quarterback was chased to his right, and barely got his pass away before being decked by defensive tackle Alan Page. "I saw linemen coming at me from everywhere and just did the best I could to escape," Harris said.

While Harris was scrambling away from the frenzy going on in his backfield, wide receiver Harold Jackson drifted into the secondary, found an open spot near midfield, and waited. Jackson caught Harris' perfect pass, juked Vikings cornerback Nate Wright, and started downfield, with the Minnesota defenders in hot pursuit (and probably at this time wishing that they had not blitzed). Fortunately for the Vikings, a few unexpected things happened on this play to save them. First, Los Angeles running back John Cappelletti trailed the play and somehow ran to the right of Jackson, who, when trying to weave to his right, had to abruptly change directions in order to avoid running into his teammate (Cappelletti). As a result, Cappelletti accidentally helped the Minnesota defensive backs draw closer to Jackson. Minnesota's Jackie Wallace appeared to have a decent angle to tackle Jackson at the Vikings' 35-yard line, but Harris sped past him. Wallace did his job though, making Jackson run farther than he intended and closer to the wide side of the field. Finally, Vikings safety Jeff Wright, who never stopped hustling on the play, caught up with the fatigued Jackson and knocked him out of bounds at the 2-yard line. "I tried to run for the corner and had to dodge several defensive backs," described Jackson.

The football gods were not done with offering a helping hand to the Vikings, however. A couple of plays later, with the ball on the 1-foot line, Alan Page plowed into Rams left guard Tom Mack prior to the snap of the ball. Page keenly noticed that Los Angeles tight end Pat Curran flinched in his stance, causing the Minnesota defensive tackle to go offside. Page protested to the referees that he was drawn offside, and they agreed. This crucial play pushed the Rams back five yards. A couple of plays later on third down from the 2-yard line, Harris rolled right and threw for Curran in the end zone. Jackie Wallace lunged for the ball and barely tipped it into the hands of his teammate, Minnesota linebacker Wally Hilgenberg, who caught it and downed it in the end zone for a touchback. The Vikings had thus been granted a reprieve. "Jackie got a hand on the ball and it came right to me," said Hilgenberg. "It's safe to say I've never had a more important interception in my career."

Minnesota capitalized on their good fortune on the very next series, when Tarkenton led a 15-play drive that resulted in a touchdown. Mixing short passes to Foreman, tight end Stu Voigt, and setback Ed Marinaro, Tarkenton willed his team to its ball-control best. The Vikings had to endure their own ineptitude on the drive, however, with a fumble and a sack. The Rams helped out, though, with two offsides penalties of their own. Finally from the 1-yard line, Minnesota running back Dave Osborn dove over just enough for a score.

The Rams to their credit came back quickly on the next series of plays. Harris once again spotted Jackson breaking free in the middle of the zone. This time, Jackson broke two tackles from Nate and Jeff Wright and jogged into the Minnesota end zone. Los Angeles would have the ball for one more series, but the Vikings re-employed five defensive linemen, and sacked Harris on consecutive plays. Minnesota's offense wound down the clock with 12 more plays, and prevailed 14–10 amidst a throng of gleeful fans who stormed the field, which was a Metropolitan Stadium tradition after a big win. "We just made too many mistakes in opportune situations," said Harris. "They [the Vikings] played better than we did and beat us. We got beat by a good football team." The Minnesota head coach felt a sense of relief after the game. "There were an awful lot of turnovers and penalties," assessed Grant. "Any one of them could have made the difference."

The difference between the Steelers and the Raiders in the AFC championship game would appear to be small too. Nineteen-severy-four marked the third straight year that the two teams would meet in the playoffs, with each team having split the first two contests. Their most recent meeting occurred back in Week 3 of the 1974 season, when the Raiders paid a visit to Pittsburgh and shutout the Steelers, 17–0. That lost lingered on the minds of the Steelers during the week leading up to the championship game, but another game seemed to carry more weight with the Steelers' psyche. After beating Miami in the divisional playoffs, *Sports Illustrated* magazine described Oakland's narrow victory over the Dolphins as "Super Bowl VIII and ½," meaning that the Super Bowl was already won by the Raiders. Oakland head coach John Madden didn't buy it, but he certainly knew his team was favored to win it all. "We have everything in our backyard," Madden said. "We have to take advantage of it."

Steelers head coach Chuck Noll, definitely not one to offer bulletin board material to fire up his opponent, did something uncharacteristic in a team meeting several days prior to the game. Noll was not a rah-rah type of coach, nor was he one who delivered pep talks. But his few words to his team would somehow resonate throughout the mid to late 1970s when people described the Steelers. John Madden called his Raiders and the team they just defeated, the Dolphins, the "two best teams in football." Noll used that remark and told his players that the "Raiders act like they just won the damn Super Bowl. They think they're the best team in the NFL. Let me tell you, the best team in the NFL is sitting right here in this room." Noll's words inspired his team like nothing else ever before. "Joe Greene was sitting right next to me," remembered Steelers veteran linebacker Andy Russell, "and he rose up out of his seat. It was as if he was ready to play right then. He was so psyched. I've never seen Chuck Noll do an emotional thing like that."

Tensions mounted prior to the game, and those tensions sporadically showed during the first half. Oakland and Pittsburgh were tied 3–3 at halftime, but both squads had good scoring drives that failed for one reason or another. In the first quarter, a fumbled punt by Lynn Swann of the Steelers led to an Oakland field goal, and a missed field goal by Roy Gerela ended a promising 13-play Pittsburgh drive. Later in the second quarter, another 13-play Steelers drive was snuffed out deep in Oakland territory by an interception from Raiders cornerback Nemiah Wilson. For their part, the Raiders offense was feeling the effects of a dominating Pittsburgh defense. Tackles Greene and Ernie Holmes were pinching inside the Oakland line and bottling up running plays almost as soon as they got started. Pittsburgh gave up zero first downs rushing all game long. "We played them man-to-man up front," explained Greene. "We felt we could beat them up there."

Oakland punter Ray Guy was getting a workout, punting four times in the first half. With just under a minute left until halftime, Oakland placekicker George Blanda missed a 38-yard field goal.

Turnovers propagated the early moments of the third quarter. Steelers fullback Rocky Bleier fumbled at the Pittsburgh 40-yard line on the first play of the quarter. The Raiders returned the favor five plays later, when a Ken Stabler pass was intercepted by the diving Pittsburgh outside linebacker Jack Ham. With almost five minutes remaining in the third quarter, Stabler threw deep down the sideline for the fleet Cliff Branch, and the Oakland wide receiver made a brilliant over the shoulder catch in the corner of the end zone over Steelers cornerback Mel Blount. The Raiders finally had a 10–3 lead to protect. They could not do it.

On the first play of what turned out to be a frantic final quarter, Steelers running back Franco Harris scored a touchdown on an 8-yard trap run up the middle for a 10–10 tie. Harris broke no less than four attempted arm tackles on the play, and tumbled into the end zone. On the Raiders' next possession, another Stabler pass interception—again by Jack Ham—ignited another Pittsburgh scoring drive. Ham returned this interception 24 yards to the Oakland 9-yard line. Pittsburgh quarterback Terry Bradshaw then saw Swann going across the middle at the back of the end zone. Bradshaw hit him with the ball in the chest, and Swann held on while getting both feet in bounds before being knocked out of the end zone by Raiders defensive back Alonzo "Skip" Thomas. The Steelers now possessed a 17–10 lead. "That was the turning point when we went the length of the field and scored after they scored," said Steelers head coach Chuck Noll.

The Raiders came right back and drove down the field, but the Steel Curtain defense stiffened up when it counted most, and permitted only a 24-yard Blanda field goal. The teams exchanged punts until the latter part of the fourth quarter. One more key interception, this one by Steelers cornerback J.T. Thomas, led to the points that put Pittsburgh in its first ever Super Bowl. Thomas caught Stabler's overthrown pass like a center fielder and returned it 42 yards to the Oakland 24-yard line. Two plays later from the Oakland 21-yard line, Franco Harris ran another trap play up the middle, and dragged a couple of Raider defenders with him into the end zone. The Pittsburgh defense shut down the Raiders offense on one more drive, and the game was over. The 24–13 Steelers victory kept Oakland out of the Super Bowl for the seventh straight year. "It was meant to be," said Bradshaw. "We were meant to win this thing. We knew we were going to win this game. We came here with the confidence to win."

The Steel Curtain defense limited the powerful Raiders to a mere 29 yards rushing. That statistic alone decided the game more than any other. "They gave us nothing on the ground," said Raiders head coach John Madden. "I can't remember when our ground game was shut down that effectively." In contrast, Pittsburgh's ground-churning offense registered 224 overall rushing yards. Franco Harris finished up with 111 yards on 29 carries and his two touchdowns. After 42 years of their existence, the Pittsburgh Steelers were one game removed from their first world title.

Super Bowl IX would be played in New Orleans, and the extravagant activities two weeks prior to the game did not disappoint. An increased number of parties and hoopla reverberated throughout the French Quarter. "Helping" out the media prior to the game were the likes of gate crashers Fred Dryer and Lance Rentzel of the Los Angeles Rams, who were wearing reporter costumes of the 1920s or so, and who humorously snuck into media sessions with the players using the pen names Cubby O'Switzer and Scoops Brannigan. No one thought to ask where Dryer or Rentzel got their press credentials.

The game itself would be played in old Tulane Stadium. It was originally expected to be played in the Louisiana Superdome, but that futuristic edifice was still not finished, thanks largely to a union construction workers strike earlier in the year, along with repeated financial woes. The Superdome did make its appearance on the front cover of the game program, however. When game day finally came around, so did the rain. Lots of rain. The saturated field was still being worked on with Zamboni machines just several hours before kickoff. The official temperature at game time was recorded at 46 degrees, but the biting winds and overcast skies made it feel colder. Fans attending the game would have to deal with the worst weather conditions that the Super Bowl had ever seen up to that date.

Despite this being their first visit to the Super Bowl, the Steelers were listed as slim four-point favorites over the Vikings, who were making their third visit to the big game and their second straight visit, all without obtaining a Lombardi Trophy. In order to avoid a third loss, Minnesota head coach Bud Grant and quarterback Fran Tarkenton planned to develop their running game. The Raiders had failed in running the ball against the Steelers in the AFC title game, but the Vikings would fare even worse in Super Bowl IX. The Steelers would permit a then–Super Bowl record of only 17 yards rushing, and they accomplished that with injuries to starting linebackers Andy Russell and Jack Lambert, and defensive end Dwight White's viral illness. White was weakened by his bout with pleurisy during the week prior to the game, but he still managed to play almost a full four quarters of the contest. "White is a good indication of the attitude of this team," said Pittsburgh head coach Chuck Noll. "He just wouldn't be denied."

Minnesota's key decision to stick with their game plan throughout the game doomed them. Tarkenton kept calling runs designed to attack the left side of the Steelers' defense. This strategic choice was foolhardy to say the least. Three Pittsburgh All-Pros (Joe Greene, Jack Ham and L.C. Greenwood) were stationed there, and all three had little trouble in plugging up the few holes that developed throughout the game. Somewhat astoundingly, the Vikings were still trying to establish their running game into the fourth quarter. A better strategy would have been for them to throw the ball on every down from the start of the third quarter on. The pinching slants of defensive tackles Greene and Ernie Holmes were not going to allow any room for Minnesota's runners.

The first two quarters of this game were a defensive struggle for both teams, however. The Steelers offense was able to move the ball on the Vikings defense, but they failed to score. Trap draw plays (Pittsburgh's calling card) were utilized to great effect. Steeler runners gained a total of 64 yards rushing in the first quarter, compared to zero for the Vikings. Placekicker Roy Gerela missed one field goal in the first quarter, however, and a fumbled snap by holder Bobby Walden ruined another. Both Steelers running backs Rocky Bleier and Franco Harris fumbled once each during the game, but it did not matter, as neither of those turnovers would lead to a Viking score. Minnesota's miscues all game long dwarfed Pittsburgh's. The Vikings committed five turnovers in the game, including three interceptions from Tarkenton. Minnesota had enough chances, but failed to take advantage of any of them.

Pittsburgh did manage to score once in the first half, and fittingly, it was their dominant defense which accrued the points. Following a Walden punt that was downed at the Minnesota 7-yard line, Tarkenton tried to pitch the ball to running back Dave Osborn, who thought that the Vikings quarterback was going to hand off to him. The ball was fumbled, then inadvertently kicked by Pittsburgh defensive end L.C. Greenwood's golden shoe (his trademark) as he was tackling Osborn, and then bounced toward the end zone. Tarkenton fell on it just inside of the end zone, and Dwight White downed him there for the first safety in Super Bowl history. Pittsburgh had a 2–0 lead at halftime. "I think that our front four won the game, they were just outstanding," said Steelers All-Pro outside linebacker Jack Ham. "They are very aggressive and got good penetration," said Tarkenton of the Pittsburgh front four.

The very first play of the third quarter produced more misfortune for the Vikings. Gerela slipped on the Poly-Turf as he kicked the ball. His squib kick bounced up against the knee of Minnesota's Bill Brown, and then continued to bounce forward. Several Steelers and a few Vikings players met the bouncing ball all at the same time. Pittsburgh's Marv Kellum came out of the pack with the ball at the Minnesota 30-yard line.

Franco Harris ran another delay play for 24 yards off of left tackle. A couple of plays later on second and goal from the Minnesota 9-yard line, Harris took a Bradshaw handoff and swept left. Steelers right guard Gerry Mullins pulled left to lead the sweep and laid a crushing block on Minnesota linebacker Wally Hilgenberg. Harris sprinted to the corner of the end zone past the chasing Vikings for the game's first touchdown. "Our offensive line just kept getting better and better," said Harris.

Pittsburgh's 9–0 lead going into the fourth quarter appeared safe enough, especially when considering how much difficulty the Vikings offense was having. But just when you thought that this game would be void of any drama, a unique series of plays changed the course of the game and eventually determined a victor. It all started when Franco Harris fumbled near midfield, and Minnesota safety Paul Krause recovered. On the very next play from the Pittsburgh 47, Tarkenton went for broke and heaved a bomb deep down the sideline. Neither Vikings receiver John Gilliam nor Steelers safety Mike Wagner could catch the ball, but line judge Ed Marion penalized Wagner for pass interference when he rode Gilliam out of bounds. On the very next play from the Pittsburgh 5-yard line, Chuck Foreman took a Tarkenton handoff and jack knifed into the line when he fumbled. Joe Greene came up with the pigskin, and a demoralized Viking offense trudged off the field. "That was the biggest defensive play of the day," said Pittsburgh head coach Chuck Noll. "They tried to run a counter play and Greene knocked the ball out of Foreman's hands. If they had scored then, they would have made it tough on us."

Minnesota's despondency would not last long, however. Pittsburgh could not gain a first down after Greene's recovery, and thus was forced to punt from their own 15-yard line. Minnesota linebacker Matt Blair broke through the line untouched and blocked Walden's punt. Vikings reserve defensive back Terry Brown scooped up the ball on a perfect bounce and trotted into the end zone. The Vikings scored a touchdown, and appeared to have life in this game after all. "I saw Blair coming and knew I didn't have a chance to get the kick away," Walden said.

Minnesota's good fortune was not meant to last, however. Vikings placekicker Fred Cox's conversion kick thudded against the left upright, keeping their deficit at 9–6. The final quarter had roughly 10 minutes remaining in it, and the game was still up for grabs. Pittsburgh's offense, however, would not wait long to resume their dominance. Steelers quarterback Terry Bradshaw would lead a 12-play drive (the longest drive of the game) to score an insurance touchdown and claim a world's championship. Key plays in the drive were provided by Rocky Bleier, who contributed a 17-yard run off right tackle, and who caught a 6-yard pass on a third and five situation.

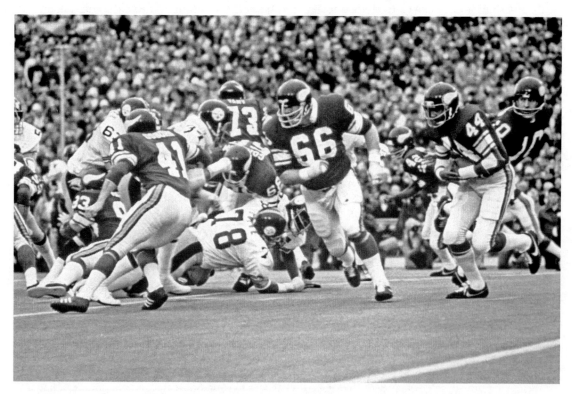

In Super Bowl IX, January 12, 1975, in Tulane Stadium in New Orleans, Louisiana, Minnesota halfback Chuck Foreman takes a handoff from Vikings quarterback Fran Tarkenton against the Pittsburgh Steelers. Foreman follows pulling guard Andy Maurer (66), and gets a crackback block from fullback Dave Osborn (41). Pittsburgh's Steel Curtain defense held Minnesota's rushing attack to a then–Super Bowl record of only 17 total yards. The Steelers prevailed 16–6, and thus won the first of four world championships that they earned in the 1970s (AP Photo/Vernon Biever).

Another key play involved the referees. Bradshaw threw a long pass on third down in the direction of his tight end, Larry Brown, who outleaped Minnesota safety Jeff Wright for the ball. Brown turned around after the catch and headed up field, when he was tackled high and low by Jackie Wallace and linebacker Roy Winston, who spun the tight end to the turf. Brown fumbled the ball, and Vikings middle linebacker Jeff Siemon recovered at the Minnesota 28-yard line. The Vikings appeared to have made the most important play of the game as the referees signaled Minnesota ball, but line judge Ed Marion had a clearer view of the play, and over-ruled his zebra-clad co-workers. Marion claimed that Brown's buttocks hit the turf a split second before the ball popped out of his hands. Looking at the play from several NFL Films camera angles from super slow motion, a case could be made that the ball was coming loose from Brown's grasp about an inch from his body hitting the turf. Nevertheless, Marion convinced his cohorts otherwise, and the Steelers retained possession of the ball. The Vikings and their coaches were visibly upset with the verdict, and in a somewhat sarcastic way blamed at least a portion of their bad luck on the officiating. "Both teams had enough chances to score and to win," said Minnesota head coach Bud Grant, "but the penalties, the interceptions and the official fumbles ... it was just a game of errors by all three teams."

Several plays later on third and goal from the Minnesota 4-yard line, Bradshaw rolled right and fired a spiral through Siemon's arms and into Brown's stomach in the end zone. The game-clinching touchdown pass gave Pittsburgh an insurmountable 16–6 lead. "I thought I had Brown covered on the rollout play," explained Minnesota safety Paul Krause. "But then Bradshaw pulled up and Brown got behind me." A few plays later in the waning seconds of the game, Pittsburgh safety Mike Wagner intercepted one more Tarkenton pass, and a new dynasty was officially born. Franco Harris was named the game's Most Valuable Player for his Super Bowl record 158 rushing yards, and beloved Steelers owner Art Rooney finally won a championship after owning the team for 42 years. The Pittsburgh Steelers would eventually be called the "team of the decade," but their first step to that glorious title was taken on a cold and grey day in New Orleans on January 12, 1975, in Super Bowl IX.

1975

A Repeating Dynasty Amidst Strong-Armed Cinderellas

The NFL's 56th season included a variety of events that made the season memorable, both on the field and off. Several important individual records would fall by the end of the 1975 regular season, and plenty of competition all year long amongst teams in the AFC Central and the NFC East Divisions would keep thousands of fans on the edge of their seats. The months prior to the start of the season also served as the grand stage for some important issues. New rule changes for 1975 included the establishment of a firm 43-man roster (down four from the previous year), and a regulation forbidding the recent trend for oversized huddles. Throughout 1974, many teams had more than the allotted 11 players (on offense or defense) linger on the field before the snap of the ball, in an attempt at confusing their opponent. As the offensive huddle broke, two or three players on either side of the ball would sprint off the field. The new rule would penalize such rule-stretching actions, and would require anyone who entered the huddle to stay on the field for at least one play.

The playoff format also underwent a change when owners agreed to reward the teams with the highest won-loss percentages by making them the hosts for the divisional playoffs. The remaining teams which won divisional playoff games and which owned the best record in each conference would then host their conference's championship game. Prior to 1975, the playoff venues were distributed each year from division to division, meaning that a team with an 8–6 record in one division would sometimes host a 12–2 team from another division in the playoffs. Finally in 1975, that injustice was corrected, as the teams with the best records would host divisional playoff and conference championship games.

The summer of 1975 also produced another short strike of one preseason game. Unfortunately, no new ideas or solutions could be found or accepted in regards to the previous year's labor dilemma. Then a week before the regular season began, several teams voted to strike once again, and several teams walked off the job. Cooler heads prevailed once again, however, and all the teams went back to the playing field almost immediately. The regular season somehow survived in spite of the ongoing disagreements between the National Football League Players Association (NFLPA) and the owners. A new contract between the two was unfortunately not signed in 1975, as the players rejected the owners' offers. Nevertheless, the players finally voted to continue and complete the season.

A new start to the season would also be seen on CBS-TV. Pregame shows had been part of a typical Sunday afternoon's television programming for many years, but in 1975, everything changed. The producers at CBS decided to come up with a show which offered more variety and more appeal than any pregame show had ever done before. The show was called *The NFL Today*, and its concept was a group of three men and one woman, each of whom would add their own particular interests to the show. Brent Musburger was the anchorman, and he would provide the outline for news of the upcoming games, the scores at halftime, and the lead-ins to various league-wide stories. Musburger also coined the iconic opening lines of each show: "You are looking live at…" whichever stadium was the first to be shown to the television audience through satellite feeds from each of that day's games. Irv Cross was a former defensive back and assistant coach-turned-broadcaster who would interview a different player each week, with an eye towards game strategy. Phyllis George, the attractive former Miss USA who was singlehandedly credited with increasing television viewership by the thousands, would also interview a different player each week, with the intentions of getting them to discuss off-the-field topics and human interest stories, such as their families, their challenges as an athlete, and their concerns away from football. Finally, Jimmy "The Greek" Snyder would help Musberger break down the one-on-one player matchups for each game, then predict the winners. *The NFL Today* was an overnight success, and it did not take too long before the NBC pregame show copied that success. "Those were some great times," admitted Musburger in a recent interview. In later years, ESPN would take CBS' idea and run with it to the tune of pregame shows which began early on Sunday mornings and last for hours. Today's pregame shows discuss virtually every topic imaginable for each of the day's contests, sometimes to the point of overexposure. What sports television producers offer viewers today originated with and are the descendants of *The NFL Today* from 1975.

Speaking of new scenes to the league, a couple of sparkling new venues appeared on the NFL landscape in 1975. The New Orleans Saints left old Tulane Stadium and finally moved into the Louisiana Superdome, and the Detroit Lions left Tiger Stadium and its miserable winter weather for the comfortable indoor confines of Pontiac Metropolitan Stadium, later to be re-named the Pontiac Silverdome. Both of these new stadiums were futuristic in design. Both had artificial turf. The Superdome rose 273 feet above the ground on a 53-acre tract of land in downtown New Orleans. It resembled a large flying circular saucer or spaceship, and it had a large, six-sided message board/gondola suspended above the center of the field. It also had a seating capacity of 72,000. The rectangular Silverdome had a roof made of a Teflon-coated fiberglass fabric that was held up by steel cables, and was inflated by compressed air. As you entered the Silverdome, you felt the rushing air blowing in your face at over 30 miles per hour. Once you were safely inside, however, you felt climate-controlled comfort. It had a large seating capacity of 80,638. "I remember that wind blowing on us when we went inside the stadium," said Buffalo offensive tackle Donnie Green after one of the Bills' visits to Detroit. "That's the thing that stands out most about it."

One thing which blew into the NFL's face in 1975 was the continued existence of the World Football League (WFL). The WFL's decisions and actions would lead to repercussions that would affect the league and every team in it. Headed by President Chris Hemmeter, the WFL continued to raid NFL rosters and lure prospective players into the WFL with outlandish (for that time) salary promises and signing bonuses. The WFL's biggest coup in 1975 came when they coaxed the offensive core of the Miami Dolphins into taking the bait. Larry Csonka, Jim Kiick, and Paul Warfield each signed with the WFL's Memphis Southmen on a $3.5 million package. Almost overnight, quite a few other NFL players also signed with the WFL, thereby weakening their former teams. Players like John Gilliam, Ted Kwalick, Pat Haden, Cecil Turner, Larry Smith, Daryle Lamonica, Jim Mitchell, Dick Witcher, and John Matuszak each signed a WFL contract in 1975. However, their experiences in the new league would be aptly described as problematic at best.

The WFL employed the "Hemmeter Plan" to attract NFL players. It was a profit-sharing plan in which most of the players would be paid one percent of their team's income. If there was no income, the players would still receive $500 a game for 20 regular season games. This was somewhat laughable, as many of the WFL players had been making more money in the NFL with their old contracts. The WFL still had the same problems as it did in 1974 with attracting fans, however, and as a result, the dollar figures of paid admission to the games were fudged by every team. The Philadelphia team could only sell 4,000 tickets for a home game at John F. Kennedy Stadium, a building that had over 90,000 available seats. Most WFL teams experienced similar low attendance numbers. Embarrassments league-wide made most of the teams look like minor league squads. The Charlotte team was evicted from its practice field because it failed to pay the rent. The Jacksonville team had its blocking sleds and tackling dummies repossessed. The Philadelphia team tried to save money by using an old school bus to travel to away games. The Southern California team tried to entice fans to buy a ticket and attend a game with the promise of giving away 10-speed bicycles at the gate. Many players were asked to take pay cuts throughout the 1975 season, and many more simply did not get paid. This whole misguided experiment of a rival league to the NFL would not even last the entire second season. By the 12th game, the WFL folded up, leaving 380 players without jobs. Many of the big-name players immediately jumped back to the NFL, but most could not. "What we needed was a strong marketing plan," said Hemmeter in a contemplative interview after the season. "You can have an exciting product, but if it doesn't have customer appeal on the shelf, it's worthless."

The WFL did manage to have some sort of worthwhile positive influence for some people, however. Players like Danny White, Jack Dolbin, and Vince Papale each got valuable pro playing experience in the fledgling league prior to making NFL rosters. White and Dolbin would incidentally go on to play against each other several years later in Super Bowl XII. Coaches like John McVay, Jack Pardee, Lindy Infante, and Marty Schottenheimer each survived their experiences in the WFL and went on to successful coaching and/or front office careers in the NFL. All tolled, the WFL was a failure in regard to most on-field and off-field aspects. But the idea of establishing a new league like the WFL was not a new idea, and it would be tried again by other new leagues in the future. Perhaps the most important result of the WFL from 1974 to 75 was the lessons that it gave future leagues like the United States Football League (USFL) and the Arena Football League. Those leagues did their best not to imitate the WFL, and tried to learn as much as they could from the WFL's myriad of financial and front office mistakes.

The league was probably not making a mistake when it decided to allow its referees to announce penalties via each stadium's public address system for the first time in 1975. The game was becoming more informative for the fans in the 1970s, and by hooking up a small Vega transmitter with a nine-volt battery to the referee's belt and attaching a small microphone to his collar, the league erased one of the last vestiges of confusion and guessing ("Who was the penalty on?") for the fans. For the players on the field, however, having their name being broadcast to thousands of fans in the stadium and millions more watching on television, the idea of announcing penalties and the guilty party was not exactly a welcome change to the game. Nevertheless, the same electronic device to announce penalties that made its first appearance in 1975 is still in use by the referees today.

The beginning of the 1975 NFL season would produce the first appearance (sort of) of a long-since-forgotten piece of offensive football strategy. Dallas head coach Tom Landry outdid even himself during the off-season with a tactical decision that would change the league's passing game forever. Of all of Landry's strategical innovations in pro football, his plan to resurrect the shotgun formation was perhaps his most ingenious. Landry did not invent the shotgun formation (it was first used by the San Francisco 49ers in the early 1960s), but he decided to look in the attic and annals of football strategy, uncover the tactic, dust it off by adding some flourishes to it, and present it to his team and to the league at the start of the season in their opening game against the visiting Los Angeles Rams. The shotgun formation (or spread formation as Landry called it) consisted of placing his quarterback Roger Staubach five to seven yards behind the center. John Fitzgerald, the Cowboys' center, would then snap the ball back to Staubach like he would to a punter. The idea behind it was to give the quarterback better sight lines to his receivers downfield, and to give his quarterback a couple of extra seconds to size up the defensive coverage downfield. Landry had Staubach use the formation to throw medium and deep passes mostly on third downs, and also to deliver short shovel passes to his running backs, which added to the opposing defense's confusion. Thanks in large part to the shotgun, Staubach was also better able to elude the oncoming pass rush.

Still considered by most fans and experts as the league's most dangerous scrambler, Staubach ran for 56 yards against the Rams, with some of those runs coming out of the shotgun formation. The Rams were fooled by the tactic as Dallas produced an 18–7 upset win. "I've always felt it was a little foolish to stay under center when everyone knows you're going to pass," said Landry after the game. "Meantime, they're putting in special defenses to stop the pass. What we're trying to do is twofold: spread the defense and give our quarterback a little more time to read the coverage. He picks up half a second or more when he's back five yards from center. And, he sees so much better. He can read defenses in a hurry." The shotgun formation resulted in higher percentages in converting third downs into first downs for the 1975 Cowboys. It also resulted in Staubach's higher completion percentage and fewer sacks. When Staubach decided to run from the shotgun formation—as he did against the Rams—he would average 7.8 yards per carry throughout the season.

Two more big factors in the Dallas win over the Rams involved the Cowboys roster and the play of the Doomsday Defense. A total of 12 rookies made the team in 1975, and their exuberance and overall speed gave Dallas a faster squad and one in which vital veterans received a needed break every now and then. The rookies became known as "The Dirty Dozen," and most contributed mightily to the Cowboys' quick resurgence into playoff contention. The defense for their part limited the Rams to 148 total yards in the season opener (128 rushing, 20 passing). Los Angeles only managed to drive across midfield once in the entire game. Ten-year veteran Dallas safety Mel Renfro intercepted two Los Angeles passes which resulted in two Dallas scores. "They just whipped our rears," said Los Angeles head coach Chuck Knox. With the defense remaining formidable, and with the rookies flying all over the place, and with the shotgun shooting holes in opposing defenses, the Cowboys would surprise many of their opponents during the course of the 1975 season, and would eventually become a Cinderella team by season's end.

No surprises were expected or delivered in San Diego on opening day, as the defending Super Bowl champion Pittsburgh Steelers crushed the host San Diego Chargers, 37–0. What the rest of the league feared appeared to be true. The Steelers were regarded by most as liable to defend their NFL title in 1975, and their showing in San Diego did nothing to alter that opinion. Pittsburgh out-gained San Diego 443 yards to 145, and accumulated 24 first downs. The Steel Curtain defense permitted the Chargers to gain only nine first downs all game long, and the San Diego offense did not penetrate past the Pittsburgh 47-yard line. Contributing to the Steelers' offensive output was quarterback Terry Bradshaw, who threw touchdown passes to wide receivers Frank Lewis and John Stallworth. "They were impressive and we were terrible," said San Diego head coach Tommy Prothro.

Both Joe Namath and Joe Ferguson threw two touchdown passes apiece in their Week 1 meeting between the Jets and the Bills in Buffalo. But that is where the similarities ended. Buffalo had superstar running back O.J. Simpson, and he ran for 173 yards on 32 carries. He also scored two touchdowns in Buffalo's 42–14 rout of New York. Buffalo was out to prove that their appearance in the 1974 AFC playoffs was no fluke. Simpson would account for five of the top nine rushing performances in the league in 1975. The Bills' efforts to make the 1975 postseason would hinge on their defense, however, a unit with more than its share of holes to fill. Yet they took the right first step by keeping the Jets under wraps. Buffalo intercepted Namath four times in the game, including a 44-yard return for a touchdown by Buffalo defensive end Pat Toomay. "I think the entire club felt this was our most important game in a long time," said Buffalo head coach Lou Saban. "They [Buffalo] out-muscled us, out-hustled us, out-fought us," said Jets head coach Charley Winner.

Another big return of sorts occurred in Milwaukee, as the Green Bay Packers played host to division rival Detroit on opening day. The Packers welcomed back a hero from their glorious past on this day. Bart Starr returned to assume the head coaching duties for his former team, and Packer Backers everywhere hoped for a return to glory for their beloved Green and Gold. Unfortunately, the loyal Packer fans would have to wait just a bit longer, as Detroit put together a spectacular performance in their 30–16 win over Green Bay. The Lions' special teams set an NFL one-game record by blocking three Green Bay punts, and returning two of them for touchdowns. Levi Johnson was responsible for two of those blocked punts off of the foot of rookie Green Bay punter Steve Broussard, and he fell on one of them in the end zone for a quick Detroit score. The Lions would improve mightily on defense in 1975, ranking number four in total defense in the NFC, compared to claiming the number 12 spot in the same category in the NFC in 1974. Their punt coverage unit also received a positive shot in the arm with their performance against Green Bay. "When you block one [punt], it just gives you encouragement to try and block another," said Detroit head coach Rick Forzano.

Another NFC Central club—the Chicago Bears—would also have their hands full with an AFC opponent on opening day, the visiting Baltimore Colts. Young and daring Baltimore quarterback Bert Jones led the Colts with two touchdown passes, and Baltimore's defense limited the Bears to a meager 121 total yards in a 35–7 Baltimore victory. "Our guys were running good routes and I had time to get the ball to them," said Jones. First-year Baltimore head coach Ted Marchibroda and veteran general manager Joe Thomas wasted no time in rebuilding the Colts from the ground up. Thomas got rid of almost two dozen veteran players during the past two seasons, drafted for need, and traded judiciously. The defensive line saw the most improvement. Young defenders John Dutton (6'7", 268 pounds), Fred Cook (6'4", 247), Mike Barnes (6'6", 260), and Joe Ehrmann (6'4", 254) became known as "The Sack Pack," a group of strong and relentless defensive linemen who contributed a league-high 59 sacks in 1975. New linebackers Tom McLeod and Jim Cheyunski came to the team via trades, and joined new defensive backs Lloyd Mumphord and Jackie Wallace, who came to Baltimore via the waiver list. The Colts defense gelled almost instantly. They intercepted 29 passes for 493 return yards and scored four touchdowns in 1975.

The Colts offense also contributed a hefty 2,217 rushing yards and 28 rushing touchdowns in 1975. Tailback Lydell Mitchell from Penn State had his best season since coming into the league in 1972. Mitchell ran for 1,193 yards and scored 15 touchdowns (11 rushing, four receiving). Mitchell also tied for the lead in the AFC in receiving with 60 catches. Bert Jones threw for 2,483 yards and 18 touchdowns. Behind Mitchell, Baltimore had three players catch 30 or more passes in 1975. They included wide receiver Glenn Doughty (39 catches for 666 yards and four touchdowns), tight end Raymond Chester (38 catches for 457 yards and three touchdowns), and running back Bill Olds (30 catches for 194 yards and two touchdowns). Roger Carr only caught 23 passes, but he accumulated 517 yards receiving, a 22.5 yards per catch average. Baltimore's offense had scored only 190 points in 1974. In 1975, they would score 395 points, the second-highest mark in the league. The Colts only won twice in 1974. That number would increase dramatically in 1975.

Teams like Minnesota and Washington were not interested in changing much in wake of their playoff appearances in each of the past two seasons. The Vikings were attempting to win their third straight NFC title, while the Redskins were hoping to wrest control of the NFC East. Both of these teams had little challenges in their respective opening games. The Vikings outlasted the San Francisco 49ers by a score of 27–17, and the Redskins squashed the New Orleans Saints, 41–3. Minnesota was as efficient as ever, using short Fran Tarkenton passes, timely Chuck Foreman runs, and their typical stalwart Purple Gang defense, which contributed four sacks, three fumble recoveries, and a 26-yard fumble return for a touchdown by defensive back Terry Brown. "We ended up playing give-away and you can't do that against a good football team," said veteran journeyman San Francisco quarterback Norm Snead.

The Redskins' thrashing of the Saints included four touchdown passes from quarterback Billy Kilmer and a 16-yard fumble return for a touchdown by linebacker Brad Dusek. On the fumble, New Orleans' running back Rod McNeill ran into a gang of Redskin tacklers who pried the ball from his grasp. Dusek was in the right spot to scoop it up and score his first pro touchdown. Washington's triumph was head coach George Allen's tenth straight opening day win. "Our team really wanted to win this game," said Kilmer. "I really wanted to play and I wanted to play good."

Two more teams which lit up the scoreboard in Week One were the Kansas City Chiefs and the Denver Broncos. The Mile High Stadium crowd witnessed several outstanding offensive plays and some explosive special teams plays in this see-saw matchup. Both the Broncos' and Chiefs' defenses were absent, however. Denver rookie Rick Upchurch accounted for 286 yards in his NFL debut. Upchurch scored on a 13-yard reverse, returned three kickoffs for 88 yards, one punt for 30 yards, and caught three passes for 153 yards, including a 90-yard touchdown reception over Kansas City cornerback Jim Marsalis. Upchurch's performance was one of the best rookie debuts in NFL history. "It's just a matter of time before he becomes a premier receiver," admitted Denver head coach John Ralston. Not to be outdone, Chiefs quarterback Mike Livingston threw for 221 yards and two scores in new Kansas City head coach Paul Wiggin's NFL debut. Rookie Chiefs tight end Walter White caught his first career touchdown in the first quarter, a 69-yard bomb from Livingston down the middle of the field. The Chiefs held a 33–24 lead midway through the fourth quarter when Denver came back in the clutch. Denver wide receiver Jack Dolbin recovered a fumble by teammate Otis Armstrong at the 2-yard line and dove into the end zone for a key fourth quarter touchdown. Denver wide receiver Billy Van Heusen then caught a 10-yard scoring pass from veteran quarterback Charley Johnson to win the game, 37–33. On the play, Van Heusen ran a quick out pattern and beat veteran Chiefs cornerback Emmitt Thomas for the score. "At least we showed a lot of character in a comeback effort," said Ralston after his team's narrow victory.

Another comeback contest was held in St. Louis' Busch Memorial Stadium, where the Cardinals played host to the Atlanta Falcons. Rookie Atlanta quarterback Steve Bartkowski led his young teammates to a 20–13 fourth quarter lead until St. Louis struck back late in the game. Quarterback Jim Hart beat a Falcons blitz and threw an eight-yard touchdown pass to wide receiver Earl Thomas which tied the game at 20 apiece. Hart then led his team on a 72-yard drive in the final 1:49, which ended with Jim Bakken's victorious 25-yard field goal with no time left on the clock. St. Louis' 23–20 win would be the first of many last-minute triumphs for a team that in 1975 would earn the nickname "Cardiac Cards." St. Louis would claim victory in seven of eight contests that went down to the final minute or overtime. "It was a very tough football game," said Hart after their narrow win over Atlanta. "Not so much physically, but mentally. I'm just glad it's over." Conversely, many of St. Louis' opponents would suffer "Hart" attacks in the waning moments of their contests with the Cardiac Cards in 1975.

Both quarterbacks in the Houston versus New England game would fail to lead their teams to scores. The game up in Foxboro would not be complete without a driving rainstorm, a bona fide Noreaster, during the middle of the struggle. Neil Graff started in place of injured Jim Plunkett for New England, and managed to do as well as Houston's Dan Pastorini. The game was won in the first quarter, when Houston's Willie Germany recovered a Mack Herron fumble and ran 48 yards with the wet pigskin for the contest's only score in a 7–0 Oilers' victory. Germany strode along the sideline until he saw an opening near the center of the field. His ability to weave his way across the slick field enabled him to score.

Rounding out the first week of the 1975 season was a Monday night meeting in the Orange Bowl between the Raiders and the Dolphins. The Dolphins had won 31 straight regular season and postseason games at home, but the streak would stop on this evening. Miami lost almost a quarter of the experienced players on their roster to teams in the WFL, and now they truly had a team of "No Names." Oakland's Harold Hart was not the least bit concerned about which Dolphins were chasing him as he returned a fourth quarter kickoff 102 yards for a touchdown that keynoted the Raiders' 31–21 victory. On the kickoff, Hart hesitated whether or not to bring the ball out of his end zone. Once he made up his mind, however, he found a hole to his left and sped through it and down the sideline untouched. Seldom-used Pete Banaszak aided Oakland's cause by rushing for 74 yards and two touchdowns. Oakland's defense also contributed to the cause with four interceptions and three sacks of Miami quarterback Bob Griese. "It was a good game for us because we've been snakebit in our openers," said Oakland head coach John Madden, whose Raiders had not won an opening game since 1969. "I'm glad we got off to a good start."

As with most NFL seasons, the 1975 campaign saw its share of new head coaches taking charge of their teams. The new men of 1975 included Ted Marchibroda (Baltimore), Forrest Gregg (Cleveland), Paul Wiggin (Kansas City), O.A. (Bum) Phillips (Houston), Jack Pardee (Chicago), and Bart Starr (Green Bay). None of these coaches were expected to do much in their first year at the helm, but a couple of them did surprisingly well. Some had quality talent to work with. Others had to build their teams from the ground up and were thus destined to rebuilding and gaining experience. Naturally, the best way to obtain experience was to learn from losing, to keep key players or most of your players healthy, and to make smart adjustments on a week-by-week basis.

Some teams made key adjustments in Week 2 which helped to propel them to victory. The Detroit Lions surprisingly remained tied for first place in the NFC Central Division with a 17–14 win over host Atlanta. The Lions came from behind in the fourth quarter with a clutch fourth-down pass from quarterback Greg Landry to wide receiver Ray Jarvis, and a 1-yard touchdown plunge by halfback Altie Taylor with 1:20 left on the clock. Taylor's score came on a daring fourth-down play when he followed fellow running back Dexter Bussey's block off left tackle and into the end zone. "I just had that feeling," said Detroit head coach Rick Forzano on going for the touchdown on fourth down. "I'm just built that way—to take chances."

The Denver Broncos took some chances in winning their second straight home game of the young season on a Monday night against the youthful Green Bay Packers, 23–13. But it almost did not happen. Denver needed two key interceptions, one by linebacker Jim O'Malley and the other by linebacker Randy Gradishar, to lead them to the winning points. Broncos quarterback Charley Johnson was ineffective during the first half, and would be replaced by backup signal caller Steve Ramsey in the second half. Ramsey did just enough to spur the Broncos offense into putting the winning points on the scoreboard. In contrast, Green Bay quarterback John Hadl completed 23 passes for 273 yards against the tough Denver defense, but the two interceptions were his downfall. "Hadl was just superb," said magnanimous Denver head coach John Ralston.

"He picked us to pieces in the second half." The Broncos came within a whisker of making the playoffs in 1973 and 1974. Their 2–0 start to the 1975 season was a good sign that they were headed to the postseason, but they would be disappointed by a few close losses and some downright humiliating defeats in subsequent weeks. Denver would take a step backward in 1975 and would finish the year with a frustrating 6–8 record.

The Houston Oilers continued to surprise the rest of the NFL with a 33–17 win over visiting San Diego in the second week of the 1975 season. Fans in the Lone Star State were optimistic following Houston's seven victories in the 1974 season. They had no idea that their team would be undefeated after the first two weeks in 1975, however. Only 33,765 attended the Oilers' win over the Chargers, which featured two Houston running backs gaining over 100 yards rushing apiece. Ronnie Coleman ran for 112 yards and Don Hardeman contributed 107 more.

Houston's defensive nose guard Curley Culp also scored his first pro touchdown when San Diego backup quarterback Jesse Frietas was hit by Houston linebacker Ted Washington and fumbled. Culp picked up the pigskin and rumbled into the end zone with a 38-yard fumble recovery return. The team and their new coach, Bum Phillips, appeared to be on the right track towards contention. "I haven't ever been 2–0 in the NFL as a head coach before," chuckled Phillips, whose friendly Texas style and down home mannerisms endeared him to his players. By the final week of the season, the growing throngs of Houston fans were endeared to him too, as the Astrodome averaged 48,065 spectators per home game.

One of the most exciting games in Week 2 occurred in Dallas, as the Cowboys and Cardinals went into overtime to decide a winner in this NFC East slugfest. Not many prognosticators were sure where Dallas would finish in the standings. Many felt that their absence from the 1974 playoffs was an anomaly, while others believed that the Cowboys' star was tarnished and on the downward spiral that most teams ride to mediocrity at one time or another. Tom Landry's club did their best to answer their critics with an exciting 37–31 victory over Don Coryell's Cardinals. The first half of this game was a defensive struggle, with Dallas taking a 7–3 lead into halftime. The second half was totally different, however, as both teams poured it on with bombs and big plays. Dallas quarterback Roger Staubach and St. Louis quarterback Jim Hart traded touchdown tosses in the third quarter. Hart's best throw came when he launched a missile to wide receiver Earl Thomas, who sped through the Dallas secondary on a quick slant pattern, caught Hart's perfect pass in stride, then raced to the end zone to complete the 80-yard play. On that play, Hart eluded a strong rush from Dallas defensive end Harvey Martin, and Thomas caught the ball just inches before Dallas safety Cliff Harris dove for a potential interception or deflection.

Immediately after Thomas' score, Dallas head coach Tom Landry and special teams coach Mike Ditka reached into their bag of tricks and came up with a gem on the subsequent kickoff return. Dallas rookie Rolly Woolsey fumbled the kick, then secured it at his 3-yard line, then handed off to fellow rookie Thomas Henderson, who was sprinting towards the sideline and away from the St. Louis pursuit lanes. Henderson was a speedy linebacker whose time in the 100-yard dash impressed the Dallas coaches at training camp. Landry and Ditka made use of this weapon at the opportune moment. Henderson raced untouched down the sideline for an incredible 97-yard touchdown which built the Dallas lead to 28–17. Henderson's description of the play lends credence to the knowledge of the Dallas coaching staff, to the will they had to take risks and use a rookie's talents in a tight ball game, and to the luck required to pull off a trick play: "But what set the play up perfectly was that Rolly Woolsey fumbled the ball. He couldn't get a hold of it, started looking for the handle. I ran toward him and finally, at the three yard line, he found the ball, handed it to me, and ran the other way. I motored along the three all the way toward the sideline where Randy Hughes picked up the first tackler on the picket fence and Cardinals were dropping like they'd been shot. I turned up field and Burton Lawless took somebody out, then finally Randy White sprung me—almost an all-rookie runback—and I went ninety-seven yards for a touchdown. I slam-dunked the ball over the goal post."

The Cardinals would not give up, however. Not in this game or in any game during the 1975 season. Jim Hart would throw for two more touchdown passes in the fourth quarter, the last one to wide receiver Mel Gray with 46 seconds remaining, thereby tying the game at the end of regulation at 31 apiece. Hart would finish the game with four touchdown passes for 314 yards. Staubach would settle for 307 yards and three touchdown passes, but he threw the one that won the game. Following a vital interception and 38-yard return by Dallas middle linebacker Lee Roy Jordan of a Hart pass midway in the overtime period, Staubach connected with tight end Billy Joe DuPree for a 3-yard score which ended the game. "I thought we'd lost it, won it, and lost it again," said Landry after the ordeal. "It was a long afternoon. It's enough to turn a man grey."

Dallas' arch-rival—the Washington Redskins—appeared to be the greyest (oldest) team in the NFL, but also the strongest team in the NFC after their 49–13 rout of the New York Giants at RFK Stadium. The Redskins scored a blistering 28 points in the second quarter and another 21 points in the fourth quarter against the young Giants. Washington quarterback Billy Kilmer and his backup Randy Johnson each threw two touchdown passes, and "The Old Dancing Bear," Redskin defensive end Ron McDole, recovered a New York fumble in the end zone for a touchdown. Larry Jones also added a 52-yard punt return for a score as well. Also in the rout, Washington wide receiver Charley Taylor caught five passes for 51 yards, and thus became the 15th player to eclipse 10,000 receiving yards in a career. The Redskins were now 2–0, and were leading the league in offense with 90 points scored, and in defense with only 16 points allowed. "I've got to give him [New York quarterback Craig Morton] credit," said magnanimous Washington defensive tackle Diron Talbert, who was credited with three sacks in the game, "because we got to him pretty good and he stood up and took it pretty well."

Finally, the Buffalo Bills had some payback in mind as they traveled to Pittsburgh to take on the defending world champion Steelers. The Bills had lost a divisional playoff game at Pittsburgh the previous December, and were eager to make amends for that defeat. Very few experts saw this one coming. In the rematch, Buffalo superstar running back O.J. Simpson took one of his first carries off right tackle and let his speed do the rest. Pittsburgh called a safety blitz on the play, and Simpson exploited it for all it was worth. Simpson flew down the sideline (and past where Pittsburgh safety Glen Edwards would have been had he not blitzed) untouched for an 88-yard touchdown that left the fans at Three Rivers Stadium and the Steelers themselves in shock. Simpson would end the day with 227 yards rushing, the most rushing yards in a game in the NFL in 1975, and the most ever surrendered in one game by the Pittsburgh Steelers. "We were in a goal line defense on Simpson's long touchdown run," said Pittsburgh head coach Chuck Noll, "and if he had been an ordinary runner we would have had him for a loss." Pittsburgh All-Pro defensive tackle Joe Greene, who helped limit Simpson to 49 yards rushing in the 1974 playoff game, added, "He [Simpson] was overdue against us. You can't keep the great ones down like that all the time. There are not enough superlatives in my vocabulary to describe him."

The Buffalo defense also contributed to the cause with a key forced turnover. Pittsburgh quarterback Terry Bradshaw lost his grip of the ball as he was attempting to pass, and Buffalo defensive end Earl Edwards plucked it out of the air. Bradshaw grabbed Edwards and tackled him, but before he hit the Tartan Turf, Edwards lateraled the ball to fellow defensive lineman Mike Kadish, who carried it 26 yards for a touchdown. "That was the first time I ever scored a touchdown in my life," said a happy Kadish.

Buffalo quarterback Joe Ferguson added two touchdown passes, one to tight end Reuben

Gant, and the other to wide receiver Bob Chandler. Gant skillfully got both of his feet inbounds before he tumbled out of the end zone with the prized ball on his score. Chandler beat Steelers cornerback J.T. Thomas on an out-and-up pattern and dove for the ball in the end zone for his touchdown. The Bills had avenged their 1974 playoff loss by giving the Steelers a 30–21 whipping. Boosted by their win over Pittsburgh, the Bills would go on to claim victory in each of their first four games in 1975.

The third week produced a few games which helped to distinguish the future identity of several teams, and served as a harbinger of what some teams were capable of during the 1975 season. The Philadelphia Eagles upset the surge of the Washington Redskins in grand fashion at Veterans Stadium, forcing six Washington turnovers and rushing for 213 yards against the Over the Hill Gang. The Eagles defense shut out the Redskin offense during the second half. A few days prior to the game, Philadelphia head coach Mike McCormack called his team a "bunch of dogs" for their lackadaisical efforts during the first two weeks of the season. Philly fans took the hint and showed up at the game against the Redskins loaded with dog biscuits, which they flung onto the field during pregame warm-ups. Philadelphia's "Boo Birds," as they were often called, were tough fans to please throughout the decade, and in years where losing was commonplace, the Eagles fans were relentless in their verbiage and vocal attacks. Fist fights in the stands were frequent, and obscene gestures during the decade were displayed as often as signals were given to grab the attention of the hotdog and beer vendors. No one was safe. The crescendo of verbal insults flowed from the upper deck on down, and included stark and profane opinions on a player's ancestry, to gynecological suggestions directed at a player's mother, wife or girlfriend. Woe be to the fan who wore an opposing team's colors or jerseys. Those poor souls were shown no mercy whatsoever. Later in the decade when sports talk radio stations came about, the colorful language and epithets heard from thousands of fans using that medium tested the patience of the Federal Communications Commission (FCC) on a daily basis in "The City of Brotherly Love."

Several other things were tested in Houston in the third week, when division rival Cincinnati strolled into the Astrodome. The Oilers held a 17–7 lead going into the fourth quarter, only to see the Bengals erupt for two touchdowns and a 21–19 victory. Houston had an opportunity to win late in the game, but after four chances from the 1-yard line, a goal-line stand by Cincinnati's defense stifled the Oilers' last chance. After the game, Houston head coach Bum Phillips talked to his team, and in classic Phillips fashion, came up with an analogy and a battle cry that lasted throughout the season: "I gave them a description of the type of guy that we wanted here. There's two mountain climbers climbing on a mountain and one of them slips and falls. We know that they guy that fell is not going to let go of the rope. W hat we wanted was someone on the other end of that rope that we knew wouldn't let go of it. So, what we did it for was an effort to make everybody realize that they guy next to them was the kind of guy that they'd bet their life on. But 'Hold on to the Rope' was something that lasted all year long."

The Buffalo Bills held on to their winning ways during the next two weeks, and they managed to score 38 points in both weeks. The Bills destroyed the visiting Denver Broncos 38–14, and outlasted the host Baltimore Colts, 38–31. O.J. Simpson ran for 138 yards against Denver, and 159 yards against Baltimore. The Bills surprisingly stood alone in first place in the AFC Eastern Division with a perfect 4–0 record.

The Pittsburgh Steelers rebounded from their embarrassment against the Bills by routing the Cleveland Browns the following week at Municipal Stadium, 42–6. The Steelers' offense accumulated 501 yards in total offense. Pittsburgh wide receivers Lynn Swann and John Stallworth each had no trouble finding success in the Cleveland secondary. Swann caught five passes for 126 yards and one touchdown, and Stallworth added four more receptions for 109 yards and one score. What made this game unique, however, was the extra-curricular free-for-all that occurred late in the second quarter. Pittsburgh defensive tackle "Mean" Joe Greene was disqualified from the game after kicking Cleveland offensive tackle Bob McKay several times in the groin. Both benches joined in the fracas. Cleveland reserve center Tom De Leone ran onto the field and was also ejected for winding up and punching Greene in the solar plexis several times while he (Greene) was on his back. "I've never seen such a ridiculous thing, a guy standing over someone and just kicking him in the groin repeatedly," said an angry Cleveland head coach Forrest Gregg after the game. "The officials should have done something before it got out of hand. There's no telling how much damage it has done to McKay. I hope Greene is proud of himself."

The Detroit Lions were proud of their 2–0 record as they closed out the NFL's third week on a Monday night in Pontiac, Michigan. The Lions would be opening their brand new Teflon-roofed stadium for the first time with a contest against the Dallas Cowboys. Both teams played a pretty even first three quarters, with Dallas holding a slim 15–10 lead. Then in the fourth quarter, the Dallas shotgun offense exploded for 21 points, propelling the Cowboys to a 36–10 triumph. The Doomsday Defense sacked Lions quarterback Greg Landry an astounding 11 times, resulting in 84 yards in losses. "It's amazing we're still unbeaten," said modest Dallas head coach Tom Landry, "considering we're in a transitional phase with so many new fellows. The veterans are keeping us going."

The Oakland Raiders kept going after opening day by winning their first three ball games. Then in Week 4, they visited arch-rival and winless Kansas City in Arrowhead Stadium. It was a bloodbath. But unexpectedly, it was the Raiders who did the bleeding. Almost everything that Kansas City's offense did succeeded beyond their most hopeful dreams in their 45–10 victory. To be fair, Oakland had several key starters injured and inactive for the game, including quarterback Ken Stabler and wide receiver Fred Biletnikoff. New Chiefs head coach Paul Wiggin quickly found himself firmly in the midst of this rivalry, regarded as one of the most intense in pro football during the 1960s and early 1970s. Wiggin did his part to build on the historic Raider-Chief clashes in this beat down. "Maybe we found it [the rivalry] again," said Wiggin after his first win as a head coach. Kansas City quarterback Mike Livingston threw for three touchdowns, and running back Woody Green ran for 101 yards and scored one touchdown. The Chiefs thus won their first game of the season, the Raiders lost their first game of the season, and an old-time football rivalry was momentarily renewed. The Raiders, however, would meet the Chiefs again in Oakland later in the season.

Another AFC West team lost more than a football game in Week 4. The Denver Broncos lost their leading rusher, Otis Armstrong, to a torn hamstring muscle against the Pittsburgh Steelers in a 20–9 defeat. Armstrong's injury occurred while he tried to cutback on a sweep along the sideline. Armstrong led the NFL in rushing a year before, and as he was taken from the field on a stretcher, Denver's hopes for a championship and a winning season went with him.

The Green Bay Packers were destined to suffer through a losing season in 1975 also, but they experienced one brief moment of elation in a surprise 19–17 win at Dallas in the fifth week of the season. The Packers caught the Cowboys overlooking them, and took advantage of it. Green Bay was trailing by five points late in the contest when center and special teams player Larry McCarren hit Dallas punt returner Golden Richards and forced a fumble deep in Dallas territory. Packers rookie defensive back Steve Luke recovered the ball at the Cowboys' 31-yard line. A couple of plays later, Packers quarterback John Hadl hit tight end Rich McGeorge in the corner of the end zone for the 26-yard winning score. The upset win marked head coach Bart Starr's first pro victory in his new role. "The credit belongs to the players," said the predictably humble Starr after the win. The Packers would only register a 4–10 mark in 1975, but they led the NFL in covering punts, allowing only 4.9 yards per punt return. The Pack also forced more fumbles (44), and recovered more fumbles (27) than any team in the league.

On Monday night, October 20, the New York Giants came from behind to defeat the previously unbeaten Buffalo Bills at Rich Stadium, 17–14. A few items about this contest made it memorable. Despite his team's loss, Buffalo's O.J. Simpson rushed for 126 yards (the 29th 100-yard game of his career), giving him a remarkable 823 yards in the first five games of the year. This broke former Cleveland Browns superstar Jim Brown's mark of 815 yards in his first five games in 1958. Another couple of instances in this game were unique due to their ridiculous nature. An inebriated fan in the first few minutes of the third quarter decided to hang on the rope which held the placekicking net in place along the west end line of the stadium. The spectacle of this fan dangling at least 50 feet above the playing surface while the game continued was unnerving to everyone, including the ABC-TV broadcast team. Howard Cosell described it as "dangerous, disgraceful, and absurd." The fan eventually made it to the "safety" of the upper deck and the stadium security personnel. In the fourth quarter, another drunken fan decided to run on the field at the 10-yard line, which halted the game action until he was arrested. These events were not new in the NFL, as many fans over the years have violated their rights as ticket-holders by running on to playing fields across the league. But in the 1970s, many fans took it upon themselves to perform this action for the television cameras and the live audiences in record numbers, most often on *Monday Night Football*, when virtually all of America was watching. Many did it minus wearing any articles of clothing, and a new phenomenon was born ... streaking. The results were the same in each instance. A delay of game, followed by an arrest. And a pretty disgusting visual offering of a naked man running. On the bright side, however, at least most streakers were not insane or drunk enough to risk hanging from a rope across the field.

The Houston Oilers kept "holding onto *their* rope" in the Astrodome when they faced the Washington Redskins in the fifth week of the season. Both teams had good defenses, and Houston's defense delivered one of its best efforts against Washington. Head coach Bum Phillips installed the 3–4 defense because he believed that it was simply more versatile than the traditional 4–3 defense that most teams relied on. "With the three-four, you can do more," explained Phillips. "It's the best run defense there is." The Redskins, who going into the game as the league's highest scoring team, could only merit one touchdown against the stingy Houston defense. It came when quarterback Billy Kilmer was tangled up by blitzing Houston linebacker Robert Brazile, who brought the veteran signal caller to the AstroTurf. Nevertheless, Kilmer was able to release the ball before being grounded, and his floated pass to wide receiver Frank Grant was caught just before Grant's feet went out of the end zone. The Oilers responded with a 1-yard scoring plunge by running back Don Hardeman. In the fourth quarter, Hardeman would score again from the 1-yard line, and that touchdown provided the winning points for the Oilers in their 13–10 upset win over Washington. The victory gave Houston a 4–1 record in the competitive AFC Central Division, just behind the undefeated Cincinnati Bengals.

Speaking of the Bengals, another tight contest occurred in rainy Riverfront Stadium. The Raiders and Bengals both had difficulty moving the ball with the poor weather conditions and the lack of decent traction all game long on the AstroTurf. The ball was slippery too, as both teams collected four interceptions apiece. The most costly and most telling turnover came when Raiders quarterback Ken Stabler tried to pick on a rookie cornerback, Marvin Cobb, who was filling in for the injured Ken Riley. Cobb intercepted a sideline pass intended for Oakland wide receiver Cliff Branch in the third quarter and speeded his way to a 52-yard touchdown. A key block by Cincinnati defensive end Sherman White on Oakland offensive tackle Art Shell allowed Cobb to reach the end zone, and allowed the Bengals to improve their record to 5–0 with a 14–10 victory.

"We know now that we don't have to be afraid to use Marvin Cobb," said Cincinnati head coach Paul Brown after the game.

By mid-season, several teams were staking claims as potential playoff contenders. Both the Dallas Cowboys and the Pittsburgh Steelers faced possible defeat against lesser competition in their Week 6 contests, yet both somehow came back from the brink and won for the fifth time. The Cowboys appeared dormant in Veterans Stadium against the Eagles, a team that had only won once at this point of the season. The Eagles were usually able to play inspired football against a hated rival, however, and that's just what they did against Dallas, at least until the final two minutes of the game. Dallas quarterback Roger Staubach had to throw a career-high 49 times (completing 27 for 314 yards) against a Philadelphia defense which shut down the Dallas running game (the Cowboys could only muster 78 rushing yards on the day). Despite Staubach's efforts and almost a dozen completions from the shotgun formation, the Cowboys still trailed the Eagles 17–10 with little more than a minute to play. Staubach responded to the challenge and managed to hit wide receiver Drew Pearson on a 21-yard slant pattern with 1:04 left to tie the game at 17–17. Dallas then miraculously recovered an onside kick and in 35 seconds drove from their 40-yard line to the Philadelphia 25-yard line in five plays. Pearson climaxed his afternoon with his second clutch catch near the sideline. The skinny (but dependable) wideout snared Staubach's final pass of the day as he leaped high over Eagles safety Randy Logan, then juked Eagles outside linebacker John Bunting prior to getting out of bounds with three seconds left on the clock. "I just fired it out there and Drew made a heck of a play," said Staubach. Dallas placekicker Toni Fritsch ended the game with a 42-yard field goal that gave the Cowboys a heart-stopping 20–17 victory and a 5–1 record. "I talked myself into it," Fritsch said of his winning kick. "I couldn't let my teammates down. It was one of the most important field goals I ever made."

The best efforts of the Pittsburgh Steelers are usually good enough to let their opponents down on a regular basis. But against the Green Bay Packers in Milwaukee's County Stadium, the Steelers had their hands full. The Packers played an inspired game on both sides of the ball, with running back John Brockington scoring twice, and with the Packers limiting the Steeler offense to zero touchdowns (the only game that the Steelers failed to score an offensive touchdown all year). Pittsburgh countered with a 94-yard kickoff return by rookie Mike Collier, and with the rugged bursts of fullback Rocky Bleier (a native of Appleton, Wisconsin), who rushed for a career-high 163 yards on 35 carries. The Steelers as a team out-rushed the Packers, 248–63. "Rocky was going well, so we kept using him," said Pittsburgh head coach Chuck Noll. Green Bay defensive back Al Randolph added, "He [Bleier] got a lot of those yards on his own."

Pittsburgh made the most of its last-minute chances, and placekicker Roy Gerela completed a difficult comeback with a 29-yard field goal (his third of the game) with 1:04 remaining to give the Steelers a 16–13 win, boosting them to 5–1 on the year, a half-game behind AFC Central Division-leading Cincinnati.

The AFC East Division had another grudge match between Miami and Buffalo in the sixth week of the season. The Bills had been competitive with the Dolphins during the past several years, and they were averaging 32 points per game in 1975 going into their first meeting of the year with Miami. The No-Name Defense was having a superior first five weeks, limiting their opponents to an average of only 14 points per game. Rich Stadium was the locale for one Miami comeback after another in this struggle. The Dolphins trailed the Bills on five different occasions before finally pulling out a tough 35–30 victory over the Bills. It took three touchdowns from Dolphins fullback Don Nottingham (each on off-tackle runs) and two scoring passes by Miami quarterback Bob Griese to produce the needed points. Buffalo scored first on a 30-yard interception return for a touchdown by rookie safety Steve Freeman, who stepped in front of a Griese pass intended for running back Norm Bulaich and sped down the sideline untouched. Buffalo's O.J. Simpson boosted the Bills' lead to 13–0 with a 26-yard run. Buffalo quarterback Joe Ferguson also had one of his best days, connecting on 20 of 29 passes for 221 yards and two touchdowns. Yet it was a costly Ferguson interception by Miami safety Jake Scott which set up the winning score, a 1-yard burst by Nottingham. "I was surprised he [Ferguson] threw just then [from deep in his own territory]. He just mis-read the coverage."

The NFC East could easily have been mis-read by most football followers by the seventh week of the 1975 season. The Dallas Cowboys, Washington Redskins, and St. Louis Cardinals were each sporting identical 5–2 records. Dallas rolled into Washington and found themselves in another tight contest with their most hated rival in their attempt to take control of the division. It did not happen, however, as the Redskins went into overtime to defeat Dallas, 30–24. Like most overtime games, this one was a nail-biter. Dallas had a 24–17 lead when Washington quarterback Billy Kilmer hit tight end Jerry Smith with a 7-yard touchdown pass with 1:52 left on the clock. Dallas responded with a drive into scoring range, but placekicker Toni Fritsch missed a 38-yard field goal attempt with nine seconds remaining in regulation. In the overtime period, Redskins safety Ken Houston intercepted a Roger Staubach pass and returned it to midfield. Nine plays later, Kilmer leaped over offensive guard Walt Sweeney and just got the ball over the goal line. The Redskins thus claimed a 30–24 victory. "It was kind of a 'boo, yea, boo, yea' afternoon," said Kilmer.

The Cardinals made the NFC East race tighter with a come-from-behind 24–17 victory over a tough New England team at Busch Memorial Stadium. St. Louis was trailing 17–10 going into the fourth quarter, when Cardinals halfback Terry Metcalf took over. Earlier in the game, Metcalf wove his way through a bevy of Patriots en route to a 69-yard punt return for a score. Late in the game, Metcalf completed two scoring drives with touchdown runs of one yard and seven yards to boost the Cardiac Cardinals to a 24–17 triumph.

The AFC Central Division mirrored the NFC Eastern Division with three teams with identical records at the end of Week 7. Pittsburgh, Cincinnati, and Houston each owned impressive 6–1 records, with the most noteworthy contest pitting the Steelers at the Bengals. The defending champs took charge early and built a 23–3 lead going into the fourth quarter. Cincinnati head coach Paul Brown built his team to be able to gain ground quickly, however, and that is just what the Bengals did. Cincinnati scored three touchdowns in the fourth quarter, all on touchdown passes by quarterback Ken Anderson. Unfortunately for Anderson, one of his fourth quarter passes was intercepted by Steelers' safety Mike Wagner, who returned the ball 65 yards, setting up the winning touchdown, a 1-yard quarterback sneak by Pittsburgh's Terry Bradshaw. "My job is to be the centerfielder on pass coverage," said Wagner. "It was the old story of being in the right place at the right time."

The time was now at hand for several teams to make playoff drives. The second half of the regular season saw some separation in the league standings, as teams like Minnesota, Los Angeles, and Miami each started to put some room between themselves and their nearest divisional challengers. The Vikings remained undefeated through the first 10 weeks of the season, and built a four-game lead over division rival Detroit. The Rams were 6–1 before being upset by a 2–5 San Francisco team in Week 8. Nevertheless, they still owned a three-game lead over the 49ers. Miami built a two-game cushion over Buffalo in the AFC East with a 7–1 mark going into Week 9. Minnesota's formula of strong defense and ball control offense was similar to Miami's, and was still proving to be successful despite newer and younger players dotting their lineup. The Dolphins had to employ nine new starters on defense thanks to a bunch of injuries to most of their veteran defenders. The Rams were winning games in spite of relying on the shared time under center of two young quarterbacks (James Harris and Ron Jaworski).

Considered at the end of the season as possibly the greatest Cinderella team of all time, the Baltimore Colts faced the Buffalo Bills at Rich Stadium on the eighth week. The Colts were a lackluster 3–4, while the Bills were 5–2. Buffalo built a seemingly insurmountable 28–7 lead in the second quarter, strengthened by three O.J. Simpson scores. By game's end, Simpson would have a mid-season total of 1,128 rushing yards, which was 24 yards ahead of the pace to break his own 2,003-yard league record which he set in 1973. The Colts were not the least bit concerned about Simpson's statistics in the second half of this game, however. Baltimore's epic comeback featured 112 ground yards from running back Lydell Mitchell (who added three touchdowns), and the passing and running abilities of quarterback Bert Jones. The "Ruston [Louisiana] Rifle" was Jones' moniker, and he proved it by throwing for 306 yards against the Buffalo secondary. Jones spiced the comeback with a 89-yard bomb to wide receiver Roger Carr, and a 17-yard touchdown scamper of his own. The Colts scored 21 points in the fourth quarter to post an impressive 42–35 win over Buffalo. "I've never been that far behind and won," said Jones. The Colts would build upon their momentum with each passing week, and would not lose again during the remainder of the regular season.

Two division rivals would make a comeback in their Week 9 contest a memorable one, and one in which the referees had a vital role in deciding the outcome. The Redskins traveled to St. Louis to take on the Cardinals. Both teams stood at 6–2. The Redskins built a 14–3 lead and controlled the game until late in the fourth quarter. Almost any lead was not safe against the St. Louis offense, however, and the Cardinals put together another of their patented comebacks in the final minutes against the Over The Hill Gang. St. Louis quarterback Jim Hart connected on a short scoring toss to tight end J.V. Cain. Trailing now by seven points with 20 seconds remaining, the Cardinals had six yards to go to tie the game. On fourth down, Hart threw a dart to his slanting wide receiver, Mel Gray, who was one yard past the goal line when he caught the ball. Washington safety Pat Fischer met Gray at precisely that point and before Gray's feet hit the turf, he dislodged the ball from Gray's grasp. Both the ball and Gray tumbled to the ground in opposite directions, and the Redskins started off the field in joy, convinced that the pass was incomplete and that they had won. Enter the referees. Several of the officials (some of whom were actually in a position to see the play) started waving their arms to signal an incompletion. A couple of other officials from a further distance ran in and waved off the incompletion, claiming that Gray had the ball for the required amount of time before it was knocked loose. Remember, his body was one yard in the end zone when all of this happened.

Confusion was seen throughout the stadium. Many players did not know what to think, as some came on the field, and others went off as in a regular change of possession. It was almost like a game of musical chairs ... without the chairs or the music. The fans in the stands were also perplexed, and because no stadium in 1975 had a scoreboard that showed quality instant replays, no one except the television audience could re-live the frame-by-frame replays available. Opinions were mixed, as a legitimate case could be made for a touchdown *or* for an incompletion. It was *that* close. The referees gathered in a small circle to discuss their dilemma. A couple of the officials tried to ward off some of the more demonstrative players who tried to plead their team's case to the zebras. After a three-minute delay, the officials signaled touchdown, and the game was tied at 17–17 going into overtime. "I've never seen them [the referees] take longer to make a decision," bemoaned Washington head coach George Allen. Referee Fred Silva explained the play to the press after the game: "Gray made the TD catch," described Silva. "The official who signaled incomplete only saw a portion of the play and the ball hitting the ground."

The Cardinals won the coin toss and capitalized upon their late momentum. The Redskins would never see the ball again. St. Louis drove down the field on the strength of eight ground-churning carries by running back Jim Otis. After seven minutes of overtime, placekicker Jim Bakken booted a 27-yard field goal to give the Cardiac Cardinals a 20–17 victory and sole possession of first place in the NFC East. St. Louis would never lose their division lead again. This penchant for such dramatic Cardinal victories actually began when Don Coryell took over as head coach in 1973, and had continued through 1974 and 1975. "I guess if there's a way to make it closer, we'll think of it," said Coryell after beating the Redskins. "I don't like some of the decisions I make, but I have a lot of trust in Jim Bakken's foot. It's better than my judgment."

In the aftermath of St. Louis' narrow win arose a clamor amongst the fans once again to institute some sort of an instant replay system to help the referees. And just as with Franco Harris' Immaculate Reception in 1972, league officials kindly refused to entertain all pleas for such a change. The Mel Gray "completion" against Washington would not be the last occasion during the 1970s for fans to petition the NFL for an instant replay system to be established, however. Indeed, there would be several more controversial plays throughout the remainder of the decade which would evoke similar sentiments from fans, players, and coaches alike.

The league's front office instead preferred to focus their attention on a rules change from the previous year which was having a big effect on the sport. The rash in overtime games saw a great surge in 1975. In 1974, there were two regular season overtime games. In 1975, that number increased to nine. Certainly competition levels depended upon how badly each player wanted to win, despite the weather conditions, and their own physical conditioning. St. Louis offensive tackle Dan Dierdorf played in two of those overtime games in 1975. "It was real warm the day we lost to Dallas," recalled Dierdorf of the Cardinals' Week 2 37–31 loss to the Cowboys at Texas Stadium. "I think their conditioning really played a factor in the game's outcome. They seemed to have a lot more left in the overtime period." Dierdorf's teammate, defensive back Roger Wehrli, had a somewhat different opinion. "I hate to play overtimes because everyone is tired and there's additional possibility of injury," Wehrli said. In any event, the overtime period gave the fans more than their money's worth, and the league's front office was more than happy to exhibit the increase in overtime games as proof that the dull, defensive struggles of previous seasons were diminishing in number.

Another tough AFC contest that gave the fans their money's worth was held in Houston's Astrodome on November 16. The Dolphins met the Oilers in a vigorous struggle. Houston wanted to prove to the nation that they were for real, just as they had done several weeks prior against the Redskins. The Dolphins had won seven straight games heading into this contest, and they still had the Bills within sniffing distance. They could ill-afford to lose this game, but lose they did. Miami won the statistical battle, gaining 350 yards to Houston's 239, but one old pro turned the tide of the game. Oilers veteran defensive end Bubba Smith blocked two of Miami's extra point attempts, and those efforts provided Houston with their winning 20–19 margin. Houston's Billy "Whiteshoes" Johnson returned a punt 83 yards for a touchdown in the third quarter (the longest punt return in the NFL in 1975), and running back Ronnie Coleman broke no less than four tackles on a sweep to the right en route to a 7-yard touchdown run in the fourth quarter for the winning points. "It had to be a great game for our fans," said Oilers head coach Bum Phillips, "because they are sure behind us."

The Cincinnati Bengals hosted the Buffalo Bills the following evening in another important AFC contest. Both defenses failed to show up, however, as both offenses put up some very impressive numbers. Buffalo's O.J. Simpson rushed for a superlative 197 yards against the supposedly tough Bengals defense. Juice now had accrued 1,325 yards in 1975, which was 122 yards ahead of his 1973 mark at the same time of that epic season. Cincinnati quarterback Ken Anderson returned the favor, throwing for a season-high 447 yards against the solvent Buffalo defensive secondary.

"Anderson was unreal," said Simpson. "We knew we'd have problems with the pass, but he just picked us apart." The Bengals accounted for a team-record 553 yards in their 33–24 win over the Bills. The victory kept the Bengals tied with the Steelers atop the AFC Central Division with an 8–1 record. The loss was Buffalo's fourth in their past five games. "We couldn't stop them and they couldn't stop us," remarked Cincinnati head coach Paul Brown after outlasting Buffalo.

A couple of important games stood out in Week 10. The Cleveland Browns pulled one of the year's biggest upsets when they upended visiting cross-state rival Cincinnati, 35–23. Cleveland quarterback Mike Phipps had his best day as a pro, throwing for 298 yards and two touchdowns. The win was Forrest Gregg's first ever as a pro head coach. "I don't have to tell you how I feel," Gregg said to reporters after the win. "That was one helluva dry spell." Cleveland's win also helped the Steelers as much as it did the Browns. Combined with Pittsburgh's 32–9 pasting of Houston on the same day, the Steelers now had the indisputable lead in the AFC Central all to themselves at 9–1. Down south in Miami's Orange Bowl, the Colts put together a great rushing performance in their 33–17 victory (their fifth straight win) over the first-place Dolphins. Baltimore star halfback Lydell Mitchell rushed for 106 yards and scored the game-clinching touchdown when he took a pitchout from reserve quarterback Marty Domres (who was filling in for the oft-injured Bert Jones), broke across the grain, and outran the Miami secondary into the end zone. The loss was even more costly to the Dolphins, as their starting quarterback, Bob Griese, was also injured trying to avoid a Colts pass rush. Griese would be lost for the remainder of the season with a broken big toe.

Perhaps the most exciting game in Week 10 was an interconference tilt between the Raiders and Redskins at RFK Stadium. Oakland's venerable placekicker/quarterback George Blanda missed an extra point in the first quarter and a 33-yard field goal attempt with eight seconds left in regulation play, but he made up for it in overtime. Blanda's 27-yard field goal in the extra period lifted the Raiders to a 26–23 victory over the Redskins. "That's what I get paid to do," said a blunt Blanda after the game. Oakland wide receiver Fred Biletnikoff caught nine passes for 113 yards, and running back Pete Banaszak ran for three Oakland touchdowns. The win—which was Oakland's fifth in a row—boosted the Silver and Black to an 8–2 record, while the loss was Washington's second straight overtime defeat, and dropped them to 6–4. St. Louis crushed the New York Jets, 37–6, to remain on top of the NFC East at 8–2, while Dallas upended the visiting Philadelphia Eagles, 27–17, to stay just one game behind St. Louis at 7–3.

The Thanksgiving weekend further stipulated which teams were hungry for playoff contention, and which teams were downright famished. The Buffalo Bills and their explosive offense was good for at least 30 points against most opponents, but their injury-plagued defense was giving up large amounts of yards and points to almost any opponent. The Bills traveled to St. Louis on Thanksgiving Day, and in a game that they simply could not afford to lose, they defeated a first-place NFC team, 32–14. The win brought Buffalo (7–4) back to one game behind AFC East-leading Miami. "This puts us back in the running," beamed Buffalo head coach Lou Saban. Pacing the Buffalo attack on Turkey Day was fullback Jim Braxton, who churned through the Cardinals defense for 160 yards and three touchdowns. "We do what we can on offense according to what the defense does," explained Braxton. The Buffalo defense simply played their best game of the season, intercepting four passes against one of the best throwing offenses in the pro game. Buffalo cornerback Dwight Harrison was guilty of picking off two of those passes. The loss was detrimental to the Cardinals, because in a few days, the Dallas Cowboys would beat the New York Giants, 14–3, thus giving them a first-place tie with the Cardinals at 8–3 in the NFC East.

The Washington Redskins found themselves in a similar position as the Bills when they took on the visiting Minnesota Vikings, who were coasting towards another NFC Central Division title with an undefeated 10–0 record. A Washington loss to the Vikings would put them a full two games behind both the Cardinals and Cowboys. Fortunately for the Redskins, it did not happen. Washington poured it on the Vikings early and often, and built a 21–7 halftime lead. Minnesota came back in the second half with three touchdowns by halfback Chuck Foreman and a 21-yard rollout touchdown run by quarterback Fran Tarkenton. One of Foreman's scores came from 31 yards out when the Redskins' defense was bunched up on the line. Foreman burst through the charging defenders, sprinted past Redskins linebacker Chris Hanburger, and raced into the end zone. The persistent Vikings had somehow come back from their deficit and retook the lead, 30–24. Washington then dug deep into their resources, as quarterback Billy Kilmer completed five straight middle-zone passes in barely over a minute, the last of which went for a 15-yard touchdown to wide receiver Frank Grant. "We worked that pattern several times against [Minnesota corner-back] Bobby Bryant," said Kilmer. "He played it pretty tough, but I decided to keep throwing it until he took it away from us." Bryant never did.

The struggle had seconds left and the Redskins possessed a 31–30 lead. Minnesota place-kicker Fred Cox lined up for a 45-yard field goal attempt, which was probably out of his range on most days. Washington defensive lineman Ron McDole was aware of that, and he figured that Cox would experiment with a low, line drive type of kick. McDole was ready for that as he bull-dozed into the Minnesota backfield and partially blocked Cox's attempt. The ball flew wide of the upright. "It looked like we were going to lose," said Washington head coach George Allen, "but we had to have it." The Redskins' playoff chances were alive for another week, but the 31–30 loss to Washington did not hurt the Vikings, who now owned a 10–1 record. Detroit's 20–0 loss to Los Angeles on Thanksgiving had secured for Minnesota their third straight NFC Central Division championship.

The Baltimore Colts won their sixth straight game on November 30 by stifling the Kansas City Chiefs at Memorial Stadium, 28–14. Baltimore's aggressive pass rush broke through the Chiefs' offensive line and registered six sacks. Baltimore halfback Lydell Mitchell racked up 178 yards on 26 carries and scored on a 70-yard dash around left end and through the struggling Kansas City defense. Few were those who could have believed at the beginning of the season that the Colts were on pace to actually make the playoffs in a few short months.

The Oakland Raiders kept pace with the rest of the AFC by winning a tight contest against visiting Atlanta in the 11th week. The Raiders were surprised by a Falcons offense which put up 34 points, and claimed a seemingly secure 34–31 lead with only 1:10 remaining on the clock. Oakland, however, owned a huge share of the patent on coming from behind late—really late—in tough games, and that is exactly what they did against Atlanta. Oakland quarterback Ken "The Snake" Stabler drove the Raiders downfield, setting up placekicker George Blanda, who converted on an 18-yard field goal to tie the game. In the overtime period both teams had chances to score, but it appeared that neither would, and time was winding down. Stabler hit wide receiver Cliff Branch, who somehow eluded the attempted tackle of Atlanta linebacker Greg Brezina, juked cornerback Tom Hayes, and got out of bounds with three seconds left in overtime. Blanda came on and for the second straight week, and won an overtime game for the Raiders with a 36-yard field goal. "That's two [games] in a row like this," said Stabler. "It sure makes for an exciting game but I wouldn't want a steady diet of it." The 37–34 Oakland victory gave them their fourth straight AFC West championship.

The Cincinnati Bengals finally put an end to Houston's dreams of a division title by upending the Oilers in rainy Riverfront Stadium on the 11th week of the season. The Bengals had to rely on backup quarterback John Reeves, who was filling in for the injured Ken Anderson, who was suffering from bruised ribs. "It was awfully slick out there," said Reeves. "I just concentrated on holding on to the ball." Reeves threw two touchdowns in the first half of the Bengals' 23–19 conquest of Houston. "He [Reeves] got protection and that really primed us," said Bengals head coach Paul Brown. The win kept Cincinnati just one game behind the dominant Pittsburgh Steelers, who would win 11 straight games before the end of the regular season. The Oilers went out like a team with a promising future, however, as they did not "let go of that rope" in winning their final three games, including a 27–26 upset at Oakland, to post an impressive 10–4 record.

No team clinched a division title or a wild card spot in the season's 12th week, but several teams won important games to keep their postseason hopes intact. One of those teams was the Baltimore Colts, who shut out the host New York Giants, 21–0. Baltimore's seventh straight win set up a Week 13 grudge match with Miami. The Dolphins, for their part, once again outscored the Buffalo Bills in the Orange Bowl, 31–21, which kept them one game ahead of the Colts at 9–3. Buffalo's O.J. Simpson rushed for 96 yards against the Dolphins, but for the first time this season, he fell below the record pace of his 1973 rushing output. Simpson would not eclipse his own 2,003-yard rushing record from 1973 this season, but he was still in prime position to break Gale Sayers' record of 22 touchdowns in a season, set in 1965. Simpson was only two touchdowns short of tying that record with two weeks remaining.

The Pittsburgh Steelers (11–1) remained a game ahead of Cincinnati by beating the Cleveland Browns at Three Rivers Stadium, 31–17. For their part, the Bengals (10–2) went to Philadelphia and crushed the Eagles, 31–0. That win put Cincinnati in the playoffs as the AFC's wild card entry. It also encouraged Eagles owner Leonard Tose to fire unsuccessful head coach Mike McCormack. Bengals quarterback Ken Anderson would eventually end 1975 as the league's top-ranked passer. Cincinnati's passing offense was tops in the NFL in yardage with 3,241 yards through the air. Not to be outdone, Cincinnati's pass defense was also the best in the AFC, giving up only 1,729 aerial yards.

The Washington Redskins had a tougher time than the Bengals as they won another challenging game at Atlanta. In a somewhat identical duplicate of the previous week's win over Minnesota, the Redskins were tied with the Falcons at 24 apiece with 1:01 left. Quarterback Billy Kilmer drove his team downfield to the Atlanta 22-yard line by completing five of six passes for 56 yards. Kilmer would end the game with 25 completions in 38 attempts for 320 yards. Redskins placekicker Mark Moseley ended the drama with a 39-yard field goal with two seconds left. The Redskins had prevailed, 27–24. "This team is like a boxer who doesn't know when to stop getting off the floor," said Moseley. "They'll have to bury us before we stop getting up."

Washington's main opponents in the NFC East, the Dallas Cowboys and the St. Louis Cardinals, had a tough fight for supremacy in Week 12 in Busch Memorial Stadium. The Cardinals avenged their earlier loss at Dallas by overpowering the Cowboys in the rematch, 31–17. St. Louis quarterback Jim Hart helped his team build a 28–3 halftime lead by throwing three touchdown passes. Hart benefited from his superior pass protection, as the St. Louis offensive line tied a league record in 1975 by only giving up eight quarterback sacks all year long. Dallas came back in the second half, but the Cardinals defense relied on frequent blitzes, several of which forced untimely interceptions. St. Louis cornerback Roger Wehrli picked off a career-high three passes, two of which came deep in Cardinals' territory in the second half. The victory gave the Cardinals a 9–3 record and at the very least a wild card berth. "We're on top but I'm having a tough time thinking about that situation," said Hart after the win. "I don't even know what the [playoff] possibilities are. All I know is I want Dallas to beat the Washington Redskins." Dallas (8–4) would meet the Redskins (8–4) the following week, with the winner almost assuring itself of obtaining a playoff spot, while knocking the loser out of the playoffs.

The 13th week of the 1975 campaign produced several moments of daring and drama. The

St. Louis Cardinals did manage to defend their NFC East title from the previous year by defeating the Chicago Bears, 34–20, in rainy Soldier Field. "We're so happy to be in the playoffs again," said St. Louis head coach Don Coryell, "we'll play anywhere." Running back Jim Otis served as the workhorse for the Cardinals in this game, as he gained 147 yards in 33 carries, which placed him in the lead amongst NFC runners with 1,007 yards. Otis also scored a pair of short yardage touchdowns. "Now I know what it [rushing for 1,000 yards in a season] feels like," said Otis, who heaped praise among his teammates. "It takes a great offensive line, great blocking, and great wide receivers. Our offensive line never quits and that's how I got my thousand yards."

The Dallas Cowboys would not quit either, as the gridiron theatrics of the NFC East race was nearing its end. The Cowboys gained revenge against the Redskins in Texas Stadium by posting a dominant 31–10 win. Roger Staubach threw two touchdown passes for the Cowboys, and safety Charlie Waters intercepted a Randy Johnson pass and carried it back 20 yards for a touchdown. The sweet win over their arch-rivals put Dallas back into the playoffs, a place where they had failed to visit the previous year. "Dallas deserved to win today because they were the better team," said disheartened Washington head coach George Allen, whose Redskins were eliminated from postseason play for the first time since 1970. Dallas head coach Tom Landry described his team's performance in 1975 as "a miraculous season. Anyone who had been to our preseason camp would agree. Now we are in the playoffs and we will play anybody … tomorrow if necessary."

A major reason why Dallas regained a playoff berth was thanks to a shrewd deal just before the start of the regular season by Landry and Cowboys' general manager Tex Schramm. The Pittsburgh Steelers had a wealth of very good running backs, and due to the league's 1975 roster limit of 43 men (down four from 1974), the Steelers had to let go of one of those backs. Dallas quickly acquired veteran Preston Pearson as soon as he hit the waiver wire, and automatically had one of the best pass-catching runners in the NFL wearing a metallic and royal blue star on the side of his new helmet. Pearson (no relation to Dallas wide receiver Drew Pearson) managed to catch 27 passes for 351 yards and two touchdowns in 1975. He also rushed for 509 yards, which was second-best on the team. Dallas quarterback Roger Staubach would by season's end call Pearson "the key to our season."

The season was nearing its end, and perhaps the greatest drama in the 13th week occurred in Baltimore's Memorial Stadium, as the Colts hosted the Dolphins in a late-afternoon game which would answer the question as to who would win the AFC East. The game was a tough defensive struggle from the opening whistle to the final gun. Miami held a slim 7–0 lead going into the fourth quarter when the Baltimore offense finally put together a scoring drive. Colts quarterback Bert Jones completed six passes on the drive, and halfback Lydell Mitchell eventually scored the tying touchdown from six yards out with 5:30 left in the game. Mitchell led the AFC in pass receptions for the second straight year, catching 60 in 1975 (along with Cleveland wide receiver Reggie Rucker, who also caught 60 passes).

The Colts fans went wild after Mitchell's touchdown, and their vociferous leader was local legend "Wild" Bill Hagy, who stood on the dugout roof (and indeed throughout the entire stadium all game long) and led the cheers for his Baltimore brethren in the stands. Hagy spelled the word C-O-L-T-S, COLTS! by forming the letters with his hands, arms and legs, a full three years before the Village People began singing "Y-M-C-A." Hagy had Memorial Stadium rocking, but neither team could break the tie in regulation, so the game went to overtime. The contest had started at 4 p.m., and by the end of the third quarter, a relentless Chesapeake Bay fog shrouded the field. Some of the players could barely see more than 20 yards in distance, and that fact caused both offenses to limit their throwing plays to shorter yardage pass patterns. Nevertheless, the Colts prevailed when placekicker Toni Linhart drilled a 31-yard field goal with just over two minutes remaining in the sudden death period. "I knew we had a long way to go," said Baltimore head coach Ted Marchibroda of his team's winning drive. "That's the kind of team we have. They've been doing what they had to do all season long."

The ensuing scene was similar to the bedlam that had been a Memorial Stadium custom in the Colts glory years of the 1950s, the 1960s, and the 1970 world championship season. Fans rushed onto the field en masse, hugging their heroic Colts (and each other), and overjoyed at the prospect of going back to the playoffs as the NFL's most noticeable Cinderella team. It was termed "The Miracle on 33rd Street" (where Memorial Stadium was located in Baltimore) for this was a team that won all of two games the previous year, and had started the 1975 season with a 1–4 record. They were now 9–4 with but one game left to play.

The 1975 season produced a miracle in the success of the Colts, but it also produced a memorable ending for one popular player. Longtime Denver running back Floyd Little called it a career after nine spectacular years. In his final game at Mile High Stadium, Little's teammates wore a special patch on their orange jerseys commemorating the 5'10" tailback. Little inspired his team through all of the losing years, but on this day, he went out a winner. The Broncos were playing another also-ran team, the Philadelphia Eagles, and in the third quarter, Little scored his first of two touchdowns on a 66-yard screen pass. "I knew as soon as I found out Max [Denver offensive coordinator Max Coley] called the screen that I could go the distance," Little said. "I couldn't believe it when I saw the blocking and the open space. I don't know how many seconds it took, but I got it down there." A throng of Denver fans carried Little off the field in triumph at game's end. Denver prevailed, 25–10, and Little retired as the seventh-leading rusher in pro football history.

The 14th and final week of the 1975 regular season saw several long-standing league individual records fall, and some teams claim deeply desired playoff berths. Washington wide receiver Charley Taylor broke Don Maynard's record of pass receptions in a career, ending the season with a career total of 635 catches. Taylor and his Redskins were upset by the woeful Eagles, however, 26–3. Taylor's record turned out to be one of the few bright spots for the Redskins. The season of 1975 was the first year under head coach George Allen that the Redskins failed to make the playoffs. "When you make as many mistakes as we did [against the Eagles], probably more than in any game this year, you can't expect to win," lamented Allen.

St. Louis halfback Terry Metcalf set a record in combined yardage with 2,462 yards in a 24–13 victory over the Detroit Lions in the Pontiac Silverdome. Metcalf claimed the new record with rushing yardage, pass receiving yardage, punt return yardage, and kickoff return yardage. Metcalf became only the third player in NFL history to contribute to scoring in five different ways in one season (as a rusher from scrimmage, as a pass receiver, as a punt returner, as a kickoff returner, and even as a passer). The Cardiac Cards completed an incredible 1975 season with 11 wins and their second straight NFC East title. The records would continue to fall in Oakland, as the seemingly ageless George Blanda would complete his 26th pro season and pass the 2,000-point scoring mark (which has since been eclipsed by several players). Blanda would retire at the end of the season. The Raiders ended the regular season with a 28–20 revenge win over division rival Kansas City (whom they lost to by a score of 42–10 earlier in the year), and posted an 11–3 record, earning yet another AFC West title.

The biggest individual records were in danger of falling on a snowy afternoon in Buffalo, however, as the Vikings took on the Bills. Minnesota quarterback Fran Tarkenton needed only two touchdown passes to break Johnny Unitas' legendary career record of 290 touchdown passes. Added to that was the dramatic duel between Minnesota running back Chuck Foreman and Buffalo running back O.J. Simpson, both of whom were competing to see who might eclipse Gale

Sayers' record of 22 touchdowns scored in a season, set in 1965. Buffalo would not make the play-offs in 1975, but on an individual basis, Simpson's 1,817 yards in 1975 were good enough for another league rushing crown, his third of the decade. Juice's running mate in the backfield, Buffalo fullback Jim Braxton, added 823 yards rushing of his own, which helped to give the Bills an NFL-best 2,640 ground yards this season. Simpson also managed to catch many more passes in 1975 (28 for 436 yards and seven touchdowns) than in the year he set the league rushing record of 2,003 yards (1973). In that year, Simpson only had six catches for 70 yards and no touchdowns.

Right from the start, the Vikings—who already secured their playoff spot by clinching the NFC Central Division way back in Week 11—played as if they needed to win this game in order to qualify for the postseason. Tarkenton shredded the weak Buffalo defense immediately with two scoring drives in the first quarter. He focused on short passes to Foreman and wide receivers Jim Lash and John Gilliam. In a span of a few minutes, the Vikings had plowed through the snow for two touchdowns. By halftime, Foreman had scored twice, Simpson had scored once, and the Vikings owned a comfortable 21–7 lead. With his 24-yard dash in the second quarter, Simpson had tied Sayers' record of 22 touchdowns in one season. But Foreman still posed a threat to that record. He caught a 1-yard touchdown pass early in the third quarter, which gave him 21 touchdowns, and which marked Tarkenton's 290th career scoring pass, equaling John Unitas' career mark. A few minutes later, Tarkenton hit Foreman again in the flat for a score from six yards out, and the NFL had a new career touchdown pass champion. "I'm just glad it's done and behind us," Tarkenton said of his successful chase to break Unitas' record. Tarkenton would also end the season as the NFC's top passer and the NFL's All-Pro quarterback. Foreman, who ended the year as the league's top pass receiver with 73 receptions, had scored four times in this contest, but a tie with Sayers' record was all that he would get … unless you count the dozens of snowballs that he received from the Buffalo fans throughout the game. One of the flying snowballs in the second half had enough velocity on it to smack Foreman in the face, giving him blurred vision for the remainder of the game. "Chuck could have had his eye put out," said Tarkenton.

Simpson and Foreman each had scored 22 touchdowns as the third quarter was winding down. Simpson, however, wasted no time in obtaining his 23rd touchdown. Immediately after Foreman scored his final touchdown, Simpson sprinted out of the backfield and caught a perfect pass from reserve Buffalo quarterback Gary Marangi. Simpson carried the ball through a couple of half-hearted tackling attempts by Minnesota defensive backs Paul Krause and Joe Blahak, and pranced into the end zone. O.J. Simpson sat out much of the fourth quarter and ended the season with 23 touchdowns in one year, a new NFL record. "It's two great players, Simpson and Foreman, and it was an interesting highlight to watch the two of them try to break the record," said Tarkenton. "O.J. got it, and he deserves a tremendous amount of credit for it."

The Bills could take solace after the game in the fact that they scored 420 points in 1975, the highest-scoring single-season mark for a team in the entire decade. Considering that they accomplished this feat in a season with only 14 games, and that no team in 1978 or 1979 (seasons in the decade with 16 regular season games), could match Buffalo's mark in 1975, and you have quite an accomplishment. Somewhat of an afterthought to all of the old records falling was the fact that the Vikings had prevailed in this contest in New York's Orchard Park, 35–13, and had dodged countless numbers of flying snowballs on their way back to the locker room.

Baltimore and Miami would end the year with identical 10–4 records. Both teams would win their final game, as the Dolphins bested the visiting Broncos, 14–13, and the Colts upended the Patriots in Baltimore, 34–21. The Broncos almost defeated the Dolphins, but a blocked field goal attempt on the last play of the game by Miami special teams player Barry Hill preserved Miami's win. The AFC East Division title belonged to Baltimore, however, based on their two previous victories over Miami. Pittsburgh ended the regular season on a losing note, falling 10–7 to the Rams on a muddy field at Los Angeles. Pittsburgh head coach Chuck Noll could not be blamed for resting many of his starters in the second half of this loss, however. The Steelers' defeat, combined with a Cincinnati win over San Diego on the final Sunday, did not harm the Black and Gold. Pittsburgh (12–2) had built up enough of a cushion during the course of the year between themselves and the Bengals to claim the AFC Central title. The Steelers had finished on top of what many experts felt was the toughest division of the decade. The AFC Central became the first division in the Super Bowl era to have three teams (Pittsburgh, Cincinnati, and Houston) to each win at least ten games during the 1975 regular season. The stage was now set for the NFL postseason.

The 1975 divisional playoffs would feature three games with a fairly predictable result, and one memorable upset. The first postseason game featured the Cinderella Baltimore Colts, owners of the most remarkable single year turn-around in the history of the NFL, venturing into Pittsburgh's Three Rivers Stadium on an overcast December afternoon. Most experts believed that the defending Super Bowl champion Steelers would have little problem with the Colts, but they were soon to have their doubts. The Colts sustained a major injury in their first offensive series, when quarterback Bert Jones was hit by Steelers cornerback J.T. Thomas. The result was a bruised throwing arm, and Jones sat on the bench until the fourth quarter. Marty Domres was Jones' backup quarterback, and he wasted no time throwing an interception. Pittsburgh outside linebacker Jack Ham stepped in front of a Domres pass intended for halfback Lydell Mitchell to set up the Steelers' first score.

Pittsburgh running back Franco Harris then went to work quickly on the Baltimore defense. Harris was sent on the requisite traps, draws, and off-tackle runs that were the mainstay of most Steeler offensive game plans. Harris scored a touchdown on an 8-yard run in the first quarter, bowling over Colt defensive backs Bruce Laird and Nelson Munsey at the goal line. He then proceeded to rack up more ground yardage. Harris would finish the day with 153 yards rushing on 27 attempts, at that time an AFC Divisional Playoff record. Harris would also finish the game with a couple of fumbles, however, and those turnovers in critical occasions helped Baltimore to stay in the game. The Colts would tie the contest in the second quarter when Pittsburgh quarterback Terry Bradshaw would throw an interception to Baltimore cornerback Lloyd Mumphord, who returned the ball 58 yards down the sideline to set up what would be the Colts' only touchdown. "I was really surprised when he [Bradshaw] threw it in my chest," Mumphord said. Quickly after Mumphord's theft, the Colts were at the Pittsburgh 5-yard line when Domres eluded a couple of Pittsburgh pass rushers in his pocket and found wide Receiver Glen Doughty uncovered in the end zone for the score.

In the third quarter, the Colts took advantage of one of Franco Harris' fumbles to produce a field goal and a surprising 10–7 lead. Baltimore would be able to move the ball on occasions in the second half, but could not produce any more points. Pittsburgh, however, would begin to make big plays on defense, and in turn would take over the game. Steelers cornerback Mel Blount intercepted a tipped Domres pass late in the third quarter and returned it 20 yards to the Baltimore 7-yard line. Pittsburgh fullback Rocky Bleier scored on the very next play on a run up the middle. Bleier dragged Mumphord with him the final three yards and into the end zone. Once again, the Steel Curtain defense had made things easy for the Pittsburgh offense. "We got a lot of pressure from our defense," said Pittsburgh head coach Chuck Noll, "and that was the difference."

Another factor which unofficially was given at least some credit to helping out the Steelers occurred off the field. Steelers radio broadcaster Myron Cope of station WTAE came up with the idea a few days before the Colts game of having fans wave a gold or black towel, much in the same tradition of Miami's handkerchief wavers. Thousands of fans complied with Cope's request, and a new tradition was born. The Steelers, according to legend, received special powers with the towel fluttering throughout the stands. Cope claimed that the towel also "inflicted unexpected problems to the opposing teams." The "Terrible Towels," as they were called, were quickly mass-produced in Pittsburgh. They have since become synonymous with the Steelers in both home and away games, and millions of them have been sold worldwide over the years since 1975. Cope donated the proceeds of his invention to charity, a tradition which has continued to this very day.

The Steelers—whether thanks to their fans and their Terrible Towels or to their talent on the field—increased their lead to 21–10 early in the fourth quarter when Bradshaw culminated a seven-play drive and scored on a 1-yard quarterback sneak over his right guard, Jim Clack. Pittsburgh's final score was part timely, part comical, and completely decisive. Bert Jones returned to the game and immediately led the Colts downfield on the strength of a 58-yard bomb down the sideline to Doughty, who had badly beaten Blount, placing the ball on the Pittsburgh 24-yard line. The Colts drove down to the 3-yard line, when Jones dropped back and cocked his arm to pass. Jack Ham of the Steelers beat his blocker, jarred the ball loose from Jones' grasp, and fellow linebacker Andy Russell picked it up at the Pittsburgh 7-yard line. Russell immediately began his journey downfield. He ran, and he ran, and he ran. A convoy of Steeler teammates ran with him, in front of him, and behind him. Russell eventually reached the end zone for a 93-yard touchdown, and miraculously did not get called for a delay of game penalty. "The bear just got on his back," laughingly exclaimed Pittsburgh wide receiver Lynn Swann.

Steelers defensive end Dwight White blocked Bert Jones three different times on the return before Russell scored and before Jones decided to stay down on the turf. "I couldn't tell if he [Russell] was running for a touchdown or running the clock out," said Ham after the game. An urban legend from unnamed sources claimed that one photographer on the sideline took a photo of Russell when he recovered Jones' fumble, and then was at the opposite goal line taking a photo of Russell as he crossed the goal line.

The Steelers ended Baltimore's Cinderella season, 28–10, and thus moved on to the AFC championship game, where they would face the winner of the Cincinnati-Oakland playoff contest. "We had a lot of mistakes and errors on offense and that hurt us a lot," Noll said. "But our defense bailed us out. I haven't seen them play with such determination in quite a few weeks." The Colts were heartbroken, as is any playoff loser, but as their head coach Ted Marchibroda told his team, "we got beat [today] by a better football team."

The pro football experts were not really sure who was the better football team when the St. Louis Cardinals would face the Los Angeles Rams in the smog-covered Los Angeles Memorial Coliseum later that day. Many people believed that the Cardinals' explosive offense stood a good chance at racking up some points against the Rams' second-ranked defense. Los Angeles head coach Chuck Knox decided to go with Ron Jaworski as his starting quarterback just three minutes before the opening kickoff, favoring "The Polish Rifle" over James Harris, who had a sore throwing shoulder. "I really didn't feel any pressure at all," said the confident Jaworski. "I am the type of person who has the confidence to go out and do a good job." Knox's confidence in Jaworski was rewarded quickly and in grand fashion. The Rams ambushed the Cardinals and built a 21–0 lead just 14 seconds into the second quarter.

Jaworski scored the first touchdown from five yards out on a rollout to his left. His score culminated a 79-yard drive that was built on the power runs of halfback Lawrence McCutcheon, who accounted for 51 yards on the drive. On the Cardinals' first offensive series, Los Angeles left defensive end Jack Youngblood stepped in front of a Jim Hart screen pass intended for running back Jim Otis, picked it off, then raced 47 yards to the end zone untouched. Youngblood—a fan favorite—chucked the ball into the stands. On the first play of the second quarter, Rams safety Bill Simpson intercepted another Hart pass, and duplicated Youngblood's feat with a 65-yard return for a touchdown. On that play, Simpson displayed his underrated speed as he raced down the sideline untouched with the prized pigskin.

Fortunately for the Cardinals, their offense was built for comebacks, something that they had done successfully all year long. Moreover, they had plenty of time in which to put scoring drives together. St. Louis scored its first touchdown on Jim Otis' 3-yard run, but reliable placekicker Jim Bakken somehow missed the extra point. Jaworski came right back to register another Los Angeles touchdown when he hit a streaking wide receiver, Harold Jackson, who was running a deep post pattern past St. Louis cornerback Norm Thompson. Jackson beat Thompson by almost five yards, and the Rams held strong to a 28–9 halftime lead.

St. Louis was determined to do their best to make a game of it, however. They scored a third quarter touchdown when Hart hit wide receiver Mel Gray on an 11-yard comeback route. Gray sidestepped the over-committed Ram safety Dave Elmendorf and waltzed into the end zone. The score was now 28–16 in favor of the Rams, who were well aware of what the Cardinals had done throughout the regular season when they were behind on the scoreboard. The Rams defense had certainly seen all they wanted to see of the St. Louis offense by this time. They would take charge during the next five Cardinals possessions, never permitting Hart and Company to penetrate the Los Angeles 37-yard line during those drives. By game's end, the Rams would force five St. Louis turnovers and would sack Hart twice. Merlin Olsen, one of the greatest and most reliable defensive tackles in league history, was given the unenviable task of trying to penetrate the wall put up by notorious St. Louis guard Conrad Dobler. Many years later, Olsen would state that he "never lost his temper throughout his entire career like he did when he played against Dobler."

The Rams' final touchdown of the afternoon occurred when McCutcheon, who set an NFC Divisional Playoff record with 202 yards on 37 carries, got to within two yards of the Cardinals' goal line when he fumbled. Los Angeles wide receiver Ron Jessie was in the right place at the right time, however, as he recovered the loose ball and strolled into the end zone.

St. Louis closed out the scoring, when running back Steve Jones, who was in the lineup for starting halfback Terry Metcalf (who spent much of the second half on the bench with severe leg cramps), completed a late Cardinals drive with a 3-yard touchdown run. The 35–23 Los Angeles victory signaled the second straight year that they would participate in the NFC championship game. For the "Cardiac Cards," the season was a great one, but one in which they would not advance any further than they did the previous year. Nevertheless, head coach Don Coryell was optimistic about his team and their chances in the future. "Even though we were behind, our people had the competitiveness to really come back and battle back," said Coryell. "I'm really proud of them for that. They've been that way all year long. We'll get better every year."

On the following day, another couple of playoff games completed the divisional round. The Dallas Cowboys versus Minnesota Vikings 1975 playoff contest is considered by many fans and experts over the years to be very similar to the 1972 playoff tilt between Oakland and Pittsburgh, where Franco Harris made his famous Immaculate Reception. Likewise, the 1975 Cowboys-Vikings contest is remembered today mostly just for one play. One very important play with its own unique name. But there was more to it than just that.

Both teams came into this game traveling different roads. The Cowboys had the tougher schedule, but somehow managed to achieve a 10–4 record. Dallas had a good deal of talent, but their youngsters had little—if any—playoff experience. They also had the knowledge of knowing that no wild card team in NFL history had ever won a playoff game, and they would love nothing more than making history by becoming the first. The Vikings (12–2) had an easier schedule than the Cowboys, playing only three teams with winning records (they suffered losses in two of those three games). Minnesota did have the top-ranked defense in the NFL, the NFC's leading passer in quarterback Fran Tarkenton, and they had plenty of playoff experience. A grey, overcast sky and 27-degree temperatures covered Metropolitan Stadium as the wild card Cowboys and their Dirty Dozen rookies were expected by most experts to let playoff pressure get the best of them and force them to make critical mistakes. In the beginning, that's exactly what happened. A score-less tie was broken in the second quarter when a Minnesota punt was mishandled by rookie Dallas offensive lineman/special teams player Pat Donovan, who mistakenly thought that Neil Clabo's punt had touched one of his teammates. Fred McNeill recovered the muffed ball for Minnesota at the Dallas 5-yard line. A couple of plays later, Minnesota halfback Chuck Foreman plowed over from one yard out to give the Vikings a 7–0 lead going into halftime.

The Cowboys' offense had gained decent amounts of yardage in the first half against the Purple People Eaters. They would continue to do so in the second half, despite the stalwart efforts of veteran Minnesota All-NFC defensive end Carl Eller, who was keeping constant pressure all game long on Dallas quarterback Roger Staubach. Dallas head coach Tom Landry had Staubach run his plays away from Eller in the second half, and that decision enabled Dallas to succeed in overall ball control. By game's end, Dallas would out-gain Minnesota, 356 yards to 215. Dallas also had a definite edge in plays from scrimmage, 75 to 57. Finally in the third quarter, Dallas tied the game on a 4-yard run by second-year running back Doug Dennison, who ran right up the middle, blasted through attempted tackles by Minnesota's Jeff Siemon and Paul Krause, and just broke the plane of the goal line for the score. Toni Fritsch then put the Cowboys in front early in the fourth quarter with a 27-yard field goal. It appeared as if the Dallas offense was starting to take over the game and build on their lead. If their defense could just hold on for a few more min-utes, the Cowboys would achieve what would be considered by many a big playoff upset.

Minnesota was in trouble, and they knew it. Their offense finally addressed their predicament late in the fourth quarter, putting together a 12-play scoring drive. Several first downs on the drive came on the strength of quarterback Fran Tarkenton's short passes to Foreman, and the running of reserve halfback Brent McClanahan, who ran an end-around for 13 yards, and a few plays later, scored the go-ahead touchdown. McClanahan's 1-yard touchdown run was the result of his own second effort. On the play, McClanahan was hit hard by forcing Dallas safety Cliff Harris. The sturdy runner managed to bounce off of Harris' attempted tackle, however, and dive into the end zone. The Vikings now owned a 14–10 lead with time winding down.

Dallas was unable to move the ball on their next series, and punted to Minnesota. The Vik-ings were in prime position to run out the clock and win the game. All they needed was one more first down and the game would be theirs. On third and five from the Dallas 47-yard line and with 2:20 left on the clock, Tarkenton bootlegged to his right, but Dallas safety Charlie Waters stayed alert, fought off a block by Foreman, and pulled Tarkenton down for a three-yard loss. To many observers, this was possibly the play of the game, for it enabled the Cowboys to get the ball back one last time. Dallas wide receiver Golden Richards made a fair catch of Clabo's ensuing punt deep in his own territory. The Cowboys now had 85 yards to go. A field goal meant nothing. They needed a touchdown, and they had 1:51 left to get one.

Premier Cowboys wide receiver Drew Pearson had been shut down by the Minnesota defense throughout the entire game. Staubach knew that he had to throw to his clutch pass catcher, and for his part, Pearson knew that he had to get open against a defense that had yet to permit him that opportunity. On first down, Pearson sprinted down the field as if on a fly pattern. The Vikings defensive backs knew that Dallas needed a lot of yards, so they figured that Pearson was going deep. As a result, they play off of him and protected against a long pass. Pearson and Staubach both read this decision correctly. Pearson broke off of his pattern and ran a quick out. Staubach hit him on the sideline for his first catch of the game and a 9-yard gain. Staubach's next pass was incomplete. On third down, Staubach hit Pearson again, this time for seven yards and a first down.

A near disaster visited the Cowboys on the next snap of the ball. Dallas center John Fitzgerald was having difficulty with the shotgun snap back to Staubach. His snaps throughout the fourth quarter were too low, and at the Dallas 31-yard line, his snap bounced off the ground and against Staubach's shin. The nimble quarterback recovered the ball for a loss of six. Coach Landry could not take anymore chances at this point in the game, so he replaced Fitzgerald with rookie center Kyle Davis.

On the next two plays, Staubach avoided a strong Minnesota pass rush, only to throw incompletions. It was now fourth-and-16 from the Dallas 24-yard line. Less than a minute remained on the clock. Both Staubach and Pearson decided to go with a play that was similar to the first play of this drive. The only difference was that Pearson had to run deeper in order to gain enough yardage to acquire the first down. The other difference was that the Dallas offensive line had to block Minnesota's surging pass rush for a longer period of time. Dallas offensive right tackle Rayfield Wright managed to drive Minnesota defensive end Carl Eller deep into the Cowboys' backfield and beyond Staubach. Kyle Davis' center snap was perfectly sent into Staubach's hands. Pearson ran his pattern, and Staubach lofted a deep pass towards the sideline. Pearson reached for it, caught it, and tried to get his feet inbounds. Minnesota cornerback Nate Wright hit Pearson almost immediately, and knocked Pearson out of bounds before he could get both of his feet inbounds. The NFL rules in 1975 (and indeed throughout the 1970s) stipulated that if a defender knocked a receiver out of bounds before he (the receiver) got both of his feet inbounds (commonly referred to as a force-out), the referee would then be called upon to judge whether or not the receiver would have made a legal catch with both feet inbounds had the defender not knocked or forced the receiver out of bounds. Thus, it was a judgment call on the part of the official. Would Drew Pearson have gotten both of his feet inbounds had he not been knocked out of bounds by Nate Wright? The head linesman on the sideline, Jerry Bergman, said yes, and signaled a Dallas first down amid the agitated complaints of the Vikings' Wright, defensive back Terry Brown, and linebacker Matt Blair. According to Minnesota head coach Bud Grant, "the official gave Pearson the benefit of the doubt."

Dallas now had a first down to work with, but they were still 50 yards away from the end zone, and there was now only 44 seconds left on the clock. Another Staubach incompletion drained the clock down to 32 seconds remaining. All during this nerve-wracking drive, Pearson said, "Roger kept asking me if I could get deep." On second down, the receiver realized the moment was at hand. "Finally we ran out of chances," Pearson said. "I told him that now was the time." Dallas head coach Tom Landry knew "our only hope was to throw and hope for a miracle," he said.

Kyle Davis once again snapped the ball back to Staubach perfectly. Running back Charles Young broke from his stance in the shotgun formation and stayed in the backfield to block. The middle of the Dallas offensive line cut down several Minnesota interior defensive linemen, and Rayfield Wright once again blocked Carl Eller out of Staubach's vision and reach. Staubach pumped a throw to draw in Minnesota deep safety Paul Krause for just enough time to allow Pearson to go against man-to-man coverage by Nate Wright. Staubach reared back and threw the ball long and deep ... deeper than any other pass that he had thrown in the game. As soon as he released the ball, Staubach said a Catholic prayer, the *Hail Mary*.

Pearson had beaten Wright down the sideline, but Staubach's pass was under-thrown. Pearson adjusted to it by slowing down for just a step. Wright did not, and both he and Pearson collided, only just slightly, but enough for Wright to start falling to the turf. The ball had now arrived by this time, and Pearson grabbed it against his hip at the 4-yard line. He then hopped over the fallen Wright. Remember Paul Krause? After being lured inside by Staubach's fake, Krause finally reached Pearson, but the swift receiver had crossed the goal line just out of Krause's reach. "Looking back I think the pump-fake helped a lot," said Staubach. "Not only did it keep Krause from being involved in breaking up the pass, but it delayed him just long enough so he couldn't tackle Drew and stop the touchdown." Pearson then threw the ball as a token of triumph at the giant scoreboard at the open end of Metropolitan Stadium ... just before he was mobbed by a bunch of his team-mates.

Wright and Krause both immediately looked around for a penalty flag, for they both felt that Pearson was guilty of offensive pass interference. No flag was to be found, however. "From our side of the field, there is no question that Nate [Wright] was pushed," said Minnesota head coach Bud Grant. "Pearson had nothing to lose. If they call a penalty on him, what had he lost? They would just line up and try another long pass. It was one chance in a hundred that he would get away with it, but it was the only chance he had." After the game, Pearson could not totally refute Grant's assertion. "It was a little bit short so I had to come back a little and that gave me a chance to get away from Nate," said Pearson. "The ball juggled around a little and I finally caught it between my elbow and my ribs.... I thought I might have gotten pass interference. It could have gone either way."

Dallas had scored a miracle touchdown with 24 seconds left on the clock, and the crowd inside Metropolitan Stadium (including many of the players on both teams) were now in a state of shock. After a few seconds of dead silence, some fans began booing the referees for their two controversial calls (or non-calls) on this drive. Others were dumbfounded by what they witnessed and remained speechless. Staubach later recalled, "You could hear a pin drop. It was as though all of a sudden we were playing in an empty stadium."

Several Minnesota players shunned any semblance of silence. They were quickly penalized for "Unsportsmanslike Conduct" for expressing their disgust to the referees by using a unique blend of colorful language and epithets. The words "blind zebra" were the two most commonly used words that were reportedly heard, but those words were also supposedly preceded by other more salty words. Dallas thus kicked off from the 50-yard line. Tarkenton took over from the Vikings' 15-yard line, and was promptly sacked by Dallas' Ed "Too Tall" Jones for a 14-yard loss. Minnesota called time out with 18 seconds left when the game took on a surrealistic quality. Tarkenton used the time out not to discuss possible strategy with his coach, but rather to berate head linesman Jerry Bergman. Several disgruntled fans then began throwing objects on the field. At the 7-yard line, field judge Armen Terzian was hit in the head by a half-full bottle of Corby's Whiskey, which flew from the stadium's lower level. Terzian went down immediately ("like he'd been shot," according to Staubach), holding his head. Trainers and doctors from both teams ran onto the field to attend to Terzian, while the stadium public address announcer admonished fans to not throw objects onto the field. After a couple of minutes, Terzian jogged off the gridiron after having his head bandaged. He would require 11 stitches at the hospital to close the gash in his forehead. "That was unforgivable," said Minnesota middle linebacker Jeff Siemon. "That could have killed him. I hope I never see anything like that again." Minnesota owner Max Winter, according to the Associated Press, "offered a $5,000 reward for information leading to the arrest and conviction of the person who threw the bottle." Mark L. Ford, President of the Pro Football Researchers Association, reported that the city of Bloomington, Minnesota, closed the investigation on the bottle-throwing incident on February 6, 1976, without ever identifying a suspect.

The game ended two plays later when Tarkenton was sacked again by Jones and fellow defensive end Harvey Martin. The Cowboys had achieved a super upset, 17–14, and had thus captured the Cinderella label surrendered by Baltimore the previous day. The game was ranked by pro football experts as the sixth-greatest game of the decade (of the top 20 games of the decade), thanks to the miracle known as the "Hail Mary Pass." Even today, a long bomb in the heat of a supposedly winless struggle against really tough odds with time running out is still termed a "Hail Mary pass." But the original occurred on a cold and grey December day in Minnesota's Metropolitan Stadium in 1975, and its author was Roger Staubach.

The Cincinnati Bengals and the Oakland Raiders completed the 1975 divisional playoff round on a sunny and warm day at the Oakland Alameda County Coliseum. The Raiders had few challenges during their 11–3 regular season, and most experts believed that they would have little trouble with Cincinnati, who ironically also sported an identical 11–3 mark. Despite the beliefs from the so-called experts, the Bengals had a good amount of confidence heading into the playoffs. They employed one of the NFL's best passing offenses, and a pretty good defense to boot. Cincinnati's offense scored 340 points, and their defense gave up only 246 points throughout the 1975 season. Oakland countered their foes with an explosive offense of their own. The Raiders scored 375 points and gave up 255 points in 1975. So both teams were fairly similar in the statistical match-up. Cincinnati had defeated Oakland earlier in the regular season at Riverfront Stadium, 14–10. But the Raiders were without several prominent starters in that game, and history proved that few teams could ever defeat Oakland twice in one season in the 1970s.

Dallas Cowboys wide receiver Drew Pearson barely holds on to the football against his hip on one of the greatest passes in NFL history. Pearson was on the receiving end of the "Hail Mary Pass," a long bomb from Dallas quarterback Roger Staubach with 32 seconds remaining in an NFC divisional playoff game at Minnesota on December 28, 1975. The incredible play resulted in a 17–14 upset victory by the Cowboys over the Vikings (AP Photo).

The Raiders took command of this playoff game right from the beginning, and kept their momentum through the first three quarters. The Bengals had been frustrated all season long at their own inability to run the ball and obtain first downs on the ground. That inability would continue in this playoff game. Cincinnati could muster only three first downs on 11 third down situations against the Raiders. Oakland's defense also had a solution to defeat Cincinnati's top-ranked passing game, that being to put intense pressure on Bengals quarterback Ken Anderson from an outside rush. Oakland was forced to use a 3–4 defense because their starting right defensive end, Tony Cline, was sidelined with an injury. Ted Hendricks was the extra Oakland linebacker in the 3–4, and he played an outstanding game. The Raiders sacked Anderson five times for 40 yards in losses, and four of those sacks came from Hendricks. The 6'7" former Colts linebacker also had four solo tackles and a blocked punt in the game.

Conversely, the Raider offense succeeded by controlling the ball. Oakland quarterback Ken Stabler had one of his most efficient days ever as a passer. Stabler connected on 17 of 23 passes for 199 yards and three touchdowns. Raider runners Clarence Davis (63 yards) and Pete Banaszak (62 yards) helped their team move the chains. Oakland's first touchdown came on a 9-yard pass to reserve wide receiver Mike Siani in the second quarter. Stabler followed that up with an 8-yard scoring pass to tight end Bob Moore, giving the Raiders a 17–7 halftime lead. "We were taking things they were giving us," said Moore of the Bengals' defensive coverages. "That's where my game comes in. I don't have the speed of [Oakland wide receiver] Cliff Branch." Cincinnati's lone first half score was a 1-yard run by fullback Stan Fritts.

Oakland's lead was 24–14 by the end of the third quarter, and it was produced when Banaszak bulled over from the 6-yard line for a third quarter touchdown. The Bengals responded with a fourth-down Lenvil Elliott 6-yard run up the gut. On that play, the Raiders figured that Anderson would throw the ball, but he out-guessed them and sent Elliott on a surprise draw for the score. Cincinnati could ill-afford to trade touchdowns with the Raiders at this point of the game, however. Things got worse for the Bengals when another Oakland tight end, Dave Casper, snared a 2-yard touchdown pass at the back of the end zone. The Raider lead now stood at 31–14 in the fourth quarter, and a blowout at this juncture was not out of the question. "Oakland just lines up one way and comes at you," said Cincinnati linebacker Ron Pritchard.

Cincinnati nevertheless started to come back and tightened the score during the next Oakland possession. Bengals cornerback Ken Riley stepped in front of a Stabler pass intended for running back Jess Phillips, intercepted it, and returned it 34 yards. "I read their zone coverage," said Stabler, "but I didn't see the guy [Riley] behind Jess. I knew he was there somewhere, but I didn't think he was that close." Two plays later, Anderson hit wide receiver Charlie Joiner for a 25-yard touchdown on a deep out pattern, beating Raiders safety Jack Tatum. Raiders head coach John Madden was visibly upset after this score, as allowing Cincinnati to gain momentum and score again was something that he desperately wanted to avoid. After a Raider punt, the Bengals scored again. Anderson led Cincinnati on a seven-play drive that resulted in another touchdown. A key play in that drive was a brilliant 37-yard catch and carry by wide receiver Chip Myers. On that second-and-20 play from the Cincinnati 40-yard line, Myers found an open crease in the middle of Oakland's zone defense, caught Anderson's throw, and ran towards the sideline for an additional 19 yards. Bengals premier wide receiver Isaac Curtis ended the drive when he finally got open in the end zone against Oakland cornerback George Atkinson, and Anderson hit him with a 14-yard touchdown pass. Suddenly, the Bengals had pulled to within 31–28 with a few minutes left.

Things looked bad for the Raiders when Banaszak fumbled on the next Oakland possession, and Cincinnati defensive end Ron Carpenter recovered at the Oakland 37-yard line. There was 4:19 left in the game at this point. All Cincinnati needed was a field goal to tie the game and send it into sudden death overtime, and they were almost within good field goal range. Yet they could not do it. On first down from the Oakland 37, Hendricks blunted Cincinnati's brief spark of momentum when he sacked Anderson again for a 6-yard loss. A short pass to tight end Bruce Coslet left the Bengals with a third-and-11 situation. An incomplete pass by Anderson resulted in a crucial fourth down. A field goal try would be from 55 yards out, and Cincinnati placekicker Dave Green simply did not have a strong enough leg to pull that off. So the Bengals tried one more pass on fourth down, and it too fell incomplete.

Oakland took over with 3:02 remaining, and the Bengals defense held them without a first down. Oakland punter Ray Guy got his fourth down punt off, but he was knocked down by Bengals special team players Brad Cousino and Jack Novak. The resulting running into the kicker penalty gave Oakland a first down, and they quickly ran out the clock. Oakland's 31–28 victory did not have to come down to the final few minutes. The Raiders held big leads throughout the game, and had amassed 27 first downs, compared to Cincinnati's 17 first downs. Oakland held on strong when they needed to, however, and advanced to their third straight AFC championship game. "We never thought for a moment the Bengals would be easy," said Stabler after the game. "We had no set plan on what we would do offensively against Cincinnati. We went with what their defense dictated."

For the Bengals, the game marked the end of Paul Brown's spectacular 41-year coaching career. The Cincinnati team founder, mentor, Hall of Famer, and game innovator had guided the Bengals from their birth to their growth as a competitive contender. He developed playoff teams in Cincinnati in 1970, 1973, and 1975, not to mention the three NFL championships that he earned in Cleveland during the 1950s. "I was proud of my team," said Brown after the game. "They never quit. But Oakland is a splendid team, especially on their home ground."

The Raiders would not be on their home ground the following week. Earning a berth in Super Bowl X would come down to two conference championship games that were chock-filled with storylines and excitement. The AFC championship game featured the Oakland Raiders making one more visit to Three Rivers Stadium to take on the Pittsburgh Steelers on Sunday, January 4. This bitter rivalry began in earnest in the 1972 playoffs when Franco Harris' Immaculate Reception defeated the Raiders in a most controversial fashion, and had continued every year since. The 1975 AFC title game would mark the fourth straight year that the two teams would meet in the postseason, and the second straight year that the two teams met in the conference championship game. The Raiders had yet to win a playoff game on the road in their storied history, a fact that they would love to erase by beating the Steelers. On the night prior to the game, the Pittsburgh ground crew covered the field with several large tarpaulins, in the event that an expected winter storm would harm the field. The winter storm did indeed come, but the tarpaulins failed to do their job properly. Several tarps split near their edges, leaving parts of the field exposed to the elements. Oakland owner Al Davis felt that the tarps were torn on purpose near the sidelines, which made those sections of the field very slick. The icy outer edges of their field most certainly did not benefit the Raiders, who relied on wide receiver Cliff Branch for his world-class speed, and fellow wide receiver Fred Biletnikoff, for his meticulous and precision moves on pass routes. Both of those men were rendered "hampered and ineffective" by the field's condition. Commissioner Pete Rozelle tried to assuage Davis' beliefs by telling him that the field "was in the same condition for both sides." Davis angrily snapped back, "Goddamn it Pete, you don't even know what you're talking about! It's not the same for both sides!" Branch would later comment after the game, "The sidelines were icy. I had no footing at all. I was too conscious of trying not to slip." With Oakland's outside receivers' effectiveness diminished, the Steelers' motto "Whatever it takes," even if one considered the loyalty of a piece of torn tarpaulin, was most appropriate.

The main role of both of these teams on this ice-chilled championship Sunday would be to hold on to the ball and eliminate turnovers. Neither team was able to do that. Pittsburgh was expected to be used to the frozen artificial turf and the cold weather (it was 16 degrees at kickoff), but they surprisingly committed more turnovers than the Raiders. Pittsburgh fumbled the ball five times, and the Raiders recovered all of them. Pittsburgh quarterback Terry Bradshaw also threw three interceptions. Oakland committed a total of five turnovers (two interceptions, three fumbles). The game was indeed sloppy, but it was also one of the hardest-hitting games of the year. Bone-jarring hits from both sides (many of which were legal) could be heard loud and clear throughout the stadium, and many of those hits by the fourth quarter resulted in a variety of injuries. Both defenses dominated in this game (as evidenced by the hard hits), especially in the first half.

The first two quarters were almost scoreless. Both teams moved the ball on occasions, but both were also stymied by their mistakes and turnovers. A dropped pass by either team's receivers would occur on almost every possession during the first half. It was one of Oakland quarterback Ken Stabler's interceptions, however, which led to the first points of the game. Stabler threw a low pass intended for his tight end, Bob Moore. Pittsburgh safety Mike Wagner dove in front of Moore and stole the pass just an inch or so above the turf. He jumped up immediately and ran 20 yards to the Pittsburgh 48-yard line. Oakland running back Marv Hubbard shoved Wagner out of bounds along the Oakland bench and pile-drove his helmet into the turf, a transgression of which Wagner took profound offense. The fiery safety tried to retaliate, but a quarry of Raiders surrounded him along the Oakland sideline and prepared to level him a second time. Wagner's teammate Mel Blount—himself no stranger to fisticuffs—pulled him out of the fray and into the "safety" of the open field during the dead ball timeout. Wagner's interception (the first of two that he would have on the day) led to a 36-yard Roy Gerela field goal. Pittsburgh would take a 3–0 lead into halftime.

Oakland placekicker George Blanda, playing in what would be the final game of his extraordinary 26-year career, would miss a 38-yard field goal in the first quarter. It would be three points that the Raiders would really need by the end of the game. More on that later, however. The Raiders were still very much in this game, and their defense started hitting even harder in the third quarter. One particular hit in the third quarter by Raider defensive back George Atkinson took one of Bradshaw's main targets away from him. Pittsburgh wide receiver Lynn Swann was running a crossing route and caught Bradshaw's bullet. He took one step and was whacked across the head by Atkinson's forearm. Both Swann and the ball fell to the turf in opposite directions, and Oakland safety Jack Tatum recovered the ball. Tatum would also intercept two of Bradshaw's passes in the game. "The Raiders secondary is the best we'll ever play," remarked Pittsburgh backup quarterback Terry Hanratty. Swann was carried off the field by a couple of his teammates and members of the training staff, then in a moment was rolled off the field on a stretcher. He would not completely recover until he was released from the hospital several days after the game. Swann's concussion was emblematic of the hitting that was going on between both teams as the fourth quartered neared. There was a total of five turnovers in the third quarter alone in this dream of a game ... for lovers of great defensive play.

An Oakland turnover late in the third quarter led to a Pittsburgh touchdown early in the fourth quarter. Stabler handed off to Raider runner Clarence Davis on a sweep to the right. Davis was quickly popped by Steelers cornerback J.T. Thomas, and the resulting fumble was recovered along the sideline by Pittsburgh middle linebacker Jack Lambert. The recovery by Lambert should have been disallowed, as replays clearly showed his feet sliding out of bounds before he fell on the ball. Nevertheless, Pittsburgh was granted possession, and commenced one of their best marches down the field in the entire game. Their five-play drive was completed when Pittsburgh running back Franco Harris swept left, broke an attempted tackle by Oakland cornerback Neal Colzie, and raced down the sideline for a 25-yard touchdown. "You come to expect those kinds of runs from Franco," said Pittsburgh head coach Chuck Noll. Key to the success of the play was a crucial crackback block by Steeler wide receiver John Stallworth, who leveled not one but two Raiders, linebacker Monte Johnson and safety Jack Tatum. Pittsburgh now led 10–0, and in this defensive struggle, that margin seemed like enough to secure a victory.

Oakland wasted virtually no time in responding with a touchdown of their own, however. Stabler led a six-play drive with six passes, three of them to reserve tight end Dave Casper. The big ex–Notre Dame target was filling in for Bob Moore, who was injured earlier in the game. The 60-yard drive concluded in the Pittsburgh end zone when Stabler connected with wide receiver Mike Siani, who ran across the middle and caught a touchdown in front of J.T. Thomas.

With the score sitting at 10–7 in favor of the Steelers midway through the final quarter, Oakland's final turnover led to what turned out to be the game-clinching touchdown for the Steelers. Oakland's Hubbard ran off right tackle and was stripped of the ball by Pittsburgh safety Glen Edwards. Lambert fell on it (his third recovery of the game) on the Oakland 25-yard line. Three plays later, Bradshaw threw a pass deep into the corner of the end zone, intended for Stallworth. Colzie had good coverage on the play, but slipped on the icy turf as the ball descended. Stallworth leaped over the fallen Colzie and snared the ball for a big Steelers touchdown. A key element in the play occurred before the ball was thrown, however. Hendricks blitzed from the outside, and Steelers left guard Sam Davis quickly turned to his left and rode the long-armed linebacker away from Bradshaw as the ex–Louisiana Tech quarterback stepped up into the pocket. Had Hendricks been able to get more than just a fleeting grasp of Bradshaw's jersey sleeve, the score would never had occurred. Pittsburgh now led 16–7 with just over nine minutes remaining in the game. "We were just looking for one big play in the second half," said Noll, "but we got a couple."

Hendricks was not about to let his failure to sack Bradshaw deter his determination, however. Several changes of possession preceded another Pittsburgh turnover, which came when Franco Harris fumbled going into the line trying to run out the clock. Hendricks recovered for Oakland at the Raiders' 35-yard line with 1:31 left. Stabler completed three passes to bring the ball to the Pittsburgh 24-yard line. One of those passes went to wide receiver Cliff Branch for a 19-yard gain, his first catch of the game. Jack Lambert greeted Branch immediately and separated his helmet from his head. On third down, Oakland head coach John Madden sent Blanda in to try a 41-yard field goal, which was good. Had Blanda converted on his missed first quarter field goal attempt, the Raiders would have only required another field goal to send the game into overtime. Madden could not worry about missed opportunities at this point, however. He reasoned that his team needed a touchdown and a field goal, and knowing that time was a critical factor, the successful field goal gave the Raiders a chance to recover the ensuing onside kick. Miraculously, reserve Steelers wide receiver and special teams player Reggie Garrett fumbled Ray Guy's perfect squib kick, and Hubbard emerged from the pile with the ball for the Raiders at their 45-yard line.

Stabler had seven seconds left to work with. The best that he could hope for was a play that would end up out of bounds and thus stop the clock with time available for one more play. He dropped back and threw deep for Branch, who caught the ball for a 37-yard gain. Mel Blount immediately tackled Branch 15 yards short of the end zone as the final gun sounded and as hundreds of gleeful Steelers fans ran onto the field. "My heart was beating pretty good in those last 25 seconds," admitted Lambert. "A lot of people didn't realize how close we were to losing." The Steelers did not lose, however, and had defended their AFC title from the previous season. They were headed back to the Super Bowl for the second straight year. "These people did everything they had to," said Noll, referring to his players. "I can't think of a team that deserves a second Super Bowl more."

The Los Angeles Rams were seeking to participate in their first Super Bowl, but before they could, they would have to dispatch the Cinderella wild card Dallas Cowboys in the NFC title game, something that most experts felt would be a mere formality. All the signs pointed to a Rams victory. No team in pro football won more games in the regular season than the Rams (12). The Los Angeles defense gave up a meager 135 points in 1975, easily the best mark in the league. Head coach Chuck Knox's team had won seven straight games heading into the NFC championship game. The Rams would be playing at home in the warm and sunny Los Angeles Memorial Coliseum. Coming off of their impressive win over the supposedly explosive St. Louis Cardinals in the divisional round of the playoffs, the Rams looked like they were only a few hours away from making reservations for Miami and Super Bowl X. Sure, Dallas had defeated the Rams in the regular season opener, but the Rams were now battle-hardened, more determined, and more familiar with the Dallas shotgun offense. The Rams were simply not going to let a lucky 10–4 team that needed a miracle to beat Minnesota defeat them at home with a conference championship at stake. A funny thing happened on the way to Super Bowl X, however.

Dallas and its Dirty Dozen rookies played unquestionably their best game of the year in the NFC championship game. They dominated the Rams in every aspect, from offense to defense to special teams to coaching, as they trounced Los Angeles, 37–7. How exactly did they pull off this stunning upset? The main priority for the Doomsday Defense was to limit the progress of star Rams runner Lawrence McCutcheon, who compiled a then–playoff record 202 yards rushing on 37 carries against the Cardinals the previous week. Dallas head coach Tom Landry's flex defense, where defensive linemen were staggered in their stances on the line of scrimmage, was geared to stopping the run first and foremost. The Rams' major offensive plan had to involve their running game, as their passing game—though strong—was relying on James Harris and Ron Jaworski at quarterback. Both men were young and fairly inexperienced in postseason games, and if there was anything that Tom Landry knew how to do, it was how to rattle the poise of young quarterbacks. Chuck Knox knew this too, so he tried to protect his quarterbacks by establishing the run early. By the time he officially gave up on that plan, Dallas had already built a 21–0 halftime lead. The Dallas front four got great penetration throughout the game, wreaking havoc in the Rams' backfield. Doomsday also accumulated five sacks, mostly during the second half while the Rams were throwing the ball on almost every down. The Cowboys limited the Ram runners to a mere 22 total yards rushing, and permitted the entire Los Angeles offense only 118 total yards all game long. "We primarily geared our game plan to stopping [McCutcheon]," said Dallas outside linebacker D.D. Lewis. "Coach Landry has done a great job with our game plans." With a defense playing as well as Doomsday did against the Rams, the Dallas offense barely needed to break a sweat. It was the Dallas offense, however, that shined as brilliantly as the Southern California sun on this day.

Preston Pearson was easily the most visible Cowboys hero of the game. After D.D. Lewis intercepted Rams quarterback James Harris' first throw of the game, Pearson caught an 18-yard middle screen pass from quarterback Roger Staubach. He then wove his way through the Rams secondary, broke an attempted arm tackle by Rams safety Bill Simpson, and pranced into the end zone. It was the first of three Pearson touchdowns on the afternoon. The Los Angeles defense simply had no answer to limiting Pearson's effectiveness. Whenever Pearson left the backfield to run a route, the Rams linebackers were rigid and stayed in their assigned zones of coverage. Pearson simply found the open areas, used his athleticism, and ended the day with seven catches for 123 yards. One of Pearson's grabs was a diving stab in the end zone. On that play, Pearson out-raced

Rams outside linebacker Ken Geddes on a short fan pattern (fan is the area for receivers and running backs between the corner area and the flat area), leaped about five feet in the air, and caught Staubach's 15-yard scoring pass as he was horizontal to the turf. "I got lucky and brought it in," said a modest Pearson. "When you keep your eye on the ball and concentrate, you can catch everything. Roger threw awfully well from the beginning today, even in the warm-ups he was on the money with everything."

Sandwiched in between Preston Pearson's first two touchdowns was another scoring pass, this one coming off play action from Staubach to wide receiver Golden Richards from four yards out. On that play, Richards slipped into the back of the end zone completely unnoticed by the Rams defense, and caught Staubach's perfect pass with virtually no one anywhere near him. "He [Richards] wasn't the primary receiver," explained Staubach, "but I saw the weak safety come up and I went to him."

The Rams tried to answer back later in the game, but they failed when rookie Dallas linebacker Thomas Henderson blocked a 34-yard Tom Dempsey field goal attempt. "I was in the gap on the outside," recalled Henderson, "I jumped the gap and blocked his [Dempsey's] field goal." Dempsey also missed a 41-yard field goal attempt in the second quarter.

Dallas scored 13 more points in the third quarter on two Toni Fritsch field goals, and another Preston Pearson touchdown reception. From the shotgun formation, Pearson caught a short shovel pass from Staubach and ran to his left, which was in the opposite direction as the flow of the play. He soon got behind Cowboys center John Fitzgerald, who made the final necessary block on the play, and out-ran Los Angeles cornerback Monte Jackson into the end zone. "We came out in the second half looking to move the football, not to run out the clock," admitted Staubach. "We didn't think we had it [the game] won at halftime."

For his part, Staubach did not just beat the Rams by throwing touchdown passes, however. He scrambled out of the pocket several times, which did not entirely surprise the Rams. Even so, like their efforts on this day against Preston Pearson, the Rams defense failed to contain the ex–Navy Midshipman. Staubach finished the game with seven carries for 54 yards, and three of Staubach's runs resulted in first downs. "We made the big third down plays and they [the Rams] didn't," said Staubach. "We hit the right play at the right time."

The Cowboys had a 34–0 lead when the Rams scored their only points in the fourth quarter on a 1-yard run by running back John Cappelletti. One more Fritsch field goal boosted Dallas to 37 points and completed this mercy killing. The team that many prognosticators at the beginning of the 1975 season felt were not going to make the playoffs somehow became the first wild card team since the merger in 1970 to reach the Super Bowl. Perhaps no other underdog playoff team in the decade was more prepared to pull off such a stunning upset as Dallas was in the 1975 NFC title game. The Cowboys did it in the grandest of fashions. "It just seemed to be our day," said a victorious Coach Landry. "We got started early with some big plays, some good catches, some good runs, and in fairness the Rams did not play that badly. As I said, it just seemed to be our day."

Most experts predicted that the Pittsburgh Steelers would have the final big day of the season when they would meet the Dallas Cowboys in Super Bowl X in Miami's Orange Bowl. True, the Steelers were a slight favorite over the underdog Cowboys to defend their world championship, but there were enough intriguing matchups in this game that would spark plenty of interest throughout the country. The Steelers were not used to playing a team like the Cowboys, who utilized a wide variety of player movements, man in motion, and shift changes before the snap of the ball. "Getting ready for them [the Cowboys] was not easy," said Pittsburgh head coach Chuck Noll. "They tried to fool you as much as beat you physically. We needed the two weeks [the time between the conference championship games and the Super Bowl] to get ready, and we used all of it."

The Cowboys also tried to fool the Steelers psychologically. The players on both teams tried to keep their comments to a minimum during the two weeks prior to the game, but one player's comments sparked some action. Pittsburgh wide receiver Lynn Swann was released from the hospital three days after the AFC title game and had a difficult time getting back in the swing of things as Super Sunday approached. He was still feeling the ill-effects of the hits he received from Oakland's George Atkinson and Jack Tatum in the conference final. Just a few days before the Super Bowl, Swann read a newspaper and discovered that Dallas safety Cliff Harris commented on the injuries that he (Swann) sustained against Oakland. "I'm not going to hurt anyone intentionally," Harris said. "Getting hit while he's running a route across the middle must be in the back of his [Swann's] mind." Harris' statements inspired Swann to get well quick and play in the game. "He [Harris] was trying to intimidate me," said Swann. "He said I'd be afraid out there. He needn't worry. He doesn't know Lynn Swann. He can't scare me or the team. I'm going to play."

This would be the tenth anniversary for the Super Bowl, giving football fans pause to reflect upon the first nine Super Bowls. Some of the previous Super Bowls were naturally historic, some were competitive, a couple were upsets, but most were one-sided. Many sportswriters and fans would consider most of the recent Super Bowls dull and to an extent even downright boring. Super Bowl X would definitely not be described in such a fashion. In fact, there are some people even today (this author included) who still considers Super Bowl X to be the best Super Bowl ever. The hoopla surrounding the game was, as usual, spectacular. NFL Commissioner Pete Rozelle wanted a patriotic theme for the event in honor of our nation's 200th birthday, and Super Bowl X would be the first big nationwide Bicentennial event. Rozelle knew that it had to be a good one. Special Bicentennial patches would be worn by members of both teams on their jerseys, and the game program and tickets featured the Vince Lombardi Trophy and the American flag. In addition, red, white and blue bunting featuring the official Bicentennial star symbol surrounded the stands of the Orange Bowl, and hundreds of red, white and blue balloons were released into the Miami sky at halftime. Even Hollywood took a part in the festivities. Actor Robert Shaw and the Goodyear Blimp were present for filming on gameday and throughout the week prior to the game for the upcoming movie, *Black Sunday*.

On the eve of the big game, CBS-TV decided to televise one of the big celebrity parties and make an entertainment show out of it. *Super Night at the Super Bowl* took place inside the Miami Convention Center, and featured hosts Jackie Gleason and Andy Williams. Other stars participating included Bob Newhart, Burt Reynolds, Dinah Shore, the Pointer Sisters, Beatrice Arthur, Hermione Baddeiey, Mary Tyler Moore, Edward Asner, Gavin McCloud, Cloris Leachman, Jimmie Walker, Joe Namath and O.J. Simpson. An audience of 1,400 attended the live event, and millions of people watched it on television. The idea to televise a Super Bowl party would be repeated several more times during the 1970s.

Other forms of entertainment were also a big part of Super Bowl X. The Dallas Cowboys Cheerleaders were supporting their Cowboys all the way back to before Super Bowl V in January of 1971. The cheerleaders would make a return trip to Miami five years later, but they sported more provocative outfits for Super Bowl X. The new sexy, cute, and classy outfits consisted of revealing royal blue tops, white vests with royal blue stars, white hot pants, and white go-go boots. The CBS ground cameramen during the game were more than happy to keep their focus on the Cowboys cheerleaders, and they received more national coverage on that day than they ever did before. According to then–cheerleader director Suzanne Mitchell, "the cameramen just seemed to fall in love with them." In 1973, Dallas general manager Tex Schramm hired Mitchell and Texie

Waterman as the squad's choreographer and coach. By 1975, the practice of choreographed dances became increasingly more the focus of the Dallas cheerleaders. They would still shout out cheers to the crowd, but their dances and pregame performances became very entertaining, and gave many fans another reason to bring binoculars to the game. The cheerleaders were actually invited to cheer for the Cowboys at the Los Angeles Memorial Coliseum for the NFC championship game two weeks prior to Super Bowl X, and they received a good amount of television coverage from that game as well. Thanks in large part to the Dallas Cowboys Cheerleaders' performance in Super Bowl X, however, cheerleading in the NFL would never be the same again.

Rozelle's halftime show was also an attempt at providing a big extravaganza to the stadium and television audience. A musical and theatrical group called Up with People made their national debut at halftime of Super Bowl X. They consisted of a cast of 300 young men and women singers, dancers, and musicians from across the country. They performed patriotic songs with the Bicentennial theme entitled "200 Years and Just a Baby," and their colorful costumes and vibrant energy was Rozelle's annual attempt to out-do and improve the Super Bowl halftime show each year. Many people derided Up with People as amateurish and even corny, and Rozelle himself in later years would regret using the group for the show. But the 80,187 fans in the stands at Super Bowl X and the millions of fans at home enjoyed the colorful spectacle of this group's first national performance.

Dallas' performance began when they won the coin toss and chose to receive the opening kickoff. Preston Pearson caught Roy Gerela's kickoff at the 3-yard line, then instead of sprinting upfield, he ran at a brisk jogging pace. What was up? In a couple of seconds, the Cowboys' plan was evident for all to see. Reserve Dallas linebacker Thomas Henderson broke towards Pearson and circled behind him, taking a handoff from him, and running a reverse down the opposite sideline. "The play was set up beautifully," said Henderson. "Steelers were toppling like ingots as I passed them." The play ended at the Pittsburgh 44-yard line, and it completely surprised the Steelers. Only a diving tackle by Gerela saved a possible touchdown. Gerela's tackle resulted in bruised ribs for the kicker, and that injury would affect him throughout the game.

No score resulted from the Cowboys' big play on the opening kickoff, but things got worse for Pittsburgh a few minutes later. Pittsburgh punter Bobby Walden fumbled a snap from center, and was pile-driven by a half dozen Cowboys into the Poly-Turf at the Steelers' 29-yard line. "I just took my eyes off the ball," Walden later said. On the very next play, Dallas used multiple movements in their backfield to confuse the Pittsburgh defense. Staubach faked a handoff to Preston Pearson, then threw a bullet down the middle to his crossing wide receiver, Drew Pearson. Staubach's pass was perfect. Pearson caught it in stride and sprinted past Steelers outside linebacker Andy Russell and into the end zone. "They went through four shifts on that play," described Pittsburgh safety Mike Wagner. "We got through three of them by the time they started the play, but there was some hesitation. We blew the play." The Dallas Cowboys thus became the first team to score a first quarter touchdown on the Pittsburgh defense all season long.

The Steelers answered the Cowboys' surprise touchdown with one of their own a few minutes later. Pittsburgh quarterback Terry Bradshaw fooled the Doomsday Defense from the Dallas 7-yard line when he had offensive right guard Gerry Mullins report to the huddle as an eligible receiver. Mullins went in motion prior to the snap. Bradshaw immediately rolled right and threw a touchdown pass to his uncovered tight end, Randy Grossman. The key play in the eight-play scoring drive was a long bomb of 32 yards to wide receiver Lynn Swann, who made a tremendous catch along the sideline over Dallas cornerback Mark Washington. Swann managed to leap high and catch Bradshaw's overthrown pass with most of his body out of bounds. Yet he was still able to get both of his feet inbounds. "Swann almost has a sixth sense," said Pittsburgh head coach

Chuck Noll. "Anybody else catching that ball would have gone out of bounds. But he S-curved his body to get his feet in."

Dallas responded on their next possession. The manner in which they drove down the field was highly unusual, however. The Cowboys ran the ball against the Steel Curtain defense (something that few teams could do), and accumulated 42 yards in a drive which resulted in a 36-yard field goal from the toe of placekicker Toni Fritsch on the second play of the second quarter. The Cowboys runners utilized trap runs, misdirection runs, and draw plays to take advantage of the surging Pittsburgh defensive line. Dallas' 10–7 lead would surprisingly hold up until early in the fourth quarter.

Late in the second quarter, another gem of a reception by Swann is worth mentioning. The Steelers were positioned at their own 10-yard line, and once again, Swann found himself in man-on-man coverage by Washington. Swann ran a deep post pattern, and he leaped for the ball near the midfield stripe. As he did, he collided with Washington, and the ball popped straight up into the air as both players began their decent to the turf. Swann latched onto the ball before he landed, making the 53-yard play one of the greatest catches in Super Bowl history. Watching Lynn Swann running a pass pattern was like watching pure poetry in motion. His ability to weave around linebackers and defensive backs in both zone and man-to-man coverages, yet all the while keeping focus on the flight of the ball and then leaping high in the air to catch it, was truly something special to observe in this special decade.

Swann's second super catch would eventually lead to a 36-yard field goal attempt by Gerela. His kick was wide left, however, and Dallas would go into halftime clinging to a 10–7 lead. Gerela would miss one more field goal at the beginning of the third quarter, but that miss would actually produce bad news for Dallas. As Gerela's kick drifted wide, Dallas safety Cliff Harris congratulated the kicker by patting him on his helmet and saying, "Way to go, Roy!" Pittsburgh middle linebacker Jack Lambert had by 1975 already earned the reputation of one of the meanest linebackers to ever play pro football. He seldom missed an opportunity to discuss how he felt about his opponents. "I don't see any sense of trying to disprove the image," admitted Lambert, who once jokingly claimed that he hailed from "Buzzard's Breath, Wyoming."

Lambert was busy walking off the field, already miffed that Gerela missed another field goal. When he heard a commotion going on behind him, he turned his head and saw what Harris was doing. Lambert's rage was—to put it kindly—palpable. He reacted instantly, ran over to Harris, grabbed him around his shoulder pads, and flung him to the turf. Dallas defensive tackle Jethro Pugh quickly escorted Harris away from Lambert, while line judge Jack Fette threatened the Steeler backer with a game ejection if he did not get back to the Pittsburgh bench. Lambert's actions fueled his own furor, as well as the momentum of his defensive teammates. "No one can be allowed to intimidate the Pittsburgh Steelers," Lambert said after the game. "We're the ones who are supposed to do the intimidating. When I see injustice, I try to do something about it. I decided to do something about it." Pittsburgh defensive tackle Joe Greene credited Lambert with reviving the Steelers' defense. "Lambert was the fellow who held us together when things weren't going good," Greene said. "He spearheaded us. He made the licks that got us going." The Steel Curtain effectively shut down the Dallas offense in the second half, and by game's end, accumulated seven quarterback sacks (a new Super Bowl record) and three interceptions.

Some of Pittsburgh's hits were unwarranted, according to the Cowboys. Many Dallas players and several Dallas coaches complained after the game that Pittsburgh received no penalties all day long, even though they could have and should have been called several times for unnecessary roughness and unsportsmanlike conduct penalties. Pittsburgh cornerback Mel Blount spent most of the second half throwing Dallas wide receiver Golden Richards around like a rag doll. Late in the game, Blount came up behind Richards after a running play was blown dead and punched him in the back. Richards went down instantly, and was eventually helped off the field. The prognosis was several cracked ribs, and Richards was done for the day. "You don't have to play the game like that," said Dallas offensive tackle Rayfield Wright. "They [the Steelers] were screaming and hollering epithets and taking cheap shots." Rookie Dallas linebacker Randy White concurred. "They had a middle linebacker [Lambert] who was hitting late and bigmouthing out there. I wasn't too impressed with him."

Yet it was neither a defensive play nor an offensive play which served as the impressive turning point of the game. The Cowboys kept their 10–7 lead going into the fourth quarter, when they lined up to punt deep in their own territory. Pittsburgh special teams player Reggie Harrison was one of 10 Steelers poised to rush rookie Dallas punter Mitch Hoopes. Harrison was wedged in between fellow Steelers Steve Furness and Dave Brown. At the snap, Harrison and Brown double-teamed Dallas blocker Roland Woolsey. In a brief moment, Harrison knifed through the line while Brown occupied Woolsey. Harrison then leaped in front of Hoopes and blocked his punt. The ball ricocheted off of Harrison's helmet and out of the end zone for a Pittsburgh safety. "I just came up the middle," Harrison said. "I knew I was going to block that one, it was mine." The Steelers now trailed 10–9.

Pittsburgh rookie Mike Collier returned Hoopes' free kick 25 yards to the Dallas 45-yard line. Several plays later, Gerela finally connected on a field goal, and the Steelers finally claimed a 12–10 lead. A few plays later, Steelers safety Mike Wagner intercepted a Staubach pass intended for Drew Pearson, and returned it 19 yards to the Dallas 7-yard line. Wagner's theft set up another Gerela field goal and a 15–10 Pittsburgh lead. "Wagner read the play and just guessed right," Staubach said.

The Dallas offense had been effectively blunted by the fierce rush of the Steel Curtain defense all throughout the second half. They could muster only 143 total net yards during the third and fourth quarters. The Steelers had fought back to take a slim lead. On third down and four yards to go from the Pittsburgh 36-yard line, Bradshaw took his regular deep drop, stepped up in the pocket to avoid a risky Dallas blitz from Cliff Harris and D.D. Lewis, and threw long and deep for Swann, who was covered once again man-for-man by Mark Washington. Swann outran Washington by a step, caught Bradshaw's perfect pass, broke a diving tackle by the beaten cornerback, and stepped into the end zone to complete the 64-yard play. "It looked as if the ball was going to be underthrown," recalled Swann. "When I looked up, it was coming right down into my arms." Washington described the play as "a perfect pass. You don't expect that against a blitz."

The greatest touchdown bomb in Super Bowl history cemented Swann as the first wide receiver to ever win Super Bowl Most Valuable Player honors. "What they were, basically, were great catches," said Washington of Swann's efforts. "It's the biggest game of the year and he comes up with those kind of receptions." The touchdown bomb to Swann was also helped tremendously by a block from Pittsburgh running back Rocky Bleier, who took out the blitzing Harris, which allowed Bradshaw enough time to throw deep. The play was not over with Swann's score, however. Dallas defensive tackle Larry Cole burrowed in on Bradshaw and planted his helmet into the quarterback's left ear hole immediately after Bradshaw released the ball. Bradshaw was helped off the field and did not return to the game. He was not coherent and able to remember the details of the play until well after the final gun. "I could hear the bells ringing," said Bradshaw after the game. "I didn't know what happened until I got to the locker room."

The championship belonged to the Cowboys going into the fourth quarter. Several minutes later, they had given up 14 points, and things appeared hopeless. Dallas was now behind 21–10 with but 3:02 left in the game. None of them were going to quit, however. Staubach had brought

In Super Bowl X, January 18, 1976, at Miami's Orange Bowl, Pittsburgh Steelers wide receiver Lynn Swann makes one of the greatest catches in Super Bowl history against the Dallas Cowboys. Swann was named the game's Most Valuable Player, and thus became the first wide receiver to ever receive that award in a Super Bowl. The Steelers came back in the fourth quarter to earn a 21–17 victory, and became the third team in league annals to win back-to-back Super Bowls (Green Bay and Miami had previously accomplished that feat) (AP Photo).

his team back from the edge of defeat against Minnesota in the divisional playoff round, and he had by 1975 developed a reputation as a reliable comeback leader. The Cowboys leaned on the memories of past victories against supposedly insurmountable odds, as they began their riposte in the waning moments of Super Bowl X. Staubach threw four quick passes worth 80 yards in just 1:14 of elapsed time. The fourth completion went to rookie wide receiver Percy Howard from 34 yards out for a touchdown. On the play, Howard, who was substituting for the injured Golden Richards, sprinted past Steelers All-Pro cornerback Mel Blount, who surprisingly fell down. Howard caught Staubach's pass falling backward himself in the end zone and cradling it into his stomach. It was Howard's only catch of his career, as an injury forced him to retire prior to the start of the 1976 season. Dallas now trailed Pittsburgh by just four points, 21–17.

Pittsburgh's Gerry Mullins recovered the ensuing onside kick. The Steelers tried to run out the clock, and they made Dallas use up all of their timeouts. On fourth down, Pittsburgh head coach Chuck Noll decided to run the ball, eschewing a punt. The decision perplexed many on both sides, but Noll knew that his punter (Walden) had already fumbled one snap, and almost had two previous punts blocked. Noll did not want to chance a similar disaster, so he had his offense run the ball one more time, gaining but two yards, and relinquishing the ball to Dallas at the Cowboys' 39-yard line. "We never even considered a punt," Noll said later. "We had confidence that our defense could hold them." There was now 1:22 left on the clock. Staubach ran for 11 yards, then threw to running back Preston Pearson for 12 yards, bringing the ball to the Pittsburgh

38-yard line. Precious time ticked away with two more incompletions. With three seconds left, Staubach threw deep down the middle one last time. Wagner leaped over the intended receiver, Drew Pearson, and deflected the ball. Pittsburgh safety Glen Edwards caught it, and ran it out of the end zone for a 35-yard return before he was downed by Dallas offensive guard Blaine Nye at the Pittsburgh 33-yard line.

The Steelers had done it. They had repeated as Super Bowl champions. Their exciting 21–17 victory over the Cinderella Dallas Cowboys in Super Bowl X was the fourth straight Super Bowl win for AFC teams. Super Bowl X was truly "super," and it would set the standard for all future Super Bowls in categories of drama, big plays, hard hits, and a frantic finish. The Pittsburgh dynasty enjoyed another memorable chapter in their illustrious history. Their goal the following year would be to win a third-straight world championship. There were plenty of other tough challengers and impassioned Cinderella teams, however, who would try their best to stop the Steelers in 1976.

1976

Bicentennial Battles

The National Football League's Bicentennial season was celebrated as part of the nation's grand and colorful year-long birthday party. Parades and patriotism enveloped the 50 states as citizens from all walks of life honored a country that turned 200 years old in 1976. In the wake of the superior spectacle that was Super Bowl X, the NFL wished for the Spirit of '76 to also become part of the new football season. Yet for whatever unknown and unspecified reasons, the official Bicentennial patch that both the Dallas Cowboys and the Pittsburgh Steelers wore on their jerseys in Super Bowl X would not be worn by any player on any team during the 1976 regular season. The speculative thought throughout the league's front office involved timing. The NFL regular season would start after July 4, 1976, so the powers that be in the NFL's Park Avenue offices decided against using the patch after the Independence Day celebrations. There were, however, two teams that did alter their uniforms somewhat to recognize the nation's 200 birthday. The Dallas Cowboys replaced one of the blue stripes on their helmet with a red stripe, thus giving them a red, white and blue stripe pattern on their helmets. The Philadelphia Eagles had a special patch on their jerseys that featured the Liberty Bell and the number 76. Today's jerseys are adorned with patches and insignias of all kinds on them, and very few teams in the 21st century ignore this new trend. All NFL teams in 1969 wore a special NFL-50 patch throughout that season to commemorate the 50th year of the league. Sadly, the NFL missed out on a great opportunity in 1976 to celebrate the memory of the Bicentennial by leaving the official Bicentennial patch off of the players' uniforms.

Two new expansion teams would help to make the 1976 season eventful, however. The Seattle Seahawks and the Tampa Bay Buccaneers became the 27th and 28th teams in the modern league. Most expansion teams in the past started out slowly, and usually took several years to become competitive. The same fate would be true for both the Seahawks and the Buccaneers. In order to fill up an expansion team's roster, the league would offer a new team a first round draft choice, plus a dozen other draft choices. The league would also require each of the other 26 teams to surrender three of their veteran players in a special allocation draft. Guys who had struggled to obtain a starting position in their team's lineup would suddenly have a really good chance at becoming a starting player with an expansion club. The trick for the other teams was to make sure that they never gave those expansion teams one of their starting players or a player with a lot of potential talent. That would be tough for a team like the defending Super Bowl champion Pittsburgh Steelers, who were solid at every position and whose lineup had a wealth of quality depth. For a team like the lackluster New York Jets, however, giving up three players would be easy, as many of their players would have difficulty making a strong team's roster anyway.

The most noteworthy veterans who joined the Seattle team were former Miami Dolphins offensive lineman Norm Evans, and former Baltimore Colts middle linebacker Mike Curtis. Both men had already earned Super Bowl rings, but both were deemed expendable by their coaches and general managers due to their advanced age. Evans was 34, and Curtis was 33 in 1976, and both of their former teams believed that they could save money by dumping them and their higher salaries. The noteworthy veterans who reported for duty in Tampa included former Pittsburgh quarterback Terry Hanratty, former San Francisco quarterback Steve Spurrier, and former Dallas and Buffalo defensive lineman Pat Toomay. While these players were good at their positions, none of them were considered great or All-Pro material.

Both Jack Patera (the new head coach of the Seahawks) and John McKay (the new head coach of the Buccaneers) knew that their chances for building a competitive team quickly would be slim at best. Patera was a hard-nosed former assistant coach for the Minnesota Vikings, and McKay was a dry-humored former head coach at the University of Southern California. Neither man had been a head coach in the NFL before, but both were up for the challenge. It is interesting to note that both new teams drafted a rookie in 1976 who would eventually be enshrined in Pro Football's Hall of Fame. Seattle wide receiver Steve Largent and Tampa Bay defensive lineman Lee Roy Selmon would each contribute spectacular careers to their teams throughout the last half of the 1970s.

The fans in Seattle were more numerous than those in Tampa Bay, based upon the numbers of early ticket sales. The Seahawks sold 59,000 season tickets before 1976 began. "We anticipated a good sale," said John Thompson of the NFL Management Council, "but no one in his right mind would have predicted this [the large number of season ticket sales before the season began]." The Seahawk colors would be blue, green and silver, and the team signed a 20-year lease to play their home games in the Kingdome, a large concrete domed stadium in the heart of the city. The walls of the circular stadium anchored the world's largest self-supporting concrete roof. The 64,757-seat Kingdome had a retractable lower level of seats, which permitted the stadium to be shared by both the Seahawks and by Major League Baseball's Seattle Mariners. The playing surface inside the Kingdome was AstroTurf.

The American Bicentennial logo was inexplicably absent from NFL stadiums and player uniforms during the American Bicentennial season 1976. A special Bicentennial patch was worn by all Cowboys and Steelers players in Super Bowl X, however (Joe Zagorski).

The Tampa Bay franchise would play their home games at Tampa Stadium, which was actually a 10-year-old stadium. The NFL knew plenty about Tampa Stadium prior to 1976, having scheduled 13 preseason games there during the first half of the decade. The stadium added over 25,000 more seats to the stadium before the 1976 season, however, giving it a total of 71,128 seats. Tampa Stadium had a large amount of sideline seats, and the seating sections curved downward near each end zone. It also had two large luxury box/press box sections with black tinted windows to provide at least some aspect of shade from the blinding glare of the hot Florida sun. Tampa Stadium sported a natural grass playing surface, and many players deemed it to be one of the best playing fields in the league. The Buccaneers' colors would be orange, white, and red trim, and they would enlist a swashbuckling pirate as their mascot.

One other team moved into a new stadium in 1976. The New York Giants had been veritable nomads since 1973, playing their home games at Yankee Stadium in the Bronx, the Yale Bowl in New Haven, Connecticut, and Shea Stadium in Flushing on Long Island during the past three seasons. In 1976, however, they moved to East Rutherford, New Jersey. The brand new Giants Stadium rose above a New Jersey swampland and stood as the welcomed home for the Giants, seating 76,891. It had an AstroTurf playing surface, and lower and upper levels that were perfectly rectangular in shape, much like the rectangular seating bowl at Arrowhead Stadium in Kansas City.

Another new addition to the NFL landscape in 1976 was a 30-second clock, the result of the league's competition committee and their efforts to help offenses avoid delay of game penalties. The clock, which received the blessing of Commissioner Pete Rozelle, measured four feet high and six feet wide, and was required to be placed at least five feet above ground in every NFL stadium. The 30-second clocks were placed behind each end zone, giving quarterbacks and referees a clear view as to how many seconds remained before the ball was required to be snapped. The fans now knew that there was a common standard by which all delay of game penalties would be called. More astute fans could sometimes be seen in the stands with stopwatches, timing the length of time it took for their favorite team to break the huddle and snap the ball.

New players would be donning new uniforms for new teams in 1976. Several trades resulted from dozens of players returning to the NFL from the now-defunct WFL. There were hopes from several teams that the new players in key positions could turn their fortunes around. A few players were able to catch on quickly with an NFL team once the WFL folded (in 1975), but most could not. They had to wait until the 1975 Pro Bowl ended, and once it did, many players returned to NFL team lineups with breakneck speed. The competition for positions was simply incredible, with each team holding a 43-man roster. New England sent quarterback Jim Plunkett to San Francisco for quarterback Tom Owen. They also received three more first-round draft picks and one second-round draft pick for Plunkett. Green Bay shipped quarterback John Hadl to Houston for quarterback Lynn Dickey. Running backs Calvin Hill and John Riggins came back to the NFL and signed with Washington, while former Dolphins and WFL refugees Larry Csonka, Jim Kiick, and Paul Warfield signed with the Giants, Broncos and Browns, respectively. Former St. Louis and Minnesota wide receiver John Gilliam left the WFL and signed on with the Atlanta Falcons in the summer of 1976.

The *Chicago Tribune* had annually started each summer by sponsoring and promoting the institution of the College All-Star Game, a preseason contest pitting the Super Bowl champions (or NFL champions prior to 1966) of the previous year playing a group of All-American college players who were recently drafted or signed as free agents by NFL teams. The game was held in late July each year since 1934 (there was no game in 1974 due to the NFL players' strike), but in 1976, the game between the world champion Pittsburgh Steelers and the College All-Star players would mark the end of the series. The Steelers held a 24–0 lead late in the third quarter when the referees (with Commissioner Pete Rozelle's agreement) suspended play due to a torrential downpour which flooded the field. The rain continued through most of the game, and just came down in buckets in the third quarter. Most pro teams and coaches were somewhat glad that the game was discontinued, as they preferred their new rookies to spend the weeks prior to the game practicing with their new NFL teams, not with each other in an exhibition game of no importance.

One thing that was not suspended was the current operational status between the league and the players' union. No new agreement could be had for the third consecutive year, although both entities (the league front office and the NFL Players Association) met several times during the season and discussed their differences. Fortunately for the good of the game, the NFLPA did not threaten to strike in 1976.

Whatever animosity that the league office and the NFLPA might have had for each other, however, was mere child's play when compared to the hostile feelings that the Oakland Raiders and the Pittsburgh Steelers had for each other. In all the years of the decade, no rivalry—and I mean no rivalry—matched the utter fierceness and the seemingly biblical proportions that were evident between the Raiders and the Steelers rivalry in the 1970s. It was bitter enmity at its most primal, and it enlivened many fans who watched the game for the simple lure of its unabashed violence. It started innocently enough, as both teams played each other twice before December 23, 1972. Both of those games were nondescript affairs. The Raiders beat the Steelers in Oakland in 1970, 31–14. The Steelers returned the favor on opening day in 1972, 34–28. Then came December 23, 1972. The infamous birthdate of this bitter rivalry, as recorded into history by Franco Harris' Immaculate Reception, or "Immaculate Deception" as the Raiders termed it. The two teams again met twice a year later, both times in Oakland. The Steelers won the regular season encounter, 17–9. The Raiders won the divisional playoff a couple of months later, 33–14.

Then in 1974, the Raiders stormed into Pittsburgh and shutout the Steelers in the third week of the season, 17–0. This was a hard-hitting affair with several late hits on display. The two teams met later that year in Oakland in the AFC championship game. Pittsburgh dominated the fourth quarter and won, 24–13. In the 1975 AFC title game in Pittsburgh, the Steelers won again, 16–10. It was during that cold-weather meeting that the rivalry really heated up. Both teams saved their most vicious hits for each other on that day, and combined with the icy and cement-like Tartan Turf at Three Rivers Stadium, several players needed help getting off of the field. One such player was Pittsburgh wide receiver Lynn Swann, who received a barbarous clothesline hit from Oakland defensive back George Atkinson, resulting in a concussion. Some players from both teams were convinced that some of the hits that were distributed in that game were after the shrill sound of referee whistles, and some career reputations for savagery were forged on that day. The Raiders may have lost the game, but they got their share of licks in, and they vowed to a man that they were not finished.

Enter the NFL's schedule makers. They sent the Steelers into the Oakland-Alameda County Coliseum in Week 1 of the 1976 regular season. Even people who were not diehard football fans sensed that there would be plenty of bloodletting in this game. Boy, were they right. Oakland safety Jack Tatum recalled, "The game itself started the way I figured—violent and brutal." The Steelers built a 21–7 lead a few minutes into the fourth quarter, thanks to a 2-yard Rocky Bleier run, an 11-yard scoring pass from quarterback Terry Bradshaw to wide receiver Theo Bell, and a 47-yard run by wide receiver John Stallworth, who received a lateral from halfback Franco Harris, who ran for 25 yards before being tackled. Things were looking pretty good for the defending champs. Earlier in the game in the second quarter, however, Pittsburgh's Swann was the recipient of yet another clothesline whack on the back of his head by George Atkinson. The hit was clearly a dirty one, as Franco Harris was busy running the ball down the middle of the field, and Swann was nowhere near the action of the play. No penalty was called on the play, mainly because the officials were busy following the action around the ball carrier. Just like in the previous AFC championship game, Swann received a concussion and would not play for the remainder of the game. Oakland went on to score two clutch touchdowns, one on a 10-yard scoring pass from quarterback Ken Stabler to tight end Dave Casper (his second touchdown reception of the game), and one on a 2-yard Stabler bootleg. Oakland linebacker Willie Hall then intercepted an ill-advised Bradshaw pass deep in Pittsburgh territory with less than one minute in regulation. Rookie Oakland placekicker Mike Steinfort capitalized on the gift by booting a 21-yard field goal, giving the Raiders a heart-stopping 31–28 victory over their most hated rival.

The live television coverage of the Atkinson-Swann incident was replayed a few times during the game. Later in the week when NFL Films' ground-level footage of Atkinson's hit was shown, the ferocity of this obvious cheap shot was clearly visible. Pittsburgh head coach Chuck Noll minced no words after he saw the film. "You have a criminal element in every society and apparently we have it in the NFL too," Noll said. "George Atkinson's hit on Lynn Swann was with intent to maim and not with football in mind. I'd like to see those guys thrown out of the league. They put a guy's whole career in jeopardy."

Atkinson did not take kindly to Noll's words, and immediately sued him and the Steelers the sum of $1 million apiece for slander. He also sued a newspaper columnist (from Oakland ironically) $1 million for writing that he (Atkinson) "could have killed Swann" with the forearm delivery. Atkinson eventually lost all three cases. NFL Commissioner Pete Rozelle levied several fines after the game, however. Atkinson was fined $1,500. Raiders safety Jack Tatum was fined $750. Steelers defensive tackle Ernie Holmes was fined $250. The charge that Rozelle determined against all three players, putting it mildly, was "being over-aggressive." Rozelle was not done, however. He also fined Coach Noll as well a total of $1,000 for his public "criminal element" comments against Atkinson and the Raiders. The whole episode gave the Raiders the label of a dirty team, whether that label was deserved or not. It also gave the Oakland-Pittsburgh rivalry of the 1970s its most emblematic and brutal chapter.

A couple of other rivalries in the league had a couple of good first week contests. The New York Giants visited the Washington Redskins and seemed to have paved the way to an upset victory over their NFC East foes. New York had lost 10 straight games to Washington heading into this contest, and despite four interceptions thrown by quarterback Craig Morton, had built a 17–12 lead late in the fourth quarter. New York scored one touchdown on a 63-yard pass from Morton to wide receiver Ray Rhodes, and a 62-yard pass from Morton to wide receiver Walker Gillette. The Giants defense seemed to put an exclamation mark on the game when they decked Redskins quarterback Billy Kilmer, who suffered a severe cut on the bridge of his nose. Kilmer came off the field, got patched up, and returned to throw the game-winning touchdown pass to setback Mike Thomas over the middle from five yards out with only 45 seconds left to play. "There was no doubt I was coming back in," said Kilmer. The Redskins made it 11 straight over the Giants, 19–17.

On *Monday Night Football*, the Dolphins and the Bills met in Rich Stadium for the first of their annual two divisional meetings. Buffalo had just signed their superstar running back O.J. Simpson (who boycotted summer training camp) to a new contract, and the still-rusty runner could gain only 38 yards rushing against the No-Name Defense. The Bills had gone through the first half of the decade without beating Miami. This game would be typical of Buffalo's past defeats. They held tight to the Dolphins and were competitive thanks to the passing of quarterback Joe Ferguson, who threw three touchdown passes. Two of those scores went to wide receiver John Holland from distances of 53 and 58 yards. Miami responded with their trademark ground control strategy. Dolphins running back Norm Bulaich churned out 107 yards. Miami placekicker Garo Yepremian booted three field goals to provide the difference in a 30–21 Dolphins win, their 13th-straight over the Bills.

As a postscript to the Week 1 contests, both of the NFL's newest teams lost their inaugural games. Tampa Bay lost to Houston in the Astrodome, 20–0, and Seattle fought hard but fell to St. Louis in the Kingdome, 30–24. This was simply the norm in the NFL. The last expansion team to actually win their first game was the Minnesota Vikings, way back in 1961.

Winning games was a pleasant surprise for the 1975 Baltimore Colts. In 1976, they were out to prove that their AFC East Division title from the previous year was no fluke. The undefeated Colts met the undefeated Cincinnati Bengals in Week 2 at Memorial Stadium. Tall and lanky Baltimore wide receiver Roger Carr had one of the best games of his career, catching six passes for 198 yards, including three touchdowns of 68, 22, and 65 yards. Baltimore quarterback Bert Jones threw for 301 yards, and Colts running back Lydell Mitchell ran for 106 yards. The Bengals fought back all game long, scoring 27 points in spite of a concussion to their starting quarterback Ken Anderson, who sat out the entire second half. A 2-yard fourth quarter touchdown run by Baltimore running back Roosevelt Leaks gave the Colts a tight 28–27 win.

The Los Angeles Rams and the Minnesota Vikings would ultimately meet each other twice in 1976. Their first meeting occurred in the second week of the regular season at Metropolitan Stadium. This was a defensive struggle from start to finish, and then through the end of an overtime period. The final score was 10–10, and many experts believed that both of these teams would end up playing each other in the playoffs, which they eventually did. The Rams were led by the rushing abilities of John Cappelletti, who ran for 125 yards against the Purple Gang. Cappelletti was a former Heisman Trophy winner from Penn State University, and was a good—but not spectacular—pro running back. The yardage that he gained against a quality defense like Minnesota's was the best single-game performance of his career. Cappelletti would finish 1976 with a career-best 688 yards rushing.

The hard hits that occurred frequently in the Rams-Vikings game left many players hurting. Veteran Minnesota outside linebacker Wally Hilgenberg was so stunned by one head-on collision that he crawled around the field for a moment, tried to stand up, then fell right back down to his knees again. "It was like tumbling around inside a giant clothes dryer," said a recovering Hilgenberg after the game.

The third week of the 1976 season was telling in fortunes for several contests. A potential preview of the upcoming Super Bowl was held in Dallas; a team of young Patriots upset a giant in enemy territory; a perpetual loser won their third straight game; and a marathon contest was held on Monday Night/Tuesday Morning Football.

Going into the Colts-Cowboys matchup at Texas Stadium, both of these division leaders stood at 2–0, and both looked very strong in all aspects of team strategy, coaching, and overall performance. The game almost went into overtime, and unlike the defensive struggle the previous week in Minnesota between the Rams and the Vikings, the Colts and the Cowboys each displayed strong passing offenses. Dallas head coach Tom Landry was also willing to pull out some gadget plays to put points on the board. In the first quarter, Dallas quarterback Roger Staubach handed off to halfback Doug Dennison, who in turn handed off to wide receiver Drew Pearson, in what appeared to be a typical reverse or end around. But Pearson was a quarterback in college, and he employed his former passing skills in tossing a perfect pass to fellow wide receiver Golden Richards in the corner of the end zone for a Dallas touchdown. Richards' score tied the Colts at 7–7, and set the stage for more scoring by both teams. The lead would change hands four times in the fourth quarter alone. Momentum? That changed with virtually every snap of the ball. "This is what pro football is all about," said Landry after the final gun.

Baltimore placekicker Toni Linhart booted a 24-yard field goal to tie the game at 27–27 with just 28 seconds left in the game. Staubach enjoyed taking on challenges, however, and he felt comfortable with the challenge brought on by the Colts on this day. The Dallas quarterback enjoyed his best statistical game in his eight years in pro football up to that point, completing 22 of 28 passes for 339 yards and two touchdowns. What is really amazing about Staubach's performance was the fact that a steady rain descended through the hole in the roof at Texas Stadium in the second half. Staubach threw two clutch passes to Drew Pearson to set up placekicker Efren Herrera's 32-yard field goal with three seconds left to give the Cowboys a thrilling 30–27 triumph over the Colts. The Cowboys now stood above the crowd in the NFC East at 3–0, and it confirmed to many observers that their 1975 Super Bowl appearance was no fluke.

Several doubters were calling the recent results of the New England Patriots a bunch of good fortune, but when they upset the defending world champion Pittsburgh Steelers in Three Rivers Stadium, even the most doubtful of critics had to take a second look. New England's meat-grinder of a schedule during the first four games (Baltimore, Miami, at Pittsburgh, Oakland) would make or break their season. The Patriots split their first two games, and were trailing the Steelers 20–9 when they suddenly went on a second half scoring spree against the Steel Curtain defense. Twenty-one points later, New England had produced an epic 30–27 upset victory. Leading the charge for the Pats was second-year quarterback Steve Grogan, who threw for two touchdowns and ran for a third against the Steelers. One of Grogan's scoring throws was a 58-yard bomb down the far end of the field to wide receiver Darryl Stingley, who tight-roped his way along the sideline stripe to the end zone. The Steelers offense fumbled the ball an incredible seven times, six of which were recovered by the New England defense. Pittsburgh fans left the stadium scratching their heads, wondering what could be wrong with their defending champs?

There was nothing wrong with the San Diego Chargers, at least not during the early stages of the new season. A team that finished the 1975 campaign with a pitiful 2–12 record somehow had managed to pull out victories in their first three games of 1976. Their third win was a 43–24 offensive shootout over the visiting St. Louis Cardinals. San Diego scored an impressive 27 points in the second quarter against the seemingly absent St. Louis defense. Chargers quarterback Dan Fouts threw four touchdown passes to pace his team. "I was just happy we won and I was able to contribute with a good day," said Fouts after the game. The San Diego defense also contributed four fumble recoveries, and limited the explosive St. Louis runners to 124 yards on the ground. The win marked the best start for San Diego since way back in 1968. The Cardinals fell to 2–1 in the NFC East, just behind the 3–0 Cowboys and Redskins.

The Philadelphia Eagles started out strong against the rival Washington Redskins on Monday night's climax to Week 3 at Veterans Stadium. It did not take long, however, for the game to shape into a struggle for field position and momentum. Throughout the game, you got the feeling that the Redskins' experience would prevail, which it eventually did. Philadelphia's offense committed key mistakes throughout the game, including five interceptions and an untimely fumble just before halftime. Washington head coach George Allen called a time out as the Eagles' offense was trying to run out the clock just before the second quarter expired. "I called time out and told them [his defensive linemen and linebackers] to blitz, [and to] try to hit them on the exchange of the ball," Allen said. Philadelphia runner Herb Lusk was hit by a couple of trucks, namely Redskins defensive tackle Dave Butz and linebacker Harold McClinton. Lusk coughed up the ball, and Redskins linebacker Brad Dusek gleefully grabbed it out of the air and rumbled 32 yards for a touchdown with just 12 seconds remaining before Howard Cosell presented the weekly "Halftime Highlights" feature on *Monday Night Football*. Despite all of their miscues, however, the Eagles offense accounted for 418 total yards against the Over the Hill Gang, and the Eagles defense limited Redskins quarterback Billy Kilmer to 90 net passing yards. The game dragged on for hours, as both quarterbacks threw plenty of incompletions, thus stopping the game clock again and again. A 41-yard Mike Boryla touchdown bomb to Philadelphia wide receiver Charles "Homeboy" Smith tied the game at 17–17 with 1:07 remaining in the fourth quarter.

What turned this struggle around was the play of the renowned Washington special teams, particularly of one special player, reserve nickel defensive back Eddie Brown. The journeyman defender returned kickoffs for a total of 110 yards throughout the night, and his key interception at the Eagles' 30-yard line late in the overtime period set up the Redskins for victory. "Eddie does everything well," said Washington defensive secondary coach Ralph Hawkins. "He does a good job of jamming and covering people one-on-one." Washington placekicker Mark Moseley (himself a former Eagle) connected on a 29-yard field goal with 12:49 elapsed in the overtime period to give the Redskins a 20–17 triumph. The game marked Washington head coach George Allen's 100th career coaching victory, and the Redskins' third win of the year (keeping them even with NFC East rival Dallas at 3–0). The game, which was the first overtime game in *Monday Night Football* history, ended at 12:59 a.m., and forced many fans to come to work late that Tuesday morning.

The New England Patriots came to work with a vengeance the following week. Doubters of their new status of contenders were shown up when the Patriots romped over the visiting Oakland Raiders, 48–17. The loss marked what would become the only blemish that the Raiders would have on their record in 1976. The 48 New England points represented the most points scored on an Oakland team since 1963. The huge Patriots win came about from the actions of their running quarterback, Steve Grogan, who made no pretense to the advantages of running the football. "Football is a physical game, and I've always played it physically," said Grogan. "I like to do anything to help us win. I like to run. I've run for a long time, ever since I was in high school. It's just something that comes natural to me. I like to do more than just hand the ball off, so I kind of enjoy it."

Grogan "enjoyed" running for 56 of New England's 468-yard offensive output against the Raiders. He also threw for two touchdowns, and scored two himself on runs of two yards and 10 yards. Grogan made great use of the naked bootleg play, where he would fake handoffs to his running backs, then whirl around and run in the opposite direction. The play is risky, as an outside linebacker or defensive end who ignores the motion of the runners and blockers and instead stays home can often pulverize a bootlegging quarterback. Grogan was swift enough to make it work on a couple of occasions against the veteran Raiders. Patriots running back Sam "Bam" Cunningham joined in on the fun as he ran for 101 yards and caught five passes worth 94 yards in the rout. The win gave the Patriots a 3–1 record and a first place tie in the AFC Eastern Division with the Baltimore Colts.

A couple of teams fell back down to earth with losses in the fourth week of the season. The San Diego Chargers were shut out by the Denver Broncos, 26–0, and the Washington Redskins were upset in grand fashion by the Chicago Bears, 33–7. But the most noteworthy defeat belonged to the Pittsburgh Steelers on *Monday Night Football*. The host Minnesota Vikings avenged their loss to the Steelers in Super Bowl IX by taking advantage of several Pittsburgh mistakes, and by playing ball control on offense to claim a 17–6 win. Minnesota was without their starting quarterback Fran Tarkenton, who was recuperating from an injury. Tarkenton's replacement was Bob Lee, who did not have an especially good performance, completing only four passes in 11 attempts. Fortunately for the Vikings, Lee was merely needed to hand the ball off to his running backs. The workhorse for the Vikings offense was halfback Chuck Foreman, who lugged the ball 27 times for 148 yards, and who scored both of Minnesota's touchdowns. Foreman's longest run was only 18 yards, so he certainly earned whatever glory he got. The Vikings defense also intercepted Pittsburgh quarterback Terry Bradshaw four times, including two interceptions by defensive back Nate Allen. "In terms of total effort, everyone is coming up with big plays," said Minnesota middle linebacker Jeff Siemon. The frustration of turning the ball over so often and being unable to sustain any legitimate drives after the first quarter acted as an ominous cloud over the Steelers offense. The Vikings now sported a 3–0–1 record with their win, while the Steelers fell to an unrecognizable 1–3 mark. "We've crawled out of holes before," said optimistic Pittsburgh running back Franco Harris. "We're too good not to do it again this year."

Speaking of good teams and good players, more big yardage numbers were being recorded by this stage of 1976 than the numbers of the previous season. Several teams were on pace to break their scoring figures from 1975, including Baltimore, New England, Denver, Detroit, Chicago, Los Angeles, and San Francisco. Several players, especially on offense, were readily increasing their yardage production. In their colossal loss to New England in Week 4, Oakland tight end Dave Casper caught 12 passes for 136 yards, and was his team's only real weapon on that day. Los Angeles quarterback James Harris threw for a career-best 436 yards and two touchdowns in the Rams' 31–28 win over host Miami in the fourth week of the season. And a tandem of rookie running backs for the New Orleans Saints were making new head coach Hank Stram look like a genius (as if he needed any more proof in that assessment). Chuck Muncie and Tony Galbreath were given the nicknames "Thunder" (Galbreath) and "Lightning" (Muncie) for their speedy and forceful running styles. Both runners had great performances for the Saints against Stram's old team, the Chiefs, in Week 3. Galbreath ran for 146 yards, and scored on runs of 74 yards and 9 yards, while Muncie accumulated 126 yards rushing. The new-look Saints upset the Chiefs in Kansas City, 27–17, and Stram got another victory ride in Arrowhead Stadium, albeit on the shoulders of the visiting team.

A couple of other visiting teams in Week 5 made impressive strides in claiming some big wins. The San Francisco 49ers went into the Los Angeles Memorial Coliseum on *Monday Night Football* and totally dominated their divisional foes on the defensive side of the ball. Veteran San Francisco defensive end Tommy Hart earned an incredible six of his team's ten sacks of Los Angeles quarterback James Harris for 97 yards in losses in the 49ers' 16–0 shutout win. "Hart is a fantastic player, he has the quickness of a linebacker," said Rams offensive tackle John Williams, who had a difficult time of blocking the speed-rushing Hart on this night. "There isn't a better defensive end in the game."

The Rams lost for the first time this season, and suffered the first shutout in the Coliseum in their storied history. San Francisco's pass rush from this game on would be known nationally as "The Gold Rush," and as evidenced by their performance against a very good offensive line in Los Angeles, the Gold Rushers were a very strong group indeed. Besides Hart, the Gold Rush consisted of fellow defensive end Cedric Hardman, defensive tackles Cleveland Elam and Jimmy Webb, and veteran backup Tony Cline. The Gold Rush registered a league-best 61 quarterback sacks in 1976, and was the key element in producing a 6–1 record for the 49ers in the first half of the season. "With Cedrick [Hardman] on the outside and Jimmy [Webb] and Cleveland [Elam] inside, they just gave the pressure and I came around and made a lot of quarterback sacks," described the soft-spoken Hart. "Sacking the quarterback is what I work for," said Hardman, who had over 90 career sacks following the 1976 season. "It's the only glamour there is on the defensive line." Incidentally, the Gold Rush's 61 sacks in 1976 were the most of any NFL team during the entire decade. Moreover, the Gold Rush were certainly not gentle in their approach towards sacking quarterbacks. More attention and notoriety went to Pittsburgh's Steel Curtain, Minnesota's Purple Gang, and Baltimore's Sack Pack during the 1970s, but no defensive line pulverized quarterbacks in the vicious and extremely hard-hitting way for one season like the Gold Rush did in 1976. According to author Dave Payne following the 1976 season, "There isn't a better front four in football."

The Kansas City Chiefs were another visiting team in Week 5 who pulled off an impressive upset for their first victory of 1976. The Chiefs used a flea-flicker pass with 1:04 left in the fourth quarter to upend the Washington Redskins, 33–30. On the winning play from the Washington 36-yard line, Kansas City quarterback Mike Livingston handed off to halfback Woody Green, who handed off to wide receiver Henry Marshall, who lateraled the ball back to Livingston, who threw into the end zone for wide receiver Larry Brunson, who made the catch for the winning points. The play fooled the Redskins so much that Brunson was all alone when he caught the ball at the 5-yard line. Neither defense showed up in this contest as evidenced by the final score. Livingston threw for a career-high 332 yards in the win, and Washington wide receiver Frank Grant caught eight passes for 138 yards and a touchdown in a losing effort.

A couple of visiting teams in Week 5 suffered bitter defeats, however. The New England Patriots were demolished by the Detroit Lions, 30–10, in the Pontiac Silverdome. Detroit defenders intercepted five of New England quarterback Steve Grogan's passes, and Detroit quarterback Greg Landry completed 15 of 18 passes, three of which went for touchdowns. The win was the first for new Detroit head coach Tommy Hudspeth, who took over for Rick Forzano, who was fired after a 1–3 start to the season.

The toughest defeat of Week 5, however, was administered to the Pittsburgh Steelers by AFC Central rival Cleveland in Municipal Stadium. Cleveland's 18–16 upset win resulted from four field goals by Browns placekicker Don Cockcroft, and a 1-yard scoring run by running back Cleo Miller. The starting quarterbacks for both teams were knocked out of this game, and a couple of rookies took over. Cleveland rookie signal caller David Mays led the 29-yard drive that resulted in Miller's touchdown in the third quarter. Steelers' rookie quarterback Mike Kruczek ran for a 22-yard touchdown with 1:05 left in the game to tighten the score. Pittsburgh failed to recover their onside kick attempt, however, and thus lost their fourth game of the season. The 1–4 Steelers were all alone in last place in their division, and with starting quarterback Terry Bradshaw injured, all hope for defending their world title in 1976 appeared lost. A period of introspection was needed. For most Super Bowl champions, complacency at some level shows itself sooner or later. The Steelers were certainly not the first team to experience a drop-off in productivity and wins after being successful, and they definitely would not be the last. The Steelers eluded complacency throughout 1975 and defended their 1974 world championship. Their slow start in 1976 was thus unexpected, and it had their coaches and players searching for answers.

"You get to thinking you're better than you are," reasoned Steelers running back Rocky Bleier. "It was a lousy training camp," said defensive tackle and team leader Joe Greene. "Pretty soon you think you can be good without the work," explained tight end Randy Grossman. "Everybody's telling you how great you are before the season has even started," recalled wide receiver Lynn Swann. "Pretty soon you start believing it." Perhaps it was Greene who summed it up best though. "Winning breeds confidence," he said. "Sometimes, over-confidence." Regardless of the reasons why the Steelers were losing, they knew that they had to go back to the basics, play sound, fundamental football, and play it one game at a time. As we shall see, that is exactly what the Steelers would do throughout the remainder of the 1976 season.

Both the Tampa Bay Buccaneers and the Seattle Seahawks were taking things one game at a time during the first half of their inaugural seasons, and both had zero wins to show for it. That statistic would change for one of those two teams in their Week 6 meeting with each other in Tampa Stadium. "The Expansion Bowl," as it was called, featured plenty of mistakes as expected, but also tough defensive showings on the part of both teams. Neither the Buccaneers nor the Seahawks wanted to lose to the other, and both felt that they had a good chance at notching their first-ever NFL victory in this contest. Penalties abounded among both of the teams. Tampa Bay gained 285 total yards, Seattle gained 253 total yards, and the officials walked off 310 total yards on an incredible 35 infractions. According to sportswriter Dave Payne, "there were more umpires' flags in the air than 727s." Seattle proved to be just a little less inept than Tampa Bay, however, and survived to claim a 13–10 win. Former Baltimore Colt great Mike Curtis leaped high and blocked a desperation 35-yard field goal attempt with 42 seconds left to play to preserve Seattle's first win. "I would have hated to go home without winning this one," Curtis admitted.

Two rivals in the opposite end of the won-loss spectrum vied for supremacy in the NFC East in Week 6. The defending NFC champion Dallas Cowboys went to Busch Memorial Stadium and played the first of their typical two tough regular season games against the St. Louis Cardinals. Dallas came into the contest sporting an undefeated record, while the Cardinals only had one loss. St. Louis relied heavily on their passing game, because the Doomsday Defense limited their running game to a total of just 90 yards. St. Louis quarterback Jim Hart threw for 346 yards and three touchdown passes to pace the "Cardiac Cards."

The Cardinals also relied on forcing the Cowboys to wear their blue jerseys. As is the established NFL rule, the home team always has the option of wearing their home or away jerseys, thus forcing the visiting team to wear the opposite. By 1974, the Cardinals came to the belief that the Cowboys suffered a jinx and often lost when they wore their blue jerseys, so the Cardinals had no qualms about wearing their white jerseys. The decision to force Dallas to wear its blue jerseys did not always work, but it did on this day. St. Louis prevailed, 21–17. Dallas had their chances, as several dropped passes and untimely penalties cost them at least two touchdowns. The Cowboys' loss dropped them from the ranks of the undefeated, and tied them with the Cardinals for first place in the NFC East with a 5–1 record.

The Pittsburgh Steelers (1–4) had their backs to the wall when the Cincinnati Bengals (4–1) came in to Three Rivers Stadium. The Steelers knew that they could not afford to lose any more games if they expected to make the playoffs. Rookie quarterback Mike Kruczek would get to start his first pro game because regular quarterback Terry Bradshaw sustained an injury against Cleveland that would keep him out of the lineup for much of the next six games. Kruczek would rely on the constant pounding of running back Franco Harris, who carried the ball a career-high and then–NFL record 41 times. "It was a lot of work," Harris admitted, "but I'll carry fifty times if necessary." Harris would gain 143 yards and scored twice with 1-yard bursts, and this formula of running the ball on an almost constant basis would mark the main offensive strategy for the Steelers offense throughout the remainder of the 1976 season. Pittsburgh's league-leading 163 rushing first downs in 1976 were earned in spite of opposing defenses who knew what was coming, yet most were unable to stop it or even slow it down. The Steelers prevailed over the Bengals, 23–6. "The offense didn't make many mistakes this week," said an understated Pittsburgh head coach Chuck Noll.

The back-to-basics approach of the Pittsburgh offense was mirrored somewhat by the Steel Curtain defense. To a man, a new determination and a new ferocity sprung forth. The front four of Joe Greene, L.C. Greenwood, Ernie Holmes, Dwight White, and reserves Steve Furness, John Banaszak, and Gary Dunn shot through the gaps in the opposing offensive lines and permitted only 69 rushing first downs all year, easily the lowest number in the league. Linebackers Jack Ham, Jack Lambert, Andy Russell, and backups Marv Kellum, Loren Toews and Greg Blankenship were extremely active from Week 6 on. The Steelers defense forced a league-high 42 fumbles in 1976. The stingy defensive secondary was up to the task as well. Mel Blount, Mike Wagner, J.T. Thomas, Glen Edwards, and reserves Jimmy Allen and Donnie Shell covered wide receivers and tight ends so well that they allowed only nine touchdown passes all year. Incredibly, Pittsburgh's defense permitted only two opposing touchdown passes from Week 6 to the end of the regular season. The Steel Curtain did not just suffocate opposing offenses during the second half of 1976. They pounded them into the ground like a blacksmith hammering his anvil.

The resurrected Steelers had finally had enough of complacency and losing. They had weathered the storms of their early season defeats. For the remainder of the 1976 campaign, the Steelers played an angry brand of football with chips on their shoulders the size of bricks, and their opponents would get to experience first hand how great this dynasty truly was. One of the strongest and most character-filled comebacks in NFL history had just begun.

The midway part of the 1976 season featured several divisional matchups in Week 7 which gave a hint as to who would contend for the playoffs. The Green Bay Packers had lost their first three games, then had won their next three straight games, taking an even .500 record into Oakland to face the 5–1 Raiders. Hardly a soul figured that the Packers would be competitive with the defending AFC West Champion Raiders, but they were. Highly competitive in fact. Green Bay limited league-leading tight end Dave Casper to just one catch, and the Packers offense burned the Raiders secondary for two touchdowns. Green Bay lost the game by a slim 18–14 score, but they surprisingly gave Oakland a very tough challenge.

More tight games followed. The Los Angeles Rams were still a half game behind San Francisco in the NFC West standings, yet they—like the Raiders—almost overlooked their Week 7 opponent. The Rams managed to hang on to a 16–10 win over the Saints in the Superdome. The anticipated battle of Florida was also closer than most experts predicted, as the injury-riddled Dolphins edged out the host Buccaneers, 23–20. New England stayed close to the surging AFC East-leading Colts with a 26–22 win over the Buffalo Bills at Rich Stadium. The Steelers traveled to New Jersey to take on the Giants. It was no contest, as Pittsburgh shut out the Giants, 27–0. Why was this result so noteworthy? It was because this marked the first of an incredible five shutouts that the Steelers defense would earn during the final eight games of the season. Clearly, the Steelers were considering every game from now on to be a playoff game.

But the most visually stimulating highlight of Week 7 occurred on Monday night, when two NFC East foes fought it out amidst a driving rainstorm. Both the Cardinals and the Redskins were behind the Dallas Cowboys in the division standings, and when they met in RFK Stadium, they met in a rain-soaked bog. St. Louis quarterback Jim Hart described the situation succinctly: "I've never played in worse conditions," Hart said. The monsoon elements tested both teams' abilities to hang on to the ball. Washington did a better job of that. The Cardinals committed a team record nine fumbles (Washington recovered eight of them for a league record which still stands), and even though they held a slim 10–6 lead early in the fourth quarter, they eventually let the ball and victory slip away from them. The game-breaking play occurred when reserve defensive back and special teams player Eddie Brown showcased his balance and determination on a 71-yard punt return for a touchdown midway through the final period. Brown dodged the would-be tacklers on his return, stayed upright, and wove his way through grasping arms and falling raindrops to the end zone. A final St. Louis fumble by halfback Terry Metcalf and a Redskins' recovery near the Washington goal line preserved a 20–10 victory for the Burgundy-clad men in the District of Columbia. "We adapted to the field while St. Louis let it bother them," explained Washington head coach George Allen. "Whether it's rain, snow, or mud, it's Redskins weather." Both the Redskins and the Cardinals were now tied for second place in their division with identical 5–2 records.

Two teams in the AFC East were trying to stay close to the first place Baltimore Colts. The New England Patriots were having one of their best seasons ever, while the injury-plagued Miami Dolphins were struggling, yet still competitive. The Dolphins had eight starters out of action with knee injuries, and by year's end, a total of 22 Miami players would miss at least one game with a variety of injuries. The Dolphins had lost 30–14 to the Patriots in the second week of the season. Now they had a chance to avenge that loss in the Orange Bowl, and pull closer to the Colts. Miami accomplished both goals, upending the Pats with a gut-checking 10–3 win. As the final score surmises, this game was great for fans of defensive football to watch. The only touchdown came on a 16-yard pass in the second quarter from Miami quarterback Bob Griese to tight end Jim Mandich, who beat New England safety Prentice McCray down the middle on a classic down-and-in pattern. New England did manage to put together a potential game-tying drive in the fourth quarter when their quarterback, Steve Grogan, drove his team down to the Miami 26-yard line. Miami defensive Tackle Don Reese quickly trapped Grogan for a 16-yard loss, however, thus ending the New England threat. Miami's win brought their record to 4–4, one game behind New England's 5–3 record, and three games behind the 7–1 Colts. "It was a game we really needed to get us back into it," said Miami head coach Don Shula. "We finally had a day when things started happening our way."

A surprise team in the NFC Central tried to make things happen their way in Week 8 by upsetting the division leaders. The second-place Chicago Bears improved their record to 4–4 by knocking the favored Minnesota Vikings out of the ranks of the undefeated with a 14–13 victory at Soldier Field. The Vikings' loss dropped their record to 6–1–1. The Bears relied on the running prowess of second-year phenomenon halfback Walter Payton, who ran through the Purple People Eaters for a 39-yard scoring run in the first quarter, and who in 1976 would come to within sniffing distance of a league rushing title with 1,390 yards. Minnesota quarterback Fran Tarkenton did his best to rally his team, however, and in the process, he obtained another individual NFL record. Tarkenton threw for 272 yards passing against Chicago, and in the process broke Johnny Unitas' all-time passing yardage mark of 40,239 yards. Try as they did, though, the Vikings could not get close enough to attempt one last field goal, and the Bears prevailed. "Now the Vikings have lost one like everyone else in the league," said Chicago head coach Jack Pardee. "We weren't in awe of this club." The Bears were on their way to an eventual 7–7 record, their best mark since 1968.

The Dallas Cowboys managed to beat the Washington Redskins in RFK Stadium in the eighth week of the season, 20–7. It was Dallas' first win in Redskin territory since 1971. Roger Staubach came into the contest with a broken bone in his throwing hand, and his right pinky finger jutted out in different directions. Regardless of his injury, his determination to beat the Redskins was as healthy as ever. Staubach led several scoring drives, and scored himself on a 1-yard plunge in the third quarter. Dallas' dominance was so complete that Washington's lone score came with but 48 seconds left in the game with a 7-yard Joe Theismann touchdown pass to wide receiver Roy Jefferson. The Cowboys' record now stood at 7–1, while the second-place St. Louis Cardinals improved to 6–2 in the NFC East with a 23–20 overtime victory over visiting San Francisco. In that game, St. Louis placekicker Jim Bakken provided the winning points on a 21-yard field goal in overtime. The 49ers fought hard with the efforts of halfback Delvin Williams, who ran for 194 yards and three touchdowns in the loss. "They [the 49ers] were better than we thought they were," said a fortunate-sounding St. Louis head coach Don Coryell following his team's narrow win.

On other news from the eighth week of the 1976 season, the Pittsburgh Steelers notched their second straight shutout with a 23–0 win over visiting San Diego. Terry Bradshaw saw action in this game in the second half despite still recuperating from his neck injury. A few hundred miles to the east of Pittsburgh, the Philadelphia Eagles scored a 10–0 shutout over the host New York Giants. It marked the first shutout in the head coaching career of Dick Vermeil, the third win of the season for the Eagles, and the eighth loss of the season for the winless Giants.

Several division leaders saw tougher games the following week, as some teams started realizing that they needed to start winning soon or making the playoffs would be an impossibility. The Miami Dolphins followed up their win over New England with a 27–7 pasting of the New York Jets. Another AFC East team, the Buffalo Bills, were not so fortunate. The Bills ran into the New England Patriots in Foxboro and got hit with a variety of hits, some of which came after the whistle. Mild-mannered superstar runner O.J. Simpson was gang-tackled in the first quarter, then shoved around by Patriot defensive lineman Mel Lunsford after the play was blown dead. Simpson took offense to the offense, a fistfight ensued, and Buffalo's best weapon was ejected from the game by the officials after gaining a mere eight yards. Simpson also suffered a gash above his left eye for his efforts at pugilism, and his team suffered a frustrating 20–10 defeat. "This is the first time in my life I've been thrown out of a game," Simpson admitted. "The whistle had blown and the play was definitely over when that guy [Lunsford] slugged me down on my head. I don't mind taking legal shots, but I'm going to let the man know when it's not a legal shot."

The Minnesota Vikings improved their shot to win the NFC Central Division with a 31–23 victory over the visiting Detroit Lions, giving the Vikes a 7–1–1 record. A spirited effort by the 4–4 Lions made this contest close, but the Vikings were able to control the ball long enough to produce the win. Throughout the 1970s, Minnesota head coach Bud Grant promoted ball control as the key to winning, and his efficient quarterback, Fran Tarkenton, was the ultimate director of that strategy. Tarkenton simply loved throwing short passes to his setbacks, and taking advantage of their abilities to elude tacklers in the open field. Minnesota once again used their running backs as receivers versus the Lions. But unlike in most of Minnesota's wins, Tarkenton was also able to have enough time to connect with rookie wide receiver Sammy White on some profitable throws deep downfield. One of Tarkenton's connections to White did not have the desired effect, however. White caught a bomb from Tarkenton and was sprinting for a score when he decided to hold the prized pigskin aloft in triumph … a full five yards before he reached the end zone. Veteran Detroit cornerback Lem Barney tripped White up at the 1-yard line, where the ball popped out of White's one-handed grasp. Fellow Detroit cornerback Levi Johnson recovered the ball in the end zone for the Lions, thus eliminating what would have been a certain touchdown for the Vikings. "If I would have had a tunnel to go into, I would have taken it rather than face the bench," White said. His head coach gave the receiver a short but stern lecture to go with his shame. "That's what happens when you showboat," said the demonstrative Bud Grant to his demoralized rookie.

White's embarrassing moment was not a first in league history, however. Dave Smith, a wide receiver for the Pittsburgh Steelers, suffered an identical fate in a 1971 game against the Kansas City Chiefs. Smith's gaffe also cost his team a touchdown. Minnesota's Sammy White did catch seven passes against the Lions on this day, however, worth an astounding 210 yards (a new team record) and two touchdowns. Despite his glaring mistake against Detroit, White would later be named the league's Rookie of the Year in 1976. White caught 55 balls worth 906 yards and 10 touchdowns in his inaugural season. The Vikings scored 305 points in 1976, the third-best mark in the NFC, and accumulated 294 first downs, the second-best mark in their conference in that category (behind St. Louis' 307 first downs).

Speaking of St. Louis, they had their hands full in Philadelphia in Week 9. Placekicker Jim Bakken booted a 20-yard field goal to give the Cards a three-point lead late in the fourth quarter. Philadelphia drove downfield with a purpose, however, and appeared to assure themselves of at the very least a field goal attempt to tie the game. But fate had other plans as Eagles setback Dave Hampton caught a swing pass and headed for the winning touchdown when he inexplicably dropped the ball. Cardinal defensive tackle Steve Okoniewski fell on the pig bladder at the St. Louis 11-yard line with less than 30 seconds to play to preserve a 17–14 win for the "Cardiac Cards." The win gave St. Louis a 7–2 record. "I'm getting tired of these cliffhangers," said St. Louis head coach Don Coryell. "But it's all right as long as we win. We were fortunate to win today."

It was quite common especially midway through a season to see teams with losing records somehow give a superior team a tough game. The Eagles had done so with the Cardinals, and another NFC East team managed to give their division-leading foes a struggle as well. The New York Giants went into Texas Stadium and almost upset the lackluster Cowboys. In a battle of field goals, Dallas prevailed over New York, 9–3. Their victory was also preserved with a fumble (just like in the Cardinals-Eagles game), as Cowboys defensive end Harvey Martin blasted into the back of Giants quarterback (and former Cowboy) Craig Morton on fourth down at the Dallas 5-yard line late in the fourth quarter. Dallas defensive tackle Randy White recovered Morton's subsequent fumble to boost Dallas' record to an NFL-best 8–1. "I feel like a man who has been reprieved," said Dallas head coach Tom Landry after the game.

An even tighter contest was held in cold and windy Chicago, as the Oakland Raiders relied on several big plays to outlast the Bears, 28–27. The Raiders also received a couple of fortunate breaks which helped them out immensely. The contest was really three games in one. The first stage belonged to the Raiders, who put together a 21–7 lead early in the third quarter thanks to a short scoring run by halfback Clarence Davis, and two touchdown passes from Kenny "The Snake" Stabler. One of those touchdowns was a 75-yard bomb to wide receiver Cliff Branch, regarded by many players, coaches, and fans as the fastest player in pro football in the mid–1970s.

The game changed direction and moved to the second phase shortly thereafter, however, as Chicago stole the momentum (and the lead) with three successive touchdowns of their own. Fleet and powerful Bears halfback Walter Payton scored on runs of 12 and 2 yards (to match his first quarter touchdown run of 5 yards), which gave his team a 27–21 lead going into the fourth quarter.

The struggle reached its third and final stage with what has been repeatedly seen (or heard) over and over in NFL history ... a referee's quick whistle. Stabler went back to pass in the fourth quarter and was hit by Bears defensive linemen Wally Chambers and Jim Osborne. Stabler twisted out of Chambers' attempted tackle, but when Osborne grasped him, he fumbled. Fellow Chicago defensive end Roger Stillwell picked up the ball at the Oakland 40-yard line and raced untouched into the end zone for an apparent touchdown. Unfortunately for the Bears, the officials blew the play dead before Stabler's body hit the turf and supposedly before he fumbled the ball. Stillwell's score was nullified, and the Raiders capitalized on that break a few plays later when Stabler threw deep again for Branch, who was guarded closely by Chicago cornerback Virgil Livers (the same player Branch torched on his earlier touchdown). Livers leaped for Stabler's pass inside the Chicago 5-yard line and tipped the ball—right into Branch's receptive arms. Branch loped into the end zone to give the Raiders a 1-point lead with 4:33 left in the game. "Livers had good position on me and I didn't touch the ball when we went up into the air," Branch described. "But he made a mistake of tipping it up instead of knocking it down. It came right to me."

To their credit, the Bears came back strong, and drove down deep into Oakland territory. Chicago's last hope for victory was a 31-yard field goal attempt by placekicker Bob Thomas, but it was not meant to be. Thomas' kick bounced off of the right upright, securing victory for the Raiders. The loss marked Chicago's fourth defeat against six straight playoff opponents in 1976, while the Raiders improved to an NFL-best 8–1 mark. "I don't think we'll lose another game this season," predicted a soon-to-be prophetic Stabler after surviving the Bears' scare. "That's the only way I can approach it. A quarterback must believe in himself and his team. We'll finish the season with a 13–1 record."

Rounding out the ninth week of the 1976 regular season were the Seattle Seahawks, who would not obtain anywhere near the victory total of the Raiders. But they did win their second game of the season and their first home game ever with a 30–13 conquest of the struggling Atlanta Falcons. "We put it all together," said Seattle head coach Jack Patera. "The offense got some yards and scores, the defense helped us out when we needed it, and the kicking game, except for one blocked punt, was good."

By the dawn of the tenth week, some interesting achievements across the NFL spectrum were being seen. Take Buffalo Bills superstar running back O.J. Simpson for example. His contract holdout at the beginning of the year resulted in him seeing very limited action during the first three games of the year. Juice was still rusty from inactivity (and movie acting and commercial filming) during the summer, and it showed during the early part of the regular season. Simpson gained only a meager 105 total yards in the first three games, but in the six weeks since then, he sprinted for 555 yards, and he most certainly would have accrued over 600 yards in that six-week span had he not been ejected in the first quarter of the November 7 game at New England. O.J. had weathered the storm of his holdout and was now well on his way to claiming another league rushing title.

Few folks were able to claim anything for certain when discussing the exploits of the Washington Redskins. One week they would play extremely well, one week they would play extremely poorly, and still another week they would defy the odds and somehow come from behind and win a game that they had no business in winning. Such a game was their encounter at Candlestick Park in San Francisco on November 7. The Skins were showing a fading 5–3 record before they used a fake field goal late in the fourth quarter to defeat the 49ers, 24–21. Backup quarterback Joe Theismann was forced to start due to numerous injuries to veteran Billy Kilmer. Theismann made the most of his chances by throwing for 302 yards and three touchdowns to tight end Jean Fuggett. On the game-winning drive, Theismann drove the Redskins into San Francisco territory with the game tied at 21 apiece, and positioned placekicker Mark Moseley for the game-winning kick. But Theismann knew that Moseley's range in the swirling winds of Candlestick Park was less than 40 yards, so he received the snap from center, rose up abruptly and ran to his right for a crucial first down inside the San Francisco 25-yard line. "I headed for the orange stick [first down marker] like a kid heads for a lollypop," described Theismann. The impromptu fake set up Moseley for a more certain 39-yard field goal. Moseley came through with the easier attempt, and the Redskins came through with yet another upset win.

The 49ers were able to take some positive accomplishments out of the loss to the Redskins, however. San Francisco halfback Delvin Williams rushed for 180 yards and scored all three touchdowns for the 49ers. He also caught four passes for 99 more yards against the Skins. Williams, a third-year runner from Kansas, would account for an impressive 1,203 yards rushing and seven touchdowns in 1976. He would also catch 27 balls for an additional 283 yards and two more scores. But the 49ers would have to deal with the fact that they were in the midst of a slump which would eventually hurt their chances to win the NFC Western Division title. Proof of this slump— if the Washington loss did not provide it—came from their loss at Atlanta the following week. The lowly 2–7 Falcons won their third game by capitalizing on two key San Francisco fumbles in the fourth quarter. Journeyman Atlanta quarterback Scott Hunter rifled two scoring tosses to wide receiver Alfred Jenkins to propel the Falcons to a 21–16 upset victory.

Besides the 49ers, a couple of other NFC teams—the Rams and the Redskins—suffered tough losses in Week 10. Los Angeles was not displaying their usual dominance through the middle of the 1976 season, but they were still in first place in the NFC West. The other three teams in their division had won a combined total of 97 games throughout the first six years of the decade. The Rams were the obvious beneficiaries of the misfortunes and the poor play of their divisional competitors (New Orleans, Atlanta, and San Francisco). The St. Louis Cardinals, on the other hand, were once again in the midst of a tight battle for supremacy in the NFC East. St. Louis—with the Cowboys and the Redskins—were winning an average of almost nine games a year by the middle of the decade. Something had to give at the Los Angeles Memorial Coliseum when the Rams met the Cards, and it was the Rams who succumbed to the pressure.

Los Angeles took an early 21–6 lead and kept it through much of the game. The Rams scored on a 4-yard run by halfback Lawrence McCutcheon, a 65-yard bomb from rookie quarterback Pat Haden to veteran wide receiver Harold Jackson, and a 90-yard kickoff return by Cullen Bryant. But true to their recent tradition of coming from behind and winning tight ball games, the Cardiac

Cards did not panic. St. Louis quarterback Jim Hart out-dueled Haden by throwing for 324 yards against the tough Rams defense. Two short touchdown runs by halfback Terry Metcalf in the second half and a 25-yard pass from Hart to tight end J.V. Cain pulled the Cards closer as the remaining time dwindled down in the fourth quarter. With only three seconds left on the clock, Hart set up a 25-yard field goal attempt for his placekicker Jim Bakken, who made the pressure kick with the greatest of poise. St. Louis thus prevailed, 30–28. It was their 15th win in the past 20 games where the margin of victory was decided by four points or less. "I'm very proud of our men because they didn't give up," said St. Louis head coach Don Coryell.

While the Cardinals' win over the Rams could not really be considered an upset, the Giants' victory over the Redskins earlier that same day certainly could. Washington had New York's number, having defeated the Giants 11 straight times before the tenth week of the 1976 NFL regular season. The Giants were in the midst of their worst season ever, unable to win a single game in their first nine. Neither the Skins nor the Giants could score a touchdown in this game, and both teams could manage only three field goals apiece until late in the fourth quarter. New York placekicker Joe Danelo contributed his fourth field goal (a 50-yarder) to give the Giants a 12–9 lead with barely four minutes left to play. Washington drove down the field to the New York 7-yard line and were destined to tie the game with 41 seconds remaining, but they got greedy at the wrong time. Redskins' quarterback Joe Theismann scrambled away from a fierce rush and threw into the end zone for setback Mike Thomas. Theismann's pass was intercepted in the back of the end zone by defensive back Jim Steinke, however, thus preserving New York's first win of the season, and their first ever against a George Allen-coached team. It was certainly one of the toughest defeats of Washington's season.

"They are a gutty bunch of guys, getting stepped on and pushed around, but still believing in each other," said Giants head coach John McVay of his defense. "They were magnificent."

Another struggle with a somewhat surprising result occurred later on November 14 when the upstart New England Patriots traveled to Baltimore to take on the Colts. The Patriots had lost a fairly close game to the Colts to open their season, but by mid-season had improved enough to upset several very good teams, including Miami, Pittsburgh and Oakland. The Colts were also playing at peak performance, and had won eight of their nine previous contests. The difference in this game were the exploits of New England rookie cornerback and future Hall of Famer Mike Haynes, who intercepted two passes and who covered standout Baltimore wide receiver Roger Carr like a blanket. "I knew Haynes was a good athlete and I knew he could run," said Carr after the game. "But I still thought I could beat him. The throws were just a little short." All of the scoring from both teams came in the first half, and the winning touchdown was scored on a 3-yard run by Patriots' quarterback Steve Grogan. New England's 21–14 victory had earned them a season split with the Colts, and would be the second of their six straight wins to close out the 1976 regular season.

The Pittsburgh Steelers were accustomed to weekly victories, now that their slow beginning to the season was a thing of the past. As the final gun sounded in their game with the visiting Miami Dolphins, they would notch yet another win (their fifth straight). What made this game unique was the fact that their opponent actually scored some points against the Steel Curtain defense. Pittsburgh's 14–3 victory over Miami was the first outing in a month where their defense gave up points. The Steelers' record of shutouts (five in their final eight games) was an outstanding accomplishment which would not be equaled in modern pro football history (the years from 1960 to the current day).

The accomplishment of winning a division title was achieved by both the Oakland Raiders and the Minnesota Vikings in Week 11. They were the first two teams in 1976 to win their respective divisions, and they were the two teams who would eventually meet each other in Super Bowl XI. Another team who would eventually be named the NFC East winners were the Dallas Cowboys. Unfortunately for Dallas, their title would have to wait a little while longer after suffering a setback in a 17–10 upset loss at Atlanta in Week 11. Dallas' lack of a rushing attack made it difficult for them to sustain offensive drives, and would ultimately be their undoing in the playoffs. Their two main rivals in the NFC East—the Redskins and the Cardinals—fought it out in Busch Memorial Stadium on November 21, and it was the Redskins who upended the Cardiac Cards for the second time this season, 16–10. "It's the biggest win we've had in six years," said Washington head coach George Allen. "It was a complete team victory … a dedicated group of forty-three men playing their hearts out." Washington's sweep of St. Louis was the determining factor in aiding their playoff ascent. "We've still got hope and we've still got a chance," said Redskins running back Mike Thomas.

The excitement level of 1976 grew in Week 12, and it began with a couple of key Thanksgiving Day contests. Neither the Buffalo Bills nor the Detroit Lions were vying for a postseason spot, but the incomparable Buffalo running back O.J. Simpson set yet another league record, as he rushed for the most yards in a game (273) in NFL history. Simpson's new record broke his old record of 250 yards that he set in 1973 (Simpson's record has since been eclipsed several times by several runners over the past 40 years). The game marked O.J.'s fifth 200-yard game of his career (also a new league record), and gave him the AFC rushing lead. Simpson's brilliance on this day was on display against a pretty tough Lions defense, which by season's end would give up only 94 rushing first downs, the second-best mark in the NFC. Although no one knew it at the time, this event would be the final great rushing achievement of O.J. Simpson's remarkable football career. "It's something that when your career is over you look back on with fond memories," said Simpson from the postgame locker room. Despite Simpson's efforts, the Bills lost to the Lions, 27–14, their tenth loss of the year. "The purpose of coming in is to win and not to set a record," Simpson stated. "If it occurs, it occurs." Detroit's Thanksgiving Day victory over Buffalo earned them a respectable 6–6 record with two weeks remaining in the season.

Fans in Texas Stadium enjoyed feasting on Cardinals as well as turkeys as their birds of fare for Thanksgiving. Dallas avenged its earlier loss to St. Louis with a 19–14 controversial win over the Cards on Turkey Day. St. Louis had four attempts to score a winning touchdown in the final minute, but four Jim Hart passes went incomplete (despite cries from the Cardinal players for defensive pass interference on two of those passes). Replays confirmed that the Dallas defensive secondary probably should have been called for pass interference on at least one of those attempts, but the referees failed to see it. Hart's final pass with but eight seconds remaining to St. Louis tight end J.V. Cain in the end zone was broken up by Cowboy safety Charlie Waters, and Dallas had increased their NFC East lead to two full games. "We had the game taken away from us," said an upset St. Louis head coach Don Coryell from deep in the bowels of Texas Stadium. "I can't amplify on that. I'm not rich like some coaches are." Coryell's inference was that he would incur a fine from the league office if he publicly bad-mouthed the referees. Throughout the 1970s, most coaches refrained from speaking publicly to reporters about referee calls that went against their team. Few were the coaches back then who wanted to receive a letter from the league office which described their monetary fine in detail. Most coaches during the decade wanted the drama to stay on the field.

But the most dramatic game of the season's 12th week—and perhaps of the whole 1976 season—involved a cold and snowy affair in Cincinnati's Riverfront Stadium. The Pittsburgh Steelers were two full games behind the AFC Central Division leaders, the Cincinnati Bengals. Pittsburgh knew that one more loss and their playoff hopes would be nonexistent. Their game with the Bengals was a defensive lover's delight. The Bengals held a 3–0 lead at halftime ... before the blizzard began. In the third quarter—during the height of the blizzard—Pittsburgh's offense finally put together a good scoring drive. It would be their only good scoring drive of the entire game, but the Steelers made the most of it. Steelers halfback Franco Harris plowed off-tackle for a 4-yard touchdown that won the game for Pittsburgh, 7–3. "This is the most satisfying win of the season," said Harris. "It was a game that meant so much." The game marked the sixth time in the past seven weeks that the Steel Curtain defense did not permit an opposing touchdown. Pittsburgh was now one game behind Cincinnati with two more games remaining.

Two more games of interesting note occurred on Week 12. One involved another snowy field, and the other a frozen one. The Chicago Bears defeated the Green Bay Packers at Lambeau Field, 16–10 (neither team was in playoff contention). The game-time temperature in Wisconsin on November 28 was five degrees, with a wind-chill factor of 19 degrees below zero. The contest marked one of the few times that the turnstiles at Green Bay's venerable stadium froze prior to the game. Many of the more limber fans had to climb over them to enter the stadium. The high school band that was scheduled to perform at halftime was sent home in the first quarter in concern for their own safety. Despite the conditions and the fact that the game was carried live by local television stations, Packer officials estimated that 54,000 of the team's 56,267 season ticket holders were in attendance. This figure represented a seemingly common trademark token of loyalty in Green Bay for their beloved 4–8 Packers.

In not as cold of temperatures as in Wisconsin—but still cold nonetheless—the Cleveland Browns recorded a big upset over the Miami Dolphins in the snow of Municipal Stadium. The 17–13 win insured Cleveland its first winning season since 1973, and it also insured Miami head coach Don Shula his first losing season as a head coach since 1959. Miami had a great chance to score a winning touchdown late in the fourth quarter as the snowflakes fell. Veteran Dolphins quarterback Bob Griese then committed a rare (for him) mental mistake which cost his team the game. Griese sent fullback Norm Bulaich on a run, then forgot that the game clock resumed ticking after a measurement for a first down following a running play. Miami's last drive thus ended at the Cleveland 3-yard line, as they scrambled to get a play off when the final gun sounded. A Don Cockcroft field goal with 1:56 left provided the needed insurance points for Cleveland in their surprising win.

Coming out of the cold and into the warm glow of a playoff spot was the reward for both the Dallas Cowboys and the Los Angeles Rams in Week 13 of the 1976 season. The Cowboys expended little effort in defeating the host Philadelphia Eagles, 26–7, behind a 259-yard passing performance from quarterback Roger Staubach. The Rams trounced the Atlanta Falcons, 59–0, behind a multi-faceted rushing attack which produced seven rushing touchdowns, including three by halfback Lawrence McCutcheon.

But the most important Week 13 game occurred on *Monday Night Football*, as the Cincinnati Bengals traveled out west to take on the Oakland Raiders. The Raiders ironically had the destiny of the Steelers in their hands. Pittsburgh needed some team—any team—to beat the Bengals, who were on top of the AFC Central Division with a 9–3 record. Pittsburgh hung close with an 8–4 mark. If Oakland lost to Cincinnati, Pittsburgh would be knocked out of playoff contention. If Oakland defeated Cincinnati, they (the Raiders) would for all intents and purposes stamp Pittsburgh's ticket to enter the playoffs. Such was Oakland's dilemma. More than just a few Oakland fans wanted them to throw the game with Cincinnati, so they would not have to face the Steelers again in the playoffs. Some members of the sports talk radio stations across the country even went so far as to suggest such an idea on the air. Pittsburgh had defeated Oakland in the previous two AFC championship games. Were the Raiders actually jinxed? Now there is no question that there have been players every year who reach the peak of their performance, and who subsequently give up on certain plays when games are unwinnable in the fourth quarter. But never in league annals has evidence been uncovered that suggest that a team agreed together to purposely throw a game. The Raiders were certainly not going to be the first. Oakland solidly defeated Cincinnati, 35–20, and thus invited Pittsburgh to the playoffs (if the Steelers could win their final game of the year at Houston, which they did). Oakland's effort against the Bengals caused Raiders head coach John Madden to remark after the game, "It was the proudest moment of my coaching career." Keep in mind that he stated that before Super Bowl XI.

Another prideful effort involved the running prowess of Buffalo's O.J. Simpson. The superstar runner started the season poorly after a prolonged contractual holdout, but was able with each passing week to get close to the top of the league rushing statistics. Simpson's attempt at defending his rushing crown brought him to Week 13, when he notched another 200-yard rushing game (203 actually, and the sixth 200-yard rushing game of his career) in Buffalo's 45–27 loss at Miami. Simpson had been creeping up to conference-leading rushers Walter Payton of Chicago (NFC) and Lydell Mitchell of Baltimore (AFC) throughout the second half of the 1976 regular season. Both Payton and Mitchell were having remarkable seasons, and both appeared to fight a duel between each other for the 1976 rushing title. That was until the last few weeks of the year when Simpson emerged from the pack. The season of 1976 would be the last full year that the original Electric Company (the name given to Buffalo's offensive line back in 1973) would be a complete unit. Trades and injuries would alter the members of that famous line in 1977. Simpson would make the most of this final year with the Electric Company, however, and in the final few weeks of the year, prove both his and his line's greatness for the nation to see.

Simpson would rush for four of the league's top six rushing performances of the 1976 season. He ran for 171 yards in the final week at Baltimore, giving him 1,503 for the year. Lydell Mitchell of Baltimore finished almost 300 yards behind Simpson, totaling 1,200 ground yards for the year. Mitchell was used as much as Simpson. He had 289 carries in 1976, compared to O.J.'s 290. Baltimore had a bevy of offensive weapons, however, and head coach Ted Marchibroda believed in spreading out the pigskin to as many of his weapons as possible. Both the Colts and the Bills played virtually the same opponents, but Simpson ran for an incredible 5.2 yards per rush average, compared to Mitchell's solid 4.2 mark. The real competition at the end of the year for Simpson came from Chicago's Walter Payton, who in reality was his team's only offensive threat. Many people in the Windy City felt that Payton *was* the team. Several fans writing in to the Chicago team public relations office to request a Bears team picture in 1976 were humorously sent an 8 × 10 glossy photo of Payton instead. Payton carried the ball 21 more times than Simpson in 1976, but gained only 49 yards before suffering an ankle injury in the final game of the season against Denver. He finished with an NFC-best 1,390 yards, thus giving Simpson the fourth and final league rushing title of his remarkable career.

The season of 1976 was a great year for many running backs. A total of 12 runners reached and/or eclipsed the 1,000-yard rushing plateau, the highest number of the decade. Included in their ranks were the likes of O.J. Simpson (1,503 yards), Walter Payton (1,390 yards), Delvin Williams of San Francisco (1,203 yards), Lydell Mitchell of Baltimore (1,200 yards), Lawrence McCutcheon of Los Angeles (1,168 yards), Chuck Foreman of Minnesota (1,155 yards), Franco Harris of Pittsburgh (1,128 yards), Mike Thomas of Washington (1,101 yards), Rocky Bleier of Pittsburgh (1,036 yards), Mark van Eeghen of Oakland (1,012 yards), Otis Armstrong of Denver (1,012 yards), and Greg Pruitt of Cleveland (1,000 yards). Harris and Bleier were the first teammate tandem to rush for at least 1,000 yards apiece in the same year since Larry Csonka and Mercury Morris of Miami did it in 1972.

The final week of the 1976 regular season completed the playoff picture. Baltimore and Pittsburgh joined Oakland, Minnesota, Dallas and Los Angeles as division champions. New England won the AFC wild card, while Washington claimed the NFC wild card. Washington had to defeat Dallas at Texas Stadium in order to make the playoffs. They did just that, thanks to the inspired efforts of former Cowboys Calvin Hill and Jean Fugett, each of whom scored touchdowns against their old team. Washington's 27–14 victory over the Cowboys denied St. Louis their third straight playoff appearance. "We were written off, pronounced dead and buried," said Redskins head coach George Allen, "but we've got some pretty gutsy guys who just kept coming back."

New England captured the AFC wild card prior to the final week, but they beat the daylights out of Tampa Bay anyway in the regular season finale, 31–14. The Buccaneers finished the season winless, the first team in modern league annals to "accomplish" that feat. "For the first time in my life, I was embarrassed to be recognized as a football player," admitted Tampa Bay defensive end Lee Roy Selmon, who in 1976 was undeniably the best player on his team. "I didn't even want to go to a grocery store. Everybody had a solution. Even the clerk would tell us what defense we should be using. Everyone had an answer ... everyone but us."

Their fellow 1976 expansion team, the Seattle Seahawks, managed to win two games in their inaugural season. The Cleveland Browns were not much better at the beginning of the year, but they enjoyed a resurrection of sorts in 1976. Head coach Forrest Gregg's team had experienced losing seasons in 1974 and 1975, and few felt that things would change that much in 1976. But change they did. Cleveland recorded an impressive 9–5 record, marked by upset wins over Pittsburgh, Miami, and a season sweep of division rival Houston.

No team, however, better symbolized the spirit of the American Bicentennial than the New England Patriots, who went from 3–11 in 1975 to 11–3 in 1976. It seemed almost fitting that the team that played its home games in the Birthplace of the American Revolution was surprising everyone in commemorating our nation's 200th birthday with its best season ever. The Patriots were this year's obvious Cinderella team, and their upset wins over Miami, Pittsburgh, Oakland and Baltimore gave one pause when thinking that head coach Chuck Fairbank's team just might make it to the Super Bowl (as Dallas had done from the wild card spot in the NFC the previous year). Fairbanks was incidentally named the consensus NFL Coach of the Year, having been selected so by seven different news and/or football organizations. The odds on the favorite team to make it to the Super Bowl (and win it) were only slightly less unanimous. Most experts believed that the Oakland Raiders (13–1) or the Pittsburgh Steelers (10–4) would hoist the Vince Lombardi Trophy in January. Both squads were so solid on paper and in their personnel that few prognosticators believed that the Colts or the Patriots would get lucky enough to squeeze into the AFC title game. The NFC playoffs, however, were more questionable. Many experts still felt that Dallas' ascendance to the top of the NFC East was a fluke, while others could not bring themselves to think that the Vikings would make it to their third Super Bowl in the past four seasons. Time would tell whether or not the Norsemen could accomplish that goal, or whether Dallas would repeat as NFC champions, or whether the Rams or the Redskins would sneak in and pull off a playoff upset or two.

The Washington Redskins began the divisional playoff round by visiting the Minnesota Vikings at Metropolitan Stadium on Saturday, December 18. The temperature was 38 degrees, not the usual chilling climate for Minnesota this late in the year. The Vikings did not seem to mind the mild weather, as they warmed things up for the Redskins, jumping to a 21–3 halftime lead. One of their touchdowns came on a superior juggling and diving catch by wide receiver Sammy White, the NFL's Rookie of the Year. White, who led the NFC in 1976 in touchdown catches with 10, got tangled up with Redskins safety Ken Houston at the 2-yard line as he waited for Fran Tarkenton's pass to descend. The ball was tipped by Houston, then by White, who dove under it and finally caught it. White then rolled into the end zone before he was touched down to complete the 27-yard play. It was the first of his two scores. Another Tarkenton touchdown pass in the first quarter went to Minnesota tight end Stu Voigt from the Redskins' 18-yard line, who plowed over Washington defenders Pat Fischer and Harold McClinton to reach paydirt.

Washington tried to stay competitive, thanks in large part to their passing game. Redskins quarterback Billy Kilmer was once again injured as the season neared its end. But he persevered through the pain, and his two fourth quarter touchdown passes to wide receivers Frank Grant and Roy Jefferson made the score respectable. Unfortunately for the Redskins, the Vikings had built up too large of a lead and prevailed, 35–20.

"The line was blocking well and that's why we ran so well," said Minnesota tailback Chuck Foreman, who lugged the pigskin for 105 yards, while his teammate, Brent McClanahan, ran for 101 yards. "Whenever your line is blocking you're supposed to run well."

Tarkenton only played three quarters of the game, but still finished with three touchdown passes. "This team has the ability to get up," said Tarkenton, "and it believes in itself and it believes it can win. We think our offense can do anything against anybody."

Earlier in the season, the New England Patriots offense did whatever they wanted to do in their first meeting with the Oakland Raiders in Foxboro (a 48–17 Patriots victory). In the divisional playoffs in northern California, the AFC wild card Patriots entered the Oakland-Alameda County Coliseum as underdogs, and few thought that they would—or could—duplicate their earlier performance against Oakland. They did manage, however, to give the Raiders a very tough time in the rematch. Oakland finished the regular season with a record of 13–1 (as Ken Stabler predicted), and they wanted desperately to avenge their embarrassing loss to New England. Although they had payback momentum going for them, the Raiders knew that they were in for a struggle by the way the first two quarters had played out. Both teams exhibited very good defensive efforts in the first half. Early in the game, the Raiders' safety Jack Tatum, notorious for his hard (and sometimes late) hits, sent a clear message to Patriot receivers when he threw a forearm into the chin of New England flanker Randy Vataha … a couple of seconds after the ball flew by him on an incompletion. No penalty was called. "The Raiders aren't the roughest team in football but they sure are the dirtiest," said New England cornerback Bob Howard.

Oakland carried a 10–7 lead going into halftime on the strength of a 31-yard pass from quarterback Kenny "The Snake" Stabler to wide receiver Fred Biletnikoff, who made a splendid catch in the corner of the end zone over the Patriots' Howard. "They [the referees] gave Fred the touchdown when they should have penalized him for pushing me," said Howard. New England scored in the first quarter on a 1-yard plunge by running back Andy Johnson.

The first half also included a couple of missed opportunities by New England. Defensive back Prentice McCray dropped a sure interception in the end zone that would have stifled an Oakland drive. A few plays later, the Raiders produced a 40-yard field goal by veteran placekicker Errol Mann. Later in the second quarter, the Patriots were driving for another score when they tried some trickery, and it cost them at least a field goal attempt. New England's All-Pro tight end Russ Francis took a handoff from quarterback Steve Grogan on an end-around. The Raiders defensed the play magnificently, and Francis found no one open as he looked to pass the ball. A better option would have been to throw the ball out of bounds and save the scoring opportunity. But Francis threw the pigskin up for grabs anyway, and down with it came Raiders safety Alonzo "Skip" Thomas, also known as "Doctor Death" for his "pleasant" demeanor towards his opponents. Thomas returned the ball 18 yards to the Oakland 24-yard line, which ignited the Oakland touchdown drive which resulted in Biletnikoff's score.

New England's offense then started to open up in the third quarter with a balanced mixture of plays. The Patriots began running the ball with success, something that they could not do in the first half. New England runners accumulated 64 yards rushing in the third quarter against the vaunted Oakland defense, and those prosperous runs allowed Grogan to make quality use of play-action passes. One such pass in the third quarter was a beautiful 26-yard strike down the middle of the Oakland zone, where Francis was running a down-and-in pattern underneath clearing receivers Darryl Stingley and Randy Vataha. Francis made up for his earlier interception and caught Grogan's third down strike in stride. He then sprinted past a half-hearted arm tackle from Jack Tatum and into the end zone. New England ended a nine-play, 80-yard drive successfully and had regained the lead, 14–10.

The Patriots were just getting warmed up, however. The Raiders were unable to adjust their defense to stop the New England running game, so the Pats just kept running the ball. Running backs Don Calhoun and Jess Phillips finished up a 10-play drive for New England with key runs for first downs. Phillips culminated the 55-yard drive with a 3-yard off-tackle run for a touchdown. The Pats now looked like they were in complete control, holding strong to a 21–10 lead as the final quarter began.

Fortunately for the Raiders, their quarterback had by 1976 built a solid reputation for inspiring comeback wins. Ken "The Snake" Stabler was already famous for guiding the Raiders to their epic come-from-behind playoff victory over the defending world champion Miami Dolphins in 1974. Now he was asked to repeat that performance. Stabler was also renown for his penchant to party late into the evening, a custom reminiscent of Bobby Layne, the former great quarterback for the Detroit Lions of the 1950s. Stabler once claimed, "I would read the game plan by the light of the jukebox." His cool and calm demeanor in the face of adversity was evident for all to see, and his teammates in the offensive huddle drew much confidence from him and from each comeback victory. Stabler wasted little time in getting Oakland moving again. He guided an 11-play, 70-yard drive which culminated with a 1-yard touchdown plunge by running back Mark van Eeghen. Key plays in the drive included two passes to Fred Biletnikoff for first down conversions. The Raiders now trailed the Patriots by a score of 21–17 with 11:03 left to play.

On the next series, New England's offense got one first down before being stopped by the Oakland defense. The Patriots defense returned the favor and immediately forced the Oakland offense three downs and a punt following a 10-yard sack of Stabler by New England defensive end Julius Adams. There was now only 6:24 left in the game, and the Patriots were in the driver's seat, cruising to one of the decade's greatest postseason upsets. A few more first downs and they could punch their own ticket to the AFC title game. The Patriots offense got one first down on a 10-yard bootleg run by Grogan. On a second and eight situation from the Oakland 35-yard line, Grogan handed off to running back Sam "Bam" Cunningham, who ran a sweep to the left. Cunningham was close to the first down marker, and in retrospect could have and should have lowered his shoulder and lunged to the marker. Instead, he stayed upright and was pushed out of bounds by Oakland linebacker Willie Hall just two inches short of a first down. This turned out to be one of the crucial plays of the game and of the season for the Pats. Grogan then employed a long count on third down, hoping to draw the Oakland defensive line offsides. Unfortunately for Grogan, several members of the left side of his own offensive line moved before the snap, inciting a 5-yard illegal motion penalty. On third-and-5-and two inches, Grogan rolled right and threw along the sideline for Francis, who was clearly being held throughout his route by Oakland linebacker Phil Villapiano. The vociferous and opportunistic Oakland linebacker dragged Francis to the ground as the ball deflected off of the tight end's right hand, causing an incompletion. Again, no penalty was called. Several Patriot players and virtually all of their coaching staff berated the officials incessantly after this play. As if New England's luck could not get any worse, their placekicker John Smith came in to save the drive with at least three points, but was just barely short on a 50-yard field goal attempt. The illegal motion penalty cost New England three points and possibly the game, because Smith's attempt was straight down the middle. One more yard and the Patriots would have increased their lead. Many critics blamed New England head coach Chuck Fairbanks for not pooch-punting the ball instead of going for the field goal, thereby forcing the Raiders to drive longer down the field. But like all other vital coaching decisions, Fairbanks went with his best judgment. Had Smith's field goal succeeded, no criticism would have been heard.

The Snake had 4:12 left to pull this one out. In retrospect, his 12-play, 60-yard scoring drive should probably have never happened, due to the previous kicking choice of Fairbanks and New England's many missed opportunities throughout the game. Stabler managed to drive his offense down to the Patriots' 27-yard line, when he dropped back to pass on a third and 18 situation. New England defensive lineman Ray "Sugar Bear" Hamilton brushed past Oakland guard Gene Upshaw and bore into Stabler's pass pocket, hitting the quarterback's facemask with his right hand as the ball was released. Stabler's pass down the sideline for setback Carl Garrett fell incomplete, but a penalty flag lay on the grass near Stabler's fallen body. Hamilton was flagged for roughing the passer, thus giving Oakland new life. It was a questionable call to say the least, and a bunch of Patriot players questioned the now surrounded officials about it, in their own "diplomatic" way. An unsportsmanlike conduct penalty was thus instantly assessed to the Patriots, and with 14 seconds left in the game, Oakland found themselves one yard away from the winning touchdown. In a couple of plays, Stabler rolled left and dove into the end zone amid a chorus of cheers and ear-piercing delirium from the partisan Raider fans. New England's Cinderella season ended abruptly and plausibly prematurely by a final score of 24–21. "Now you know what it means to us to have the home field edge [in the playoffs]," said Oakland head coach John Madden after the game. "We did what we had to do."

To say that the disconsolate Patriots disagreed with the way the game was called by the referees was an obvious understatement. "I'll tell you I was held [by Oakland's offensive linemen] plenty," said Ray Hamilton after the bitter loss. "I used to think Santa Claus wore red and white," said New England offensive guard John Hannah. "Those guys who gave the game to Oakland wore black and white." Jack Costello, the sports editor for the *Lowell Sun* newspaper, was even more spiteful in his rhetoric. "In order to beat the champ, you gotta knock him out," Costello wrote after the game. "In order to win in Oakland you gotta knock out the officials."

The next day, the other two AFC playoff teams did battle, but the game at Baltimore's Memorial Stadium between the Steelers and the Colts had virtually none of the drama that was seen in Oakland. The Steelers had ended Baltimore's own Cinderella season in their 1975 divisional playoff game. Today, they would duplicate that conquest in grand fashion. Pittsburgh wasted little time in taking the lead with a beautiful 76-yard bomb deep down the middle of the field from quarterback Terry Bradshaw to reserve wide receiver Frank Lewis. The play occurred on the third snap of the game, and it set the tone for what was to follow. The Steelers would build a 26–7 halftime lead on the strength of another scoring pass from Bradshaw (to wide receiver Lynn Swann), a touchdown run by backup runner Reggie Harrison, and two Roy Gerela field goals. Baltimore managed to score once in the first quarter on a 17-yard pass from quarterback Bert Jones to wide receiver Roger Carr, but throughout the remainder of the game, the Colts struggled mightily against the Steel Curtain defense. Greene, Greenwood, Lambert, Ham and Company parlayed their momentum from the last half of the regular season into this playoff matchup. It was as if the Steelers had read Baltimore's playbook all week prior to the game, and knew where to be on virtually every play. "Our defense is just too potent to crack," said Pittsburgh cornerback Mel Blount after the game. The Colts were held to 71 rushing yards and 144 passing yards, while the Steelers ran for 225 yards and their quarterbacks completed 19 passes for 308 yards.

There was no scoring by either team in the third quarter, but in the fourth quarter, the Steelers put two more touchdowns on the scoreboard. Bradshaw hit Swann for another score from 11 yards out, and Harrison ran up the middle of the Colts line for 10 yards and another touchdown. Reserve Pittsburgh center and 14-year veteran Ray Mansfield was needed to kick his team's final extra point after regular placekicker Roy Gerela suffered an injury. It was Mansfield's first score of any kind in his career. The Steelers crushed the Colts, 40–14. "That is the kind of game we needed to have for the playoffs," said Bradshaw.

Unfortunately for Pittsburgh, what they absolutely did not need was having two vital members of their starting offensive backfield suffer injuries which would keep them out of their next game. Both Franco Harris (bruised ribs) and Rocky Bleier (fractured toe) could barely walk after the game in Baltimore. Both were the heartbeat of the Pittsburgh offense, and missing both of them would turn out to be very detrimental to the Steelers' Super Bowl hopes. Fifteen minutes following the game, one last episode put an exclamation mark on the day. A Piper Cherokee airplane flew into the upper deck of Memorial Stadium, destroying a portion of seats and causing smoke and flames to burst into the evening Baltimore sky. The pilot, 33-year-old Donald Kroner of Baltimore, was taken to Union Memorial Hospital unconscious. He managed to survive with just lacerations and contusions, however. Three Baltimore policemen were also taken to the hospital, overcome by smoke from the plane as they tried to rescue the pilot. Fortunately as far as everyone's safety was concerned, the game was a blowout, and many fans had already exited the stadium before the final gun. Only a token number of fans remained in their seats after the game to witness the accident, and none of those fans were injured by the plane crash.

The final playoff game of the divisional round in this Bicentennial year was held in Dallas. The Cowboys had enjoyed one of their usual good seasons (they finished with an 11–3 record), even though their starting quarterback Roger Staubach sustained an injury to his throwing hand in the eighth week of the season in a victory over the Chicago Bears. After Staubach's injury, Dallas was upset by both the Atlanta Falcons on November 21 and the Washington Redskins on the final Sunday of the regular season. This was definitely not the time to be in a slump. The losses to the Falcons and the Redskins proved that the Cowboys were not immune to a fatal upset defeat in the postseason. The Rams were banking on this as they came into Texas Stadium, and hoped that the Cowboys would continue their recent trend of uninspiring play. "It all went downhill after Roger got hurt," admitted Dallas head coach Tom Landry in a reflective moment after the game. Los Angeles also had a huge chip on their shoulder. They were brutally ousted in last year's NFC championship game by the Cowboys (by a score of 37–7), and nothing would make them happier than returning the favor.

The game was a defensive struggle, with neither team able to run the ball very well. The Rams accrued 120 total ground yards, while the Cowboys could muster only 85. A similar fate for both teams came through the air. Rookie Los Angeles quarterback Pat Haden managed to pass for only 152 yards. He also tossed three interceptions. Dallas' Staubach was held to a paltry 150 passing yards. He also was guilty of throwing three interceptions. Despite their mistakes, Tom Landry's squad held on to a shaky 10–7 lead going into the fourth quarter.

Los Angeles converted a Drew Pearson fumble into a short touchdown drive in the final stanza, and benefitted from another Dallas mistake in the drive. Cliff Harris of the Cowboys ran into Rams placekicker Tom Dempsey on a 24-yard field goal attempt. The penalty gave Los Angeles head coach Chuck Knox the option of keeping the three points and a 10–10 tie, or gaining a first down at the Dallas 3-yard line. Knox chose the latter option, and it proved to be the winning decision. Two plays later, Rams halfback Lawrence McCutcheon burrowed into the end zone for a 14–10 Los Angeles lead. All three Dallas linebackers that were on the field—Lee Roy Jordan, D.D. Lewis, and Thomas Henderson—protested vehemently to the officials that McCutcheon had not crossed the goal line. Their complaints fell on deaf ears, however, and McCutcheon's score stood.

Dallas would have the ball for four more possessions in the game. One ended in a punt, one ended with a Staubach interception, one ended on an incompletion on fourth down, and the final Cowboys possession ended on a fourth down Staubach completion to tight end Billy Joe DuPree, who came up just one yard short of a first down. "We just made too many errors," lamented Landry. "Both teams made mistakes, it was just a matter of who made [them] at the wrong time."

Punter Rusty Jackson of the Rams sealed the win when he caught a center snap on the last play of the game, and ran out of the end zone for a Dallas safety. Los Angeles' 14–12 victory was very disheartening to Cowboys safety Charlie Waters, who blocked two of Jackson's earlier punts, and who also intercepted one of Haden's passes. Coach Knox's decision to have Jackson avoid a third blocked punt may have given Dallas a couple of meaningless points, but it also gave the Rams a ticket to the NFC championship game and a big revenge win over the hated Cowboys. "It was a great victory for our players," Knox said. "This victory was a team effort. Everyone wanted to win and we played hard enough to win."

The 1976 NFC championship game was fought on December 26 in frigid Bloomington, Minnesota. The scene was repeated several times in the late 1960s and throughout the 1970s. Metropolitan Stadium offered no real defense from the cold weather in December, and Minnesota head coach Bud Grant did not help matters for his team. His refusal to allow heaters along the players' benches in the 12-degree weather was psychological in nature. Grant believed that if his players showed their opponents that the cold weather did not bother them, they would present an aura of strength and invincibility. The plan worked often enough for the Vikings to record eight NFC Central Division championships throughout the decade of the 1970s. The plan also worked against the Rams on this day, despite the fact that the Rams allowed their players to make use of heaters along their bench.

Minnesota got off to a startling lead when it appeared as if the Rams would draw first blood. Los Angeles marched down the field on their second possession, only to have endured epic misfortune on one single play. Unable to pierce the Vikings' end zone, the Rams settled for a 17-yard field goal attempt. Placekicker Tom Dempsey kicked the ball soundly, but Minnesota cornerback Nate Allen rushed into the backfield untouched and blocked the ball, which bounced across the field and into the inviting arms of fellow Minnesota cornerback Bobby Bryant. Never before had Bryant been offered such a gift, as he ran 90 yards untouched into the Rams end zone. "There was a little misfire between the center, holder, and myself," said Dempsey, "drawing us off a tenth of a second or so, but it obviously gave Allen enough time." Minnesota's personnel had a well-earned reputation for blocking kicks. "We've got the people who believe they can kick it, catch it, block it, or whatever has to be done," said Minnesota head coach Bud Grant. According to Bryant, "We just tried to get a good jump on the ball and Nate [Allen] does that very well. My main responsibilities are to check for the fake and move into position should the kick be blocked in my direction. Sure enough, Nate made the block and the ball bounced right into my arms as I was in stride at the 10-yard line. I continued up field and there wasn't anyone within 10 yards of me. There wasn't any way I couldn't score."

A blocked punt by Minnesota linebacker Matt Blair set up a 25-yard Fred Cox field goal in the second quarter, which gave the Vikings a 10–0 halftime advantage. Minnesota added to that lead early in the third quarter, thanks to the talents of halfback Chuck Foreman. The All-Pro

Vikings runner burst off-tackle for a 62-yard dash, then followed that run up with a 1-yard dive into the Rams' end zone. The Vikings now owned a seemingly insurmountable 17–0 advantage.

The Rams earned a 10–3–1 record in 1976, and they were a veteran team. They had the NFC's highest-scoring offense with 351 points scored, and they would not be held down in this game for long. Los Angeles put together their first scoring drive midway through the third quarter. It culminated with a 10-yard run up the middle by halfback Lawrence McCutcheon, who broke an arm tackle by Minnesota defensive end Carl Eller, then bowled over Viking safeties Paul Krause and Jeff Wright as he crossed the goal line. The Rams had secured control of the momentum a little over three minutes later when they scored their second touchdown. Rookie Rams quarterback Pat Haden threw a 5-yard scoring pass to veteran wide receiver Harold Jackson, closing the Rams' deficit to 17–13 with a whole quarter left to play. By game's end, the Rams would out-gain the Vikings in total yardage, 336–267. "They [the Rams] could have rolled over," said Grant after the Vikings took an early lead. "They could have surrendered earlier and they didn't. They were every bit as good, maybe even better, as we thought they were going into the game."

Despite their resilient toughness and determination, the Rams were unable to put together another scoring drive. Minnesota's Foreman made another game-breaking play late in the fourth quarter, when he caught a short Tarkenton screen pass and romped down the sideline for 57 yards, thereby setting up reserve running back Sammy Johnson for a 12-yard touchdown run up the middle. Johnson's score clinched a 24–13 victory for the Vikes, and sent them to their fourth Super Bowl in the past eight years. "You've got to give them [the Vikings] credit," said Los Angeles head coach Chuck Knox after losing his third straight NFC championship game. "They know how to win."

The Oakland Raiders had not been to a Super Bowl since 1967, and there were critics who believed that they might never get back there. Managing General Partner Al Davis' team was seemingly jinxed over the past several years. They had lost the AFC championship game each of the past three years. Their losses in 1974 and 1975 were to their most bitter rival, the Pittsburgh Steelers. But 1976 was a special season for the Raiders. Their playoff win over the Patriots in the divisional round gave them some measure of momentum. True, they would meet a Pittsburgh team which had won their previous 10 games in dominant fashion, surrendering a total of only 28 points in those 10 games (including an astounding five shutouts). But the Raiders were at home, and the Steelers were greatly wounded, missing both of their starting running backs to injuries. The odds were finally leaning in Oakland's favor, and on this day, there would be no Immaculate Reception.

Oakland took a 3–0 lead into the second quarter when they took full advantage of a key Pittsburgh turnover. Oakland linebacker Willie Hall dove for a deflected Terry Bradshaw pass and made the interception at the Steelers' 26-yard line. Hall then bounced up and ran 25 yards to set up the game's first touchdown. Oakland halfback Clarence Davis ran off tackle for a yard and a score. Pittsburgh answered back on the next series with an eight play, 75-yard drive that culminated with a 3-yard run by reserve running back Reggie Harrison. Both Harrison and John "Frenchy" Fuqua could earn only 68 total rushing yards on this day, however, as they substituted for Pittsburgh's injured running backs, Franco Harris and Rocky Bleier.

"You take 2,000 yards away and its got to affect a team," said Oakland linebacker Monte Johnson, referring to the sidelining of both Harris and Bleier, each of whom ran for over 1,000 yards during the regular season. "You know a lot of people will be saying that we couldn't have won if Harris and Bleier had been in there. Well, I don't know about that … and I guess we'll never know."

The Raiders were not about to allow the Steelers to gain a foothold of momentum in this game. The men in Silver and Black responded quickly after Harrison's score with another touch-down of their own, a 4-yard pass from quarterback Kenny "The Snake" Stabler to seldom-used setback Warren Bankston (who was also a former Steeler). Bankston's tally boosted Oakland to a 17–7 halftime lead. A key play in the nine-play Raider scoring drive was a 13-yard sweep left by veteran running back Pete Banaszak, who was one of only four Oakland players remaining from their Super Bowl II team in 1967 (Fred Biletnikoff, Willie Brown and Gene Upshaw were the others).

The game's second half would see further proof that the Raiders were just healthier than the Steelers. Pittsburgh's offense was unable to obtain another first down until barely three minutes were left in the third quarter. By that time, Oakland's offense had scored another touchdown, this one coming on a 5-yard pass from Stabler to Banaszak. Oakland's defense took over from there, and never allowed the Steelers to get in scoring range again. Pittsburgh's last play of the season, a 24-yard pass from Bradshaw to wide receiver Lynn Swann, was halted by hundreds of Oakland fans who ran onto the field, much as the Steeler fans had done at the conclusion of the previous year's AFC title game in Three Rivers Stadium. Oakland's 24–7 victory over Pittsburgh was surprising by one ironic statistic. The Steelers actually out-gained the Raiders in total net yards, 237 to 228. But the Raiders had finally vanquished the Steelers, and were headed to Pasadena to play in Super Bowl XI.

"I know it sounds trite," said Oakland head coach John Madden, "but if you do everything right, you've got to win. We knew if we just did the things we always do as well as we could, that we would win."

Neither the Minnesota Vikings nor the Oakland Raiders had won a Super Bowl prior to 1976. The Vikings had lost each of the three previous Super Bowls in which they played. The Raiders had lost six AFL/AFC championship games after they appeared in Super Bowl II. History would change forever with a very happy chapter for one of these teams on January 9, 1977. Super Bowl XI would be played for the first time ever at the Rose Bowl Stadium in Pasadena, California. The 100,421 people who attended the game would set a new Super Bowl record, as would the 81 million television viewers to watch a sporting event. Super Bowl XI would also be the final Super Bowl which began in the afternoon. Every Super Bowl thereafter would start later in the day, and would end in the evening on the east coast. This would also be the first Super Bowl in which the spectators in the stands would play a major part in the game's halftime entertainment activities. Because of the game's proximity to Walt Disney Land in Southern California, the Disney theme would be prevalent. To the sounds of the Los Angeles Unified School District's All-City Band playing "It's a Small World After All," the fans would hold up colored placards (which were distributed to them during the first half), while dancers on the field would unfurl colored streamers amidst a giant globe. This colorful spectacle, where organized symmetry would be seen from the middle of the field to the top row in the stands, was the first of its kind at a pro football game, and variations of it would be repeated at many halftime productions in the league in the future. Commissioner Pete Rozelle's vision of quality entertainment reached a new and higher level with this halftime performance.

The performance of the Minnesota Vikings special teams produced the game's first big play midway through the first quarter when they performed their specialty ... blocking kicks. Minnesota blocked an NFL-high 13 kicks in 1976, and early in Super Bowl XI, they were at it again. Linebacker Fred McNeill became the first player ever to block a Ray Guy punt. The ball, however, took a backwards bounce away from the Oakland end zone. McNeill managed to recover it at the Oakland 3-yard line. The Oakland defense had their backs to the wall, but they displayed the poise of a champion two plays later. They blunted two Minnesota running plays and delivered a statement that they were not about to concede anything to the Vikings. Minnesota running back Brent McClanahan was hit hard at the line of scrimmage on second down and fumbled the ball. Raiders linebacker Willie Hall dove in the pile of humanity and made the recovery at the Oakland 3-yard line. Minnesota's best chance to score early in a Super Bowl had been denied, and it would cost them in both points and momentum.

Oakland's offense would drive 90 yards on their next possession, but failed to score a touchdown. They moved the ball through the Vikings defense primarily by running the ball on sweeps and off-tackle runs to their left behind All-Pro blockers Art Shell (left tackle) and Gene Upshaw (left guard). "They were in a formation where they ran the same play every time," said Minnesota defensive tackle Alan Page, "and we knew it. Or at least we should have known it." Oakland's first major drive was culminated with a 24-yard field goal from the toe of veteran placekicker Errol Mann. They certainly were not satisfied with just a field goal, however. The Raiders continued their next drive by continuing to run to their left, and the constant pounding against the right side of the Vikings defense was beginning to take its toll. Oakland quarterback Ken Stabler also tossed in a few passes to keep the Norsemen off balance. The Snake completed five passes in five attempts on the 10-play drive, which ended in successful fashion with a 1-yard touchdown lob to tight end Dave Casper. The Raiders were now in firm control of this contest. On their next possession, they would add another touchdown to the ledger. A key 17-yard pass to the game's eventual Most Valuable Player, Oakland wide receiver Fred Biletnikoff, would set up long-time Raiders running back Pete Banaszak, who burrowed into the end zone on a 1-yard run. The Raiders took a 16–0 lead into halftime.

Minnesota had been in this identical situation before. In fact, in each of their four Super Bowl appearances throughout the 1970s, the Vikings had failed to score even one single point during the first half of those games. In each of their previous three Super Bowls, the Vikings had been unable to come back in the second half. Minnesota's defense would have to shore up their right side and limit Raider runners Clarence Davis and Mark van Eeghan from gaining ground yardage at will if they were to become competitive in the second half of Super Bowl XI. Moreover, their defensive secondary would have to keep Fred Biletnikoff from making key catches, which in the first half had provided key first downs in Oakland's scoring drives. Unfortunately for Minnesota, their defense would not be up to the challenge. The Raiders increased their lead in the third quarter on the strength of a 40-yard field goal by Errol Mann.

Minnesota quarterback Fran Tarkenton had learned his lesson from Super Bowl IX, however, when he kept trying to run the ball against the dominant Steel Curtain defense of Pittsburgh. The Steelers limited the Viking runners to a then–Super Bowl record of just 17 yards on the ground. In Super Bowl XI, Tarkenton sensed by halftime that his running game was unable to succeed against the Raiders run defense, just as they were unable to run against the Steelers two years ago. He was right. Minnesota managed to accumulate only 71 net yards rushing against the Raiders in Super Bowl XI. Tarkenton thus relied on the pass almost exclusively from the third quarter on. His decision finally resulted in a touchdown late in the third quarter. Tarkenton dropped back and threw to rookie wide receiver Sammy White, who was running an out pattern in the Oakland end zone. White leaped high over reserve Raiders defensive back Neal Colzie and snared the pass, producing Minnesota's first score. The Vikings trailed 19–7 as the third quarter ended.

Minnesota's defense was seemingly inspired by their offense's touchdown. They quickly held the Raiders offense to their only three-and-out series of the second half. Tarkenton then once again drove his offense downfield, but on one of the plays in the drive, Oakland safety Jack Tatum delivered one of the hardest and most resounding hits in pro football history. "It was one of those collisions defensive people dream about and offensive people have nightmares over," Tatum later said. Tarkenton threw a strike down the middle of the field, and Sammy White caught it cleanly. As soon as he did, however, Tatum blasted the rookie wideout with a shattering helmet-to-helmet blow. White's helmet flew off of his head in one direction, and his chin strap flew away in another direction. To his extreme credit, White somehow managed to hold on to the ball at the Oakland 44-yard line, but he was knocked out cold. "I wanted to make a statement that the game was over," Tatum later said. "That type of devastating hit has a tendency to discourage other receivers and running backs from trying anything over our middle. I had just wasted Sammy White."

White's catch gave Minnesota a much needed first down, however, but on a subsequent third and three situation from the Oakland 37-yard line, Tarkenton was chased out of the pocket and lofted a pass down the middle of the field, intended for Vikings running back Chuck Foreman. Oakland linebacker Willie Hall sprinted in front of Foreman, intercepted the pass, and returned it 16 yards to near midfield. Just as soon as it flourished, Minnesota's momentum sank in the aftermath of Hall's interception.

Stabler squandered no time in driving the Raiders downfield. His 48-yard pass down the middle to Biletnikoff ended up at the Vikings' 2-yard line, where Biletnikoff was tackled by Minnesota cornerback Bobby Bryant. Banaszak dove over for his second touchdown on the next play, thereby giving the Silver and Black an insurmountable 26–7 lead midway through the fourth quarter.

Tarkenton's last gasp was another drive deep into Oakland territory, and that drive also ended with disaster for the Vikings. Veteran Oakland cornerback Willie Brown stepped in front of a square out pattern along the sideline and picked off Tarkenton's quick throw, intended for Sammy

The Oakland Raiders won their first Super Bowl on January 9, 1977, when they defeated the Minnesota Vikings in Super Bowl XI at the Rose Bowl in Pasadena, California. Here Raiders running back Pete Banaszak plows through the Minnesota defense, while Vikings defensive back Bobby Bryant prepares to make the tackle. Banaszak scored two touchdowns in Oakland's 32–14 thrashing of Minnesota (AP Photo/NFL Photos).

White (who somehow recovered from Tatum's vicious hit from earlier in the fourth quarter and returned to the game). Brown was not the fastest cornerback in the league anymore, but it did not matter. There was no one near him and no one in front of him as he ran down the sideline and scored on a then–Super Bowl record 75-yard interception return. "I felt comfortable after Willie Hall's interception," said Raiders head coach John Madden after the game. "And I felt very comfortable after Willie Brown's."

The dejected Vikings scored one more meaningless touchdown with less than a minute to play on a 13-yard pass from reserve quarterback Bob Lee to tight end Stu Voigt. Oakland had prevailed, 32–14, and thus had won the first world championship in their history. They had finally won the big one, and had thrown away the "choker" label forever. The Raider players gave head coach John Madden a victory ride off of the Rose Bowl turf, something that NBC-TV broadcaster Curt Gowdy humorously described as "the toughest job that the Raiders had to do all day." The decisive Oakland victory made history in one aspect: The Raiders became the first team that employed the 3–4 defense as their full-time defense to ever win a Super Bowl. The Vikings, however, also made history. They remained winless in the big game, losing their fourth Super Bowl. It took several decades before another team would equal and eventually exceed that level of futility in pro football's world championship game.

Summing up Super Bowl XI for both teams, perhaps it was John Madden who said it best in his pregame speech to his players. Instead of regaling his athletes with a pep talk diatribe or a soliloquy on the honor to play in this game, Madden only verbalized one sentence. His statement is as true today for any team or any man playing in a Super Bowl, as it was on January 9, 1977, in a crowded Rose Bowl locker room. "Today will be the best day of your lives," said Madden to his players, "but only if you win."

1977

Missing Pieces Found
and Broncomania Born

The 1977 season in the NFL was a year which saw a Cinderella team from the AFC West achieve an outstanding accomplishment. The Denver Broncos enjoyed their greatest season ever (up to that time), and enjoyed their first visit ever to the NFL postseason tournament. The 1977 season also represented the final year in pro football before a bevy of new rules changed the league's strategical, statistical, and scheduling landscapes. The 1977 season marked the last year in which the regular season would remain 14 games in length. It was also a year in which a regular trend of the decade's ultimate victory met an abrupt—if only for a season—end. In addition, followers of the NFL would notice a seemingly regular annual occurrence during the early and middle years of the decade of the 1970s: The American Conference teams were dominating the National Conference teams, in both head-to-head matchups during the regular season, and also in the Super Bowl. The AFC in 1977 marked its fourth straight year as winners of the league's interconference regular season games in head-to-head matchups with NFC teams, collecting 19 wins against 9 losses. The Super Bowl measuring stick proved a little less of an example of AFC dominance, as two Super Bowl winners of the first half of the decade—the Baltimore Colts and the Pittsburgh Steelers—were actually former NFL teams prior to the merger in 1970. But both the Colts and the Steelers moved to the AFC when the merger took place, and their three accumulated world championships prior to 1977 were earned under the banner of the AFC. In 1977, however, a true blue (metallic blue and silver, to be precise) NFC team would win a Super Bowl, thereby ending AFC dominance in the big game for at least a year.

Changes to the norm were made off the field too. An agreement between the players union (NFLPA) and the league owners finally took place prior to the beginning of the 1977 season. The ratified agreement would last until July of 1982, and the total cost of the agreement was estimated to be $107 million. A college draft was continued in the new agreement to 1986, as well as a no-strike, no-suit clause for the players to adhere to. But the players also got their share of benefits with the new contract. Increases in minimum salaries, and increases in money for preseason and postseason games were welcomed by the players, as was improved insurance, and medical and dental benefits. Like any contract between the league owners and the NFLPA, the ability to compromise was the key to success, and in 1977, both managed to make enough compromises to satisfy each other.

The annual institution of off-season rule changes also occurred in 1977, with the emphasis being on limiting player injuries and opening up the passing game. The head slap was finally outlawed, a move that was greeted with glee by all offensive linemen in the league. The head slap was a defensive lineman's most dangerous tool, a surprise whack with a forearm and an open palm across an offensive lineman's head. The head slap could seldom be avoided by offensive linemen without giving up too much ground while blocking. Naturally, the rule change was derided by defensive linemen all across the league. "Offensive linemen are not going to stop holding, you can bet on that," said Atlanta defensive end Jeff Merrow. "The head slap was the great equalizer." The results of too many head slaps incurred were too many concussions and too many punctured eardrums. Without worrying about the threat of head slaps in 1977, offensive linemen could now achieve better success in keeping their foes away from their quarterback, hence giving passers more time to locate and throw to receivers downfield.

Another rule change which was implemented to aid the passing game involved forbidding defensive backs and linebackers from hitting receivers more than once. This rule was only lightly enforced, but in the following year, it would be greatly enhanced and regulated. The rule changes of 1977 did take a solid step in opening up the passing game, but the rule changes in 1978 would take a sprinting broad jump toward establishing a league-wide aerial onslaught, and we'll read more about that in the next chapter. Naturally, the defenders were not happy with all of these new rules. Most cornerbacks felt it was difficult enough trying to guard gazelle-like wide receivers, without giving them an extra rules advantage. In an attempt at throwing a bone to the defensive players, the rules committee in 1977 made it illegal for wide receivers to clip defensive players, even in the area where receivers would sometimes deliver crackback blocks. This rule did not see much enforcement, namely because there were not too many coaches in the NFL who wanted to see their skilled receivers end up on the injured reserved list. A 190-pound receiver was simply no match for a ferocious 245-pound linebacker, and only teams that ran the ball continuously would require their receivers to perform crackback blocks against opposing outside linebackers. Clipping a linebacker? That was pretty much out of the question, and only the foolhardy or revenge-minded receivers ever tried it.

A question that was popping up from some scribes across the nation over the decade involved the realignment of teams to more geographically-sensible areas of the country. It still made no sense to some people why a team like the Atlanta Falcons were in the NFC West Division, or why a team like the Dallas Cowboys were in the NFC East Division. The league office decided not to tackle the pesky inquiry of overall realignment in 1977, but they did find a permanent home for the league's newest teams. The Tampa Bay Buccaneers would be permanently placed in the NFC Central Division, and the Seattle Seahawks would be permanently moved to the AFC West Division. Permanence in this case did not mean infinity, however, as both of these teams moved to different divisions again in 2002, when a league-wide realignment of most of the teams took place.

Speaking of the Buccaneers and the Seahawks, they were each granted rights to the first two choices in the 1977 NFL player draft. The Buccaneers selected Ricky Bell as the first pick in the draft. Bell was a big and talented tailback from the University of Southern California, and a player that former USC head coach and current Tampa Bay head coach John McKay was well acquainted with. The Seahawks, on the other hand, decided to make a trade with their selection. The Dallas Cowboys offered Seattle a first-round draft choice and three second-round draft choices in exchange for Seattle's first-round pick, which was the second overall selection. The Seahawks accepted the offer, and the Cowboys took halfback Tony Dorsett as their first pick. Dorsett, who won the Heisman Trophy in 1976, was a darting and dashing runner from the University of Pittsburgh. He was as fast as he was elusive, and even though it took him a while to learn head coach Tom Landry's complicated offensive system, he proved to be the missing ingredient in Dallas' quest to win the Super Bowl. The Seahawks? They used their four draft choices from Dallas in 1977 on offensive lineman Steve August, guard Tom Lynch, and linebackers Terry Beeson and

Pete Cronan. None of these players went on to superlative careers. Dorsett, on the other hand, went on to rush for 12,739 career yards on his way to enshrinement in the Pro Football Hall of Fame.

While the trade for Tony Dorsett proved to be the biggest coup of the season in the NFL, several more trades in 1977 also provided a few teams a chance to improve their fortunes. One such team was the Philadelphia Eagles, who sent disgruntled tight end Charles Young to Los Angeles in exchange for quarterback Ron Jaworski. This trade benefitted both teams, as Young would give Rams quarterback Pat Haden an explosive passing target, while Jaworski would give the Eagles an athletic signal caller with plenty of potential. The New York Giants obtained another quarterback, Steve Ramsey from Denver. To get Ramsey, the Giants offered the Broncos their supposedly injured and over-the-hill veteran quarterback, Craig Morton. As we shall see, Morton was not as banged up and over-the-hill as the Giants might have believed. The 1977 season also marked the first year since 1964 that the New York Jets would not have Joe Namath on their roster. Namath was obtained by the Rams during the off-season, despite his long-running history of injuries throughout the decade. Nevertheless, several media outlets throughout the country believed the hype that Namath would be the main reason why the Rams would finally reach the Super Bowl. Unfortunately for Namath and the Rams, the future Hall of Fame quarterback would continue his string of injuries and would see action in only four games in 1977. The Rams would thus ultimately continue to be absent from the Super Bowl.

A couple of new head coaches in Atlanta and in Denver provided much-needed changes for their respective franchises. Leeman Bennett immediately took a losing Falcons squad that registered only four wins in 1976 and mightily improved their defense. The 1977 Atlanta defense would go on to make superlative headlines as they confounded many offensive coordinators around the league. Robert "Red" Miller was selected as the new head man in Denver, and he wasted absolutely no time in converting the Broncos from a competitive team with a 9–5 record in 1976 to a dominant team in 1977. Both men got the best efforts out of their rosters, both were able to help new players get adjusted to new game plans and strategies, and both were able to inspire their players to make big plays throughout the 1977 season.

Another change in the head coaching ranks occurred in New York City. Walt Michaels took charge of the New York Jets, but unlike Bennett and Miller, he could perform no new miracles. The Jets finished 1977 with a 3–11 record, which was identical to their 1976 record under Mike Holovak, who replaced Lou Holtz after 13 games in 1976. Rebuilding seemed to be an annual occurrence for the Jets throughout the decade.

One of Oakland's seemingly annual occurrences was losing their first game of the season, something that they did throughout the first five years of the decade. Then in 1975 and 1976, the Raiders won their first game. Head coach John Madden called it "a good omen." The Raiders continued their new trend of opening day victories with an impressive 24–0 shutout win over visiting division rival San Diego, despite having a bull's-eye on their backs due to their status as defending Super Bowl champions. Oakland's roster in 1977 was virtually unchanged from their 1976 roster, and bringing back that continuity would be vital to the team to repeat as world champions. Oakland's formula for victory was once again the accurate passing of Kenny "The Snake" Stabler, who tossed two first half touchdowns against the Chargers, one each to wide receiver Cliff Branch and to tight end Dave Casper. The Raiders' win marked their 18th straight victory against San Diego.

A few other teams started the new season in a fashion similar to the Raiders. The Philadelphia Eagles won their first season opener since 1967 by beating the lowly Tampa Bay Buccaneers, 13–3, in Veterans Stadium. Second-year head coach Dick Vermeil was making strides with his reclamation project, trying to turn a perennial loser into a winner. Vermeil was a tough, no-nonsense type of coach, who worked his players harder during the summer training camp than any other coach in the league. But he also wore his emotions on his sleeve, and his love for his players was evident for all to see. He soon started to fill his roster with men who would play their hearts out for him. The Eagles were easily one of the league's most improved teams by season's end. They may have only earned a record of 5–9, but their young and stalwart defense gave up only 207 points, the fourth-best mark in the National Football Conference. A team which drew plenty of media interest in the first week of the 1977 season was the Los Angeles Rams, primarily because everyone was interested in how Joe Namath would do with his new team. There was a lot of speculation among players and fans alike, wondering if "Broadway Joe" still had the capability to lead a team to victory. But the team that Namath and the Rams had to play in Week 1 delivered a stunning upset. The Atlanta Falcons started their season by upending the Rams, 17–6. New Atlanta head coach Leeman Bennett realized that the oft-injured Namath simply could not run anymore and could not drop back into his pocket quickly anymore. The Falcons blitzed their linebackers and safeties often to force Namath into quick, off-target throws. Atlanta's defense even utilized a nine-man line, with every one of those nine defenders blitzing Namath. The "Grits Blitz," as Atlanta's defense would be called, began the season with promise and productivity. They would be heard from throughout 1977.

Another team which started the season on a winning note was the Denver Broncos, who earned a 7–0 victory over visiting St. Louis. This rather nondescript triumph over a good team showcased Denver's much improved defense, which surrendered 221 passing yards versus the Cards, but did not allow their opponents to visit the Broncos' end zone. "We've been saying all along that our defense has to take another step up, and today we did that," said new Denver head coach Robert "Red" Miller. "We beat a good team today." The win marked Miller's first career coaching victory, and it was also the first win in orange and blue for new Broncos quarterback Craig Morton. Unexpected victories would become welcomed and familiar in Denver during the course of the regular season, and they would become a dominant team in a very short amount of time. The positive results were a Godsend for their loyal fans.

Fans of pro football have established loyal followings of their favorite teams for many years. In 1977, however, fans in Denver, Colorado, demonstrated a rabid following for their team. The Bronco fans were always supportive of their Rocky Mountain players since their birth in 1960, regardless of the team's record. Now as the 1977 season came around, Mile High Stadium increased its seating capacity from 63,500 to 75,087. Those extra seats (most of which were in the upper deck along the visitor's sideline) were filled quickly with extra loud voices, cheering heartily for their team, and all wearing orange and blue. Virtually every business in Denver added to the football fever during each week by going crazy for the Broncos, displaying banners and posters all along the streets of the city. Every local television and radio station responded in similar fashion, and promoted the team with a bevy of player stories, interviews, and team highlights every single day of the season. It was a growing phenomenon called Broncomania. It was filled with vocal passion among the entire Denver populace, and it grew like a rolling and rumbling snowball with every Broncos victory. As we shall see, Denver would experience some really exciting moments as the year went on.

Finally, the Dallas Cowboys won their first game of the year at Minnesota. The buzz in this game was the speculation surrounding the Cowboys' rookie runner, Tony Dorsett. He was fresh off of his Heisman Trophy, and much was expected from him. Yet he did not start the game, and he carried the ball only four times for 11 minimal yards against the veteran Purple Gang. That did not seem to matter too much to Dallas, a team that possessed a wealth of superior athletes. Starting Dallas tailback Preston Pearson caught a 7-yard touchdown pass from quarterback Roger

Staubach in the fourth quarter, and the Doomsday Defense caused the Vikings to turn the ball over five times. The game was highly competitive, however, and was tied 10–10 at the end of the fourth quarter. Staubach won the game with 6:14 left in the overtime period when he ran around left end and dove into the end zone. Staubach was hit hard on the play at the goal line by Vikings middle linebacker Jeff Siemon, but he managed to hold onto the ball as he tumbled in for the score. Dallas prevailed in a tough opening game, 16–10.

"Both offenses had trouble," said Dallas head coach Tom Landry. "What I liked about our offense was that it didn't quit."

Another overtime game on *Monday Night Football* in the second week of the season brought on more drama, and it would be the first overtime game in history for both the New England Patriots and the Cleveland Browns. Cleveland's Municipal Stadium was the scene for this offensive slugfest. The Browns were testing themselves to gauge their improvement against a playoff-caliber team like the Patriots. It was a see-saw contest with nine different lead changes, and with both teams trading scores and big plays throughout. The game also featured a matchup between two of the best young quarterbacks in the league, Brian Sipe of Cleveland and Steve Grogan of New England. Both quarterbacks led their respective offenses to important scores late in the game. Grogan and the Pats were trailing by three points and had less than a minute to play in regulation. The lanky and poised Grogan quickly took his offense downfield with short passes to set up a 34-yard field goal. New England placekicker John Smith was true with his attempt with no time left in regulation, and the game was tied, 27–27. Cleveland won the coin toss at the beginning of the overtime period, and that proved to be the difference. Sipe drove his offense downfield with short passes also, and set up a 35-yard field goal attempt to win the game. Cleveland head coach Forrest Gregg decided to try the field goal on second down instead of waiting until fourth down. "Let's take our three points and go home," Gregg said to Sipe along the sideline. Cleveland placekicker Don Cockcroft successfully kicked the ball through the uprights with 4:45 elapsed in overtime, and the Browns had an exciting 30–27 win over a playoff team from a year ago. "We're hard to discourage," Gregg said of his team following their marathon win in one of the greatest *Monday Night Football* games of the decade.

A couple of familiar rivals met a day earlier in Pittsburgh to renew their seemingly annual rivalry. The Raiders came in to Three Rivers Stadium in an unusual position, that of defending world champions. The Steelers were anxious to avenge their discouraging loss to Oakland in the previous year's AFC title game. Unfortunately for Pittsburgh, their discouragement would continue on this Sunday. The Raiders defense was in mid-season form, forcing five Steeler turnovers and sacking Pittsburgh quarterback Terry Bradshaw five times. Three Errol Mann field goals and an 8-yard touchdown run by Oakland running back Mark van Eeghan was more than enough to post a 16–7 win. "We're not happy," said Pittsburgh head coach Chuck Noll following the loss. "But when somebody beats your tail, what can you do except go back to the drawing board and start over."

Although neither the Raiders nor the Steelers knew it at the time, this game marked the final time that they would meet each other in the decade. No fights broke out in this final contest between the two bitter rivals, and in subsequent years and decades, other rivalries between other teams would draw the attention and the focus of the league. But even though its ending was rather undistinguished, the Steeler-Raider rivalry of the 1970s would always be remembered as one of the most malevolent and memorable in a short span of time in all of sports history.

One NFL team trying to make history in 1977 was the Baltimore Colts, a team which had won the AFC Eastern Division in each of the past two seasons. They started the 1977 campaign off with five straight wins against Seattle, the New York Jets, Buffalo, Miami, and Kansas City.

Head coach Ted Marchibroda's team scored 128 points through those first five games. Baltimore's offense was once again led by quarterback Bert Jones, the "Ruston [Louisiana] Rifle." Setback Lydell Mitchell and wide receivers Roger Carr and Glenn Doughty were three of the most explosive players in the league. The Colts' defensive line, known as "The Sack Pack," was as formidable as any in the NFL. Baltimore looked like they would coast to another division title, but as the season wore on, the road for them would get rockier.

Speaking of rocky roads, a couple of potential playoff clubs in the NFC did not experience the fast start to 1977 that the Colts did. Both the Washington Redskins and the St. Louis Cardinals struggled through perhaps what was the toughest division in the league, the NFC East. The first meeting of the year between these two clubs came in Week 3 at RFK Stadium. The Redskins swept the Cards in 1976, and it appeared that they would have no trouble in adding to that streak during the first three quarters of this contest. Washington owned a 14–0 lead going into the fourth quarter, but true to their comeback pedigree, St. Louis began coming back. A 7-yard touchdown pass from Cardinals quarterback Jim Hart to tight end J.V. Cain brought the Cardiac Cards back into contention. The Redskins quickly responded in the final quarter, however, with a gut-checking 53-yard scoring pass from Washington quarterback Billy Kilmer to setback John Riggins, who ran a short circle route, cut back against the grain, and outraced Cardinals safety Roger Wehrli to the end zone. The play provided enough of a spark to produce a key 24–14 Redskins victory. "We needed a good game," Riggins said afterward. "We couldn't afford to lay another egg." With their early win over the Cardinals, the Redskins took a step forward in the tough NFC East.

Speaking of the NFC East, the Dallas Cowboys were busy giving their prized rookie runner, Tony Dorsett, more time on the field. Dorsett scored his first two pro touchdowns in a 41–21 romp over the visiting New York Giants in the second week. Yet he took a step back in his progress in the following week against Tampa Bay. Dorsett's fumble in the second quarter was returned 37 yards by Buccaneers linebacker Richard Wood for Tampa's lone score in a 23–7 Dallas win at Texas Stadium. It appeared as if Dallas would have to adjust to Dorsett's growing pains on a week-to-week basis.

The New England Patriots were hoping to grow out of their Week 2 loss to the Browns when they visited Shea Stadium to take on the Jets in Week 3. Head coach Chuck Fairbanks' team had built a large lead in the fourth quarter, thanks to a spectacular 100-yard kickoff return by Raymond Clayborn (which was a then–Patriots record), and two more touchdowns from running back Don Calhoun and wide receiver Darryl Stingley. But the Patriots allowed New York to come back strong in the final quarter with a 44-yard interception for a touchdown by linebacker Greg Buttle, and a 25-yard scoring pass from young quarterback Richard Todd to wide receiver Wesley Walker. A 32-yard field goal by placekicker Pat Leahy with 23 seconds left in the game boosted the Jets to a surprising 30–27 win. "We made so many errors it was impossible to overcome them, no matter who we were playing against," said Fairbanks. The Pats suddenly found themselves mired in the middle of their division with a 1–2 record. They could place the blame for their failures on fumbles and penalties, but also on their faltering defense, which allowed 77 points in those first three games. The Jets (who were also now 1–2) for their part really needed to win this game if they hoped to stay somewhat close to the surging Colts and Dolphins.

Speaking of the Dolphins, they jumped off to a great start in 1977, as they posted an undefeated record after their first three games. Head coach Don Shula's squad suffered through a 6–8 record in 1976, their first losing mark since 1969. Shula was the type of coach who simply would not tolerate another season-long letdown, and his Dolphins were probably more fearful of their coach's wrath after losing a game than they were of taking on their opponents on the field. Miami shut out the Bills in the 1977 season opener, 13–0. They then edged San Francisco, 19–15, in

Candlestick Park in the second week. In the third week, Miami romped over the Houston Oilers in their home opener, 27–7. Shula's team needed that quick start, because their opponents in the AFC East had all gotten tougher over the past couple of years. A case in point occurred the following week in Baltimore, when the first place Dolphins took on the (also) first place Colts. Both of these undefeated teams knew that this game would be vital in each of their plans to win the AFC East. The first half of this struggle produced a scoring track meet. Miami took a 28–10 lead midway through the second quarter. Freddie Solomon returned a Baltimore kickoff 90 yards for the first Dolphins touchdown. A few minutes later, Miami running back Benny Malone added a 52-yard scoring run on a power sweep down the right sideline. Malone's backfield teammate, Leroy Harris, ran in from the 1-yard line for another touchdown. Just before halftime, Malone broke free for a 66-yard score—again on a power sweep to the right—and the Dolphins went to their locker room with confidence and a big lead.

Making halftime adjustments in strategy and personnel is the mark of any good coach in the NFL. One of Shula's trademarks over the years was to successfully adjust his game plans at halftime and coach his team to many come-from-behind victories. Baltimore head coach Ted Marchibroda, however, was the coach who made enough of those similar adjustments on this day to produce a powerful Colts win over their divisional adversaries. Baltimore scored three touchdowns in the second half on two touchdown passes from quarterback Bert Jones, and a 1-yard scoring run by fullback Don McCauley. Earlier in the game, their versatile halfback Lydell Mitchell ran 64 yards for the Colts' first touchdown. Equally as important as those touchdowns was the fact that the Dolphins were held scoreless during the final two quarters. The Colts rumbled to an impressive 45–28 victory over the stunned Dolphins. "We couldn't contain the Colts when we had to," lamented Shula after the game. "It's no accident that Bert Jones was voted the Most Valuable Player [in the AFC] last year."

But all was not well with the Colts. Their best wide receiver—Roger Carr—had suffered a debilitating knee injury earlier in the year, and would be unable to play in seven games. Carr would catch only 11 passes all year, and would score only one touchdown in 1977, compared to the 11 touchdowns that he scored in 1976. The Colts earned an uninspiring 17–6 win at Kansas City in Week 5, and continued to pileup injuries. Defensive end John Dutton was sidelined during the entire first half of the season, and his loss limited the efforts of the rest of the Sack Pack. Baltimore's winning streak ended in New England on the sixth week of the season by a score of 17–3. The Patriots completely dominated the Colts (now 5–1), limiting Bert Jones to just six completions in 18 attempts. Baltimore's offense could generate only 86 total yards in this lopsided affair. New England finally put together a strong effort on both sides of the line of scrimmage against Baltimore. Quarterback Steve Grogan completed 11 of 16 passes for 214 yards and one touchdown, a 31-yard catch-and-carry to tight end Russ Francis. New England now improved its record to 4–2, just one game behind both Baltimore and Miami. The AFC East would be a tough challenge for any of its teams to win in 1977.

The AFC West was once again thought to be securely in the grasp of the defending Super Bowl champion Oakland Raiders. The Silver and Black steam-rolled to a 4–0 start, and for all appearances, they looked like they were determined to win another division title. They had no major injuries to speak of at the beginning of the 1977 season, and their defense gave up only six touchdowns in their first four games. A surprise team in their own division, however, rose up in 1977 to give the Raiders an unexpected and most difficult challenge. The Denver Broncos built upon their quick start with consecutive victories in each of their first six games. Following their opening day win against the Cardinals, the Broncos defeated Buffalo, Seattle, and Kansas City. Their early competition was not a true gauge to measure how much Denver had improved, however. The Broncos traveled to Oakland to take on the Raiders in the fifth week. This contest would be a more realistic measuring stick for the Broncos. Were they a dominant contender, or were they just another average team that over-achieved in previous wins against below-average competition?

Head coach Red Miller's squad left no doubt as to their answer to that question. Denver posted an impressive 30–7 win over the defending champion Raiders, and dominated in every facet of the game. Their offense scored on a 10-yard pass from veteran quarterback Craig Morton to tight end Riley Odoms; a 16-yard touchdown run by Lonnie Perrin; and a surprise fake field goal which gave the Broncos a 21–7 halftime lead. On that memorable play, holder and backup quarterback Norris Weese took the snap, jumped up, and rolled to his right. He then stopped dead in his tracks and turned around to see a sight which must have sickened the Raiders and their entire coaching staff. Denver placekicker Jim Turner faked his kick, then ran unmolested and unnoticed to his left and down the sideline. Weese lofted a rainbow into Turner's inviting arms as a collective gasp—and a collective expletive—were heard throughout the Oakland-Alameda County Coliseum. Turner caught the pass and jogged into the end zone to complete the 25-yard scoring play. "I've been playing against the Raiders for fourteen years and I'm sure they never thought the ball would be thrown to me," Turner said. Weese was equally surprised. "Jim was so wide open I couldn't believe it," said the Broncos' second-string quarterback. "I threw it high and soft, realizing that he's not used to catching passes and he's slow."

Denver's not-so-slow defense was vibrantly inspired by this opportunistic bit of trickery, as they intercepted Oakland quarterback Ken Stabler a team-record seven times, including three thefts by Broncos linebacker Joe Rizzo. "We've played together for a year," said Denver linebacker Randy Gradishar of his linebacking teammates. "You need to play together to become good. We've gotten to know each other, and I think that's why we improved." Rizzo and Gradishar helped to produce Stabler's worst game ever, and it proved to be the end of Oakland's 17-game winning streak (dating back to its start in the fifth week of 1976). Oakland was able to move the ball throughout much of the game, but the interceptions would be their undoing in this crushing defeat. "They kicked hell out of us," Stabler admitted afterward. Before this game, Denver's defense was given the moniker the "Orange Crush" defense. Following this game, the rest of the league readily accepted that description.

While Denver was enjoying its newly-earned 5–0 record and its lone position in first place in the AFC West, the Dallas Cowboys were starting to renew their annual push towards another NFC East division title. They visited Busch Memorial Stadium in the fourth week of the season for the first of their two annual contests with the St. Louis Cardinals. The Cowboys wore their blue jerseys for the first (and as it turned out last) time this year, and unfortunately for the Cards, the "blue jersey jinx" did not apply on this day. Dallas matched St. Louis score for score through the entire game in what was an offensive shootout. The two teams traded field goals in the first quarter. Then St. Louis' elusive tailback Terry Metcalf broke free on a 62-yard jaunt through the middle of Dallas' flex defense. Later in the second quarter, St. Louis wide receiver Mel Gray caught a 60-yard scoring strike from quarterback Jim Hart down the near sideline. The Cowboys responded with their rookie runner Tony Dorsett, who experienced his best day thus far in his brief pro career. Dorsett broke three attempted arm tackles on an off-tackle run en route to a spectacular 77-yard touchdown. Later in the game, Dorsett added a 1-yard touchdown dive to boost his total to 141 yards rushing for the day. "Now that I'm getting some time to play," said Dorsett, "I'm getting real comfortable in the offense." Dorsett was beginning to resemble the missing ingredient to the winning formula that Dallas was concocting.

But Dallas needed some of their patented comeback magic to win this contest, and there was no one better to supply that than the other Heisman Trophy winner in their backfield, quarterback Roger Staubach. With 6:53 remaining in the game, Staubach lofted a fade pass in the end zone for wide receiver Golden Richards, who peeled back underneath the blanket coverage from Cardinals cornerback Lee Nelson, then somehow managed to catch the ball in between his left forearm and his chest as he fell to the AstroTurf. Richards' sensational grab gave Dallas a 30–24 victory, their fourth in four games.

Another team from down south besides Dallas in the NFC was also winning on a regular basis. The Atlanta Falcons earned narrow victories in three of their first four games, defeating the Rams, Giants, and 49ers. Their defense gave up a miserly 19 overall points in their first four contests. Leading the Atlanta defense was future Hall of Fame defensive end Claude Humphrey, and speedy defensive back Rolland Lawrence, who would end up leading the NFC in 1977 in interceptions with seven. The Falcon linebacking corps of Greg Brezina, Rick Kay, Fulton Kuykendall, Ron McCartney, Dewey McClain, Ralph Ortega, Robert Pennywell, and Andy Spiva were a veteran group which filled holes in the line better than any other linebackers in the league. Atlanta surrendered only five opposing rushing touchdowns all year, and gave up an average of only 9.2 points per game in 1977. Even many of their losses were extremely close. Atlanta lost to Washington by a score of 10–6 in Week 2, and to Buffalo in Week 5 by a score of 3–0. The loss to the Bills was extremely disheartening to the Falcons. A fumbled snap by quarterback Scott Hunter near the Buffalo goal line cost Atlanta a touchdown and a victory. The trend of giving few points but also scoring few points would define the Falcons throughout the year. Their success simply relied on how well their defense could play, and if their offense could somehow catch a few breaks. "We're still playing sound defense," said Atlanta head coach Leeman Bennett.

The Washington Redskins also suffered a disheartening loss in the fifth week of the season at Dallas. Head coach George Allen's Over the Hill Gang was fighting to keep pace with the Cowboys in the competitive NFC East, and the Redskins defense was certainly doing their part to stay competitive. Washington had given up only 40 total points in the first four games of the season, and a win over Dallas would pull them even with the Cowboys in the standings. Dallas had a really strong defense too, however, and it was their Doomsday Defense which decided this, the first of their two annual meetings with Washington. The Cowboys sacked Redskin quarterbacks eight times, permitted only one net yard passing, and injured George Allen's entire starting offensive backfield. Dallas' 34–16 win boosted their record to a perfect 5–0, while Washington fell to 3–2. Pacing the Cowboys on this day was the passing of quarterback Roger Staubach, who threw for 250 yards and two touchdowns. One of those scores was a beautiful 59-yard bomb to wide receiver Drew Pearson, who got behind second-year Redskins cornerback Gerard Williams on a simple but effective straight fly pattern down the sideline. The play was successful more by luck than by design. "They [the Redskins defense] gave us a blitz look," said Staubach, "and the cornerback moved up to cover Drew right at the line. I was already into my snap count, so I couldn't audible. I made a motion with my hand and Drew understood what I meant. He ran a streak right down the sideline." Pearson's account of the play confirmed the connection that both he and Staubach had achieved during their five years on the field together. "I saw him [Staubach] motion and I knew what it meant," said Pearson. "The ball was perfectly thrown, a little to the inside like you want it."

The other Staubach six-pointer was a splendid 50-yard catch and carry to his other wide receiver, Golden Richards, who also defeated cornerback Williams on the play. Dallas fullback Robert Newhouse also bulled in for two touchdowns of his own to complete the conquest of their hated rivals. "It feels great," said Dallas head coach Tom Landry. "Anytime you beat Washington it feels good."

Rounding out the fifth week of the 1977 regular season were a couple of noteworthy games and another record achieved by a famous running back. The Seattle Seahawks met the Tampa Bay Buccaneers in the Kingdome for the second meeting between these two expansion teams in their history. Seattle won their inaugural meeting last year, and they prevailed once again this year, this time by a score of 30–23. It was the first of five wins that Seattle would earn this season. Tampa Bay's all-time record following this loss stood at 0–19. Would the Buccaneers make history by failing to win at least one game in two consecutive years, or would they finally notch a victory? There were now nine weeks left in the 1977 season to discover the answer.

The Minnesota Vikings discovered a new answer in how to defeat visiting division rival Chicago in Week 5. Here's a hint: It involved some trickery. The Bears played the Vikings to a 16–16 tie at the end of regulation. Minnesota forced a Chicago punt in overtime, then drove 80 yards for the winning score, which came on a fake field goal attempt. Holder Paul Krause positioned the ball for the placement for placekicker Fred Cox. But Krause pulled the ball off the grass before Cox could kick it, much like Lucy did to Charlie Brown in the *Peanuts* comic book series. Krause then rose up and ran to his right, then passed the ball 11 yards to tight end Stu Voigt for the winning score in a 22–16 Minnesota victory. "I don't think the Bears were expecting it," said Voigt of the winning play. "It seemed like the time to do it," admitted Grant. "I figured it was a super call," said Krause. The win gave the division-leading Vikes a 4–1 record in the NFC Central. The Bears fell to third place with a record of 2–3.

O.J. Simpson's 138 yards rushing on October 16 over Atlanta made him the second man ever to rush for over 10,000 yards in a career. Cleveland Browns great Jim Brown was the first. Simpson was one of only two runners who would surpass 100 yards rushing in a game against the 1977 Atlanta defense. Los Angeles halfback Lawrence McCutcheon was the other, running for 152 yards versus the Grits Blitz defense in a 23–7 Rams victory over the Falcons in Week 13. Simpson would endure a half season worth of injuries in 1977, however, missing over seven full games. Nevertheless, Simpson's 557 ground yards in 1977 would be enough for him to lead the Bills in rushing this year, incredibly the ninth straight season in which he did so.

The sixth week of the 1977 season saw a couple of supposedly "weak" or "mediocre" teams play tougher competition, and almost come out with upset wins. Take the New York Jets, for example. They were still trying to get used to seeing a different University of Alabama product at quarterback in their lineup. Richard Todd would be the New York signal caller instead of the departed Joe Namath when the Jets met the Oakland Raiders in Shea Stadium. The Jets were thought by many to be nothing more than a .500 team at best, but unknown to many, they were beginning to lay a firm foundation for success. Head coach Walt Michaels' players gave the Raiders one of their toughest games ever on this sunny day, as the young Richard Todd gave the Silver and Black a multitude of headaches. Todd connected on 17 of 29 passes for an incredible 396 yards and four touchdowns to four different receivers against the vaunted Oakland defense. "I think Todd silenced some of his critics today," said Michaels. The Jets held a 27–14 lead going into the fourth quarter, but as was their custom, the Raiders came back strong in the fourth quarter. Oakland's Ken Stabler, himself an Alabama alum, led a comeback with two touchdown passes. Old reliable Fred Biletnikoff caught one of those scores from seven yards out on a curl pattern, and reserve receiver Mike Siani caught the winning score from 24 yards out in the near corner of the end zone. Oakland running back Mark van Eeghen also contributed 143 rushing yards and a touchdown as the Raiders barely prevailed over the Jets, 28–27.

The Philadelphia Eagles also had a new quarterback. Ron Jaworski was improving on a weekly basis, but it was the Eagles defense which once again kept their team highly competitive. Philadelphia owned a tight 7–6 lead going into the fourth quarter in their game versus the visiting

Dallas Cowboys on October 23. Dallas also possessed a come-from-behind pedigree (like the Raiders), and they did it again on this day. Cowboys quarterback Roger "The Dodger" Staubach ran for his career-long of 33 yards on one play, which provided a comical edge to this contest. Before the snap of the ball, Staubach noticed a switch in the Philadelphia defensive formation. He immediately called an audible at the line of scrimmage, in effect telling his backfield to run to the left. Eagles middle linebacker Bill Bergey noticed Staubach's change of plays, and instantly yelled out to his defensive teammates, "Don't believe him! Don't believe him!" Unbeknownst to Staubach and to the Eagles defense, most of the Dallas blockers and both Dallas running backs failed to hear Staubach's audible. At the snap of the ball, the vast majority of the Dallas players went in the wrong direction. All of the Eagles defenders went in the wrong direction too. Staubach composed himself quickly and carried the ball instead of handing it off (which he had originally planned to do, except his running backs ignored him and ran away from him). Staubach "raced" down the right sideline for 33 yards. "Frankly," said the dry-witted and exaggerating quarterback, "I was amazed that anyone was able to catch me. I was sure I was going in for six. I had up a full head of steam. I don't know who it was who finally caught me but he must be some fast dude." According to then–Dallas public relations director Doug Todd, "It was the first time in NFL history that 11 players from a defensive unit were credited with simultaneously making a tackle. Every man they had caught Roger."

The game-breaker play was supplied by the Dallas special teams, however. Jay Saldi blew through the middle of the line, sacrificed his body, and blocked a Spike Jones punt head-on. Dallas safety Charlie Waters returned the recovered ball 17 yards amidst a convoy of blockers for the winning touchdown. "It was a gutsy play by Saldi," said Waters afterward. "We came up with the big play when we had to have it," said Dallas head coach Tom Landry. Dallas' 16–10 victory over the Eagles was their sixth straight win, and it boosted their lead in the NFC Eastern Division to three full games.

The sixth game for a couple of other teams foretold a future playoff matchup. The Los Angeles Rams had lost several playoff contests to Minnesota during the past few years, but on this day, the Rams beat the daylights out of the Vikings, 35–3, in the Los Angeles Memorial Coliseum on *Monday Night Football.* It was a mercy killing. Rookie Rams runner Wendell Tyler ran for 102 yards and his running mate, Lawrence McCutcheon, added 81 more. Rams quarterback Pat Haden threw for two scores and also ran for one in the one-sided win. Vikings quarterback Fran Tarkenton could never get on track, as he threw two interceptions and was sacked four times. "This was a very satisfying win because we played well against a real good team," said Los Angeles head coach Chuck Knox. "The offense moved the ball, the defense did a great job, and the special teams played with a lot of enthusiasm."

Despite Knox's compliments, this was perhaps the first time in the decade where the Vikings in large part began to show their advanced age, as they were never really in this contest. Minnesota's defeat to Los Angeles dropped them to a record of 4–2 in the NFC Central. The Rams' victory gave them a first-place tie in the NFC West with the Atlanta Falcons, who outlasted the Chicago Bears, 16–10, on the previous day. Atlanta permitted only its third touchdown of the year on a Brian Baschnagel kickoff return with but five seconds remaining in the game.

The seventh week marking the mid-season point of 1977 turned out to be a day of revenge for several teams. The New Orleans Saints, for many years a whipping boy for their divisional foes, got a chance to deliver some payback against the visiting Los Angeles Rams on October 30. The Saints hung tough to the Rams throughout their second meeting (the Rams won the first one in Los Angeles by a score of 14–7 on October 16), and were able to match them score for score. The Saints had to resort to a trick play to help them defeat the Rams in this game, however.

New Orleans defensive end Elois Grooms reported into the huddle as an eligible receiver. The unlikely and unexpected Grooms somehow managed to get his 6'4", 250-pound body into the end zone unnoticed. He then clutched a 3-yard scoring pass on a fake field goal attempt for a touchdown. New Orleans reserve quarterback Bobby Scott (who was filling in for the injured Archie Manning) added to Grooms' touchdown by driving his offense deep into Rams territory later in the fourth quarter. New Orleans placekicker Rich Szaro delivered a 31-yard field goal with just over three minutes remaining to lift the Saints to a 27–26 upset win over their divisional rivals. "This was a game we had to win," declared New Orleans head coach Hank Stram. "This is a stepping stone for our program."

The defending world champion Oakland Raiders were the victims of a huge upset by the Denver Broncos on October 16 by an embarrassing score of 30–7, and they were chomping at the bit for a chance to return the favor. Virtually the whole city of Denver, Colorado, seemed to be present at the rematch on October 30. It was declared "Orange Sunday" by the governor, and every fan was asked/advised/required to wear an orange shirt or jacket to the game to cheer on their 6–0 Broncos. Mile High Stadium resembled a giant orange rectangle surrounding a green playing field, as the fans poured out their encouragement to their team both visually and audibly. Oakland was surprised by Denver's strength and big-play abilities in the first meeting. They would be much more prepared for the Broncos in this second meeting, however. Oakland had history on their side going into the rematch. The Raiders had not lost in Denver since 1962.

Oakland's defense rose up to stifle Denver head coach Red Miller's offense, permitting them to cross midfield only once during the first three quarters, and sacking Denver quarterback Craig Morton eight times. Oakland's offense was led by their rushing game, which accumulated 200 total yards versus the Orange Crush defense. Tailback Clarence Davis rushed for 105 yards, and teammate Mark van Eeghen added 82 more. Raiders quarterback Ken Stabler was intercepted an astounding seven times in the first meeting between these two teams. On this day, Stabler only completed seven passes in 14 attempts. One of those completions, however, was a 21-yard pass on a simple down-and-in pattern in the first quarter to wide receiver Cliff Branch for a touchdown. Short scoring runs by Davis and van Eeghen boosted Oakland's lead to 24–0 going into the final quarter. Denver scored two touchdowns in the final stanza on an 11-yard pass from Morton to wide receiver Jack Dolbin, and a 7-yard run by halfback Otis Armstrong, who was held to a mere 37 yards rushing on the day. The Raiders had gained revenge over their upstart divisional foes in their own Orange stadium, 24–14. Both teams were now tied for first place in the AFC Western Division with identical 6–1 records.

"The one thing we didn't want to give them was life," said Oakland head coach John Madden. "We wanted to keep their backs to the wall and have them starting at eighty yards each time they got the ball."

Revenge was finally achieved by the Baltimore Colts on the same Sunday as well. Their post-season nemesis during the past two years was in town for another game. This time, the Colts managed to defeat the Pittsburgh Steelers in Memorial Stadium. Baltimore's offense was working on all cylinders throughout the first half and the early part of the third quarter, registering a 24–0 lead over the surprised Steelers. Baltimore quarterback Bert Jones completed his first seven passes, and finished the day with two touchdown passes and one touchdown run. Jones hit running backs Roosevelt Leaks and Lydell Mitchell on his scoring tosses. Baltimore reserve runner Ron Lee then displayed his skills by breaking no less than three attempted tackles on his 25-yard touchdown run up the gut of the Steel Curtain defense. The Colts defense also came to play, as they forced six Pittsburgh turnovers en route to a 31–21 Baltimore victory. The win gave the Colts a 6–1 record, good enough for first place in the AFC East, while the loss dropped Pittsburgh to 4–3, which was good enough for second place in the AFC Central. "We got our butts beat in every phase of the game by a darn good football team," lamented Pittsburgh head coach Chuck Noll.

The team which owned the first place designation in the AFC Central Division was a surprise to almost everyone. The Cleveland Browns had somehow put together an inspiring 5–2 record at mid-season. The Browns had defeated some pretty good teams early on, including Cincinnati, New England, and Houston. On the seventh Sunday, the Browns routed the visiting Kansas City Chiefs, 44–7. Everything worked for the Browns on this day as the score indicated. Tailback Greg Pruitt rushed for 153 of his team's 322 ground yards, including a 78-yard touchdown sprint in the third quarter, which was the longest run from scrimmage of his career. Cleveland's offense accounted for 526 total yards and a team record 34 first downs (which was broken in 1986). Kansas City head coach Paul Wiggin was fired in the aftermath of this crushing defeat, and was replaced by assistant coach Tom Bettis.

Rounding out Week 7 were some highly competitive contests. The New England Patriots defeated the visiting New York Jets, 24–13, while their counterparts in the AFC East, the Miami Dolphins, lost a tough one to the visiting San Diego Chargers, 14–13. An AFC Central battle was fought out in Cincinnati, where the Bengals out-muscled the Houston Oilers in overtime, 13–10. But the weekend ended on a flagrant note on *Monday Night Football*, when the St. Louis Cardinals easily defeated the New York Giants, 28–0. This game is remembered not so much for the final score or for who won the game, but for the fistfight that Conrad Dobler started. Dobler, as you may recall, was one of the league's most capable and most willing bullies. He recovered a teammate's fumble in the Giants end zone for a touchdown, and then went to work. The extra curricular activities began with fervor and ferocity. "I saw the ball, grabbed it, and they [the New York players] tried to grab it from me," Dobler described. "Two guys kicked at me and I kicked back." Dobler did not stop kicking, however, and his offensive teammates came to his aid. Future Hall of Fame tackle Dan Dierdorf "picked up one [New York Giants linebacker Brian Kelley], carried him ten yards, and shishkabobbed him on the goal post," according to Dobler. After the game, Dobler reflected on the donnybrook. "Most people score a touchdown and spike the ball," Dobler said. "I score one and start a fight."

Several teams were in the mood to fight for first place in the standings in the eighth week. The result of heated competition produced a couple of key upsets and one great struggle on Monday night. First the upsets. The Buffalo Bills were on a downward slide throughout the first half of the year. They suffered a major indignity by losing to Seattle, 56–17, in one of their previous six defeats. Nevertheless, they managed to upend the host New England Patriots on November 6. The Bills proved the old adage "On any given Sunday, any team can beat any other team." Buffalo surprised New England with two quick first quarter touchdowns, including a 7-yard pass from quarterback Joe Ferguson to tight end Reuben Gant (who caught seven passes for 97 yards in the game), and a 2-yard Jim Braxton scoring run. Buffalo halfback Roland Hooks was in the lineup in place of the injured O.J. Simpson, and he made the most of his opportunity. Hooks ran for 155 yards, including a 66-yard run which set up Buffalo's second touchdown. "We had something to prove—that we weren't the worst team in pro football," declared Hooks after the game. New England responded with a 93-yard kickoff return for a touchdown by speedster Raymond Clayborn, but the Bills regained the momentum immediately. A second quarter field goal and a 24-yard interception return for a score by Buffalo safety Doug Jones in the third quarter proved to be enough of a cushion for the Bills to outlast the Patriots, 24–14. "It was a humiliating type of loss," said New England head coach Chuck Fairbanks. "It shows that all teams in this league can play well if they're mentally ready." It was a brief and fleeting moment of glory for a Buffalo team which experienced only three victories all year long.

Another big upset occurred in Minnesota, where two very competitive teams were expected to produce a very competitive game. But the Vikings failed to give the Cardinals a challenge, as St. Louis won an easy 27–7 contest against the Norsemen in Metropolitan Stadium. The field was muddy and the sky was overcast, but no legitimate excuses could found for the Purple People Eaters, who were eaten up by the St. Louis rushing attack. Second-year fullback Wayne Morris was quickly becoming the perfect complement to veteran halfback Terry Metcalf. Morris ran for 182 yards against Minnesota. He also scored two touchdowns, as did Metcalf, who contributed 83 rushing yards. "This was by far our best game of the year," said St. Louis head coach Don Coryell. "It was a game we had to win and maybe we caught them [the Vikings] a little bit flat."

The Vikings suffered through a difficult season in 1972 when they failed to make the playoffs, but they came back quickly in 1973 and won the NFC championship. The season of 1977 appeared to once again emulate the failures of 1972, as they would struggle against strong competition. But in 1977, various injuries also abounded, and it looked as if Minnesota's misfortunes would catch up with them. The Vikings owned a 5–3 record after eight games, but their offense had scored only 98 points during those weeks, and their defense had allowed 118. Moreover, both Detroit and Chicago were right behind them and offering strong challenges to the Norsemen. Detroit shut out the visiting San Diego Chargers, 20–0, in the eighth week, to pull to within one game of the Vikings.

The Washington Redskins were dealing with a similar situation as Minnesota's. The Redskins were in a competitive fight in the NFC East, and they had a chance to tie the second-place Cardinals and pull closer to the division-leading Cowboys in Week 8. They met their neighbors, the Baltimore Colts, in Baltimore on *Monday Night Football,* under not-so-optimum circumstances. A driving rainstorm covered Memorial Stadium throughout the night, signaling a low-scoring, defensive struggle. This was the type of game that the aging Redskins were usually successful in winning, but on this evening, the Colts were able to hold the struggling Washington offense to just a field goal. Baltimore's offense was also held to only three points by the Over the Hill Gang during the first three quarters. The Colts finally pierced their opponents' end zone in the fourth quarter, however, as Bert Jones tossed a 12-yard touchdown pass to Freddie Scott on a simple slant pattern. "Scott came in on a crucial situation and made a big play for us," said Baltimore head coach Ted Marchibroda. Baltimore running back Lydell Mitchell was once again the workhorse of his team's offense, rushing for 112 yards on this night in the Colts' 10–3 victory over the Redskins. Mitchell would also go on to lead the NFL in pass receptions in 1977 with 71.

Leading the Colts defense was safety Lyle Blackwood, who would finish the year with a league-high 10 interceptions. Blackwood was an integral part of a pass defense which was busy stifling most of the quarterbacks that they faced in 1977, as the Colts intercepted 30 passes, the second-highest mark in the AFC (behind Pittsburgh's 31 interceptions). Baltimore boosted their record to 8–1 following their 31–13 romp over Buffalo in Week 9. But their AFC East-rival, the Miami Dolphins, stayed close to them with a surprising 17–5 conquest of New England in the Orange Bowl. "It wasn't very artistic but it ended up right," admitted Miami head coach Don Shula. "We still don't seem to be able to put teams away when we have them on the ropes. We had a heckuva goal line stand and we needed it." The win improved the Dolphins' record to 7–2, and dropped the Patriots down to a mediocre 5–4. New England's disappointing record was due in large part to injuries to starters Steve Nelson and Steve Zabel on defense, and All-Pro tight end Russ Francis on offense. The Patriots would recover, however, and would claim victories in their next four games.

The Steelers claimed a victory over a divisional rival and moved into a first-place tie in the ninth week as a result. Pittsburgh's 35–31 offensive shootout win over Cleveland on November

13 was played at Three Rivers Stadium, where a snowstorm descended in western Pennsylvania in the final quarter. The Browns were similar to the Patriots, in that they were also playing without some of their star players. Cleveland starting quarterback Brian Sipe had injured his throwing shoulder in the first half against the Steelers. Little-used backup David Mays replaced him, and did a very respectable job against the Steel Curtain defense. Mays threw for 269 yards and three touchdown passes in the game, all to setback Larry Poole in the fourth quarter. Mays ducked and dodged a typically formidable Pittsburgh pass rush as time wore down to a frantic finish, but he fell just one play short of achieving what would have been an incredible upset. Pittsburgh quarterback Terry Bradshaw was ailing too with a sore left arm and bruised ribs, but he helped his team build a 28–3 halftime lead with touchdown tosses to wide receivers John Stallworth and Lynn Swann. Pittsburgh's defense bent quite a bit in the final quarter, but they held on at the end to preserve a tough win against an unexpectedly tough Browns team. "They [Pittsburgh] won the first half," said Cleveland head coach Forrest Gregg. "We won the second half. They just won the first half a little bit bigger."

The Denver Broncos were also able to prove their mettle in their game later on the same day at San Diego. The late-game heroics in this contest were supplied by the Denver offense, in particular veteran quarterback Craig Morton, who threw two touchdown passes to wide receiver Haven Moses. The first scoring toss to Moses was from 33-yards out in the third quarter. The second touchdown pass to Moses was from San Diego's 8-yard line, and it came on a fourth-and-four situation with only 1:36 left in the game. Denver's Orange Crush defense shut out the Chargers in the second half, and the Broncos prevailed, 17–14. "We always find some way to win, one way or the other," said Denver head coach Red Miller, "and this was the other."

Another veteran quarterback, Fran Tarkenton of Minnesota, had by this time made a career of late-game victories. No real heroics were needed against the visiting Cincinnati Bengals, however, as the Vikings soundly defeated them, 42–10. The real drama of this game occurred when Tarkenton was chased around in the pocket by Cincinnati defensive end Gary Burley late in the third quarter. Burley trapped him for a sack which would greatly change Minnesota's season. A gasp was heard from the crowd throughout Metropolitan Stadium, as Tarkenton lay on the turf. The diagnosis was a fracture of his right fibula (a small bone in his lower leg). "He tried to plant his leg and spin," recalled Burley of Tarkenton's injury. "He was going down on a spin when I hit him. I had my weight on him when he went down. There was no way I could stop and let his leg out. I hate to be the one to hurt Fran Tarkenton. I don't like to have that kind of stuff on my mind." Tarkenton was done for the season, marking the first time in his 17-year career that he suffered a serious injury. Backup Vikings quarterback Tommy Kramer came in for Tarkenton and did an admirable job, as he engineered three more touchdown drives in the fourth quarter. But Minnesota was suddenly in an even tougher race to contend for a division title, now that Tarkenton was sidelined for the rest of the year.

The Chicago Bears would become a big reason for the increased competition in the NFC Central Division. They managed to overcome a 17-point halftime deficit against the visiting Kansas City Chiefs to post a 28–27 victory. The Chiefs took a 27–21 lead with just 24 seconds remaining in the game on the strength of a 14-yard touchdown sweep by halfback Ed Podolak. But the Bears responded quickly with a couple of long passes by Chicago quarterback Bob Avellini, the last of which went for 37 yards and a touchdown to tight end Greg Latta with just three seconds left. Chicago halfback Walter Payton rushed for 192 yards and three touchdowns in the victory. "You win some games like that, and you lose some games like that," said Avellini in describing his team's frantic finish in a seemingly hopeless situation.

It appeared as if the Dallas Cowboys were going to be able to avoid any similar kind of drama during their 1977 season. A Monday night contest in Dallas put an end to the Cowboys' season-long winning streak, however. The rival St. Louis Cardinals came from behind to defeat Dallas, 24–17. St. Louis simply had to win this game if they hoped to contend for a playoff spot. Quarterback Jim Hart was the catalyst for his team's crucial win. Hart threw the winning touchdown pass to tight end Jackie Smith with 3:10 left in the fourth quarter. A few minutes before, he hit wide receiver Mel Gray with a beautiful 49-yard bomb down the near sideline to bring the Cardinals to a 17–17 tie. Dallas had the game well in hand, but they seemed to let up late in the game, and it cost them a potential undefeated season. Dallas' record was now 8–1 in the NFC East, two games ahead of the second place Cardinals, who were now 6–3. "This was a great game for us to win," said St. Louis head coach Don Coryell. "It was a game we wanted real bad. To be behind like we were and come back the way we did, I think was just super."

"Super" would be a fairly apt description of the Week 9 game at the Oakland-Alameda County Coliseum, where the Raiders took on the visiting Houston Oilers. The defending champs were fresh off of a 44–7 rout of Seattle the previous week. The Oilers were still unable to regain the momentum that they built in 1975 when they went 10–4. So far in 1977, Houston was little more than mediocre, as they owned a 4–4 record when they went up against the Raiders. But they played hard and gave Oakland all that they wanted. Houston quarterback Dan Pastorini threw two touchdown bombs, a 41-yard pass to sprinter Ken Burrough, and a 71-yard strike to Billy "Whiteshoes" Johnson, one of the best punt and kickoff return specialists of the decade. But Pastorini also threw four interceptions in the game. Included among those were two key pickoffs in the fourth quarter by Oakland defensive backs Jack Tatum and Willie Brown, each of which stifled promising Houston drives. Oakland placekicker Errol Mann scored the only points in the fourth quarter on a 25-yard field goal as the Raiders prevailed, 34–29. "That was a gutbuster," exclaimed Oakland head coach John Madden from a victorious Raiders locker room. The Oilers would rebound, however, and would lose only once more for the rest of the season.

The Dallas Cowboys lost once more in Week 10, their second loss in a row. The host Pittsburgh Steelers were responsible for that defeat, as their running game did what few running games could do against the Dallas flex defense … accumulate over 200 yards on the ground. Steeler halfback Franco Harris ran for a single game career-best 179 yards through the heart of Doomsday. He also scored two touchdowns, one of them coming on a 61-yard sprint. The Steelers held a 14–13 lead at halftime, then shut down the Dallas offense in the second half. Rookie Cowboys tailback and former University of Pittsburgh star Tony Dorsett had his Pittsburgh homecoming spoiled by the Steelers, but he did manage to score once on a 13-yard run in the first quarter. The Steelers' 28–13 conquest of the visiting Cowboys improved their record to 6–4, good enough for a first-place tie in the AFC Central Division with Cleveland. Dallas' lost dropped them to 8–2, and signaled for them a legitimate slump. "Franco Harris was the difference in the ball game," said Dallas head coach Tom Landry. "He is just a great runner. Dorsett [who ran for 73 yards on 17 carries] ran hard and ran well. His whole future is ahead of him."

Another outstanding rushing performance from another outstanding young runner occurred earlier the same day in Chicago. Bears halfback Walter Payton broke the NFL single-game rushing record when he ran for 275 yards against the Minnesota Vikings in rainy Soldier Field. Chicago narrowly defeated the Vikings, 10–7, giving them a 5–5 record, one game behind Minnesota's NFC Central Division-leading 6–4 record. Payton's record eclipsed the 273-yard performance by Buffalo's O.J. Simpson from the previous year. Payton ran the ball 40 times on this day (averaging almost seven yards a carry), a day in which he was still trying to recover from a week-long flu. "I didn't think I could put on a Walter Payton performance when I left the dressing room for the game," Payton admitted. The Chicago offensive line, consisting of guards Revie Sorey and Noah

Jackson, tackles Dennis Lick and Ted Albrecht, center Dan Peiffer, and tight end Greg Latta, were the under-publicized and underrated group which paved the way for the new record. "Anyone could run behind them," said Payton of his blockers. "I had no idea I was anywhere near it [the single-game rushing record]. I don't like my teammates running up to me and telling me I've done this or that. It breaks my concentration."

Concentration was required of the Oakland Raiders as they met the San Diego Chargers in San Diego on November 20. The Raiders unfortunately could not muster enough concentration to keep the Chargers from pulling off a 12–7 upset win over their California rivals. The Chargers overcame a 7–6 halftime deficit by scoring two field goals in the second half, and shutting down Oakland's powerful offense during the final two quarters. In what seemed to be the year for injured quarterbacks, Oakland signal caller Ken Stabler twisted his knee in the first quarter, and was replaced by seldom-used quarterback Mike Rae, who failed to generate any meaningful offensive threat for the remainder of the game. The Raiders could account for only 142 yards of total offense throughout the game, including only 30 net passing yards. "It was really frustrating," said disappointed Oakland head coach John Madden in describing his team's performance. Halfback Rickey Young paced the San Diego offense against Oakland with 83 yards rushing and a 4-yard touchdown jaunt in the second quarter. Young was joined by rookie quarterback (and punter) Cliff Olander, who in his first start for the injured Dan Fouts, led the Chargers on a 44-yard, eight-play drive which ended with Young's score. "I think Olander did a very credible job for a rookie," assessed San Diego head coach Tommy Prothro. Oakland's loss dropped them to 8–2 on the season, a game behind the 9–1 Denver Broncos, who narrowly defeated Kansas City at Arrowhead Stadium, 14–7.

St. Louis had to manufacture one heck of a comeback on November 20 if they were to defeat the surprising Philadelphia Eagles, who built a 16–0 lead over the host Cardinals. New Philadelphia quarterback Ron Jaworski led the Green and Silver with 211 passing yards and two touchdown passes. Wide receivers Harold Carmichael and Charles Smith were the recipients of those scoring tosses. But the Cardinals did not get the moniker Cardiac Cards for nothing. They chiseled away at the Eagles' lead with the bulwark running of fullback Jim Otis, who ran for 97 yards and who broke off a 25-yard touchdown run in the third quarter. St. Louis quarterback Jim Hart shortly thereafter hit wide receiver Mel Gray with a 69-yard touchdown bomb to pull the Cardinals to within two points of the Eagles. Otis climaxed the comeback with a 1-yard off-tackle scoring run with 38 seconds left to play to give St. Louis a thrilling 21–16 victory. The win was St. Louis' sixth straight triumph, giving them a 7–3 record, which was good enough for second place in the competitive NFC East standings. Unfortunately for the Cardinals, this victory over Philadelphia would mark their last win of the year. St. Louis would go on to lose their final four games to finish 1977 with a depressing 7–7 record, which was only good enough for third place in their division. Cardinals head coach Don Coryell would receive a pink slip following the end of the regular season.

Both the Miami Dolphins and the Cincinnati Bengals were trying to avoid a similar fate as the Cardinals when they met each other in Week 10 in Riverfront Stadium. The Dolphins (7–2) were in good shape for a potential wild card spot in the playoffs, and were still in contention for the AFC East title. The Bengals were in a tougher situation, as they sported a lackluster 4–5 record going into their game with the Dolphins. But the Bengals were fortunate in that in their division (the AFC Central), both the Cleveland Browns and the Pittsburgh Steelers were in a first-place tie and both were only one game ahead of Cincinnati in the standings. The Bengals won this evenly-matched game against the Dolphins 23–17, with a trick play that somehow succeeded. Cincinnati quarterback Ken Anderson called for a triple-reverse, which culminated with a flea-flicker pass with 2:35 left to play. Cincinnati tight end Bob Trumpy was the recipient of the winning toss, which came from 29 yards out. On the trick play, Anderson handed the ball off to fullback Pete Johnson, who in turn handed the ball off to wide receiver John McDaniel, who in turn quickly handed the ball back to Anderson, who rolled right and threw to the open Trumpy in the end zone.

Rounding out the tenth week of the 1977 season was a tight contest in the Louisiana Superdome. The Saints managed to score three touchdowns against the Atlanta Falcons and their Grits Blitz defense in a 21–20 New Orleans victory. In dealing with the formidable Falcons defense, New Orleans quarterback Archie Manning claimed, "I really threw them a lot of formations out there and a lot of different motions. I tried not to ever give them the same thing twice." Those three Saints touchdowns were the most that the Falcons had given up in one game all year. In their next-to-last game, however, Atlanta would surrender 23 points to the Rams.

Surrendering a divisional lead in Week 11 was on the minds of several teams. The Denver Broncos (9–1) would host the Baltimore Colts (9–1) in one of the most anticipated games of the week. Both of these squads were stacked with young and athletic talent, and both were considered by many experts at this point of the season to be shoo-ins for the playoffs. Denver had one important factor going for them in this contest: Broncomania. The crowd at Mile High Stadium provided enough loud noise to rattle the Baltimore offense during the entire first half. The Orange Crush defense fed off of the frenzy of their fans, and limited the powerful Colts offense to a mere three points in the first 30 minutes. The game got tight after halftime, however, as Baltimore came back strong in the third quarter. A second field goal by Baltimore placekicker Toni Linhart and a 15-yard pass from Colts quarterback Bert Jones to setback Lydell Mitchell pulled Baltimore to within one point at 14–13 going into the final quarter. Mitchell's extra effort in breaking the attempted tackles of defensive backs Louis Wright and Bernard Jackson, and linebackers Joe Rizzo and Randy Gradishar, was the key to the score. Mitchell would catch nine of Jones' passes in the game, and his fellow setback, Don McCauley, would catch 11. Throwing to his running backs was Jones' only real option, as the Orange Crush pass rush was blasting in on his pocket too quickly for him to spend more time locating receivers deep downfield.

Two valuable defensive plays in that final quarter pointed the way to victory for the Broncos, however. The first one occurred during a Baltimore drive deep in Denver territory. Jones threw down the middle for McCauley on a short circle route. Broncos linebacker Tom Jackson stepped in front of the pass, intercepted it, and sprinted 73 yards for a touchdown. It was at that time the longest interception return for a touchdown in team history. "Jones was gaining confidence in the flat pass," said Jackson. "I just decided to come underneath. I don't think Bert ever saw me." Denver cornerback Louis Wright then picked off another Jones pass and returned it 59 yards to set up the final Broncos score, a 6-yard touchdown run by veteran quarterback Craig Morton. Denver survived this competitive test, 27–13, and thus secured the best record in the NFL at 10–1. The Colts fell to 9–2, still good enough for them to remain in first place in the tough AFC Eastern Division.

Another competitor in the AFC East was striving to get close to Baltimore, however. The Miami Dolphins traveled to St. Louis to take on the Cardinals in a rare Thanksgiving Day game. Neither team had a regular custom of playing on Thanksgiving, although the Cardinals took on the Buffalo Bills on that holiday in 1975. The league wanted to try a Turkey Day visit to St. Louis again this year in place of the regular Thanksgiving Day game at Dallas. The Dolphins were led by Bob Griese, who at this time in his career was wearing eyeglasses instead of contact lenses. Griese certainly had no problems seeing his open receivers on this Turkey Day, as he threw for a career-best six touchdown passes against the Cards. Miami scored a 55–14 rout of St. Louis, and improved their record to 8–3 (now just one game behind the Colts). "I thought they went out and showed a lot of fire," said Miami head coach Don Shula of his players' performance against the Cardinals. "That's one of the finest football games that any team I've been associated with played." Dolphins wide receiver Nat Moore stood out by catching three of Griese's touchdown tosses. Miami's 55 points was the most that the Cardinals had given up in one game in their 58-year history. The humiliating defeat left St. Louis with a 7–4 record in the standings.

The Cardinals' loss helped their main divisional foes—the Dallas Cowboys—secure a stronger lead in the NFC East. The Cowboys went to Washington as they tried to stop the bleeding in their current two-game losing streak. The Redskins were hoping to cause more Dallas blood to be shed in their hopes to keep pace for a potential wild card spot in the playoffs. The Redskins defense frustrated Dallas throughout the first half, but the Cowboys offense finally capitalized on two scoring drives in the second half to win, 14–7. Dallas wide receiver Golden Richards caught a 4-yard touchdown pass from quarterback Roger Staubach in the back of the end zone in the third quarter, and the now-starting rookie tailback Tony Dorsett scored the game-winning touchdown on a 1-yard burst in the final quarter. Dallas now held a 9–2 record, while the Redskins fell to 6–5. "Our whole team picked it up in the second half," said Dallas head coach Tom Landry. "We played the second half the way we should, to the point where we dominated the game. We can play better than we played today. That's got to be our objective."

Several other teams had the same improvement objective as the Cowboys in their Week 11 games. Bitter weather presented itself in varying degrees in Ohio and in Wisconsin, where winter presents more challenges than just a football opponent on a gridiron. In Cleveland, the Browns were in the thick of the fight in the AFC Central race as they took on the visiting Los Angeles Rams, who were trying to build on their two-game lead over Atlanta in the NFC West. The cold winds off of Lake Erie and a light and sporadic snowfall failed to help the Browns, however. Los Angeles registered their fourth straight win in a 9–0 shutout victory over Cleveland, marking the third shutout for the Rams' defense in 1977. "Getting out of Cleveland with this one is very big," said Los Angeles head coach Chuck Knox. The loss was only the fifth shutout in Cleveland's storied 367-game history. The Rams record thus improved to 8–3, while the Browns' record fell to 6–5.

Down the road in Cincinnati, a heavier snow fell on Riverfront Stadium. This snow, however, was friendlier to the home team, as the Bengals roughed up the visiting New York Giants, 30–13. Cincinnati quarterback Ken Anderson was one of the most accurate passers throughout the decade, and he proved it on this day by throwing three touchdown passes in the first half through the falling flakes. What really makes Anderson's performance against the Giants so remarkable was the fact that he attempted a total of only four passes in the first half. Anderson struck early and often. His first touchdown came on a 58-yard bomb on a deep fly pattern to wide receiver Billy Brooks, who streamed past a diving Giants cornerback, Bill Bryant. His next touchdown came on a 30-yard pass to Brooks, who beat the other Giants cornerback—Ray Rhodes—on a post pattern. Anderson's third scoring toss came on a quick 47-yard strike to tight end Jim Corbett, who snuck behind Giants linebacker Brad Van Pelt, caught Anderson's look-in dart, then raced to the end zone. The win lifted Cincinnati's record to 6–5, keeping them just one game behind the Steelers in the AFC Central Division. "We thought we had to throw early," said Cincinnati head coach Bill Johnson. "We knew the weather was going to change."

Finally in Green Bay, a blizzard affected both the Vikings and the Packers, as both teams struggled to run or throw in the foot-deep snow. The Vikings—like most teams—relied on keeping the ball on the ground when playing in snowy conditions. Minnesota running back Chuck Foreman ran almost exclusively to his right behind All-Pro offensive tackle Ron Yary and All-Conference offensive guard Ed White. Foreman finished the game with 101 yards on 26 carries.

Minnesota quarterback Bob Lee got to start in place of the injured Fran Tarkenton, and he managed to throw a 40-yard touchdown pass to Sammy White. "Even in a snowstorm, you have to throw the ball sometimes," claimed Lee. The Vikings Purple Gang preserved their lead with key interceptions by safety Paul Krause and cornerback Bobby Bryant. Minnesota prevailed 13–6, and thus remained a game ahead of the pesky Chicago Bears, who defeated the Detroit Lions on Thanksgiving, 31–14.

Rounding out the 11th week of the season were Pittsburgh's 23–20 win over the New York Jets in Shea Stadium; New England's 14–6 win over visiting Philadelphia; and Atlanta's 17–0 win over host Tampa Bay. The Steelers' win kept them alone in first place in the AFC Central with a 7–4 record, while the Patriots' win gave them a 7–4 record also. Unfortunately for the Pats, they were in what was probably at this particular moment the most competitive division in the league, the AFC East. New England's record was only good enough for third place in their division with three weeks remaining. Atlanta's shutout over Tampa Bay boosted the Falcons to a 6–5 record, two games behind the NFC West-leading Rams.

By the time the 12th week of the 1977 season came about, talk about tie-breaking procedures were being heard throughout the NFL. There were a couple of divisions at this stage of the season with two teams in contention for their divisional championships. There were also a couple of divisions with three teams still fighting for a divisional title. And in the AFC Central, each of the four teams in that division was still within one game of each other as fans entered their serious Christmas shopping mode. The first tie-breaking procedure in 1977 to decide a division winner involved the best won-loss percentage in head-to-head competition. The second tie-breaker was the best won-loss percentage in games within the division. The third tie-breaker was the best won-loss percentage in games within the conference, provided that the teams that were tied played an equal number of intraconference games. The fourth tie-breaking procedure was the best point differential in head-to-head competition. There were a total of eight tie-breaking procedures all together, the last of which was a coin flip. There were also tie-breaking procedures to help determine the wild card winner in each conference. By the final week of the 1977 regular season, these tie-breaking procedures would get a serious workout in both the AFC and the NFC.

The first competitive contest in Week 12 started out as a blowout. The San Francisco 49ers had built a seemingly insurmountable 24–0 lead over the Minnesota Vikings in the third quarter at Metropolitan Stadium. San Francisco running back Delvin Williams ran for 107 yards and scored twice on touchdown runs of two and five yards, and return specialist Dave Williams returned the kickoff to begin the third quarter 80 yards for another touchdown. Williams also returned a punt 60 yards a few minutes later to set up another San Francisco touchdown. Minnesota finally scored in the latter moments of the third quarter on a 15-yard pass from quarterback Bob Lee to running back Brent McClanahan. But Lee was greatly ineffective while he was playing during the first three quarters, so head coach Bud Grant decided to replace him in the fourth quarter with rookie signal caller Tommy Kramer. Grant had previously planned on giving Kramer some snaps in the game, and he figured that now would be as good a time as any, with his team's deficit seemingly too large to overcome. Grant wanted to give his rookie some game time experience. What he really gave him was a memory that would last a lifetime.

Kramer had only 12 minutes to work with, so he went right to work. A short drive led to an 8-yard scoring toss from Kramer to wide receiver Ahmad Rashad on a quick slant pattern. After an exchange of possessions, Kramer led the Vikes to another touchdown, coming on another 8-yard pass, this one going to tight end Bob Tucker. Suddenly, the 49er lead looked tenuous at best, as the Vikings trailed by just three points at 24–21. The 49ers tried to put an end to the sudden Minnesota upsurge by moving the ball downfield. The Purple People Eaters prevented another

San Francisco touchdown, but 49ers placekicker Ray Wersching connected on a 31-yard field goal to give his team a 27–21 lead with barely two minutes to play. Kramer had been relying on the tried and true trademark of veteran (but injured) Minnesota passer Fran Tarkenton, which was to use the short pass to his running backs to move the ball downfield in bits and pieces. The 49ers defense knew that with time dwindling, Kramer would have to go deep sooner or later. The Minnesota offensive line prepared for one more self-sacrificing team effort to keep the Gold Rush off of their rookie quarterback. Kramer dropped back and threw long down the middle for wide receiver Sammy White, who was running a deep fly pattern. The ball landed perfectly in White's hands, and despite the 49ers' secondary trying desperately to catch him, White sprinted across the goal line on a 69-yard score with 1:38 left to play. Tommy Kramer had thrown three touchdown passes in the fourth quarter, completed 9 of 13 passes for 188 yards, and produced one of the greatest comebacks in NFL history. "When you go in there you gotta think you're hot," Kramer said from a victorious Vikings postgame locker room. Minnesota's record improved to 8–4, and kept them a game ahead of Chicago, who had shutout the Buccaneers 10–0 on the same day.

Another long play in Dallas helped propel the Cowboys to a 24–14 victory over the Philadelphia Eagles at Texas Stadium. Dallas runner Tony Dorsett had his best day yet, rushing for a team record 206 yards on 23 carries for an incredible 8.9-yard average, including a beautiful 84-yard sprint for a touchdown. On that play, the Dallas offensive line never blocked better, as every man on the line managed to block every Eagle defensive linemen, several of whom were blasting in through the gaps and into the Dallas backfield. Trap blocks by guard Herbert Scott, veteran tackle Ralph Neely, and tight end Jay Saldi took out blitzing Eagles middle linebacker Bill Bergey and surging defensive end Art Thoms, which in turn sprung Dorsett through the line of scrimmage. Clearing blocks by Dallas offensive tackle Pat Donovan (on Philadelphia defensive lineman Manny Sistrunk) and tight end Billy Joe DuPree (on Eagles linebacker John Bunting) made an alley for Dorsett to break into the secondary. A final shield block by wide receiver Drew Pearson on Philadelphia cornerback Herman Edwards opened the seam in the secondary for Dorsett to use his natural speed to sprint past the vain Eagles pursuit to the end zone. "Dorsett's play broke our backs," said Philadelphia head coach Dick Vermeil. "You just give him [Dorsett] a crack and he's in the secondary," said Dallas offensive guard Tom Rafferty. Dorsett also scored an earlier touchdown for the Cowboys on a 1-yard run. The win over Philadelphia improved Dallas' record to 10–2, and clinched the NFC East title for the boys in metallic blue and silver. It marked the fifth division championship for the Cowboys in the decade.

Two more teams managed to clinch division titles in Week 12. One was the Los Angeles Rams, who defeated their visiting northern California neighbors, the Oakland Raiders, 20–14. The Rams defense intercepted Oakland quarterback Ken Stabler four times. Los Angeles quarterback Pat Haden had better luck, tossing a 43-yard touchdown pass to wide receiver Harold Jackson with 2:10 left in the fourth quarter for the winning points. It was Los Angeles' fifth straight win, and their fifth straight division title. "This was the kind of game that we knew it would be," said Los Angeles head coach Chuck Knox. "It was a knockdown, dragout fight against the world champions. It clinched the division title for us and I'm very happy about that for the players and the organization."

Oakland's major divisional nemesis—the Denver Broncos—were the other team that clinched a division title in Week 12. Denver scored a 24–14 victory over the Houston Oilers in the Astrodome. Oft-injured Denver quarterback Craig Morton was in and out of the lineup with a sore shoulder, but managed to complete 13 of 22 passes for 187 yards and two touchdowns. Reserve Bronco quarterback Norris Weese did mop-up duty for Morton, and scored on a 5-yard run in the fourth quarter for added insurance to Denver's lead. The win (Denver's 11th against only one loss) marked the first division title ever for the Denver franchise. Broncomania was on fire, and after greeting their victorious heroes in the Denver airport later that night with screams, signs, banners, and hugs and kisses, both players and fans partied well into the early morning hours. "I thought the players were going to tear the plane apart," said Denver head coach Red Miller upon landing. "They were stomping and throwing champagne in the air." The Mile High Denver Broncos were finally—after 17 fruitless years of existence—in the NFL playoffs.

The Miami Dolphins had a somewhat similar feeling of euphoria (on a somewhat lower altitude level than the Broncos), as they defeated the Baltimore Colts on *Monday Night Football* in the Orange Bowl, 17–6. Miami quarterback Bob Griese threw a 15-yard touchdown pass to tight end Andre Tillman in the second quarter, and Miami running back Leroy Harris rushed for 140 yards, including a 77-yard jaunt for a touchdown in the fourth quarter. Harris' incredible effort included breaking two tackles from Baltimore linebackers Ed Simonini and Tom MacLeod at the line of scrimmage, then breaking two more tackles from Colts defensive backs Norm Thompson and Lyle Blackwood. A strategical cutback by Harris at the Baltimore 25-yard line led to a final broken tackle through the arms of Colts cornerback Nelson Munsey at the 1-yard line and into the end zone for the score. "I never did have the feeling I was going to go all the way," said the modest Harris, whose run at that time was the longest in team history. "I was looking for a filling station to gas up." The No-Name Defense made a key recovery of a Baltimore fumble in the final quarter to preserve the win. Miami was now tied for first place in the AFC East with the Colts, with both teams owning 9–3 records. Their rivals—the New England Patriots—also kept pace by defeating the host Atlanta Falcons, 16–10. The Patriots thus improved their record to 8–4.

Pittsburgh improved its record to 8–4 too, as they defeated the visiting Seattle Seahawks, 30–20. Cincinnati remained a game behind the Steelers with a 27–7 win over the host Kansas City Chiefs. Chicago kept to within one game of the Minnesota Vikings in the NFC Central Division with a 10–0 shutout win over the host Tampa Bay Buccaneers, who were now 0–26 in their history. Would the Buccaneers *ever* win a game? That was one cynical question that would be answered as the dramatic ending to the 1977 regular season approached.

NFL standings since the AFL-NFL merger in 1970 have shown increased competition down the stretch as the promise of the playoffs appeared on the horizon. One big reason for this was due to the increased number of teams in the NFL. It was not uncommon to find at least one division each year where three teams in that division would vie for a playoff spot. Such was the case in 1977. The AFC Eastern Division was a pure logjam entering Week 13. The Miami Dolphins, Baltimore Colts, and New England Patriots were all tied with each other at 9–4, thanks to the results of their Week 13 contests. The Colts played host to the Detroit Lions, and the Dolphins met the Patriots up in New England. Baltimore was favored to beat the mediocre 5–7 Lions, but the Colts played one of their least inspired games of the year. Baltimore trailed Detroit most of the way, but finally pulled ahead late in the fourth quarter when quarterback Bert Jones hit setback Lydell Mitchell over the middle for a 34-yard touchdown. Mitchell's score gave the Colts a seemingly safe 10–6 lead. Baltimore got the ball back and had a fourth down situation deep in their own territory with only nine seconds to play. The Lions were out of time outs, and they knew that their only faint chance to win was to block the ensuing punt, recover the ball, and carry it in to the end zone. Colts punter David Lee could have received the snap from center and downed the ball in the end zone for an intentional safety, thereby giving the Lions two more points, but preserving a victory for Baltimore. Instead, Lee tried to punt the ball in the midst of the oncoming rush. Reserve Detroit wide receiver Leonard Thompson broke through the line and blocked Lee's punt. The ball bounced off the hard dirt surface of Memorial Stadium and nestled perfectly in Thompson's arms as he waltzed into the end zone for the winning touchdown. The Lions prevailed,

13–10. "When you have two people hitting into one gap like we did on that play, someone has to come free," said Detroit head coach Tommy Hudspeth. "It was Leonard."

The stunning loss was the Colts' third straight defeat. It forced them to share the lead in the AFC East with both the Dolphins and the Patriots. The contest between those two teams in the bitterly cold Schaefer Stadium was really two games, separated mostly by halves. The first half was dominated by the Patriots, as they scored two quick touchdowns in the first quarter on 1-yard runs by running backs Ike Forte and Sam Cunningham. The Dolphins then started to take control. A 28-yard field goal by placekicker Garo Yepremian late in the second quarter and a 23-yard touchdown pass from Miami quarterback Bob Griese to wide receiver Nat Moore in the third quarter narrowed the Dolphin deficit to 14–10. But the stubborn New England defense throttled the Dolphin offense throughout the final quarter, and limited the Dolphin runners to a minimal 25 yards rushing, the lowest total in Miami head coach Don Shula's tenure with the Dolphins. Miami had several opportunities to score the winning touchdown from deep in Patriot territory, however, but New England's defense forced key incompletions down the stretch to preserve a 14–10 victory. "The turning point was the fact that we were able to dominate at the beginning," said New England head coach Chuck Fairbanks.

New England's win gave them a 9–4 record, and tied them with the Colts and the Dolphins. Enter the NFL tie-breaking formulas. The Colts—despite losing their past three games—could still win the AFC East title with a win in Week 14 against the Patriots. "So it's all irrelevant," said Baltimore linebacker Stan White. "It all comes down in the fact that we have to beat New England." New England's chances for a playoff spot were more daunting. Not only did they need to beat the Colts, but they also needed the Buffalo Bills to beat the Dolphins in the final week. Miami could make the playoffs with a win over Buffalo and a Patriot win over the Colts. The most ironic of these postseason ironies came from the Detroit-Baltimore game in Week 13. It actually helped the Colts more by *losing* to the Lions than by winning, because New England's road to the playoffs through the applicable tie-breaking procedures suffered more from Baltimore's loss. The Patriots were now at the mercy of the Bills, who had won only three times all year. A Buffalo loss to the Dolphins would eliminate New England, regardless of what happened in the Patriots-Colts game in Week 14. The stage was now set for one of the truly remarkable and memorable games of the decade in the final week of the 1977 season, when the Colts met the Patriots with the playoffs on the line. This type of competition late in a season is now an annual occurrence in the NFL. But that was not always the case. In actuality, the excitement that resulted from the competition in pro football really got its start during the 1970s, as new rivalries flourished throughout the league, thanks mostly to the AFL-NFL merger in 1970.

The rivalries in the AFC Central Division presented its own examples of success and failure down the stretch. The Browns held a division-leading 5–2 mark at mid-season, then went on to collapse and lose all but one of their last seven games, finishing in last place with a 6–8 record. Cleveland head coach Forrest Gregg lost his job at season's end. The Steelers entered Week 13 at 8–4, good enough for first place in the division. They met the 7–5 Bengals in frozen Cincinnati and suffered a debilitating loss, 17–10, thanks to a beautiful 43-yard touchdown bomb in the third quarter to punter and reserve wide receiver Pat McInally, who beat the seemingly faster Pittsburgh cornerback J.T. Thomas down the far sideline. "My assignment was to run deep and distract them," said McInally. The original target on the play was fullback Pete Johnson, but Cincinnati quarterback Ken Anderson found McInally open and hit him in stride with the game-winning pass. The Bengals were now tied with the Steelers for first place in the AFC Central with a record of 8–5, and could win the division outright with a win in their final game of the year. The Houston Oilers were mathematically ineligible for the playoffs by Week 13, but they won anyway, defeating the

Cleveland Browns, 19–15, on a cold and snowy day at Municipal Stadium. The Oilers would be resoundingly heard from again in Week 14.

Another team that was ineligible for a playoff spot late in the 1977 season was the 0–12 Tampa Bay Buccaneers, who were 0–26 overall in their history. Few football fans today realize that Tampa Bay's offense in 1977 was even worse than their offense in 1976 (if that was even possible). The 1977 Bucs had accumulated just four offensive touchdowns in their first 12 games, and they were shut out six times. Their quarterbacks in 1977 combined to throw a grand total of three touchdown passes and 30 interceptions during the year. Tampa Bay would travel to the Louisiana Superdome in their next-to-last game of the regular season, with virtually no hope of winning. But somehow, someway, the Bucs left New Orleans with the first win in their existence. Tampa's defense provided the impetus for victory, as they returned three intercepted passes for touchdowns in their 33–14 victory over the Saints. No team in the modern era of the league would ever equal the Buccaneers' 0–26 start over almost two full seasons. "We [the Tampa Bay coaches] just read the article to them [the Tampa Bay players] where Archie [Manning, the New Orleans quarterback] said it would be disgraceful to lose to Tampa Bay," said Buccaneers head coach and major league quipster John McKay. "Whatever Archie Manning said, I agree with him. He said it would be disgraceful to lose, and it is. If we can get some more guys to make statements like that…." Several Buccaneers players were seen and heard jeering Manning at the final gun with the phrase "It's disgraceful! It's disgraceful!"

The performances of both the Chicago Bears and the Minnesota Vikings in 1977 were certainly not disgraceful. Both of those teams gave the NFC Central Division a tight finish to the season. The diligent and determined Bears finally managed to catch the Vikings in the standings in mid–December. A 21–10 Bears win over their hated rivals, the Green Bay Packers in Week 13, gave the Bears an 8–5 record. It was Chicago's fifth win in a row. The Vikings also had an 8–5 record after they fell hard in Oakland to the Raiders, 35–13. Both the Bears and Vikings had split their two-game series with each other, but the Vikings owned the tie-breaker, thanks to the point differential that they earned between the two clubs in their first meeting. That fake field goal in overtime in Week 5 not only gave the Vikings a 22–16 win over the Bears on October 16, it also provided Minnesota with enough points in point differential to eclipse Chicago's 10–7 win over the Vikes on November 20. Those extra points gave Minnesota the inside track to the division title.

Finally, the Washington Redskins would read numerous reviews of how they would eventually be knocked out of the playoff picture from mid-season on. Most experts expected the Cardinals to put the final nail in the Redskin coffin in St. Louis on December 10, but once again, the Over-the-Hill Gang refused to lie down and accept what many thought to be the inevitable conclusion. Washington's defense managed to hold on just long enough to defeat St. Louis, 26–20. The key play occurred when reserve Washington defensive back Eddie Brown made a diving interception of a Jim Hart pass deep in the St. Louis end zone late in the fourth quarter to preserve the win. "I'm really proud of this football team," said Washington head coach George Allen. "We beat the Cardinals in their own backyard." The Redskins were still alive in the playoff race with an 8–5 record. All they needed to do was beat the Los Angeles Rams in the final week (a pretty tall order considering that the Rams were 10–3 and had already clinched the NFC West title) and hope that the Bears (who shared an 8–5 record with the Redskins) fell to the 5–8 New York Giants. Those two resulting scenarios would produce another playoff appearance for Coach Allen's Over-the-Hill Redskins.

It all came down to the final week of the season. The Redskins did manage to defeat the Rams, 17–14, at RFK Stadium. The Rams had nothing to play for except to spoil the Redskins' season. They almost succeeded in that mission, but Rams placekicker Rafael Septien missed two field goal attempts in the final minutes of the game. Washington's win proved to be futile, however, because the Chicago Bears defeated the New York Giants in Giants Stadium on the following day. The strategy in that contest was dictated by the weather and the slippery playing surface. There was ice, sleet, freezing rain, and snow, all of which limited both teams' offenses. Chicago halfback Walter Payton entered the game hoping to eclipse O.J. Simpson's season rushing record, but was held to just 47 yards by the Giants defense and the icy field. "The biggest disappointment was the condition of the field," Payton admitted afterward. Nevertheless, Payton's 1,852 rushing yards in 1977 were enough to win the league rushing title, and at that time were the third-best mark in league history.

A battle of field goals produced a 3–3 tie as the fourth quarter began. Chicago fullback Robin Earl scored the game's lone touchdown on a 4-yard run in the final quarter. New York responded when placekicker Joe Danelo sent the game into overtime with a 27-yard field goal at the end of regulation. Both the Bears and the Giants had several chances to score in overtime, but missed field goals kept the game tied at 9–9. "These are the worst conditions for field goals and extra points," exclaimed Chicago head coach Jack Pardee. If the overtime period would end without a score, the game would end in a tie, and the Redskins would enter the playoffs instead of the Bears. Chicago placekicker Bob Thomas had one last chance from 28 yards out with nine seconds remaining in the overtime period. Thomas had missed two earlier field goals and an extra point conversion throughout the game (thanks in part to a couple of low center snaps which proved too difficult for his holder to field), but he came through for his team when they needed him most. His final field goal attempt was successful, the Bears were finally in the playoffs for the first time since 1963, and there was unabashed joy in Chicago. The Bear players mobbed Thomas on the field following Chicago's 12–9 victory, and several other Bear players rolled around in the snow like gleeful children who just learned that school was cancelled for the day. Bears owner, patriarch, and the acknowledged Father of the NFL, George Stanley Halas, was caught up in the euphoria. "Thank You Lord," Halas said to reporters as he wiped tears from his face after the game, "and thank You for these fans."

The Minnesota Vikings had to give thanks too, as they were able to hold off the surging Bears in the NFC Central Division with a 30–21 victory over the Detroit Lions in the Pontiac Silverdome. Minnesota was led by running back Chuck Foreman, who rushed for 156 yards and two touchdowns. Foreman also eclipsed the 1,000-yard rushing mark for the third straight season. The Vikings also benefitted from the play of reserve quarterback Bob Lee, who passed for two touchdowns. The Vikings held off the inspired efforts of Detroit's Eddie Payton (Walter Payton's little brother), who scored twice on a 98-yard kickoff return and a 87-yard punt return. The win gave the Norsemen their seventh NFC Central title in the decade.

Elsewhere in the NFC, the Atlanta Falcons defeated the New Orleans Saints, 35–7, in Atlanta. That win gave the Falcons a respectable 7–7 record to close out the season. The Grits Blitz defense gave up a league-low 129 points in 1977, a modern-day NFL record which still stands today. Tampa Bay ended the season on a winning streak, as they won their second straight game with a 17–7 victory over visiting St. Louis on the season's final Sunday.

Several teams in the AFC also needed to win their final game if they were to make the playoffs. One of those teams was the Cincinnati Bengals, who traveled to the Astrodome to take on division rival Houston. The Oilers were not playoff bound, but they were bound to spoil the Bengals' hopes for the postseason. Houston upended Cincinnati, 21–16, thus stopping the Bengals from obtaining the AFC Central title. "We said after our first game in Cincinnati that we were better than they were," recalled Houston head coach O. A. "Bum" Phillips. "In order for us to prove it, we had to win today." The Oilers did, and Cincinnati missed out on the playoffs for the second straight year.

The honor of winning the AFC Central thus belonged to the Pittsburgh Steelers once again, as they barely squeaked past the host San Diego Chargers, 10–9. The Oakland Raiders had already secured the AFC wild card spot, but they won their final regular season game anyway. Oakland edged the visiting Kansas City Chiefs, 21–20. The Denver Broncos took their nearly perfect 12–1 record into Dallas and received their second blemish of the season, this one coming from the Cowboys, 14–6. Both of those teams were substituting reserves for starters by the second quarter. Winning this contest would not alter either team's standing in the upcoming playoffs. "Emotionally, I guess this wasn't a big game," admitted Denver safety Steve Foley. Both Dallas and Denver entered the 1977 playoffs with identical 12–2 records, and both owned the top seed in their respective conferences.

The main focus of drama on the regular season's final Sunday occurred in the AFC East, and specifically in Baltimore, where the Colts would take on the Patriots. A New England win would give the Miami Dolphins the division title, while a Baltimore win would give them the title. Miami put this must-win pressure on Baltimore when they defeated the Buffalo Bills a day earlier, 31–14. Miami and their head coach Don Shula would now be spectators to their own fate, and would watch the Colts-Patriots game with the nervousness of an expectant father. "We got it done," said Shula after his team defeated the Bills. "Now we'll have to watch … to see if New England can give it their best shot."

The Patriots were indeed giving it their best shot, as they wasted little time in taking the lead. A 5-yard touchdown pass from New England quarterback Steve Grogan to All-Pro tight end Russ Francis and a 1-yard touchdown dive by Grogan himself gave the Patriots a 14–3 halftime advantage. That lead increased with the second half kickoff, as New England return specialist Raymond Clayborn caught Baltimore placekicker Toni Linhart's kick one yard deep in his end zone, ran to his right, and began a textbook return. Clayborn first eluded attempted arm tackles from Colt players Jimmie Kennedy and Doug Nettles. New England's Steve King then wiped out another would-be Baltimore tackler, as Clayborn veered back to the middle of the field. New England's Doug Beaudoin then blocked out Baltimore's Nelson Munsey, the last real opponent that had a legitimate chance to make a tackle. Clayborn's 9.4 speed in the 100-yard dash did the rest, as he sprinted past Baltimore's Sanders Shiver and into the end zone. The Patriots now owned a 21–3 lead. A multitude of Dolphin fans in Miami were now in preliminary celebration mode.

Baltimore responded with a third quarter touchdown on a 14-yard pass from quarterback Bert Jones to flanker Glenn Doughty. New England placekicker John Smith then added a 30-yard field goal to boost the Patriots' lead to 24–10 as the fourth quarter began. Baltimore's 9–1 start to the 1977 season now appeared to be a distant memory. If they were to salvage their season, they would have to score several times in the final quarter against a Patriots defense that salivated at the chance to end the Colts' season. Baltimore quarterback Bert Jones knew full well that time was of the essence, so he quickly spearheaded the Colts comeback as the game clocked ticked away. Jones hit tight end Raymond Chester deep down the middle of the Patriots zone defense on a third-and-18 situation from his own 22-yard line. Chester caught the ball in stride and ran for his life. He barely crossed the goal line with a 78-yard touchdown before being tackled.

The Colts defense then forced a New England punt, and Jones accelerated his dropbacks as he went back to work. The Baltimore quarterback would eventually finish the game with 340 passing yards, and as time dwindled, he hit wide receiver Freddie Scott for another touchdown from 12 yards out. Baltimore now trailed the Patriots by only a single point, 24–23. The Baltimore fans were now wholeheartedly believing that their team could actually comeback and win this game. They were believing it even more when the Colts defense shut down the Patriots offense once again with barely two minutes remaining in the struggle. Jones took over and once again drove his offense down the sodded field. Baltimore was at the New England 6-yard line when a gift from the heavens (or from the animal species known as zebras) was bestowed upon them. Jones took the snap from center and pivoted to his right to hand the ball off. The problem was that neither halfback Lydell Mitchell nor fullback Roosevelt Leaks went the way that Jones expected them to go. Jones immediately saw his dilemma and whirled to his left. The New England defense also immediately saw Jones' quandary, and Patriot linebackers Steve Zabel and Pete Barnes hit the Colt quarterback simultaneously. The ball immediately popped out of Jones' grasp. New England linebacker Sam Hunt picked up the pigskin and started running towards the opposite goal, and only stopped when he heard the referee's whistle. The play had incredibly been blown dead. "The quarterback was in the grasp of the tackler and I blew the whistle," said referee Fred Silva after the game. "The ball came out. That's it."

Silva's simple explanation of Jones' non-fumble did not sit well with the Patriots. "I thought it was a fumble," said New England head coach Chuck Fairbanks. Baltimore's Jones declared, "It's a judgment call and the officials gave it to us." And Miami's Don Shula, watching from his home in Florida, required a full day before he could calm down long enough to address the press.

Baltimore's comeback ended successfully a couple of plays later when running back Don McCauley ran off right tackle from three yards out and into the New England end zone. The Colts managed nothing short of a miracle as they scored 14 fourth quarter points and pulled out a 30–24 win, thus giving them the AFC East title. Baltimore's victory also dashed the hopes of the Dolphins, who were one quarter—or at the least one quick referee's whistle away—from the playoffs. The bizarre fumble or non-fumble incident in the Patriots-Colts game would unbelievably repeat itself once again, albeit with different participants, in just a few weeks in the AFC championship game.

The 1977 postseason finally arrived after a regular season chock-filled with excitement. The divisional playoff game in Dallas had a predictable conclusion, where the heavily favored NFC East Champion Cowboys routed the wild card Chicago Bears, 37–7. The Doomsday Defense flexed its muscle and made mincemeat of the Bears offense, as they shutdown the Chicago playmakers, and frolicked in the Bear backfield. Dallas limited Walter Payton, the league's leading rusher, to 60 yards on 19 carries and zero touchdowns. Payton also suffered a concussion later in the game when he was hit head-on by Dallas strong safety Cliff Harris. Chicago quarterback Bob Avellini had a tough outing as well, as he threw four interceptions, three of which were collected by Dallas free safety Charlie Waters for a team playoff record.

The Dallas offense dealt with no such difficulties. Cowboys quarterback Roger Staubach threw a second quarter touchdown pass of 28 yards to tight end Billy Joe DuPree, but more often than not, he relied on his runners to move the ball and score the points. Dallas halfback Tony Dorsett scored twice on runs of 23 and 7 yards, and reserve tailback Doug Dennison contributed a 2-yard touchdown run in the first quarter. Dallas placekicker Efren Herrera booted three field goals as well. "This has to be our best game of the year," said Dallas head coach Tom Landry from a victorious locker room. "Every phase of our game was excellent, from our offense to the defense and specialty teams. Right now we are playing good ... we feel confident right now."

Avellini led the Bears to their only score late in the fourth quarter on a 34-yard touchdown pass to wide receiver Steve Schubert, who beat Cliff Harris on an out pattern. By that time, however, the game had long since been decided, and quite a few reserve players were on the field for Dallas. "They're [Dallas] a real good team, there's no doubt about it," said Avellini after the abrupt conclusion to Chicago's season of contention. The Cowboys' playoff experience proved too much for the young and inexperienced Bears on this day, however, and was the main factor in sending Dallas to the 1977 NFC championship game.

Another team with a huge amount of playoff inexperience—as in none—would be playing in the first playoff game in their history on December 24. The Denver Broncos earned the best record in the league at 12–2 (tied with Dallas' 12–2 record), and they hoped that the momentum that grew for them throughout the regular season would continue in the playoffs. They would host the Pittsburgh Steelers at Mile High Stadium, and were out to prove that they belonged in the postseason. Most experts believed that the playoff-savvy Steelers would duplicate what Dallas did to Chicago and finally bring the Broncos back down to earth. Nevertheless, the oddsmakers listed the Broncos as three-point favorites to beat the Steelers. They had defeated Pittsburgh in Week 8, 21–7, and many prognosticators felt that they could do it again despite the playoff pressure. Denver quarterback Craig Morton was dealing with a myriad of injuries, however, and was purely a pocket passer at this stage of his 13-year career. His knees, back, hip, shoulder, and throwing arm were all ailing as the season wore down, keeping Morton in a weekly regimen of repeated convalescing. The pro football writers and experts all knew this, but they also knew that Denver had large amounts of emotion on their side, and a pretty good defense to boot. That emotion, stemming from the vociferous shouts and screams from Broncomania's maniacs in the stands, would resound throughout the game and would filter down to the playing field. The Broncos seemed to feed off of the noise and play harder as the game wore on, and that emotional style of play by Denver proved to be Pittsburgh's undoing.

Denver scored first in this competitive matchup in the first quarter. Rookie running back Rob Lytle burst through the middle of the Steeler defensive line for a 7-yard touchdown run. Lytle's score was set up by a blocked punt. Pittsburgh responded in the second quarter with a 1-yard quarterback sneak by Terry Bradshaw. The trading of touchdowns continued in the second quarter. Denver linebacker Tom Jackson returned a Franco Harris fumble 30 yards. Broncos running back Otis Armstrong followed that up with a 10-yard touchdown run on a play similar to Lytle's earlier score. Pittsburgh closed out the second quarter with a 1-yard scoring run by halfback Franco Harris. By this time in the contest, however, both teams were involved in a couple of extra-curricular activities after the whistle. Pittsburgh's All-Pro defensive tackle Joe Greene punched Denver offensive guard Paul Howard in the solar plexus. This action from "Mean Joe" resulted from what Greene described as "constant holding," an infraction which was seldom called by the referees (according to Greene). Greene's punch to Howard's gut was missed by the officials, but on the very next play, Greene again punched Denver center Mike Montler in the stomach. The referees did see that punch, however, and penalized Greene 15 yards for unsportsmanlike conduct. It took a few minutes to separate the combatants after Greene's actions.

Denver head coach Red Miller did not accept the ensuing fights on the field with aplomb. He decided to go after the officials as the first half ended. Miller voiced his disdain to the referees for their failure to penalize the Steelers efficiently enough to suit the punches that he saw Greene deliver to his players. Miller was not satisfied with yelling at the officials, however. He also decided to yell at Pittsburgh head coach Chuck Noll and Pittsburgh defensive line coach George Perles in the hallway separating the two locker rooms underneath the stands. "To tell you the truth, I'd have been surprised if Red *hadn't* gone after somebody," said Denver placekicker Jim Turner after the game. "He's a tiger. You mess with one of his boys, you're messing with his family. That's what he preached all season. Today he practiced it."

Things changed for both teams in the third quarter. For one thing, the fights on the field stopped. For another, Pittsburgh failed to score a single point during the third quarter, but Denver just kept rolling along. Morton hit Denver tight end Riley Odoms for a 30-yard touchdown, and it seemed as if the pressure was now on the Steelers to answer. Could the Black and Gold come back again? True to their success-driven pedigree, the Steelers tied the game at 21–21 in the fourth quarter when Bradshaw hit his tight end, Larry Brown, with a 1-yard touchdown pass.

Denver's defense then started to display the poise of a champion. Broncos outside linebacker Tom Jackson made two interceptions in the fourth quarter which pointed the way to an eventual victory for his team. His first interception set up Denver's Jim Turner, who connected on two field goals from 44 and 25 yards, boosting the Broncos' lead to 27–21. Jackson's second interception set up the Denver offense for a clinching touchdown. Broncos wide receiver Jack Dolbin, himself a former sandlot minor league player for the Pottstown (Pennsylvania) Firebirds, beat Pittsburgh reserve defensive back Jimmy Allen to the corner of the end zone. Dolbin caught Morton's perfect pass over his shoulder to complete a 34-yard touchdown, giving Denver too large of a margin for the Steelers to overcome as the final quarter waned. "It was great protection by our offensive line," admitted Morton in describing his touchdown pass to Dolbin. "I had an unbelievable amount of time to throw."

The Broncos had won the first playoff game in their history, 34–21, thereby cancelling what would have been Pittsburgh's fourth straight championship game appearance. "We gave them too many opportunities in the first half," said Chuck Noll. "You can't make that many mistakes against a good team in the playoffs. The interceptions really hurt us. It was a hard fought, physical football game. Denver played well." Denver's fans were in complete agreement with Noll's opinion. They serenaded their beloved Broncos as they left the field on this magical Christmas Eve by singing in unison, "I'm Dreaming of an Orange Crushmas." The Broncos were headed to their first ever conference championship game. Coach Miller had the last word. "Our team is earning the respect of the entire league," Miller assessed. "We showed we can hang in there with anybody. After today, nobody should doubt us."

Most people doubted the chances that the Minnesota Vikings had going up against the Los Angeles Rams on December 26. The Rams had defeated the Vikings earlier in the season by a score of 35–3, and there was little hope that the Vikings would be able to do much better in their second meeting. The Vikes were still without their injured starting quarterback Fran Tarkenton, and his replacement, Bob Lee, was considered by most experts to be little more than a fair backup. But history was on Minnesota's side, as they had never lost to the Rams in a postseason game. The Vikings defeated the Rams in 1969 in the NFL divisional playoffs, and in 1974 and 1976 in the NFC championship game. Another factor would also be on Minnesota's side on this day— the weather. A rare Los Angeles tropical storm afflicted the area throughout the entire day, inundating the field with 1.5 inches of rain. Even after removing the tarp which covered the natural grass surface, the rain continued to drench the sod. Los Angeles' perceived overall team speed over Minnesota was now rendered even.

The Rams were still favored to win this game by 10 points, however, and they began as if they would pile-drive the Vikings into the mushy field. The Los Angeles offense, led by second-year quarterback Pat Haden, moved briskly down to the Minnesota 31-yard line, where they were faced with a fourth-and-two situation. Rams head coach Chuck Knox decided to go for it, and it proved to be a costly decision. Rams tailback Lawrence McCutcheon slammed into the pile of humanity, only to be met by the supposedly aging Minnesota defensive line as they filled the rather small hole. Minnesota defensive end Mark Mullaney and defensive tackle Alan Page administered the point of impact, thereby putting an immediate stop to McCutcheon's progress. The chain gang came out for a measurement, and the ball was short of a first down by less than a yard. The Vikings defense had done their job well. Minnesota's offense took over from there.

Minnesota head coach Bud Grant decided to start Bob Lee at quarterback instead of rookie

Tommy Kramer, mainly because of Lee's overall edge in experience. Lee did not disappoint his coach. He immediately led the Vikings on a 70-yard scoring drive, highlighted by completions of 12 and 25 yards down the near sideline to Minnesota wide receiver Ahmad Rashad. A 5-yard off-tackle run by Vikings tailback Chuck Foreman behind the right side of the offensive line completed the drive successfully in the Los Angeles end zone. Minnesota lead 7–0. "The field gets worse as you play on it," observed Grant. "If we were going to get anything passing, we had to get it early."

The next two quarters would see a multitude of punts and exchanges of possessions from both teams. Bob Lee would call an incredible 28 straight running plays during a stretch of the second and third quarters. The Rams got within easy scoring range in the second quarter, but an unforeseen dilemma showed up to confound their offense. Pat Haden was one of the smaller quarterbacks in the league, standing only 5–11. His hands were small too, and in dealing with a wet ball all game long, his grip on the pigskin was slippery at best. His toss on a first and goal situation from the Minnesota 5-yard line drifted to the back of the end zone, where Vikings defensive back Nate Allen caught it and kept both of his feet in the end zone before falling out of it. The second Rams threat was thus quickly diffused. "A lot of people say our defense is old but they can play," said Minnesota running back Chuck Foreman.

It was not until early in the fourth quarter for another score to occur. Minnesota fullback Sammy Johnson did the honors, plunging in from one yard out to culminate a 10-play, 40-yard drive. The Vikes now had a 14–0 lead with less than a quarter to play. Haden threw his second interception several minutes later. Minnesota safety Paul Krause stepped in front of Haden's floating pass deep in Viking territory to end another Rams drive. By this time, the majority of the umbrella-clad crowd in the Coliseum were calling for Joe Namath to replace Haden. Namath was mostly healthy for this, the final game of his pro career. He also had larger (and dryer) hands than Haden, which could have made a difference when gripping and throwing the ball. But Coach Knox ignored the suggestion from a couple of assistant coaches on the Rams' sideline that Namath go in the game. "I told Knox three times that Namath was throwing the ball better of the two on the sidelines, and he was ready to go in," said Rams quarterback coach Kay Stephenson. "Every time I told him, [Knox] he just nodded and walked away. Chuck never called on him [Namath]." Rams receivers coach Lionel Taylor concurred with Stephenson's claim. "I was shocked Joe didn't get the call," Taylor said. The decision to keep Haden in the game would be one unfortunate factor (albeit a small one when comparing it to his major inability to win a conference championship or a Super Bowl) in Knox's dismissal after the season was over.

The Rams finally scored with less than a minute to play in the game when Haden hit wide receiver Harold Jackson for a 1-yard score on a lob at the edge of the end zone. The Vikings' lead was now 14–7, and if they could recover the ensuing onside kick, they would win the game. They could not do so, however. Los Angeles special teams player and reserve running back Jim Jodat recovered Rafael Septien's slippery onside kick, and the Rams were still faintly alive. Haden managed to quickly drive his offensive teammates down the field. He used up all of his time outs, however, to get within scoring range as the precious seconds ticked off the clock. Haden's last-gasp pass with three seconds remaining was intercepted by Minnesota safety Jeff Wright, thus securing a 14–7 upset victory for the Vikings. Once again, the Rams failed to defeat the Vikings in the playoffs. Minnesota added yet another chapter to their storied history as a team that plays extremely well in bad weather conditions. They did not have a single turnover in this game. The Vikings thus earned another ticket to the NFC championship game, their fourth such ticket in the decade. "Bud Grant knew what to do," wrote sportswriter Jim Murray in his editorial following the game. "Get seven quick points and then take the football out in the backyard and bury it like a bone. A half-hour went by and the Rams didn't see the ball." Despite his team's loss, Knox was avoiding excuses in looking for the reasons why his team came up short in another playoff game. "The field conditions were terrible for both teams," Knox admitted. "We can't blame the defeat on the weather."

Indeed there were elements of drama in the Vikings-Rams mudfest, but the best divisional playoff game of the weekend pitted the Oakland Raiders and the Baltimore Colts in Baltimore's Memorial Stadium. Some experts considered it to be the best divisional playoff game of the decade. It finished with a ranking of eighth best in a poll of the greatest games of the decade conducted by sportswriters and NFL experts at the end of the 1970s. The game was filled with a multitude of dramatic plays, stellar offensive production, nine different lead changes, and pivotal special teams efforts which helped to change the game's momentum on several occasions. The outcome was not decided until 43 seconds had elapsed in the second overtime period, making it (at that time) the third longest game in NFL history.

The Raiders entered the contest as the AFC's wild card team, but they were also the defending Super Bowl champions, and they won 11 games in 1977. Still, they had incredibly never won a playoff game in their entire history as a visiting team. The Colts had somehow managed to win their third straight AFC East title, but it definitely was not easy. Only a miraculous win over New England in the final game of the season lifted Baltimore to a 10–4 record. The Colts had lost three of their final four games, so they were definitely not peaking at this time of the year. A sunny and somewhat warm day (47 degrees at kickoff, rising to 51 degrees later in the day) greeted both teams at Baltimore's Memorial Stadium. The balmy (for December in Maryland) weather seemed to baffle both teams in the first quarter, as five punts signaled a possible defensive battle and an even standstill in the statistics. Indeed, both teams held the ball for an equal amount of minutes and seconds (7:30) in the first quarter.

Oakland drew first blood towards the end of the first quarter, however, and they did it thanks to their running attack. The left side of the Oakland offensive line featured All-Pro tackle Art Shell and All-Pro guard Gene Upshaw, both of whom would become future Hall of Famers. Shell and Upshaw paved the way for a 30-yard touchdown run by halfback Clarence Davis, giving the Raiders a 7–0 lead. Also providing a key block on the play was Davis' running mate Mark van Eeghen, who wiped out forcing Baltimore linebacker Stan White, which helped spring Davis into the secondary.

The Raiders' first possession of the second quarter met with a much different result, however. Oakland quarterback Kenny "The Snake" Stabler was intercepted by Baltimore strong safety Bruce Laird, who baited Stabler into throwing for van Eeghen in the right flat. Laird stepped in front of van Eeghen, intercepted the ball, and raced untouched into the Oakland end zone. "We were in a strongside zone rotation and I was assigned to cover the flat," said Laird. "I just read the flood pattern, and when van Eeghen ran into the flat, I looked at Kenny. He cocked his arm, I read his release, and I stepped in front of van Eeghen, who was falling down, and picked it right off his hip." Laird's 61-yard interception return for a touchdown and a 36-yard field goal by Colts' placekicker Toni Linhart gave Baltimore a slim 10–7 lead going into halftime.

Oakland seized the momentum and the lead early in third quarter. Stabler launched a Silver and Black trademark long bomb to wide receiver Cliff Branch, good for 41 yards down the far sideline. Stabler then hit his All-Pro tight end Dave Casper three plays later for what would be the first of three touchdowns for the former Notre Dame standout. Stabler benefitted from the quality time given to him in the pocket by his offensive line. That group allowed only one sack all game long against Baltimore's vaunted Sack Pack. Casper's 8-yard scoring reception down the middle of the Colts' short zone gave the Raiders a 14–10 lead, but they would not enjoy that slim advantage for very long.

Baltimore kick returner Marshall Johnson caught the ensuing kickoff at his own 13-yard line, followed the blocking wedge to his left, and broke into the clear for an 87-yard touchdown dash. "We knew when we drafted him that he had speed," said Bert Jones, "but we didn't know that he had *that* kind of speed." The game now resembled a see-saw affair, and most viewers expected Oakland to answer Baltimore's quick score with one more of their own. The Raiders did not disappoint those expectations, but they endured a small speed bump along the way. Laird intercepted another Stabler pass at 10:39 of the third quarter, but Oakland's defense forced a punt in three plays. That punt appeared to be a game-breaking play. Colts' punter David Lee was rushed quickly by three Oakland defenders, one of whom was linebacker Ted Hendricks, who took a swipe at Lee's punt and blocked it. "Actually, I was running by the punt," recalled Hendricks, "so I stuck my arm out to the side, and my forearm hit the ball solid." Reserve Oakland linebacker Jeff Barnes snared the ball as it descended and returned it to the Colts' 16-yard line before being driven out of bounds. Three plays later, Stabler hit Casper for another touchdown. Stabler once again displayed his customary poise in the pocket on this 10-yard scoring play, as he flung the ball with a sidearm delivery with Baltimore lineman Fred Cook draped all over his legs, trying in vain to pull him to the ground. The Raiders thus once again took the lead, 21–17.

Baltimore answered Oakland's score by launching their best scoring drive of the game at the beginning of the fourth quarter. A 13-play, 80-yard march was culminated with a fourth and goal run from the 1-yard line by burly Colts running back Ron Lee, who used his brawn and muscle to dive up and over the goal line. Baltimore's advantage now stood at 24–21, but there was still over ten minutes left in the fourth quarter, and that was plenty of time for the Raiders to put more points on the scoreboard. This they did on their very next possession. Oakland kick returner Carl Garrett returned Linhart's kickoff 44 yards. A few plays later, Stabler threw deep once again for Branch, but Baltimore cornerback Nelson Munsey was called for pass interference in the end zone. On the very next play, reserve Raiders running back Pete Banaszak plowed over right guard from the 1-yard line to score. Oakland had once again recaptured the lead, 28–24.

By this time, two probable scenarios appeared to be the impetus for the climax to this game. Either the team that had the ball last would win, or the defense that was able to stop the opposing offense just once in the final quarter would produce a victory for their team. The Colts wasted no time as the final quarter neared its midway point. Baltimore went through the Oakland defense like a rigid hot knife through a soft Maryland crab in four quick plays to score once more. Jones hit his tight end, Raymond Chester, for a 30-yard pass across the middle. Ron Lee then took over for the Baltimore offense. He caught one pass for 16 yards and a first down, then ran a sweep to his left for 14 yards and another first down. Lee completed the drive on a brilliant cutback run for a 13-yard touchdown. The Colts moved back in front, 31–28, with 7:45 left in the fourth quarter.

Two more exchanges of possessions from both teams left only 2:55 on the clock. The tension and pressure of the moment mounted on the backs of the Baltimore defense as the fourth quarter was grinding to an end. They had made some great plays earlier in the game to thwart Oakland drives. Just a few more defensive stops and the Colts were bound for the AFC title game. One more forced Oakland punt and Baltimore would win the game. They were unable to accomplish this, however. The Raiders were 70 long yards away from the winning score, and they faced a crucial third down situation. Oakland desperately needed one big play, and fortunately for them they got it. Stabler saw that both of his primary receivers were covered, so he threw deep for Casper, who was running a deep post route. Casper had to readjust his route to the flight of the ball, however. He managed to do so, and made a splendid over-the-back-of-his-head catch as the ball descended into his arms. The 42-yard play was forever labeled as "Ghost to the Post," paying homage to Casper's nickname ("Ghost") and identifying his pass route. "When Casper made that catch, it kind of took the wind out of our sails," said Laird. Oakland linebacker Monte Johnson expressed his optimism in contrast to Baltimore's dejection. "I just had that feeling we were going to win," said Johnson. "I felt it when Kenny threw that pass to Casper and he made that all-pro play." Casper's great catch still left Oakland head coach John Madden with a major decision to make, however. His Raiders were trailing by three points with 29 seconds left on the clock. They had moved the ball down to the Baltimore 5-yard line after Casper's miraculous grab, and it soon became fourth and goal for the Pride and Poise boys. Madden discussed the matter on the sideline with his assistant coaches and Stabler during a timeout, then decided to go for the tying field goal instead of the winning touchdown, hoping that his team would be able to win the game in overtime. Oakland placekicker Errol Mann booted the 22-yard field goal, thus tying the game at 31–31. Regulation was over, and ready or not, both teams headed into the overtime period.

Sudden death overtime in the playoffs during the 1970s declared that the first team to score in any manner would win the game. Both teams would play as many 15-minute periods as needed in the postseason until a team scored the winning points. Neither the Raiders nor the Colts could manage to score during the first 15-minute overtime period. Both had a couple of chances, but both defenses stiffened up and stopped the opposing offenses. Yet it was the Oakland offense which continued to move the ball better than their foes, and that consistency proved to be the deciding factor in this contest. Raiders wide receiver Cliff Branch converted a key third-and-19 situation with a 19-yard diving reception late in the first overtime period. Several plays later in the early stages of the second overtime period, the Raiders found themselves on the Baltimore 10-yard line. Coach Madden disdained a field goal for the win, and instead allowed Stabler to throw a play-action pass to the end zone. Oakland's Dave Casper caught his third touchdown pass of the game with another over-the-shoulder catch, and this pivotal AFC playoff game was in the history books. "The final play was designed for Casper all the way," Stabler described. "He's as good a receiver as there is. He was open. I saw him beat his man right away." Casper described his strategy on the game-winning play in simple terms. "I just had to run to the corner of the end zone as fast as I could," said Casper. "It was a play-pass. You just hope the cornerback is sucked up on the fake." Baltimore cornerback Nelson Munsey did indeed bite on Stabler's fake, and this final mistake ended the Colts' 1977 season.

The Raiders had prevailed, 37–31, and thus had won their first road playoff game since their inception in the old AFL in 1960. The game lasted 75 minutes and 43 seconds, making it one of those marathon games for the ages. "It was a great football game," said an understated Madden afterward. It also marked the last time that a playoff contest would be held in Baltimore's Memorial Stadium. Sadly for the Colts, their loss to the Raiders would also mark their final taste of the playoffs in the decade, as they failed to reach the postseason in 1978 and 1979. The Raiders advanced to the AFC championship game for the sixth time in the past eight years, thanks to their gut-check performance in a game labeled for posterity as the Ghost to the Post game.

The Raiders' opponent in the 1977 AFC title game was none other than their divisional rivals, the upstart Denver Broncos. The game would be played at Denver's Mile High Stadium on Sunday, January 1. The temperature topped off at a cold 18 degrees, and the puffing breaths of the players resembled two teams of train engines spewing smoke all game long. A bright Rocky Mountain sunshine was emblematic of how the game would be remembered by Colorado fans for generations. Both teams had won once in their head-to-head meetings during the regular season. This game would be for all of the marbles, however. A ticket to Super Bowl XII was the prize, and it would become one of the most memorable games in Broncos history.

Oakland's first drive showcased their playoff game experience. The Raiders put together an

18-play, 54-yard drive to begin the game. Denver's Orange Crush defense kept the Silver and Black out of the end zone, however. Oakland placekicker Errol Mann culminated his team's initial possession with a 20-yard field goal, giving the Raiders a 3–0 lead.

Denver would strike for its first big play just moments later. Broncos quarterback Craig Morton came out of a hospital bed to play in this game, and even though he still had painful injuries to his hip and to several of his other joints and muscles, he still proved capable of dropping back and throwing short passes before a charging defensive line like Oakland's could sack him. On second down from the Denver 26-yard line, Morton sent wide receiver Haven Moses on a medium-length pattern which caused him to cut towards the sideline, just in front of Raiders safety Alonzo "Skip" Thomas. Morton's pass was perfect, and it arrived in Moses' grasp quickly enough to give the receiver a chance to react to Thomas' hit. Thomas, known to many by his "affectionate" nick-name "Doctor Death," tried to arm-tackle Moses' shoulders, and at the very least, drive him out of bounds, because Moses was skirting the sideline. But Moses was a little too quick for Thomas, and he broke free from the cornerback's grasp. From there, Moses sprinted untouched to the end zone to complete the 74-yard scoring play. "It was a zig out and Haven ran it perfectly," said Morton. The Broncos took a 7–3 lead amidst their cheering fans, and would keep that lead going into halftime.

Prior to intermission, however, Oakland wide receiver Fred Biletnikoff suffered a dislocated shoulder injury going across the middle on a pass pattern. The loss of Biletnikoff would affect the Raiders' passing attack throughout the entire second half, and would force Stabler to rely on other options if his team was to move the ball against the Denver defense. Neither team was able to move the ball via their ground attacks through much of the game. But it was one particular running play in the third quarter which garnished plenty of attention. So much so, in fact, that the play is still remembered even today for its outcome.

Reserve Denver defensive lineman Brison Manor recovered a Clarence Davis fumble deep in Oakland territory a few plays into the third quarter. Denver then quickly drove the ball down to the Oakland 2-yard line and were looking to increase their lead. Then came a play which would live forever in infamy and NFL lore. On first and goal, Morton handed off to rookie running back Rob Lytle on a quick dive play. Oakland safety Jack Tatum immediately met Lytle at the line of scrimmage and delivered a powerful hit, knocking Lytle dizzy and knocking the ball loose. "That was one of the hardest hits I've ever seen or heard," admitted Oakland defensive lineman John Matuszak. "Lytle got the crap knocked out of him and fumbled the ball." Oakland reserve defensive tackle Mike McCoy recovered the ball and immediately got up and ran for the opposing goal line. Head linesman Ed Marion's whistle blew the play dead, however. The officials did not see the fumble, and claimed that Lytle's forward progress was stopped prior to the fumble that they failed to observe. Instant replays on television proved otherwise, and the clamor among fans, players and coaches alike (especially Raider fans, players and coaches) resumed their shouts for an instant replay system to finally be installed in the league. Such a permanent change to the way referees officiated games was years in the future, however. The pleas to keep the "human element" in the game still resounded just a bit louder than the hue and cry for modern electronics to make on-field decisions. Nevertheless, the Rob Lytle fumble in the 1977 AFC title game would add yet another example that pro-instant replay advocates referred to when arguing their position before the league's competition committee in the off-season, and in many off-seasons after 1977.

The groggy Lytle was helped off the field after the play, and the referees added salt to the Oakland wound after they gave the ball back to Denver by penalizing Raider linebacker Floyd Rice for unsportsmanlike conduct. Rice apparently mentioned his displeasure with the officials, and they in turn mentioned their displeasure with his vocabulary by showing him a yellow hanky.

Denver now had the ball at the 1-yard line. Morton quick-pitched the ball to running back Jon Keyworth, who ran a sweep to his right and followed a tremendous block by running mate Otis Armstrong into the end zone for a touchdown. The Broncos now possessed a 14–3 lead.

The Raiders were still miffed at Lytle's "non-fumble," and they answered Denver's touchdown with one of their own on the second play of the fourth quarter. Stabler hit tight end Dave Casper for a 7-yard score to culminate a 48-yard drive. Casper was double teamed all game long, and was held to zero catches in the first half. He finally broke into the open on his touchdown, beating Denver linebacker Joe Rizzo on a down-and-in pattern. Oakland now trailed by a score of 14–10. There was still plenty of time remaining in the game, as Denver got the ball back following Casper's touchdown with 14:11 left. Both teams then traded interceptions, but when Denver linebacker Bob Swenson picked off Stabler, he set up the Broncos for the winning touchdown. Facing a third-and-five situation with the ball on the Oakland 12-yard line, Morton dropped back and avoided the Oakland pass rush just long enough to find Moses breaking free of coverage deep in the end zone. Morton fired a dart which Moses caught low to the ground for his second touchdown. "That last touchdown was set for [tight end] Riley Odoms," Morton explained, "but he slipped and then was double-teamed. Haven ran his pattern, then saw it break, so he went to the left and I fired and he made a great catch." Denver placekicker Jim Turner missed the extra point (he had also missed three field goals in the game), but the Broncos now owned a 20–10 advantage halfway through the final quarter.

It took the Raiders just eight plays to answer Denver's touchdown with one of their own. Once again, Stabler found Casper in the end zone for a 17-yard score to complete a 74-yard drive. Casper made another spectacular grab, this one coming in between Denver linebacker Tom Jackson and Denver defensive back Bernard Jackson. Oakland's Mann converted on his extra point attempt, however (unlike his opponent Jim Turner), leaving the Raiders a mere field goal from a tie. Time was of the essence at this point in the contest, though. For Denver to hold on to their 20–17 lead, they would need to run off the final 3:08 left on the clock. The Broncos kept the ball on the ground, with reserve runner Lonnie Perrin carrying the ball three times and converting one third down play into a first down. Oakland was forced to use up all of their time outs, but the Broncos still maintained possession of the ball. A short run for another first down by halfback Otis Armstrong and a final kneel down by Morton ended the greatest game in Denver history (up to that time), as the Broncos prevailed 20–17, thus winning their first ever AFC championship. Denver head coach Robert "Red" Miller got a glorious victory ride on the shoulders of his players, and one of the most unpredictable Cinderella teams finally made it to the big dance, otherwise known as the Super Bowl. "You have to play hard and we did," said Moses, who did his share of leading the Broncos to the promised land. "This is a big, big day for the team and for Denver."

After the AFC title game, most of the talk in the Oakland locker room dealt with Rob Lytle's fumble, which was strangely similar to Baltimore quarterback Bert Jones' fumble during the Patriots-Colts game on December 18. The result on both occasions was a play that was blown dead, and the ball returning to the possession of the offense. There was no arguing the fact that no team during the 1970s saw or endured more controversial calls than the Oakland Raiders. Some went in their favor, but many did not. Oakland head coach John Madden—to his credit—refused to criticize the referees and preferred not to dwell on Lytle's fumble after the game when speaking to the reporters. "Sure I felt we should have had the ball," said Madden. "But it's a sixty-minute game. It doesn't boil down to one play or one person."

The Dallas Cowboys brain trust certainly felt that one person was the reason why they were back in the NFC title game. Rookie running back Tony Dorsett finished his inaugural year in the NFL with 1,007 yards rushing. He was named Rookie of the Year, and the threat of him breaking long runs on virtually every carry put fear in the hearts and minds of all defensive coordinators in the NFL. Dorsett himself never felt like he was the key to the success of the Cowboys, but it was generally felt that without the former University of Pittsburgh star, the Cowboys would not have dominated the league like they did in 1977. The Dallas attack would be taking on the Minnesota Vikings in the NFC championship game. The Vikings were considered by most experts to be lucky to have gotten this far in 1977. Virtually no one thought that their aging squad could have returned to the Super Bowl, especially after losing quarterback Fran Tarkenton to injury for the second half of the season. Yet the Vikings persevered, won several close games, came from behind to win some others, and somehow pulled off an upset over host Los Angeles in the divisional playoffs to get to within one game of Super Bowl XII.

The 1977 NFC championship game included a couple of instances of pathos to go with the action on the field. Some Viking fans coming down from Minnesota for the game decided to bring suitcases filled with snow from the Northland. Some of those fans were successful in bringing those suitcases into the stadium, and they were seen throwing snowballs at Dallas players during the pregame warm-ups. They were quickly informed of the error of their ways by the Texas Stadium security personnel. Then a frightening accident occurred early in the second quarter. The temperatures in Dallas on January 1 were a frigid (for Texas) 30 degrees. According to the *Dallas Morning News*, a spectator named Daniel Yoder was walking down an aisle in Section 9 when he brushed against a flaming can of Sterno held by a 16-year-old girl, who was selling hot chocolate in the stands. Yoder wore a snowman costume to the game, and that costume caught fire around his shoulders. A panic in the stands occurred immediately. Yoder stumbled into the girl, and the liquid fuel from the Sterno can poured down the front of his costume. He ended up with second degree burns over 15 percent of his body, mostly on his legs and neck. He was released from the hospital six days later. Another spectator was the main person credited with putting out the fire. Clarence Walters covered Yoder with his coat to extinguish the flames. The fire burned off Walters' moustache, some of his hair on the right side of his head, and the fur collar of his coat. Walters was apparently not hurt, however, as he sat down after the incident and watched the rest of the game. As is the custom with most accidents, Yoder's lawyer announced a lawsuit against Texas Stadium and the costume company, but it was either never officially filed or it was settled quietly.

The Cowboys caught on fire figuratively in the early moments of the first quarter. Dallas All-Pro defensive end Harvey Martin followed up his 23-sack regular season by recovering a fumble by Minnesota running back Robert Miller, who never quite got a handle on the handoff from Vikings quarterback Bob Lee. Two plays later from the Minnesota 32-yard line, Dallas quarterback Roger Staubach hit wide receiver Golden Richards for a touchdown. Richards snuck behind Vikings cornerback Bobby Bryant, who took the bait on the pump fake screen by Staubach. "I almost started to run on that play," said Staubach. "I was so close to the line of scrimmage and then I saw Golden open." Dallas placekicker Efren Herrera missed the ensuing extra point. Herrera had an excellent regular season, hitting 39 of 41 extra point attempts. But he would have his share of problems in the postseason.

The 6–0 Dallas lead held up throughout the remainder of the first quarter. In the second quarter, Dallas fullback Robert Newhouse completed an eight-play, 46-yard drive with a 5-yard touchdown run. Veteran Viking placekicker Fred Cox then kicked two field goals (of 32 and 37 yards) to answer the Dallas touchdowns. Herrera booted a 21-yard field goal for Dallas with five seconds left to end the second quarter. The Cowboys went to the warmth of their locker room owning a 16–6 halftime lead. A couple of Dallas Cowboys Cheerleaders also warmed up during halftime by joining the indoor CBS-TV location set in the Stadium Club of Texas Stadium. They provided some on-air scenery and chatted with the NFL Today's television crew of Brent Musberger,

Irv Cross, Jimmy "The Greek" Snyder, and Phyllis George. The halftime show on the field featured the Thomas Jefferson High School Band of Minneapolis, Minnesota, and it seemed that they— along with the Vikings—brought the cold weather down south with them.

The third quarter of the game produced no new scoring, but quite a few punts. One punt midway through the fourth quarter, however, pointed the way to victory for the Cowboys. Minnesota punt returner Manfred Moore attempted to return Danny White's 40-yard punt. Moore was hit hard as soon as he turned upfield by Dallas linebacker Thomas Henderson (who came in high) and by Dallas defensive back Mark Washington (who came in low). Henderson flew into Moore's body with the speed and velocity of a torpedo, thereby dislodging the ball from Moore's grasp. Reserve Dallas tight end Jay Saldi dove for the ball and secured it before it went out of bounds. "Well, it was being in the right place at the right time," said Saldi. Five plays later, Dorsett took a handoff from Staubach and ran right behind pulling guards Herbert Scott and Tom Rafferty. Dorsett was hit hard by Dallas defensive back Nate Wright at the goal line, be he managed to hold on to the ball and score from 11 yards out, giving the Cowboys an insurmountable 23–6 advantage. "I thought it was an excellent call," said Dorsett. "We were in the spread [formation] and I knew they [Minnesota] expected the pass. I was hungry for the ball. When I broke through the line and saw the flag, I knew we either had six [points] or the ball was on the one-inch line."

The 23–6 score remained unchanged as the final gun sounded, and Dallas found themselves back in the Super Bowl for the fourth time in the past eight years. "It's a happy new year for us," said Dallas head coach Tom Landry. "We're very happy to be going to the Super Bowl. Overall, our defense was outstanding this year."

Super Bowl XII would be a matchup of Denver's Broncomania versus the calm, cool, and collected Cowboys of Dallas. The game would be played in New Orleans in the Louisiana Superdome, and would make history as the first Super Bowl to be played indoors. It would also be the first Super Bowl to have an early evening kickoff time, slated for 6 p.m. on the east coast. Denver used the historic opportunity of their first visit to the Super Bowl to honor their past as an original member of the AFL. Several Broncos players wore brown and gold striped socks, used by the first Denver team in 1960, in their pregame warm-up. Speaking of history, a pair of former teammates quarterbacked both clubs in Super Bowl XII. Craig Morton once played for Dallas, and was on their roster in Super Bowls V and VI. Now in an ironical twist of fate he was the signal caller for the Denver Broncos, as he tried to defeat his old team for a championship. Roger Staubach led the Cowboys to a Super Bowl VI victory, but his most recent exposure to the Super Bowl was a loss to the Pittsburgh Steelers in Super Bowl X. There was no doubt that Staubach wanted to erase that memory somewhat, and a victory over his old friend Morton in Super Bowl XII would go a long way in obtaining that goal.

Both teams had excellent defenses. Both Orange Crush for Denver and Doomsday for Dallas would make their marks in this game, and cause a bunch of turnovers. There were a total of 10 turnovers among both teams in Super Bowl XII, which was just one fewer than the record set between the Cowboys and the Colts in Super Bowl V. There were also several more fumbles which were recovered by the fumbling team, as well as a total of 20 penalties among both teams, making this one of the more sloppier Super Bowls ever played. The Dallas flex defense did its usual good job stopping the opposing running attack, but it outdid itself in shutting down the Denver air game. "Doomsday" permitted a Super Bowl record of only 35 net passing yards by Denver all day. The Dallas defensive line blew into Morton's pocket, sacked him twice, and hurried his passes on virtually every one of his dropbacks. "Rushing the passer was the key to it, as far as we were concerned," said Dallas head coach Tom Landry. "We knew if we gave Craig time, he could hurt us. So we wanted a big rush. Craig didn't have a chance. Our rush was on him before he could respond."

The Cowboys defensive secondary also intercepted four of Morton's passes, the first of which on a second-down play midway through the first quarter led to the first score of the game. Dallas safety Charlie Waters blitzed and hit Morton in harmony with a hit on the Denver quarterback from Cowboys defensive tackle Randy White. Morton's wounded duck of a pass was intercepted by reserve Dallas defensive back Randy Hughes at the Denver 25-yard line. Hughes would go on to recover two fumbles in the game to go with his interception. "They took away everything we had," lamented Morton. "Even when I audibled their defense made an adjustment to the play I called."

The Cowboys capitalized on their first gift from Morton when they drove down to the Denver 3-yard line. Dallas halfback Tony Dorsett ran over Denver defensive backs Bernard Jackson and Bill Thompson on a fourth and goal play and scored standing up. Two more Broncos turnovers resulted in two field goals from Dallas placekicker Efren Herrera. Dallas took a 13–0 lead into halftime, but it could have been worse for the Broncos. Herrera missed on three other field goal attempts in the first half, the longest of which was from 44 yards out. Had Herrera made those three kicks, Dallas would have taken an insurmountable 22–0 lead into halftime. As it was, Denver still had a chance to come back. The spirit that had sustained them throughout the regular season and their two postseason victories was needed now more than ever.

Denver got to work immediately in the third quarter with an eight-play drive that concluded with a 47-yard field goal from veteran placekicker Jim Turner. The Orange Crush defense had delivered a sound performance in the first half, as they sacked mobile Dallas quarterback Roger Staubach four times (Staubach would be sacked once more in the second half). That defense would continue to blitz Staubach in the third quarter, so the Dallas running backs stayed in the backfield to block, allowing Staubach a precious extra second or two in the pocket to locate his receivers. Staubach utilized that extra time when he delivered a pinpoint pass to streaking tight end Butch Johnson for 45 yards and a touchdown midway through the third quarter. The spectacular play increased Dallas' lead to 20–3. On the scoring play, Johnson outraced Denver defensive backs Bernard Jackson and Steve Foley, dove for the ball and caught it with his fingertips, then incredibly twisted his body in mid-air, which enabled him to land on his back one yard past the goal line. As Dallas radio station KRLD play-by-play announcer Verne Lundquist aptly described, "It was a *sensational* catch." The ball popped loose out of Johnson's grasp after his body rolled on the AstroTurf for a brief moment, causing Foley to complain that Johnson did not have possession of the ball long enough for a valid reception, but field judge Bob Wortman ruled otherwise, as once Johnson had the ball in his grasp as the ball crossed the plane of the goal line, a touchdown was scored. Anything that Johnson did with the ball (as in fumbling it) after the goal line was crossed was irrelevant. "That catch took a lot of air out of us," admitted Denver defensive lineman Lyle Alzado. "I've never seen one like it." Referee Jim Tunney said afterward, "He [Johnson] caught the ball in the air, in flight, and crossed the goal line in possession and came to the ground in the end zone. Then he released the ball. He didn't fumble the ball—he hit the ground, then released it." Johnson's catch was even more amazing when considering that he made it after his right thumb was broken earlier in the second quarter while blocking a Denver defender.

It seemed as if Dallas had taken Denver's best punch and had delivered a better one right back at them. The symbolic punches continued on the ensuing kickoff, as Denver kick returner Rick Upchurch dashed and darted through several missed tackles for 67 yards, giving the Broncos their best starting field position of the game at the Dallas 26-yard line. Denver head coach Robert "Red" Miller decided at this moment to replace Morton at the quarterback position with Norris Weese, who unlike Morton had the ability to escape the Dallas pass rush with his two younger and healthier legs. Weese led the Broncos downfield to score their only touchdown of the game.

Denver running back Rob Lytle burrowed into the mass of humanity at the line of scrimmage and ended up in the end zone for a 1-yard scoring run. Denver now trailed Dallas 20–10 at the end of the third quarter.

Both teams exchanged possession of the ball several times until midway through the fourth quarter. Denver faced a third-and-four situation from their 30-yard line when the unrelenting Dallas pass rush struck once again. Dallas defensive end Harvey Martin wrapped Weese up and forced another fumble, this one recovered by Dallas cornerback Aaron Kyle (who also intercepted a Morton pass earlier in the game). Kyle's recovery set up the clinching score of the game. Tom Landry sent in a gadget play that according to the Cowboys, failed to work at all during the two weeks of practices prior to the game. Staubach pitched the ball to fullback Robert Newhouse, who was running left as if on a sweep. Newhouse abruptly stopped and turned to face the end zone, however. He threw an arching pass into the hands of Dallas wide receiver Golden Richards, who beat Denver safety Steve Foley just inside the end zone. Richards squeezed the ball to his chest for a 29-yard touchdown, and Dallas squeezed the final drops of competition out of the Orange Crush defense. Robert Newhouse thus became the first running back in NFL history to throw a touchdown pass in a Super Bowl. "It was a perfect pass," said Richards. "I was nervous about throwing the ball," confessed Newhouse, who had to lick a bunch of stickum substance off of his hands in the huddle prior to the play so he could release the ball properly. "I was tempted to run, but then I remembered it was one of Coach Landry's all-or-nothing plays so I threw. There's no way the Broncos would have expected me to throw running left."

The Cinderella season of the Broncos met with a losing ending, but the Broncos and their

Ed "Too Tall" Jones of the Dallas Cowboys hits Denver Broncos quarterback Craig Morton in Super Bowl XII, January 15, 1978, in the Louisiana Superdome. The Dallas Doomsday Defense forced eight Denver turnovers, as the Cowboys prevailed, 27–10 (AP Photo/Vernon Biever).

fans were nevertheless proud. They had proved that spirit and desire could take an unlikely under-dog team to within a few touchdowns of pro football's summit.

As the final few minutes of Super Bowl XII wound down, the Dallas Cowboys Cheerleaders were on the sidelines cheering, "We're number one!" and "Super Bowl champs!" A bevy of Orange Crush soda cans lie crushed and dented on the AstroTurf section of the Dallas bench area. The 27–10 Dallas victory was complete with a victory ride off the field for Tom Landry, his second such glory ride of the decade. A pair of Dallas defensive linemen—Randy White and Harvey Martin—were named co–MVPs, the first (and so far only) time in Super Bowl history for such an honor to be bestowed upon two players. For only the second time in the decade, an NFC team won a Super Bowl. On both instances, it was the Cowboys who captured the Lombardi Trophy, their first coming in 1971 in Super Bowl VI. The Cowboys had compiled an NFC-best 18 wins over AFC teams from 1970 to 1977, and they had won 82 regular season games during the same time period, which was the second-best mark in their conference. Dallas general manager Tex Schramm mentioned prior to the 1977 NFL draft, "If we can get Dorsett, we can win the Super Bowl." The Cowboys did indeed get Dorsett, and Schramm's prediction came true. The missing piece to the Cowboys' Super Bowl puzzle was finally in place, and the Dallas dynasty appeared to be stronger than ever.

1978

The Game Adjusts and Renews Itself

The 1978 NFL season would see more lasting and important rule changes in how the game was played on the field than in any other season during the entire decade of the 1970s. The new rules would test each coaching staff's ability to refine and rewrite their playbooks to incorporate the new rules. Coaching staffs throughout the league were rushing to help their players adjust to the new regulations. Each team would try to restructure their rosters in order to obtain more faster and athletic players, many of whom would be in the best position to take advantage of the new rules. The 1978 season would also see more coaching changes and more major player trades than in any other year in the decade, ignited at least in part by the addition of the new rules. The rule reforms that originated in 1978 are incredibly still affecting the way the game is played today, almost 40 years later. One of those big changes involved the season itself; most notably, the length of the season. NFL teams during the formative years of the 1920s would often play an irregular number of games. The Duluth Eskimos played a total of 29 games in one season (1926), with 27 of those contests coming on the road. The Eskimo players practically lived in passenger trains as they barnstormed the nation. The league became more organized as the years went on, however, and the 14-game regular season schedule became the norm in 1961. That norm lasted until 1978, when a shortened preseason melded with a lengthened regular season. The preseason went from six games to four for most teams. The two teams chosen to play in the annual Hall of Fame Game in Canton, Ohio, would each have an extra preseason game on their slate. The regular season was increased to 16 games in 1978, and its effect was immediate and lasting. As was predictable, many players and coaches were opposed to the two extra regular season games.

"It's bad for the players for a couple of reasons," said Los Angeles Rams defensive back Dave Elmendorf. "For one thing, we don't get any more money for playing two extra games. The other thing is that the veterans will end up playing more because the preseason has been reduced. Now, we will have to play more in the third and fourth preseason games to get ready for the season. Simply, we're playing more for the same money." Denver Broncos head coach Red Miller worried that the new 16-game schedule would put too much strain on the 45-man team rosters, which fortunately increased by two players over the 43-man team rosters from the previous three seasons. "Boy, it's going to take its toll," Miller said.

Trying to make a professional roster with two less preseason games would also be more difficult for the bevy of rookies throughout the league. "I have seen rookies start out slow, then really come on from the third or fourth week of preseason," said Oakland Raiders reserve running back Warren Bankston. "The way it's going to be now, a rookie will no longer have that luxury. If you're a low draft choice or a free agent, you had better show something early or you'll be gone." Bankston's head coach, John Madden, concurred with Bankston's opinion. "The difference is we're going to have eight fewer quarters to get everybody ready," Madden said. "That means I won't be able to play some of my backup people as much as I would like."

The longer regular season schedule would benefit the owners and the fans, however. The league signed new contracts with the three major television networks (ABC, CBS, and NBC), and each team was slated to make an extra $5 to $6 million from those deals, thanks to the two extra regular season games, which would attract much more revenue than the two lost preseason games. The new television contracts also called for several prime-time games on Thursday and Sunday nights. The fans were still shelling out a tidy sum of money to go to the games, but those fans who owned season tickets now no longer had to spend the same amount of money for two more meaningless preseason games. Instead, each season ticket holder would see eight home regular season games, as opposed to seven home games from the previous years.

The structural makeup of the new 16-game regular season schedule was also new in 1978. There would still be the usual home and away contests between teams in each division, but now there would also be a system in place where all teams in each division would play teams from another conference and division on a round-robin format. For example, teams from the NFC East would play teams from the AFC West. The following year, they would play teams from the AFC East. The year after that, they would play teams from the AFC Central. If a team finished in second place in their division, they would play a second place team from another division. The same was true when teams from one division played a team from another division in their own conference. The system did have its share of inequities, though. A fourth-place team would end up playing five divisional champions, while a fifth-place team would face three first-place teams and four fifth-place teams. Despite this, the structure still had more balance than schedules from previous years. It also let the fans know what opponents their favorite teams would face in the upcoming season as soon as the current regular season concluded. Finally, the 1978 season called for the addition of another wild card team in each conference, thereby increasing the total number of playoff teams from eight to 10. The two wild card teams in each conference would face each other the week after the conclusion of the regular season. "Before, there were questions about where the schedule came from," recalled Madden. "Now you know exactly where you're going to be. At least now we all understand it."

Many players on the offensive side of the line of scrimmage eventually understood that the two extra games could be beneficial, especially if they were trying to break team or league records. Scoring, yardage, and receiving records would all fall by the wayside in time with those two extra games. Aiding the increased offensive output would be 12 new rules changes in 1978. Two of the major rules changes would revolutionize the pro game for years to come. The first involved offensive linemen, who were now allowed to extend their arms to pass block. Prior to 1978, they were required to keep their elbows bent and their hands completely out of view of the referees. The new blocking technique in 1978 also stipulated that the offensive linemen were now allowed to grasp the jersey of the defensive linemen that they were blocking, as long as their grasp stayed within the frame of their shoulders. These obvious advantages gave offensive linemen an enormous edge in pass blocking, and as a result, it also gave their quarterbacks more time to throw the ball. Moreover, it lessened the amount of quarterback sacks from the defense. Every defensive lineman was understandably miffed at this new direction in rule changes, most of whom called it "legalized holding." According to former Cleveland Browns head coach Nick Skorich, who served as the assistant supervisor of NFL officials in 1978, the new blocking rule would help the offenses in several ways. "Basically in giving offensive blockers more leeway, we feel the number of holding calls should go down," Skorich claimed, "and there should be fewer injuries to quarterbacks. It could possibly help make the scrambler even more effective."

The second new rule on the field involved defensive backs. From 1978 on, defensive backs could only hit or obstruct receivers for five yards past the line of scrimmage. After five yards, defensive backs were required to keep their hands off of the receivers. The "illegal chuck" rule— as it was called—was also commonly referred to as the "Mel Blount rule." Mel Blount was an All-Pro cornerback for the Pittsburgh Steelers who was generally recognized as the toughest cornerback in the NFL in the latter part of the decade, and the one who made it most difficult for receivers to run their routes. Receivers with the new rule in place could now run their patterns unimpeded after five yards and with relative safety. The rule makers were not done with those two epochal rule changes, however. Another new rule permitted a ball to be deflected from one offensive player to another. Such an occurrence would have been declared an illegal catch prior to 1978, unless a defensive player touched the ball in between the two offensive players. The new deflection rule would be on display in a crucial game later in the season between Atlanta and New Orleans. Finally, the league decided to prohibit the use of tear-away jerseys, claiming that they (the tear-away jerseys) were not supporting a player's shoulder pads adequately, and that the constant changing of torn jerseys created undue delays in the game. Cleveland halfback Greg Pruitt was the league's accepted spokesman for tear-away jerseys, as he usually had anywhere from 10 to 15 of them torn in every game. The Browns typically had 20 jerseys prepared for Pruitt every Sunday. Now he only needed one. Incidentally, Pruitt's 960 rushing yardage in 1978 was 126 yards less than his 1086 ground yards in 1977.

Miami Dolphins head coach Don Shula was a member throughout the decade of the NFL's Competition Committee. He fought against the addition of new rules for many years, but he eventually relented and voted for them in 1978. "I'm a defensive coach with a defensive background," Shula explained, "but I was willing to compromise. The owners wanted to do something to produce more offense and the fans indicated that they wanted more scoring. To me, it was great the way we had it. But I had to look at the entire picture and I was willing to compromise as long as the integrity of the game was not violated. [With] the changes will be more scoring, more TD passes and more touchdowns." Dallas defensive secondary coach Gene Stallings concurred with Shula. "The plain and simple fact," admitted Stallings, "is that the new rule was designed to open up the passing game. It's going to make it a lot harder to play defense. I know that."

Needless to say, the defensive backs across the league were upset by the new rule concerning wide receiver coverages. "Next year they'll probably rule that you can have a maximum of only three [defensive backs] in the secondary," said a disgruntled and slightly sarcastic Dallas cornerback Aaron Kyle. "There is no way you can disguise what the defense is trying to do under the new rule. When you have to cheat a man up close to the line so he can get that bump in within the legitimate area, you've given away any advantage you might have had."

Perhaps the thought of making it tougher on defensive backs was going through Oakland safety Jack Tatum's mind. Maybe it was just his way of saying that he was not going to change the way he played the game, with all-out abandon and complete disregard for his (or anyone else's) physical well being. Regardless of his reasons, in a preseason game against the visiting New England Patriots on August 12, 1978, Tatum hit Patriots wide receiver Darryl Stingley head-on as Stingley ran a pass pattern across the middle of the field. The pass was overthrown and sailed over Stingley's head by several feet, but Stingley—being the pro that he was—leaped for it anyway. Tatum leaped too, and launched his body into Stingley's head and chest. Stingley crashed to the turf, and his body was not moving. To many nearby observers, it appeared that the motionless receiver was not even breathing. Panic and prayers filled the fans in the stands and the players of both teams. This horrific scene saw Stingley being placed very gently on a stretcher, then being taken away in an ambulance and rushed to a nearby hospital. Within hours, it was determined that his neck was

New England Patriots team trainers and doctors attend to wide receiver Darryl Stingley, injured by Oakland Raiders safety Jack Tatum in a preseason game at Oakland on August 13, 1978. Stingley was paralyzed from the neck down for the rest of his life as a result of Tatum's hit, and players and fans all across the country were once again suddenly reacquainted with the dangerous nature and innate risks of playing pro football (AP Photo).

broken in two places and that there was serious damage to his spinal cord. Stingley would be paralyzed from his chest down for the rest of his life. His football career was over in an instant, and his life was changed forever. Tatum's life was changed also.

"It was one of those pass plays where I could not possibly have intercepted," Tatum described, "so I automatically reacted to the situation by going for an intimidating hit. When the reality of Stingley's injury hit me with its full impact, I was shattered. I didn't know if I could ever play football again. I had some very trying hours talking with doctors about Darryl's condition. That was constantly on my mind and tearing at my insides. I am tough, but I'm not a brutal animal."

Many people blamed Tatum, claiming that the safety could have and should have held up prior to hitting the receiver. Many people said that because the game was a preseason game, Tatum should not have launched his body into Stingley's upper torso, because the game did not mean anything in the standings, and because neither player was in jeopardy of losing their job. Some people blamed the way Tatum was coached to hit his vulnerable opponents—with reckless abandon. This was the type of incident that the NFL wanted to avoid at all costs, and almost immediately, more thoughts on overall player safety began to work its way into the player's union (NFLPA) and the league office. Stingley's injury was a sobering reminder that football was and is a violent game, and each player assumes a risk in suiting up and going on the field. Very few players decided to quit after witnessing Stingley's fate, however. Almost to a man, they agreed that the advantages of playing pro football outweighed the risk of possible injury.

Another couple of important events also occurred in the 1978 preseason. The rule makers finally relented—at least somewhat—in the discussion on the topic of instant replays. They observed that the Rob Lytle fumble in the 1977 AFC championship game was just too glaring to overlook. They decided to form an exploratory study on the use of instant replay as an officiating aid. The plan was to use a basic, no-frills instant replay system in seven nationally televised pre-season games. The results were inconclusive, but the hopes among the members of the league's competition committee was that this action would at least provide some useful data and possibly quell the active voices pleading for the addition of an instant replay system to be installed in all league games. Unfortunately for the competition committee, even more glaring examples of blown calls on the field and referee indecisions later in the 1978 season would increase the yelps from the populace for a permanent instant replay system to be used in the NFL—as soon as possible.

The other big news story during the 1978 preseason involved the continued growth of the game to extend to foreign countries. An NFL preseason contest was held for the first time ever in Mexico City, Mexico. This was not the first time that two NFL teams played a game outside of the United States. The St. Louis Cardinals played the San Diego Chargers in a 1976 preseason game in Tokyo, Japan. That overseas visit came off without a hitch, but such was not the case in Mexico City in 1978. The New Orleans Saints defeated the Philadelphia Eagles, 14–7, but the result of the game was a mere afterthought to the overall excursion. The big news from that afternoon involved the field conditions. Philadelphia quarterback Ron Jaworski's memories of that trip were probably not what the league hierarchy had in mind when they wanted the pro game to expand into a new market which had never seen the sport before. But both the Eagles and the Saints were guinea pigs, and any amount of misfortune on this visit to Mexico City would not deter the league from scheduling more preseason games (and eventually regular season games) in the future in foreign lands. Jaworski's take on his team's trip included the following: "It was, without a doubt, one of the worst weekends I've ever had in my life. You could see it [Mexico City] wasn't a beautiful city. All you could see were slums, some of the worst slums I'd ever seen. We got to the stadium and we walked about 100 yards through this tunnel that was very dark and very old. On the right we looked down and there were all the bulls for the bullring next door. You can imagine how it smelled. We [then] came out on the worst field that I've ever played on. On the sidelines there were lumps, rocks and gravel. It was a cow pasture. In one end zone there was a mound two feet higher than the rest of the end zone. The goal posts were crooked. The biggest cheer of the trip came when our back wheels [of the team plane] left the ground. A stewardess was passing out sodas and hit offensive lineman Stan Walters with one. That was an indication of what the trip [was] like."

Despite the Eagles' experiences in Mexico City, the league was in a mode of change, as they searched for positive results on many fronts. Overall, the NFL's best pass catchers would take immediate and full advantage of the new blocking and pass coverage rules, and receiving totals and yardage totals would go up exponentially for most teams in 1978. Oakland wide receiver Cliff Branch caught 16 more passes in 1978 than he did in 1977, worth 169 more yards. Minnesota pass catcher Ahmad Rashad caught 66 passes in 1978, an increase of 15 more receptions than the 51 balls he caught in 1977. Rashad's yardage went up too, from 681 yards in 1977 to 769 yards in 1978. Most receivers achieved similar results as Branch and Rashad, but two receivers *really* profited from the new rules. Philadelphia's Harold Carmichael caught nine more passes in 1978 than he did in 1977, but his yardage total skyrocketed from 665 yards in 1977 to 1,072 yards in 1978. Seattle's Steve Largent caught an AFC-best 71 passes in 1978, which was an amazing 38 more than his 33 receptions in 1977. His yardage totals increased dramatically from 643 yards in 1977 to 1,168 in 1978. These new receiving totals simply could not be ignored, and fans of offensive football and point scoring were very gleeful.

The league also did not ignore the idea to improve the quality of officiating during the off-season. They decided to add an extra referee called a side judge to help the other six officials on the field. Their reasoning being that an extra pair of eyes might help in seeing potential fumbles (like the Rob Lytle fumble in the 1977 AFC title game) and calling the play correctly. The side judge would be positioned on a typical play from scrimmage directly opposite across the field from the back judge, and would stand along the sideline in the defensive secondary.

Many new head coaches would also be standing along the sidelines in 1978. Perhaps the most surprising was Don Coryell's replacement in St. Louis. The Cardinals hired former legendary University of Oklahoma head coach Bud Wilkinson, considered one of the greatest college coaches in history. Wilkinson was a thoughtful teacher of the sport who led the Sooners to 145 victories (including 47 in a row) and three national championships from 1947 to 1963. He was also a gentlemanly competitor, much in the similar fashion as Tom Landry of Dallas. But many fans and pro football experts considered Wilkinson's time away from the game (he never coached pro football before 1978) to be detrimental to his chances. Time would tell if Wilkinson could adjust on the fly to the pro game. "I think I'm relatively current," said the 61-year-old Wilkinson, who spent his years after collegiate coaching as an analyst on the ABC network telecasts of college football. "Pro football is a high level of sophistication, but I think the factors are the same at any level."

Don Coryell had no problems adjusting to his new team, the San Diego Chargers. Coryell was a former head coach of San Diego State University prior to joining the Cardinals in 1973. He joined the Chargers after head coach Tommy Prothro resigned in the middle of the 1978 season. It would not take long for Coryell to infuse his pass-happy offensive schemes into the Chargers' playbook. Moreover, combined with the aforementioned new rules helping offenses and a strong-armed quarterback on the Chargers roster in the form of Dan Fouts, San Diego would soon be breaking many old team and league passing and receiving records. Fouts benefitted from the likes of rookie wide receiver John Jefferson, who rose like a meteor to become one of the league's most dangerous deep threats and who had a pair of the best hands in the game. Jefferson caught 56 passes for 1,001 yards and a league-leading 13 touchdowns in 1978. Only nine other players had more receptions, and only three players had more receiving yardage than Jefferson.

While Coryell moved out west, Chuck Knox moved east to be the head coach of the Buffalo Bills, who fired Jim Ringo after the 1977 season. "Our immediate goal is to be competitive," said Knox, "so week in and week out we'll play good, consistent football." George Allen moved back to Los Angeles to take Knox's old position. Allen was the head coach of the Rams previously, from 1966 to 1970. He was back for a second try in 1978, but unfortunately, Allen would last only two preseason games before the Rams ownership decided to fire him and replace him with assistant coach Ray Malavasi. The Rams front office was definitely in a state of flux; or at the least, continual change. They had announced during the spring that the team would be moving from Los Angeles to Anaheim in 1980. This team movement would be the first of several relocations by NFL franchises in the near future.

Jack Pardee, the former head coach of the Chicago Bears, moved back to coach the Washington Redskins, the team that he spent so many productive seasons as a player for George Allen. "Everybody has one job in their profession they would consider just about perfect for them," Pardee said, "and that's Washington for me." Neill Armstrong, a former Minnesota Vikings assistant coach, replaced Pardee in Chicago. Another longtime assistant coach, Marv Levy, was named the new head coach in Kansas City. Sam Rutigliano, a longtime assistant coach for several teams, took over for Forrest Gregg as the new head coach of the Cleveland Browns. "There isn't a coach who doesn't think he'll win," said Browns owner Art Modell of Rutigliano's chances. "This is a new era for the Browns." The San Francisco 49ers also began a new era when they fired Ken Meyer and hired former Redskins assistant, Pete McCulley. "The place the 49ers have to make some improvements is in the passing game," said McCulley. "You make the big play with a passing game. You win in the NFL with a passing game." McCulley was not the only one with that opinion. Another San Francisco head coach in 1979 (Bill Walsh) would end up revolutionizing the pro passing game in the 1980s.

More coaching changes followed. Tommy Hudspeth was fired in Detroit, and was replaced by Monte Clark. Hank Stram was fired by New Orleans and was replaced by Dick Nolan. That decision was not unanimously appreciated by most New Orleans players. "I'm really disappointed, and shocked," said New Orleans quarterback Archie Manning, who admitted to weeping when he heard the news of Stram's dismissal. "I didn't think they'd do this to Hank, who is one of the most thoughtful men in the world. He treats football players like men." And Homer Rice replaced Bill Johnson in Cincinnati after the first five games of 1978. Only one of the new head coaches— Malavasi of the Rams—was able to get his team into the 1978 postseason.

Quite a few players also changed teams in 1978. Some were household names, and some were not. They included superstar running back O.J. Simpson, who finally went from Buffalo to San Francisco after several years of pleading for a trade to take place. The 49ers traded promising running back Delvin Williams to Miami for wide receiver Freddie Solomon, cornerback Vern Roberson, and two draft picks. Washington traded away a first-round draft pick to get veteran Cincinnati defensive back Lemar Parrish and veteran defensive lineman Coy Bacon. Miami tight end Jim Mandich was traded to the Redskins, who in turn quickly traded him to the Steelers. Notorious offensive guard Conrad Dobler was traded from St. Louis to New Orleans. Long-time punter Jerrel Wilson was traded from the Chiefs to the Oilers. Finally, Tampa Bay traded away their first-round selection to Houston for tight end Jimmie Giles and a first and second-round draft pick in 1978 and a third and fifth-round pick in 1979. The Oilers in turn got a franchise superstar when they chose 5'11", 224-pound University of Texas running back Earl Campbell with their first selection in the 1978 NFL draft. Campbell was a Heisman Trophy–winning power back with exemplary speed who would help Houston's offense in much the same way that Tony Dorsett helped the Dallas offense the season before.

The opening of the 1978 NFL season featured several telltale contests which gave fans a hint as to what to expect during the year. Earl Campbell was one highly-touted rookie who wasted no time in making his mark in the league for the Oilers. He rushed for 136 yards in his pro debut against the tough Atlanta Falcons "Grits Blitz" defense in Week 1 at Atlanta. Included in Campbell's totals was a 73-yard sprint down the far sideline for a touchdown on a lateral. The Oilers lost to the resurgent Falcons, 20–14, but Houston's offense now had a game-breaker in their backfield. The Oilers with the addition of Campbell would become a much-improved team in 1978. Defensive coordinators around the NFL would now have to contend with not only the new pass coverage rules, but also with a runner like Campbell, who in physicality and pure athletic ability resembled the great Jim Brown of the Cleveland Browns of the 1950s and 1960s. The Oilers would rebound from their first loss in subsequent weeks, and would achieve more success in 1978 than they ever had since the 1970 merger. The Falcons would also achieve success, as they would continue to excel and provide the league with many exciting moments in 1978.

Another up and coming team in the NFC also came within a play or two of defeating a perennial playoff team in Week 1. The Philadelphia Eagles fought hard against the visiting Los Angeles Rams, and even took a 14–13 lead late in the game on a weaving 57-yard punt return by Wally Henry. But the Eagles had a time-honored penchant for self-destruction, and the Rams had the ability to take full advantage of just one mistake. Los Angeles defensive back Rod Perry blocked Spike Jones' punt, and his Rams teammate, Nolan Cromwell, dove on the rolling pigskin for a touchdown just before the ball toppled out of the end zone. Los Angeles placekicker Frank Corral completed the Rams' comeback with a 46-yard field goal with seven seconds left in the game to give his team a 16–14 comeback victory over a surprisingly tough Eagles squad. Philadelphia Eagles head coach Dick Vermeil was a master motivator, however, and his innate abilities to inspire his club would make the 1978 season a year that both players and fans in the City of Brotherly Love would never forget. Despite their narrow loss to the Rams, the Eagles would build on the lessons learned with every succeeding game. "Guys, you don't have to be embarrassed about your performance," Vermeil told his players after the game. "That Los Angeles Rams team has as much talent as anybody in football. You give them a blocked punt for a touchdown, you can't win. But damn it, we're a good football team ... and don't let anybody tell you different."

Another first week surprise occurred in the tough AFC East, where the New York Jets, clad in their new kelly green helmets and jerseys, upset the Miami Dolphins at Shea Stadium, 33–20. Quarterback Richard Todd led the Jets with two touchdown bombs of 47 and 43 yards to wide receiver Wesley Walker. Todd also threw another touchdown pass to tight end Mickey Shuler from one yard out. The Dolphins were without injured starting quarterback Bob Griese, but the backups did a reputable job. Miami quarterbacks Don Strock and Guy Benjamin each threw a scoring pass against the Jets defense. New Miami tailback Delvin Williams began his Dolphins debut with 119 yards rushing, including a 58-yard run for a touchdown. The main difference in the game was four field goals from the foot of Jets placekicker Pat Leahy.

The difference in Washington's surprising 16–14 victory over the host New England Patriots was an untimely fourth quarter fumble by Pats running back Horace Ivory, who was hit hard on a sweep by Redskins defensive lineman Dave Butz. Ivory quickly lost control of the ball, and Washington outside linebacker Brad Dusek picked up the pigskin and returned it 31 yards for the game-winning touchdown with just 2:40 left to play. "I hesitated at first," said Dusek of his recovery. "I wanted to be sure I could pick it up on the run." Apparently there was more to the Redskins' success in this game than what was seen on the field. "The Redskins seemed to know every play we were going to run," claimed New England quarterback Steve Grogan. "We'd run a play and they'd be there waiting for us." There was a good reason for this. Several copies of New England's game plan were mistakenly and mysteriously left in the visiting locker room, giving the Redskins an early Christmas present. The Redskin coaches quickly helped their players to adjust to the clues from the discovered playbooks, and their advantage was indeed fortunate. Washington's defense held on to the lead after Dusek's touchdown to preserve the upset.

The Denver Broncos preserved their recent superiority over division rival Oakland in the opening game of the year with a 14–6 win over the Raiders at Mile High Stadium. The Broncos were led by their Orange Crush defense, which held the Raiders to merely two Errol Mann field goals. Denver's offense pierced Oakland's defense with touchdowns from a 6-yard pass from veteran quarterback Craig Morton to wide receiver Haven Moses in the second quarter, and a 1-yard run from halfback Otis Armstrong in the fourth quarter.

While the Oakland dynasty appeared to be faltering, the Green Bay Packers were attempting to revive their dynasty from the 1960s. The Packers edged the host Detroit Lions on opening day, 13–7, behind the consistent runs of halfback Terdell Middleton, who rushed for a game high 91 yards on 28 tough carries. Two Chester Marcol field goals and a 1-yard scoring dive by Packers running back Barty Smith teamed with a stubborn Green Bay defense to secure the win. Middleton would go on to lead the Pack in rushing in 1978 with 1,116 yards and 11 touchdowns. He would also set a Packers record for rushing attempts in a season (284). It looked as if after years of searching, Green Bay head coach Bart Starr finally had the runner to build his offense around. "We were pleased with him from the day he came to camp," Starr said of Middleton. "Even though he had pulled a hamstring, he wanted to run. We already knew about his speed and strength, but that showed us something about his heart."

The heart of the Pittsburgh Steelers for years had been pounding in their defense. In 1978, however, their offense seemed to get a beat stronger from the new pass coverage rules in their opening game at Buffalo's Rich Stadium. Steelers wide receivers John Stallworth and Theo Bell each scored touchdowns on passes from quarterback Terry Bradshaw. Stallworth juked Buffalo cornerback Charles Romes at the 14-yard line, then proceeded to break arm tackles from Romes, linebackers Doug Becker and Dan Jilek, and cornerback Mario Clark en route to his 28-yard scoring reception. Bell simply caught a quick slant pass from 15 yards out for his six-pointer. The Steelers running game also contributed to the win. Franco Harris and Sidney Thornton each scored from short distances. Harris rushed for 96 yards in the win and thus became the league's eighth all-time leading rusher.

A couple of upsets also made headlines on opening day. The lowly New Orleans Saints surprised the defending NFC Central Champion Minnesota Vikings at the Louisiana Superdome, 31–24. Veteran Saints safety Tommy Myers set a team record with three interceptions, and returned one of them off of a deflection 97 yards down the far sideline for what turned out to be the winning touchdown in the fourth quarter. Minnesota quarterback Fran Tarkenton was playing in his first meaningful game since his leg injury in the ninth week of the 1977 season. Even though he completed 28 passes for 287 yards, he also threw four interceptions, and that was all New Orleans needed to secure their first win. On a bright note for the Vikings, Rickey Young set a team single-game record for running backs by catching 12 passes, two of them for touchdowns.

The final game of the first week was a telling contest on *Monday Night Football*. The evening started out with a one-hour ABC television special/variety show about the Dallas Cowboys Cheerleaders entitled *The 36 Most Beautiful Women in Texas*. The show ended with a live pregame performance from the cheerleaders at Texas Stadium, just before the defending Super Bowl champion Cowboys took on the defending AFC Eastern Division Champion Baltimore Colts. The Dallas offense performed as beautifully as their female counterparts on the sidelines, as they decimated the listless Colts. The Cowboys compiled 587 total yards, and limited the Colts, who were missing injured quarterback Bert Jones, to a mere 181 yards. Dallas quarterback Roger Staubach blistered the Baltimore pass defense by throwing four touchdown tosses in the victory, but the real offensive star was sophomore running back Tony Dorsett, who rushed for 147 yards and scored on a 1-yard run in the second quarter. Dorsett also caught three passes for 107 yards, including a brilliant 91-yard catch and carry through the heart of the Baltimore defense for a touchdown. "[Dallas wide receiver] Tony [Hill] just cremated somebody to shake me loose," described Dorsett, "and I have the ability to cut against the grain with a lot of speed."

The measured results of the new pass protection and pass coverage rules did not depend upon speed. But nevertheless, they were taking effect all throughout the league almost immediately. Teams that had struggled throwing the ball in the past were now succeeding beyond their most optimistic expectations. Take the New York Jets, for example. Their daring and youthful quarterback Richard Todd threw three touchdown passes in New York's Week 1 victory over Miami, and he threw three more touchdowns in Week 2 as the Jets came from behind to defeat the Buffalo Bills at Rich Stadium, 21–20.

Similar to the Jets' success, the Green Bay Packers were also winning games through the air. Young quarterback David Whitehurst teamed up with wide receiver James Lofton, a gazelle-like pass catcher who had the speed to outrun many defensive zones or man-to-man coverages. Few were the defenders who could keep pace with him on longer and deeper pass routes. The Packers were 2–0 after their 28–17 victory over the New Orleans Saints at Milwaukee County Stadium,

The Dallas Cowboys Cheerleaders were becoming famous across the nation by the middle of the decade. Soon after Dallas won Super Bowl XII, the DCC were on their way to two television movies, their own one-hour television special, several appearances on television's *The Love Boat*, and many annual USO shows to entertain the American troops across the world. The success of the DCC was soon to be imitated throughout the NFL (©1978, Shelly Katz Photo).

which was Green Bay's second home in Wisconsin for usually three or four of their home games each year during the decade. Loften caught three of Whitehurst's four touchdown passes against the Saints, coming from 47 yards, 42 yards, and 18 yards out. Green Bay tight end Rich McGeorge also caught a 9-yard scoring pass from Whitehurst. The Packers running game did its share as well. The Green Bay runners contributed to 220 team rushing yards, including 114 by halfback Terdell Middleton. The victory marked the best start to a season for the Packers since 1969. "We've been working together a lot," Whitehurst said of his teamwork with Loften. "He [Loften] knows my limitations. I don't think he has any." Whitehurst was quite correct and quite prophetic in his assessment of his star wide receiver. In 2003, Loften would be measured for a gold jacket from the Pro Football Hall of Fame in Canton, Ohio.

Several other team offensive units would also achieve much success in the second week of the season. The Miami Dolphins registered a 42–0 thrashing of the host Baltimore Colts, thanks to the passing efficiency of reserve quarterback Don Strock, who completed 13 of 20 passes for 151 yards and three touchdowns. Miami's No-Name Defense also registered six interceptions in the rout. The Colts were shut out for the second straight week, with their defense giving up 80 total points in that span.

The Washington Redskins and the Philadelphia Eagles each had little difficulty in finding the end zone when they met each other on September 10. The Redskins were led by quarterback Joe Theismann, who threw for three touchdowns, two of which went to tight end Jean Fugett.

Theirmann also ran for a score. The Eagles countered with the inspired play of young halfback Wilbert Montgomery, who scored four touchdowns. Theismann's 37-yard touchdown pass to wide receiver Danny Buggs on a gadget play early in the fourth quarter provided the margin of victory. The Redskins prevailed, 35–30, and thus improved to 2–0. Philadelphia fell to a worrisome 0–2. Thanks in part to the longer regular season in 1978, however, the situations for both of these teams would change as the push for the playoffs continued.

The Chicago Bears were out to prove that their playoff record from a year ago was no fluke. They began the 1978 season with an impressive 3–0 record, surrendering only 23 total points in victories over the Cardinals, 49ers, and Lions. It appeared to most observers in the Windy City as if the Bears would continue their rise to contention. Chicago halfback Walter Payton was once again the team's accepted leader, and by season's end, he would once again lead the NFC in rushing.

The Oakland Raiders easily led the league in unbelievable endings to many of their games over the years. They added one more incredible ending in 1978, as good fortune smiled on them. The Raiders were trailing the Chargers in San Diego late in their Week 2 meeting, 20–14. Oakland quarterback Ken "The Snake" Stabler dropped back to pass on the game's final play and was rushed quickly by San Diego linebacker Woodrow Lowe. It appeared as if Stabler just chucked the ball underhanded as he was being tackled to the ground by Lowe. The referees, however, determined that it was fumble. "I tried to fumble," Stabler admitted afterward. "I know damn well I did. If I get sacked, the game is over." Oakland running back Pete Banaszak tried to recover the ball, but as he was in a crouch and prepared to pick it up, he picked it up and heaved it towards the San Diego goal line just before he did a face plant on the ground. "Sure I batted it [the ball]," confessed Banaszak. "I could see a San Diego guy right alongside me. If I pick it up, he would have tackled me and the game would have been over."

Oakland tight end Dave Casper was the next closest player to the bouncing ball, and he basically stumbled as he was chasing the ball. He then inadvertently kicked the ball forward. By the time that Casper tried to grasp the ball, however, it crossed the goal line, and both Casper and the ball were in the Chargers end zone. Casper fell on it there, and 14 yards after Stabler fumbled (or chucked, whichever version you believed) the pigskin, the Raiders had scored the game-winning touchdown. Oakland prevailed in a wild finish after Oakland placekicker Errol Mann kicked the extra point, 21–20. San Diego head coach Tommy Prothro protested the play, claiming that the ball was illegally flipped forward by both Stabler and Banaszak. Referee Jerry Markbreit disagreed, basically claiming that the ball did all of that on its own, and ruled the play a legal touchdown. The game's ending was so unbelievable that it earned its own nickname: the "Holy Roller." Like the Immaculate Reception in 1972 and the Hail Mary Pass in 1975, the decade of the 1970s had another implausible and miraculous ending to another game. The Holy Roller thus became an icon moment in league history, and a much-repeated highlight on NFL Films. Perhaps just as amusing and as dramatic as the play itself was the radio broadcast of the event by Raiders play-by-play announcer Bill King. "Madden is on the field," exclaimed the excited King immediately after the conclusion of the play. "He [Madden] wants to know if it's real. They [the referees] said yes! Get your big butt out of here! He does! There's nothing real in the world anymore! The Raiders have won the football game! This one will be relived ... forever!"

Once again, proponents of developing an instant replay system to be used in helping the officials now had yet one more piece of evidence that they could point to in affirming their opinion. The NFL's Competition Committee did their duty during the following off-season, however, and ruled that players could not throw or chuck a ball forward on purpose following a fumble. Unfortunately for the Chargers, that new rule came one year too late to help them.

Some teams were able to adjust to the new rules better than others. Altering defenses to include more blitzes and to design more intricate zone coverages was the order of the day for all defensive coordinators. A few teams with very athletic personnel were more successful in keeping their opponents out of the end zone. Many experts felt that teams such as Atlanta, Dallas, Pittsburgh, and Los Angeles (each of which had great defenses) would adapt to the new rules more quickly than most of the other teams. Two such defensive-minded squads met on *Monday Night Football* on September 11. The Denver Broncos and their Orange Crush defense met the Minnesota Vikings and their Purple Gang in Metropolitan Stadium, and both defenses flustered the opposing offenses all game long. The Vikings eventually won, 12–9, in a battle of field goals.

As was suggested earlier, Pittsburgh's stellar defense was in good shape to adjust to the new rules. The Steel Curtain paved the way to seven straight wins to start the season. They gave up a total of only 77 points in those seven games, easily making their defense the best in the league. The Steelers defeated AFC Central foes Cincinnati and Cleveland (twice) in the first half of the season, and also registered wins over Seattle, the New York Jets, and Atlanta in the early going. Those first seven wins laid a foundation for a formidable team that was built to mirror the city in which they played … tough, hard-nosed, determined, and strong in all phases of the game. Pittsburgh and the blue-collar Steelers were simply made for each other. "Pittsburgh is a tight community," said Steelers defensive tackle Joe Greene. "The fans are with you all the way."

The way was getting a little tougher for the defending world champion Dallas Cowboys, however. They lost to the Rams in a rather non-competitive contest in Week 3, 27–14. After a nondescript 21–12 win over St. Louis, the Cowboys met the Redskins on *Monday Night Football* in Week 5. The game was a defensive battle at RFK Stadium with little scoring, but the attendance of one person made the game memorable. President Jimmy Carter became the first sitting President in American history to attend a *Monday Night Football* game. Whether or not President Carter brought the Redskins some good luck was debatable, but they certainly did not suffer from the upstaging of their fight song ("Hail to the Redskins") by the President's favorite tune, "Hail to the Chief." Washington placekicker Mark Moseley booted three field goals, while the Cowboys could muster only one field goal and a safety on the last play of the game. That particular play featured Redskins quarterback Joe Theismann taking the snap from center, holding the ball aloft in triumph, running around in the back of his end zone to run out the clock, and being tackled by Dallas defensive tackle Randy White. Washington's 9–5 win over Dallas shook up the standings in the NFC East. The Redskins stood alone at the top of that division with a perfect 5–0 record, while the despondent Cowboys fell to 3–2.

The Baltimore Colts fell from the ranks of the quality teams in the league when they left the field after their second straight shutout loss in Week 2 . Most people figured that the Colts would lose their third game of the season also, as they played the Patriots on *Monday Night Football* in New England. A light drizzle fell during the first half of this game, and that drizzle increased to a steady rainfall in the second half. A young and diminutive 5'10" Colts halfback by the name of Joe Washington got a chance to see some action in this game, and by game's end, his stellar performance earned him a lasting place in the history of *Monday Night Football*. On his first big play early in the fourth quarter, Washington took a handoff and ran to his left. He stopped behind the line of scrimmage and threw a 54-yard bomb to Colts wide receiver Roger Carr down the far sideline. "A lot of teams are conscious of me going to the outside," Washington explained. "They [the Patriots] were looking for a sweep." A few minutes later Washington caught a 23-yard touchdown pass from reserve Colts quarterback Bill Troup. Following the second of two straight New England touchdowns which tied the game at 27–27, Washington finished this game of a lifetime by returning the ensuing kickoff 90 yards through the raindrops and the slipping Patriot players for the game-winning touchdown. Baltimore prevailed, 34–27, for their first win of the year. The Patriots fell to 1–2. "We showed a lot of character out there tonight," said Baltimore head coach Ted Marchibroda. "All I can say is that you can talk about all kinds of victories, but this was a tribute to our club."

New England used their shocking and humiliating defeat by Baltimore to inspire them to win their next seven straight games. The Patriots went to Oakland in Week 4 and defeated the Raiders, 21–14. They won their next two games over San Diego (28–23) and Philadelphia (24–14) with steady offensive outputs. Their defense took over in Week 7, allowing a meager field goal in their 10–3 win over the Bengals in Cincinnati. Prior to the start of the season, many experts predicted that New England would represent the AFC in the Super Bowl. By mid-season, it looked as if those predictions might be accurate. The Patriots outscored Miami, 33–24, for their sixth win. They then trounced the visiting New York Jets, 55–21, and upended the Bills over in Buffalo, 14–10. New England's streak of victories earned for them an 8–2 record, good enough for first place in the competitive AFC East.

The Miami Dolphins to their credit kept pace with the Pats all the way into November. Head coach Don Shula kept his team on track in the midst of another year of continued injuries to key personnel, namely starting quarterback Bob Griese, who missed the first six regular season games. Backup quarterback Don Strock did an admirable job in replacing Griese during the first half of the 1978 season, throwing for 10 touchdowns before Griese re-entered the huddle. The Dolphins sported a 7–3 record going into the 11th week of the season, good enough for second place in the AFC East, just one game behind the Patriots.

There were several big surprises in the standings during the first half of the season. The New York Giants built a 5–3 record at mid-season, thanks to the stalwart play of a defense that allowed an average of only 11 points a game in their five victories. Unfortunately for the Giants, their early wins were achieved against mediocre or weak teams. Once they started to play tougher competition, they started to lose. The Giants would win only one more game for the remainder of the season, and finished in last place in the NFC East with a record of 6–10.

Another early surprise team was the Green Bay Packers, who somehow won six of their first eight games. The Pack stood alone in first place in the NFC Central Division, otherwise known as the Black and Blue Division, named for the tremendous hitting and smash-mouth competition among the teams in that division. The Packers swept divisional foe Detroit for two wins, then defeated New Orleans, San Diego, Chicago and Seattle. In their 24–3 victory over the host Chargers, Packer defensive back Willie Buchanon intercepted a single-game league record four passes, and returned one of them 77 yards for a touchdown. By season's end, Buchanon would go on to lead his team in interceptions with nine, which was good enough for first place in that category in the NFC. "He's the premier cornerback in the NFL," said Green Bay defensive coordinator Dave Hanner of Buchanon. Unfortunately for the Packers, they would also—like the Giants—lose more games during the second half of the year.

The Houston Oilers were also a surprise team in the AFC, yet most observers predicted that they would have a contending 1978 season. Houston achieved a major upset in the eighth week of the season by defeating the previously undefeated Pittsburgh Steelers in Three Rivers Stadium on *Monday Night Football.* The Oilers relied on their brutish and bullish rookie running back Earl Campbell, who scored all of his team's touchdowns in their 24–17 win. Campbell ran through the Steel Curtain defense for 89 yards, plunged into the end zone for his touchdowns on short yardage situations, and kept several scoring drives alive with key first downs. The Steelers were cruising through the first half of the season, but this was an upsetting loss. Both the Oilers and the Steelers would meet again later in the year in the midst of the drive for the playoffs.

Pittsburgh's in-state neighbors, the Philadelphia Eagles, had a tough 0–2 start. Both of those losses were games that they lost by only a small margin. The Eagles began to put together some key victories as mid-season approached, however. They defeated one of the strongest teams in the league in the Miami Dolphins at Veterans Stadium on September 24 by a score of 17–3. Philadelphia's defense was quickly becoming regarded around the league as a very formidable one after permitting only one field goal against the talented Dolphins. The Eagles also edged previously unbeaten Washington at home a few weeks later, 17–10. In that game, Philadelphia cornerback John "Deke" Sanders intercepted a Joe Theismann pass along the sideline and returned it 19 yards for a touchdown. The Eagles' offense put the game away in the fourth quarter on a 12-yard sweep run by tailback Wilbert Montgomery. "This is the one win we were looking for," said Vermeil after his team beat the Redskins. "Our defense kept us in the game, but we also had a certain amount of luck." Although they were only 4–3 and in third place in the NFC East, Philadelphia would build on the luck and momentum gained from those two early upsets to stay competitive in the second half of the regular season.

It seemed as if imposing upsets would be the norm during the early part of the 1978 season. The league's most auspicious losers—the Tampa Bay Buccaneers—somehow managed to defeat the defending NFC Central Division Champion Minnesota Vikings at Metropolitan Stadium in the third week of the season, 16–10. It was Tampa's first win of the year, and the loss dropped Minnesota's record to 1–2. The Buccaneers then upset the Atlanta Falcons and their Grits Blitz defense in Week 4, 14–9. It appeared as if the embarrassment of Tampa's 0–26 franchise start was behind them for good. According to author and pro football historian Denis M. Crawford, "A win like this [against the Vikings] really served notice to Tampa Bay fans that there was something different about their team. There was a mental toughness to this team that was forged during their 26-game losing streak."

Losing streaks were somewhat foreign to several teams as they took on their Week 5 and Week 6 opponents. Many favored teams during those weeks did what they were expected to do—defeat less-talented opponents. Teams like the Denver Broncos maintained their lead in the AFC West with a 28–7 victory over visiting Seattle on October 1. Division leaders New England, Pittsburgh, Washington, Green Bay and Los Angeles each won in Week 5. Philadelphia traveled down the I-95 Interstate Highway and defeated the Colts in Baltimore, 17–14, thanks to the running ability of halfback Wilbert Montgomery, who ran for 144 yards and scored the winning touchdown in the fourth quarter on a 14-yard run. The Eagles were held scoreless by the Colts until the fourth quarter, when they erupted for their two touchdowns and a 26-yard field goal from the foot of placekicker Nick Mike-Mayer.

A highly competitive game at Foxboro took place in the fifth week when the San Diego Chargers took on the New England Patriots. The Chargers were busy taking full advantage of the new pass blocking and pass coverage rules. Rookie wide receiver John Jefferson was small but he was also "lightning" fast, and his hands were magnets for the football. Teaming up with Jefferson at wide receiver was veteran Charlie Joiner, one of the best route runners and pass catchers in the game. San Diego traded for Baltimore halfback Lydell Mitchell in the off-season, and he contributed speed in the backfield and another pair of excellent hands. Chargers quarterback Dan Fouts was a six-year veteran with the strength, poise and the ability to become one of the league's best passers. Finally, the Chargers named Don Coryell as their head coach just prior to the fifth game of the season. Coryell's genius in developing a dominant air game was a custom fit for the Chargers' personnel. The Patriots on the other hand had some of the best athletes in the NFL at most of the "skill" positions, like All-Pro tight end Russ Francis, and veteran wide receiver Harold Jackson. Moreover, their 3–4 defense regularly distributed a plethora of hard hits and permitted only minimal yardage totals in every game. Defenders like linebackers Steve Nelson and Sam Hunt, defensive backs like Mike Haynes and Tim Fox, and defensive linemen like Ray "Sugar Bear" Hamilton and Julius Adams, each provided plenty of problems for their offensive opponents every Sunday.

The Chargers built a 20–14 lead going into the fourth quarter before the Patriots struck with a 6-yard touchdown toss from quarterback Steve Grogan to tight end Russ Francis and a 4-yard touchdown run by Grogan himself. New England won this battle of quarterbacks, 28–23. Grogan ended the day completing 17 passes in 29 attempts for 231 yards and three scoring passes. "I may have ulcers soon," suggested Grogan after New England's last-minute win over the Chargers. San Diego quarterback Dan Fouts also contributed fairly good numbers (for him) in the game, as he went 14 of 18 for 173 yards and three touchdown passes. The abilities of Fouts and the Chargers offense was even more visibly noticed when they went up against the Denver Broncos and their Orange Crush defense a week later. The Chargers "crushed" the Broncos, 23–0, and sent a message to the rest of the NFL that San Diego was a team to be reckoned with. Fouts only threw one touchdown pass in the win, a 14-yard toss to setback Hank Bauer. Nevertheless, Fouts commanded long drives in every quarter which resulted in a score of one kind or another, and the inspired San Diego defense intercepted three passes and recovered two fumbles. Another key factor in the Chargers' win was due to their defense limiting the Broncos offense to just 90 yards passing for the day.

Not to be outdone, another team in the AFC West also had a tough contest in the fifth week of the season, but they managed to survive. The Oakland Raiders defeated the Chicago Bears at Soldier Field, 25–19, but it took them an overtime period to do it. Oakland placekicker Errol Mann booted a 29-yard field goal with five seconds left in regulation to tie the score at 19–19. Oakland's defense then took charge. The Raiders employed a sixth defensive back, Neal Colzie, who intercepted a Bob Avellini pass in overtime and returned it 24 yards. Oakland running back Arthur Whittington then swept to score on a 2-yard touchdown for the winning points. "That was the first time we used six defensive backs," said Oakland head coach John Madden, referring to Colzie's interception. "It was not an element of surprise, just another type of prevent defense."

One team that was surprised in Week 6 was the Minnesota Vikings, who were upset by the Seattle Seahawks in the Kingdome, 29–28. The Vikings were having difficulty in 1978 maintaining the regular stretch of victories that they had achieved throughout the decade, and were now dealing with head coach Bud Grant's decision to keep his older players on his roster while they were past their prime. The Norsemen had quality young backup players, but they rarely had chances to play with so many veterans on the team. Clearly, the Vikings defense was a shadow of its former self. They permitted young Seattle quarterback Jim Zorn to scamper 12 yards and 22 yards for two touchdowns. Zorn also threw 44 yards to wide receiver Sam McCullum (himself a former Viking) for another score. Zorn completed his stellar afternoon by leading his team on a 70-yard drive late in the fourth quarter which resulted in the winning field goal off the foot of placekicker Efren Herrera, who was cut by Dallas in the preseason and picked up by the Seahawks to provide an improvement in their special teams.

Like the Vikings, the Cincinnati Bengals were also experiencing a season of troubles. The Bengals went through the entire first half of the year winless, and they definitely did not look like the competitive team that they were during the early years in the decade. The Bengals were horrendous on both sides of the line of scrimmage, and lost games by both wide and small margins to supposedly inferior teams like Kansas City, New Orleans, and Buffalo. Homer Rice took over as head coach after the fifth game of the season, replacing the fired Bill Johnson. It was not until late in the year when the Bengals started to play like the Bengals of old, winning their final three games of the regular season to finish with a depressing 4–10 record.

Quite a few games in the sixth week of the 1978 season had more predictable results. Pittsburgh routed the visiting Atlanta Falcons, 31–7. Dallas upended the New York Giants in the New Jersey Meadowlands, 24–3. Los Angeles outlasted San Francisco at the Los Angeles Memorial Coliseum, 27–10. Finally, New England defeated upstart Philadelphia up in Foxboro, 24–14. There were also several unexpected results in Week 6. The New York Jets were expected to defeat the Buffalo Bills in Shea Stadium, but few experts could have predicted them to rout the Bills by a final score of 45–14. Virtually every facet of New York's offense was clicking on all cylinders. Running back Kevin Long scored three touchdowns and rushed for 91 yards. New York's special teams shined too. A blocked punt and a fumble recovery on a kickoff led to 14 unanswered points. Reserve Jets halfback Bruce Harper returned a punt a spectacular 82 yards right down the middle of the field for a touchdown, at that time the second longest punt return in team history. The New York defense also contributed to the rout. Safety Burgess Owens returned an interception 40 yards for a score in the first quarter to set the tone for the afternoon. The Jets offense took over with three touchdowns in the second quarter. New York's offense had been excelling in recent weeks with the play of quarterback Richard Todd. In this game, however, Matt Robinson took the snaps in place of Todd, who was injured and who threw only nine passes in this game before leaving to the bench. Robinson came in and relied mostly on his running game, which pounded out an impressive 231 ground yards against the porous Buffalo defense. New York's record improved to 3–3 with their win over the Bills.

Week 7 saw several teams do whatever it took to win close games. The defending Super Bowl champion Dallas Cowboys went in to Busch Memorial Stadium and endured another tough outing with the St. Louis Cardinals. Dallas had won the first game between the two clubs back on September 24 by a score of 21–12. This next meeting on October 15 would be even more competitive. The Cowboys needed to employ another one of head coach Tom Landry's gadget plays to score a touchdown in the third quarter. Landry called for a flea-flicker pass which went from quarterback Roger Staubach, who handed the ball off to tailback Tony Dorsett, who handed the ball to wide receiver Drew Pearson (who was going in the opposite direction as Dorsett). Pearson then lateraled the ball back to Staubach, who threw the ball 37 yards downfield to wide open wide receiver Tony Hill, who trotted into the end zone. Staubach would throw for three touchdowns in the game, including a second scoring toss to Hill.

The Cardinals responded with two short touchdown runs by running back Jim Otis, and a 1-yard touchdown pass from quarterback Jim Hart to setback Wayne Morris. Cardinals placekicker Jim Bakken had a 33-yard field goal attempt bounce off the left upright with 2:54 left in the fourth quarter which would have put St. Louis in the lead. Not to be outdone, Dallas placekicker Rafael Septien had his 49-yard field goal attempt blocked with two seconds left. Septien got another chance in overtime, however, as he nailed a 47-yard field goal to give the Cowboys a 24–21 victory and a season sweep of the Cardinals. "You have to definitely be cool," said Septien after the game. "If you let your emotions control you, you don't have a chance." The win boosted Dallas to a 5–2 record in the tough NFC East, a game behind the 6–1 Redskins. The loss left the 0–7 Cardinals and their new head coach, Bud Wilkinson, still searching for their first win.

The other Texas team—the Houston Oilers—also had a struggle on their hands in Week 7 when they took on the lowly Buffalo Bills in the Astrodome. Houston was in a fight to wrest control of the AFC Central Division from the Pittsburgh Steelers, and they had to win every game that they were "expected" to win. The Bills were not willing to go down easily, however. Keith Moody returned a punt 82 yards for a touchdown to give Buffalo a 10–7 halftime lead. Houston quarterback Dan Pastorini then drove his team 97 yards in 11 plays for the winning touchdown. Houston running back Rob Carpenter ran 18 yards through the Bills defense for the winning score as the Oilers prevailed, 17–10. Houston rookie Earl Campbell continued to accumulate ground yardage, rushing for 105 yards on 19 carries against the Bills. "We'll just give the ball to Earl and let him make his own plays," said the homespun Houston head coach Bum Phillips.

Perhaps the toughest defensive battle in Week 7 took place at Riverfront Stadium, where the New England Patriots edged the Cincinnati Bengals, 10–3. New England head coach Chuck Fairbanks watched his team struggle against the winless Bengals, as they entered the fourth quarter with only one field goal to their ledger. It required a 66-yard drive late in the game to set up Sam Cunningham's 3-yard touchdown run for the win. This game was simply a case of a superior team playing down to the level of their competition, something that every good team was guilty of at least once in a while during the decade.

Two good teams played lesser competition in their Week 7 games, and they both took care of business and won by comfortable margins. The Pittsburgh Steelers defeated the Cleveland Browns at Cleveland Municipal Stadium, 34–14, and the Oakland Raiders swatted down the Kansas City Chiefs in Oakland, 28–6. Another team—the Los Angeles Rams—enjoyed a small token of revenge by beating the host Minnesota Vikings, 34–17. The Rams had lost to the Vikings in the 1977 divisional playoffs, not to mention losses in the postseason to Minnesota in 1969, 1974, and 1976. So the redemptive win over the Vikings in 1978 must have felt good to them. Rounding out Week 7 was the defending AFC champion Denver Broncos, who sent the visiting Chicago Bears down to defeat on *Monday Night Football*, 16–7.

The eighth week of the 1978 season produced a bunch of impressive defensive efforts, where point production was minimal. Week 8 also had a few surprising upsets. The Buffalo Bills shut out the visiting Cincinnati Bengals, 5–0. Bills running back Curtis Brown ran for 100 yards in the win. The Baltimore Colts barely edged the Denver Broncos at Baltimore's Memorial Stadium, 7–6. A deflected 19-yard touchdown pass from reserve Colts quarterback Bill Troup to wide receiver Glenn Doughty produced the winning points for Baltimore. The Dallas Cowboys were expected to win and allowed only one touchdown in their 14–7 victory over the rival Philadelphia Eagles at Texas Stadium. But it was a tough, hard-hitting game. "We hit 'em good and peppered 'em," said Dallas outside linebacker D.D. Lewis. "When you see three and four guys piling into [Eagles tailback Wilbert] Montgomery, that's an indication what's happening." Montgomery entered the game as the league's leading rusher, but was held to just 57 yards on the ground by the Doomsday Defense. Philadelphia quarterback Ron Jaworski also suffered five sacks in the game. "It was a tough defensive game and we hung in there," observed Dallas head coach Tom Landry. The game might have been easier for the Cowboys had their star halfback Tony Dorsett not overslept the day before the game, causing him to be late for Saturday's practice. Coach Landry benched him against the Eagles until only six minutes remained in the first half. The official excuse given by Dorsett was a broken alarm clock.

But perhaps the primary scene for excuses in Week 8 occurred in the Los Angeles Memorial Coliseum, where the New Orleans Saints surprised the Los Angeles Rams, 10–3. The Saints defense played a whale of a game, as they intercepted three passes, recovered three fumbles, and blocked a field goal. It was a game where the Rams simply did not come to play as a team, and it showed. Virtually none of the Rams were able to put together their usual strong effort. Saints quarterback Archie Manning took advantage of Los Angeles' listless performance, as he rolled out and threw a 19-yard touchdown pass to setback Tony Galbreath for the winning points. It marked New Orleans' first win ever at the Coliseum, and it ended the Rams' 12-game home winning streak.

A few other large upsets also took place on that Sunday. The New York Giants surprised the Washington Redskins in the Meadowlands, 17–6. The Tampa Bay Buccaneers had a fine offensive outing as they pounded the visiting Chicago Bears, 33–19. But virtually no one could have predicted what occurred in the Kingdome, where the Seattle Seahawks trounced the Oakland Raiders, 27–7. The Seahawks defense limited the Raiders to only 70 overall rushing yards in this game, and Seattle running back Sherman Smith scored twice in the second quarter on two short touchdown runs. "I think this is the best we've played both offensively and defensively," admitted Seattle head coach Jack Patera. "In fact, I know it is." The win gave Seattle a 4–4 record in the AFC West, while the loss dropped the Raiders to 5–3 and a first-place tie with the Denver Broncos in the same division.

The upsets continued to flourish in Week 9. It started on a special Thursday night contest between the Minnesota Vikings and the Dallas Cowboys on October 26 at Texas Stadium. It was a rematch of last year's NFC title game, but the result was much different. The Vikings finally had a healthy Fran Tarkenton in their lineup, and he befuddled the defending champs, 21–10. Tarkenton relied on his full repertoire of small check-off passes to his setbacks, a bevy of screen passes, and many quick-out passes along the sidelines. The results were that Tarkenton only threw for a total of 139 yards against the Doomsday Defense. Nevertheless, the Vikings kept moving the ball because their star halfback Chuck Foreman was also healthy, and he contributed 101 rushing yards in one of his best games of the year. But it was the Purple Gang who gave up only 10 points and secured the unexpected win. "Defensively, we played well," said Minnesota head coach Bud Grant. "Dallas is a big play team, and we contained them. They didn't make the big play on us."

The Atlanta Falcons made enough big plays on October 30 to notch an upset victory over the visiting Los Angeles Rams on *Monday Night Football*, 15–7. The Falcons benefitted from the performance of free agent placekicker Tim Mazzetti, who just a few weeks prior to this game was serving drinks as a Philadelphia bartender. The Falcons signed this "Walter Mitty" to a basic minimal contract. Mazzetti lived a dream and booted five field goals, including three in the fourth quarter, for all of Atlanta's points. The Grits Blitz defense in 1978 had failed to display evidence of its dominance from the previous season. But in this contest with their division rivals, the Falcons defense came alive and intercepted three Los Angeles passes, recovered one fumble, and their special teams blocked a punt. The win was the third straight for the 5–4 Falcons, while the loss was the second straight for the 7–2 Rams.

In the time between the Minnesota and Atlanta victories in the last weekend in October, a couple of winless teams finally won. The Cincinnati Bengals upended the visiting Houston Oilers, 28–13. The Bengals offense at last started to achieve a measure of success, as they accumulated 436 total yards against the Houston defense. Cincinnati quarterback Ken Anderson completed 11 of 16 passes for 268 yards and one touchdown. Bengals wide receiver Isaac Curtis caught four of Anderson's throws for 130 yards, including a 45-yard score. Houston running back Earl Campbell continued to have success despite his team's loss. Campbell rushed for 102 yards on 18 carries, marking his fifth 100-yard rushing game of the year.

The St. Louis Cardinals and their "rookie" head coach Bud Wilkinson also notched their first win of the year, and Wilkinson's first win in the professional coaching ranks. The Cards defeated the Philadelphia Eagles at Veterans Stadium, 16–10, as Cardinals quarterback Jim Hart completed 12 of 24 throws for 260 yards. Included in those statistics was a 55-yard touchdown toss in the second quarter to wide receiver Dave Steif. Philadelphia wide receiver Harold Carmichael also found success. Carmichael caught seven passes for 126 yards, including a 33-yard touchdown from quarterback Ron Jaworski. Carmichael also extended his consecutive game receiving streak to 89 in the losing effort. After the final gun, there was relief, sentimentality, and emotion on display in the St. Louis locker room, as a tearful and thankful Bud Wilkinson accepted the game ball from his victorious players, stating, "I've never been prouder to be associated with any group of men in my life." His players were equally proud of him. "I've been in this league seventeen years," said Cardinals placekicker and captain Jim Bakken to Wilkinson. "I can tell you that other coaches would have quit on us. But you stayed with us and gave us inspiration. A lot of coaches would have berated us, called us on the carpet. But each week you told us we were getting closer." Tears were shed amongst many of the Cardinal players during Bakken's speech, and every man embraced Wilkinson as he congratulated his players.

The Green Bay Packers were embracing the possibility of obtaining a winning season. Green Bay notched their seventh win of the year with a 9–7 triumph over Tampa Bay in sunny Florida. Packers placekicker Chester Marcol kicked a 48-yard field goal with 41 seconds left in the game for the lead. Green Bay's defense then hung on for the win. The Packers' 7–2 record was their best start to a season since 1966. "I was having a horrible day," admitted Marcol after the game, "and I was hoping for another chance." The Packers' lead in the NFC Central was now a full two games over the 5–4 Minnesota Vikings. One more win for Green Bay, and they would be guaranteed at the very least to obtain a .500 season.

New England owned the same record as the Packers at 7–2 following their 55–21 rout of the visiting New York Jets. Patriots quarterback Steve Grogan led his offense to scores on its first seven possessions, as New England built a very comfortable 41–7 halftime cushion. Grogan ended the afternoon completing 15 of 19 passes for 281 yards and four touchdown passes. In other Week 9 contests, the Pittsburgh Steelers barely escaped an upset at the hands of the Kansas City Chiefs at Three Rivers Stadium, 27–24. Pittsburgh improved to 8–1 with the win. Kansas City dropped to 2–7. The Chicago Bears succumbed to an upset from their NFC Central rivals, the Detroit Lions, 21–17. The Bears were halted twice in the fourth quarter deep in Lions territory by Detroit's determined defense. The win was Detroit's second in a row and improved their record in the NFC Central Division to 3–6, while the Bears, a playoff team from a year ago, fell to an identical 3–6 last-place record.

The San Diego Chargers had an even worse record than the Lions and the Bears, but they were building a foundation for success, despite their 2–6 record. They were more than capable of upsetting contending teams by the latter part of the 1978 season, and on October 29, they did just that as they came from behind to stun the Raiders at the Oakland-Alameda County Coliseum, 27–23. Oakland owned a 20–7 halftime lead, but the clutch passing of Chargers quarterback Dan Fouts resulted in 13 fourth quarter points to produce the win. Fouts was definitely not a scrambling or a running quarterback, but he had a very strong arm, which was a necessity for a passer who stayed in the pocket. Most importantly, Fouts had the mindset of a linebacker. He was a dynamic and courageous team leader, and his demonstrative nature in the huddle and at the snap of the ball inspired his teammates to achieve great things, beginning in 1978. By the end of the decade, Fouts and the San Diego offense would rewrite the league record books.

The season's tenth week featured a very close margin of victory for all of the teams. Incredibly, an average total of a mere six points separated the winner and the loser in all 14 games. The Chicago Bears continued their tailspin into the cellar of the NFC Central Division by losing to the visiting Seattle Seahawks, 31–29. Seattle's offense produced points in long-distance drives of 70, 73, 72, and 73 yards. Left-handed Seattle quarterback Jim Zorn paced the Seahawks with 208 passing yards and two touchdown tosses, both to his reliable wide receiver Steve Largent. Seattle moved up to even their record at 5–5 with their victory. The fast-crumbling Bears dropped to 3–7 and were virtually out of the playoff chase.

Another surprisingly tight contest took place at the Los Angeles Memorial Coliseum, where the Rams barely survived their meeting with the Tampa Bay Buccaneers. It took four field goals from Rams placekicker Frank Corral, the last one coming with but three seconds left in the game, to give Los Angeles a narrow 26–23 victory over the Buccaneers. John McKay, the dry-witted head coach for Tampa Bay, was once the successful head coach for the University of Southern California, and he desperately wanted to avoid any embarrassment in returning to his old stomping grounds. His Bucs surprised many folks in this one, as they scored two touchdowns in the fourth quarter to tie the game. Tampa Bay's defense also kept the explosive Rams offense to just two touchdowns. "McKay knew his team would always be within a score of winning as long as his defense played to their potential," observed author and pro football historian Denis M. Crawford. Two former USC players notched touchdowns for Tampa Bay in this contest, as both halfback Ricky Bell and John McKay's own son, flanker J.K. McKay, crossed the goal line in the same stadium where they once experienced so many victorious collegiate memories. The Rams' defense performed admirably, however, and proved to be too much in the end for the Buccaneers to handle. They sacked reserve Tampa Bay quarterback Mike Rae nine times, intercepted three of his passes, and recovered two Buccaneer fumbles, thereby giving the Rams enough scoring chances to win. The Rams now owned an 8–2 record, which was the best mark in the NFC. Tampa Bay, though vastly improved from their multitude of embarrassing performances since 1976, fell to 4–6.

Improvement was on the minds of the New York Jets, as they traveled to Denver to take on the favored Broncos at Mile High Stadium. The Jets played what was possibly their best game of the season against the defending AFC champions, as they upset Denver, 31–28. The New York defense shut out the Broncos offense in the second half, and reserve Jets quarterback Matt Robinson threw touchdown passes to wide receivers Derrick Gaffney and Wesley Walker. Gaffney's 4-yard scoring reception precluded Walker's 75-yard touchdown catch with 5:45 left in the fourth quarter. "I just took off," said Walker after securing the pigskin on his long distance score. Denver placekicker Jim Turner missed a chance to tie the game with eight seconds remaining in the game when his 42-yard field goal attempt fell just short of the crossbar. The win boosted the Jets to a 6–4 record, while Denver's loss dropped them to an identical 6–4 record, which was also the same record as their AFC West foes, the Oakland Raiders, who defeated the Kansas City Chiefs on November 5 by a final score of 20–10.

A pivotal game in Miami's Orange Bowl helped in an indirect way to decide a divisional champion. The defending world champion Dallas Cowboys took on the Miami Dolphins in an interconference game between two tough contenders. The Cowboys were in the midst of a mid-season slump. They would appear to be on the verge of a dynasty one week, and then look like an also-ran the next. Dallas rarely lost to AFC teams during the decade, but Miami took advantage of the Cowboys' current drop-off by building an early lead, then holding on to win, 23–16. The lost left the Cowboys with a 6–4 record, a game behind the rival 7–3 Washington Redskins in the NFC East. A period of soul searching was due in Dallas. They were certainly not the first champion to suffer from complacency in the year following a Super Bowl title, and they would certainly not be the last. "I don't think they were playing with emotion," observed Miami defensive tackle Bob Baumhower after the game. The Cowboys knew that they had to right their ship if they expected to return to the playoffs. "The challenge is there right now," said Dallas tailback Tony Dorsett. "If we don't rise to it now, if this isn't the incentive, then something's wrong." The Cowboys as we shall see, would use this loss as a motivational factor for the remainder of their regular season. Like many defeats, it would inspire their surge to the playoffs.

Another team that had to surprisingly struggle in their tenth game was the New England Patriots, who tangled with the Bills at Rich Stadium. The Pats held on to survive this AFC East matchup, 14–10, thanks in large part to the rushing abilities of running back Horace Ivory, who ran for 128 yards on 16 carries, and who also scored both of New England's touchdowns on runs of 19 and 5 yards.

But perhaps the most important game in the league's tenth week occurred on *Monday Night Football* at Baltimore's Memorial Stadium. The I-95 Beltway neighbors—the Redskins and the Colts—met in a tough contest which in the end would keep the standings tight in the NFC East. The Colts were languishing in fourth place in the AFC East, but often-injured quarterback Bert Jones came off the bench and threw for three touchdown passes. Jones' inspirational play in the midst of the pain from his continued shoulder separation spurred his teammates to compete strongly, especially in the fourth quarter. His 27-yard scoring toss to wide receiver Roger Carr with 3:08 left in the game produced the winning margin, 21–17. Carr also caught a 78-yard touchdown pass from Jones in the third quarter. The win improved Baltimore's record to 4–6, while the loss dropped the Redskins to a record of 7–3. Washington's loss also kept them from increasing their slim one-game lead over the rival Dallas Cowboys in the NFC East.

"We all know Bert is hurt," said Carr. "Bert is the heart and guts of this team. I've caught him enough that I know when he's right. Tonight he wasn't right until the fourth quarter and then that last touchdown—the ball had all the old-time zip." Even so, Jones was seen grimacing in pain after every throw. The jury was out as to how much pain Jones would be able to tolerate to keep his team in contention.

The pain of having a glorious upset win in your grasp, only to lose to a hated rival on the last play of the game, was a pain that the New Orleans Saints had to experience in their 11th contest of the season at the Louisiana Superdome. The Saints were playing host to the Atlanta Falcons, who desperately needed to win in order to stay alive for a potential wild card berth. New Orleans had the spoiler role and played it well, as they built a 17–3 lead at halftime. Atlanta mounted a comeback in the fourth quarter, and trailed 17–13 with less than a minute to play. The Falcons were at their own 43-yard line as the clock wound down to ten seconds remaining in the game. The situation caused the Saints to instantly and automatically revert to having their defensive players assume the prevent defense, a formation which has most (if not all) defensive backs playing back deep to prohibit a long pass completion. The prevent also sometimes includes extra defensive backs coming off the bench and substituting for linebackers or even defensive linemen, thereby giving the defense more coverage deep down the field. Many coaches swore by the prevent defense in the 1970s, but some did not. Oakland head coach John Madden once declared, "The only thing that the prevent defense prevents is victory." Such would be the unfortunate outcome for the Saints on this day.

The play was called "Big Ben right," and it was installed in the Atlanta game plan just after their tenth game. The Falcons placed a couple of receivers—Alfred Jenkins and Wallace Francis—on the weak side of the formation, and had them both run deep fly patterns. Atlanta quarterback Steve Bartkowski received great protection from his offensive line, and after a couple of seconds, he threw the ball deep down the field. By this time, New Orleans defensive backs Clarence Chapman, Ralph McGill, and Tom Myers had recognized what the play would be, and they congregated quickly around Jenkins and Francis around the 15-yard line. The ball descended and was tipped by both Chapman and Francis at the same instant. Jenkins was near the sideline at the 12-yard line, and he caught the deflected ball with no interference from McGill or Myers, both of whom had fallen over the falling Francis. "All I know is we all went up for it," described Chapman, "it was batted up in the air, and they [the Falcons] came down with it." Jenkins ran untouched into the end zone as time expired, setting off a raucous victory celebration by the Falcons. To the casual observer, the play appeared to be nothing more than a wild streak of good luck. In reality, the play was planned as it occurred, including the tipping of the ball to a teammate. The new rule established in 1978 that permitted an offensive player tipping or deflecting the ball to another offensive player thus saw its first major example of being used and of actually working to perfection in this game in New Orleans. Atlanta's "Big Ben" play—as it was known for posterity—gave the 7–4 Falcons a 20–17 win over the Saints, and thus kept them alive for a possible playoff berth.

A couple of other teams during that weekend were also forced to come from behind to win tight contests. The Houston Oilers found themselves trailing the New England Patriots in Foxboro, 23–7 at the half. Stopping the explosive New England offense was a tough chore for most good defenses, but the Houston defense outdid themselves in the second half, as they shutout the Patriots after halftime, and limited them to a mere 43 yards in the last two quarters. The Houston offense began chipping away at their deficit in the third quarter with the first of two touchdown runs by running back Rob Carpenter. Houston quarterback Dan Pastorini connected on 15 of 28 passes for 200 yards in the game, and threw a 10-yard pass for the winning touchdown to veteran tight end Rich Caster with 2:29 left to play. The Oilers prevailed, 26–23. "Throughout the second half, on every play in the huddle, Pastorini kept saying, 'we're gonna score, we're gonna win,'" said Houston wide receiver Ken Burrough. "It got infectious."

Winning close games over contending opponents had been somewhat infectious for the Los Angeles Rams throughout the better part of the decade. The Rams took their 8–2 record into a struggle against the visiting 9–1 Pittsburgh Steelers. It was a game where both stalwart defenses took control on a soft and muddy field, limiting the opposing offenses to just one touchdown apiece. The Steelers scored on a 14-yard third quarter touchdown pass from quarterback Terry Bradshaw to wide receiver Lynn Swann. Los Angeles placekicker Frank Corral answered a few minutes later when he booted a 37-yard field goal. That score was followed in the fourth quarter by a 10-yard scoring pass from Rams quarterback Pat Haden to wide receiver Willie Miller, which proved to be the winning touchdown. The Rams defense performed admirably, so much so that the Steelers' running backs were held to a meager 59 total yards on 25 carries. Pittsburgh's offense was held to a yardage total of minus 13 yards in the Steelers' final seven series with the ball. Los Angeles endured in this muddy struggle, 10–7. "The Rams are a super team," said Steelers head coach Chuck Noll. "There is no question about that. The difference was we couldn't run and they could. Except for our touchdown drive, our offense couldn't get anything going."

Several other tight games in Week 11 included Baltimore's 17–14 win over Seattle, Miami's 25–24 victory over Buffalo, San Diego's 29–23 overtime triumph over Kansas City, Minnesota's 17–14 narrow win over Chicago, and Washington's 16–13 overtime conquest of the New York Giants. None of these games could have been considered an upset, but the Dolphins, the Vikings, and the Redskins each could ill-afford to lose the aforementioned contests. Miami never lost to Buffalo during the course of the decade, but the Bills played them tough in several of their meetings, including on November 12, 1978. Dolphin halfback Delvin Williams rushed for 144 yards and scored on touchdown runs of 25 and 26 yards. Williams' efforts enabled him to eclipse the 1,000-yard mark for the year, and gave Miami their 18th straight win over Buffalo.

Minnesota's veteran roster was by 1978 expected to annually lose to younger, faster, and healthier teams in their division ... like the Bears. The Vikings managed to sweep their season series with the Bears, however, with the second win pulling the Norsemen even at 7–4 with the Green Bay Packers for first place in the NFC Central Division. Chicago tailback Walter Payton— like Miami's Delvin Williams—also went over the 1,000-yard rushing mark for the year, thanks to his 127-yard effort against Minnesota. But Payton's performance could not out-shine the play of Minnesota quarterback Fran Tarkenton, who completed 24 passes in 37 attempts for 245 yards against the Monsters of the Midway.

The Redskins were able to stay a game ahead of the Cowboys in the NFC East with their overtime win over the Giants at RFK Stadium. Washington tried throughout the game to give control of the contest to New York, and then tried desperately in the final minutes to come back and secure the lead. Washington halfback Mike Thomas managed to tie the game at 13–13 with a 1-yard run with 1:05 left in regulation. Washington placekicker Mark Moseley then had two chances to win the game in overtime. His first attempted field goal from 35 yards out failed, but his second opportunity from 45 yards out with 8:32 elapsed in overtime won the game for the Redskins, 16–13. The Redskins were now boasting an 8–3 record in their division, a game ahead of the Dallas Cowboys, who appeared to finally resuscitate themselves with a 42–14 romp over the Green Bay Packers in Milwaukee. The Cowboys ran the ball for a then–club record 313 yards against the Packers defense, with halfback Tony Dorsett rushing for 149 yards, and fullback Robert Newhouse rumbling for 101 more. Both Dorsett and Newhouse scored two touchdowns apiece in the massacre. "You saw a team [Dallas] today play like a Super Bowl team," said Green Bay head coach Bart Starr.

Hopes for an invitation to the Super Bowl were still alive for several teams by the time Week 13 of the 1978 season rolled around. Key victories during this week would keep those hopes alive for three teams in the AFC Western Division. The San Diego Chargers evened their record at 6–6 with a 13–7 surprise upset win over the host Minnesota Vikings. The victory was San Diego's fourth straight win, and it was earned surprisingly through the strength of their defense, which limited the Vikings to 63 rushing yards. The Chargers' defense also intercepted two passes from Minnesota quarterback Fran Tarkenton, and recovered two fumbles to preserve their lead in the fourth quarter. San Diego wide receiver John Jefferson caught a somewhat comical 10-yard touchdown pass from quarterback Dan Fouts for the winning score. Fouts fell down while dropping back to pass, got up, and threw a dart to Jefferson who was triple covered by three Minnesota defensive backs. "It was a delay pattern," Fouts quipped when describing the play. "I just had to get up and throw it." The loss to the Chargers did not hurt the Vikings, however, as they remained in first place in the NFC Central Division with the Green Bay Packers, who also lost at Denver's Mile High Stadium to the Broncos, 16–3.

The Oakland Raiders improved their record to 8–4 with a 29–17 win over the visiting Detroit Lions. The Raiders and the Broncos were both now holding strong with identical records in the AFC West as the season neared the home stretch. Oakland's win over the Lions was due primarily to the play of Raiders running back Mark van Eeghan, who scored twice on two short touchdown runs, and who recovered teammate Cliff Branch's fumble in the end zone for another touchdown.

Recovering another fumble earlier on the same day in Giants Stadium turned out to be historic for the visiting Philadelphia Eagles. The Giants were playing the role of spoilers to the hilt, as they were defeating the favored Eagles, 17–12, late in the fourth quarter. New York had possession of the pigskin, and all they needed to do was to have quarterback Joe Pisarcik fall down on the ball for three successive plays to run out the clock and claim the victory. On first down, Pisarcik fell on the ball as everyone expected, but on second down the Eagles defenders crashed into the Giants backfield and hoped to plow right into the turf-bound quarterback. But Pisarcik handed off to fullback Larry Csonka instead. Giants offensive coordinator Bob Gibson quickly decided after that play that the possibility of a fumble would be decreased if he had Pisarcik hand the ball off to Csonka one more time. There was now only 28 seconds left on the clock and a third-and-two situation from the New York 29-yard line. Gibson sent in the play "Pro 65 Up," which was a basic straight ahead dive run by the fullback, a play which every team runs when trying to gain a yard or trying to run out the clock. Most of the Giants players in the offensive huddle vocally tried to get Pisarcik to disregard Gibson's play, and instead just fall on the ball again. Pisarcik refused to change the play, however, mainly because he was reprimanded earlier in the season for not following Gibson's orders. At the snap, Pisarcik had difficulty handling the ball. He turned to hand the ball off to Csonka, but the ball brushed against Csonka's hip instead of lodging into his stomach. The ball fell to the turf and bounced once as Pisarcik tried to recover it. Unfortunately for the Giants quarterback, the ball slipped out of his arms as if it had liquid grease all over it. Philadelphia cornerback Herman Edwards had by this time entered the Giants backfield. He picked up the pigskin and nestled it in his arms as if the two were meant for each other. Edwards was probably just as surprised at laying claim to his good fortune as everyone else on the field and all of the 70,318 fans in the stands. He raced 26 yards untouched into the end zone for the winning touchdown and was immediately mobbed by his joyous teammates. "I looked back for a flag," Edwards recalled, "but everyone was jumping on me so I knew it was good." The Eagles had won, 19–17. "That's the most horrifying ending to a ball game I've ever seen," said a dejected Giants head coach John McVay from the New York locker room.

The play went down in history as "The Miracle in the Meadowlands," and besides making Edwards famous and Pisarcik infamous, it kept the Eagles alive in their hunt for a playoff spot with a 7–5 record. New York fell to 5–7 and was now for all intents and purposes out of the post-season chase. Giants offensive coordinator Bob Gibson was fired immediately after the game, and McVay and the remainder of his coaching staff were fired as soon as the regular season ended.

A few other postscripts surrounded this miraculous ending. Many people blamed New York fullback Larry Csonka as much as Pisarcik for the fumble, but the media was not buying it. "They [the media] preferred to blame a guy [Pisarcik] who was not as famous as Csonka," opined Pro Football Hall of Fame Vice President of Media Operations Joe Horrigan. Also, an unreported (at that time) irony involved a short discussion before the snap of the ball between Giants center Jim Clack and Eagles noseguard Charlie Johnson. "Usually when the quarterback is just going to fall on the ball," said Clack, "we tell the other team to take it easy and not bury him. When Charlie Johnson, the guy I was playing opposite, asked me if he were to take it easy, I said, 'No, we're running a play.'" Clack's honest answer was fateful indeed. NFL coaches made adjustments quickly in the aftermath of the Giants' gigantic miscue. From the following week to this very day, all teams that are running out the clock at the end of a game will put a player 10–15 yards behind the quarterback, in the event that an opponent recovers a fumble and starts to return it to the end zone, just as Edwards had done against the Giants on November 19, 1978. Finally, the two most notable opponents in the Miracle at the Meadowlands experienced another irony, as they both eventually got to wear the same uniform. Pisarcik was traded to the Eagles in 1980 and became a teammate of Edwards as both men took the field for Philadelphia in Super Bowl XV.

New York's other team—the Jets—also lost a close game when they were upended by the visiting New England Patriots by the same score that felled the Giants in the New Jersey Meadowlands, 19–17. The Patriots required a 24-yard field goal from placekicker David Posey with 2:30 left in the game to give them their ninth win of the season against three losses. The Pats ran for 225 yards as a team against the Jets defense, and kept a slight grasp of their one-game lead over the Miami Dolphins in the AFC East standings. New York wide receiver Wesley Walker caught another touchdown pass, this one coming from 56 yards out from reserve quarterback Matt Robinson. Walker would end the 1978 season with 48 receptions worth 1,169 yards and eight touchdowns, and his 24.4 yards-per-catch average was the best average in the league for receivers with more than 20 receptions. Walker would be unanimously named to the All-Pro team in 1978.

Another unanimous All-Pro in 1978 was rookie Houston running back Earl Campbell, who was having an outstanding season. So outstanding in fact, that Campbell would become the first rookie runner to lead the NFL in rushing since the great Cleveland Browns Hall of Famer Jim Brown did it in 1957. Campbell's most memorable moment occurred on *Monday Night Football* to close out the Week 12 games, when the Oilers took on the Miami Dolphins at the Astrodome. The "Eighth Wonder of the World," as the Astrodome was called in the sporting world during the 1970s, reverberated with the loudest noise in its history, and the ABC-TV cameras captured over 50,000 fans waving blue pom-poms and blue placards with the words "Luv Ya Blue" on them. The fans also sang a song called "Luv Ya Blue" all night long after every Houston score. The song was sung to the tune of the Beatles' hit "Love Me Do," albeit with a bit of a country and western flair. It was a raucous night, and both teams fought hard all game long. The score was tied at 21–21 as the final quarter began. The Oilers and Campbell saved their best for the end however, and like their new theme song, they were quite a hit on this night. Campbell rushed for a conference-best 199 yards and four touchdowns in the game, the last of which late in the fourth quarter came on an 81-yard dash down the far sideline. Campbell took a pitchout from quarterback Dan Pastorini, swept to his right, and out-raced the Miami defenders to the end zone. "If he [Campbell] keeps up this pace, you can be damned sure that he'll be the NFL's best player ever," said a rather biased Houston head coach Bum Phillips. "He is the ultimate team player. He wants to do everything in his power to help the team."

Houston's defense was carved up by Miami quarterback Bob Griese, however, to the tune of 349 yards and two touchdowns passes. Nevertheless, time ran out on the Dolphins at the end. Houston's 35–30 triumph over Miami gave the Oilers and the Dolphins identical 8–4 records, as both teams held on to second place in their respective divisions. The Dolphins-Oilers game also made the list among the greatest games of the decade as determined by an esteemed group of pro football writers and reporters just prior to 1980, as it ranked number 15 in the top 20 games of the 1970s.

The Thanksgiving Day weekend brought forth more excitement, and some upsets as well. The first upset happened on Turkey Day inside the Pontiac Silverdome, as the host Detroit Lions upended the defending AFC champion Denver Broncos, 17–14. As the score indicated, both defenses were able to stymie the opposing offenses for most of the game. The Lions defense managed to sack Denver quarterback Craig Morton six times, thus increasing their NFL lead in that category to 48 sacks. Detroit running back Horace King culminated one of the few impressive scoring drives of the game in the fourth quarter. King dove into the end zone for a 1-yard touchdown, thus completing an 11-play, 77-yard scoring drive. Denver placekicker Jim Turner had a chance to tie the game at the end of regulation, but his 51-yard field goal attempt fell just short. Detroit once again excelled in the role of Thanksgiving Day spoilers, defeating Denver and thereby dropping the Broncos' record to 8–5.

The Broncos did not lose their lead in the AFC West, however, because the Seattle Seahawks pulled off a similar surprise in Oakland. Seattle had defeated the Raiders up in Seattle on October 22, and no team since 1965 had beaten Oakland twice in one season, making Seattle's accomplishment in this game even more astounding. Seattle quarterback Jim Zorn won this second battle of left-handed signal callers (Oakland quarterback Ken Stabler was also left-handed) by leading three distinct scoring drives against the Raiders. The first one went for 80 yards and ended with a 38-yard touchdown pass from Zorn to wide receiver Steve Raible. The second big Seahawks drive went for 84 yards, and culminated with a 27-yard scoring pass from Zorn to wide receiver Steve Largent. The final Seattle scoring drive came right after Oakland took the lead late in the fourth quarter with a 31-yard pass from Stabler to tight end Dave Casper. Zorn then connected on five passes worth 51 yards of real estate to position placekicker Efren Herrera to kick the game-winning 46-yard field goal with two seconds left. Seattle won 17–16, had swept Oakland in their season series for the first time ever, and had boosted their record to 7–6. "Don't forget," said Zorn to reporters in the postgame Seattle locker room, "this is the first time we've *ever* been over .500."

The Buffalo Bills were certainly not going to go over .500 in the standings in 1978, but on the same day that Seattle swept Oakland, the Bills enjoyed their best game of the year. O.J. Simpson was no longer on the team, having been traded to San Francisco before the start of the season. Simpson's replacement was rookie Terry Miller out of Oklahoma State. Miller had yet to surpass the 100-yard mark in any of his first 12 games with the Bills, having accumulated a 50 yards-per-game rushing average during those first 12 contests. His 13th game against the visiting New York Giants was different, however. Miller rushed for 208 yards against the Giants on 21 carries. His single-game yardage totals were the highest individual mark in the league in 1978. Miller also scored twice on runs of 39 and 13 yards. Roland Hooks was Miller's running mate, and he chalked up an additional 115 yards on 12 carries in the same game, including a touchdown of his own as the Bills crushed their cross-state adversaries, 41–17. The victory would be a much needed ray of light in an otherwise underachieving season for the Bills, who finished the 1978 campaign with a 5–11 record.

Several other upsets in Week 13 were unique for several reasons. Miami's Orange Bowl was the scene where the New York Jets stunned the Dolphins for the second time this season. The Jets' 24–13 win on November 26 was indicative of how much they had improved since Walt Michaels became their head coach back in 1977. The win boosted the Jets to a 7–6 record, and revived their faint hopes for a wild card spot. The loss dropped the Dolphins to 8–5, a full two games behind the AFC East–leading New England Patriots, who were cruising along with a 10–3 record. Miami's loss also displayed the depths of their current slump. "I'm the leader of the offense," said Miami quarterback Bob Griese, who fumbled the ball in a critical situation and who threw three interceptions against the Jets, "and the offense scored six points. Draw your own conclusions." Miami head coach Don Shula knew that time was running out for his team. "It [the loss to the Jets] really puts us in a situation where we've got to win them all [their remaining three games] to get into the playoffs," surmised Shula.

A conclusion in the AFC Western Division left plenty of football experts scratching their scalps. The Kansas City Chiefs notched their first shutout win at Arrowhead Stadium by blanking the San Diego Chargers, 23–0. The Chiefs found a way to read and react well to the Chargers' passing game by intercepting reserve quarterback James Harris five times. Harris was filling in for the injured Dan Fouts. The win was Kansas City's third of the year, while the loss dropped the Chargers to 6–7 and virtually out of the playoff picture.

Another big surprise in Week 13 was Cleveland's upset of the Los Angeles Rams at Municipal Stadium in Cleveland. The Browns had no trouble scoring against one of the NFL's best defenses, and posted a 30–19 victory. "It was our first good game against a competitive team," admitted Cleveland head coach Sam Rutigliano. Cleveland quarterback Brian Sipe threw for 246 yards, which included a 31-yard touchdown toss to wide receiver Reggie Rucker. Cleveland tailback Greg Pruitt added a scintillating 57-yard touchdown run in the victory. Finally, Cleveland's defense limited the Rams to just four field goals until late in the fourth quarter, and knocked star Los Angeles running back Lawrence McCutcheon out of the game with a torn hamstring injury. Cleveland thus improved to 7–6 with this win, while the Rams dropped to 10–3, which was still two games ahead of their next closest competitors in the NFC West. "Now that we've conquered adversity, we've got to see if we can handle success," added Rutigliano.

A couple of other successful teams were also surging towards divisional championships with victories in their Week 13 contests. The Dallas Cowboys defeated the Washington Redskins at Texas Stadium, 37–10, while the Pittsburgh Steelers crushed the San Francisco 49ers at Candlestick Park on *Monday Night Football*, 24–7. The Cowboys had lost a tough game to the Redskins earlier in the season, and their vengeful answer to that previous loss came on Thanksgiving with the stellar play of all aspects of their team. The Doomsday Defense limited the Redskins to 201 total yards, and Dallas' multi-talented offense racked up 507 total yards of their own. Reserve

Dallas fullback Scott Laidlaw filled in nicely for injured teammate Robert Newhouse by rushing for 122 yards and scoring two touchdowns. Dallas now held control of first place in the NFC East with a 9–4 record, while the Redskins fell into a tie for second place in the division with the 8–5 Philadelphia Eagles.

The Steelers' win over San Francisco showcased their aerial attack. Pittsburgh quarterback Terry Bradshaw was continuously taking advantage of the new rules which helped out his pass receivers. Bradshaw threw for three touchdowns against the 49ers, two of which went to wide receiver Lynn Swann, and the other of which went to wide receiver John Stallworth. The Steel Curtain defense chipped in with five pass interceptions in the win, which was Pittsburgh's 11th of the year. No team in the league had a better record than the 11–2 Steelers at this stage of the season.

Prior to 1978, the regular season would have been completed by this juncture, but the two extra games beginning in 1978 would extend the chances of success for the 14 teams who were still alive for a berth in the postseason. The race to make the playoffs was over for three teams in the NFL, as the Dallas Cowboys, the Los Angeles Rams, and the Pittsburgh Steelers each clinched their respective division titles, the first teams to do so this year. The age-old belief that defenses win championships was proven once again for these three division winners. The Cowboys defeated the New England Patriots in Texas Stadium by a score of 17–10, in what many experts described as a possible preview of Super Bowl XIII. This highly competitive matchup saw the Cowboys come from behind in the second half. Their Doomsday Defense shut out the powerful Patriots offense in the third and fourth quarters, and Dallas quarterback Roger Staubach threw two touchdown passes to provide the winning margin. One of Staubach's scoring tosses came from 40 yards out as the result of a gadget play. Staubach handed the ball off to running back Scott Laidlaw, who ran close to the line of scrimmage, then quickly turned around and flipped the ball back to Staubach, who then threw it deep downfield to wide receiver Tony Hill. New England defensive back Tim Fox caught up to Hill just after Hill caught the ball at the 3-yard line, but Hill managed to break the plane of the goal line for the touchdown. "They were doubling me with the cornerback short and the safety [Fox] deep," described Hill. "Fox is as aggressive as [Dallas safety] Cliff Harris on running plays, which is saying a lot, so he came zooming up when he saw Laidlaw going into the line. I ran right by him." It took plays like that for the Cowboys to defeat a truly strong Patriots team, because the game was so evenly matched. Dallas' record improved to 10–4 with the win, while New England's loss dropped them to an identical 10–4 record, which was still good enough for the Pats to maintain their sole ownership of first place in the AFC East.

Losing was not taken so well in New Jersey, however. The ramifications from the Miracle in the Meadowlands game on November 19 was having its effects a couple of weeks later for many disgruntled New York Giants fans. Ron Freiman, a Giants season ticket holder for the past 23 years, placed an ad in the local newspapers asking fans to send him their tickets for their next home game on December 3 against the Los Angeles Rams. The frustrated Freiman wanted to obtain the tickets so he could burn them in a pile in front of Giants Stadium before the Rams game. Apparently he burned about 100 tickets in a bedpan, with Giants owner Wellington Mara's name printed on the front. Despite rumors to the contrary, Freiman's bedpan is not a part of the collection of exhibits at the Pro Football Hall of Fame in Canton, Ohio.

The Rams' 20–17 win over the Giants that day did little to assuage Freiman's disgust at his team's performance. The strength of the Rams defense decided the winner, in particular their pass defense. Los Angeles cornerback Pat Thomas was covering New York receivers tight all day. He intercepted a fourth quarter pass and returned it 33 yards for a touchdown. Rams safety Dave Elmendorf also recovered a Giants fumble a few minutes later, and that recovery led to a key Frank Corral field goal for the eventual winning points. The Rams now owned an NFC-best record of 11–3. The Rams would eventually go on to earn the home-field advantage in the playoffs in the NFC, thanks to finishing the 1978 season with the best record in the conference (12–4). Dallas also finished the regular season with an identical record, but their loss to the Rams on September 17 gave Los Angeles the right to play all of their postseason games at home.

The AFC's Pittsburgh Steelers would also end up playing their playoff contests at home, thanks to their impressive record. By 1978, everyone in the league was used to seeing their Steel Curtain defense punish opponents, just as they have done since their first playoff season in 1972. They did so again in Week 14 by limiting the Houston Oilers to just one meager field goal. Pittsburgh's offense did just enough to outscore the Luv Ya Blue Oilers in the Astrodome, 13–3. Pittsburgh now sported the best record in the entire NFL with a mark of 12–2. Houston's loss dropped them to 9–5, but they were still very much alive in the mix for a possible wild card spot in the playoffs. Time was running out, however, on teams who had winning records, but were still behind in the standings.

A rather unique situation was occurring in the NFC Central Division, as both the Minnesota Vikings and the Green Bay Packers were both tied with each other for first place in the standings with identical 7–5–1 records. These two teams met in Week 13 at Lambeau Field and fought to a 10–10 tie after a full period of overtime. The Packers actually had the game in hand, but the Vikings scored on a 5-yard touchdown pass from quarterback Fran Tarkenton to wide receiver Ahmad Rashad in the corner of the end zone in the waning seconds of regulation. "They [Green Bay] had us in the bag and they couldn't keep us there," said Tarkenton. Both teams missed field goals in the overtime period. This tie would have far-reaching implications in the NFC playoff picture as the season-concluding weeks went by. In Week 14, the Packers traveled to Tampa Bay and upended the Buccaneers, 17–7, which gave the Packers their eighth win of the season, and which guaranteed them their first winning season since 1972.

The Vikings on the same day were visited by the Philadelphia Eagles, who were still on a proverbial high following their Miracle in the Meadowlands victory a couple of weeks earlier against the New York Giants. The Eagles ambushed the Vikings in the first half of their matchup with three touchdown passes from quarterback Ron Jaworski to wide receivers Charlie Smith and Harold Carmichael. The lanky Carmichael caught two of the scores from 56 and 21 yards out. The Eagles took a 27–14 lead into halftime.

Minnesota came back strong in the second half, however, thanks to the strength of their defense, which refused to bend in the final stages of the game and which shut out the Eagles in the final two quarters. Minnesota quarterback Fran Tarkenton made full use of his defense's ability to get the ball back for their offense. Tarkenton completed 30 passes in 56 attempts against the Eagles. "I've pitched a lot of innings this year," chuckled Tarkenton. Four of his completions went for touchdowns, including a 20-yard scoring pass to wide receiver Ahmad Rashad with 1:49 left, giving the Vikes a thrilling 28–27 victory. Minnesota thus was once again tied for first place with Green Bay at 8–5–1. Philadelphia's loss dropped them to 8–6, and left them with a tough but simple road ahead. If the Eagles won their final two games (against Dallas and New York), they would be in the playoffs. If they did not, they would need some help from some other teams to reach the postseason.

One team which helped itself immensely in Week 14 was the Denver Broncos, who traveled to Oakland and dominated their arch-rivals in the second half to produce a 21–6 victory, thereby giving the Orange and Blue sole possession of first place in the AFC West. Denver linebacker Randy Gradishar clinched the win with a 30-yard return of a fumble by Raiders running back Mark van Eeghan for a touchdown. The Broncos now owned a 9–5 record, while Oakland fell to 8–6 in the standings.

Other teams still in contention and posting big wins in their 14th game were the Seattle Sea-hawks, who beat the Cleveland Browns by a score of 47–24; the New York Jets, who defeated the Baltimore Colts 24–16; and the Miami Dolphins, who shut out the Washington Redskins, 16–0. Seattle was enjoying its best season ever, and their multi-faceted offense had no trouble with the Cleveland defense. Seattle fullback David Sims rushed for three touchdowns in the romp, and defensive lineman Bill Gregory recovered two key fumbles leading to Seattle scores. "David [Sims] is a fine football player," assessed Seattle head coach Jack Patera. "Anytime he's in there, we're stronger." The win marked Seattle's third straight triumph and guaranteed them at least a break-even season.

The history between the Jets and the Colts has had many important chapters, but in 1978, the Colts were in the midst of a depressing year, while the Jets were on the upsurge. New York swept their AFC East rivals from Maryland with a 33–10 win in the seventh week and a 24–16 triumph in the 14th week. A key player in the Jets' resurgence was wide receiver Wesley Walker, who caught two more touchdown passes in the second meeting with the Colts. Reserve Jets quarterback Matt Robinson connected with Walker on scoring passes of 38 and 48 yards. Walker thus became the first Jets pass receiver since Don Maynard in 1968 to eclipse 1,000 yards in pass receiving yardage in a year.

Rounding out Week 14 was a stellar performance from the playoff-hungry Miami Dolphins, who desperately wanted to avoid a repeat of the embarrassing loss that they endured in their previous game to the Jets. Miami sent Washington to their third straight defeat with their No-Name Defense, which picked off four of Washington quarterback Joe Theismann's passes. The Dolphins thus became the first team to shut out the Redskins in seven years. "It certainly was sudden death for us," said Miami head coach Don Shula of his team's victory over Washington, and of their need to win the rest of their games in order to have a chance at the playoffs.

A shutout victory by the Chicago Bears over the Green Bay Packers in Week 15 was also important to the playoff chase. The Bears were relegated to the role of spoiler, and they played that role perfectly against Green Bay, defeating the Packers 14–0 at Soldier Field. The loss did not eliminate the Packers from playoff competition, but it made their entry into the postseason quite a bit tougher. Fortunately for the Pack, their primary competitors in the NFC Central, the Minnesota Vikings, also lost on this day to the host Detroit Lions, 45–14. A win by either Minnesota or Green Bay was a virtual must in their final game of the season, but the Vikings held the tie-breaker. If they finished the regular season with an identical record as the Packers, the division title would go to Minnesota, based on the fact that the Vikings defeated Green Bay back in the eighth week of the season, and their second meeting resulted in a tie on November 26.

The Philadelphia Eagles were still in the playoff chase too, despite suffering a 31–13 trouncing at home at the hands of the Dallas Cowboys, who jumped to an early lead and dominated the Eagles throughout much of the game. Dallas running backs Tony Dorsett and Scott Laidlaw each scored two touchdowns apiece, and the Dallas Doomsday Defense racked up eight sacks, three interceptions, and two fumble recoveries in the rout. The Eagles still held an inside edge to a wild card spot in the NFC playoffs, however, based on their better overall record over a few other NFC teams. Because of the way things worked out with the other contending teams in the NFC, all the Eagles needed to do now was defeat the New York Giants at home in their final game of the year to make it to the postseason as a conference wild card entry.

Several teams in the AFC guaranteed themselves a ticket to the playoffs with victories in Week 15. New England played host to a potential spoiler in the Buffalo Bills, but they somehow managed to clip the Bills by a close score of 26–24, giving the Patriots an 11–4 record in the AFC East. New England took advantage of their opponent's poor clock management to position themselves for the winning 21-yard field goal, which came with eight seconds left in the game from placekicker David Posey. After several years of being a contending team, New England finally tasted the ownership of a division title. "Somebody could beat me up tonight and I wouldn't care," said a gleeful Posey from the victorious Patriots locker room. The excitement and happiness was shared by the members of the Patriots' offensive backfield. Running backs Sam Cunningham (768 yards rushing), Horace Ivory (693 yards rushing), Andy Johnson (675 yards rushing), and quarterback Steve Grogan (539 yards rushing) became the first quartet in league history to rush for more than 500 yards each in the same season. New England's total of 3,165 yards rushing as a team in 1978 also set a league record which has yet to be equaled. The New England Patriots were crowned as the new AFC East Champion, for the first time in their history.

The Miami Dolphins remained just a game behind the rival Pats, however, by powerfully dismantling the not-so-impressive Oakland Raiders at the Orange Bowl, 23–6. The win guaranteed the Dolphins possession of one of the two wild card spots in the AFC playoffs. A key player in Miami's victory was linebacker Larry Gordon, who intercepted three of the five passes that Oakland quarterback Ken Stabler errantly threw into the Dolphins secondary. "How can a linebacker play better than Larry Gordon did today?" asked Miami head coach Don Shula, who himself did a masterful job of getting his team back into the playoffs following a three-year absence from the postseason. "Stabler's receivers were really getting creamed," added Miami safety Tim Foley, "and he had a lot of deflected balls and tipped passes. But we made the breaks and took advantage of them."

The Houston Oilers took advantage of their opportunities and earned the other wild card in the AFC by defeating the New Orleans Saints in the Louisiana Superdome, 17–12. This contest was probably closer than it should have been, but the Oilers had to deal with several starters who were suffering injuries which kept some of them out of the lineup. A quick-out pass from Houston quarterback Dan Pastorini to rookie wide receiver and Olympic sprinter Robert Woods provided the Oilers with a spectacular highlight. Woods caught the ball near the far sideline at his own 28-yard line, broke to the inside to avoid the attempted tackle from New Orleans cornerback Maurice Spencer, and then raced down the field untouched to score an 80-yard touchdown for the winning points. Houston's win signaled their first trip to the playoffs since 1969. Despite his team's loss, New Orleans quarterback Archie Manning profited from the new passing rules instilled at the beginning of the year. Manning completed 25 of 37 passes for 251 yards against the Oilers, thereby giving him over 3,000 yards passing in a season, the first time that he eclipsed that mark in his pro career.

Some teams were in the midst of the playoffs already, as they found themselves in must-win games at the end of the regular season to reach the playoffs. The Atlanta Falcons and the Washington Redskins were two such teams, and they met each other in Week 15 in Atlanta. The Falcons had been a very lucky team during the last half of the 1978 season, having won three games already in the final minutes. Their meeting with the Redskins would make four heart-stopping triumphs for Atlanta. Placekicker Tim Mazzetti's 32-yard field goal with no time remaining won it for the Falcons, 20–17. The victory kept Atlanta alive for a wild card spot in the NFC with a 9–6 record. The Redskins dropped to 8–7, and needed to win their final game against Chicago, and then hope that Philadelphia and either Green Bay or Minnesota both lost their final games. The AFC playoff picture was already set by the end of Week 15, as New England, Miami, Pittsburgh, Houston, and Denver were all successful in making the postseason.

The final week of the 1978 regular season brought some surprises that virtually no one saw coming. It started with the shocking announcement from New England head coach Chuck Fairbanks six hours prior to the start of his team's game against the Dolphins in Miami. Fairbanks announced that he was quitting the team in order to become the head coach of the University of Colorado, effective immediately after the Patriots season ended. New England owner William H. Sullivan, Jr., suspended Fairbanks immediately, and assigned two of the team's assistant coaches— Ron Erhardt and Hank Bullough—to act as co-head coaches against the Dolphins. The Patriot players were naturally shocked by this unexpected development, and it showed on the field. Miami crushed New England, 23–3, thereby giving both teams an 11–5 regular season record. The Patriots already owned the AFC East championship, however, based on their better record against teams in their own division.

The Philadelphia Eagles did not have a problem with the absence of their head coach. Indeed it was quite the opposite. Dick Vermeil was labeled by the press as a "workaholic" for his 20 or more hours of work each day during the football season. Vermeil often slept on a cot in his office, and poured his heart and soul into his team. He reminded his players in a trembling voice just prior to their final game of the regular season against the visiting New York Giants about how far they had come as a team, and about the confidence that he had in their abilities. "Well guys ... twelve years ... twelve years have gone by since the Eagles have been a winner," Vermeil informed his players. "We're gonna come out winners today. You've worked like winners. You've played like winners. Sure, we've won a couple we should have lost, but we've lost a few we should have won. We're right where we ought to be, playing for the first winning season since 1966. Hey, God love all of you."

The Eagles took an early lead in cold and windy Veterans Stadium, and never lost it. Halfback Wilbert Montgomery scored twice in the first quarter. His second touchdown came when he gashed through the line on a trap draw and cruised into the end zone standing up from seven yards out. Later in the game, the Giants found themselves fighting not just the Eagles but their fans as well. An overzealous and most likely intoxicated Eagles fan ran onto the field and dove head-first into a couple of New York players who were standing—innocently enough—in their team's huddle during a television timeout. Luckily, no Giants player was injured in this blatant display of poor fan behavior. A few minutes later, Philadelphia linebacker Frank LeMaster's interception of a Joe Pisarcik pass and his 9-yard return for a score clinched Philadelphia's 20–3 victory. The Eagles were finally in the postseason for the first time since they won the 1960 NFL championship. "It's like a dream come true," said Coach Vermeil from a victorious Eagles locker room. "Just to be able to say we are winners, let alone a playoff team. It's a real warm, warm feeling."

The feelings of Minnesota Vikings head coach Bud Grant were a little different than Dick Vermeil's, but they were the result of similar news. The Vikings had not won an NFL championship since 1969, and they had been unsuccessful in their four Super Bowl appearances. Nevertheless, the Vikings claimed their eighth NFC Central Division title of the decade, despite their 27–20 loss in Oakland to the Raiders on the last Sunday of the season. Minnesota made the playoffs because the Green Bay Packers, who finished the season with an identical 8–7–1 record, also lost their final game. Green Bay fell down in the mud of the Los Angeles Memorial Coliseum to the Rams, 31–14. The term "backing into the playoffs" received another example in the fate of the Vikings, but Coach Grant was not depressed at how his team made it to the postseason.

"We achieved our goal," Grant said. "If we had a better record, it wouldn't give us any better shot of winning in the playoffs. Getting to the playoffs [as a division winner] makes us one of the six best teams in the NFL. I have no mixed emotions about getting in."

Minnesota was not alone in backing into the playoffs. The Atlanta Falcons also lost their last game to the St. Louis Cardinals in Busch Memorial Stadium, 42–21. But the Falcons were beneficiaries of both the Packers' loss and the Redskins' 14–10 loss to the Chicago Bears. So for the first time in their history, Atlanta was in the postseason tournament. Washington, on the other hand, was in first place in the NFC East after 11 weeks of the regular season with an 8–3 record. They would go on to lose their next five straight games and finish 1978 with an 8–8 record, good enough for third place in their division, and good enough to keep them out of the playoffs.

The NFL playoffs undertook a new look beginning in 1978. A new "wild card round" was held the week after the regular season ended. The two wild card teams in the AFC (Houston and Miami) would play each other, as would the two wild card teams in the NFC (Philadelphia and Atlanta). Those would be the only two games during that first postseason weekend. This was highly beneficial to the six division winners of both conferences, as the extra week off would give them a chance to rest their injured players and devise more diligent and detailed game plans for the second round of the playoffs, known as the divisional round. Was it an unfair advantage? Possibly. But it was earned legitimately through a better regular season record.

The first wild card game was held at Atlanta's Fulton County Stadium, where an overcast and rainy Christmas Eve afternoon saw the Eagles and the Falcons meet each other on a wet and muddy field. The Eagles began the contest with a first quarter touchdown to take the lead. Philadelphia quarterback Ron Jaworski hit wide receiver Harold Carmichael on a quick slant pattern from 13 yards out for a score. On the play, Carmichael brushed aside an attempted tackle by Atlanta defensive back Rolland Lawrence inside the 5-yard line, and waltzed into the end zone. The Falcons defense then decided to double and even triple-team Carmichael, and as a result limited him to just three more short receptions for the remainder of the game. The other Philadelphia wide receiver, Charlie "Homeboy" Smith, took advantage of the single coverage on his side with seven catches for 108 yards. Unfortunately for the Eagles, a season-long kicking problem manifested itself once again when placekicker Mike Michel missed the extra point after Carmichael's score. The Eagles defense, however, had been the team's strength all throughout the 1978 season, and they were strong once again during the first three quarters of this game, permitting zero points, and collecting four Falcon turnovers. Philadelphia tailback Wilbert Montgomery capitalized on one of those turnovers when he dove over from the 1-yard line to boost the Eagles' lead to 13–0 going into the final quarter. Montgomery's moment of success would be fleeting, however. He managed to run for 1,220 yards during the regular season, but in this game, the Atlanta defense held him to a paltry 19 yards on 16 carries.

Nevertheless, the Eagles appeared to have the game sewn up. Atlanta had failed to score a single point, and there was only five minutes left on the clock. The Falcons had been accustomed to coming from behind in several big games this season using the long pass, however, and they would miraculously do so once again on this day. Atlanta quarterback Steve Bartkowski took to the air. He hit wide receiver Wallace Francis with a 49-yard controversial completion to the Philadelphia 26-yard line. Francis had pried the ball away from Eagles defensive back John Sanders, but many felt that Francis was guilty of pass interference before the ball was caught. "That was the key play," said Philadelphia head coach Dick Vermeil. "It should have been offensive interference." Francis naturally disagreed. "There was no scuffling until we both had the ball," described Francis. "Maybe I'm a little stronger or maybe I wanted it badder."

Francis' catch set up Atlanta's first score. Falcons tight end Jim Mitchell ran a quick slant pattern four plays later and caught a 19-yard touchdown pass from Bartkowski to make the score 13–7. Atlanta was not done. They wasted little time when they got the ball back. Francis ran a deep post pattern and caught a 37-yard touchdown pass from Bartkowski with but 1:39 left in the game. On the play which sent the partisan Atlanta crowd into a frenzy, the Philadelphia defensive secondary misread their keys and left Francis unguarded deep down the middle of the field. It was the biggest and most costly mistake of the game. Atlanta placekicker Tim Mazzetti made good on the extra point conversion, and the Falcons led for the first time all day, 14–13.

Jaworski frantically drove the Eagles downfield, however, and positioned his offense for a game-winning field goal attempt from 34 yards out. Unfortunately for the Eagles, Michel's kick barely missed staying inside of the right upright with 13 seconds left, and the Falcons had notched yet another miracle win to their ledger, 14–13. It was the first playoff victory in their history, dating back to their first year in the NFL in 1966. In a somber Philadelphia postgame locker room, Coach Vermeil commented, "Mike Michel missed a chance to win it for us, but he sure didn't lose it for us." Indeed, the Eagles defense bore the brunt of the blame. They held Bartkowski to 82 passing yards during the first three quarters. Bartkowski ended up with 243 passing yards at the final gun.

The AFC wild card contest later that December 24 afternoon featured the Houston Oilers and the Miami Dolphins at the Orange Bowl. For the last half of the season, Houston quarterback Dan Pastorini's injuries were a common topic of discussion amongst fans and media alike. His injuries got even worse when he suffered three broken ribs in Houston's final game of the regular season, and was stuck in a hospital bed for several days. Fears among the fans and coaches alike abounded, as most believed that there was no way that Pastorini would be able to play in the wild card game. But in an eclectic mix of Hollywood fiction, modern science, plastics, and answered prayers, a couple of strangers entered the quarterback's hospital room. At first, Pastorini "became nervous" when one of the men, who was wearing a trench coat, handed a baseball bat to his partner, who opened a bag that he was carrying. The man in the trench coat was Byron Donzis, and this moment in Pastorini's hospital room would change the world for football quarterbacks everywhere. Donzis strapped on a padded and plastic contraption around his torso. His partner then began taking whacks at Donzis' ribs with the baseball bat. Nothing happened. Donzis was not phased in the least at the successive hits to his ribs. "I've got to get one of those," an amazed Pastorini said. The "Flak Jacket" that Donzis invented could cushion the blow of a charging defensive lineman with the aid of air pockets under a clear plastic cover, which distributed the shock of a blow evenly throughout the device. The flak jacket would soon become a regular piece of football equipment for all quarterbacks throughout the league to this very day. The grateful Pastorini would wear that first flak jacket in his team's playoff game at Miami, and throughout the rest of his career.

Pastorini would need his new flak jacket, along with a brace, multiple pads, and plenty of athletic tape in the postseason. His injuries included broken ribs, a wrenched knee, a sprained ankle, and a swollen elbow. He was a stationary quarterback, prone to staying in the pocket for his lack of running ability. His wrenched knee required a special knee brace, meaning that he was practically a sitting duck. Enemy defenses were well aware of this, and often blitzed the Oilers in the hopes of sacking or pressuring Pastorini. Conversely, Miami quarterback Bob Griese was not in much better health. Griese entered the wild card game against the Oilers with rib and knee problems also, and he too would be fitted for a knee brace.

The game was a nearly identical standoff throughout the first three quarters. Both teams scored a touchdown on short passes. A muffed punt in the first quarter by Houston kick returner Robert Woods led to Miami's score when Griese hit his tight end, Andre Tillman, down the middle for six points on a 13-yard pass. Pastorini responded in the second quarter with a 12-yard touchdown toss to running back Tim Wilson, who was left uncovered by the No-Name Defense. Wilson benefitted from a fake handoff from Pastorini to running back Earl Campbell, and a fake handoff on a reverse to tight end Mike Barber. By the time that the Dolphins defense realized what had happened, Wilson was holding the ball aloft in the end zone.

Both defenses took charge during the third quarter, however, as both offenses failed to mount a scoring drive. Finally in the fourth quarter, Houston managed to advance the ball deep enough into Miami territory to take the lead. Houston placekicker Toni Fritsch booted a 35-yard field goal for a 10–7 Oilers advantage. Houston linebacker Gregg Bingham then intercepted a Griese pass, thereby igniting a game-clinching scoring drive. Pastorini stood resilient in the pocket and drove the Oilers 50 yards downfield in ten plays. Campbell culminated the drive in a most bullish fashion. Campbell, who led the NFL in rushing in 1978 with 1,450 yards, did not have the leaping ability that a Walter Payton of Chicago or a Sam "Bam" Cunningham of New England had. Nevertheless, Campbell attempted to dive over the line of scrimmage once he was given the ball at the 1-yard line, but he could only leap about a foot or so off the ground. Fortunately for the Oilers, Campbell's strength and power was enough to plow through the Dolphins front line to push the pigskin past the goal line. Miami defensive back Tim Foley tried to make the tackle on Campbell with a head-on collision. Foley bounced off of Campbell like a rubber ball bounces off of a concrete wall. To be fair to Foley, most of the Miami defenders were also hit pretty hard by Campbell all game long, and most of them also suffered the brunt of his powerful charges through the line. Campbell's clutch score boosted the Houston lead to 17–7.

Houston head coach Bum Phillips relied on a smart strategical choice as the game neared its end. The Oilers got the ball back, and rather than risking a fumble or an interception deep in their own territory, Phillips instructed Pastorini to take an intentional safety by running out of the end zone with the ball, thus giving the Dolphins two points, but insuring a free kick and ultimately, victory. Houston's 17–9 win was their first playoff triumph of the decade, and it was mostly the result of the spectacular effort by the Oiler defense, and by Pastorini's 306 yards passing. The sore-ribbed signal caller completed 20 of 29 passes in the game, and was given the game ball from his grateful teammates for his inspiring efforts. But perhaps the most poignant and joyful feelings that this playoff victory provided were felt by long-time Houston veteran defensive end Elvin Bethea, who endured many years of failure with the team. "We thought we were losers, and would always be losers," said Bethea. "Teams would come into town knowing they would beat us, then go home and laugh about it. I've waited for this for 11 years. I'm really happy for the first time since I got here."

The Falcons and the Oilers had thus survived the wild card round to advance to the divisional playoff round with the other six playoff teams. The team with the best record in each conference would receive an added perk, as they would have home games for as long as they remained alive in the divisional round and the conference championship round. In the AFC, the Pittsburgh Steelers had the best record with a mark of 14–2. They would face the 10–6 Denver Broncos at Three Rivers Stadium in the divisional round. In the NFC, the Los Angeles Rams had a 12–4 record, and based on their Week 3 win over Dallas, would own the tie-breaker for the best record in their conference. The Rams would meet the 8–7–1 Minnesota Vikings in the divisional playoff round at the Los Angeles Memorial Coliseum. Rounding out the divisional playoff round were the 10–6 Houston Oilers at the 11–5 New England Patriots in the AFC, and the 9–7 Atlanta Falcons at the 12–4 Dallas Cowboys in the NFC.

The Steelers had defeated Denver on the last weekend of the regular season at Mile High Stadium, 21–17. Pittsburgh had won five straight games going into their playoff meeting with the Broncos, and most experts believed that they would have little trouble in defeating Denver again. The experts were right. Pittsburgh's offense rarely looked better than it did against the Orange Crush defense. Quarterback Terry Bradshaw passed for 272 yards, and running back Franco Harris churned out 105 yards rushing, marking the sixth postseason game in his career with over 100 yards rushing. Harris also scored two touchdowns from 1 and 12 yards out, giving him 12 postseason touchdowns in his career. On his 12-yard jaunt to the end zone, Harris broke Denver cornerback Louie Wright's diving tackle, and tip-toed down the sideline for the score. The Denver defense decided to double team Pittsburgh wide receiver Lynn Swann in the game, and hope that the other Steeler wide receiver—John Stallworth—would not hurt them too badly. Their strategy failed miserably, as Stallworth grabbed 10 passes for 156 yards. Both Swann and Stallworth caught touchdown passes in the fourth quarter, but Stallworth's 45-yard score should not have counted, as his right foot was slightly over the end line when he came down with the ball. Field judge Dick Dolack was right there to make the call, but he missed it and declared Stallworth to be inbounds. Regardless, that score would not affect the outcome of the game. Swann's 38-yard catch had no questions about its legality, but it was a leaping grab of beauty. The graceful Swann jumped high for the ball, and came down with it while being held upside-down by Denver safety Bill Thompson, who carried Swann out of the end zone and planted him head first onto the Tartan Turf's 1-yard line. Swann kept his grasp on the ball, however, and his momentum helped him cross the goal line before he came down. "Swann and Stallworth are as good as any combination in the league," exclaimed Denver cornerback Steve Foley after the game. "And Bradshaw was putting it right in there. There really wasn't much I could do."

The Steel Curtain defense limited the Denver offense to 218 total yards, and shut out the Broncos in the third and fourth quarters. Pittsburgh's dominant 33–10 victory sent them to the AFC championship game for the fifth time in the past seven years.

Later that day in Dallas, the Cowboys and the Falcons played a surprisingly competitive playoff game in Texas Stadium. Dallas took a slim lead against Atlanta in the first quarter, thanks to a 34-yard field goal by placekicker Rafael Septien, and a 13-yard touchdown run by fullback Scott Laidlaw on a quick trap-draw up the middle. On that play, Falcons safety Tom Pridemore blitzed and actually ran right past Laidlaw. Atlanta responded shortly thereafter with a 14-yard scoring run on a trap-draw play by running back Bubba Bean. The Falcons were not finished though. They mounted several other scoring drives in the first half, which concluded with two Tim Mazzetti field goals and a 17-yard touchdown pass from quarterback Steve Bartkowski to wide receiver Wallace Francis on a quick slant pattern. Atlanta owned a surprising 20–13 lead with but 38 seconds left in the second quarter when an overzealous play by a member of their Grits Blitz defense changed the course of the game. Falcons linebacker Robert Pennywell hovered around the line of scrimmage at the snap of the ball. When his defensive linemen cleared out of his way, he rushed forward and hit Dallas quarterback Roger Staubach after the ex–Navy star had thrown the ball. Pennywell instantly hung onto Staubach's chest and drove him into the ground. Staubach's helmet bounced off of the Tartan Turf, thereby giving him a concussion which knocked him out of the game.

The Dallas Doomsday Defense watched their quarterback get injured, and they took umbrage at Pennywell's action. They responded with an inspired and ignited effort in the second half. The Cowboys shut the Falcons out in the final two quarters, and limited their offense to a mere 85 yards of total offense in the second half. They also sacked Bartkowski five times in the game, and gave up only one Atlanta first down in the third quarter. Reserve Dallas quarterback Danny White replaced the groggy Staubach and did an admirable job, completing 10 of 20 passes for 127 yards. "White has great poise," affirmed Dallas head coach Tom Landry. "His ability is unlimited." White also led Dallas on two clutch scoring drives. In the third quarter, White rolled out to his right and hit veteran tight end Jackie Smith in the corner of the end zone for the tying touchdown from two yards out. That scoring drive lasted seven plays and garnished 54 yards. Then in the fourth quarter, White benefitted from a shanked punt by Falcons punter John James, which positioned the Cowboys at the Atlanta 30-yard line. Dallas drove down to the Falcon 1-yard line, where Laidlaw dove into the end zone behind a key block from offensive tackle Pat Donovan.

Dallas finally enjoyed their first lead since early in the first quarter, and Doomsday made it last. The Dallas defense had registered an NFL-high 58 sacks in 1978, and they poured into Bartkowski's passing pocket in the second half like they had throughout most of their opponents' offensive backfields during the regular season. The Falcons had made a living all year on winning games in the last minute, but there were no miracle finishes for them on this day. Dallas defenders like Larry Cole and Randy White stuffed Falcon runners in the second half, and the Dallas defensive backs intercepted three passes and effectively covered Atlanta's receivers in the final two quarters. Bartkowski could complete only eight passes all game long. The Cowboys gained 242 of their 369 total yards in the second half, and held on at the end to win this tough battle, 27–20. "They [Atlanta] came to play," said star Dallas tailback Tony Dorsett, who was held to only 65 yards rushing against the Falcons defense. "We got fired up in the second half because we were behind. That's enough to motivate any team." The motivated Cowboys would thus enter their seventh NFC title game in the past eight years.

The following day was Sunday, December 31. The Houston Oilers were up in Foxboro, Massachusetts, to take on the New England Patriots in a playoff contest that most felt would be a classic and close contest. But the side effects of former New England head coach Chuck Fairbanks' resignation were enduring. Patriots owner William Sullivan, Jr., dismissed Fairbanks as soon as the coach announced his decision to leave the Patriots in favor of coaching at the University of Colorado. "I told him to get out," Sullivan said of his discussion with Fairbanks. "He asked me if I wanted to fire him. I said no, I didn't want to set him up for a settlement." Sullivan took the time in between his team's final regular season game and their first playoff game (a span of two weeks) to contemplate his impulsive decision, however. He eventually decided to reinstate Fairbanks for the remainder of the postseason. Sullivan's change of heart did not sit well with New England's fans, who lambasted Fairbanks on local radio sports talk shows, and who spared no verbal invective on Fairbanks when he ran onto the field at Schaefer Stadium for the playoff game with the Oilers. Several of the signs and posters that the fans displayed on game day had Fairbanks' name emblazoned on them, along with at least a few salty references with the word "quitter" to go with it.

Besides the owner and the fans, the Patriot players were also miffed that their coach abruptly quit on them. Their play on this day was emblematic of their disdain for Fairbanks, their confusion over the game plan, and their obvious and clearly visible lack of effort. Despite being injured in several positions and being listed as a seven-point underdog, Houston's players took full advantage of New England's situation, and exploded for an early and lasting lead. Houston quarterback Dan Pastorini's ribs were still hurt and he was still wearing his flak jacket, but he had his best playoff game ever against the Patriots on this day. He completed 12 of 15 attempts for 200 yards and three touchdowns. Both teams traded several possessions in the first quarter. In the second quarter, Pastorini beat a blitz by New England linebacker Rod Shoate and lofted the ball deep down the sideline for his fastest wide receiver, the lean and stream-lined sprinter, Ken Burrough. Covering Burrough on this particular play for the Patriots was another speed merchant, cornerback Mike Haynes. Both players jumped for the ball, but Burrough was in a better outside position to catch it, which he did. Haynes lost his balance and fell down, and Burrough almost lost his balance too. But Burrough tight-walked the sideline stripe with an official just two yards behind him to make sure that he (Burrough) stayed inbounds. Once he got his balance back, Burrough sped down the sideline untouched for Houston's first touchdown. "I didn't know what happened until I got up," described Pastorini. "I know what I hoped."

The Oilers were not done yet. Houston tight end Mike Barber also had one of his best games ever. He caught Pastorini's next two touchdown passes, both coming in the second quarter. The first one was from 19 yards out, and on it he cut across the middle and juggled the low pass, but he finally held onto the ball around the 10-yard line. From there, Barber chugged towards the goal line, breaking a couple of diving arm tackles from Patriots linebacker Sam Hunt and from Haynes, who had the last (but futile) chance to trip him up before he reached paydirt. Barber's second score came from 13 yards out, and it required hardly any athletic ability on his part. Pastorini once again barely beat a blitz, but this time his arm was hit by New England defensive lineman Richard Bishop. His wobbly pass landed in Barber's hands at the 2-yard line. Barber walked into the end zone from there.

Houston owned a 24–0 lead in the third quarter until the Patriots finally overcame their list-lessness and started to show signs of life. New England halfback Andy Johnson threw a beautiful 24-yard option pass for a touchdown to veteran wide receiver Harold Jackson. Later in the fourth quarter, superstar Patriots tight end Russ Francis caught another 24-yard scoring pass near the back of the end zone from reserve quarterback Tom Owen. But Houston's rookie sensation Earl Campbell spent most of the contest keeping drives alive, and that as much as anything else proved to be New England's undoing. Campbell carried the ball 27 times for 118 yards, and he closed out the game with a 2-yard touchdown run. The Oilers won their second straight road playoff game, 31–14, and sent New England head coach Chuck Fairbanks out of the pro ranks with a depressing loss. "We play better with our backs against the wall," said Pastorini, "and our backs have been against the wall all year."

The divisional playoff round reached its completion on New Year's Eve at the Los Angeles Memorial Coliseum, where the Rams would take on the Minnesota Vikings for the fourth time in the decade in the NFL playoffs. The Vikings had won each of the previous three meetings, despite being listed as underdogs in all three. Many people were beginning to think that the Rams were jinxed when they played the Vikings in postseason games, even though they had no trouble defeating Minnesota in regular season games. No amount of luck or good fortune would be needed by Los Angeles in this playoff contest, however. The Rams decided not to take any chances though. They wore their white road jerseys instead of their usual home blue jerseys, in a superstitious attempt at changing their destiny from that of their previous playoff results. Both teams played a competitive first half, but the Rams dominated the Vikings in the second half to win going away, 34–10. "No way we were going to lose this game," said Los Angeles safety Bill Simpson after the game.

Insuring the Ram victory was a defense which permitted zero Viking points in the second half, and an offense which capitalized on virtually every break that their defense and special teams units gave them throughout the game. The Los Angeles defense allowed Minnesota's runners a scant total of only 36 rushing yards all game long, while in contrast the Ram runners churned out a robust 200 yards rushing. The Rams scored two touchdowns in the third quarter on a 3-yard run by fullback John Cappelletti and a 27-yard pass from quarterback Pat Haden to wide receiver Ron Jessie. On Jessie's score, Haden sent him on a simple down-and-out pattern. Jessie caught the pass at his 20-yard line, broke a tackle from Minnesota cornerback John Turner, then raced down the far sideline to the end zone. The entire Rams effort on both sides of the ball was praised by their head coach, Ray Malavasi. "I thought our defense played exceptionally well in the third quarter," said Malavasi, "and Pat Haden was super. Our players felt that we could beat Minnesota. In the past we beat ourselves when we have played them, but today we didn't. [We] played a great second half."

The Los Angeles offense closed out the scoring in the fourth quarter with a 28-yard field goal by placekicker Frank Corral and a short run by reserve running back Jim Jodat. On Jodat's touchdown, he ran off-tackle through a huge hole on his left and scored untouched from three yards out. "Once they got their offense in high gear, there wasn't much that we could do," admitted Minnesota middle linebacker Jeff Siemon. "They [the Rams] controlled the line of scrimmage," said Vikings halfback Chuck Foreman. "We couldn't run and when you can't run you are in big trouble." It became readily apparent by the end of the third quarter that the jinx which had supposedly did the Rams in throughout the 1970s was finally over. "I never believed in that jinx business anyway," said Rams offensive guard Tom Mack. "We finally ran out of ways to lose."

The next week, the conference championship games were two of the most one-sided title games of the decade. The Houston Oilers traveled to Pittsburgh to take on the Steelers. These two teams split their regular season meetings, with Houston winning up in Pittsburgh on October 23. That victory must have given the Oilers at least some degree of confidence, but they also knew in the back of their minds that the Steelers were very tough to beat twice in a season. The Steelers were favored to win, and they were much healthier than the Oilers. The weather at Three Rivers Stadium on January 7 also slightly favored the Steelers. The elements on this day in the Steel City were much worse than anything that the Oilers were used to. Houston's players were conditioned to playing half of their games inside the climate-controlled Astrodome, but the freezing rain, the patches of ice on the cement-like Tartan Turf, and the 26-degree temperature at kickoff of this AFC championship game, would test the abilities of both teams to hold onto the ball and to keep their footing. Houston fared poorly in their efforts to combat the elements.

Pittsburgh's Steel Curtain defense shut down the Oilers early, as they permitted only two Houston first downs in the first quarter. Pittsburgh's offense experienced much more success against the Oilers defense. Steelers running back Franco Harris began his team's scoring deluge with a 7-yard off-tackle touchdown run. Harris scored standing up on the play. Harris' running mate in the Steelers backfield—fullback Rocky Bleier—followed that up with a hydroplaning run to the right worth 15 yards and another touchdown. Bleier just barely reached the near corner of the end zone, but he made it thanks to a splash dive into the puddle-filled turf. Pittsburgh's 14–0 lead going into the second quarter received a small dent when Houston linebacker Robert Brazile recovered a Franco Harris fumble deep in Steeler territory. Houston placekicker Toni Fritsch converted the turnover into a 19-yard field goal. Houston's sudden surge of good luck continued during the next two Pittsburgh possessions, as Oilers cornerback Greg Stemrick intercepted a Terry Bradshaw pass, and defensive end James Young recovered another Harris fumble. Unfortunately for the Oilers, their offense was unable to turn those breaks into points against the stubborn Steelers defense.

Pittsburgh received the rest of the breaks in the second quarter. Steelers outside linebacker Jack Ham recovered a fumble by Houston running back Ronnie Coleman. Four plays later, Bradshaw threw a 29-yard touchdown pass to wide receiver Lynn Swann, who ran a deep post pattern and beat Houston cornerback Willie Alexander on the play. The Steelers' lead thus increased to 21–3. The freezing rain by this time was turning to slush on the field and iced stalactites on the crossbars of the goal posts. The ball was also icing up and becoming very difficult to grip. Rookie Houston kick returner Johnny Dirden fumbled the ensuing Pittsburgh kickoff before he was ever hit, and Steelers special teams player Rick Moser recovered the slippery ball at the Houston 17-yard line. Two plays later, Bradshaw threw another touchdown pass, this one going to wide receiver John Stallworth. The game was getting out of hand as Pittsburgh now led, 28–3, with time waning in the second quarter.

Things immediately got worse for the Oilers on their next play from scrimmage, however, as they attempted to run out the clock and end this miserable first half. Ronnie Coleman fumbled the ball once again, however, and Pittsburgh defensive lineman Steve Furness recovered. Steelers placekicker Roy Gerela booted a 37-yard field goal to give the Steelers a 31–3 lead going into their warm and dry halftime locker room. The second half proved to be somewhat anticlimactic, as there was little scoring from both teams. The Steelers wanted to run down the clock as much as possible, so they ran the ball 25 times in the second half, and threw the ball only four times during the final two quarters. Pittsburgh's Gerela added another field goal to boost the Steeler lead to 34–3. Roughly four minutes later, Pittsburgh's Rocky Bleier was tackled in the end zone by Houston outside linebacker Ted Washington for a safety. That was it for the scoring. The Steelers decisively earned their third conference championship in the past five years with a 34–5 conquest over the Oilers. The Steelers allowed Houston's offense to gain only 142 total yards all day. In a reflective mood after the game, Pittsburgh defensive tackle Joe Greene commented, "I don't know if they [Houston] even had a chance."

A big key to Pittsburgh's win was their ability to stop Houston's main weapon, All-Pro running back and NFL rushing champion Earl Campbell. In Campbell's first meeting with the Steel Curtain defense back in October, he scored all three of Houston's touchdowns and rushed for 89 yards in a 24–17 Oilers win. On this day, Campbell was held to 62 yards on 22 carries, which averaged out to 2.8 yards per carry. Campbell also fumbled the slick ball three times. The Steelers benefitted from a total of nine Houston turnovers in this title game. And so ended the Cinderella season of the 1978 Houston Oilers, a young team that few—if any—experts believed would challenge for a title.

The romp notwithstanding, virtually every Steeler had praise for the courage displayed by Houston quarterback Dan Pastorini, who played the whole game with broken ribs. "Dan Pastorini has more guts than any quarterback I've ever seen," said Joe Greene after the game. Pastorini was sacked four times and threw five interceptions, but those mistakes resulted more from the Steel Curtain's brilliance and the miserable weather conditions than the quarterback's failures.

The Los Angeles Rams had failed to reach a Super Bowl all throughout their history, despite having three straight chances to do so in three straight NFC title games from 1974 to 1976. They had earned another chance at the end of the 1978 season on January 7. Their opponents on this day would be the defending Super Bowl champion Dallas Cowboys at the Los Angeles Memorial Coliseum. The Rams were favored to win the game by a small margin, but they refused to take any chances. For the second straight week, the Rams wore their white jerseys, thereby forcing the Cowboys to wear their blue jerseys. Many people, including the Rams management, still believed that Dallas was jinxed by wearing those blue jerseys. Those thoughts were put to rest for some skeptics on this day.

The first half ended in a scoreless tie, but both teams moved the ball and had several scoring chances. Los Angeles placekicker Frank Corral missed two field goals in the second quarter, and Dallas missed a sure touchdown on an unusual fumble right in front of the Rams goal line. Dallas fullback Scott Laidlaw ran off-tackle and was hit by Rams linebacker Bob Brudzinski. Laidlaw fumbled the ball just before he crossed the goal line. Three Cowboys—Laidlaw, offensive tackle Pat Donovan, and tailback Tony Dorsett—each crashed into each other as they all tried to recover the fumble simultaneously. The ball seemed to have other plans, however, and bounced out of their grasps and towards the back of the end zone, where Rams defensive end Jack Youngblood recovered it.

The Cowboys were not deterred by this mishap, however. Dallas safety Charlie Waters intercepted a Pat Haden pass early in the third quarter and returned the ball 20 yards to the Los Angeles 10-yard line. Five plays later, Dorsett followed a sweep to his right and waltzed into the end zone for a 5-yard touchdown and a 7–0 Dallas lead. Very early in the fourth quarter, Laidlaw made up for his first half fumble in a big way. Laidlaw sprinted out to his left from his backfield position and was left virtually unguarded in the flat. Dallas quarterback Roger Staubach saw him immediately and rifled a swing pass to the fullback, which he caught and then broke an arm tackle by Rams safety Dave Elmendorf. Laidlaw quickly tumbled into the end zone for a 4-yard touchdown reception and a 14–0 Dallas lead. The way the Cowboys defense was playing, that lead looked fairly safe. The Doomsday Defense intercepted five passes and recovered two Los Angeles fumbles by the final gun.

It was a fumble recovery by Dallas defensive end Harvey Martin at the Dallas 11-yard line which led to a third Cowboys touchdown. Dorsett began the scoring drive with a 53-yard dash on a sweep to his left. Six plays later, Staubach connected on a misdirection rollout and hit tight end Billy Joe DuPree from 11 yards out for a touchdown. The play fooled the Rams defense so well that DuPree was all alone in the end zone when he caught Staubach's pass. The game was now out of reach for the Rams. Nevertheless, Dallas added one more salt in the wound touchdown when outside linebacker Thomas "Hollywood" Henderson intercepted a Vince Ferragamo pass in the right flat and sprinted 68 yards for a conclusive touchdown. Henderson, who claimed before the game, "Dallas would destroy the Rams," barely had enough energy left after running across the field to flip the ball over the crossbar of the goal post after crossing the goal line. The Cowboys' 28–0 shutout victory over the Rams successfully defended their conference championship, and earned them their fifth trip to the Super Bowl, more than any other team (at that time) in NFL history. "This was not really a 28–0 game," said Staubach from a victorious Dallas locker room. "We were just able to make the most of our opportunities and convert the turnovers. If we could not have done it we might still be on the field now." Like his quarterback, Dallas head coach Tom Landry knew that his team would have to find a way to overcome their mistakes if they were to win. "I was a little anxious after the first half," admitted Landry after the game. "I thought turnovers would make the difference and that someone would take charge in the third quarter. It was a great defensive battle."

NFL Films would describe Super Bowl XIII as a "Battle of Champions," which was a most apt description. There was little doubt that the Pittsburgh Steelers and the Dallas Cowboys were the two best teams in the league going into the Super Bowl. Both squads had explosive offenses and formidable defenses. Plenty of ironies surrounded this title game, however, and plenty of storylines surfaced too. Both the Steelers and the Cowboys had each won two Super Bowls prior to Super Bowl XIII, but the Cowboys entered the game on January 21 as the defending champs. Both of these teams had met each other in Super Bowl X, which was held in Miami's Orange Bowl. This would be the first ever Super Bowl re-match, and it would once again be played in Miami's Orange Bowl. The stadium's natural grass field surface in 1978, however, had replaced the Poly-Turf surface from Super Bowl X. The first championship meeting between Pittsburgh and Dallas in Super Bowl X was generally regarded by most fans and experts as the most exciting Super Bowl ever played … at least until the final gun sounded at the end of Super Bowl XIII.

The pregame hoopla and media frenzy that was typical of most Super Bowls was certainly visible in this 13th edition of the fight for the Vince Lombardi Trophy. But this year an instigator of sorts was added to the mix. Dallas linebacker Thomas "Hollywood" Henderson took center stage and talked to dozens of reporters prior to the game. Henderson spared few Pittsburgh players with his bravado and insults. Besides guaranteeing a Dallas victory, his most condescending remarks were reserved for Steelers quarterback Terry Bradshaw. Henderson claimed that Bradshaw "is so dumb, he can't spell cat if you spotted him the c and the a." Henderson's penchant for verbal sparring and his hot-dogging on the field and on the sidelines was certainly not the image that Dallas head coach Tom Landry desired for his players to display. But Henderson produced plenty of big plays for Doomsday in 1978 when he went up against the toughest competition. Moreover, he also made many hits and tackles while on special teams, so Landry tolerated his antics. Indeed, winning will get a coach to overlook a lot of things.

Both the Steelers and the Cowboys did a lot of winning in 1978. The Steelers went 14–2 in the regular season, while the Cowboys finished with a 12–4 mark. Bradshaw had his best season ever, throwing for a career-high and NFL-best 28 touchdowns. Dallas quarterback Roger Staubach finished the year as the league's highest-ranked passer with 3,190 yards through the air and 25 scoring tosses. Although both teams had excellent defenses, most experts expected an offensive shootout. That's exactly what they got.

Dallas received the opening kickoff and immediately established its running game. Halfback Tony Dorsett surprised everyone by successfully running the ball on the Steelers defense to the tune of 38 yards on his first three carries. With the ball on the Pittsburgh 34-yard line, however, Dallas head coach Tom Landry called for a gadget play that he immediately regretted. Staubach handed off to Dorsett, who attempted to hand the ball off to wide receiver Drew Pearson, but Pearson fumbled the ball. Pittsburgh defensive tackle John Banaszak fell on the ball near midfield. Pearson was expected to throw the ball after receiving the handoff from Dorsett, and if he had not fumbled, Dallas tight end Billy Joe DuPree was all alone downfield near the Pittsburgh end zone. This was just one of several mistakes which would haunt the Cowboys throughout the game.

Pittsburgh capitalized on this first Dallas miscue with a seven-play drive that resulted in the game's first touchdown. Bradshaw lobbed a 28-yard touchdown pass to wide receiver John Stallworth, who caught it and got both of his feet inbounds in the corner of the end zone just before he got knocked out of bounds by Dallas defensive backs Aaron Kyle and Cliff Harris. Dallas responded later in the first quarter with a short drive which resulted in the tying touchdown. Staubach faced down a maximum Steeler blitz on the final play of the first quarter and fired a 39-yard scoring pass to wide receiver Tony Hill. It was the first time all year that Pittsburgh's defense had allowed a touchdown by any opponent in the first quarter. On the play, Hill ran a quick out pattern and caught Staubach's pass along the far side of the field, then outran Steelers defensive back Donnie Shell to the end zone. Pittsburgh cornerback Mel Blount was oblivious to Hill's catch and run, as he was focused on guarding the other Dallas wide receiver—Drew Pearson—man-to-man. Hill ran right past the out-smarted Blount to tie the game at 7–7.

The Doomsday Defense then gave the lead to the Cowboys in the second quarter. Bradshaw rolled to his right but fumbled the ball when he brushed against the hip of Pittsburgh running back Franco Harris. Bradshaw quickly recovered his fumble, but was soon caught in the grasp of Dallas linebackers Thomas Henderson and Mike Hegman. As Henderson brought Bradshaw to the turf, Hegman ripped the ball out of the quarterback's hand. Hegman then sprinted 37 yards for a touchdown, giving the Cowboys a 14–7 lead. Bradshaw slightly hurt his shoulder on the play as Henderson drove him into the ground, but as soon as Bradshaw got the ball back, he would get even with the Dallas defense. On third down from his 25-yard line, Bradshaw threw a quick square-out pass to Stallworth, who displayed his speed and his ability to break tackles. Stallworth first broke an attempted tackle around his knees from Dallas cornerback Aaron Kyle. He then received a key block downfield from fellow Steelers wide receiver Lynn Swann. Stallworth cut back towards the middle of the field and broke an attempted diving arm tackle from Dallas defensive back Randy Hughes. All that was left was a sprint down the middle of the field to the end zone. Stallworth's gazelle-like stride allowed him to outrace Dallas safety Cliff Harris as he reached the end zone to complete the 75-yard play. Stallworth's spectacular effort would tie the record for the longest touchdown reception in Super Bowl history (up to that time).

Pittsburgh's offense was not done there, however. They managed one more scoring drive following a Staubach interception late in the second quarter. Bradshaw rolled out to his right from the Dallas 7-yard line, and was soon under pressure from Dallas defensive lineman Larry Cole. Bradshaw lobbed a pass to the end zone, where Steeler running back Rocky Bleier outleaped Dallas linebacker D.D. Lewis for the ball. Bleier landed on his back with the pigskin snugly in his grasp, and Pittsburgh had a 21–14 lead at halftime. "I thought I'd have an angle on the ball if Terry would throw it up and back," Bleier said after the game. "That's exactly what he did. I reached for it and it stuck between my hands. That's as high as I can jump."

Dallas dominated the third quarter on both offense and defense, but would get only three points to show for it. Their defense limited the Steelers offense to only one first down all quarter long. The Dallas offense would account for a drive of eight plays and a drive of nine plays during the third quarter. The eight-play drive resulted in a punt, but the nine-play drive resulted in their greatest and most disastrous mistake of the game, and quite possibly, the greatest mistake in Super Bowl history. The situation was a third down at the Pittsburgh 10-yard line. Dallas head coach Tom Landry called for a pass play which was designed for veteran Cowboys tight end Jackie Smith, who was required to run a simple down and in pattern. The Steelers actually called a blitz on the play, but the Cowboys picked it up extremely well. Dallas fullback Scott Laidlaw planted his helmet right into the sternum of blitzing Pittsburgh middle linebacker Jack Lambert, and even though Lambert threw Laidlaw down, the running back did his job. Lambert played the rest of the game with bruised ribs from this encounter. With no linebackers in the area to speak of, Smith found himself alone as he ran his pattern. "He was so open, I could have punted the ball to him," observed Staubach. Smith reached the goal line and turned his head to look for the ball. Staubach threw the ball straight on a line, but Smith had to wait for the ball to arrive, and then inexplicably slid to the ground as he adjusted his body to smother the ball to his chest. The ball bounced off of the number 81 on the front of Smith's jersey, and the Cowboys lost what would have been the game-tying touchdown. "I was just wide open and I missed it," lamented Smith, who was surrounded by a horde of sportswriters around his locker after the game. "It might have been a matter of my being overcautious. Maybe I would have caught it with my hands, but in that situation you are trying to be sure, so you want to use your chest." To his credit, Staubach magnanimously accepted partial blame for the dropped pass. "I tried to take a little bit off the pass," said Staubach, who finished the game with three touchdown passes. "I tried to just lob it. If I'd thrown it in there, he [Smith] would have had an easy catch."

A field goal by Dallas placekicker Rafael Septien salvaged three points for the Cowboys, and narrowed their deficit to 21–17. Smith's dropped pass was followed by more strikes of misfortune for the Cowboys, however. Doomsday had the Pittsburgh offense on the ropes on their first possession of the fourth quarter. Pittsburgh was faced with a third and eight situation at their own 17-yard line. A stop here would have resulted in another Pittsburgh punt, and probably very good field position for the Cowboys. It did not happen. Bradshaw hit his tight end Randy Grossman for nine yards, thereby igniting a eight-play touchdown drive. The most controversial moment of the drive and of the game occurred three plays after Grossman's clutch catch. Bradshaw lofted a high-arching bomb down the near sideline for Swann, who was running a long fly pattern, and who was guarded closely by Dallas cornerback Benny Barnes. Swann was actually behind Barnes, who was running towards the ball, which was descending away from the sideline and closer towards the middle of the field. Swann tried to adjust to the ball when he ran up the back of Barnes and tripped over the cornerback's feet. Both players tumbled to the turf, with the ball bouncing off the ground. The official closest to the play was back judge Pat Knight. He called the play an incomplete pass, thereby declaring the fender-bender between Swann and Barnes to be incidental contact. But field judge Fred Swearingen, who was closer to the middle of the field, threw his penalty flag. To even the casual observer, Swann tripped over Barnes while the defensive back was already face down on the ground. Therefore, there could have been no intentional tripping on the play. Yet Barnes was penalized—not for tripping—but for defensive pass interference.

"Benny Barnes went to the ground on the play," said Dallas safety Charlie Waters. "What does the ref think happened to make him go to the ground?" Barnes naturally agreed with his teammate. "I was turning to look for the ball, and I felt the push [from Swann] and I went down," described Barnes. Swann, of course, told a completely different story. "I don't recall ever putting my hands on Benny Barnes," said Swann. "He tripped me and then he kicked me."

The Steelers received 33 yards from the penalty, and then quickly took advantage of the break to score a touchdown four plays later. Pittsburgh benefitted from another stroke of good luck when Franco Harris rumbled 22 yards up the middle on a trap play for a score. Umpire Art Demmas screened Charlie Waters from making the tackle on Harris on the play, and even though it was a matter of unlucky positioning, the Cowboys were once again stuck playing the role of the victim. Waters was the last Dallas player who had a chance to make the tackle, but fate intervened. "The official played a vital role in the block," said Waters. "I don't know what I could have done except to knock him [Demmas] flat, or knock him into Franco. I couldn't make the guy invisible, so I had to play around him, and that opened me up for the block [from Steelers right tackle Ray Pinney]."

Dallas defensive tackle Randy White probably wished that he had been invisible on the following kickoff. White was on the Dallas kickoff return team, but he had a cast on one of his hands. He had fractured his thumb in the NFC championship game against the Rams, when he not-so-gently inserted it inside Los Angeles quarterback Pat Haden's face mask, causing a key interception. White's cast would hinder his ability to grip and tug opposing jerseys throughout the Super Bowl, however. It would also play a part in the kickoff following Harris' score. Pittsburgh placekicker Roy Gerela accidentally slipped as he approached the tee, and kicked a low, bouncing ball downfield. White picked it up, then tried to carry it in his cast-encased hand. The ball slipped out of his grasp before he was even hit. Steelers reserve linebacker Dennis Winston emerged from the pile of players with the pigskin at the Dallas 18-yard line. On the very next play, Bradshaw took advantage of Doomsday's lack of alertness and confusion by throwing a touchdown pass to a leaping Swann, who caught Bradshaw's bullet in the middle of the end zone and came down with the ball just before he stepped over the end line. The Steelers now owned a seemingly insurmountable 35–17 lead with just under seven minutes left in the game.

The Cowboys may have been upset at all of their misfortune, but they did not show it in the closing minutes of the fourth quarter. The Dallas offense quickly drove down the field on a eight-play drive which resulted in a 7-yard touchdown pass from Staubach to tight end Billy Joe DuPree, who plowed through an attempted tackle by Steelers cornerback Ron Johnson and dove into the corner of the end zone. The Cowboys' special teams then chipped in with an onside kick that was recovered by reserve Dallas defensive back Dennis Thurman. On that play, the ball went right through the hands of Pittsburgh defensive back Tony Dungy, and into Thurman's mitts. Staubach drove his offense downfield again on a nine-play drive to score on a 4-yard pass to reserve wide receiver Butch Johnson, who was left all alone by the Steeler defenders in the end zone.

There was now only 22 seconds left on the clock, and the Cowboys were all out of timeouts. Dallas attempted another onside kick, but Bleier easily recovered Septien's squibbler in the middle of the field. One of the greatest Super Bowls of all time was history, with Pittsburgh prevailing, 35–31. The Steelers had thus become the first team to win three Super Bowls, and the first team to win a Super Bowl rematch. Ironically, Pittsburgh's four-point margin of victory was identical to their four-point margin of victory over Dallas in Super Bowl X (21–17). Pittsburgh quarterback Terry Bradshaw was honored with the game's Most Valuable Player award, thanks to his record four touchdown passes and his 318 yards passing. Bradshaw's stellar and victorious accomplishments against Dallas overshadowed his two fumbles and his lone interception, each of which occurred in the first half of the game.

Pittsburgh quarterback Terry Bradshaw prepares to take the snap from center Mike Webster in Super Bowl XIII, January 21, 1979, against Dallas in the Orange Bowl Stadium in Miami, Florida. Bradshaw threw four touchdown passes and earned the game's Most Valuable Player award, as the Steelers held on to defeat the Cowboys, 35–31. Pittsburgh thus became the first NFL team in history to win three Super Bowls (AP Photo/Al Messerschmidt).

Super Bowl XIII left many questions, discussions, and opinions in its aftermath. Both teams played well at times, and both teams made several mistakes. The Cowboys were certainly not the beneficiaries in this game when it came to lucky or unlucky breaks. The Cowboys just ended up making more mistakes, and the Steelers managed to capitalize on several of them during key moments of the game. Some of Dallas' mistakes came not with their execution on the field but from play-calling decisions from the sidelines. Why did Coach Landry fail to call more running plays, considering the success that Tony Dorsett had experienced to start the game? Dorsett would emerge as the game's leading rusher with 96 yards, but he carried the ball only 16 times in the game, with only seven of those carries coming during the entire second and third quarters combined. Why did Landry decide to call a double reverse play after opening the game with a flurry of basic and successful running plays? Even more answers were lacking regarding the refereeing decisions, which garnered a large amount of postgame discussions. Why did back judge Pat Knight refuse to argue his call of incidental contact to his fellow official, Fred Swearingen, on the errant fourth quarter Bradshaw pass, which caused the Benny Barnes interference penalty? That decision gave the Steelers 33 yards of real estate and a boost of momentum which they did not have up to that time and which they never lost. Dallas general manager Tex Schramm said that the interference call was what beat his team. Even NFL Commissioner Pete Rozelle responded to a letter from a disgruntled Cowboys fan and claimed that the penalty flag should have stayed in Swearingen's back pocket.

Umpire Art Demmas then throws a key block to spring Franco Harris on his touchdown run. Who could have planned or predicted that fateful occurrence? Of course, the Cowboys themselves made the most crucial errors. Dallas tight end Jackie Smith drops what would have been the tying touchdown pass in the third quarter, which he probably would have caught nine times out of ten. A fumbled kickoff by Dallas defensive tackle Randy White, who was never used by the Cowboys as a ball handler, but who naturally tried to pick up the ball as it came to him. That fumble invited another Steelers touchdown. Pittsburgh's miscues and misfortune paled by comparison. It all added up to a bottom-line Pittsburgh victory, and gave voice and credibility to their claim as the team of the decade.

Super Bowl XIII was the top-viewed sporting event of all time (up to 1979), thanks primarily to the popularity of the two championship teams which took the Orange Bowl field that day. Although no one knew it at the time, Super Bowl XIII marked the final Super Bowl for the Tom Landry-led Cowboys. Dallas ended the decade of the 1970s with the most Super Bowl appearances (five) in NFL history. The 1978 Steelers had picked up the mantle of champions left by the Cowboys as the decade drew to a close. Pittsburgh transformed its offensive identity (due mostly to the new 1978 passing rules) from a running team to a passing team, probably better than any other team in the league. As a result, they were back at the top of the NFL hill once again. Their victory in Super Bowl XIII was their third world title in the past five seasons. In 1975, they defended their first world title. As the decade was about to end, the year of 1979 would see if they could repeat as world champions once again.

1979

The Curtain Descends
on a Super Decade

The decision was perhaps fitting and certainly expected throughout the final months of the 1979 regular season. The game's historians, writers, and various media outlets all attempted to look back on the previous nine seasons of the decade, much like New Year's Eve revelers recall the moments that made the previous year memorable. The process of rediscovery of the 1970s in the NFL produced the expected results. You started to see articles and stories that featured the "best of" categories during the 1970s. Names and games that were forgotten by many would suddenly come back to refresh our memories in several sports magazines and newspapers. As you looked at the decade on a year-by-year basis, the 1970s was making a strong claim by 1979 as the greatest decade in pro football's history. The sport had grown increasingly in many different ways during the 1970s, from overall attendance at the games, to the number of teams in the league, to the number of superstar players and their incredible exploits, to the incredibly large and growing television audiences and revenues … all of these examples vividly pointed to the obvious maturation of pro football. There seemed to be no end to how big the NFL might grow as the decade of the 1980s loomed ahead.

The 1979 season would be the league's 60th year, and like all the other years during the decade, 1979 would mix exciting plays, dramatic endings, and telling stories. Great careers from several great players would mark their ends at the conclusion of 1979. They included the likes of household names such as O.J. Simpson, Roger Staubach, and Jim Marshall. Great careers of future stars like Ottis Anderson, Mark Gastineau, Joe Montana, Phil Simms, and Kellen Winslow would also be launched in 1979. The 1979 season would mark a definitive ending and a clear turning of the pages of pro football history. Like all previous decades, the 1970s naturally laid the foundation for what was to happen in the 1980s. The game's popularity by 1979 was growing annually, and it was brought on by the game's action and excitement, its controversies, its heroes and its villains, and a multitude of stories of successes and failures. The game was now by 1979 more of a human drama than ever before, and one in which many fans could relate to and draw correlations to in the midst of their own lives. Maybe that was the most important reason why the decade was regarded in such high esteem.

The 1979 NFL season started like every other year, in the off-season, where activity off the field dominated the news wires. The league's competition committee was busy coming up with a whole new batch of rule changes. Following the tragic injury to former Patriots wide receiver Darryl Stingley during the 1978 preseason, the competition committee wanted to focus on more rules to help protect the players. They started with altering the blocking techniques on kickoffs, punts, and field goal and extra point attempts. No longer were blockers on the receiving side of the ball permitted to block below the waist, in the hopes that knee and groin injuries would decrease in 1979. They then restricted the area where crackback blocks could be made. Prior to 1979, crackback blocks by offensive players were permitted anywhere outside of the offensive tackles along the line of scrimmage. Starting in 1979, however, crackback blocks would be forbidden from three to five yards past the offensive tackles along the line of scrimmage. This move would hopefully curtail the injuries caused by blindside blocks on defensive players.

Both player and referee uniforms were also subjected to changes. The players were forbidden to wear tear-away jerseys in 1978, not so much because the teams had to buy more of them, but because after those jerseys were torn during the course of a play, the plastic padding underneath the jerseys would often cause contusions and sometimes bruises to the players. That rule was reaffirmed in 1979, and the officials on the field were given more authority in 1979 to check the players' jerseys prior to kickoff to confirm that they (the players) were not wearing tear-away jerseys. The officials' jerseys also changed a little. The officials were now required to wear in small lettering the name of their position (i.e., Head Linesman) and their number on the back of their striped jersey, and an abbreviation of their position (i.e., HL) and a smaller rendering of their number on the front chest pocket of their jersey. The referee in each game would also now wear a black cap with white piping, while the rest of the officials on the field would wear a plain white cap. The changes to the officiating crew's uniforms across the league were designed mostly to aid television and radio broadcasters to better identify the individual officials on the field.

The competition committee naturally tried to address the subject of controversial plays from the previous year, most notably the "Holy Roller" play between Oakland and San Diego during the second week of the 1978 season. The committee now declared that a fourth down fumble anywhere on the field could only be recovered by the player who fumbled the ball. It also stipulated that any fumble on any down after the two-minute warning of each half could be advanced only by the player who fumbled the ball. On the "Holy Roller" play on September 10, 1978, Oakland quarterback Ken Stabler fumbled the ball, which was then picked up by Raiders running back Pete Banaszak, who flipped it towards the goal line, where his teammate, Oakland tight end Dave Casper, practically dribbled the ball before he fell on it in the end zone for the winning touchdown. This new rule would eliminate the possibility of that type of fluke play from happening again.

In the end, however, the competition committee reverted back to the subject of player safety. They instructed officials to blow their whistles quicker when they saw the quarterback in the grasp of a defensive player in the pass pocket. This new rule took a swipe at the physicality element of the game. Once informed of the new rule, Pittsburgh middle linebacker Jack Lambert would infamously suggest that quarterbacks "should now wear dresses." This new rule was undoubtedly instilled following the physical beating that Houston quarterback Dan Pastorini took in the AFC playoffs in 1978. Yet many taller and stronger quarterbacks who were often able to break tackles and run for yardage were against the new rule. Quarterbacks who were successful runners such as New England's Steve Grogan, Baltimore's Bert Jones, and Pittsburgh's Terry Bradshaw, would now be losing yardage totals because a referee would deem them to be in the grasp of a defender, thus whistling the play dead. Despite complaints against this rule, it has withstood the test of time and is still being used today, although many officials today allow the bigger and more physical signal callers several extra seconds to break away from the grasp of defensive players.

The league office made another decision in the 1979 off-season which would change the environs of the game for many years. The AFC-NFC Pro Bowl Game, which was traditionally held the weekend after the Super Bowl, would now be held at Aloha Stadium in Honolulu, Hawaii. It would mark the first of 30 straight years that the Pro Bowl Game would be held in Hawaii. The

50th state welcomed the game and the opportunity to see NFL players in person, and sellouts for the game would become common.

Also common in the spring of 1979 was the increase in players and personalities who left the game. Retirees included Los Angeles guard Tom Mack, Dallas defensive tackle Jethro Pugh, Minnesota quarterback Fran Tarkenton and center Mick Tinglehoff, and Kansas City punter Jerrel Wilson (among many others). Tragically, Rams owner Carroll Rosenbloom also left the game when he died in the off-season in a drowning accident. Rosenbloom had been swimming off the coast of Florida when the undercurrent tide took him under the waves. His wife Georgia Frontiere would take over the ownership of the team, thus becoming the first woman in history to own an NFL team. She would also oversee the team's move out of Los Angeles at the end of the 1979 season to their new home in Anaheim, California. The move would be regarded as profitable for the team's finances, mainly because thousands of seats in the cavernous Los Angeles Memorial Coliseum (which seated 92,604) were commonly empty throughout the regular season during the 1970s. Anaheim Stadium had a smaller seating capacity (69,006 for football), which would insure more sellouts. Moreover, the lighting facilities there also presented a vast improvement over the diminished lights for night games at the Coliseum.

Rosenbloom's drowning was not the only fatality in the NFL in 1979. Another tragic death occurred in the St. Louis Cardinals summer training camp, when tight end J.V. Cain collapsed after running a play and suffered a heart attack. He caught a pass and was jogging back to the huddle when he suddenly dropped to the ground. "It looked like he had been shot by a sniper," said Cardinals head trainer John Omohundro, who tried unsuccessfully to revive Cain in the midst of many players gathering around their fallen teammate in prayer. Cain was quickly rushed to a local hospital where he expired. The league acknowledged in the autopsy report that Cain had been suffering from a heart condition, which was labeled as the cause of his death. Nevertheless, they also admitted that the heat and humidity that was a constant feature of summer training camp could also have played a part in his death. The league office immediately began instructing team trainers and doctors to be aware of the signs of dehydration and heat-stroke illnesses during summer training camps. Players were soon urged by their coaches not to skip water breaks in order to prove their toughness, and water caddies (large water jugs on wheels which were located several feet away from groups of players at practice) were introduced at training camps. Sadly, Cain's death would be repeated in 2001, when Minnesota offensive lineman Korey Stringer would also die in summer training camp, specifically from a heatstroke.

While the league was busy making changes to the game, several teams were also making annual changes to their coaching staffs and to their player rosters. Ron Erhardt was named the new head coach at New England in the wake of Chuck Fairbanks' departure at the end of 1978. Oakland head coach John Madden retired at the end of 1978, thanks in large part to the ill effects that the game was delivering to his stomach lining. Oakland assistant coach Tom Flores took over for Madden. Across the San Francisco Bay, Bill Walsh was named the new head coach for the 49ers. Former Baltimore Colts wide receiver Ray Perkins was named the new head coach for the New York Giants, after John McVay was fired after the 1978 season ended. Walsh would eventually end up in the Pro Football Hall of Fame for inventing the "West Coast Offense," and for building one of the most formidable champions in league history in the 1980s. Flores' successes were also significant. He would lead the Raiders to two Super Bowl wins in the 1980s.

Speaking of Super Bowls, the Dallas Cowboys' loss in Super Bowl XIII did not seem to diminish their notoriety during the off-season. Every spring, NFL Films produced a highlight film for each team, depicting and illustrating their exploits from the previous year. Bob Ryan was a veteran editor at the company, and had been writing and producing the Cowboys' annual highlight film for years. But what Ryan spliced together for the Cowboys before the 1979 season began was an epic which would make him famous. "We had noticed that wherever the Cowboys played, regardless of the city, we would film hundreds and thousands of Dallas fans each week in visiting stadiums. Their popularity throughout the nation was so evident, that I decided to give them *America's Team* as the title for their 1978 highlight film." Little did Ryan know of the ramifications that his film would have over the years. The other 27 teams in the league immediately took umbrage at Dallas' new title, and would now have another reason to knock the Cowboys off of their lofty perch. "I thought it was a joke and they'd bring in the *real* highlight film next," said Dallas quarterback Roger Staubach upon viewing the film for the first time. "The [Cowboys] players hoped that the America's Team thing would remain an inside joke. But what we feared came true: It didn't. Pretty soon the tag was everywhere. I'm sure it bothered other teams because they couldn't wait to rub it in after they beat us." Beating "America's Team" would now become a weekly challenge for every competitor on the Dallas schedule. Although the tag has stuck like a badge of honor to the team for several decades, most of the Cowboys players back then would have easily traded their new moniker for something less inciting to their opponents.

Several teams attempted to trade a player or two in the hopes of trading for better fortunes in 1979. The Detroit Lions sent veteran quarterback Greg Landry to Baltimore for some draft choices. The Los Angeles Rams sent outside linebacker Isiah Robertson to the Buffalo Bills for draft choices. The Bills wasted their first pick in the draft when they selected All-American Ohio State linebacker Tom Cousineau, who opted to play football in the Canadian Football League instead of the NFL. Washington running back Mike Thomas was traded to the San Diego Chargers for a draft choice. Key rookies who enjoyed successful 1979 seasons included a tandem of running backs for the Atlanta Falcons, William Andrews and Lynn Cain. Andrews toted the pigskin for a team-best 1,023 yards, while Cain contributed 295 rushing yards in spot duty. Dan Hampton of Chicago, Jerry Robinson of Philadelphia, and Marty Lyons of the New York Jets, all turned in admirable rookie seasons on the defensive side of the ball for their respective teams. Buffalo made up for the Cousineau debacle by drafting defensive lineman Fred Smerlas and linebacker Jim Haslett, both of whom had superb rookie seasons for the Bills. Rookie tight end Dan Ross made the starting lineup in Cincinnati and contributed 41 receptions for 516 yards.

Rookies like Ross proved to provide immediate help for their teams from the very beginning of the 1979 season. Week 1 showcased a dynamic new runner in St. Louis who was named after a dynamic older runner who was still playing. Ottis "O.J." Anderson was nicknamed after O.J. Simpson, and displayed some of the speed and moves similar to Simpson's, but he also injected the brute power of a Jim Brown in his running abilities. Anderson experienced one of the best opening games ever as a rookie against the visiting Dallas Cowboys by rushing for 193 yards on 21 carries, including a 76-yard jaunt through the Doomsday Defense in the fourth quarter, which gave St. Louis a 21–19 lead. "I'm just a running back trying to make a name for myself," said the modest Anderson.

Dallas was anxious to reclaim the title that they had begrudgingly lost the year before when they lost Super Bowl XIII. But the 1979 season took on an ominous tone early, and falling behind in the scoreboard to the Cardinals on opening day was the least of their problems. The Cowboys' hopes for the new season took a hit before summer training camp. One of their best defensive players—defensive end Ed "Too Tall" Jones—decided to abruptly retire from pro football in order to begin a career in professional boxing. This move turned out to be little more than an experiment on Jones' behalf to see if he could excel at two sports. He would return to the Cowboys in 1980, and by then he was fully committed to football. Problems occurred for Dallas on the offensive side of the line of scrimmage as well. Star halfback Tony Dorsett accidentally fell off a horse during the summer. He also dropped a wall mirror on his foot just before training camp began. That embarrassing accident sidelined him for several weeks with a broken toe. Fortunately for Dallas, rookie runner Ron Springs replaced Dorsett and filled in nicely. Springs helped the Cowboys come back against St. Louis in the fourth quarter when he threw a 30-yard halfback option pass to wide receiver Tony Hill, who was all alone in the Cardinals end zone as he caught Springs' perfect pass. Dallas was still trailing late, however, but they managed to drive downfield with time waning. Dallas placekicker Rafael Septien booted a 27-yard field goal with 1:15 left in the game to give the Cowboys a narrow 22–21 victory over the Cardinals. The win was the 15th straight opening day win for the Cowboys, still an NFL team record. "This wasn't a game that could make us or break us," said Dallas head coach Tom Landry, "but it was a key game for us to win, no doubt about it."

There were also several other close and exciting finishes in the first week of the new season. The Cleveland Browns outlasted the New York Jets at Shea Stadium, thanks in part to another kicker, Don Cockcroft of the Browns. Cockcroft connected on a 35-yard field goal which tied the game at 22–22 with four seconds left in the fourth quarter. Cockcroft then kicked the winning 27-yard field goal with 15 seconds left in the overtime period, lifting Cleveland to a 25–22 victory. Few kickers throughout the decade were as dependable as Cockcroft, who led the league three times in field goal percentage, and who scored an incredible 1080 points in his 13-year pro career.

Miami relied on the help from a prodigal son to lift them over the Buffalo Bills in their opener at Rich Stadium. Dolphins running back Larry Csonka was welcomed back to the team by head coach Don Shula after several years in exile in the now-defunct World Football League, and later with the New York Giants. Csonka was obviously not the same player that he was during his early years with Miami, but he provided the team with 87 yards rushing on 16 carries, and scored what would be the winning touchdown on a 1-yard burst in the fourth quarter. The Dolphins 9–7 victory was guaranteed when Buffalo placekicker Tom Dempsey missed a 34-yard field goal attempt with four seconds left in the game. Csonka's effort on this day moved him into sixth place all-time in NFL rushing yardage, and one step closer to the Pro Football Hall of Fame. The win marked the 19th straight victory for Miami over Buffalo.

Another close contest on opening day with even less scoring than the Miami-Buffalo game occurred in Chicago, where the Bears outlasted their NFC Central Division rivals, the Green Bay Packers, in a battle of field goals, 6–3. Chicago running back Walter Payton rushed for 125 yards on an incredible 36 carries, and journeyman quarterback Mike Phipps completed 15 passes in 25 attempts for the Bears. But perhaps the biggest indicator of victory was the Chicago defense, which limited the Green Bay offense to 149 total yards and sacked Green Bay quarterbacks six times. This win over the Packers would be vital to Chicago's possible playoff chances as the season neared its end.

The Houston Oilers would also play an important interconference game when they visited RFK Stadium to take on the Washington Redskins on opening day. The Redskins had built a 27–13 lead in the fourth quarter when the Oilers finally started to drill. Houston quarterback Dan Pastorini threw a 14-yard touchdown pass to Billy "Whiteshoes" Johnson to draw the Oilers closer. Then following a 26-yard field goal off the foot of Houston placekicker Toni Fritsch, the Oilers defense recovered a Redskins fumble in Washington territory, and the Oiler offense mounted a game-winning drive. Houston's star running back Earl Campbell ran for 166 yards on 32 carries, and scored two rushing touchdowns, the second of which from three yards out gave the Oilers a 29–27 victory. It definitely was not a thing of beauty, but it counted six just the same. "I just slipped, and everybody just stood there," said Campbell in describing his game-winning score. "It was the best slip I've ever had." Both of these contending teams would not slip much throughout the 1979 regular season.

Most people felt that the Atlanta Falcons would continue their success from the previous season and also have a strong 1979 season. Their coaches, however, felt that the team may have over-achieved in 1978. The Falcons were a young team, but the inexperience of their multitude of younger players was seldom seen in their playoff season of 1978. Many teams throughout the decade had regressed in the year following a winning season, and the Falcons wanted to avoid that fate at all costs. Atlanta's foe on opening day was the team that they had miraculously defeated twice in 1978, the New Orleans Saints. The Louisiana Superdome was the venue for their first meeting of the 1979 campaign, and both teams arguably accounted for even more excitement in this game than they delivered in their two games in 1978. Both defenses were several steps behind the opposing offenses, so scoring would be fast and furious in their first encounter of 1979. New Orleans scored quickly with a 5-yard touchdown pass from quarterback Archie Manning to wide receiver Ike Harris. The Saints' other wide receiver, Wes Chandler, then caught a 40-yard score on a halfback option pass from running back Chuck Muncie. Both teams contributed an incredible combined total of 41 points in the second quarter. Atlanta's air game took wing when quarterback Steve Bartkowski threw a 20-yard touchdown pass to wide receiver Alfred Jenkins, and two touchdown passes to his other wide receiver, Wallace Francis. Mixed in with Bartkowski's scoring tosses were two field goals from Falcons placekicker Tim Mazzetti, and a 4-yard touchdown run by running back William Andrews.

The Saints responded with two ground touchdowns by Muncie, one from four yards out, and the other on a spectacular 69-yard run. New Orleans rookie placekicker Russell Erxleben also booted two field goals, the second one of which from 38 yards out tied the game at 34–34 at the end of regulation. Erxleben would play a major role in the overtime period, but not in a way that he would have liked. Erxleben's talents also permitted him to split time between place-kicking and punting, and with 8:22 left in the overtime period, he was standing back near his 23-yard line, readying for a punt. The snap from New Orleans center John Watson on fourth down flew over his head, however, sending off a mad rush to recover the ball. Erxleben picked it up at his 2-yard line and was immediately corralled by Atlanta safety Tom Pridemore. Falcons rookie running back James Mayberry was trailing the play, and simply found himself in the right place at the right time. Erxleben attempted to throw the ball, but he was in the process of being flung to the ground by Pridemore. He also did not have a good grip on the ball, and his end-over-end toss from his goal line only flew a few yards in the air. Mayberry caught the errant throw at the New Orleans 6-yard line and strolled into the end zone untouched for the winning touchdown. "I didn't see the bad snap," recalled Mayberry, "but I heard the crowd and I knew something was wrong. I saw the ball back there, and I just took off after it. I ran back there expecting to tackle him [Erxleben]. A pass was the last thing on my mind." Mayberry was mobbed by his teammates in the end zone following Atlanta's incredible 40–34 win over their arch-rivals, and the Falcons' miraculous season of 1978 seemed to be right on schedule for an encore in 1979.

A more controversial finish at Metropolitan Stadium occurred on opening day between the San Francisco 49ers and the Minnesota Vikings, and the controversy would involve one of the new rules adopted for 1979. The 49ers built a 9–0 lead in the third quarter on the strength of three field goals from placekicker Ray Wersching. The contest then took on a see-saw quality, as both teams hit paydirt through the air. Minnesota quarterback Tommy Kramer threw three straight touchdown passes to wide receiver Ahmad Rashad, from 52, 32, and 8 yards out. San Francisco quarterback Steve DeBerg then tossed a 44-yard scoring pass to wide receiver Freddie Solomon. A 4-yard touchdown run by 49ers running back Lenvil Elliott gave San Francisco a 22–21 lead late in the fourth quarter. Kramer responded when he put together a 56-yard scoring drive on nine plays, which culminated with a 25-yard pass to Rashad for the game-winning touchdown. It was Rashad's fourth scoring reception of the game, and is still a Vikings team record. But the play was protested by the 49ers, as they claimed that Rashad had lost possession of the pigskin before he crossed the goal line. Fellow Minnesota wide receiver Sammy White recovered the ball in the end zone, but the new 1979 fumble rule would have made the recovery illegal. The new rule specified that a fumble inside of the last two minutes of each half would have to be recovered by the player who fumbled the ball. San Francisco protested the play, saying that White's recovery should be disallowed. The officials disagreed, claiming that the ball had crossed the goal line while still in Rashad's possession. "I'm sick about the loss," said rookie 49ers head coach Bill Walsh.

The defending NFC West Champion Los Angeles Rams also were inflicted with a sickening loss in their Week 1 contest against their visiting Northern California neighbors, the Oakland Raiders. The Rams scored all of their points in the first half on a 1-yard touchdown run by halfback Wendell Tyler, a 17-yard pass from quarterback Pat Haden to wide receiver Willie Miller, and a 46-yard field goal by placekicker Frank Corral. The opportunistic Raiders defense then shutout the Rams in the second half, intercepting three passes and recovering one fumble. The Oakland offense also began to find the end zone in the final two quarters. Scoring for Oakland was tight end Raymond Chester, who caught two touchdown passes in the third quarter from quarterback Ken Stabler, and reserve tight end Derrick Ramsey, who caught another scoring pass from Stabler from one yard out. Oakland prevailed 24–17, marking their 17th win against NFC opponents in their last 18 interconference games.

Another upset of sorts was registered the night before the league openers. The Tampa Bay Buccaneers defeated the visiting Detroit Lions on a Saturday night in Tampa Stadium, 31–16. The reason why the game was moved to the evening before the rest of the games was due to the sweltering Florida weather. According to author and pro football historian Denis M. Crawford, the decision to move the kickoff was beneficial for both players as well as fans. "From 1977–1981 the Bucs would play early season home games on Saturday nights or Sundays at 4:00," said Crawford. "Owner Hugh Culverhouse requested the exception because of the intense heat and humidity in Tampa in late summer. Tampa Stadium was a one-level concrete bowl with aluminum bleachers. At one o'clock in 90 degree heat and 90% humidity, patrons were cooked like baked potatoes. Players on the field could see temps of 110 degrees or more."

Perhaps due to their daily summer practices in the Florida heat and humidity, the Buccaneers seemed to have more stamina than the Lions, particularly in the first half. Rookie Tampa Bay running back Jerry Eckwood rushed for 121 yards as the Bucs built a 24–7 halftime lead. "All I wanted to do was play well," admitted the understated Eckwood. Tampa Bay defensive end LeeRoy Selmon added a touchdown to the cause when he returned a Detroit fumble 29 yards for a touchdown. The surprise victory over the rival Lions was the beginning of what would become the greatest year in the early history of the Tampa Bay franchise.

Undoubtedly the most poignant moment of the first week of the 1979 season occurred on *Monday Night Football* in Foxboro, Massachusetts. During the second quarter of the Steelers-Patriots game, former Patriot Darryl Stingley made his first visit to Schaefer Stadium since his tragic injury in a 1978 preseason contest at Oakland. The stadium's public address announcer and the *Monday Night Football* television broadcasting crew informed the fans that Stingley was in the press box. The officials on the field stopped the game, and the fans and players alike from both teams faced the paralyzed former Patriot and gave him an extended standing ovation, which lasted for several minutes. Stingley's presence at the game inspired the New England squad, and they played one of their best games of the season. Unfortunately for the Patriots, several crucial penalties at key moments in the game helped to defeat them. The struggle was tied at 13–13 at the end of regulation, but the defending world champion Steelers produced a 16–13 victory in overtime on a 41-yard field goal by placekicker Matt Bahr.

The numerous amount of tight contests in Week 1 of the 1979 regular season was not duplicated in Week 2 ... well, at least not as much. There were a few mismatches, a couple of which involved AFC East teams. The Buffalo Bills routed the visiting Cincinnati Bengals, 51–24. Buffalo running back Roland Hooks carried the ball five times for 70 yards. But four of his carries were for touchdowns in the victory. "I got out in the open a lot and got to work one on one," said Hooks. "That's my job—to beat people in the open field." The New England Patriots runners and receivers experienced plentiful amounts of open field too, as they rebounded from their depressing loss to the Pittsburgh Steelers in the opener to crush the visiting New York Jets, 56–3. New England quarterback Steve Grogan completed 13 of 18 passing attempts for 315 yards. He also threw five touchdown passes, three of which went to veteran wide receiver Harold Jackson. The Patriots piled up 597 yards in total offense, and their 56 points was the highest amount of points scored in one game in their franchise's history.

Two other divisional games produced two more one-sided games. The San Diego Chargers were at home when they trounced the Oakland Raiders, 30–10, in one of their two annual AFC West contests with the Silver and Black. The Chargers offense showed a glimpse of future success as quarterback Dan Fouts threw three touchdown passes, one each to wide receiver John Jefferson, veteran tight end Bob Klein, and rookie tight end Kellen Winslow. The San Diego defense also contributed a stellar effort. Chargers linebacker Woodrow Lowe intercepted a Ken Stabler pass in the second quarter and returned it 32 yards for a touchdown. San Diego's pass rush gave Stabler plenty of problems, as the Raiders were able to put together only two sustained drives all afternoon long. "We had him [Stabler] a little gun-shy," said San Diego defensive end Leroy Jones. "He threw some up for grabs, and he knew it. We were coming at him. After three or four times, he started throwing it up because he didn't want to take the pounding."

The Pittsburgh Steelers delivered one of their traditional poundings in their home opener with a 38–7 drubbing of the team that they defeated in last year's AFC title game, the Houston Oilers. Leading the Steeler attack was a defense which limited Houston to only 124 net yards of total offense, and which permitted star Oilers running back Earl Campbell a meager total of only 38 ground yards. Pittsburgh linebacker Dennis "Dirt" Winston accounted for one of five Steeler interceptions and returned it 41 yards down the far sideline for a touchdown. Houston quarterbacks Dan Pastorini and Gifford Nielsen completed a combined total of only eight passes in 27 attempts. "The defense has had some great games in the past few years," admitted Pittsburgh middle linebacker Jack Lambert, "and today was one of them. We held one of the great running backs to less than forty yards." Pittsburgh would begin the 1979 season by winning their first four games, which gave them a good start in the highly competitive AFC Central Division.

The competition level for teams which were trying to make improvements was evident in several tough second week contests. The Cleveland Browns improved their record to 2–0 with a 27–24 win over the Kansas City Chiefs in Arrowhead Stadium. Cleveland quarterback Brian Sipe authored an epic comeback, but midway through the third quarter, few thought that a comeback by the Browns would be necessary. Cleveland had built a 20–0 lead over the Chiefs on the strength of a 17-yard touchdown pass from Sipe to Browns wide receiver Reggie Rucker, and a 20-yard scoring pass from Sipe to tight end Ozzie Newsome. Kansas City showed their mettle, however, by scoring several times in the second half on a 17-yard touchdown pass from quarterback Steve Fuller to wide receiver J.T. Smith, and touchdown runs by running backs Tony Reed and Ted McKnight. Sipe was not phased by Kansas City's resilience, though, and rallied the Browns down to the last minute. His 21-yard touchdown pass deep in the end zone to Rucker with 52 second left lifted Cleveland to a 27–24 victory. The St. Louis Cardinals were labeled the Cardiac Cards during the mid–1970s for their monumental late-game comebacks. Now the Cleveland Browns had claimed that mantle, and it fit them nicely. The "Cardiac Kids" of Cleveland would account for several more come-from-behind victories as 1979 continued.

The Tampa Bay Buccaneers duplicated the Browns' effort when they came from behind to defeat the Baltimore Colts in overtime in Memorial Stadium, 29–26. Tampa spotted the Colts a 17–0 first quarter lead, then responded with two touchdowns of their own in the second quarter on a 1-yard run by star tailback Ricky Bell and a 9-yard scoring pass from quarterback Doug Williams to wide receiver Isaac Hagins. The third quarter was scoreless, but in the fourth quarter, the Tampa Bay defense increased the pressure on the Colt offense. Buccaneers cornerback Mike Washington stepped in front of a Greg Landry throw and returned his intercepted pass 49 yards for a touchdown. Tampa defensive end LeeRoy Selmon also provided constant pressure inside the Baltimore pass pocket. Landry was sacked ten times in the game, and Selmon was responsible for his share of those sacks. Selmon also caused a key fumble by Landry deep in Baltimore territory in the overtime period, which eventually set up the winning score. A 31-yard field goal by Tampa Bay placekicker Neil O'Donoghue early in the sudden death period gave the Bucs a surprising 2–0 record.

Another NFC Central team was enjoying a perfect beginning as well. The Chicago Bears improved their record to 2–0 following their 26–7 conquest of their main rivals, the Minnesota Vikings, at Soldier Field. The Bears were led by their superstar halfback Walter Payton, who rushed for 141 of his 182 yards in the second half. Payton scored on runs of 43 and 26 yards in the second half, as he simply wore down the Purple Gang. "We were feeling them out in the first half," admitted Payton, "and that's dangerous to do against a team like the Vikings. But in the end it was youth and conditioning against age."

It was age against age in a special Thursday night game at Mile High Stadium, where the Los Angeles Rams took on the Denver Broncos. Both teams had veteran squads and both had superior defenses. It was not surprising, therefore, that one of those defenses decided this game. Seasoned Los Angeles safety Dave Elmendorf blitzed deep in Denver territory in the fourth quarter and hit Denver quarterback Craig Morton, causing him to fumble. Rams linebacker Jack "Hacksaw" Reynolds picked up the ball and stumbled four yards into the Broncos end zone for the winning points in a 13–9 win for Los Angeles. "It was a normal safety blitz," described Elmendorf. "I was amazed to see the ball pop out," admitted Reynolds. "I concentrated on falling on the ball. Everybody [as in Reynolds' defensive teammates] down there just picked me up and moved me on my way."

A rematch of 1978 playoff teams completed the second week of the 1979 regular season on *Monday Night Football*. The Atlanta Falcons visited Veterans Stadium and managed to repeat their playoff victory over the Philadelphia Eagles to the tune of 14–10. The Grits Blitz defense once again performed admirably, as they limited the Eagles offense to just 97 total yards and zero points in the second half. Atlanta quarterback Steve Bartkowski threw a 12-yard touchdown pass to wide receiver Wallace Francis in the fourth quarter to provide the winning points. "Francis has a tremendous knack to work himself open," said Bartkowski in describing the deciding score. "He saw the outside blocked and worked his way inside."

Late-game heroics were needed by several more teams in Week 3. Leading the charge in this category was once again the Cardiac Kids of Cleveland, who spotted the Baltimore Colts ten points in the first quarter, then shut them out the remaining three quarters. Cleveland quarterback Brian Sipe was quickly becoming a hero to Browns fans, as he threw a 35-yard touchdown pass to wide receiver Dave Logan in the third quarter, then threw a 74-yard pass to tight end Ozzie Newsome late in the fourth quarter. Newsome's catch set up Cleveland placekicker Don Cockroft for a 28-yard field goal attempt with 1:51 left in regulation. Cockroft's kick was good, and gave the Browns a heart-pounding 13–10 triumph over the Colts. "It was unartistic, but it was a win," said Cleveland head coach Sam Rutigliano. Cleveland was now 3–0 in the AFC Central Division, and ailing fans of the Cardiac Kids started shopping for pacemakers.

Another team in Cleveland's division also required a dramatic finish to claim victory in Week 3. The Pittsburgh Steelers made a rare appearance at Busch Memorial Stadium in St. Louis to take on the upstart Cardinals. The Cards jumped out to an early lead in the first half of this inter-conference game, then were virtually shut down by the Steel Curtain defense in the second half. The Pittsburgh maulers held St. Louis to just 37 net yards during the final two quarters. But it looked as if such a comeback would probably never happen. Steelers star quarterback Terry Bradshaw was injured and carried off the field on a stretcher in the first half. The Steelers were behind by 17 points in the fourth quarter when they finally started to play like defending Super Bowl champions. A 4-yard scoring run by Pittsburgh fullback Rocky Bleier trimmed the Steelers' deficit, then the gutty Bradshaw returned to the game to throw a 5-yard touchdown pass to tight end Bennie Cunningham. A 20-yard field goal by Pittsburgh's rookie placekicker Matt Bahr with 13 seconds left in the struggle gave the Steelers their third win of the season in dramatic fashion, 24–21. "Our whole football team, I think, came back from adverse circumstances," assessed Pittsburgh head coach Chuck Noll.

An almost identical final score later that day was the verdict in Dallas, as the Cowboys came from behind to defeat the previously undefeated Chicago Bears at Texas Stadium, 24–20. It took a 22-yard touchdown pass from Dallas quarterback Roger Staubach to wide receiver Tony Hill with 1:53 left in the game to beat the Bears. On the winning score, Hill caught a quick square out pass from Staubach along the near sideline, waited for blocks from offensive tackle Pat Donovan and offensive guard Herbert Scott, juked past Chicago safety Lenny Walterscheid, and broke an arm tackle from Bears linebacker Tom Hicks inside the 5-yard line. Hill pranced into the end zone, and Dallas continued their strong start with a 3–0 record. "I'm grateful for Donovan making that block," said Hill. "As for that linebacker [Hicks]—no way is an arm tackle going to keep me out of the end zone."

In their on-again, off-again NFC West rivalry, the Los Angeles Rams survived a late surge by the visiting San Francisco 49ers to pull out a 27–24 win. San Francisco quarterback Steve DeBerg connected on two touchdown passes to wide receiver Mike Schumann in the fourth quarter, but two Frank Corral field goals late in the game provided the Rams (now 2–1) with the margin of victory. The loss to the Rams dropped the improving 49ers to a somewhat depressing 0–3 record.

Speaking of depressing, the formerly intimidating Oakland Raiders traveled to Seattle to take on the Seahawks. It turned out to be a surprising mismatch, as Seattle quarterback Jim Zorn threw for 277 yards and three touchdowns in his team's 27–10 victory over the Silver and Black. Seattle wide receiver Steve Largent caught two of those scoring passes from Zorn, on distances of 40 and 21 yards. Oakland quarterback Ken Stabler eclipsed Zorn's yardage total, as he threw for a career-high 343 yards. But Stabler was intercepted twice, and the ever-alert Seattle defense also recovered two fumbles en route to victory. "If you don't win, it [the 343 passing yards] doesn't really mean a damn," said a discouraged Stabler after the game. "We stopped ourselves a lot."

The Miami Dolphins stopped the host Minnesota Vikings in a game that was closer than the final score indicated. Miami reserve quarterback Don Strock helped his team erupt for 20 points in the final 15 minutes to post a 27–12 victory over the Norsemen. Strock threw touchdown passes from six yards out to both wide receiver Jimmy Cefalo and to running back Larry Csonka, while fellow Dolphin runners Norm Bulaich and Delvin Williams each added a short scoring run. Miami now owned an impressive 3–0 record to start the season.

Rounding out some other key games in the third week of the 1979 season were strong wins by the Washington Redskins over the visiting New York Giants. The Redskins shutout their NFC East rivals, 27–0. Washington's defense did yeoman's work, as defensive end Karl Lorch intercepted a Joe Pisarcik screen pass and romped 31 yards untouched for a touchdown in the second quarter. Redskins quarterback Joe Theismann also ran for one score and threw for another in the most lopsided win of Washington's season. The Redskins were now 2–1, while the Giants fell to 0–3. The Tampa Bay Buccaneers kept on winning on the strength of their defense, and as a result continued to surprise everyone, perhaps even themselves. The Bucs traveled to Lambeau Field to take on the Green Bay Packers, a team that was also young and eager to change their trend over five of the last six years of finishing with a losing record. Tampa took command in the second quarter and stayed in control throughout the remainder of the game. Both Jerry Eckwood and Ricky Bell contributed over 90 yards each to bolster the Tampa Bay rushing attack, and each man also rushed for a touchdown in the 21–10 victory over the Pack.

The Buccaneers were one of four teams which managed to remain perfect a week later. Tampa was welcomed home to a raucous and now optimistic crowd at Tampa Stadium. Those Tampa fans had never seen their team own an undefeated record during the first month of a season, and with each victory came fewer and fewer available tickets. The Buccaneers took on the Los Angeles Rams at Tampa Stadium on September 23. Head coach John McKay's team now entered a game owning at least some measure of momentum with wins during the previous three weeks. They would next play one of their best games of the year against a truly formidable opponent. Los Angeles jumped on top in the first quarter on a 31-yard interception return for a touchdown by Rams linebacker Jim Youngblood. That was practically the only mistake that the Bucs made all day. Tampa Bay quarterback Doug Williams made up for his interception by throwing for two touchdowns in the second quarter, part of the Buccaneers' 21-point barrage prior to halftime. Williams threw a 15-yard touchdown pass to wide receiver Larry Mucker, and a 29-yard scoring toss to tight end Jimmie Giles. Adding to the Tampa scoring was a 5-yard touchdown run by tailback Ricky Bell. Tampa Bay triumphed over the Rams, 21–6, and earned a few big firsts in their history. It was the first time that they ever won four straight games, and it was the first time in their young history that their defense did not surrender a single point against an opponent. The Buccaneers were now the only team in the NFC to be 4–0, while the Rams dropped to 2–2 with the loss. "We played as good in the second quarter as we can play football," exclaimed Tampa Bay head coach John McKay. "As long as we are healthy, I think we can play with most people."

The Buccaneers were not the only Florida team that owned a perfect record. The Miami Dolphins also won their fourth game against zero losses with a 31–16 win over the Chicago Bears at the Orange Bowl. Miami fullback and prodigal son Larry Csonka scored three touchdowns in the victory. Csonka's scoring spree was eclipsed on the same day in Buffalo by rookie wide receiver Jerry Butler of the Bills, who caught four touchdown passes from quarterback Joe Ferguson in Buffalo's 46–31 win against the visiting New York Jets. Butler's 10 receptions for 255 yards set a team rookie record, and his scoring catches of 5 yards, 75 yards, 74, yards, and 9 yards helped to produce the majority of a 34-point Buffalo scoring surge in the second and third quarters. At that time, Butler's efforts produced the seventh-best receiving day in league history. Typically, 31 points is often enough to defeat most opponents in the NFL, but not in this contest, and seemingly not in many of the pass-happy games that 1979 produced. Ferguson finished the game with a club-record five touchdown passes, and a career-best 367 yards passing. Buffalo now evened its record at 2–2.

Another defenseless contest took place in Denver on September 23, where the Broncos scored 27 unanswered points in the second half to post a 37–34 victory over the Seattle Seahawks. Veteran Denver signal caller Craig Morton came off the bench to throw three touchdown passes in a span of less than three minutes to aid the Broncos attack. Morton's efforts produced plenty of late-game drama, and in Foxboro, Massachusetts, a pair of other strong AFC quarterbacks did the same. San Diego's Dan Fouts dueled with New England's Steve Grogan in a highly competitive matchup which required a key defensive play to secure a win. The Patriots built a 20–0 lead into the second quarter, but the Chargers responded with a 19-yard touchdown pass from Fouts to wide receiver John Jefferson, and a couple of 1-yard touchdown runs by running back Clarence Williams. New England went ahead in the fourth quarter on a 5-yard touchdown pass from Grogan to Patriots tight end Russ Francis. Fouts then quickly led his offense down the field late in the final quarter, but his pass intended for Jefferson across the middle was intercepted by New England linebacker Steve Nelson at the Patriots' 2-yard line with 1:33 remaining, thus preserving New England's 27–21 victory. Jefferson appeared to be wide open on the play, but Nelson drifted across the field to make the biggest play of the game. "Football makes a kid of you," said Nelson in a contemplative mood after the game, "and I feel like a fifteen-year-old with a six-pack and his best girlfriend."

Both the Broncos and the Patriots avoided overtime periods in their wins, but a couple of games in Week 4 were destined for overtime excitement. In Minnesota, the annual battle between the Vikings and the Packers was decided when Vikings quarterback Tommy Kramer threw his second touchdown pass of the day with 3:18 elapsed in the overtime period. On the receiving end of Kramer's game-winning pass was Minnesota wide receiver Ahmad Rashad, who broke a couple of tackles en route to the 50-yard score which gave the Vikes a 27–21 triumph over their NFC Central Division rivals. Rashad ended the day with nine catches for 136 yards and two touchdowns, and Minnesota running back Chuck Foreman carried the ball only six times all day, but he nevertheless became the all-time leading rusher in Vikings history. "You get Ahmad Rashad to catch the ball and it makes the quarterback and the coaching staff look great," admitted Minnesota head coach Bud Grant.

The other overtime contest in Week 4 took place in Cincinnati's Riverfront Stadium, where the Houston Oilers improved to 3–1 with a 30–27 win over the Bengals. Houston placekicker Toni Fritsch ended the game with a 29-yard field goal with just 32 seconds left in the overtime period. Early in the second quarter, it appeared to most observers that the Oilers were destined to lose this contest. Cincinnati bolted to a 24–0 lead in the second quarter before the Oilers started hitting gushers. Houston quarterback Dan Pastorini threw touchdown passes of 35 yards to wide receiver Ken Burrough and 22 yards to fellow wide receiver Rich Caster to spur the Houston comeback. Both defenses recovered from a faulty first half to play strong in the second half. Cincinnati placekicker Chris Bahr booted a club-record 55-yard field goal which sent the game into overtime, but he also missed a field goal attempt from 32 yards out earlier in the fourth quarter which would have given the Bengals their first win of the year.

Cincinnati's 0–4 record was in direct contrast to the two teams at the top of the AFC Central Division. Both the defending world champion Pittsburgh Steelers and the upstart Cleveland Browns remained perfect with big wins. The Steelers took on the visiting Baltimore Colts and listlessly played down to the level of their winless competition. The struggling Colts took a surprising 13–10 lead into the fourth quarter of this game, only to lose when Pittsburgh quarterback Terry Bradshaw connected with tight end Bennie Cunningham for a 28-yard touchdown with 5:41 left in the struggle. Pittsburgh seemed to be able to win a lot of close games in 1979, usually the mark of a good team. But the 1979 Steelers were also committing a lot of turnovers (52 in all), up 13 more from the amount that they committed in 1978 (39).

Up in Cleveland's Municipal Stadium on *Monday Night Football*, the resurgent Browns sent a message to Pittsburgh and to the rest of the league, as they dominated the defending NFC champion Dallas Cowboys, 26–7. It was Dallas' first loss of the year, and they were never really competitive throughout the contest. Cleveland quarterback Brian Sipe threw two touchdown passes in the first quarter, one from 23 yards out to wide receiver Dave Logan, and one from 52 yards out to tight end Ozzie Newsome. Cleveland defensive back Thom Darden added a 39-yard interception return to increase the Browns' scoring barrage. "It was 20–0 before we knew what was happening," opined disgusted Dallas defensive end Harvey Martin. Cleveland's defense recovered three Dallas fumbles in the onslaught, and also blocked a Dallas field goal attempt. "We played opportunistic football," said Cleveland head coach Sam Rutigliano. The outcome marked an unusual ending for the Cardiac Kids, as the one-sided ending permitted Rutigliano to put in several of his substitutes late in the game. The Browns would play in 12 games in 1979 that ended with a margin of victory of seven points or less, including three games that went into overtime and seven games which were decided in the final minute or in overtime. Their victory over Dallas was a rare respite from those nail-biters. The ABC-TV camera crew concluded the evening in an unforeseen way when they captured a moment of disgorging distress on live television, as Dallas wide receiver Drew Pearson was seen bending down to his waist and throwing up after an incomplete pass late in the game.

The Oakland Raiders to a man probably felt like vomiting the day before after falling to their historical rivals, the Kansas City Chiefs, 35–7. Marv Levy was in his second year as the head coach at Kansas City, and the offense he used for his offensive personnel was called the Wing-T. It was an old college offense designed to run the ball and to keep gaining first downs, and Levy used it in order to keep his deplorable defense—which gave up an average of 24 points per game in 1978—off the field. It utilized three running backs in odd formations in the offensive backfield, and usually included a myriad of fakes and misdirection runs. Levy described the Wing-T as "grueling" and "consistent." The key to its success was its deceptive nature. One or more of the backs usually shifted into a position next to the outside offensive tackle or tight end just before the snap of the ball. The most common strategy was to attack a defense's flanks with sweeps and reverses. According to Chiefs team historian Bob Moore, "Ball-handling was crucial here, especially with the dimension of a third back, and what caused confusion for the defense was the number of flows and split flows the offense ran." In 1978, Levy's offense racked up 2,986 rushing yards, the second-most in the NFL. In 1979, the Chiefs' rushing offense was still strong, gaining 2,316 yards. But the rest of the league's defenses caught on to the strategy by the end of the 1979 season, and the Wing-T would quickly go back on the shelves of history.

Nevertheless, the Chiefs used the Wing-T to build an insurmountable 28–0 lead against the Raiders into the fourth quarter of their first meeting in 1979. Kansas City scored on the strength of a 19-yard touchdown pass from quarterback Steve Fuller to wide receiver Steve Gaunty; a club-record 88-yard punt return by J.T. Smith; a 70-yard interception return by Kansas City safety Gary Barbaro; and a 1-yard touchdown run by running back Arnold Morgado, who would also add another 3-yard rushing score in the fourth quarter. The Chiefs defense also played one of its best games in team history, recording seven sacks, three interceptions, and limiting the Raiders offense to a meager 121 total yards. "We executed poorly, and they beat the hell out of us," said a despondent Oakland quarterback Ken Stabler after the game. "We did not expect their pass rush to be that good, but it was. I'm not perplexed about it. We're just not playing well."

The Detroit Lions finally played well enough to win their first game of the year, a 24–23 upset over the visiting Atlanta Falcons. The Lions relied on the formula for victory that was a Falcons trademark from the year before. Detroit came from behind in the fourth quarter, thanks to a 13-yard touchdown pass from reserve quarterback Jeff Komlo to wide receiver Luther Blue, and a 26-yard scoring run by running back Rick Kane. Komlo threw for 289 yards in the win, and the loss dropped Atlanta to 2–2, which was good enough for a tie in the NFC West with the Los Angeles Rams. Both the Washington Redskins and the Philadelphia Eagles were tied for first place in the competitive NFC East with victories in the fourth week. The Redskins upended the host St. Louis Cardinals, 17–7, and the Eagles managed to outlast the New York Giants in the New Jersey Meadowlands, 17–13. Both the Redskins and the Eagles looked like they were ready to offer strong challenges to the Dallas Cowboys, as all three were 3–1 in their division. As the season wore on, all three would settle the issue of winning the NFC East with plenty of hard hits and spectacular plays, but it would take until the final week of the season for a champion in that division to be crowned.

The Tampa Bay Buccaneers could be crowned as the NFL's best team at the end of the fifth week of play. They reigned as the only 5–0 team in the NFL, and were probably as surprised of their success as was anyone else. Their fifth win came at the expense of the Chicago Bears on a bright, sunny day at Soldier Field, and it required a comeback in the final quarter. An 8-yard touchdown pass from Buccaneers quarterback Doug Williams to wide receiver Isaac Hagins with 5:08 left in the game lifted Tampa Bay to a 17–13 victory. Tampa's 3–4 defense was the catalyst for most of their team's five wins, and this triumph over their divisional rivals was no different. The Bears could gain only 82 yards on the ground all afternoon, and their great halfback Walter Payton could earn only 46 of those yards. "I guess we're ahead of our plan for five weeks," said Tampa Bay head coach John McKay after his team's win over Chicago, "but we still have a long way to go."

Another key defensive effort was needed in a key AFC East contest at Shea Stadium. The youthful New York Jets were taking on the undefeated Miami Dolphins in what appeared to be a David versus Goliath game. New York's defense managed to come up with several key plays, however, including a 58-yard interception return for a touchdown in the third quarter by cornerback Bobby Jackson, and a recovery of a blocked George Roberts punt in the end zone by fellow Jets cornerback Johnny Lynn earlier in the game. Not to be outdone, the Dolphins had built their winning record through the strength of their dynamic offense. They managed to take advantage of the poise of their veteran quarterback Bob Griese, who threw three touchdown passes against the Jets. Yet it was a 71-yard touchdown bomb from Jets quarterback Richard Todd to his fast and fluid wide receiver Wesley Walker which provided New York with the winning points. "I told him I was open the whole game," said Walker of his discussions to his quarterback in the huddle. "All day long I kept going deep and getting open. I'm glad Todd finally saw me and got it to me." The Jets prevailed, 33–27, improving their record to 2–3, while the loss dropped the 4–1 Dolphins from the ranks of the undefeated.

The Cleveland Browns and the Pittsburgh Steelers were also undefeated going into their fifth game, and both suffered their first loss. The Browns ran into a buzzsaw inside the Houston Astrodome, as the Oilers leveled a 31–10 pasting on their division rivals from Ohio. The Oilers built a 24–10 lead at halftime, and shut out the Browns in the second half. Houston running back Earl Campbell contributed three short rushing touchdowns in the rout, and Oilers defensive back J.C. Wilson added a 34-yard interception return for a score in the second quarter. "We played some good, all-around football," assessed Houston nose guard Curley Culp after the victory.

The Philadelphia Eagles played pretty good football also in their win over the visiting Pittsburgh Steelers in the Battle of Pennsylvania. Both of these teams played each other annually in the preseason, but contests in the regular season between each of these teams occurred only every few years. The site for this meeting was Veterans Stadium, where the Eagles were in the midst of building a strong home-field advantage in the late 1970s. The overcast and rainy skies foreshadowed a dismal day for the defending world champion Steelers. The Eagles "Gang Green" defense caused several key Pittsburgh turnovers, the most crucial of which occurred near the end of the game at the Philadelphia goal line. Eagles defensive tackle Ken Clarke recovered a fumble which preserved a 17–14 Philly victory over their Keystone State rivals. The loss had to be examined in its total scope of details, however, as the Steelers were playing minus the services of starters Lynn Swann, Gerry Mullins, Steve Furness, and L.C. Greenwood, each of whom were not suited up due to injuries. Several other Pittsburgh starters only saw brief action in the game, and they included running backs Franco Harris and Rocky Bleier, and cornerback Ron Johnson. Those facts did not matter to Philadelphia head coach Dick Vermeil, who counted this win over the defending champs as a great accomplishment by his young team. "It was as good as the Rose Bowl," said Vermeil, referring to his UCLA squad which won the 1976 Rose Bowl over Ohio State. Vermeil's Eagles thus remained in a three-way tie for first place in the NFC East with both Dallas and Washington.

The Cowboys rebounded from their embarrassing loss to Cleveland the week before to take apart another Ohio team—the Bengals—by a score of 38–13 at Texas Stadium. Dallas built a 21–6 halftime lead and never looked back. Reserve Dallas running back Scott Laidlaw scored two short rushing touchdowns, and Dallas defensive backs Randy Hughes and Aaron Mitchell each chipped in big interceptions which set up two more touchdowns. Star Dallas halfback Tony Dorsett rushed for 119 yards in the win. "This helps us because it builds up our confidence," said Dallas head coach Tom Landry. "This is the first game this year that we had a good feeling like last year. Everything clicked."

The Washington Redskins' offense also clicked in several key moments of their 16–7 win over the Falcons in Atlanta in Week 5. Despite the low score, the Redskins accounted for 359 total yards against the Grits Blitz defense, including 233 yards passing from Washington quarterback Joe Theismann. "I felt today I threw the ball as well as I ever have as a pro," said Theismann. The same could not be said for Theismann's counterpart, Atlanta quarterback Steve Bartkowski, who threw three costly interceptions. Washington's defense took over from there, and limited the Falcons offense to a paltry 29 total yards and zero points in the second half.

Strong defensive performances were also seen in the fifth week of the season by the Oakland Raiders and the Los Angeles Rams. The Raiders crushed the defending AFC West Champion Denver Broncos at the Oakland-Alameda County Coliseum, 27–3. The stingy Raiders defense kept the Broncos from sustaining scoring drives, while the Oakland offense relied on ball control to win their second game of the year. Down the west coast about 370 miles, the Rams won their third game of the year with a 21–0 shutout of the St. Louis Cardinals, who were still struggling in the second year of Bud Wilkinson's head coaching tenure. Before the end of the 1979 regular season, the Cardinals would achieve a few upsets but would finish with a 5–11 record, and Wilkinson would be released. The Los Angeles coaches had difficulties as well during the season, but against the Cardinals, their defense played strong. They limited the Cardinals to 47 total yards in the first half. The Rams offense also chipped in and kept moving the ball on the ground for much of the game.

The 1979 San Diego Chargers offense in contrast was definitely not rooted in their ground attack. Chargers quarterback Dan Fouts piloted an offense labeled "Air Coryell" after the San Diego head coach and passing guru. The Chargers were following up on their record-setting 1978 season by continuing to drop bomb after bomb on their opponents. The Chargers' victim in Week 5 of the 1979 season was the visiting San Francisco 49ers, a team that would remain winless following their 31–9 loss to the Chargers. The catalyst for the San Diego win was once again Fouts, who would have little trouble solving the coverages from San Francisco's youthful defense. Fouts completed 26 passes in 34 attempts for 251 yards and two touchdowns. The only bright spot for the 49ers was the play of veteran running back O.J. Simpson, whose 89 yards rushing brought his career total to 11,006 yards.

Rounding out the fifth week was an unlikely upset on *Monday Night Football,* when the visiting New England Patriots fell to the Green Bay Packers, 27–14. The Patriots were showing off their new road uniforms on national television on this Wisconsin evening, which included new red pants in place of their old white pants. Over the course of the decade of the 1970s, only a few teams made slight changes to their uniforms, preferring instead to retain their common identity and tradition. Such is not the case in the NFL of today, as many teams experiment with new uniform designs at least twice in the span of every 10 years. The main reason behind the changes in team logos and uniforms involves money. The arm of the league known as NFL Properties has made millions of dollars over the past several decades by producing new jerseys, sweatshirts, and t-shirts (among a variety of other team merchandise) for fans to purchase, all with new team logo designs every few years. New clothing items and souvenirs for the fans every few years results in much more money for the league every few years.

In its tenth season in 1979, the specter of *Monday Night Football* was still having a measured effect on underdog teams, particular when they were playing at home. The Packers were just such a team. They had fallen on many a bad year following their last playoff appearance in 1972. Nevertheless, the Packers knew that all of America was watching, so they did their best, and made the most of the early momentum that they built. Green Bay's porous defense had one of its better outings, as they intercepted New England quarterbacks Steve Grogan and Tom Owen a total of five times. The Packers defense also managed to shut out the Patriots in the second half. "That was as inspirational, as emotional a victory as I have ever been a part of," admitted Green Bay head coach Bart Starr, who throughout the 1960s as the Packers quarterback authored more than his share of big wins. "New England has one heck of a team. We were grateful just to be on national TV against them. To win is a huge bonus."

There were two shutouts in the sixth week of the 1979 season, and both were by identical 7–0 scores. The Chicago Bears went up to Buffalo in desperate need of a win to keep pace with the surging Tampa Bay Buccaneers in the NFC Central Division. Neither the Bears nor the Bills displayed a strong offense in this game, but the Bears had a weapon that the Bills lacked. Chicago running back Walter Payton rushed for 155 yards on 39 bone-rattling carries, and he managed to score the game's lone touchdown. On fourth down from the Buffalo 1-yard line in the fourth quarter, Payton leaped up and over the Bills defensive line and landed on his head in the end zone. The Chicago defense complemented Payton by playing its best game of the year in the Bears' victory, limiting the Bills offense to just seven first downs and 106 total yards.

A much more surprising 7–0 win was achieved in Denver by the Broncos, who bushwhacked the pass-happy San Diego Chargers at Mile High Stadium. The Chargers gained their seemingly weekly allotment of over 300 yards on offense, but the Broncos defense threw up a concrete barrier at their goal line. The big standout here for the Orange Crush defense was veteran safety Bill Thompson, who intercepted two passes and recovered a key fumble in the third quarter, which set up the game's lone score. Reserve Denver quarterback Norris Weese ran a naked bootleg to his left for a 3-yard touchdown. The win lifted the Broncos to a 4–2 record, which tied them for first place in the AFC West with the Chargers and the upstart Kansas City Chiefs, who pulled out a 10–7 win over the hapless (and winless) Cincinnati Bengals at Riverfront Stadium.

One team that was winless going into Week 6 would be winless no more following their surprising victory over a team that no one believed would be undefeated going into their sixth game of the 1979 season. The New York Giants managed to upset the visiting Tampa Bay Buccaneers, whose winning binge to start the year was halted after five games. Most of the fans in Giants Stadium were undoubtedly shocked by the result, as their defense actually performed well, and their offense managed to put together a couple of strong scoring drives against a defense that was gelling in the early part of the season. Little-known Giants running back Billy Taylor rushed for 148 yards on 33 carries. He also scored both of New York's touchdowns on short runs in the second quarter. "The offensive line did a tremendous job," noted Taylor. "It's just a matter of timing, and the offensive line was a little off on coordination until today." Tampa Bay came back with a couple of scoring tosses from quarterback Doug Williams. One of those touchdown passes went to wide receiver Larry Mucker, who caught a 14-yard tipped pass as he fell in the Giants end zone. New York placekicker Joe Danelo booted a 47-yard field goal in the fourth quarter to give the Giants a 17–14 win. There were now no undefeated teams left in the league.

A few more games in Week 6 produced upsets, tight final scores, and potential playoff implications. The 1–4 St. Louis Cardinals visited the Astrodome to take on the 4–1 Houston Oilers. They left the Astrodome with their second victory. The Cards accumulated a total of 447 total yards against a pretty fair Oiler defense. St. Louis rookie running back Ottis "O.J." Anderson carried the ball for 109 yards, and his teammate in the backfield, Wayne Morris, scored two short touchdowns in the fourth quarter to provide the winning points. The Cardinals' 24–17 triumph was also due to the passing prowess of quarterback Jim Hart, who completed 23 passes in 38 attempts for 253 yards. Houston's loss dropped them to second place in the AFC Central with a 4–2 record. "St. Louis outplayed us and they deserved to win," admitted Houston head coach Bum Phillips. "That doesn't mean that our season is over."

The New England Patriots owned an identical 4–2 record after struggling to beat the visiting Detroit Lions in Week 5. The Lions had only one win to their credit, but they played the Patriots tough all day, and even took a 17–14 lead into the fourth quarter. New England's superior athletes came through at the end, however, as reserve quarterback Tom Owen hit running back Don Calhoun for a 6-yard touchdown pass, and placekicker John Smith kicked a 29-yard field goal to aid his team. New England's 24–17 win gave them a first place tie in the AFC East with Miami, who dropped a 13–3 decision in Oakland to the Raiders.

There was a two-team tie for first place in the NFC East as well. Both the Dallas Cowboys and the Philadelphia Eagles won their respective contests in Week 6. The Cowboys invaded Metropolitan Stadium and defeated the Vikings, 36–20. Dallas halfback Tony Dorsett enjoyed one of his better games of the year, as he rushed for 145 yards and scored three touchdowns. "I'm blessed with an offensive line that loves to block, lay their hats on people and just wipe them out," Dorsett said. The Eagles loved to wipe people out too. They played host to the division rival Redskins, and began showing their offensive potential. Philadelphia halfback Wilbert Montgomery rushed for 127 yards and scored all four of the Eagles' touchdowns, three on rushes and one on a 11-yard pass from quarterback Ron Jaworski. The Eagles defense allowed Washington to score twice in the final quarter, but Philadelphia's lead was big enough by then to outlast their foes from the District of Columbia, 28–17.

Scoring would not be a problem for the Pittsburgh Steelers in their game at Cleveland. The Steeler runners accounted for a club record 361 ground yards. But the Cleveland offense was also able to gain yards, mostly through the air. Cleveland quarterback Brian Sipe threw for a career-high 351 yards, and tied a team record with five touchdown passes. The scoring for both teams came in waves, as neither defense managed to show up for the game. The Steelers jumped on top early with 21 points in the first quarter, built on two touchdown passes from quarterback Terry Bradshaw, and a 71-yard scoring run by halfback Franco Harris. By game's end, Harris would rush for 153 yards and would score two touchdowns. Cleveland responded in the second quarter with touchdown passes from Sipe to wide receiver Reggie Rucker and to tight end Ozzie Newsome. Six more touchdowns were scored in the second half, three by each team. Perhaps the most incredible was a 70-yard dash for a touchdown in the fourth quarter by Steelers fullback Rocky Bleier, who broke through a trap draw play right up the middle. Cleveland's defensive backs were busy near opposite sidelines as they double covered the Pittsburgh wide receivers. By the time that they reacted to Bleier's run, they were already behind him. By the final gun of Pittsburgh's 51–35 victory over Cleveland, a total of 980 combined yards were gained by both teams. Pittsburgh head coach Chuck Noll called his team's 522-yard performance "a rebirth of our offense." Noll also came to terms with the unusual play of his defense. "The defense is banged up," Noll admitted. "That's why we gave up so many yards. But our offense more than offset it." Cleveland head coach Sam Rutigliano commented afterward that the game might have been closer had not his offense given up three drive-killing interceptions and two costly fumbles. "We made mistakes," Rutigliano said bluntly. "We helped create things for them [the Steelers]. You can't do that against Pittsburgh—they'll capitalize."

Capitalizing on your opportunities would be common in the seventh week of the 1979 season. The tables would be turned on the Steelers against another division foe; three teams in the NFC East would continue to win; a couple of teams in the AFC East and AFC West started to break away from the congestion in the standings; and the Raiders and the Buccaneers reverted back to preseason expectations. Pittsburgh head coach Chuck Noll's hope was that his defense would be more focused following their breakdowns against the Browns in the previous week. Unfortunately for Noll, those hopes were dashed in their game against the previously winless Cincinnati Bengals at Riverfront Stadium in Week 7. Pittsburgh's defense could not be blamed in whole for the Bengals' surprising 34–10 victory. The Steelers offense did more than their part in the defeat by fumbling the ball … over and over again. The Bengals recovered seven Steeler fumbles, many of which occurred in Pittsburgh territory. Two of Pittsburgh's fumbles were recovered by Cincinnati linebackers Howard Kurnick and Jim LeClair. Both of those Bengal players returned their prizes for touchdowns. "You've got to be up to play the world champions," said Kurnick, a rookie on the Bengals squad. "We took it to them." The Steelers were never competitive, and Coach Noll was not in an understanding mood following his team's embarrassing performance. "We aided and abetted them considerably," said Noll. "I don't care what the reasons were, just as long as we straighten them out."

The reasons why the Dallas Cowboys won in decisive fashion against the visiting Los Angeles Rams had to do mainly with the play of their offense. Dallas quarterback Roger Staubach threw three touchdown passes, and tailback Tony Dorsett became the first player in team history to rush for over 100 yards in three straight games when he ran for 103 versus the Rams. Of course, the Dallas Doomsday Defense also did their share of the work, limiting the Rams to just 59 total ground yards and two field goals. The Cowboys' 30–6 romp over Los Angeles kept them in first place in the competitive NFC East with an impressive 6–1 record. "The Rams didn't seem as intense as they did the last time," said Dallas safety Cliff Harris, in reference to the way the Rams played the Cowboys in the 1978 NFC championship game. A much different Rams team, however, would go on to meet the Cowboys again later in 1979.

The intensity of Dallas' main rivals in the NFC East continued to grow stronger as midseason neared. The Philadelphia Eagles continued to win close games and stay even with the Cowboys. On October 14 at Busch Memorial Stadium, a battle of birds took place as the Eagles met the Cardinals. Philadelphia was in the midst of building a strong rushing attack. Halfback Wilbert Montgomery rushed for 117 yards against St. Louis, and scored on a 5-yard touchdown run in the third quarter. Long-time pro coach Sid Gillman, agreed upon by many as the father of the modern pro passing game, was signed on by head coach Dick Vermeil to be a consultant, and to help quarterback Ron Jaworski gel into a polished passer. Gillman's advice, coaching and counseling helped the Eagles' offense improve immensely and immediately. Jaworski would finish the season with 2,669 yards passing and 18 touchdowns. But the pride of the Eagles seemed to be their opportunistic defense, which would account for 22 interceptions and 11 fumble recoveries in 1979. In the Cardinals game, however, an unlikely contributor in the form of diminutive kick returner Wally Henry stole the show. Henry returned five Cardinal kickoffs a total of 142 yards, and his 34-yard punt return in the fourth quarter set the Eagles up for the winning touchdown. Reserve Philadelphia halfback Billy Campfield ran 11 yards for the deciding score as the Eagles won, 24–20. It was Philadelphia's fifth straight victory. "I've said it all along, we've got character and talent," exclaimed Eagles head coach Dick Vermeil.

The Washington Redskins were right behind the Cowboys and the Eagles in the NFC East, thanks to their 13–9 win over the host Cleveland Browns. The Redskins' only touchdown came with only 27 seconds left in the final quarter on a 14-yard pass from quarterback Joe Theismann to setback Clarence Harmon. Washington's win improved their record to 5–2, as their defense improved to tops in the NFC with only 104 points allowed in seven games.

Two teams in the AFC East also sported 5–2 records. The Miami Dolphins won a tight contest at the Orange Bowl against the Buffalo Bills, 17–7, and in doing so, they set a league record. This victory marked the 20th straight win for Miami over Buffalo, giving the Bills a winless record against the Dolphins for the entire decade. No other team in the NFL throughout the 1970s had an opponents' number quite like Miami did over the Bills. Besides the Dolphins, no other team in league history has defeated a division rival 20 straight times. The Dolphins defense ranked as second best in the AFC by this stage of the 1979 season, but it was a big play by their special teams which ignited their second win of the season over Buffalo. Dolphins rookie Tony Nathan returned a punt a team record 86 yards for a touchdown in the first quarter. Veteran Miami running back Larry Csonka would eventually be named the league's Comeback Player of the Year. He would add another touchdown against the Bills on a 7-yard run, thereby giving the Dolphins a lead in the second quarter which they never lost.

Miami's foremost rival in the AFC East, the New England Patriots, also defeated an inferior team. The Patriots offense proved too much of a challenge for the Chicago Bears at Soldier Field. New England's 27–7 victory came about thanks to three touchdown passes from quarterback Steve Grogan, who connected with wide receivers Stanley Morgan on a 10-yard touchdown, and Harold Jackson on a 19-yard score, both of which came in the first quarter. Grogan hit tight end Russ Francis in the final quarter with a 4-yard touchdown pass. Taking the time to pay a visit to his former teammates on the sidelines was former Patriots wide receiver Darryl Stingley, who was paralyzed in a 1978 preseason game at Oakland. Stingley's presence in a wheelchair undoubtedly inspired the Patriots to win their fifth game of the year.

Both the Denver Broncos and the San Diego Chargers also won their fifth games of the season. The Broncos defeated the Kansas City Chiefs at Arrowhead Stadium, 24–10, and the Chargers upended the Seattle Seahawks at San Diego Stadium, 20–10. The top two teams in each of the three divisions in the AFC all now owned identical 5–2 records. The logjam of tight divisional races would also be prominent in the NFC, albeit with more mediocre records. The fervor and fan excitement ignited by the Tampa Bay Buccaneers was finally starting to level out, as the Bucs lost their second straight game. The culprit in Week 7 was surprisingly the New Orleans Saints, a team which had only won twice before meeting Tampa Bay at Tampa Stadium on October 14. The Saints offense had no trouble solving what had been the league's best defense … at least in the game's second half. A scoreless first half precipitated a big turnaround with six New Orleans touchdowns in the final 30 minutes. Five of those scores came on the ground with Saints quarterback Archie Manning running two yards for one touchdown. Saints halfback Tony Galbreath then scored twice, as did fellow runner Mike Strachan. When the onslaught was finally over, the Saints posted a 42–14 rout of the Buccaneers. "I thought we could win, but not that big, not against that [Tampa Bay] defense," said a surprised New Orleans head coach Dick Nolan. "You don't do this to them [the Buccaneers] everyday," admitted Manning.

A few routs in Week 8 could also have been regarded as "statement" games, as several team began to gel on both offense and defense as the season reached its midway point. One such team which showcased its abilities was the San Diego Chargers, who easily defeated their California neighbors, the Los Angeles Rams, at the Los Angeles Memorial Coliseum. The Chargers' 40–16 pasting of the Rams came about unsurprisingly with the aid of their dominant passing attack. San Diego's offense was the third-highest scoring offense in the NFL at this stage of the season, and with a quarterback like Dan Fouts and receivers like John Jefferson and Charlie Joiner (both of whom were destined to eclipse the 1,000-yard mark for receiving yardage in 1979), the Chargers were tough for even the strongest of defenses to stop. San Diego head coach Don Coryell was the kind of mentor who believed in keeping scoreboard operators in business. Sure, the Chargers did run the ball on occasion, but their real offensive strength came through the air. Against the Rams, Fouts threw for 326 yards and two touchdowns. Fouts' performance made him the seventh player in league history to record three straight 300-yard passing games. Under publicized in this game was the play of the San Diego defense, a unit which forced eight Los Angeles turnovers. The win boosted the Chargers to an AFC-best 6–2 record, while the loss dropped the Rams to 4–4 in the NFC West, easily the worst division in the NFL, at least as far as team records were concerned.

The Pittsburgh Steelers remained on top of the AFC Central Division, regarded by most experts as the best division in the NFL. The Steelers crushed Denver's Orange Crush, 42–7, at Three Rivers Stadium in Week 8. The Steel Curtain defense gave up a 64-yard touchdown pass in the first quarter from veteran Denver quarterback Craig Morton to wide receiver Haven Moses, then held the Broncos scoreless for the remainder of the game. Pittsburgh running backs Franco Harris and Sidney Thornton each scored two touchdowns in the romp. The Steelers now owned a division-leading 6–2 record, and seemed to have gotten most of their starting lineup back from the injuries that they sustained earlier in the year.

One of Pittsburgh's chief rivals took quite a beating in their eighth game of the season. The Houston Oilers ventured into Seattle's Kingdome and were humiliated by the Seahawks, 34–14. Seattle quarterback Jim Zorn threw for 252 yards and three touchdowns against the Oilers, two of which went to wide receiver Steve Largent from distances of 45 and 55 yards. Houston's loss dropped them to second place in the AFC Central with a 5–3 record. A couple of other AFC divisional battles also altered the standings. The Battle of Ohio was held in Cleveland, where the Browns took a physical beating from the Bengals, but still held on to defeat their cross-state rivals, 28–27. The Bengals were in the midst of a woeful season in which they only had one win to their credit by mid-season. But they played the Browns tough, and even owned a 20–14 lead going into the fourth quarter. Cleveland had lost its previous three straight games, but they managed to end that streak with four touchdown passes from quarterback Brian Sipe, two of which came in the final quarter to give the Browns their fifth victory of the season. Sipe spread his throws out to seven different teammates, with four different Cleveland players making touchdown receptions against the Bengals. Aiding the Browns' passing attack was a ground game which featured Mike Pruitt, who ran for 135 yards and kept several key Cleveland drives alive with clutch first down runs. "Mike Pruitt is becoming more and more of an instinctive football player," said Cleveland head coach Sam Rutigliano after the game.

The AFC East saw a battle for first place when the New England Patriots played host to the Miami Dolphins on October 21. Each team owned identical 5–2 records going into this contest, but the Patriot offense had scored almost 50 more points than Miami through the first seven games. It would once again be the Patriot offense which would decide this game. New England spotted Miami a 13–0 lead in the first half, then went on to score four unanswered touchdowns the rest of the way. Leading the Patriots' scoring barrage was quarterback Steve Grogan, who directed drives of 69 and 59 yards through the No-Name Defense. Grogan also threw a 15-yard touchdown pass to substitute wide receiver Ray Jarvis, and New England running backs Horace Ivory and Sam "Bam" Cunningham each scored on 1-yard dives. The Patriots' 28–13 win gave them sole possession of first place in their division.

Another tight struggle was occurring in the NFC East, where the Dallas Cowboys managed to move ahead of both the Philadelphia Eagles and the Washington Redskins in the standings. The Cowboys eked out a tight win against the St. Louis Cardinals in Texas Stadium, 22–13. The Doomsday defense recorded seven quarterback sacks, but it was a rookie Cardinals defensive back who made the play of the day, albeit in a losing effort. Roy Green returned a Dallas kickoff 106 yards for a touchdown, tying a league record for the longest kickoff return in history. That record has since been broken several times. Dallas quarterback Roger Staubach offset Green's effort by throwing touchdowns passes to tight end Billy Joe DuPree and wide receiver Tony Hill. Dallas now owned a league-best 7–1 record. "We've got a much better record than I thought we would in the first half of the season," said Dallas head coach Tom Landry. "We usually start slowly. We're seldom 7–1 at the halfway mark."

Neither were the Eagles and the Redskins, but both were having excellent years themselves. The Eagles visited RFK Stadium to see which of these two rivals would get a key divisional win. The game was surprisingly not close, despite the final score. Washington's defense limited the Eagles to one lone touchdown in the fourth quarter on a 40-yard Ron Jaworski pass over the middle to tight end Keith Krepfle. The Redskins permitted star Eagles tailback Wilbert Montgomery only 33 yards rushing, and they sacked Jaworski seven times. "You stop number thirty-one, and you stop the Eagles," confirmed veteran Redskins defensive tackle Diron Talbert, in referring to his team's success in halting Montgomery's progress. Leading the Redskin offensive attack was running back John Riggins, who rushed for 120 yards. Washington's 17–7 triumph over Philadelphia gave them a 6–2 record, while the Eagles fell to 6–2 with the loss.

Two rivals in the NFC Central were in a similar situation as the Redskins and the Eagles. Both the Minnesota Vikings and the Chicago Bears were trying to stay close to the division-leading Tampa Bay Buccaneers. The Vikings managed to avenge their Week 2 loss to the Bears by defeating them at Metropolitan Stadium in Week 8, 30–27. Minnesota required virtually every player in their roster to win this game, and their big plays came just in the nick of time. The Vikings scored the winning touchdown on a 5-yard pass from quarterback Tommy Kramer to set-back Rickey Young with but 13 seconds left on the game clock. It marked the fourth scoring pass of the game for Kramer. One of Minnesota's biggest stars of the game did not score any touchdowns, but return specialist Jimmy Edwards returned 10 kickoffs and punts for a total of 217 yards, including a 56-yard kickoff return in the fourth quarter to set up one of Minnesota's touchdowns. The win evened the Vikings' record to 4–4, while the Bears fell to a lackluster 3–5.

The San Francisco 49ers owned an abysmal record during the first half of the season, as they went without a win until Week 8. New head coach Bill Walsh finally won his first pro game when the 49ers upended the visiting Atlanta Falcons, 20–15, on October 21. Standing out for the 49ers was wide receiver Freddie Solomon, who took a reverse 56 yards for a touchdown in the first quarter. San Francisco running back Paul Hofer added two short scoring runs in the second half.

Despite the fact that this was only the third win for the 49ers in the past two years, Coach Walsh was certainly not overenthusiastic after the game. "I'm trying to be casual about this [win]," said Walsh. "[It's] just your typical Sunday."

Your typical Sunday in Week 9 of the 1979 NFL season involved a smattering of high scoring games, low scoring defensive struggles, and a few blowouts. Perhaps the most anticipated contest of the week was a rematch of Super Bowl XIII in Three Rivers Stadium. The result would be the same this time around, but the excitement from the previous meeting between the Steelers and the Cowboys was missing in this 1979 battle. Pittsburgh's defense was playing at a very high level, as they limited the Dallas offense to a mere three points. Pittsburgh defensive end L.C. Greenwood knocked Cowboys quarterback Roger Staubach out of the game early in the fourth quarter. Staubach was running out of the pocket for yardage and was tripped up just a fraction of a moment before the 6'6", 250-pound Greenwood dove head-first for the quarterback's knees. As it turned out, Greenwood's helmet met Staubach's helmet, and Greenwood's helmet won. He hit Staubach so hard that Staubach's left shoe popped off and the football popped out of Staubach's grasp. Several minutes passed before the groggy Staubach was able to walk to the bench with help from the Dallas trainers. Any hope for a Cowboys comeback left as Staubach took a seat on the bench. "We expected Roger to be running," said Greenwood after the game. "He's been running this year when he had to, but I don't think he saw me coming. It was helmet against helmet."

Pittsburgh's offense was much more basic than what they showed in the previous year's Super Bowl. In this game against Dallas, Pittsburgh running back Franco Harris *was* the Steeler offense, rushing for 102 yards and both of his team's touchdowns on runs of 1 and 48 yards. The Steelers won, 14–3, and thus improved their record to 7–2. Dallas' loss would be the beginning of what head coach Tom Landry referred to as "going down in the valleys." The Cowboys would lose three of their next four games.

The were two other teams in the NFC East who had a great chance to tie Dallas for the division lead. Unfortunately for the Washington Redskins and the Philadelphia Eagles, neither of them were able to beat lesser teams in their Week 9 games. The Redskins fell at home to the New Orleans Saints, 14–10, and the Eagles traveled to Cincinnati, where they were ambushed by the Bengals, 37–13. Washington had only themselves to blame for being unable to tie Dallas in the standings. The Redskins failed to cross the Saints goal line an incredible 18 different times in goal line situations, and their offensive line permitted quarterback Joe Theismann to be sacked seven times in the game. Philadelphia's failures against Cincinnati were numerous and all-consuming. The Eagles defense allowed more points in this game than in any game up to this point in Dick Vermeil's tenure as Philadelphia head coach. The Eagles offense turned the ball over four times and scored their first and only touchdown in the fourth quarter after the Bengals had built an insurmountable 31-point lead. It would be Cincinnati's second win in a season where they would post only four victories overall.

The Miami Dolphins posted a key victory earlier the same day as they downed the visiting Green Bay Packers, 27–7. Miami's win brought them right back into a first place tie with the New England Patriots in the AFC East. The Pats lost their edge in the division by losing a tight game in Baltimore, 31–26. Baltimore tailback Joe Washington scored three touchdowns, and quarterback Bert Jones made several key plays by throwing and running out of the pocket to keep Baltimore scoring drives alive. "He's their key," admitted New England head coach Ron Erhardt when discussing Jones after the game. "We know that, everybody knows that, but that doesn't make it any easier to stop him."

Both Cleveland and Houston also remained close to the AFC Central-leading Steelers. Cleveland defeated the St. Louis Cardinals at Busch Memorial Stadium, 38–20, and Houston outlasted the visiting New York Jets in overtime, 27–24. Houston placekicker Toni Fritsch kicked the game-winning field goal from 35 yards out with 5:10 elapsed in the overtime period. Denver pulled even in the AFC West standings with the San Diego Chargers later in Week 9. The Broncos beat the Kansas City Chiefs at Mile High Stadium, 20–3, while the Chargers lost to Oakland in a special Thursday night game at Oakland, 45–22. Raiders kick returner Ira Matthews returned a kickoff 104 yards for a touchdown in the third quarter to spark the Oakland attack. "They [the Raiders] were fired up," said an understated San Diego linebacker Woodrow Lowe after the game, "and they just beat us." Despite their efforts, the San Diego defense was unable to keep pace with the San Diego offense, a fact which would remain emblematic of the Chargers in the coming decade. On a good note for the Chargers, their quarterback Dan Fouts became the first quarterback in NFL history to throw for at least 300 yards in four straight games.

In the NFC, the Los Angeles Rams appeared to cash in their chips in what looked like a failed season. The Rams played poorly in a 20–14 loss to the visiting New York Giants. The loss dropped the Rams to a dismal 4–5 record. To be fair to the Rams, they had more than their usual share of injuries to key personnel. Several important players would return, however, to their starting lineup a little bit at a time during the second half of the regular season. Aiding the Rams' fortunes was the fact that they were a member of what was currently the worst division in the league, where most of the teams hovered at or below the .500 mark. Only time would tell if the Rams could respond with more wins in the last half of the year.

One team that seemed to take a couple of losses and respond with a victory surge was the Tampa Bay Buccaneers, a team that no one expected to see at the top of the NFC Central standings. Tampa Bay's strength was its defense, a unit which ranked as the best in the NFC after Week 9. The Buccaneers went into Metropolitan Stadium and scored a come-from-behind 12–10 win over the rival Vikings, and as a result, improved their record to 7–2. Tampa halfback Ricky Bell's 2-yard run in the fourth quarter provided the margin of victory. After the win, Tampa Bay head coach described his team's chances on making the playoffs. "Well, I'm not going to talk too much about the division race anymore," said McKay, hoping to avoid any jinx. "But this [win] puts us in a position to do some bad things now and still be in first place. I don't think we'll panic now. We have a little more confidence and a little more experience [than last year's team]."

Rounding out the ninth week was an exciting game between two teams which would not factor into the chase for a championship. The Seattle Seahawks defeated the Atlanta Falcons on *Monday Night Football* at Atlanta Fulton County Stadium, 31–27. Seattle's trademark in 1979 was their penchant for using trick plays, and they left no stone unturned in doing so in this contest. A vivid example of this came when Seattle placekicker Efren Herrera lined up to kick a field goal in the second quarter. Atlanta was alert for a gadget play, but they still could not stop it. Herrera went through the motions of kicking the ball, but his holder, quarterback Jim Zorn, picked the ball up much like the Lucy and Charlie Brown comic strip. He immediately started running around in the backfield. The Atlanta defenders began to chase Zorn, but while they did, Herrera slipped through the middle of the line of scrimmage and ran down the field. Zorn lofted the ball over the rushing Falcons and into Herrera's stomach. The kicker caught it and ran with it downfield. He gained a first down before he was tackled, and thereby kept a Seahawks scoring drive alive. A critical end zone interception of a Steve Bartkowski pass by Seattle defensive back Dave Brown with 35 seconds left in the game preserved the Seahawks' victory. It marked an exciting conclusion to Seattle's first game ever on *Monday Night Football*. "The turning point wasn't the gambles though," explained Seattle head coach Jack Patera. "The turning point was Dave Brown's interception." To Bartkowski's credit, he brought the Falcons back from a 24–14 fourth quarter deficit, but his effort fell just short. "I can't remember a pass [the Dave Brown interception] that was any more disappointing than that one," lamented Bartkowski.

More disappointments were in store for several teams in Week 10 of the 1979 season, as a separation of sorts between the pretenders and the contenders began to take place. Two inter-conference games were detrimental to both the Philadelphia Eagles and the Washington Redskins. The Cleveland Browns strolled into Veterans Stadium, fell behind the Eagles, then came back in the fourth quarter as was their custom. Cleveland was trailing 19–10 with but 3:21 remaining in the game when they finally started to get their offense in gear. Cleveland quarterback Brian Sipe threw a 5-yard touchdown pass to tight end Ozzie Newsome. The Browns defense then quickly forced a Philadelphia punt. Sipe took over at his own 29-yard line with less than two minutes on the clock. He mixed in several runs with short passes along the sidelines. Cleveland running back Mike Pruitt then climaxed this comeback with a 24-yard touchdown run on a sweep to his left, giving the Browns an important 24–19 win. Cleveland's third straight triumph now gave them a 7–3 record in the AFC Central Division, one game behind the 8–2 Pittsburgh Steelers.

Philadelphia's loss to Cleveland dropped them to 6–4 on the year, but a couple of side notes are important to mention. The 6'8" veteran Eagles wide receiver Harold Carmichael set a new league record against the Browns when he became the first player in NFL history to catch at least one pass in 106 consecutive games, breaking the old mark of 105 consecutive games set by former New Orleans Saints and San Francisco 49ers wide receiver Danny Abramowicz. "I'm very happy about getting the record," Carmichael said, "[but] it's like empty without the win." The lanky pass catcher was awarded with a giant trophy at halftime to honor his achievement. The trophy measured over 22 feet in height and weighed an incredible 800 pounds, and it eventually found a home at the Pro Football Hall of Fame in Canton, Ohio. Philadelphia halfback Wilbert Montgomery also found a home across the Cleveland line of scrimmage, as he rushed for a robust 197 yards on 30 carries in the game, one of which went for a 52-yard touchdown run.

The Washington Redskins once again duplicated the Eagles' result, as they also failed to pull out a victory. The Redskins lost in a big way to the Pittsburgh Steelers at Three Rivers Stadium, 38–7. It was a total team victory for the Black and Gold with plenty of highlight reel material. Pittsburgh quarterback Terry Bradshaw threw four scoring passes; Steelers halfback Franco Harris became the fifth player in NFL history to gain over 8,000 career rushing yards; and the Steelers won their 11th straight home game. The contest was not as close as the final score indicated, as the Redskins could never get on track against the Steel Curtain defense. But it was the Pittsburgh offense which really kept the loyal Steeler fans waving their Terrible Towels in standing ovation mode. Pittsburgh wide receiver John Stallworth added six pass receptions for 126 yards and two touchdowns, as the Steelers improved their record to an NFL-best 8–2.

Sharing that won-loss mark with the Steelers was the Dallas Cowboys, who somehow managed to combat 57 minutes of lethargy and mistakes against the host New York Giants with a few of minutes of never-say-die football. Dallas trailed 14–6 when quarterback Roger Staubach threw a deep post pattern pass to wide receiver Drew Pearson, who caught the ball at the Giants 2-yard line and then carried both his tackler (Giants cornerback Terry Jackson) and the ball into the end zone. Pearson's 32-yard scoring reception and a suddenly stalwart Cowboys defense forced a quick New York punt. Dallas now had the ball at their own 9-yard line with 1:21 remaining in the game. Staubach knew that he had no time to waste, so in a few plays and a very short amount of time he connected once again with Pearson on a 27-yard pass, which placed the ball at the New York 44-yard line. Staubach then threw a 32-yard screen pass to setback Tony Dorsett, who broke several tackles before being pulled out of bounds inside of the Giants' 10-yard line. Placekicker

Rafael Septien ended the drama with a 22-yard field goal with three seconds left which won the game for Dallas, 16–14. "They [the Dallas offense] gave me a chip shot to work with," explained Septien. "I just did my job." Dallas head coach Tom Landry commented that this type of comeback situation was not new for his team. "We only played the final few minutes," said a relieved Landry after the game.

Another Texas team also needed a field goal to defeat their opponent in Week 10. The Houston Oilers met the Miami Dolphins in the Orange Bowl, and required three field goals from placekicker Toni Fritsch to win the game, 9–6. Miami's loss dropped them to 6–4 in the AFC East, a game behind the 7–3 New England Patriots, who easily defeated the Buffalo Bills, 26–6. Unfortunately for the Oilers, they would not leave Miami unscathed. As the Oilers were playing the Dolphins, someone managed to break into the visiting locker room at the Orange Bowl and steal a bunch of valuable personal items from the Oilers players, such as their wallets and keys. Houston head coach Bum Phillips sardonically quipped afterwards "I've heard of poor losers, but this is something else."

Three contending teams in the AFC West also avoided losing in their Week 10 games, but a couple of them barely escaped defeat. Denver, San Diego, and Oakland each won their contests, with both the Broncos and the Chargers requiring extra efforts to pull out a win. Denver survived against a vastly improved New Orleans Saints club at Mile High Stadium, 10–3. The game's lone touchdown came in the fourth quarter on a 12-yard scoring pass from Denver quarterback Craig Morton to wide receiver Rick Upchurch. At the same time, the Chargers held on for dear life against the Chiefs at Arrowhead Stadium. San Diego built a 13–0 lead going into the fourth quarter, then watched the Chiefs score twice to make it close. San Diego defensive back Glen Edwards intercepted a last gasp Kansas City pass, however, thereby preserving a 20–14 Chargers win. "You have to have a strong heart, or you die," exclaimed San Diego head coach Don Coryell. "Kansas City's people just wouldn't give up."

The Oakland Raiders did not have to deal with the drama that Denver and San Diego experienced, as they easily defeated the visiting San Francisco 49ers, 23–10. One other AFC West team suffered the worst tenth game of the season, however. The Seattle Seahawks played host to the struggling and injury-riddled Los Angeles Rams in the Kingdome in what many folks believed would be a fairly competitive contest. What occurred was either the NFL's greatest example of defensive team play, or the worst example of offensive team play, depending upon how you looked at it. The Rams shut out the Seahawks, 24–0, but the real story was that the Rams defense held the Seattle offense to an incredible total of minus seven yards for the game. It was a league record which still stands today. Seattle's futility was also evidenced by the number of first downs that they were able to get by game's end: one. The Seahawks had been averaging 350 yards a week, so this shocking result was difficult for many statisticians to believe. Leave it to Los Angeles defensive end (and future television actor) Fred Dryer, who was seldom at a loss for words, to sum it up best using his own inimitable verbiage: "Know what this win feels like?" Dryer asked a group of postgame reporters. "Like when the perfect woman walks into the bar at 1:55 a.m. and smiles at you."

Fate was definitely not smiling at the Tampa Bay Buccaneers, as they lost their third game of the year at Atlanta. The Falcons started to play like the playoff team that they were the previous season, as they registered a 17–14 win over the Buccaneers. Two fourth quarter Atlanta touchdowns provided the margin of victory for the 4–6 Falcons. Atlanta quarterback Steve Bartkowski threw a 4-yard scoring pass to tight end Jim Mitchell, which was followed by a 60-yard touchdown run from Falcon tailback Bubba Bean with 1:22 left in the game. Tampa Bay now owned a 7–3 record, which was still two games better in the NFC Central standings than their next closest competitor, the 5–5 Chicago Bears.

A group of competitors in Week 11 of the 1979 season rose up and sprung some upsets on their unsuspecting opponents, while a few other underdogs came extremely close to pulling out narrow victories, but fell just a play or two short. The St. Louis Cardinals took their 3–7 record into wet and muddy RFK Stadium and gave the 6–4 Redskins all that they wanted to deal with. But the Redskins came back strong in the second half and won the game by a score of 30–28 on a 39-yard field goal off the foot of placekicker Mark Moseley with just 36 seconds left to play. Moseley's kick successfully answered three St. Louis touchdowns in the fourth quarter which gave them (the Cardinals) a 1-point lead before Washington's final offensive possession proved fruitful. The winning kick almost did not happen, however, as Redskins center Ted Fritsch bounced his snap of the ball on the mushy field to holder Joe Theismann, who was able to make a somewhat miraculous recovery of the slippery pigskin. "Joe has great hands," confirmed Moseley. "My leg was in motion by the time he got the ball down."

Another near upset took place in the Pontiac Silverdome, where the Detroit Lions came within a hair of beating the new beast of the NFC Central Division, the Tampa Bay Buccaneers. Detroit held a 14–6 fourth quarter lead until Tampa Bay came back with a 28-yard field goal by placekicker Neil O'Donoghue and a 23-yard touchdown pass from Buccaneers quarterback Doug Williams to wide receiver Larry Mucker. Indeed, coming from behind to win games was a treasured trademark of contending teams, and failing to hold a lead late in a game was a sobering example of a struggling or a losing team. The Cincinnati Bengals were in the midst of a two-win season, when they lost another lead in the fourth quarter, this time to the visiting San Diego Chargers. Contending teams like the Chargers would often rely on a different player each week to play a key role in a victory. One such player for San Diego was their placekicker Mike Wood, who kicked four field goals against the Bengals, including one from 32 yards out with 19 seconds left to give the Chargers a 26–24 triumph. It gave San Diego an 8–3 record, good enough for a first place tie in the AFC West with the Denver Broncos. Despite his late-game heroics, Wood was more relieved than anything else. "I hate games like this," he admitted, "because they make me older than twenty-five. I would just as soon blow them [the Chargers' opponents] out by twenty or thirty."

Speaking of blowouts, an unexpected one happened in Mile High Stadium. The Denver Broncos crushed the New England Patriots in a driving Rocky Mountain snowstorm, 45–10. Both teams had identical 7–3 records going into this game, but the Broncos proved that they were certainly more ready to play in the elements than the Patriots. Denver bolted to a 24–0 lead in the first quarter, and by halftime, that lead grew to 38–7. It was a mercy killing in the second half, as Denver substituted a bevy of players, yet still only permitted a mere field goal in the final two quarters. "It was just one of those games," said Denver quarterback Craig Morton. "Maybe everything was just going right for us and nothing went right for them. Again, I had great pass protection and when that happens, I can do anything I want." Denver punt returner Rick Upchurch seemingly did anything he wanted, as he set a new punt return yardage record in the game, breaking the previous record of former New York Giants and Green Bay Packers great Emlen Tunnell. New England's loss forced them back into a tie with the Miami Dolphins (7–4), who easily defeated the upset-minded Baltimore Colts, 19–0.

Several teams did manage to pull stunning upsets in Week 11. One such team was the Chicago Bears, who defeated the visiting Los Angeles Rams, 27–23. The Rams were hindered by injuries, especially at the quarterback position, where rookie third-stringer Jeff Rutledge stood behind center for the first start of his career. His untimely interception in the fourth quarter set up the Bears for the winning touchdown on a 2-yard run by halfback Walter Payton with 1:12 left in the game. The loss dropped Los Angeles to a woeful 5–6 mark, a game behind the NFC West leading New Orleans Saints, who upended the San Francisco 49ers in the Superdome, 31–20.

The race in the NFC East drew closer too, thanks in large part to the Philadelphia Eagles' 31–21 upset win over the Dallas Cowboys on *Monday Night Football* at Texas Stadium. The Cowboys took a quick lead on their first possession with a 48-yard bomb from quarterback Roger Staubach to wide receiver Tony Hill. The Doomsday Defense then injured Philadelphia quarterback Ron Jaworski. Reserve Eagles quarterback John Walton replaced Jaworski and played like an All-Pro, as he led his team to a 17–7 halftime lead. Undoubtedly the biggest play of the first half came with no time left on the clock, as rookie Eagles placekicker Tony Franklin booted a 59-yard field goal, which at that time stood as the second-longest in NFL history behind Tom Dempsey's 63-yard field goal for New Orleans against Detroit in 1970. Franklin was unique in that he was the first of several kickers in league history who preferred to kick the ball barefoot. "When he kicked that field goal right before the half, it just took something out of us," said Dallas head coach Tom Landry. "It was just a spectacular kick. We couldn't believe it."

The Cowboys also could not believe Philadelphia's determination in the second half. Jaworski returned to action and threw his second touchdown pass to wide receiver Harold Carmichael, and tailback Wilbert Montgomery added a 37-yard sprint for a score in the fourth quarter. Even though the Cowboys came back with two more touchdown passes from Staubach (who threw for 308 yards in the game), the Eagles survived to improve their record to 7–4, which tied them for second place in the NFC East with the Redskins, while the Cowboys fell to 8–3, which was still good enough for first place in the division.

In the AFC Central Division, Pittsburgh and Houston each won, but Cleveland dropped a tough game at home to Seattle, 29–24. The Steelers romped over the host Kansas City Chiefs, 30–3, while the Oilers proved themselves to be stronger than the Oakland Raiders inside the Astrodome, 31–17. Pittsburgh now stood alone with the best record in the league at 9–2, while Houston owned an 8–3 mark, and Cleveland still had hopes for the playoffs with a 7–4 record.

Pittsburgh's momentum was unexpectedly interrupted in their 12th game at San Diego, however, where the Chargers played perhaps their best game of the year against the defending Super Bowl champions. The Chargers owned a 21–0 first half lead against the Steelers, as quarterback Dan Fouts threw touchdown passes to wide receiver John Jefferson and veteran tight end Bob Klein. The San Diego defense chipped in mightily with five interceptions off of Steelers quarterback Terry Bradshaw, two each coming from linebackers Woodrow Lowe and Ray Preston. One of Lowe's interceptions ended 77 yards later in the Pittsburgh end zone. "The only people open were *their* linebackers," said disgruntled Pittsburgh head coach Chuck Noll after the game. There was a basic and sound strategy behind the Chargers' interceptions, but it required a premium effort from their defensive line. "We don't blitz," admitted San Diego defensive tackle Wilbur Young. "We go with four of us [his fellow defensive linemen]. We just rush and let the linebackers drop back." San Diego's 35–7 romp over Pittsburgh kept the Chargers in first place in the AFC West with a 9–3 record, while the Steelers fell to 9–3 and a first place tie in the AFC Central with the Houston Oilers.

The Oilers took advantage of the Pittsburgh loss as they drilled the Cincinnati Bengals at the Astrodome, 42–21. Houston benefitted from the play of their All-Pro running back Earl Campbell, who recorded his seventh 100-yard rushing game of the season, and who scored the first two Oiler touchdowns in the rout of Cincinnati. Houston was not the only team in the AFC Central who were glad to see the Steelers lose, however. The Cleveland Browns (a.k.a. the Cardiac Kids) won a drama-filled contest at home against the Miami Dolphins, 30–24. Cleveland quarterback Brian Sipe tossed a 39-yard touchdown pass deep down the middle of the field to wide receiver Reggie Rucker early in the overtime period to obtain the win. The decision on the winning score came from Rucker himself, who noticed what would work best against Miami's rotating zone coverages. "I brought the play to [assistant coach] Jim Shofner at halftime," said Rucker. "He had the same play on his mind." Sipe ended up throwing for 358 yards and three touchdowns against one of the best defenses in the league. Prior to facing the Browns, the Miami defense had given up only 142 points in 11 games (an average of only 13 points per game). The Browns were now 8–4, and were still very much in the hunt for a postseason berth. "I don't know of anything that would give our team more impetus for the Pittsburgh game next week," said Cleveland head coach Sam Rutigliano of the way his team defeated Miami. The Dolphins dropped to 7–5, and if they were to make the playoffs, they would have to treat the rest of their remaining contests as must-win games.

Another reason why the loss to Cleveland was so detrimental to Miami was because the New England Patriots recovered quickly from the sound beating that they took the previous week at Denver to post a 50–21 win against the visiting Baltimore Colts in Week 12. The victory gave the Patriots an 8–4 record and a slight edge in obtaining at least a wild card berth. They would need that edge, as the remaining four teams on their schedule had a 23–25 combined won-loss record, while Miami's next four foes had a combined 18–30 won-loss mark.

The tightness in the AFC East race, however, could not measure up to the taut drama that was being played out in the NFC East. After Week 12, Dallas, Washington and Philadelphia each owned identical 8–4 records. The Cowboys had a strong lead at the beginning of November. Now past the midway point of the month, that lead was gone and Dallas was becoming unhinged. The Cowboys fell to the Redskins at RFK Stadium, 34–20. Washington played its best game of the year against their traditional rivals. Their defense forced five Dallas turnovers and recorded six quarterback sacks. Redskins quarterback Joe Theismann threw for 210 yards and three touchdown passes. The bitterness of this rivalry suddenly went dormant for the past couple of years, but the brutal contention between these two enemies finally returned to the surface in this game. With the Redskins up by 14 points with just a couple of seconds to play, Washington head coach Jack Pardee had his placekicker Mark Moseley attempt a short field goal instead of having Theismann take a knee and running out the clock. Moseley missed the attempt, but several of the Cowboys were angered by the gesture. "When they get us down, they want to rub it in our face," exclaimed Dallas defensive end Harvey Martin. "The Redskins have no class. It was totally an insult. It just got me in a frame of mind to hate the Redskins."

Pardee defended his decision by stating that point differential is one of the tie-breaking procedures in determining a playoff team, and thus he wanted his team to score as much as possible should the Redskins need to rely on point differential at the end of the season. As fate would have it, Pardee would be prophetic in his beliefs at the end of the regular season, albeit not in the way that he would have wanted.

Dallas head coach Tom Landry wanted his team to recover quickly from their loss, and in order to aid that recovery, Landry cut a suspected cancer from his team. Linebacker Thomas "Hollywood" Henderson was making more plays recently off the field than on it, as he made it a point to ham it up on the sidelines in front of any television camera that he could find. Landry accepted Henderson's behavior since his rookie year in 1975, but he (Landry) finally decided to place Henderson on waivers in 1979 after his lackluster performance against Washington. Henderson immediately announced his involuntary retirement. "I'm still the greatest linebacker, bar none," said the not-so-modest former pro football player. "I love the Dallas fans and I love the Cowboys. I don't want to play for a lower-echelon team. I don't want to be passed around the league. I've decided [to] make beer commercials." Henderson would play again in 1980 for a total of eight games in both San Francisco and Houston, but for all intents and purposes, his NFL career was all but over the day he was cut by the Cowboys.

The Philadelphia Eagles were delighted by Henderson's departure (Henderson had given them headaches on the field since 1975) as well as by Dallas' loss in Washington. The Eagles were a contender for the NFC East title, but they were not yet a superior team. They were challenged at home by the lowly St. Louis Cardinals, who currently had only three wins to their name. Yet the Cards played strong on defense, and it took a 40-yard fourth quarter touchdown pass from Eagles quarterback Ron Jaworski to tight end Keith Krepfle to secure Philadelphia's eighth win.

The top two teams in the NFC West were tied with each other in the standings once again following their Week 12 games. The New Orleans Saints lost to the Seattle Seahawks in the Kingdome, 38–24. Seattle quarterback Jim Zorn was the difference, as he threw for 284 yards and four touchdowns, two of which went to wide receiver Steve Largent, who caught nine passes for 146 yards against the solvent New Orleans defense. The Los Angeles Rams tied the Saints in the division by defeating the Atlanta Falcons at the Los Angeles Memorial Coliseum on *Monday Night Football*, 20–14. The Rams handed the controls of the starting quarterback position to youngster Vince Ferragamo, who had only three years of pro experience as a substitute. Ferragamo threw for two scores in the Rams' victory over the Falcons. He would gain more vital experience as the regular season winded down.

The Thanksgiving Day games once again signaled that the regular season was nearing the home stretch. It seemed that regardless of their record, the Detroit Lions always played well on Turkey Day, and they did so again in 1979. Detroit recorded their first shutout in over two years as they downed the division rival Chicago Bears, 20–0. The win was only the second all year for the Lions, who were led by a stalwart defensive effort. Defensive end Al "Bubba" Baker accounted for four sacks in the game. "You know, anytime you play shutout football you've done a job in this league," said a gleeful Baker after the win. Down in Texas Stadium, the Dallas Cowboys were desperate to change their current course and win again on Thanksgiving. The Cowboys had not lost on this holiday since 1973, but the Cowboys were playing their in-state rivals, the Houston Oilers, who were right in the hunt for a playoff spot themselves in the AFC. The Oilers were playing a better brand of football than the Cowboys throughout November, and their current overall balance on offense proved to be too much for the Cowboys by game's end. Houston's Earl Campbell rushed for 195 yards, and scored touchdowns on runs of 61 and 27 yards. With apologies to Chicago's Walter Payton, Campbell was quickly becoming the toughest running back in the league to tackle. "When Earl runs the ball now, the bruises belong to the other people," said Houston head coach Bum Phillips. Oilers quarterback Dan Pastorini also contributed a 47-yard touchdown pass to wide receiver Mike Renfro, and a 32-yard touchdown pass to wide receiver Ken Burrough. Houston won this battle of Texas, 30–24, and took the sole lead in the AFC Central Division.

That lead would only last for a few days, however, as the Pittsburgh Steelers came from behind to defeat the Cleveland Browns in overtime at Three Rivers Stadium on Sunday, November 25. The Browns played hard and smelled a victory throughout the game. They held a 27–13 lead going into the fourth quarter of this, their second meeting of the year with Pittsburgh. Cleveland head coach Sam Rutigliano had impressed upon his players prior to the opening kickoff of the importance of winning against a rival that had dominated the league for so long, and a team which felt that it was superior to all the others in the NFL. "There's nothing greater than to knock a thing down when it's cocked at an arrogant angle," Rutigliano told his team, "and that's Pittsburgh. It's a deep delight to the blood." But the Steelers—whether they were arrogant or not—managed to score 17 points late in the game to send the contest into a sudden death period. Pittsburgh placekicker Matt Bahr's steely-eyed calm in the midst of the clamoring din from the crowd decided the winner. His 37-yard field goal won the game for the Steelers, 33–30. "We tried not to put any pressure on him," said Steelers quarterback Terry Bradshaw after the game. "We just said, 'Miss it and you're cut.'" Bahr's teammates mobbed him on the field after he came through for them. Both Houston and Pittsburgh were now tied atop the division with 10–3 records, while Cleveland dropped to 8–5.

Both the Miami Dolphins and the New England Patriots were once again tied for first place after 13 weeks in the AFC East. Miami edged the stubborn Baltimore Colts at Memorial Stadium, 28–24, while the Patriots suffered a debilitating 16–13 loss to the Buffalo Bills at Foxboro in over-time, 16–13. Like Matt Bahr in Pittsburgh, Buffalo placekicker Nick Mike-Mayer booted a 29-yard field goal with 9:15 gone in overtime for the win. But the Bills offense did not wait to drive the ball closer for their kicker. Instead, the coaching staff decided to try the kick on first down. "We didn't run the ball three times before kicking," said Buffalo head coach Chuck Knox. "We weren't taking any chances. It was a hell of a hard-fought football game. Our players came back. For a team that's learning how to win, it was a great accomplishment." This loss was difficult for New England to stomach, because even though they were still tied for first place with Miami, they would have to play the Dolphins in a few days at the Orange Bowl in a special Thursday night game. "It's a tough loss, one that shouldn't have happened," said Patriots head coach Ron Erhardt. "We've got our backs to the wall now."

The Denver Broncos could sympathize with Erhardt and his Patriots. They also lost a game at home to the Oakland Raiders that they probably should have won, 14–10. Despite showing little if any offensive output during the first three quarters, the Denver offense scored twice in the fourth quarter on a 30-yard Jim Turner field goal and a 1-yard run by running back Rob Lytle. The Broncos' final efforts were stopped twice by the Oakland defense with less than two minutes to play, however. With the loss, Denver now found themselves in second place in the AFC West at 9–4. The first place team in that division was none other than the surging San Diego Chargers, who had no trouble whatsoever defeating the Kansas City Chiefs, 28–7. San Diego quarterback Dan Fouts threw for 350 yards and three touchdowns in the win. It was the fifth time this season that Fouts had thrown for more than 300 yards in a game. Such high offensive passing yardage totals simply could not have been accomplished by *any* quarterback in the league prior to the epochal 1978 rules changes. San Diego now stood strong with a 10–3 record.

Over in the NFC, no team could lay hold of a 10–3 record. But one team managed to take possession of the NFC East for the first time since the seventh week. The Philadelphia Eagles strode into Lambeau Field and defeated the Green Bay Packers, 21–10. The New York Giants—of all teams—helped the Eagles' cause by beating the visiting Washington Redskins on the same day, 14–6. Philadelphia now had a 9–4 record, while both Dallas and Washington were tied for second place with 8–5 records.

The Tampa Bay Buccaneers were only one victory away from claiming the NFC Central title, but they reverted back to repeat several error-filled scenes from their winless inaugural season (1976) in their second meeting of the 1979 season with the visiting Minnesota Vikings. The Buc-caneers lost the game, 23–22. The Vikings special teams blocked four different kicks in the game, including a field goal, a punt, and two extra points. Tampa Bay scored a touchdown with nine seconds left in the game on an incredible 13-yard touchdown scramble by quarterback Doug Wil-liams. The Bucs were setting up for the tying extra point conversion attempt when a bit of savvy Vikings strategy won the game for the Norsemen. Minnesota had blocked two of Tampa Bay placekicker Neil O'Donohue's earlier attempts with outside rushes. On this attempt, the Bucs decided to keep their focus on the outside flanks, thereby all but ignoring the middle of their line. Vikings linebacker Wally Hilgenberg noticed the change in attention and rushed through the mid-dle to block O'Donohue's attempt. Caustic Tampa Bay head coach John McKay was inconsolable after the loss. "We stunk," exclaimed McKay. "We could not kick a field goal, a punt, an extra point. We couldn't do anything." Tampa Bay's inpatient fans were learning adroitly from McKay how best to insult their team. "Neil O'Donohue tried to commit suicide after the game by putting a gun to his head," said one disgusted Buccaneers fan, "but somebody blocked it." Tampa Bay still had a two-game lead in the NFC Central over Chicago, however, with only three games to play. So there was no real urgent need for alarm … at least not yet.

Unless, that is, you were a fan of either the New Orleans Saints or the Los Angeles Rams. Both of those teams owned 7–6 records after 13 games, but the Rams owned the head-to-head tiebreaker by defeating the Saints in Week 6. Now in the homestretch of the regular season, neither team could afford another loss. The Rams eked out a tough 26–20 win over the San Francisco 49ers at Candlestick Park on November 25. It was a couple of big plays which won the game for the Rams, including a 71-yard touchdown pass from quarterback Vince Ferragamo to setback Wendell Tyler, and an 80-yard return of a blocked 49ers field goal attempt by Los Angeles' Sid Justin. The Saints also produced a win in Week 13, as they defeated an old nemesis of theirs, the Atlanta Falcons at Atlanta-Fulton County Stadium, 37–6. The Saints offense accumulated 415 total yards in the rain-filled contest, and the New Orleans defense forced six Atlanta turnovers. "It's very special to beat the Falcons here [in Atlanta]," said New Orleans quarterback Archie Manning, "because of the rivalry and because Atlanta won the last three [meetings] in the final seconds."

By the 14th week of the 1979 season, no team had clinched a division title yet, and there were no less than 16 teams that were still in the running for a playoff berth. The Miami Dolphins would come the closest to securing a postseason spot when they defeated the visiting New England Patriots, 39–24. Veteran Dolphins running back Larry Csonka continued to add glory to his come-back performance in Miami by scoring three 1-yard touchdown runs against the Patriots. Csonka would end the evening by becoming the sixth rusher in league history to eclipse the 8,000-yard rushing mark. By season's end, Csonka would lead the Dolphins in rushing with 837 yards, and he would score 13 touchdowns (12 rushing, 1 receiving). Miami quarterback Bob Griese did not start the game, but after New England took a 17–13 lead going into the third quarter, Dolphins head coach Don Shula decided to insert his veteran signal caller into the offensive huddle. It was a wise decision. Griese completed 8 of 10 passes for 101 yards, including a 38-yard scoring toss to Miami wide receiver Nat Moore. Like Csonka, Griese also eclipsed a statistical milestone when he cleared the 24,000-yard mark for career passing yardage. The win would give the Dolphins a 9–5 record, and although they did not know it at the time, it would prove to be the key win in earning them a division title. "We don't think we're home free for a playoff berth," said a cautious Miami head coach Don Shula afterward, "but I have a great feeling our team is on the upswing and this is the right time for it." New England, despite the 350-yard passing performance of quarterback Steve Grogan, dropped to 8–6, a game behind the Dolphins in the standings.

A similar result occurred in the AFC Central. The Pittsburgh Steelers took sole control of the division by combining a dominating win against the visiting Cincinnati Bengals, 37–17, with a loss by the Houston Oilers, who fell to the Cleveland Browns at Municipal Stadium, 14–7. Pittsburgh quarterback Terry Bradshaw had his usual solid performance against the Bengals, as he threw for 339 yards and two long touchdowns to wide receiver Lynn Swann. By game's end, Bradshaw's efforts made him the first Steeler quarterback in history to pass for over 3,000 yards in a season. Pittsburgh running back Franco Harris ran for 92 yards against Cincinnati, and thus tied the great Jim Brown's mark of seven seasons with over 1,000 yards rushing. The Cleveland Browns, however, did not concern themselves with records in their meeting with the Houston Oilers at Cleveland Municipal Stadium. Cleveland simply had to win this game to remain in contention for a chance at the playoffs, and they relied on ball control to produce a 14–7 victory. Cleveland running back Mike Pruitt scored both of his team's touchdowns, the second of which capped an 87-yard drive and came on a 1-yard run early in the final quarter to break a 7–7 tie. Cleveland's defense also played strong, as they limited the Oilers offense to a mere four plays in the third quarter. The Browns' win improved their record to 9–5, while Houston fell to 10–4.

Over in the AFC West, the Denver Broncos rebounded from their loss against Oakland the previous week to upend the Buffalo Bills at frozen Rich Stadium, 19–16. It was a game of turnovers, as both teams accounted for 11 fumbles. There were four fumbles in the first quarter alone, and by game's end, the Bills would lose six of their fumbles. Several of them set up the Broncos for pivotal points. Denver placekicker Jim Turner finally settled the affair on a 32-yard field goal with three seconds left in the game. Buffalo's loss dropped them from playoff contention with a 7–7 record. In contrast, the win lifted Denver (10–4) into a first place tie with the San Diego Chargers, who were taking on the Atlanta Falcons at home. A win would have given San Diego their first playoff berth since 1965. The Chargers had the most prolific passing offense in the league at this stage of the season, while the Falcons were woefully poor in pass defense. But on this day, the Falcons were good enough. Atlanta gave up big plays, but they made their share of them too, the biggest of which was a 6-yard touchdown pass from Falcons quarterback Steve Bartkowski to wide receiver Wallace Francis in the back of the end zone with 21 seconds remaining to win the game, 28–26. "We could have come down here and just laid down," said Francis. "We knew we had to be tough and we didn't hang our heads." San Diego's hopes for a playoff berth would have to wait at least one more week.

The playoff hopes of the youthful Philadelphia Eagles received a jolt of energy after they completely demolished the visiting Detroit Lions, 44–7. It was a most welcome rout for the Eagles. The tough Philly defense limited Detroit to a mere five first downs and only 180 total yards. The Eagles now owned an impressive 10–4 record, which was good enough for first place in the NFC East with just two more games left to play. The win also clinched at least a wild card berth for Philadelphia for the second straight year. "We really can't let up," cautioned veteran Philadelphia defensive end Claude Humphrey. "I think we now have more pressure on us. Our goal is to win the division. If we can do that, we can lay off for a week and get all of our guys rested and healthy."

Both of Philadelphia's prime challengers for division superiority also won on this day. The Washington Redskins came from behind in the fourth quarter at RFK Stadium to defeat the Green Bay Packers, 38–21, while the Dallas Cowboys vanquished the visiting New York Giants, 28–7. Green Bay's 21–7 halftime lead over Washington was blunted in the second half, as the Redskins defense limited the Packers offense to an incredibly low 23 total combined yards in the third and fourth quarters. The Redskins, on the other hand, accumulated 305 of their 437 total yards in the second half. Washington quarterback Joe Theismann threw a career-high four touchdown passes in the victory. The Redskins now owned a 9–5 record.

The Dallas Cowboys owned a similar record, thanks to their big win against the Giants. Some degree of action took place even before the opening kickoff of this game, however. The Giants decided to name all of their players as team captains, and as a result, all of the Giants players met the three Cowboys captains at midfield for the opening coin toss. This attempt at building team momentum and togetherness did not sit well with Dallas defensive end Harvey Martin, who as a Dallas captain spent his time at the coin toss yelling and gesturing at any New York player who would listen. "They were trying to intimidate us here in Dallas, man," explained Martin. "You can't do that. The whole team was out there for the coin flip. What is that?" New York's ploy failed to work, as the Cowboys delivered a workmanlike performance in their win. Dallas quarterback Roger Staubach connected with wide receiver Drew Pearson for three touchdown passes. One of those receptions had an unfortunate ending, however. Pearson leaped high after scoring and tossed the ball into the stands. When he landed, however, his left knee buckled. Pearson managed to continue playing (in pain) in the game, but his overzealous expression of glee had unfortunate ramifications, as it kept him out of the Dallas lineup for their pivotal meeting the following week at Philadelphia.

The lineup for the Chicago Bears proved to be too much for the Tampa Bay Buccaneers to handle on December 2 at Tampa Stadium. Chicago's defense recorded five interceptions, and their special teams blocked a Tampa Bay punt, which led to a 1-yard Walter Payton touchdown. The Bears thus stayed alive in their hopes for a postseason berth with a 14–0 victory. The race in the NFC Central Division was now quite tighter, with the Buccaneers still in first with a 9–5 mark, and the Bears right behind them with an 8–6 record. Neither team could afford to lose again, however, and like most divisional races in December, the playoff pairings would not be completely determined until the end of the regular season. "They're not going to hold the season up for us," reasoned Tampa Bay quarterback Doug Williams. "Clinching has been on everybody's mind. I think about it, too, but even if we don't win another game we've had a hell of a year."

The Minnesota Vikings were already out of hope for the playoffs by Week 14 with a 6–7 record, and they had nothing to play for except personal pride, to be a spoiler, or to accomplish an individual or a team record. The Vikes lost to the Los Angeles Rams in overtime on December 2 at the Los Angeles Memorial Coliseum by a score of 27–21. But one Vikings veteran set a standard that several decades later has yet to be equaled. Minnesota free safety Paul Krause broke the NFL's career interception record of former Giants and Packers great Emlen Tunnell. Krause had tied Tunnell with 79 interceptions in the fifth week of the season in a win at Detroit. On the last play of the second quarter against the Rams, Krause caught a Vince Ferragamo pass that was tipped by Rams tight end Charle Young, and began his return while holding the ball aloft in triumph. A new interception king had crowned his career with one of the most important defensive records in NFL history. Krause would go on to make his 81st interception later in the fourth quarter. "I never take a chance," admitted the safety-conscious safety. "I go for the interception only when I'm convinced that I can get it."

In the overtime period, everyone in the Coliseum was convinced that the Vikings would try their utmost to block Los Angeles placekicker Frank Corral's short field goal attempt. Minnesota had enjoyed much success during the decade in blocking kicks, and to some degree, almost had the practice down to a science. As the Rams set up to attempt the kick, however, holder Nolan Cromwell pulled the ball off the ground, whirled around to his left, and sprinted into the Minnesota end zone from five yards out for the winning touchdown. Minnesota did indeed send most of their defenders into the Rams' backfield to block the kick, but all they saw was Corral standing alone, as Cromwell ran past the shocked Vikings almost completely unnoticed.

The win over Minnesota proved vital to the Rams. It gave them an 8–6 record, which was good enough for first place in the NFC West with just two weeks left in the regular season. The New Orleans Saints had a tie with the Rams for the top spot within their grasp. They owned a 35–14 lead going into the fourth quarter of their Monday night contest against Oakland at the Superdome. All they had to do was hold on to their swelled lead for 15 more minutes, and a big upset victory would be theirs. They were unable to do so. The Raiders were not regarded as the "Kings of *Monday Night Football*" for nothing, and their comeback magic by this time of the decade was already legendary. Another chapter would be added to that legend on this night. The Raiders scored four touchdowns in the second half, including three in the final quarter, to obtain one of the greatest comebacks in NFL history, and the greatest comeback win in *Monday Night Football* history (until the year 2000). Oakland's 42–35 victory was secured with the passing prowess of quarterback Kenny "The Snake" Stabler, who proved to many doubters that he was not yet over the hill. The Snake hissed two of his scoring tosses to wide receiver Cliff Branch (including the game winner from eight yards out with 1:54 left in the contest), and one each to tight ends Derrick Ramsey and Raymond Chester. The win boosted Oakland's *Monday Night Football* overall record to 13–1–1, easily the best mark in the NFL. It also kept the Raiders faintly alive for a playoff spot with an 8–6 record. The loss decimated the Saints, who were now 7–7, and who could ill-afford any more losses if they were to make the playoffs. "This is one of my most disappointing losses ever," said Saints head coach Dick Nolan. "When you've got a 21-point lead, you've got to keep it."

A total of six more teams crossed the postseason threshold after their Week 15 games. In the NFC, Dallas and Los Angeles each earned a playoff berth, while in the AFC, Houston, Miami, Pittsburgh and San Diego punched their ticket to the postseason tournament. The underdog Cowboys limped into cold and windy Veterans Stadium in Philadelphia minus two injured veteran starters (Charlie Waters and Drew Pearson). The Eagles were 60 minutes away from winning their first divisional championship since 1960. Emotion and momentum belonged to the Eagles and to their rabid fans, while Dallas' woes continued to mount when their tailback, Tony Dorsett, suffered a slightly separated shoulder in the first quarter, and would not play for the remainder of this game, nor for their final regular season game the following week against Washington. But Dallas managed to make some big plays early which silenced the crowd, beginning with a tipped interception return of a Ron Jaworski pass by Cowboys safety Randy Hughes. Dallas fullback Scott Laidlaw plowed over from the 1-yard line a couple of plays later for the game's initial score. The scoring ebbed back and forth between both teams until another tipped pass in the fourth quarter paved the way to a Dallas victory. Cowboys quarterback Roger Staubach threw a pass down the middle on third down from his 17-yard line. The ball was tipped by Eagles linebacker Frank LeMaster, and began its downward descent to the AstroTurf. Reserve Dallas wide receiver Butch Johnson, who was filling in for the injured Drew Pearson, immediately broke off of his intended route for the middle of the field. Johnson dove for the plummeting pigskin just one yard inside of the end zone, made a fingertip catch, and gave the Cowboys a 24–17 gut-check victory. "Our team has never really jelled this season until this game," said Dallas head coach Tom Landry. "The offensive line was the outstanding part of our team," assessed Staubach. "They were a solid wall up there, run or pass, with no leaks."

The Washington Redskins also were solid against Cincinnati, as they defeated the Bengals at RFK Stadium, 28–14. Veteran Redskins defensive lineman Coy Bacon, whose journeyman career in the NFL included stops in the past for the Bengals, the Chargers, and the Rams, recorded four sacks against his former team. The Redskins, the Cowboys, and the Eagles all now shared identical 10–5 records. Both the Eagles and Cowboys were in the playoffs at this stage of the season, but the Redskins' fate would have to wait to be determined until the season's final week. Washington could win the NFC East with a victory over Dallas in the final game. Even if they lost that game, the Redskins' chances were still good to make the playoffs. A Chicago loss against St. Louis in the final week would put the Redskins in the playoffs, and if both the Redskins and the Bears finished with 10–6 records, Washington owned the tie-breaker between the two clubs based on net point differential. That tie-breaker amounted to a seemingly insurmountable edge for Washington. In order for the Bears—and not the Redskins—to make the playoffs, the Bears would have to defeat the Cardinals by more than 32 points, and the Redskins would also have to lose at Dallas. It all made for some incredible drama during the last weeks of the 1979 regular season.

Speaking of the Bears, they eked out a 15–14 win over the Green Bay Packers at Lambeau Field on the second-to-last week of the season, thanks in large part to a 66-yard interception return of a Lynn Dickey pass for a touchdown by Bears linebacker Tom Hicks. A desperate 52-yard field goal attempt by Packers placekicker Tom Birney with 32 seconds remaining in the game fell just short of the crossbar. The win gave the Bears a 9–6 record, which was good enough for a first-place tie with the Tampa Bay Buccaneers, who at the same time were busy losing their third game in a row. The San Francisco 49ers, who had only one win to their name going into Week 15, defeated the Bucs by a score of 23–7 at Candlestick Park. Several weeks prior, Tampa Bay appeared to be a shoo-in for the NFC Central Division title. Now with but one game left, they appeared primed and ready to own one of the biggest collapses in NFL history.

Over in the NFC West, the Los Angeles Rams finally overcame their multitude of injuries and bad luck to earn their seventh division title of the decade (which tied a league record at that time). The Rams crushed the Atlanta Falcons in Atlanta, 34–13. Four Rams touchdowns in the second quarter, including a 34-yard interception return for a score by linebacker Jim Youngblood, insured Los Angeles' ninth win of the season. The Rams defense recorded six sacks and forced five Falcons turnovers. The Rams offense was led by halfback Wendell Tyler of UCLA, who rushed for 138 yards and one touchdown. "Maybe we can sneak into the Super Bowl," an optimistic Tyler said after the Falcons game. "You never know."

The New Orleans Saints, who for a time toyed with the opportunity to unseat the Rams in the NFC West, soundly fell in their second-to-last game to the San Diego Chargers in the Superdome, 35–0. New Orleans would finish the 1979 season with their best record in the decade, however, earning a respectable 8–8 mark. San Diego's win over the Saints guaranteed the crew with a lightning bolt on the sides of their helmets a playoff berth for the first time since 1965. Reserve Chargers running back Hank Bauer scored three touchdowns against New Orleans, each one coming from one yard out in the first half. San Diego quarterback Dan Fouts only played in the first half of this game, mainly due to his team's large lead gained by halftime. Fouts would end the season with 4,082 yards passing, becoming the first quarterback in the decade to pass for more than 4,000 yards in a season. The measuring stick for that grand statistic originated with Joe Namath of the New York Jets, who threw for 4,007 yards in 1967 (in a 14-game regular season). The Chargers now laid claim to an 11–4 record, and would finish the 1979 season with their best mark of the decade at 12–4.

San Diego was indirectly aided in their efforts to win the AFC West. Surprisingly, that help came from none other than their main adversaries in the division, the Denver Broncos, who collapsed during the end of the year. Denver lost three of their final four games, and finished with a 10–6 record. Denver had played well enough during the first half of the year, however, to somehow manage to earn a wild card spot in the AFC playoffs. The Seattle Seahawks won their final two games of the year to give them a winning season at 9–7 for the second straight year.

The AFC Central would also end up in a fight to the finish. The defending champion Steelers visited the Houston Astrodome on *Monday Night Football* on December 10 and got another chance to see and hear the Luv Ya Blue fervor. By 1979, the "Luv Ya Blue" song had become the accepted trademark song of the city of Houston. The Oilers earned that type of fan adulation. They had improved even more since the previous year, where they made it to the 1978 AFC title game. But just as in the previous year, the Oilers were unfortunately suffering from a plethora of key injuries to key players. That did not matter on this night, however, as the Oilers gained a token of revenge against the Steelers by holding on for a 20–17 win. Houston relied once again on the efforts of their bell cow, the great running back Earl Campbell, who toted the ball 33 times for 109 yards against the tough Steel Curtain defense. In the end, a Pittsburgh onside kick attempt was ruled by the referees to have not traveled 10 yards, and the Oilers prevailed. "We showed the country tonight that we're a class organization," exclaimed Houston head coach Bum Phillips.

"Three points, ten points, thirty points … any kind of win against these folks is a big one." Both the Oilers and the Steelers were now tied for first place in their division with 11–4 records.

The only team in the AFC who had first place all to themselves after Week 15 was the Miami Dolphins, who went into the Pontiac Silverdome and defeated the Detroit Lions, 28–10. It was another efficient game for the Dolphins, as quarterback Bob Griese threw two first quarter touchdown passes to set the tone for his offense. The No-Name Defense complimented Griese and the Dolphin offense by registering four sacks in the game. Miami's victory cemented the championship of the AFC East because the New England Patriots imploded on the same day against the host New York Jets, 27–26. The Jets were fighting for a break-even season (which they would get by winning their final game), but they had revenge in mind, thanks to their embarrassing 56–3 loss to the Pats in Week 2. New York placekicker Dave Jacobs' 25-yard field goal in the fourth quarter provided the winning margin.

A couple of longtime veterans would complete the 15th week of the 1979 season by celebrating the final home game in their extraordinary careers. Although he played the vast majority of his career in Buffalo, O.J. Simpson was one of those men. The San Francisco 49ers held a pregame ceremony for the most prolific running back of the decade, and Simpson said a fond goodbye to the fans from his Northern California hometown. "Over the years, I have heard your applause and appreciated your cheers," said Simpson. "I already know that's what I'm going to miss the most." The NFL's oldest defensive lineman would probably agree with Simpson's sentiments, as he also suited up for his final home game. Minnesota's Jim Marshall culminated an incredible 20-year NFL career, in which he played in every game in Vikings history. His teammates carried him off on their shoulders following Minnesota's 10–3 win over Buffalo at Metropolitan Stadium, for one more glorious memory for the NFL's recognized ironman.

Another old pro had his career extended by at least one more game following a couple of miraculous results in the final week of the regular season. Veteran Chicago linebacker Doug Buffone was prepared to end his 14-year NFL career as the Bears took on the St. Louis Cardinals at Soldier Field. Buffone intercepted a pass in what he thought was his final game, which was a nice retirement memento to be sure. But a funny thing happened to Buffone and his buddies in this game. The Bears were still mathematically alive for a wild card playoff spot, but in order for them to obtain that spot, they would have to beat the Cardinals by more than 32 points (due to the tie-breaking formula that was required), and the Washington Redskins would have to lose to the Dallas Cowboys later that day. The odds of both of those occurrences happening were very slim, almost impossibly slim. Incredibly, both of those stipulations miraculously came to pass on this day.

Sunny but frigid weather greeted the Bears and Cardinals for their early afternoon game at Soldier Field on December 16, which suited the Chicago players just fine. They erupted for a 42–6 pasting of the Cards, as they scored three touchdowns in each half. The Bears were led by the NFC's leading rusher, halfback Walter Payton, who ran for 157 yards and three touchdowns against St. Louis. "Sweetness," as Payton was called by his teammates, the press, and the fans, finished the year with 1,610 rushing yards. Bears quarterback Mike Phipps also threw for 233 yards and two scoring passes in the rout of St. Louis. Chicago (10–6) had unbelievably accomplished the most difficult part of the formula that they needed for the playoff invitation by beating the Cardinals by 36 points. They would now be spectators to their fate, as the issue now rested in the hands of the Cowboys and the Redskins at Texas Stadium. The entire city of Chicago would immediately become Dallas Cowboys fans for the next several hours.

Dallas had already earned at least a wild card spot in the NFC playoffs. A win by Washington would give the Redskins the NFC East title, and it would send the Bears home for the holidays.

A Cowboys victory would mean their fourth straight division championship, as well as an early Christmas present to the folks in Chicago. Washington had defeated Dallas earlier in the season at RFK Stadium by a score of 34–20 in Week 12. In their second meeting, the Redskins jumped to an early 17–0 advantage, sparked by a 55-yard pass from Washington quarterback Joe Theismann to setback Benny Malone. Dallas responded in the second quarter with three straight touchdowns, including a 26-yard scoring pass from Cowboys quarterback Roger Staubach to setback Preston Pearson. The Cowboys owned a 21–17 lead going into the fourth quarter, but the fireworks were just beginning. Both offenses erupted for big scores in the final period, but it would be a critical play by an old-time defensive player which set the stage for ultimate victory.

The fourth quarter began with another Redskins scoring barrage. Washington running back John Riggins plowed through Doomsday for a 1-yard touchdown, then followed that effort up a few minutes later with a dynamic 66-yard power sweep down the far sideline for another score. On that touchdown, Riggins proved that he had not lost a step since his rookie year in the league in 1971, as he outraced second-year Dallas defensive back Dennis Thurman to reach paydirt. Dallas was now facing a 34–21 deficit with only four minutes left in the game. Fortunately for the Cowboys, they had a quarterback who was born to win seemingly winless games in the clutch. Roger Staubach would do just that one more time in his glorious career on this day. Staubach drove his offense down to the Washington 26-yard line, and with just over two minutes left to play, he noticed rookie setback Ron Springs streaking down the middle of the field past Redskins linebacker Brad Dusek. Staubach hit Springs in the hands, and the young Ohio State standout plowed through Dusek and Washington defensive backs Mark Murphy and Ray Waddy at the goal line to score. Dallas was now down by only six points at 34–28.

Dallas head coach Tom Landry opted not to try an onside kick at this time, preferring instead to give his defense one last attempt at stopping the Washington offense. Doomsday had been having difficulty all afternoon long trying to halt the Redskin advance, but on a third-and-short situation late in the game, an old pro defensive end for Dallas named Larry Cole shot through a gap in the Washington offensive line and tackled Riggins behind the line of scrimmage as he (Riggins) tried to secure the game-winning first down on another sweep. Cole's play turned out to be the play of the game, as it gave Staubach one last opportunity with under two minutes left to move his offense towards the winning score. Staubach would throw for 336 yards in this game, and with less than 40 seconds to play, he would throw the winning touchdown on an 8-yard lob pass in the back of the end zone to wide receiver Tony Hill, who beat Redskins cornerback Lemar Parrish on a straight stutter-step and go pattern. As soon as Hill made the grab, you could almost hear the roar of Bears fans from dozens of bars and thousands of homesteads over 900 miles away in Chicago cheering in wild exhilaration, as their Bears would receive the unexpected gift of a playoff berth after all. The Cowboys' 35–34 victory over the Redskins was later described by Staubach as "the most exciting game I've ever played in."

The excitement of a playoff berth had been on hold in Tampa for almost a month before the Buccaneers would get one last chance at winning the NFC Central Division on the last Sunday of the 1979 regular season. They had been poised to claim their first ever divisional championship during the last quarter of the season, and all they needed was one more win or one more Chicago loss. Three consecutive Tampa losses and Bear wins later, and the Bucs were down to their last chance on December 16. The conditions at Tampa Stadium could not have been worse on that day for their game against the Kansas City Chiefs, however. A day-long deluge of rain showers would make throwing the ball very difficult. The relentless downpour would also make holding on to the ball almost impossible. The Chiefs were busy having their best season in years, and a win over Tampa Bay would give Kansas City a break-even record at 8–8, which would be their best record since 1973 when they went 7–5–2. The Chiefs could also be spoilers on this day, as another Tampa Bay loss would give Chicago the NFC Central Division title, and would eliminate the Buccaneers from advancing into the playoffs.

Predictably, there was not much scoring in this soaking contest, as in none. At least not until midway through the fourth quarter, when Tampa Bay placekicker Neil O'Donoghue booted a 19-yard field goal, which proved to be the only score in the game. Tampa's defense permitted the Chiefs to gain only 58 yards rushing, while Buccaneers accumulated 224 ground yards, 137 of which came from running back Ricky Bell. "I don't really feel too tired," said Bell after the game. "I was caught up in the game. They just kept giving me the ball." Tampa Bay's 3–0 victory culminated with the one-time laughing stock of the league only a few short years ago going from worst to first, their motto for their best season ever. Several Buccaneers players were seen splashing around the field after the game in rapture and glee, as if the previous 60 minutes of getting waterlogged were not enough time to get drenched.

The remainder of the postseason pairings were set with the following wins and losses. The Miami Dolphins lost for the second time this year to the New York Jets, 27–24. The Jets thus finished 1979 with an 8–8 record, which was identical to their 1978 record. The Dolphins finished the year with a 10–6 mark, and would get a week off before taking part in their playoff game at Pittsburgh on December 30. Speaking of the Steelers, they shut out the Buffalo Bills in their final regular season game of the decade, 28–0. The decisive win marked head coach Chuck Noll's 100th pro victory. Pittsburgh's main nemesis in the AFC Central Division, the Houston Oilers, lost their final regular season game at the Astrodome to the Philadelphia Eagles, 26–20. It was an anticlimatic game, as both teams had already secured a wild card spot in the playoffs.

Two teams from the AFC West would also make the postseason tournament. The San Diego Chargers defeated the visiting Denver Broncos in the final *Monday Night Football* game of the decade, 17–7. The Chargers thus won the division with an impressive 12–4 record, which tied Pittsburgh for the best record in the NFL. Despite losing, the Broncos still won 10 games, which was good enough for a wild card spot in the AFC playoffs. The term "backing in" to the playoffs was appropriate for the Broncos in this case, but teams like the Saints, Redskins, and Patriots wished that they would have had similar luck. New Orleans soundly defeated the Rams in their final game of the season, 29–14, but the Saints' 8–8 record caused them to miss the postseason by one game. Washington's 10–6 record would have been competitive in any division, but their one-point loss to Dallas sent them back to the drawing board to plan for 1980. New England earned a winning record (9–7), but losing several games to lesser teams held them back from participating in the playoffs.

There were a few final sentimental goodbyes as the 1979 regular season ended. O.J. Simpson of the San Francisco 49ers played his final pro game in a 31–21 loss at Atlanta, and Minnesota's Jim Marshall did likewise in a 27–23 loss at New England. The Patriots displayed a fond moment of class to a fellow warrior by having all of their players gather on the field to greet Marshall as he was announced to the Schaefer Stadium crowd. But perhaps the most unusual of endings occurred in Los Angeles, as the Rams played their final game at the Los Angeles Memorial Coliseum. The team had played there since 1946, but they would be moving to the suburb of Anaheim in 1980. Despite the fact that the Rams had made the 1979 playoffs, all of their playoff games would be on the road based on their 9–7 record. So the Rams' final game at the old Coliseum saw the sentimental words "Good Bye" painted by the grounds crew in both end zones. The Rams lost to the Saints in their last regular season game, a contest that if they had won would not have helped their positioning in the playoffs one bit. Most Ram fans felt that there was little hope for their team to succeed in the playoffs.

The playoffs began the following Sunday with two wild card games. Both home teams managed to emerge victorious. In one of those contests, the Philadelphia Eagles came from behind at Veterans Stadium to outlast the Cinderella Chicago Bears, 27–17. The Bears took a 17–10 lead into halftime, thanks to a couple of short touchdown runs by their superstar halfback, Walter Payton. Yet it was another Payton run early in the third quarter which proved to turn the tide of momentum in this game. On that play, Payton took a handoff at the Chicago 15-yard line from Bears quarterback Mike Phipps and ran to his right, followed a solid block from fullback Dave Williams on Eagles safety Randy Logan, then began a determined sprint down the far sideline. Payton soon escaped a diving attempted tackle by Eagles outside linebacker Jerry Robinson, and greatly benefitted from a shielding block downfield from Chicago wide receiver Rickey Watts on Eagles defensive back John Sciarra. Philadelphia cornerback Herman Edwards caught up with Payton at the Eagles' 22-yard line, but quickly found out that arm tackles were useless against Sweetness. Payton's speed proved too much for Edwards, and 85 yards after the snap of the ball, the Bears had a game-breaking touchdown ... or so they thought. An illegal motion penalty at the line of scrimmage against Chicago wide receiver Brian Baschnagel cancelled Payton's third score and a potential 14-point Bears lead. Chicago's offense visually let down from that point on, while Philadelphia's offense finally woke up.

Eagles quarterback Ron Jaworski did not really have a great first half. He threw one 17-yard touchdown pass to wide receiver Harold Carmichael in the first quarter, but he also fumbled a snap from center which resulted in a Chicago field goal just before halftime. Jaworski came back strong in the second half, however. He threw another scoring toss to Carmichael from 29 yards out in the third quarter, tying the game at 17–17. In the fourth quarter from his 37-yard line, Jaworski threw a short square-out pass to reserve setback Billy Campfield in the right flat. Campfield ran past three Chicago defenders along the far sideline to complete a 63-yard game-deciding touchdown. Philadelphia head coach Dick Vermeil addressed Jaworski's problems in the first half and his response to correct them in the second half. "I just went up to him [Jaworski] and told him 'You've got yourself a problem, now fight your way out of it.' I knew he would, and he did," Vermeil said later. The Philadelphia "Gang Green" defense also solved the problems that the Bears' offense had caused them in the first half. Two big interceptions by Eagles defensive backs Bobby Howard and Herman Edwards combined with a key fumble recovery by Philadelphia nose guard Charlie Johnson to eliminate Chicago's hope for victory. The Eagles would thus overcome their halftime deficit and survive this gut-check. They would continue their season with a ticket to the divisional round of the playoffs, a step further than they traveled the previous year.

Both the Denver Broncos and the Houston Oilers were hoping to do the same in their AFC wild card game in the Houston Astrodome later that day. This game would be a defensive battle from start to finish. Only two touchdowns were scored all day, one by each team. The Oilers scored first on a 31-yard field goal by placekicker Toni Fritsch. The Broncos followed that up a few minutes later in the first quarter when reserve running back Dave Preston ran out into the left flat uncovered. He caught a quick 7-yard pass from Denver quarterback Craig Morton, cut back against the grain, and dove into the end zone to give the Broncos a 7–3 lead. Preston's score ended an 80-yard drive, easily Denver's longest drive of the game. The Oilers defense would buckle down from this moment on, however, and would not allow the Broncos to score another point for the remainder of the game.

Houston's offense, however, did not do much better. The Oilers suffered the loss of three of their most important starters to injury in this game, including quarterback Dan Pastorini, running back Earl Campbell, and wide receiver Ken Burrough. The Oilers did manage to score a touchdown late in the second quarter on a 3-yard plunge by Campbell, who fumbled the ball just after he crossed the goal line. The referees confirmed that Campbell did indeed score, but the burly runner also suffered a groin injury on the play, and would be sidelined for the rest of the day. Houston's 10–7 lead held up, though, thanks to six sacks of Morton, and a key fourth quarter interception by Oilers linebacker Gregg Bingham, which set up another field goal by Fritsch, this one coming from 20 yards out. Following Houston's 13–7 victory, virtually all of the talk in the Oilers' postgame locker room surrounded the injuries they sustained, most notably Campbell's injury. "You guys keep asking about Earl," commented Houston head coach Bum Phillips to the gathering of reporters. "But you might have forgotten about how good a back Rob Carpenter is." Carpenter was a third-year pro who filled in for Campbell in the second half, rushing for a game-high 59 yards on 16 carries.

Denver head coach Robert "Red" Miller was dumbfounded by his team's sudden loss to a team that allowed 69 more points to opponents than his team did in the regular season. Yet it was his offense's lack of success which foretold the misfortune of his team. "You can't win many games with seven points," Miller lamented. "I never dreamed they [Houston] could beat us without Campbell and Pastorini."

Neither would the San Diego Chargers, who would be salivating at the thought of playing the injury-riddled Oilers in the divisional playoff round the following week. The Chargers were listed as 8 and ½-point favorites to win the game. They would be playing in front of their home fans at San Diego Stadium, and they had the second-best offense in the league in 1979, scoring 411 points (an average of 26 points per game). Overall team health added to the factors that were also in San Diego's favor. Certainly the Chargers were much more healthier than the Oilers, who had to do without the likes of starting quarterback Dan Pastorini, premiere running back and NFL rushing champion Earl Campbell, and gazelle-like wide receiver Ken Burrough, for the entire game. The situation appeared hopeless for Houston. The only element that the Oilers could possibly point to as a plus mark in their favor was that the Chargers had not been to the playoffs since 1965, while Houston had almost reached the Super Bowl the previous season. By the final gun, however, the Chargers and their fans were left scratching their heads and were virtually speechless. Many pro football experts claimed that Houston's 17–14 upset victory over San Diego was the most stunning and unexpected playoff outcome of the decade.

There were several keys which pointed the way to victory for Houston. One was the spectacular play of their defense. Going up against the most powerful passing game in the league, the Oilers felt that they had to contain Chargers quarterback Dan Fouts from gouging their defensive secondary. Fouts ended up throwing for 333 yards against the Oilers, which was a typical amount of yardage for him in one average afternoon. What was definitely not typical for Fouts, however, was his five interceptions, four of which nestled into the willing arms of rookie Houston strong safety Vernon Perry, setting a league postseason record for an individual defender. Perry's thefts were a big contribution, but not his only ones. He also blocked a Mike Wood field goal attempt in the second quarter and returned the ball 57 yards. Perry's return eventually led to a 26-yard field goal from Houston placekicker Toni Fritsch, which provided Houston with the eventual margin of victory. "They [the Chargers] kept throwing at me and I kept intercepting passes," said Perry. "Picking on a rookie isn't such a bad idea in a passing scheme. This just happened to be one of those times where it worked out better for me."

San Diego's offense was not working out better for them, because they simply were not used to playing in a low scoring game. Chargers head coach Don Coryell prided himself in seeing his offense put up bunches of touchdowns every week. Perhaps the extra week off after their final regular season game did them more harm than good. Perhaps the discontinuing of the repetition of daily practices threw off the important timing of the Chargers offense. Regardless of the reasons, the Chargers offense probably felt that all they needed was a quick score to revive their fortunes. San Diego halfback Lydell Mitchell's timely 8-yard run off left tackle for a touchdown early in the third quarter seemed to solve their problems and got them back into their regular scoring rhythm. They now had a 14–10 lead, and were ready to put up more points. All indications appeared that more San Diego points was only a few minutes away from being registered.

Reserve Houston quarterback Gifford Nielsen had up to now played an average game, and he would finish with 10 completions in 19 attempts. But his counterpart, San Diego's Dan Fouts, had thrown 47 passes, and completed less than half of them. With three minutes left in the third quarter, Fouts threw a crucial interception to Oilers cornerback J.C. Wilson, which fatefully set up the winning score. Wilson made an incredible, one-arm catch on the play. A few minutes later on a third-and-11 situation from the San Diego 47-yard line, Nielsen completed the most important pass of the game. He hit reserve Houston wide receiver Mike Renfro on a quick slant pattern over the middle. Renfro broke an arm tackle from Chargers safety Mike Fuller, which accidentally helped to make the play a success. Fuller's fateful grab twirled Renfro's body around so that the receiver's momentum now had him going in the opposite direction of the flow of San Diego's pursuers. Renfro then cut back against the grain and easily eluded Charger cornerback Willie Buchanon and linebacker Ray Preston. A key block by Oilers tight end Mike Barber allowed Renfro to get to the far sideline. From there, Renfro outraced Chargers safety Glen Edwards and linebacker Woodrow Lowe to the pylon of the end zone. This game-breaking play proved to be the Chargers' undoing.

"That play was designed to go for the first down," said Houston head coach Bum Phillips. "He [Renfro] just did a good job of running—and he got some blocking downfield." San Diego middle linebacker Bob Horn had seen his defense give up some big plays during the regular season, but Renfro's back-breaker of a play was difficult for the Chargers to stomach. "We haven't been hurt too often like that," Horn admitted. "Usually, if a guy catches a pass like that, he doesn't go far. Someone missed a tackle, and we were all spread out. He had a lot of room to run."

Fouts had a lot of time to bring his team back again, however. He had in fact all of the fourth quarter to do so. But he failed in this mission, and his final last-gasp attempt of the year was intercepted by none other than Vernon Perry for the icing on the cake. The Oilers survived once again, and thus earned a ticket to the AFC championship game for the second straight year.

The other AFC divisional playoff game—unlike the battle in San Diego Stadium—had virtually no elements of suspense. The Miami Dolphins traveled to Three Rivers Stadium to take on the defending world champion Pittsburgh Steelers. Miami had won the AFC East for the first time since 1974, and had put together one heck of a year with a 10–6 record. But the Steelers had won the AFC Central for the sixth straight year in 1979, and their obvious strength took the heart out of Miami's attack right from the start. The Steelers scored three touchdowns in the first quarter on a 1-yard burst by fullback Sidney Thornton, a 17-yard touchdown pass from quarterback Terry Bradshaw to wide receiver John Stallworth, and a 20-yard scoring toss from Bradshaw to his other wide receiver, Lynn Swann. Stallworth's touchdown showcased his innate abilities to escape would-be tacklers and run with the ball. Stallworth broke four arm-tackles from Miami defensive backs Neal Colzie, Gerald Small, and Norris Thomas, and a final diving attempt from reserve Dolphins linebacker Earnest Rhone. He then tight-roped his way down the near sideline for a few yards before prancing inside of the end zone pylon for six points. Both teams traded touchdowns in the third and fourth quarters. Pittsburgh running backs Rocky Bleier and Franco Harris each scored on runs of short distances, and Miami running back Larry Csonka ended his illustrious pro career with a 1-yard touchdown run late in the game. The Steelers' 34–14 romp over the Dolphins was not unexpected. Pittsburgh's defense had traditionally played with wild abandon during the playoffs, and they did so on this day as well. The Steel Curtain held Miami's offense to just 35 total yards in the first half, including only a meager seven rushing yards. By game's end, the Dolphins had accumulated a total of only 25 net rushing yards. Pittsburgh defensive tackle Joe Greene bluntly and somewhat boastfully remarked, "We're just better than other teams."

The Dallas Cowboys were better—at least on paper—than their foes in the divisional playoff round, the Los Angeles Rams. Dallas had easily defeated the Rams on October 14 by a score of 30–6, and few experts believed that the injury-riddled Rams would offer much competition in this meeting either. But the Rams had learned some profitable lessons from that earlier drubbing. They knew that Dallas quarterback Roger Staubach threw for three touchdowns and completed 13 of 18 passes in their previous meeting. They also knew that Dallas halfback Tony Dorsett was playing for the first time in three weeks due to a separated shoulder injury that he sustained late in the regular season, and they hoped that he would be a little rusty in this contest. So the Los Angeles defense devised a strategy to virtually ignore the Cowboys' rushing game. They decided instead to focus on confusing Staubach by using seven defensive backs on almost every second and third down situation throughout most of the game. Their strategy worked quite well, especially in the first half. "I wouldn't say that Roger was confused by our strategy," opined Rams defensive coordinator Bud Carson. "After all, Roger is never really confused. I'd say we just made it very difficult for him to operate." Staubach finished the game with only 13 completions in 28 attempts for a mere 150 total passing yards.

The Rams would rely on the youthful Vince Ferragamo as their quarterback. Ferragamo was filling in for injured starter Pat Haden during most of the last few games of the regular season. Indeed, many Rams players at a variety of positions were substituting for starters who were injured earlier in the season. Ferragamo had completed only 48 percent of his passes in 1979, and had twice as many interceptions (10) as touchdown passes (5). The Rams entered the postseason tournament with the worst record of all the playoff teams at 9–7. But the Rams disregarded all of those facts and were motivated to win. The memory of their 28–0 loss to the Cowboys in the 1978 NFC title game was still giving their veteran players a bad taste in their mouths, and they wanted nothing more than a little payback. All-Pro Dallas defensive tackle Randy White managed to delay that payback somewhat when he sacked Ferragamo in the Los Angeles end zone for a first quarter safety. After that, however, the Rams offensive line began to pass block more effectively, and Ferragamo decided to get rid of the ball quicker with shorter drop-backs.

But the main ingredient in Los Angeles' comeback early in the second quarter was tailback Wendell Tyler, who ripped off a 35-yard run on a sweep to his right. Tyler would account for a team-high 82 rushing yards on the day, and he was also very valuable to his team as a pass receiver. Tyler culminated a 92-yard Rams scoring drive in the second quarter when he circled out of the backfield, raced past Dallas outside linebacker D.D. Lewis, and caught a 32-yard touchdown pass from Ferragamo for a 7–2 Los Angeles lead.

Dallas came back on their next possession late in the first half when placekicker Rafael Septien booted a 33-yard field goal to draw the Cowboys closer at 7–5. The Rams had just 50 seconds left on the clock and the ball at their own 30-yard line. Most people felt that with a slim lead, the Rams offense would just sit on the ball and not risk a turnover. But the Rams applied what has become over the years one of the most acknowledged coaching axioms in the NFL … if you want to win in the playoffs, you have to be willing to take risks. The Rams took a chance with their limited available time and threw deep in the face of the Cowboys' prevent defense. From the Dallas 43-yard line, Ferragamo barely got his long pass away before being belted by the onrushing Randy White. Los Angeles wide receiver Ron Smith reached the end zone before the arching ball descended. Smith had only a moment to out-maneuver Dallas defensive backs Randy

Hughes and Aaron Kyle, then out-jump both of them for the ball. The 6' Smith did just that, and came down with the prize for a dramatic touchdown. The Rams took a surprising 14–5 lead into halftime. "It was thrown up there and I just didn't make the play," Hughes admitted. "We let them have three big plays. That's what killed us."

Midway through the third quarter, the Cowboys tried to postpone their death. They responded to the Rams' advantage by putting together a six-play drive which resulted in their first touchdown. Dallas benefitted from a pass interference penalty in the end zone on Rams linebacker Jim Youngblood. One play later, rookie Cowboys running back Ron Springs dove over from the 1-yard line for a score which brought Dallas to within two points of the Rams at 14–12. It now seemed like the Cowboys had finally figured out what Los Angeles was trying to do strategically on both ends of the line of scrimmage. Dallas safety Cliff Harris intercepted a Ferragamo pass with just under five minutes left in the third quarter. The Cowboys immediately went on their longest scoring drive of the game, lasting for 11 plays. Reserve Dallas tight end Jay Saldi did the honors, catching a 2-yard touchdown pass from Staubach. Saldi's score gave the Cowboys a 19–14 lead.

The onus was now on the Doomsday Defense to put the clamps on the Rams offense in the fourth quarter. A 12-play Los Angeles drive died at the Dallas 32-yard line when on a fourth-and-eight situation, Ferragamo's pass for wide receiver Drew Hill fell incomplete. On the next Rams possession, they were forced to punt from their own 41-yard line. There was now just 2:45 left in the game. The Rams defense did its job on the next Dallas series, forcing another Dallas punt after three plays. With 2:16 left to play and with the ball at midfield, the Rams turned in the play of the day. Ferragamo dropped back to pass and threw deep down the middle for Rams wide receiver Billy Waddy. The pass was thrown ahead of Waddy, however, and would have either been incomplete or intercepted. But fate intervened in the form of leaping Dallas linebacker Mike Hegman, who managed to tip the ball just slightly, which slowed it down and changed its trajectory to drop down ... right into Waddy's waiting hands. Waddy was probably just as surprised by his good luck as the Dallas defense was. He immediately streaked past Cowboys defensive backs Dennis Thurman and Cliff Harris, both of whom were converging on the area where Waddy caught the ball. Waddy ran down the near sideline untouched to complete the 50-yard scoring play. "I kept my eye on the ball," Waddy said. "I said, I ain't gonna let that son-of-a-gun get past me." According to Harris, "He [Waddy] never broke stride [after catching the ball]."

The Cowboys would get one last chance to retake the lead. They had the ball at their 21-yard line with 1:57 left to play. Unfortunately for Dallas, the Rams defense played its best series of the game, causing four of Staubach's passes to fall incomplete, thus ending the game. Los Angeles prevailed in one of the greatest upset wins in their history, 21–19. It marked the second time in the decade (with 1976 being the first time) that the Rams won a divisional playoff game at Texas Stadium. "I've been around football all my life. That's the best damn effort I've seen any team in my whole career ever give," exclaimed Rams head coach Ray Malavasi from the victorious postgame locker room. "It was a great win. Probably the greatest since I've been in L.A. Our guys just played a super game. They never gave up and neither did I."

One Los Angeles player certainly did not give up and contributed a truly super game. Defensive end Jack Youngblood suffered a broken left leg between his knee and ankle (his fibula) on a double-team block just before halftime. He incredibly returned to the contest in the third quarter with wads of ace bandages and padding on his leg, and he somehow managed to finish out the game. "Playing in pain is part of the game," Youngblood said later. "I guess one of the reasons I did play on my leg was that I believe that the mind controls the body. And that's not saying that I have total control over my body because of my mind, but that I do know that it does work. If you want something bad enough and you want to overcome something, the mind can do it. That's basically what I believe. It had me out there playing in the situation I was in."

The situations for both the Oilers and the Rams involved achieving upset victories in the 1979 playoffs, which they both accomplished. Most experts, however, believed that the Philadelphia Eagles would be one team that would not fall victim to an unexpected loss when they strolled into Tampa Stadium to face the Buccaneers. The Eagles were favored to win, having slightly more postseason experience than the Buccaneers. That experience factor was often the true measuring stick in determining the winner in a playoff game throughout the decade. Teams which had more years of playoff experience won 64 percent of the time over teams which had less playoff experience during the course of the 1970s. Philadelphia's offense was rated slightly better than Tampa Bay's, as they managed to score 66 more points during their 16 regular season games than what Tampa Bay's offense could accumulate. Added to these elements was the fact that the Buccaneers did not possess any degree of confidence going into this contest with the Eagles, having lost three of their previous four games.

Despite all of the factors which were going against the Bucs, they wasted no time in securing an early lead against the Eagles. Tampa Bay running back Ricky Bell had 11 carries on his team's first drive of the day, which consumed over nine minutes off the clock and took up an incredible 18 plays. Bell culminated the 80-yard drive with a 4-yard touchdown run on an end sweep to his right. He would finish the game with 142 rushing yards and two touchdowns. Bell also earned a new NFL playoff record with 38 carries, which is still a record to this day for a non-overtime playoff game. "I don't care if I carry the ball 10 times as long as we win," Bell said. "It wasn't really in the game plan for me to carry the ball that much."

A 40-yard field goal midway through the second quarter by Tampa Bay placekicker Neil O'Donoghue increased the Buccaneers' lead to 10–0. The Bucs added to their advantage just a little over a minute later when Philadelphia tailback Wilbert Montgomery fumbled on a run up the middle. Tampa Bay nose tackle Randy Crowder recovered Montgomery's miscue at the Eagles' 4-yard line. On fourth and goal from the 1-yard line, Bell plowed through for his second score and an impressive 17–0 Tampa Bay lead.

The Eagles knew that they had to answer back with a score of some kind soon if they were to stay competitive in this game. It took a turnover for them to do so. Philadelphia linebacker Jerry Robinson intercepted a Doug Williams pass and returned it 37 yards to the Buccaneers' 11-yard line with 1:37 left in the second quarter. Philadelphia quarterback Ron Jaworski threw a slant pass to wide receiver Charlie Smith for a touchdown a couple of plays later, and the Eagles had drawn to 17–7 at halftime. Philadelphia's momentum continued in their first drive of the third quarter, when Eagles bare-footed placekicker Tony Franklin booted a 42-yard field goal to narrow the visitor's deficit to 17–10.

There was no more scoring in the third quarter, but midway through the final period, Williams put together a 9-play drive which ended with another Tampa Bay touchdown. On third and goal from the Philadelphia 3-yard line, Williams rolled right and threw a dart to his tight end Jimmie Giles, who was clearing out the deep corner of the end zone. Giles snagged the touchdown pass and the Bucs grabbed a 24–10 lead with seven minutes left to play. The Eagles came right back, however, on their next possession. Jaworski dropped back from his 37-yard line and threw over the middle to his 6'8" wide receiver, Harold Carmichael, who caught the pass at the Tampa Bay 14-yard line and sprinted into the end zone. The Eagles now trailed 24–17 with 3:25 left to play. Philadelphia tried an onside kick, but it failed. Their "Gang Green" defense held the Bucs to just two yards on their next three plays, though, and the Eagles offense had the ball back after a Tampa Bay punt with 2:11 left. Philly was deep in their own territory at their 19-yard line, and they had to pass. The Buccaneers defense prepared for this, but Jaworski managed to complete two different fourth-down tosses which resulted in first downs. The game clock nonetheless was now quickly becoming a relentless foe to the Eagles. Jaworski had to deal with one more fourth down situation at the Tampa Bay 45-yard line with just 43 seconds left. His final pass of the 1979 season was overthrown, however, and the Buccaneers had won their first playoff game ever, 24–17.

"I think we outplayed them," said victorious Tampa Bay head coach John McKay. "I thought we could move the ball on Philadelphia and we did. We have a fairly young team [and] we have good players. I think we can play most anybody."

The Buccaneers would end up playing the Rams for the NFC championship a week later. Thanks to the Bucs' better regular season record (10–6 over the Rams' 9–7 record) and the fact that they beat the Rams earlier in the year (on September 23 by a final score of 21–6), the NFC title game would be held in Tampa Bay. The home field advantage would appear to be a great edge for the Buccaneers. Nobody—and I mean nobody—believed for even one moment at the beginning of the year that the Buccaneers would reach this very point, just one win away from the Super Bowl. This story was not just your average Cinderella story. Instead, it was a Cinderella story where Cinderella has a chance to wave a conference championship trophy in the face of her evil stepsisters. The Bucs were just two years removed from their 0–26 franchise start. Now they were four quarters away from setting off a victory party the likes of which had not been seen in western Florida since the invention of the air conditioner.

The Rams had planned for victory parties since 1973, only to lose in the playoffs each year. They were not as healthy as the Tampa Bay squad, but they certainly had more postseason experience. Because of that experience, they were listed as slight favorites going into the NFC championship game. The Bucs had beaten a Philadelphia team the previous week in the divisional round of the playoffs that also had more experience than they did. They were not awed by the Rams, or by any team for that matter. The game was settled more by the opposing defenses than by anything else. Los Angeles defensive end Jack Youngblood postponed the surgery that he needed on his broken fibula and played the whole game. Youngblood's show of courage obviously motivated his teammates, and the Rams defense rarely played better. Their pass defense would allow Tampa Bay quarterbacks only four completions in 26 attempts, worth a paltry 54 total yards. Buccaneers halfback Jerry Eckwood did manage to complete a 42-yard pass to wide receiver Larry Mucker in the third quarter, but it amounted to no points.

To be fair, the Rams offense also struggled, at least in one aspect. They had no problems moving the ball against Tampa Bay's defense. They just had problems putting the ball in the end zone. A first quarter touchdown run by Rams running back Cullen Bryant was called back due to an illegal procedure penalty. Los Angeles placekicker Frank Corral did manage to salvage a 13-play drive by kicking a 19-yard field goal early in the second quarter to give his team a 3–0 lead. Later in the same quarter, Corral added a 21-yard field goal to give the Rams a 6–0 edge heading into halftime.

The third quarter was scoreless, thanks to another missed field goal attempt by Corral. The Rams, however, kept running the ball well, and would end the game with 216 rushing yards against a very strong Buccaneers defense. A series of punts ensued until Corral was called upon again to try a 23-yard field goal with 8:09 left in the game. Corral's kick was good, and the Rams now owned a 9–0 lead. The way their defense was playing, that might be enough. By this time, reserve Buccaneers quarterback Mike Rae was now under center, having filled in for the injured Doug Williams. But Rae was unsuccessful, and each of his deep throws into the Los Angeles end zone fell incomplete. His final attempt with 2:18 left in the fourth quarter was overthrown, and the

Buccaneers' remarkable "Worst to First" season was finally over. The Rams held on to the ball for the remainder of the game, and won their first ever NFC championship, 9–0. It was the lowest-scoring conference championship game in NFL history. The Rams had been to the NFC title game four previous times during the 1970s, all without success. Now they had finally put together a winning effort and claimed a ticket to the promised land—the Super Bowl.

As the victorious Rams celebrated in the visiting locker room in Tampa Stadium, thoughts among many of their veteran players and coaches went from a sentimental journey through their recent failed past to the challenges and travails that they all had endured during a tumultuous 1979 season. "It's been so long, it's been frustrating," said Los Angeles head coach Ray Malavasi in referring to the Rams' heartbreaking playoff losses throughout the 1970s. "I feel really good, not just for myself but for all of our other players," exclaimed Rams linebacker Jim Youngblood. "We've been through hell this year ... we really have. But we stuck together." Their momentum and inspiration wore number 85, and he was embracing his teammates in blissful relief. "There's something different about this team [the 1979 Rams]," said their free spirit defensive end Fred Dryer. "It's this guy [pointing his finger at Jack Youngblood]. He's playing with a goddamn broken leg [which was later diagnosed to be a hairline fracture of his fibula]. He was there." Malavasi added, "He [Youngblood] wasn't 100 percent, but he gave 100 percent." Dryer summed his teammate's effort by simply stating, "There's nothing more you can ask of the guy."

Houston Oilers head coach O.A. "Bum" Phillips asked for one more win from his 1979 team, and they would have to accomplish the task in the most formidable venue in the league—Pittsburgh's Three Rivers Stadium. The Oilers had lost the previous year's AFC title game at the same location by a score of 34–5. They were more determined than ever to right that wrong, but they were nowhere near as healthy as they were in 1978. Both injured Houston quarterback Dan Pastorini and injured running back Earl Campbell would play in this game, however. Both knew that they were going to have to play the game of their lives in order to pull off an upset.

The Oilers received a couple of breaks early. One involved the weather. It was 22 degrees and overcast in Pittsburgh on January 6. But it was not raining, and the threat of freezing rain and ice on the field was not present as it was the previous year. The second break that fell into Houston's lap happened on the seventh play of the game. Pittsburgh quarterback Terry Bradshaw threw deep down the middle, intending his pass for tight end Bennie Cunningham. Houston safety Vernon Perry, the big hero of the Oilers' previous playoff game against San Diego, stepped in front of Cunningham, intercepted Bradshaw's pass, and ran 75 yards untouched to score. It was the longest interception return for a score in AFC championship game history at that time.

The Steelers managed to shorten their deficit when placekicker Matt Bahr booted a 21-yard field goal a few minutes before the end of the first quarter. Houston got that field goal right back early in the second quarter when they drove 72 yards in eight plays. Houston placekicker Toni Fritsch connected on a 27-yard field goal to boost the Oilers' advantage to 10–3. It would be the last good drive of the first half for the Oilers, however. Pittsburgh dominated the remainder of the second quarter with two touchdowns, an interception, and a recovered fumble. A 10-play drive culminated with a 16-yard touchdown pass from Bradshaw to his tight end Cunningham which tied the game at 10–10. Cunningham leaped over Vernon Perry, and just barely got both of his feet inbounds to secure a legal catch. A little later in the game, another player in this dramatic contest would have a similar catch questioned ... almost beyond belief.

Six plays after Cunningham's touchdown, Houston quarterback Dan Pastorini threw over the middle for wide receiver Mike Renfro, who caught the ball, then was immediately hit by Steelers safety Donnie Shell and fumbled the pigskin. Pittsburgh cornerback Mel Blount recovered it and advanced it five yards to the Houston 49-yard line. Seven plays later, Bradshaw threw another touchdown pass, this one coming from 20 yards out to wide receiver John Stallworth, again in the back of the end zone. The Steelers owned a 17–10 lead at halftime.

No scoring occurred in the third quarter, but the Houston contingent sure felt that there was a score. One of the decade's most controversial plays convinced them of this. It was a play in which most of the proponents clamoring for an instant replay system in pro football pointed to in the years since as the most obvious example of their argument. They felt that the legitimacy of the game was in question, and that by 1979 there was a dire need to help out the referees. There was just a few minutes left before the gun would sound to end the third quarter between the Oilers and the Steelers. Houston had put together a 10-play drive with the ball at the Pittsburgh 6-yard line. They had a first and goal situation, and they appeared assured of scoring the tying touchdown. Pastorini lobbed the ball for Mike Renfro deep in the far corner of the Steeler end zone. Renfro was covered closely by Pittsburgh cornerback Ron Johnson, but still managed to get behind him and get in position to make the catch. Renfro did indeed make the catch, and did indeed get both of his feet inbounds before falling out of the end zone. Renfro got up, fully expecting to see the officials signaling a touchdown. The zebras did no such thing, however. Both side judge Don Orr and field judge Bill O'Brien looked quizzically at each other like a pair of deer which just got caught looking into a pair of automobile headlights.

Confusion reigned among players, coaches, fans, and the rest of the officials alike. Was it a touchdown? Did Renfro have complete possession of the ball before he slid out of the end zone? Those were the two main questions. The fans watching the game on television were given the chance to see several instant replays of the catch. The officials on the field had no such luxury. The zebras huddled in the end zone for about a minute, then referee Jim Tunney signaled incomplete pass. The Oilers and their coaches were immediately livid. Once they saw the television instant replay from their perch in the booth, NBC broadcasters Dick Enberg and Merlin Olsen both admitted back and forth that Renfro got both feet in and had full possession of the ball. "I hate to see the biggest plays of the game not made by the players on the field, but by the officials," said Olsen. "There's no doubt that was a Houston touchdown," said Enberg. "The Oilers were cheated out of a touchdown," Olsen added. Bum Phillips erupted in anger on the sidelines. "Bum could just eat that Cowboy hat," Enberg said. The play seemed to take the wind out of Houston's sails. They failed in succeeding plays to get their "lost" touchdown, and settled for another field goal at the beginning of the fourth quarter. It would fatefully be their final points of the 1979 season.

Pittsburgh's offense answered immediately with another field goal of their own to make the score 20–13. The Oilers had to respond quickly in this stage of the game if they had any hope of victory. Reserve Houston wide receiver Guido Merkens caught a pass from Pastorini for a first down with under six minutes to play, but fumbled the ball. Pittsburgh safety Donnie Shell made the recovery. Nine plays later, Steeler fullback Rocky Bleier churned into the Oiler end zone from four yards out for the game-clinching touchdown. The Steelers survived this struggle, 27–13, and had won their fourth conference championship in the past six years. In the Houston postgame locker room, Renfro's controversial "non-catch" was the main topic of discussion. "It was a touchdown," said Pastorini. "I know it was a touchdown, no matter what they say. But what I say doesn't count. I'm not an official. If we get that touchdown, the balance shifts. We can come out and run in our next possession instead of throwing like we had to. It's tough to take." Houston placekicker Toni Fritsch minced few words. "It was robbery," said Fritsch. Pittsburgh defensive tackle Joe Greene and Houston head coach Bum Phillips were both a little more contemplative and magnanimous about the reality of the play's outcome and the day's final result. "This isn't a flap at the officials," said Greene. "It just shows that they need help." Phillips added, "I'm not going to blame the officials. They're human. We had 59 other minutes in the game to beat Pittsburgh and we didn't. I don't think anybody can beat Pittsburgh except Houston ... and we didn't do it today."

The Los Angeles Rams had beaten Pittsburgh four times during the course of the decade. This is quite notable, considering that the two teams met each other only four times during the course of the decade. Going into Super Bowl XIV, however, the Steelers were favored by most experts to win. Los Angeles' mind set going into this game was still in a state of flux from the previous spring. They were still dealing with the tragic death of their former owner, Carroll Rosenbloom, who tragically drowned in April. The discord following Rosenbloom's fate remained a trying problem for the team. Rosenbloom's wife—Georgia Frontiere—inherited the majority ownership of the team, and she soon fired Rosenbloom's son Steve, who had served the club as an advisor and special counsel to his father. She also moved the team's headquarters out of Los Angeles to Anaheim, California. In 1980, she would oversee the Rams' move out of the Los Angeles Memorial Coliseum to Anaheim Stadium. All of the players and coaches on the team were trying their best to ignore these off-the-field issues, as they prepared for their chance to pull off what most people would consider one of the greatest upsets in NFL history.

The Rams would go into the big game with the worst record ever (9–7) of any team to have ever made it to a Super Bowl. One fact that might be considered a good omen for the Rams, however, involved the game's location. Super Bowl XIV would be played in the Rose Bowl Stadium in Pasadena, California, making this a virtual home game for the Rams. Moreover, the Rams felt that their personnel matched up well with the Steelers, despite the fact that they still had more injuries than the Steelers. No less than six starting Ram players on offense had to be replaced by the time the playoffs came around. The team was resilient, though, as exhibited by their big wins in the postseason over Dallas and Tampa Bay. This was the first time that the Rams had ever made it to a Super Bowl, and their enthusiasm was evident for all to see. Veteran Pittsburgh defensive tackle Joe Greene certainly took notice of it by the end of the game. "We got into that game and, right away, we knew we were in for a war," admitted Greene. "The Rams were a fired-up team. And it wasn't one of those superficial, locker-room highs that lasts about three minutes. They were *pumped*." Los Angeles head coach Ray Malavasi expressed the feelings of his team as they prepared for the biggest game of their lives. "We're not afraid of anything or anyone," said Malavasi.

The defending world champion Steelers were equally as fearless, having won three of the past five Super Bowls. So were their fans, who followed the team to Pasadena in huge numbers, and who unveiled a large Terrible Towel on the field before the game. As was the case with Super Bowl XI in the Rose Bowl Stadium, every fan in the stands at Super Bowl XIV was given special placards to hold during the pregame and halftime shows, which shimmered brilliantly in the Southern California sun. The Super Bowl continued to be the foremost spectacle in professional sports, and its popularity was reaching new heights in 1979, and growing more and more with each passing year. Popular celebrities naturally abounded throughout the stadium, and Cheryl Ladd of ABC-TV's *Charlie's Angels* fame delivered a beautiful rendition of the National Anthem.

Pittsburgh's offense delivered its multi-faceted attack right from their very first possession, driving 55 yards in 10 plays. Placekicker Matt Bahr booted a 41-yard field goal to give the Steelers an early 3–0 lead. The Los Angeles offense responded with one of their best scoring drives of the year against one of the best defenses in the league. Rams tailback Wendell Tyler spurred the drive with a spectacular 39-yard run around left end. On that play, Tyler broke through a diving tackle by Pittsburgh cornerback Mel Blount, then juked the other Steelers cornerback J.T. Thomas. He then cut back to avoid the grasp of linebacker Dennis "Dirt" Winston, and was finally caught from behind by Pittsburgh safety Donnie Shell. Tyler's success on this run would not be repeated during

Pittsburgh Steelers running back Rocky Bleier is gang-tackled by a group of Los Angeles Rams defenders in Super Bowl XIV, January 20, 1980, at the Rose Bowl in Pasadena, California. The Steelers won their second straight world championship with a 31–19 triumph over the Rams to close out the 1970s (AP Photo/Vernon Biever).

the rest of this game, however. He would carry the ball 16 more times in for a mere 21 more yards, and would suffer a series of nagging leg cramps and minor injuries several times in the second half. Despite Tyler's fate, the Rams did manage to take the lead in the first quarter with a 1-yard plunge by fullback Cullen Bryant. This would be the first of seven different lead changes throughout this contest.

The most unsung hero of Super Bowl XIV returned the ensuing kickoff. Pittsburgh kick returner Larry Anderson's 45-yard return set the Steelers up near midfield for their next scoring drive. Anderson received a total of five Los Angeles kickoffs in the game, and returned them for a total of 162 yards (a 32-yard average per return). Early in the second quarter, Pittsburgh running back Franco Harris swept to his right and outraced the Los Angeles pursuit into the corner of the end zone for a touchdown. The Rams did not trail for long, however. Los Angeles quarterback Vince Ferragamo led his team on a 10-play drive which resulted in a 31-yard field goal by place-kicker Frank Corral. The game was now tied at 10–10 midway through the second quarter.

The Rams defense then made its first big play of the contest a few minutes later. Los Angeles strong safety Dave Elmendorf intercepted a Terry Bradshaw pass and return the theft 10 yards to the Steelers 39-yard line. Corral booted a 45-yard field goal to give the Rams a surprising 13–10 lead going into halftime. Bradshaw would later be named the Most Valuable Player of the Game, the second straight year that he would receive this esteemed award. But he would throw a total of three interceptions in the game, a statistic which usually did not usually equate to an MVP trophy. Bradshaw would have better luck later in the game, however, but his offense had struggled through a tough first half. Pittsburgh's offensive strategy had to change, and Bradshaw knew it. The Rams defense was shutting down the Steelers running game, and by the final gun would limit Franco Harris to 46 yards on 20 carries, and his running mate Rocky Bleier to 25 yards on 10 carries. Bradshaw recognized his need to throw the ball early enough following halftime to revive his offense. On the fifth play of the third quarter, Bradshaw beat a delayed blitz by Rams linebacker Jack "Hacksaw" Reynolds and launched a perfect 47-yard touchdown bomb deep down the middle of the field to Steelers wide receiver Lynn Swann. The graceful Swann made yet another one of his trademark leaping catches over Rams defenders Nolan Cromwell and Pat Thomas and tumbled into the end zone. "I guess I jumped a little early," said Cromwell. "I was on the way down when the ball arrived." Pittsburgh thus once again regained the lead, 17–13.

Ferragamo and the Rams came right back, however. The young Rams passer threw a long pass from his own 26-yard line to wide receiver Billy Waddy, who made a splendid catch 50 yards downfield. On the very next play, Ferragamo handed the ball off to Rams halfback Lawrence McCutcheon, who swept to his right, straightened up, and threw an option pass to reserve wide receiver Ron Smith. The ball nestled into Smith's arms inside the near corner of the end zone, and the Rams had incredibly retaken the lead. Corral's point after touchdown conversion failed, but Los Angeles gleefully took their 19–17 lead into the final quarter.

By this time, two more Pittsburgh drives were thwarted by interceptions in Los Angeles territory. Moreover, Steelers wide receiver Lynn Swann was knocked out of the game with a concussion. Bradshaw was running out of options, and he was also running out of time. He decided to throw caution to the wind and throw long to his only remaining healthy wide receiver, the tall and fleet John Stallworth. On a third-and-eight situation from his own 27-yard line, Bradshaw dropped back and launched a deep, arching pass down the middle of the field. Stallworth found himself single covered by Rams cornerback Rod Perry, who should have had help from reserve safety Eddie Brown. But Brown was too intent watching the action in the Pittsburgh backfield, and allowed Stallworth to run right by him without so much as a glance. Perry leaped in an attempt to knock the ball down, but he barely missed. Stallworth caught the pass in stride and loped untouched into the Los Angeles end zone. "I saw Rod Perry's hand over me just as I was about to catch the ball," Stallworth said. "He came very close to making a damn good play." The Steelers now owned a 24–19 lead.

An exchange of punts left less than half of the fourth quarter remaining. Ferragamo and the Los Angeles coaching staff knew that with one more touchdown, the Rams stood a good chance to win. Their offense started at their own 16-yard line and began a clutch drive, moving the ball with three pass completions and a Wendell Tyler run to the Pittsburgh 32-yard line. There was now just a little over five minutes remaining when Ferragamo committed his only real mistake of the game. Rams receiver Billy Waddy ran a deep post pattern and was left uncovered by the Pittsburgh defensive secondary. Ferragamo failed to see him, and instead threw the ball down the middle to his other wide receiver, Ron Smith, who ran a slant pattern about 15 yards past the line of scrimmage. Pittsburgh middle linebacker Jack Lambert made the most important play of his career when he stepped in front of Smith and intercepted the ball. Lambert's return of 16 yards ignited the final Steelers drive of the game. "Lambert is a very rangy guy," admitted Ferragamo.

Bradshaw again took what the Rams defense gave him, namely the long pass. On a third-and-seven situation from the Pittsburgh 33-yard line, the "Blonde Bomber" let loose with his final long bomb of the decade. Stallworth was once again the target, but on this occasion, he was adequately covered by Perry and Elmendorf. Regardless of the coverage, Stallworth made perhaps the greatest catch of his career, as he leaned backwards and caught the ball over his left shoulder with two defenders draped all over him. His 45-yard reception was followed five plays later by a

1-yard touchdown dive by Franco Harris, who barely stretched the ball across the goal line. It was the fourth Super Bowl touchdown of Harris' illustrious career, and it insured the Steelers of their fourth world title. The game ended less than two minutes later with no more scoring, as the Steelers won back-to-back Super Bowls for the second time in the decade with a 31–19 victory. "We knew how good the Rams were," said Bradshaw, "and they were playing at home. I knew it would be very, very tough. Never in my life was I so happy to see a game end."

Super Bowl XIV marked a fitting end to the decade of the 1970s. Pittsburgh's dynasty reached its grand zenith with their fourth world championship in the past six years. They were unanimously named the Team of the Decade. The Rams gave them a good challenge and kept the pressure on them throughout the game. "We had 'em on the ropes," assessed Rams defensive end Fred Dryer afterwards. "We played the hell out of those guys [the Steelers]. I guarantee those guys know they've been in a football game." Steelers defensive tackle Joe Greene lauded the effort that the Rams presented in the final Super Bowl of the decade. "They [the Rams] played their hearts out," admitted Greene. According to NFL Films in their highlight film of Super Bowl XIV, the Rams "earned a dignity in defeat that they had never achieved in victory." Debatable as that statement was, one thing that everyone agreed on was the bravery of Rams defensive end Jack Youngblood, who played his third straight game with what amounted to a broken leg. In all the annals of athletic competition and organized sports, few examples of courage and determination can match what Youngblood did in the 1979 postseason. "There'a a lot of pride on this team," said a modest Youngblood after the game.

Looking back at the 1970s would give the NFL as a whole a lot of pride. The league now had a solid foundation for growth in the 1980s. The league underwent a variety of changes—some good and some bad—during the 1970s. The next decade would bring further changes and even more growth. But the 1980s would also bring more challenges and more problems. One thing was for sure, however. The NFL in the 1970s was more exciting and enjoyable than it had ever been before. And there were more than just a few fans who were sad to see it go. We would never again see another decade in pro football quite like it. Perhaps "Dandy" Don Meredith summed up the 1970s best when he sang late in the fourth quarter of most *Monday Night Football* games in which he was broadcasting: "Turn out the lights, the party's over, they say that all good things must end." Even if the game was a blowout, many fans stayed up late on Monday nights just to hear Dandy Don sing. Meredith always was a good entertainer.

Epilogue

The decade of the 1970s in professional football concluded abruptly, with the sound of the final gun at the end of Super Bowl XIV. The excitement encountered during those preceding ten years were in and of themselves a proper epitaph for a sport which experienced a wealth of changes and growth during that time span. Those of us who lived through the 1970s and enjoyed it knew that those remarkable years went by fast … almost too fast. I admit that I spent the 1979 season trying to reminisce about the decade in pro football. All the while I knew in my head and in my heart that this game that I first fell in love with at the beginning of the decade had changed over time, and would never be the same again. The 1970s ended amid the fanfare that one would suspect at the end of any decade. Even before the completion of the 1979 season, it was almost a given requirement that NFL Films would produce a documentary on the decade, just like they did in 1969 when they produced a 24-minute film called *The Sensational Sixties*. The creative minds at NFL Films knew full well that 24 minutes would certainly not be long enough to properly portray the 1970s, however. So they settled on a 48-minute film, and in reality, even that was not long enough to adequately depict the decade. The tough part was to divide the decade of the 1970s up equally and to focus on each year and each important event equally. This is what I've tried to do with this book, but keep in mind, I've had many more years to digest the events of the 1970s than the folks at NFL Films did in 1979.

Just as the publications on the sport increased as the decade wore on, so too did my sources increase with each chapter of this book. I indeed had more information to draw upon for the year 1979 than I did for the 1970 NFL season. Similarly, everyone involved with pro football in the 1970s could trace the growth of the game with each passing year. It was a decade of continual adjustments, where coaches, players, and teams in general learned from their mistakes. Sometimes they did not. Washington Redskins head coach George Allen made a career of annually trading away his team's draft choices in order to obtain established but older players from other teams. Allen's stubborn front office moves made the Redskins instant contenders, however, and playoff participants in five of his first six seasons in Washington. Despite this, he was never able to win a Super Bowl, and his veteran leaders eventually became too old to play the game effectively. The Redskins were definitely not as powerful during Allen's later years with the team as they were when he first took charge of them in 1971. He never did learn from his mistakes and used his draft choices on college talent, but many of the league's opposing coaches did. Many of them often traded players, but certainly not to the frequency that Allen did. The Pittsburgh Steelers of the 1970s built their juggernaut exclusively through the draft, and rarely traded anyone … except to obtain future young players through the draft. The Steelers ended up winning four Super Bowls in the decade.

Sometimes a single play or two in a big game served as a fitting stage to judge a player's ability to make amends for an earlier mistake. This happened all throughout the decade, and often with spectacular results. Take the case of Pittsburgh Steelers safety Mike Wagner, for instance. Early in Super Bowl X against the Dallas Cowboys, Wagner "played it safe" by dropping back during a series of shifts initiated by the Dallas offensive personnel on a first-and-10 situation at the Pittsburgh 29-yard line. Dallas wide receiver Drew Pearson filled the middle of Wagner's voided area, caught a perfect pass from Cowboys quarterback Roger Staubach, and zipped into the end zone for the game's first touchdown. "I screwed up," admitted Wagner. "If they [the Cowboys] do this [play] again, I'm not going to hesitate. I'm going to go." The Cowboys did indeed try that play again midway through the fourth quarter. This time, Wagner made a quick decision, and jutted in front of Pearson to intercept the ball and return it deep into Dallas territory. Wagner's quick adjustment (or gamble if you will) helped the Steelers to come back from a fourth quarter deficit to defeat the Cowboys, 21–17, and thereby winning their second straight Super Bowl.

My mistakes in this book did not come from an instant decision like Wagner's, but rather, they are largely due to the space available. I always wanted to include as much information as possible about this all-inclusive effort about the 1970s in the NFL. My greatest fear was leaving anything of significance out in the ten chapters of this book. Despite all of the countless hours I spent on research, I know that there will be some aspects of this subject that I've neglected to mention. For that, I am truly sorry. But I did my best. So too did the players of the 1970s. I had the privilege of interviewing quite a few of them for this book, and it was their efforts on the football field during that decade which gave me the inspiration that I needed to write about their exploits. Mike Brown, the President of the Cincinnati Bengals and the son of Pro Football Hall of Fame head coach Paul Brown, once claimed, "Your heroes as a 12-year-old boy remain your heroes all throughout your life," and that is definitely the case with me. I idolized these men that I write about in this book, and I'm honored to get to know them many years later, and to bring their stories back to print here in these pages.

Many of the players and coaches that I've interviewed for this book were not considered great enough to make the Hall of Fame, but some of them were. Many of them never participated in a playoff game, but some of them played in multiple playoff games. Regardless of their successes or failures, each player and each team had a say in how the decade evolved, and how the competition on any given Sunday could produce a moment or two of sheer excitement. One instrument to gauge the importance or the greatness of a decade in pro football history is to simply count the number of incredible moments of those ten years which many years later are still vividly recalled or talked about by fans and sporting personnel alike. In the 1970s, events such as the Immaculate Reception, the Sea of Hands game, the Ghost to the Post game, the Rob Lytle fumble, O.J. Simpson's 1973 season, and the exploits of the Pittsburgh Steelers dynasty, are just some of the most memorable events of the 1970s. Try to list an equal number of memorable events in any decade before or since. It's not that easy. But somehow, the 1970s are still being talked about today.

A case in point involves a flawless moment. Perhaps no other team in NFL history is discussed more than the 1972 Miami Dolphins, the only pro team in the modern era of sports to achieve a perfect season. The Dolphins went 17–0, and their greatness would become an annual reminder for all teams since 1972 to aspire to. Now several decades after their achievement, the surviving members of that undefeated Miami club gather together every fall or winter when the final previously undefeated team finally (and so far ultimately) loses. Those old Dolphin pros then drink a champagne toast to their unequaled accomplishment from so many years ago. Mention the 1972 Miami Dolphins, and every football fan can tell you that was the team that went undefeated and untied throughout a full season. Former Dallas Cowboys Hall of Fame wide receiver Michael Irvin once claimed that he would be willing to give up two of his three world championship rings if he knew that his remaining Super Bowl ring came as a result of achieving a perfect season like Miami did in 1972. That's how memorable that 1972 Dolphins team is … even today.

On rare occasions in the 1970s, a split-second decision on behalf of one player on the field of battle changed the life of another player forever. A case in point came in 1978. Oakland Raiders safety Jack Tatum, in a preseason game against the New England Patriots, decided to launch his helmet into the face mask and upper torso of Patriots receiver Darryl Stingley. The resulting injury left Stingley paralyzed for the rest of his life. Many fans admit that Tatum was so shocked by the aftermath of his hit on Stingley, that he was never able to play with the same vigor and reckless abandon again. It was the most notable injury of the decade, and one in which still gets discussed whenever a player in the years since gets carted off the field on a stretcher. Stingley never was able to forgive Tatum for that hit on August 12, 1978 … at least not publically. Both men died at young ages. Tatum suffered as a diabetic in his later years and eventually had to have one of his legs amputated prior to his death. The sadness of this unfortunate event was not unique to just these two men, however, as other decisions by players involving drug usage would receive its first bout of publicity in the 1970s, and would ultimately also help to destroy the lives of several players in the league.

The fate of many players of the decade was sometimes tied to their intense desire to make a team roster, or to become a superstar player. "The competition for jobs and big money is making the game immensely more violent," claimed former journeyman center Jon Morris. "You see it especially among the younger players. They'll do anything to get into the NFL." The effects of anabolic steroids helped to make a player bigger, faster, and stronger. If enough players on one team used them, a very strong team would often be the result. But after a player retired from the game, the effects of taking those steroids were usually detrimental to his physical health, causing heart attacks, a frequent brain aneurism, and even in some cases, a premature death. Today there are numerous stories of players who took steroids in the 1970s, and the results serve as an unmistakable lesson for all current players. Today's athletes for the most part have learned from the errors of the past with steroids. If they don't, the league has instilled some pretty definitive punishments, some of which have included fines and multi-game suspensions.

Sometimes the decisions made in the 1970s were not hasty ones, but ones which came about during the course of several years of thought and contemplation. Player movement thanks to more liberal free agent policies increased as the decade wore on. Players increasingly had to decide to stay with their current team after their initial contract, or ask for a trade. More and more players by the end of the 1970s would decide to change uniforms, believing that the grass might be greener on a different team. Some teams were willing to trade a player, and some were not. By the 1990s, free agency among players became the norm, and it eventually led to a salary limit amongst every team. Today, leaving one team for another usually involves leaving for a higher salary. Long-time veterans in the current age will often leave their initial team (especially if it is a losing team) for a better chance to win a Super Bowl with a contending team.

Individual players were not the only ones who moved to a new city in the 1970s. The Boston Patriots moved to Foxboro, Massachusetts in 1971, and became the New England Patriots. But that was just a meek prelude to what would happen at the end of the decade. The Los Angeles Rams moved to Anaheim, California, to begin the 1980 season. The Rams' change of residence ignited a fervent squabble between Oakland Raiders Managing General Partner Al Davis and NFL Commissioner Pete Rozelle as soon as 1979 ended. Multiple court cases which dominated the headlines throughout 1980 and 1981 were the unfortunate result. Putting it succinctly, Davis wanted to move his team to Los Angeles to fill the void in that city when the Rams left for Anaheim. Rozelle wanted him and his Raiders to stay in Oakland. A federal district court judge sided with

Davis, and the Oakland Raiders became the Los Angeles Raiders to begin the 1982 season. Davis and the Raiders would ironically move back to Oakland in 1995 when the Oakland Alameda County Coliseum was improved with new luxury boxes and increased overall seating capacity.

Davis surprisingly happened to be on the same side as Commissioner Rozelle in at least two instances in 1970 and 1974, when the players and their union decided to go on strike. The 1970 strike amounted to little more than an airing of player grievances before the athletes returned to their teams. But the 1974 strike put forth a plan of action among the players in their hopes for a new collective bargaining agreement. Many of the players followed through on that plan by carrying picket signs during training camp and during the league's exhibition season. The annual Chicago All-Star Game was cancelled due to the strike, and many of the early preseason games featured nothing but rookies on every team. Those two strikes in the decade of the 1970s would pale in comparison to the lengthy player strikes of 1982 and 1987, however. More and more, instances off the playing field began to mirror the situational examples seen in the lives of all Americans. We all wanted to make more money and provide for our families and our futures, and so did the players in the National Football League. Those guys were just like us, except that many of them were just a little more famous than the rest of us fans, and as the decade reached its end, most of them made more money than the average citizen.

Also by the end of the decade, the new avenue for television viewing called "Cable TV" would make its debut. American televisions would require antennas to receive a minimum of basic channels throughout much of the 1970s, but those few channels would be greatly multiplied by 1979, thanks to Cable TV. The Home Box Office (HBO) cable channel would begin with premium movies seven nights a week. It would eventually include a weekly program called *Inside the NFL*, featuring former Kansas City quarterback Len Dawson and former Miami middle linebacker Nick Buoniconti as the hosts. The show would feature weekly highlights from NFL Films, and before long, millions of Americans would start seeing a thin black cable emerge from their streets, and hooked into the back of their television sets. ESPN, the 24-hour-a-day sports network, soon followed suit, and thanks to ESPN, the NFL quickly received even more coverage than the Pittsburgh Steelers' defensive backs covered opposing pass catchers. One of the best advantages of having Cable TV was that unlike antenna stations, all of the channels would come in clear, regardless of the weather outside.

In the end, the winds of change were evident, but one could also surmise that the decade of the 1970s still continued to walk a familiar path along a fine tradition. The 1970s repeated what the decade of the 1960s did, namely add to the previous foundation of the game with more excitement and more overall growth. The decade of the 1980s and each of the following decades would add still more of those factors on many occasions. But no decade in my opinion could match the overall greatness of the 1970s, and perhaps none ever will. Leave it to the gang at NFL Films to provide a fitting and somewhat "holy" ending to the decade. By 1979, pro football was becoming to many fans somewhat of a religious experience, an autumnal expression of a hallowed tradition. The directors and producers at NFL Films knew this (and indeed were a proponent of it). They used for their annual *NFL Game of the Week* programs a group of consecrated words at the end of the Lord's Prayer, spoken by players who were recorded in a random team locker room, that can be aptly paraphrased here at the conclusion of this super decade. "For thine is the kingdom, the power, and the glory...." While the players reciting this prayer were obviously referring to thanking God for His protection in battle and perhaps for victory over their opponents, at least a little part in me thinks that they could also for a brief moment have been referring to the game of pro football itself. The glory of the NFL ... in the 1970s.

Bibliographic Essay

Pro football writers grew in dramatic numbers during the 1970s, much as the game itself grew. The public's thirst for more in-depth knowledge of the NFL during the decade resulted in increasing numbers of books, football-only newspapers, and a wide variety of magazine articles. Reporters reveled in the growing accessibility of the coaches and players, and delved deep into the lives and jobs of these men. The first book in the decade which could be considered required reading for the NFL aficionado was Paul Zimmerman's *A Thinking Man's Guide to Pro Football*. First published in 1970 with a revised edition in 1971, the book opened the game up to the public like none ever did before. Zimmerman tackled each of the positions on the field, the coaches, the strategies, the training camps, and even the growth of the television industry covering the game. Zimmerman's work served as a primer for fans who wanted to learn more about the nuances about the pro game, as well as a platform of anecdotes which destroyed the myth that football players were "dumb." Zimmerman's success caused many new writers to branch out with their own interests in the pro game. It was the book which really got me interested in the details of the game as a youngster.

One of those new writers was Tom Bennett, who in 1976 wrote *The Pro Style: The Complete Guide to Understanding National Football League Strategy*. Bennett's book was a stylish, polished piece which explored football strategy from a historical standpoint. *The Pro Style* displayed diagrams and color and black and white photos in abundance, and disclosed secrets in terminology and tendencies. Bennett wanted the book to be a research tool, and indeed it was. A section on great coaches and their advances in football strategy preceded a chronological movement-by-movement series of plays and plans by both offenses and defenses. Bennett's work was a watershed in the realm of pro football strategy, and has yet to see a comparable book in all the years since its publication. *The Pro Style* served as a natural bridge for me and for most fans to go from the simple enjoyment of watching a game to analytically learning more about the game's strategy.

The Pro Style was one of the many books that were published through the authorship and direction of NFL Properties, an arm of the league which owned copyrights to game programs, fan merchandise, and team trademarks. NFL Properties published quite a few good books about the game in the 1970s. Some dealt with historical aspects of the game. Perhaps the most noteworthy of these types of books were several versions of *The NFL's Official Encyclopedic History of Professional Football*. The *Official Encyclopedia* contained segments on the history of each team, as well as defunct teams. It also included a chronological year-by-year look at the pro game from its earliest years in Pennsylvania and Ohio. The modern era is also well represented in the *Official Encyclopedia*. Photos and information on all the stadiums, team records and rosters, and championship and Super Bowl sections are just some of the important items in this book. There had been encyclopedias of pro football written in the 1960s, most notably Roger Treat's version. None of those were officially sanctioned by NFL Properties, however. The *Official Encyclopedia* served as a must volume in any of its versions for dedicated fans and those who considered themselves to be historians of the pro game.

Other NFL Properties books in the 1970s which highlighted specific teams came during the years of 1973 and 1974. The *Great Teams' Great Years* series of books focused on past histories of the following teams: The New York Giants, Washington Redskins, Los Angeles Rams, Kansas City Chiefs, San Francisco 49ers, Dallas Cowboys, Detroit Lions, Cleveland Browns and Pittsburgh Steelers. A different author wrote each team's book, and these volumes went further into details of the great players and the great games of that specific team. Other books from NFL Properties delved into the artistic side of the game, in the form of photos and paintings. A book like *The Pro Football Experience* (1974) showcased a multitude of color photos, and mixed with text from NFL Properties boss David Boss, glorified a typical Sunday afternoon in the fall, from the perspective of fans, players, and coaches. Another NFL Properties book titled *More Than a Game* (1974) addressed various facets of the game that were part human interest stories, part artwork, and part game strategy. John Wiebusch, a long-time editor at NFL Properties, edited the 48 different segments of the book. Later in 1980 a book called *The Professionals* featured paintings of popular current and former players from renown artists across America. NFL Properties was just getting warmed up. *The Professionals* also included a forward by famous sportswriter Tex Maule, and text by another famous sportswriter, Ray Didinger. Another noted author, Jack Clary from Massachusetts, would write a number of football titles, but his book called *The Gamemakers* (1976) was undeniably his best. *The Gamemakers* was another book from NFL Properties, and it featured in-depth stories on eight head coaches. Clary interviewed each of them with a plan to discover what aspects made each man successful. The results gave readers a focused look into the world of head coaches, where each man's personality, thoughts on game strategy, and crucial decisions in the midst of championship games were profoundly shared with readers. I relied greatly on *The Gamemakers*, primarily for great quotes from these head coaches, but also for background information on the coaches themselves.

The Players were not bashful about writing books themselves in the 1970s. In fact, many of their books, which were written by accompanying and/or ghost authors, became very popular and newsworthy. Books from superstars like Roger Staubach, Terry Bradshaw, and O.J. Simpson were seen throughout bookstores and libraries, but so were books from supposed NFL villains like Jack Tatum and Thomas Henderson. Tatum's *They Call Me Assassin* (1980) was written mostly in response to his paralyzing hit to New England wide receiver Darryl Stingley during the 1978 preseason. Tatum attempted to justify his hard-hitting play in the book, and his stance on the violence that the game produced must have awakened many fans to a side of the game that they knew existed but never really read much about. Henderson's *Out of Control* (1987) was an extremely honest portrayal of his years as a member of the Dallas Cowboys (1975–1979). Henderson's book was one of the most in-depth efforts to open up to the public the world of an NFL linebacker. Henderson documented his difficulties with drugs, sex, coaches, opponents, prison … in short, anything that he survived during his life. Henderson was one of those authors who was brave enough to tackle the "me" generation of the 1970s with acceptance and brutal honesty, and who fortunately came out the better for it. I used both Tatum's and Henderson's books for specific information on several dramatic moments in NFL history. It was not long before several players and coaches on a Super Bowl championship team would annually write books, and the total number of player-written books would increase each year throughout the 1970s.

Naturally, those who did most of the writing on a typical football Sunday were the beat writers from the local newspapers throughout the country. The beat writers represented the backbone of the media. Their role was to cover their city's team on a day-by-day basis, and this non-stop job was regarded by most in the profession as a necessity. Although players and coaches even back in the 1970s bad-mouthed the newspaper reporters, they also knew that such men (and eventually women) were making them famous. In this book, I used stories from a wide variety of reporters, who represented a wide variety of newspapers. Some of those authors included Jack Bluth, Joe Carnicelli, Bruce Lowitt, Tom Seppy, Gordon Forbes, and Vito Stellino. Some of the more noteworthy newspapers that I used included *The Frederick News, The Santa Fe New Mexican, The Hutchinson News, The Independent Press-Telegram,* and *The Huron Daily Plainsman.* Stories from the Associated Press and United Press International were the backbone of this book. I found most of the material quotes for this book from beat writers and newspaper reports.

Football magazines, weekly newspapers, and game programs were in their zenith during the 1970s. The most important to me growing up and even now for this book was *Football Digest,* which served as a compilation of news stories on the game from all over the country. Also being published on an annual basis each summer was *Street and Smith's Pro Football Annual,* and *Prolog,* a classy NFL Properties magazine which recounted the previous season and previewed the upcoming year in the NFL. Weekly publications like *Pro Football Weekly, The Sporting News,* and *Sports Illustrated,* all helped to give a needed fix to the football addict of the 1970s. There was an added bonus to a fan attending an NFL game (preseason, regular season, or postseason) in the 1970s … the chance to purchase a game program. Once again, NFL Properties took charge of the game programs with a flashy magazine called *Pro!* Regardless of which stadium you attended, you could always count on *Pro!* to give you a preview of the game, photos of the players, and very interesting national articles. I referred back to *Prolog* and *Pro!* throughout all of the chapters of my book for background information and an occasional quote.

Later in the decade of the 1970s, a few teams came out with weekly newspapers which covered their respective teams in depth. Some of the most notable were the *Dallas Cowboys Weekly,* Ray Nitschke's *Packer Report,* and Doug Buffone's *Bear Report.* These newspapers by the mid–1980s were seen all over the league, but they got their birth in the 1970s. They employed beat reporters, and had features on all of the players. The *Dallas Cowboys Weekly* even had features on their world famous cheerleaders.

Last but not certainly not least, I would be delinquent in this bibliographic essay if I did not mention the work of NFL Films. Almost all fans of the NFL in the 1970s were familiar with the various films shown on syndicated television from NFL Films. I referred to annual highlight films from every team for this book, as well as the weekly *NFL Game of the Week, This Week in Pro Football, This Week in the NFL, Pro Football Perspective,* and various other offerings from NFL Films. In the mid–1970s, NFL Films began to branch out with specialty films that dealt with game strategy and the history of the game. Films like *The Defenders, Old Leather,* and *A Glorious Game* helped to tell the story of the pro game in cinematic fashion with sideline sound, music, and the unmistakable noise of popping pads. I owe a debt of gratitude to Ed and Steve Sabol (the founders of NFL Films), editors Bob Ryan, Phil Tuckett, Mike Adams, Bob Angelo, Todd Schmidt, David R. Morcom, and James Green (among many), historian Chris Willis, and so many others who took a kid's game and made it into a million dollar industry. I viewed a great deal of NFL Films footage in describing hundreds of plays in this book, and I'm sure I will again in future books.

The following is a chapter-by-chapter review of some of the more prominent sources that I used as I traveled back to the NFL in the 1970s.

1970

My information on Super Bowl IV came mainly from the following: *A Thinking Man's Guide to Pro Football (Revised Edition)*. New York: E.P. Dutton, 1971, Zimmerman, Paul. *Kansas City Chiefs: Great Teams' Great Years*. New York: Macmillan, 1974, Connor, Dick. *The Super Bowl: Celebrating a Quarter-Century of America's Greatest Game*. New York: Simon & Schuster, 1990. National Football League Properties, Wiebusch, John, Editor-in-Chief. There are plenty of other quality resources that one can find on Kansas City's 23–7 victory over Minnesota in the final Super Bowl before the two leagues (AFL and NFL) merged.

Speaking of the AFL-NFL Merger, it too is tackled through a variety of sources, most notably from an editorial by Kansas City Chiefs quarterback Len Dawson: *The Kansas City Times*, June 9, 1966, Dawson, Len. Also informative were the following: "Vets Won't Be Hurt." *The St. Louis Post Dispatch*, June 9, 1966, Morrison, Robert. "Kemp Says Players Back Merger." *The Washington Post*, October 23, 1966, Brady, Dave. *The Scrapbook History of Pro Football (Expanded and Updated)*. Indianapolis: Bobbs-Merrill, 1979, Cohen, Richard M., Deutsch, Jordan A., and Neft, David S., also provided good factual information. Finally, NFL Commissioner Pete Rozelle was a major proponent of the merger and the growth of the pro game in the 1970s. A good article on his efforts is "Pete Rozelle, Architect." *Super Bowl XIV Program*, January 20, 1980, 31–37, McGrane, Bill.

The Players' Strike of 1970, although brief in time, is addressed in the following: "NFL Players Strike for Benefits." *The Columbus (Nebraska) Telegram*, July 30, 1970, 10. "NFL Pro Vets Issue Strike Call." *The Steubenville (Ohio) Herald Star*, July 31, 1970, 10, Rappoport, Ken. Also informative was "NFL Owners, Players Reach Accord." *The Bucks County (Pennsylvania) Courier Times*, August 3, 1970, 29, and "Strife-Torn NFL Arrives at Truce." *The Arizona Republic*, August 4, 1970, 27.

Information on the Birth of *Monday Night Football* was found through the following sources: *Prolog: The National Football League Annual*. Chicago: Follett, 1971, Oates, Bob, Jr. Also "Pro! Q and A: A Conversation with Roone Arledge." *Pro!*, September 22, 1974, 15A–17A, Felser, Larry. A good retrospective article on the best *Monday Night Football* games of the decade is "*Monday Night Football '*S 10 Most Memorable Games." *Football Digest*, November 1980, 34–43, Payne, Dave. You should also check out the following two articles: "Monday Night!" *Pro!* December 4, 1978, 37, Freeman, Don; and "Prime Time Football." *Pro!* November 26, 1978, 2C–10C, Natal, Jim. The lightning rod of *Monday Night Football* was sportscaster Howard Cosell. A good interview on the controversial Cosell is "The Ubiquitous One." *Pro!* September 21, 1975, 5A, Herskowitz, Mickey.

The Chiefs-Raiders Rivalry in 1970 was documented in the following sources: "Davidson's Sweet Foul." *The Oakland Tribune*, November 2, 1970, 40, Newnham, Blaine. *Kansas City Chiefs: Great Teams' Great Years*. New York: Macmillan, 1974, Connor, Dick, and "The Game I'll Never Forget." *Football Digest*, August 1978, 78–82, Keating, Tom, as told to Payne, Dave. *Sunday Zebras*. Lake Forest, IL: Forest Publishing, 1980, Holst, Art, provided an in-depth account to a referee's view of this great rivalry.

George Blanda's miracle season has several sources, but these were some of the best: "Blanda Does It Again as Browns Fall." *The Portsmouth (Ohio) Times*, November 9, 1970, 18, Prewitt, Eric; *30 Years of Pro Football's Great Moments*. New York: Rutledge Books, 1976, Clary, Jack; "When 2 Wrongs Right for Raiders." *The Oakland Tribune*, November 2, 1970, 40, Ross, George; "Better Let George Do It." *The San Francisco Chronicle*, November 10, 1970, Fimrite, Ron; "Old Quarterbacks Never Die." *Football Digest*, January 1972, 56–64, Twombly, Wells, and "George Blanda: 1970 Miracle Worker." *Football Digest*, March 1976, 74–79, Campbell, Jim.

New Orleans Saints placekicker Tom Dempsey kicked a record-breaking 63-yard field goal against the Detroit Lions on November 8, 1970. His record for the league's longest field goal stood for 43 years before it was broken by Matt Prater, who booted a 64-yard field goal in 2013. A good article on Dempsey's feat can be found by reading: "Tom Dempsey Kicks 63-Yard FG." *Football Digest*, October 1976, 76–80, Olney, Ross R.

Paul Brown and the Cinderella Cincinnati Bengals had their first great season in 1970. The following source was helpful: "Bengals Wrap Up Title by Overwhelming Boston, 45–7." *Appleton Post Crescent*, December 21, 1970, 30.

The postseason games from 1970 has many good sources including: "Colts Gallop Past Raiders for AFC Title." *The Santa Fe New Mexican*, January 4, 1971, 63. "League Winners Await Super Bowl." *The Santa Fe New Mexican*, January 4, 1971, 63, and *Prolog: The National Football League Annual*. Chicago: Follett, 1971, Oates, Bob, Jr.

Super Bowl V, one of the NFL's most unique Super Bowls, has a lot of good sources. These include: "Eleven Big Mistakes." *Sports Illustrated*, January 25, 1971, 12–17, Maule, Tex. *Prolog: The National Football League Annual*. Chicago: Follett, 1971, Oates, Bob, Jr. National Football League Properties, *The Super Bowl: Celebrating a Quarter-Century of America's Greatest Game*. New York: Simon & Schuster, 1990, Wiebusch, John, Editor-in-Chief. A good article from a player's perspective on that Super Bowl is "The Game I'll Never Forget," *Football Digest*, September 1972, Smith, Bubba, as told to Billings, Bob. Finally, "Super Bowl V and the End of the AFL," *Coffin Corner*, November/December 2013, 4–10, by Bert Gambini, is a great article on how Super Bowl V was the end of an era in pro football.

1971

The Growth of NFL Stadiums increased greatly during the 1971 season. Helpful information on this topic can be found inside the pages of: *The Official NFL Encyclopedia of Pro Football*, New York: NAL Books, 1982, Barron, Bill, et al., eds. Also informative is "Pro Stars Rate the Playing Fields." *Football Digest,* November 1976, 30–36, Bortstein, Larry. Another good article about seating preferences in the newer stadiums is "Where Watching Football Is the Living End ... Zone." *Pro!*, October 17, 1976, 3D–6D, Pollack, Joe. A good pictorial article on the league's stadiums is "Like a Living Thing." *Pro!* December 10, 1972, 3B–12B, Boss, David. Finally, a good article focusing on the building of new stadiums is "Designs on Football's Future." *Pro!* October 9, 1977, 3B–14B, Stillwell, Paul.

Willie Ellison of the Los Angeles Rams set a new league rushing record on December 5, 1971, when he ran for 247 yards against the New Orleans Saints. A good article is "The 247-Yard Rushing Day." *Football Digest*, December 1973, 60–61.

The NFL's Longest Game was an epic playoff matchup on Christmas Day in Kansas City. Great sources are found in these articles: "Garo Makes Up for Pro Bowl Snub." *The Independent Press-Telegram*, December 26, 1971, S-4. "Yepremian, Miami Take Big Step." *The Montana Standard*, December 26, 1971, 9. A chapter in *Kansas City Chiefs: Great Teams' Great Years* is a must read. It is published by New York: Macmillan, 1974, Connor, Dick. A great article on sudden death epics in pro football is "O, Sudden Death, Where Is Thy Sting?" PRO! December 22, 1974, 3B–7B, Bennett, Tom. Ed Podolak was the main hero of that unforgettable playoff contest, albeit in a losing effort. His story "I Remember." *Pro! Magazine*, November 30, 1975, 34, Podolak, Ed, is a great first-person story. Also a couple of good accounts of the game is "The Game I'll Never Forget." *Football Digest*, October 1972, 63–66, Dawson, Len, as told to Billings, Bob; and "The Game I'll Never Forget." *Football Digest*, November 1974, 32–35, Lanier, Willie, as told to Billings, Bob. "Overtime Games: Good or Bad for Pro Football?" *Football Digest*, October 1976, 44–53, dissects how the coaches and players adjusted to overtime games after a few years of dealing with them. Also be sure to check out "How the Chiefs Lost Longest Game in History." *Football Digest*, April 1972, 27–37, by Frank Ross, for a good drive-by-drive report on the game. Finally, three more good articles are "The Game I'll Never Forget." *Football Digest*, April 1976, 70–74, Podolak, Ed, as told to Payne, Dave; "Jan Stenerud: He Can't Help but Remember." *Football Digest*, April 1976, 76–78, Luksa, Frank; and Pro! Talk. "A Con-

versation with Garo Yepremian." *Pro!* Divisional Playoff Edition, December 22, 1974, 15A–17A.

The Rise of the Dallas Cowboys in their first championship season is chronicled within the following: *The Dallas Cowboys: Winning the Big One.* New York: Grosset & Dunlap, 1972, Perkins, Steve. Also informative is *Dallas Cowboys: Great Teams' Great Years.* New York: Macmillan, 1974, Meyers, Jeff. The best book that I found on Dallas head coach Tom Landry is *The Man Inside ... Landry.* Waco: Word, 1979, St. John, Bob. *The Dallas Cowboys: An Illustrated History.* New York: Harper & Row, 1981, Whittingham, Richard, is a good book to tie-in all of the history of the club.

Super Bowl VI saw Dallas finally win a world title. Good sources on that game include: "A Cowboy Stampede." *Sports Illustrated*, January 24, 1972, 10–15. Also *The Dallas Cowboys: Winning the Big One.* New York: Grosset & Dunlap, 1972, Perkins, Steve. Dallas quarterback Roger Staubach recalls his success in the game in *Time Enough to Win.* Waco: Word, 1980, Staubach, Roger with Luksa, Frank. Also, National Football League Properties, *The Super Bowl: Celebrating a Quarter-Century of America's Greatest Game.* New York: Simon & Schuster, 1990, Wiebusch, John, Editor-in-Chief, gives great information on this game. Some good articles on Super Bowl VI includes: "Dallas Had Edge in Talent and Team Effort." *Football Digest*, April 1972, 14–16, Markus, Robert; "Cowboys' Front Line Made Big Difference." *Football Digest*, April 1972, 17–20, Young, Dick; "John Niland the Cowboys' Unsung Hero." *Football Digest*, May-June 1972, 16–20, Bortstein, Larry; and "The Game I'll Never Forget." *Football Digest*, November 1975, 40–44, Staubach, Roger, as told to Luksa, Frank.

1972

Changing of the Hashmarks: Perhaps no single change in the way that the game was played in the decade occurred in 1972, when the hashmarks on the playing fields were moved in closer to each other. The idea behind the change was to give wide receivers more room to run their routes, but the game's running backs would get more room too, and it is they who profited the most over the years from the change. A good source for the results of running backs who succeeded thanks to the change in the hashmarks can be found in a statistical analysis in PRO!, August 18, 1973, "The Magic Numbers: 1000 and 100." You can also find an excellent chart on comparative statistics between 1971 and 1972 in the August 1973 issue of *Football Digest*, on page 62. A good article on the success of the pro running game is "In 1972 the Running Game Came Alive Again." *Football Digest*, February 1973, 17–19, Durslag, Melvin. Conversely, a good article on why the movement of the hashmarks harmed the pro passing game can be found by reading "How Hashmarks Rule

Hurt the Passing Game." *Football Digest*, February 1974, 48–50, Oates, Bob.

The Namath-Unitas Duel: I found that the best source of information on this famous matchup which occurred on September 24, 1972, comes from the NFL Films' NFL Game of the Week footage. The NFL Films special order catalog includes the highlights of this game for public sale. A very informative article on that game comes from the recipient of many of Namath's passes on that day, Rich Caster (as told to Payne, Dave), "The Game I'll Never Forget." *Football Digest*, February 1978, 36–38.

The Pack is Back was a bumper sticker slogan seen in Wisconsin in response to the 1972 season. Green Bay's sudden success in 1972 is documented in the following articles: "John Brockington: Green Bay's Td Weapon." *Football Digest*, November 1972, 48–50, Bledsoe, Terry, and "Pack Has Reversed NFL Image." *The Capital Times*, December 11, 1972, 23, United Press International. Another good source is "Lane Lauds Packs Great Team Effort." *The Capital Times*, December 11, 1972, 23, United Press International. Also informative is a recap of Green Bay's 1972 season in "Season of Change: The 1972 Packers." *PFRA Annual*, 1988, 83–96, Zagorski, Joe; and an editorial from John Kuenster in *Football Digest*, March 1973, 4–7.

Washington's super season was the hallmark of George Allen's coaching career. Good sources for the 1972 Redskins season include: "Larry Brown: The Redskins' Superstar." *Football Digest*, March 1972, 32–39, White, Russ, and *Washington Redskins: Great Teams' Great Years*. New York: Macmillan Publishing Company, Inc., 1974, Clary, Jack. A good article on Washington's victory in the 1972 NFC title game is "The Game I'll Never Forget." *Football Digest*, October 1981, 76–79, Kilmer, Billy, as told to Payne, Dave.

The Immaculate Reception was the name that was given to Franco Harris' miracle catch and touchdown in the Steelers' first playoff game ever. Sources on the play include "Frenchy Fuqua Remembers Franco's Miracle Catch." *Football Digest*, January 1975, 28–30, Stellino, Vito, and "Great Games of the 1970s." *PRO!*, August 16, 1980, Rollow, Cooper. "A Football Life: The Immaculate Reception." *NFL Films*, 2013, is a concise visual look at key memories of the epic play from the players, coaches, and fans involved. A good article from Jack Tatum's point of view is "The Game I'll Never Forget." *Football Digest*, December 1975, 32–38, Tatum, Jack, as told to Payne, Dave. Another good article is "The Game I'll Never Forget." *Football Digest*, January 1974, 29–31, Russell, Andy, as told to Billings, Bob. One of the most answer-filled articles that I found on the Immaculate Reception is "Former NFL Official Fred Swearingen Speaks Out." *Football Digest*, April 1982, 78–85, Dwyer, Bill. In the end, you really have to see the film (who hasn't?), then decide for yourself if either Jack Tatum or John Fuqua was the last

player to touch the deflected ball before Harris made his signature play.

Dallas' Playoff Comeback in 1972 took a back seat in history to Pittsburgh's Immaculate Reception victory (both of which occurred on the same day), but the following articles describe the Dallas win over San Francisco in detail: "Staubach Rallies Dallas, 30–28." *The Daily Review*, December 24, 1972, 17, Tonelli, Charles. Also *30 Years of Pro Football's Great Moments*. New York: Rutledge Books, 1976, Clary, Jack, and "Great Games of the 1970s." *PRO!*, August 16, 1980, Rollow, Cooper.

The Undefeated Dolphins are as much a study of a spectacular team as a study of a spectacular coach. Reading *The Gamemakers: Winning Philosophies of Eight NFL Coaches*. Chicago: Follett, 1976, Clary, Jack, is a must to learn how Don Shula prepared his team for perfection. A good source for the 1972 AFC title game is "Number 16 … On the Way to 17–0." *PRO!* January 1, 1978, Berger, Dan. Another good article which tackles each game of that glorious season is "Remember When…." *Football Digest*, March 1983, 70–79, Strother, Shelby.

Super Bowl VII has plenty of good articles, including: *Prolog: The Official National Football League Annual for 1973*. Los Angeles: Dell, 1973, Oates, Jr., Bob, and *the Sporting News Super Bowl Book*, St. Louis: The Sporting News, 1987, Reidenbaugh, Lowell and Attner, Paul. Miami All-Pro offensive guard Larry Little describes the game in "The Game I'll Never Forget." *Football Digest*, March 1979, 80–83, Little, Larry, as told to Payne, Dave.

1973

Blackout Rule: I could not find a lot on this topic, but the best article that I discovered was "NFL Issues a 'Yellow Paper' on TV Blackouts." *The Washington Post*, February 17, 1973, Brady, Dave. Fans of losing teams would rarely get a chance to see their teams on television except when they played their road games. The idea of blacking out home games if they were not sold out at least 72 hours prior to kickoff was intended to get the public to buy more tickets. If a game was blacked out, the local market would televise a different game, usually from a contending team. Small wonder why so many fans in the New York audiences started to become Cowboys and Steelers fans in the 1970s. A good article on how fans at the games accepted television's impact on the pro game is "How Television Affects Pro Football Spectators." *Football Digest*, November 1977, 36–39, Queenan, Bob.

Ray May and Holding Hands in Denver: Yes, it was certainly unique and for some observers, somewhat strange … the sight of seeing grown men holding hands in the huddle. Today, it is commonplace. "Broncos: Right Spot, Right Time." *The Colorado Springs Gazette Telegraph*, November 19, 1973, 3-B, Associated Press, is a good article on the subject. Also informative is information on

Denver head coach John Ralston from *The Gamemakers: Winning Philosophies of Eight NFL Coaches.* Chicago: Follett, 1976, Clary, Jack.

Rookies helping several teams succeed: Some key rookies helped to resurrect teams like Chicago and Cincinnati. The Bears drafted defensive lineman Wally Chambers, and he immediately lent strength to Chicago's pass rush. The Bengals drafted a virtual nobody in running back Boobie Clark, but no one could have predicted his worth to the Bengals in 1973. Check out "Rookie All-Stars of 1973." *Football Digest*, March 1974, 30–37, Billings, Bob; "How Bengals' Boobie Clark Bounded Out of Obscurity." *Football Digest*, March 1974, 38–41, Eldridge, Larry, Jr.; and "Wally Chambers: Big Man for the New Chicago Bears." *Football Digest*, November 1975, 21–26, Pierson, Don.

Minnesota comes back to the top: "Vikings Full of Surprises." *The Huron Daily Plainsman*, December 31, 1973, 10, Associated Press. "Tarkenton Sheds Tag with Touch of Bitterness." *The Danville (Virginia) Bee*, December 31, 1973, 8, Associated Press. Minnesota was absent from the playoffs in 1972, but they came back strong in 1973, as they won the NFC Central Division, and then the conference championship.

Cincinnati comes back to win the AFC Central: Check out the legacy of the great Hall of Fame coach Paul Brown in *The Gamemakers: Winning Philosophies of Eight NFL Coaches.* Chicago: Follett, 1976, Clary, Jack. The 1973 Cincinnati Bengals team highlight film entitled *Here Come the Bengals*, written and directed by Louis Schmidt, is also worth a view. The 1973 season marked Cincinnati's second division championship of the decade.

O.J. Simpson's 2003-yard Odyssey: "O.J. Simpson: Player of the Year." *Football Digest*, March 1974, 18–23, Kuenster, John. An extensive article on Simpson's spectacular year and his offensive line can be found in an official NFL publication called *Profile*. Another couple of good articles: "The Game I'll Never Forget." *Football Digest*, September 1974, 32–36, Simpson, O.J., as told to Billings, Bob; and "The Electric Company: Buffalo's Big Blockers." *Football Digest*, March 1974, 48–53, Felser, Larry. For a good gauge on Simpson's best games, check out "O.J. Simpson's Six Greatest Performances." *Football Digest*, June 1977, 82–92, Baker, Jim. Finally, a good retrospective article is "I'll Never Forget … 2003: O.J.'S Odyssey." *Gameday*, September 5, 1983, 12D, Thalman, L. Budd.

Miami Repeats as World Champions: National Football League Properties, *The Super Bowl: Celebrating a Quarter-Century of America's Greatest Game.* New York: Simon & Schuster, 1990, Wiebusch, John, Editor-in-Chief. Miami head coach Don Shula talks extensively on the subject in the book *The Gamemakers: Winning Philosophies of Eight NFL Coaches.* Chicago: Follett, 1976, Clary, Jack. Two good articles on Super Bowl VIII are "How

Miami Zonked Minnesota." *Football Digest*, April 1974, 18–23, Oates, Bob; and "An Inside Look at the Super Bowl." *Football Digest*, April 1974, 28–30, Butkus, Dick.

1974

The unparalleled 1974 draft of the Pittsburgh Steelers is still being talked about today. One of the most recent sources worth watching is NFL Films' *Caught in the Draft 1974*, which details the Steelers' selections of Lynn Swann, Jack Lambert, John Stallworth, and Mike Webster. It was the only time in league history where one team obtained four future Hall of Famers in the same draft. A good article on the supposed success of the draft is "Who Won the 1974 Player Draft?" *Football Digest*, June 1974, 18–26, Felser, Larry.

The New Rules Changes of 1974 did much to aid the offenses throughout the NFL. A short but informative article on the subject is "NFL Coaches Discuss New Rule Changes," *New Castle News,* May 22, 1974, 44, UPI. Another good article is "Getting a Kick Out of the New Rules." *Pro!* September 22, 1974, 3C–7C, Oates, Bob, Jr.

The emergence of the World Football League left an undeniable legacy on the 1970s in pro football. The struggling WFL failed to last two full seasons due to a lack of overall funds, but it did eventually bring about higher player salaries. Bob Billings contributed a good article describing the main points in the new league in "How the WFL Will Change Pro Football." *Football Digest*, August 1974, 20–25. Jack Clary added a good article on the failure of the WFL in "The World Football League Had a World of Troubles." *Football Digest*, November 1983, 28–31. Also a good article which described an individual player's decision to jump to another league is "Why Paul Warfield Left Miami." *Football Digest*, September 1975, 60–63, Coughlin, Dan. Finally, a good retrospective article is "WFL Flashback." *Football Digest*, June 1978, 60–71, MacLean, Norm.

The Players' Strike of 1974 was unique in that it was (at least as far as I could research) the first pro football strike in America where the players were seen all across the land actually holding picket signs and walking picket lines, much like the rank and file members of the Teamsters Union, among others. It was an unusual scene to say the least. The public would gain an insight into labor relations in the NFL during the summer of 1974. Several informative articles include: "NFL Players Agree to Strike If Demands Aren't Met." *The Asbury Park (New Jersey) Evening Press*, March 7, 1974, 37; "Eagle Vet Picket Line Fails to Stop Rookies." *The Philadelphia Inquirer*, July 10, 1974; and "Player Agreement Likely, with No Strike, NFL Told." *The Philadelphia Inquirer*, February 27, 1974, Forbes, Gordon. A good video to watch is "Rebels in the NFL," *Double J Films*, 2011. Produced by Jay Meyers. It gives a good background to the strike and includes many good insights from the players involved. Also, there were some players who disagreed with the decision to strike. Check out "Curtis Would Ignore Strike." *The Baltimore Sun*, March 30, 1974, Snyder, Cameron C. Player representatives from the 26 teams discuss their votes for a strike in: "Ex-Player Reps Recall the 1974 Player Strike." *Football Digest*, January 1983, 50–61, Jackson, Derrick. Finally, a good retrospective on several important elements of the strike can be read in an article on one of the foremost proponents of the strike: "Alan Page Proved the Vikings Wrong." *Football Digest*, June 1980, 50–55, Green, Ted.

The outstanding 1974 season of Denver running back Otis Armstrong was an anomaly of sorts. It was the only year that he led the NFL in rushing, as he interrupted the four years that O.J. Simpson led the league in rushing (1972, 1973, 1975, and 1976). A great film to watch Armstrong's feats is the 1974 Denver Broncos team highlight film, entitled *Across the Great Divide*, written and directed by Bob Carmichael. Also providing insight is the chapter on Denver head coach John Ralston in the book *The Gamemakers: Winning Philosophies of Eight NFL Coaches*. Chicago: Follett, 1976, Clary, Jack.

The Cinderella 1974 season of the St. Louis Cardinals is chronicled nicely in the website Pro Football Reference.com. The Cardinals 1974 team highlight film *Big Play Big Season* also shows plenty of the great plays which helped St. Louis reach the playoffs for the first time in the decade. The film was written and directed by Louis Schmidt. A good editorial on this dynamic teams can be found in the January 1975 issue of *Football Digest* magazine. Look for John Kuenster's *Out of the Huddle* editorial on pages 5–8. Another good article focusing on the St. Louis offense is "The Big Surprise of 1974." *Football Digest*, February 1975, 18–23, Meyers, Jeff. Finally, the main catalyst for the St. Louis offense was multi-purpose back Terry Metcalf. A good article on his exploits is "Terry Metcalf: Pro Football's Most Exciting Player." *Football Digest*, November 1976, 23–28, Barnidge, Tom.

Clint Longley's Thanksgivings Day Miracle: Check out the book *The Dallas Cowboys: An Illustrated History*. New York: Harper & Row, 1981, Whittingham, Richard. Also be sure to watch the 1974 Dallas Cowboys highlight film, entitled *A Champion in Waiting*, written and directed by Bob Ryan. In what was the worst season of the decade for the Cowboys, Longley's performance in that Thanksgivings Day victory over the hated Washington Redskins was one of the few bright spots that the team had in 1974.

The Sea of Hands Game was an obvious choice for NFL Films to showcase in their weekly NFL Game of the Week series. The Oakland Raiders managed to end the three-year reign of the Miami Dolphins as the standard bearers of the American Football Conference championship. Some other good sources on this AFC Divisional Playoff Game include *The Scrapbook History of Pro*

Football (Expanded and Updated). Indianapolis: Bobbs-Merrill, 1979, Cohen, Richard M., Deutsch, Jordan A., and Neft, David S. A great article on Oakland quarterback Ken Stabler's two-minute decisions in that game can be found by reading "NFL Playbook Two-Minute Offense." *Pro! Magazine*, August 25, 1979, 15D, Cassady, Steve.

The first world championships for the Pittsburgh Steelers was 42 years in the making, but it finally happened in 1974. The Steelers highlight film that year entitled *Super Steelers* provides a good introduction to the team, as does NFL Films' *America's Game* series. More good information can be found in the book *The Sporting News Super Bowl Book*, St. Louis: The Sporting News, 1987, Reidenbaugh, Lowell and Attner, Paul. Another source of good information comes from the National Football League Properties book, *The Super Bowl: Celebrating a Quarter-Century of America's Greatest Game*. New York: Simon & Schuster, 1990, Wiebusch, John, Editor-in-Chief.

1975

The Louisiana Superdome and Pontiac Stadium were two of the leagues newest and most modern venues which opened in 1975. Many new stadiums were unveiled in the 1970s, and these two had features which were futuristic, to say the least. The facts and figures on these two arenas can be found in the book *Total Football: The Official Encyclopedia of the National Football League*. New York: HarperCollins, 1997, Carroll, Bob, Gershman, Michael, Neft, David, and Thorn, John.

Offensive Strategy in the NFL got a boost over the defenses in 1975 when Dallas head coach Tom Landry resurrected the old "Shotgun" offense. Several good articles on Landry's decision are "Is the Dallas Shotgun a Rinky-Dink Offense?" *Football Digest*, October 1976, 20–26, Luksa, Frank; "Using the Spread Is a Loaded Expression." *Pro!* November 1981, 25–26, Madden, John, with Cassady, Steve; and "Why the Dallas Offense Worked So Well in '75." *Football Digest*, February 1976, 40–42, Didinger, Ray. Another good article which traces the history of the formation from its earliest days in 1960 is "Riding Shotgun." *Pro!* August 1981, 98–106, Fox, Larry.

Mel Gray's controversial catch against the Washington Redskins in Week 9 of the 1975 season provided audiences with one of the more memorable questionable plays of the decade. The referees discussed the play, then declared that Gray had possession of the ball long enough to score a legitimate touchdown. Members of the opposing Washington Redskins disagreed with the decision. The best source of information for this play comes from an Associated Press article "Allen Can't Believe It." *Oakland Tribune*, November 17, 1975, 95. Another good source is the Cardinals 1975 highlight film, entitled *Car-*

diac Cards, and written and directed by Louis Schmidt. You'll have to decide for yourself if you think the referees blew it or not.

The Dallas Cowboys rebounded to win the NFC championship in 1975. Good stories on that remarkable team can be read in Richard Whittingham's book *The Dallas Cowboys: An Illustrated History*. New York: Harper & Row, 1981; and in Thomas Henderson's autobiography (with Peter Knobler) *Out of Control: Confessions of an NFL Casualty*, New York: G.P. Putnam's Sons, 1987.

The Hail Mary Pass became one of those iconic plays, similar in importance in league history to the Immaculate Reception. It's origin is best described by its inventor, Dallas quarterback Roger Staubach. A good read on this subject are from the following books: *Time Enough to Win*. Waco: Word, 1980, Staubach, Roger with Luksa, Frank; *Dallas Cowboys: The First 25 Years*. Dallas: Taylor, 1984, Stowers, Carlton. A good Associated Press article can be found with "Did Pearson Push Viking in Miracle?" *Star News*, December 29, 1975, 42.

The NFL cheerleaders were around for many of the league's teams prior to the 1970s, but in 1975, the television networks started to pay more attention to these beautiful young ladies on the sidelines. The Dallas Cowboys cheerleaders were (and still are) the NFL's most popular cheerleading squad. More information on them and the rise of the NFL cheerleaders can be found in *A Decade of Dreams*. Dallas: Taylor Publishing Company, 1982, Evans, Mary Candace. The magazine *Dallas Cowboys Cheerleaders "A Touch of Class."* Jordan & Company Publishers, Inc., 1979, is also worth a look. An article by Bill Sullivan in *Dave Campbell's Dallas Cowboys Magazine (1978 Outlook)* entitled "The Dallas Cowboys' "Other" Super Team" is a nice article as well. Other cheerleader squads across the league can be discovered by reading: "NFL Cheerleaders: The Hottest New Teams in Pro Football." *Pro!* September 9, 1978, 3B–9B, Natal, Jim; and "Girls of the Game." *Pro!* September 9, 1977, 9B–14B, Brock, Ted.

Super Bowl X was the decade's first truly great Super Bowl. Many people still regard it as one of the best ever. Good books that cover the game include *The Sporting News Super Bowl Book*, St. Louis: The Sporting News, 1987, Reidenbaugh, Lowell and Attner, Paul; National Football League Properties. *The Super Bowl: Celebrating a Quarter-Century of America's Greatest Game*. New York: Simon & Schuster, 1990, Wiebusch, John, Editor-in-Chief. A great article on this game can be found in the following year's Super Bowl game program: "Super Bowl X." *Super Bowl XI Game Program*, January 9, 1977, 37–44, Oates, Bob, Jr. There are plenty of other good articles on the game. Some of them are "How We Won!" *Football Digest*, April 1976, 14–21, Swann, Lynn, as told to Payne, Dave; "This One Was Super." *Football Digest*, April 1976, 22–26, Zimmerman, Paul; "Should Dallas Have Run More?" *Football Digest*, April 1976, 28–31, Roswell, Gene; and "Cowboys

Blast 'Cheap Shot' Steelers." *Football Digest*, April 1976, 34–37, Forbes, Gordon.

1976

The NFL expanded in 1976 with two new teams, the Tampa Bay Buccaneers and the Seattle Seahawks. The Buccaneers started their franchise with a record of 0–26, yet within four years, they would make it to the NFC championship game. The best source for everything on the Tampa Bay team is author and pro football historian Denis M. Crawford. A great read is his book *Hugh Culverhouse and the Tampa Bay Buccaneers: How a Skinflint Genius with a Losing Team Made the Modern NFL*, Jefferson, NC: McFarland, 2011. I found a great source on the origins of the Seattle Seahawks' Kingdome in *The Kingdome Magazine*, March 1976. Several good articles on the subject of expansion teams include: "Expansion Teams: The NFL's Biggest Winners & Losers." *Football Digest*, April 1977, 58–67, Bortstein, Larry; "Year One—An Evaluation: The Seattle Seahawks." *Football Digest*, April 1977, 68–73, Fair, Don; "Year One—An Evaluation: The Tampa Bay Buccaneers." *Football Digest*, April 1977, 74–80, McEwen, Tom; "No Respect for Their Elders." *Pro!* August 25, 1979, 7D–13D, Clary, Jack; and "An Expansion Year: Seattle." *Pro!* December 14, 1975, 3D–8D, Rockne, Dick.

The American Bicentennial: The best source for pro football's celebration of the 1976 is welcomed in the Super Bowl X Game Program. Not only is the Vince Lombardi Trophy majestically placed next to a draped American flag on the cover of the program, but some of the information in the program describes the Bicentennial celebration to be seen at the game.

Pittsburgh's Steel Curtain Defense in 1976: Few defenses could compare to this defense during the course of the decade, particularly during the second half of the season. A good source to chart Pittsburgh's week-by-week progress is *Prolog: The Official National Football League Annual for 1977*. Los Angeles: Dell, 1977. In today's score-a-minute pro offenses, it is doubtful if any future team could come close to duplicating what the 1976 Steeler defense accomplished, namely five shutouts in their final eight regular season games.

New England's Spirit of '76: Few people felt that a team like New England, who had only three wins in 1975, would be able to win much more than that in 1976. But they surprised everyone in this Bicentennial season, winning the AFC wild card spot with 11 victories. The best information on this team can be found in their 1976 highlight film entitled *The Second Revolution*, written and directed by Bob Ryan.

No rivalry in the decade matched the brutal rivalry seen between the Steelers and the Raiders. A couple of great articles on the organized bloodletting between these two teams can be found in the October 1977 issue of Football Digest. Check out "The Raiders Say … 'We Beat 'Em Last Year, We'll Beat 'Em Again.'" *Football Digest*, October 1977, 24–36, Payne, Dave; "The Steelers Say … 'We've Got Some Paying Back to Do.'" *Football Digest*, October 1977, 24–36, Stellino, Vito; and "Inside Free Safety with Oakland's Jack Tatum." *Football Digest*, December 1976, 46–54, Payne, Dave.

The Raiders "Steal" one in the playoffs: The New England Patriots easily defeated the Oakland Raiders in the fourth week of the 1976 regular season, and it appeared that they were ready to beat them again in the first round of the playoffs. But the Raiders benefitted from a couple of questionable calls by the referees, and lost a game that they probably should have won. The best source for reviewing Oakland's 24–21 playoff win over New England is NFL Films' *NFL Game of the Week*, which was produced immediately following the game on December 18, 1976. A good article on the game is "The Game I'll Never Forget." *Football Digest*, February 1979, 86–90, Hamilton, Ray, as told to Payne, Dave.

Super Bowl XI: Oakland wins their first Super Bowl over the Minnesota Vikings. The following books provide good information: *The Sporting News Super Bowl Book*, St. Louis: *The Sporting News*, 1987, Reidenbaugh, Lowell and Attner, Paul; National Football League Properties. *The Super Bowl: Celebrating a Quarter-Century of America's Greatest Game*. New York: Simon & Schuster, 1990, Wiebusch, John, Editor-in-Chief. Several good articles on the game include: "How Oakland Pulverized the Vikings." *Football Digest*, April 1977, 14–17, Guback, Steve; "How Art Shell and Gene Upshaw Whipped the Minnesota Defense." *Football Digest*, April 1977, 18–22, Payne, Dave; "Sensational Is Routine for Fred Biletnikoff." *Football Digest*, April 1977, 26–27, Didinger, Ray; "Clarence Davis: The Raiders' Unsung Hero." *Football Digest*, April 1977, 38–39, Elderkin, Phil; "Linebacker Willie Hall: Key to the '76 Raiders' Success." *Football Digest*, April 1977, 40–45, Payne, Dave; "The Game I'll Never Forget." *Football Digest*, January 1979, 48–54, Biletnikoff, Fred, as told to Payne, Dave; and "The Game I'll Never Forget." *Football Digest*, June 1981, 74–77, Brown, Willie, as told to Payne, Dave.

1977

"Broncomania": The fervor unleashed by the city of Denver, Colorado, in the midst of Denver's Cinderella 1977 season, is captured best in the book *Broncos! The Team That Makes Miracles Happen*, New York: Stein & Day, 1978, Sahadi, Lou. A good article on Denver's glorious victory in the 1977 AFC championship game is "The Game I'll Never Forget." *Football Digest*, September 1980, 72–77, Swenson, Bob, as told to Payne, Dave. Author Dick Connor aptly describes the infectious feel-

ings of the Bronco fans during the 1977 season in: "Painting the Town Orange." *Pro!* September 3, 1978, 3C–11C.

The Chicago Bears made the NFL playoffs in 1977, and it was their first playoff appearance since they won the NFL championship in 1963. Their main (and some say only) weapon on that team was their terrific and future Hall of Fame halfback Walter Payton. On November 20 of that year, Payton rushed for 275 yards against rival Minnesota, and thus broke O.J. Simpson's single-game rushing record. The Bears needed an incredible and frantic victory over the Giants on the season's final Sunday to earn their ticket to the postseason. Check out the Associated Press article "Bears Playoff Bound After Overtime Win." *Panama City News Herald*, December 19, 1977, 18; and the Bears 1977 highlight film entitled *A Season in the Sun*, written and directed by Mike Adams.

The Rams lost another playoff game to Minnesota in 1977, this time in Los Angeles. The game was played in a quagmire, much to the Vikings' delight. To see just how much mud was on the Coliseum field that day, watch NFL Films' *This Week in Pro Football* Vikings-Rams segment following the December 26 game.

The Epic 1977 AFC Divisional Playoff: See "Casper's Few Catches Count Most." *Argus*, December 25, 1977, 22. NFL Films' *Ghost to the Post* in the NFL's Greatest Games series is also a fine depiction of the double overtime contest between the Raiders and the Colts. A superlative article on the game is "Shootout on Christmas Eve." *Pro!* January 7, 1979, 3B–14B, Zampa, Mike. Oakland defensive lineman John Matuszak saw his share of great games, but the 1977 playoff win over the Colts was his most memorable. His recollections of that contest can be read here: "The Game I'll Never Forget." *Football Digest*, November 1982, 78–81, Matuszak, John, as told to Janoff, Barry.

The Dallas Cowboys ended Denver's dream of a world championship when they defeated the Broncos in Super Bowl XII. A key ingredient to helping the Cowboys win their second world title was a flashy Heisman Trophy–winning halfback named Tony Dorsett. Good information on Dorsett and his rise to greatness can be found in: "Tony Dorsett Rookie of the Year." *Football Digest*, March 1978, 28–33, Luksa, Frank; and in the book *Dallas Cowboys: The First 25 Years*. Dallas: Taylor Publishing Company, 1984, Stowers, Carlton. You can also get direct information from Dorsett himself by watching NFL Films' *America's Game* series, featuring the 1977 Dallas Cowboys.

Good sources on Super Bowl XII include: *Dallas Cowboys: The First 25 Years*. Dallas: Taylor, 1984, Stowers, Carlton; *The Dallas Cowboys: An Illustrated History*. New York: Harper & Row, 1981, Whittingham, Richard; *Time Enough to Win*. Waco: Word, 1980, Staubach, Roger with Luksa, Frank; "Newhouse Wiped Stickum, Stuck 'Em." *Dallas Cowboys Weekly*, January, 21, 1978, 3, 27, St. John,

Bob. A referee's point of view on Super Bowl XII is Art Holst's book, *Sunday Zebras*. Illinois: Forest Publishing, 1980. Also good information can be found by reading "How We Won!" *Football Digest*, April 1978, 12–17, Martin, Harvey, as told to Buck, Ray; and "How the Cowboys Crushed the Broncos' Dreams." *Football Digest*, April 1978, 18–31, Paige, Woodrow Jr.

1978

A bunch of new rule changes were introduced to the league in 1978, and they opened up the offenses like never before. See "New Blocking Rules Give an Edge to Scrambling QBs." *Football Digest*, October 1978, 38–40, Guback, Steve; and "It's Time to Change the Rules and Protect the Quarterbacks." *Football Digest*, December 1977, 30–36, MacLean, Norm, for information on the new rules. Miami head coach Don Shula was against the majority of the new rules changes. See "We Should Have Left the Rules Alone." *Football Digest*, October 1978, 41–43, Lincicome, Bernie, for information on Shula's opinions. Also sharing Shula's point of view was Oakland All-Pro tight end Dave Casper. Check out "Even Dave Casper Doesn't Like the New 'Dave Casper Rule.'" *Football Digest*, November 1978, 62–63, Miller, Ira.

The New Schedule for 1978 included two more regular season games and two less preseason games. It also increased the league's playoff participants to five teams for each conference. Information on these changes can be found by reading "How the 16-Game Schedule Will Change Pro Football." *Football Digest*, August 1978, 28–34, Payne, Dave. Another good article discussing the results of the 1978 season is "1978 Wrap-Up: A Wild and Crazy Season." *Football Digest*, April 1979, 78–85, Jeansonne, John. Finally, NFL Commissioner Pete's Rozelle's descriptions of the new schedule-making process can be found by reading: "Game Plan '78." *Pro!* December 4, 1977, 3B–4B, Rozelle, Pete.

Oakland safety Jack Tatum hit New England wide receiver Darryl Stingley in a preseason game which affected both players forever. Indeed the majority of what was written about the incident surrounded Tatum. A good read is *They Call Me Assassin*. New York: Everest House Publishers, 1979, Tatum, Jack, with Kusher, Bill. Good articles include: "Talking Football With ... Jack Tatum." *Football Digest*, September 1980, 56–60, Lundgren, Hal; and "'I Don't Play Dirty,'—Jack Tatum." *Football Digest*, January 1979, 32–37, Hersh, Phil.

The unexpected success of the 1978 Atlanta Falcons included hiring a former Philadelphia bartender named Tim Mazzetti to be their regular placekicker. Mazzetti's success was observed for the first time when he almost singlehandedly defeated the rival Los Angeles Rams on *Monday Night Football*. Check out the postgame article "Falcons Kick Rams." *Altoona Mirror*, October 31, 1978,

39, Smith, Walt. A good article on Mazzetti is "Tim Mazzetti: The Placekicker Who Wouldn't Quit." *Football Digest*, October 1979, 64–69, Sheeley, Glenn. Another good source is the 1978 Atlanta Falcons highlight film entitled *Mighty Men and Magic Moments*, written and directed by Bob Smith. A good article on Atlanta's very first playoff game is "The Game I'll Never Forget." *Football Digest*, April 1980, 76–79, Mitchell, Jim, as told to Payne, Dave.

Dan Pastorini's secret weapon is now a common piece of equipment for many quarterbacks to wear. The flak jacket that Pastorini first wore in 1978 helped him to play, and play well despite badly injured ribs that he sustain near the end of the season. A good story on the original football flak jacket can be found in the United Press International article "Donzis' Creations Save Oilers from Collapsing." *New Castle News*, November 17, 1979, 15.

Super Bowl XIII was the highest scoring Super Bowl of the decade. It was also one of the most exciting, with a wealth of pivotal plays. There is no shortage of quality information on this game, but I found these sources to be some of the best: "Was It Interference or Not?" *Football Digest*, April 1979, 37–41, Zimmerman, Paul; *The Super Bowl: Celebrating a Quarter-Century of America's Greatest Game*. New York: Simon & Schuster, 1990, Wiebusch, John, Editor-in-Chief. National Football League Properties; "Superduper Bowl." *Super Bowl XIV Program*, January 20, 1980, 43–55, Cassady, Steve; *Out of Control: Confessions of an NFL Casualty*. New York: G.P. Putnam's Sons, 1987, Henderson, Thomas "Hollywood" and Knobler, Peter; and *Time Enough to Win*. Waco, Texas: Word, Inc., 1980, Staubach, Roger with Luksa, Frank.

1979

Harold Carmichael breaks the consecutive game receiving record: On Sunday, November 4, 1979, Philadelphia Eagles wide receiver Harold Carmichael set a new NFL record by catching at least one pass in 106 consecutive games (the record has since been broken several times by several different players). The Cleveland Browns spoiled the Eagles party by beating them in the final seconds. A good editorial on the game is "Birds Couldn't Deliver on Carmichael's Biggest Day" from Mike Gibson of *The Doylestown Intelligencer*, November 5, 1979, 43.

Minnesota safety Paul Krause broke Hall of Fame defensive back Emlen Tunnell's all-time NFL career interception record in 1979. Read up on Krause in "Paul Krause: Minnesota's Quiet Thief." *Football Digest*, November 1975, 52–53, Hartman, Sid; and *Prolog: The Official National Football League Annual for 1980*. Los Angeles: Dell, 1980, Boss, David.

Vernon Perry's classic playoff conquest of San Diego was the main ingredient in pulling off one of the league's greatest playoff upsets. A good article on Perry's game of a lifetime is from the Associated Press entitled "Oilers,

Buccaneers Pull Off Upsets." *Paris News*, December 30, 1979, 13. Perry's own recollections can be read at: "The Game I'll Never Forget." *Football Digest*, December 1981, 72–76, Perry, Vernon, as told to Lundgren, Hal.

The Mike Renfro "Non" catch helped to define the 1979 AFC championship game. The play was one of the most prominent examples given by advocates of using an instant replay system to help the referees. Two good articles describing this event are "NFL Playoffs Suffer Blurred Vision Attack," *Santa Fe New Mexican*, January 7, 1980, 50 (from the Associated Press), and "Controversial Call Makes Loss Bitter One." *Clearfield Progress*, January 7, 1980, 14 (from United Press International). Several differing opinions on the worth of instant replay can be read at "Why Instant Replays Won't Solve Controversial Plays." *Football Digest*, June 1976, 90–92, Guback, Steve; "Let's Keep Instant Replay Out of Pro Football." *Football Digest*, June 1980, 6–7, Meyers, Georg N.; and "NFL Refs Should Use Instant Replay." *Football Digest*, April 1982, 4–5, Boesch, Barry. A good retrospective article on referee mistakes during the latter part of the decade can be found by reading: "Zebras: On the Spot Again This Year." *Football Digest*, January 1979, 66–69, Scholl, Bill.

Tampa Bay's "Worst to First" 1979 season: The best source for information on Tampa Bay's incredible turnaround comes from Denis G. Crawford's book, *Hugh Culverhouse and the Tampa Bay Buccaneers: How a Skinflint Genius with a Losing Team Made the Modern NFL*. Jefferson, NC: McFarland, 2011. A good article to read on the subject is "How Tampa Bay Became a Winner." *Football Digest*, January 1980, 32–37, Oates, Bob. Finally, a good

article on stalwart Buccaneer defensive end Lee Roy Selmon is "Big Buc Lee Roy Selmon: Tampa Bay's Tower of Strength." *Football Digest*, June 1980, 22–28, McEwen, Tom.

The Courage of Jack Youngblood was exhibited throughout the 1979 postseason, as he played on what amounted to a broken leg, and led the Rams to their first Super Bowl berth. A good article on Youngblood can be found in the league's annual *Prolog* magazine: *Prolog: The Official National Football League Annual for 1980*. New York: NFL Properties, 1980. Also good is "Injured Youngblood 'An Inspiration' to Rams." *Santa Fe New Mexican*, January 7, 1980, 50, Oberjuerge, Paul.

Super Bowl XIV: The NFL's final Super Bowl of the decade was a David versus Goliath matchup, with the defending champion Steelers winning their fourth world title. Check out: "IV for XIV." *Super Bowl XV Program*, January 25, 1981, 39–48, Cassady, Steve; *The Super Bowl. Celebrating a Quarter-Century of America's Greatest Game*. New York: Simon & Schuster, 1990, Wiebusch, John, Editor-in-Chief. National Football League Properties; *The Sporting News Super Bowl Book*, St. Louis: *The Sporting News*, 1987, Reidenbaugh, Lowell and Attner, Paul. A group of interesting articles on the game include: "How Pittsburgh Won Again." *Football Digest*, April 1980, 18–25, Oates, Bob; "Vince Ferragamo Proved Himself Against the Steelers." *Football Digest*, April 1980, 40–41, Hershey, Steve; "George Allen and Merlin Olsen Analyze Super Bowl XIV." *Football Digest*, April 1980, 26–33, Payne, Dave; and "The Rams Can Be Proud of Their Performance." *Football Digest*, April 1980, 44–50, Green, Ted.

Bibliography

Articles

Alfano, Pete. "Flashback: How the AFC Was Born." *Football Digest*, March 1981, 92–96.

Allen, Larry. "Nolan Cromwell: An Unsung Star of the Strong Rams' Defense." *Football Digest*, February 1981, 48–50.

Ames, Steve. "John Brodie—Most Deadly Arm in NFL." *Football Digest*, November 1971, 14–18.

Anderson, Dick, as told to Billings, Bob. "The Game I'll Never Forget." *Football Digest*, October 1975, 40–43.

Anderson, Ken, as told to Payne, Dave. "The Game I'll Never Forget." *Football Digest*, September 1977, 43–46.

Antonucci, Mike. "Yesterday's Heroes." *Football Digest*, August 1982, 86–89.

Armstrong, Jim. "Their 15 Minutes." *Super Bowl XXXV Program*, January 28, 2001, 102–110.

Associated Press. "Allen Can't Believe It." *Oakland Tribune*, November 17, 1975, 95.

_____. "Anderson's Aerials Deflate Bills." *Newark Advocate*, November 18, 1975, 12.

_____. "Bakken Kick Lifts Big Red." *Edwardsville Intelligencer*, November 1, 1976, 8.

_____. "Baltimore Rips Bears 35–7." *Benton Harbor Herald Palladium*, September 22, 1975, 19.

_____. "Bears Playoff Bound After Overtime Win." *Panama City News Herald*, December 19, 1977, 18.

_____. "Bengal Victory Revives Reeves." *Anderson Herald Bulletin*, December 1, 1975, 16.

_____. "Bengals Wrap Up Title by Overwhelming Boston, 45–7." *Appleton Post Crescent*, December 21, 1970, 30.

_____. "Bills Put Patriots on the Hooks." *Greenfield Recorder*, November 7, 1977, 14.

_____. "Blitz Brings on Fumble, Rams Beat Denver, 13–9." *Alton Telegraph*, September 7, 1979, 22.

_____. "'Blocked Punt Disastrous'—Skorich." *The Independent Press-Telegram*, December 25, 1972, 76.

_____. "Bradshaw's Career Peaks in Steelers' Rout of Bills." *Charleston Daily Mail*, December 23, 1974, 18.

_____. "Branch's Catches Help Raiders Erase Pair of 21-Point Deficits." *Madison Capital Times*, December 4, 1979, 16.

_____. "Broncos: Right Spot, Right Time." *The Colorado Springs Gazette Telegraph*, November 19, 1973, 3-B.

_____. "Browns Close on High Note." *The Lima News*, December 20, 1971, 20.

_____. "Bucs Stay Unbeaten with Win Over Rams." *Daily Herald Suburban Chicago*, September 24, 1979, 26.

_____. "Campbell Even Stumbles Well." *Big Spring Herald*, September 3, 1979, 9.

_____. "Cardinals Died Hard." *The Danville Bee*, November 26, 1976, 36.

_____. "Cards Overcome Errors, Oilers, 24–17." *Alton Telegraph*, October 8, 1979, 55.

_____. "Career High for Braxton." *Charleston Daily Mail*, November 28, 1975, 32.

_____. "Chargers Surprise Raiders, 12–7." *Santa Ana Orange County Register*, November 21, 1977, 28.

_____. "Chiefs Come Close." *The Iola Register*, September 22, 1975, 6.

_____. "Colt Coach Is Worn Out." *The Frederick News*, December 14, 1970, 29.

_____. "Colts Gallop Past Raiders for AFC Title." *The Santa Fe New Mexican*, January 4, 1971, 63.

_____. "Colts Stunned by Thrashing." *The Hutchinson News*, January 3, 1972, 8.

_____. "Colts Win in Sudden Death." *Edwardsville Intelligencer*, December 15, 1975, 6.

_____. "Colts' Jefferson Happy Catching Unitas' Passes." *Port Arthur News*, December 27, 1970, 18.

_____. "Conrad Dobler Thinks He'll Be Watched Closely Sunday." *Mt. Vernon Register News*, November 5, 1976, 1B.

_____. "Dallas Decks Chargers, Almost Glides Too Soon." *The Odessa American*, November 6, 1972, 17.

_____. "Dejected Brodie Snaps Answers." *The Hutchinson News*, January 3, 1972, 8.

_____. "Departing Dolphins Reflect on Reign." *Bakersfield Californian*, December 22, 1974, 24.

_____. "Desperation Pass Destroyed Colts." *The Danville (Virginia) Bee*, October 23, 1972, 25.

_____. "Did Pearson Push Viking in Miracle?" *Star News*, December 29, 1975, 42.

_____. "Dolphins Stop Patriots, 39–24." *Mount Carmel Daily Republican Register*, November 30, 1979, 4.

_____. "Double Defeat for Packers." *Stevens Point Daily Journal*, September 20, 1971, 4.

_____. "Eagle Vet Picket Line Fails to Stop Rookies." *The Philadelphia Inquirer*, July 10, 1974.

_____. "Eye Injury May Force Foreman Out." *Hagerstown Daily Mail*, December 22, 1975, 35.

_____. "Falcons Halt Vikings Streak, 20–14." *The Walla Walla Union-Bulletin*, November 20, 1973.

_____. "Falcons Still Pull Them Out." *Daily Globe*, September 11, 1979, 11.

_____. "Fans Say Pack Is Back, but Starr Still Not Convinced." *Daily Globe*, October 2, 1978, 13.

_____. "Feisty Young Bucs Claim 12–10 Win Over Vikings." *Albert Lea Evening Tribune*, October 29, 1979, 10.

_____. "For Unitas, a Fitting Home Town Farewell." *The Salisbury (Maryland) Daily Times*, December 4, 1972, 7.

_____. "Garo Makes Up for Pro Bowl Snub." *The Independent Press-Telegram*, December 26, 1971, S-4.

_____. "Giants Out-Kick Redskins." *Annapolis Capital*, November 15, 1976, 24.

_____. "Grant Call Surprising to Everyone." *Jacksonville Courier*, October 17, 1977, 9.

_____. "Griese Connects Six Times During Rout of Cardinals." *Midland Reporter Telegram*, November 25, 1977, 18.

_____. "Hart Made It Look Simple." *Edwardsville Intelligencer*, December 8, 1975, 7.

_____. "Hill, Garrison Gain Revenge for Dallas in Redskin Romp." *The Journal News*, December 10, 1972, 28.

_____. "Houston Rally Beats Browns." *Dover Times Reporter*, December 16, 1974, C1.

_____. "Houston Shakes Off Loser Image." *Walla Walla Union Bulletin*, December 26, 1978, 12.

_____. "Interception 'Big Play.'" *Star News*, December 26, 1971, 31.

_____. "Jim Otis Bulls Cards Over Bears." *Edwardsville Intelligencer*, December 15, 1975, 6.

_____. "Kilmer Cruises Past Saints." *Biloxi Daily Herald*, September 22, 1975, 15.

_____. "Landry Praises Aggressive Skins." *The Abilene Reporter-News*, January 1, 1973, 46.

_____. "Late Scramble by Tarkenton Gives Vikes Win Over Cards." *Great Bend Tribune*, November 12, 1974, 7.

_____. "League Winners Await Super Bowl." *The Santa Fe New Mexican*, January 4, 1971, 63.

_____. "Lennie the Cool Steals Blanda's Act." *The Hutchinson News*, December 13, 1971, 9.

_____. "A Lineman's Game." *The Danville (Virginia) Bee*, December 31, 1973, 8.

_____. "Lions Block Three Punts, Rip Packers." *Benton Harbor Herald Palladium*, September 22, 1975, 19.

_____. "Lions Got Their Turkey but Without Juice." *The Danville Bee*, November 26, 1976, 35.

_____. "Luck Enough for Atlanta." *Santa Ana Orange County Register*, October 10, 1977, 4.

_____. "Madden Had Hopes Until Late Gamble Backfired." *The Danville (Virginia) Bee*, December 31, 1973, 8.

_____. "Miami Win Nets East Crown." *The Stevens Point (Wisconsin) Daily Journal*, December 20, 1971, 18.

_____. "Minnesota Edges Eagles." *Doylestown Intelligencer*, December 4, 1978, 8.

_____. "More Playoff Appearances in Future for Bengals?" *Piqua Daily Call*, December 29, 1975, 11.

_____. "New Dallas Hero Cool Under Rush." *Abilene Reporter*, November 29, 1974, 1C.

_____. "New Miami Yell." *Southern Illinoisan*, December 26, 1971, 14.

_____. "NFL Players Add Demands." May 21, 1974.

_____. "NFL Players Agree to Strike If Demands Aren't Met." *The Asbury Park (New Jersey) Evening Press*, March 7, 1974, 37.

_____. "NFL Playoffs Suffer Blurred Vision Attack," *Santa Fe New Mexican*, January 7, 1980, 50.

_____. "NFL Quotes." *Syracuse Herald Journal*, November 28, 1977, 39.

_____. "NFL Upset Day." *Southern Illinisan*, November 11, 1974, 9.

_____. "NFL's Dirtiest Player." *The Danville Bee*, October 11, 1976, 14.

_____. "Oilers Waive Curry, NFL Players President." *The Sheboygan (Wisconsin) Press*, August 31, 1974, 16.

_____. "Oilers, Buccaneers Pull Off Upsets." *Paris News*, December 30, 1979, 13.

_____. "Opportunism Crucial to NFL Hopefuls." *Naples Daily News*, November 7, 1977, 37.

_____. "Overtime Answer to Blanda." *Lumberton Robesonian*, December 1, 1975, 18.

_____. "Patriots with Plunkett Stun Raiders." *The Newport Daily News*, September 20, 1971, 15.

_____. "Pittsburgh Finally Makes Title Tilt." *Hutchinson News*, December 30, 1974, 19.

_____. "Plastic Man' Landry Has Last Laugh." *Abilene Reporter News*, December 14, 1975, 143.

_____. "Raider, Oiler Quotes." *The Daily Review*, November 14, 1977, 24.

_____. "Raider Victory Party Has Cautious Attitude." *High Point Enterprise*, December 22, 1974, 41.

_____. "Raiders Run to Super Bowl." *The Danville Bee*, December 27, 1976, 8.

_____. "Raiders Spared Many a Sleepless Winter Night." *Bakersfield Californian*, December 22, 1974, 24.

_____. "Raiders, Vikes NFL Winners; Miami Ousted." *Journal News*, December 22, 1974, C3.

_____. "Redskins Are Paced by Kilmer, Moseley." *Panama City News Herald*, December 11, 1977, 27.

_____. "Rooney, Steelers Savor Big Moment." *Racine Journal Times*, January 13, 1975, 13.

_____. "Saints Explode Past Tampa Bay." *Laurel Leader Call*, October 15, 1979, 9.

_____. "San Francisco Defense Forces Redskin Miscues." *Montana Standard*, December 27, 1971, 12.

_____. "Seahawks Outlast Atlanta." *Cedar Rapids Gazette*, October 30, 1979, 18.

_____. "Stabler-to-Davis TD Pass Ends Miami Title Chances." *Hattiesburg American*, December 22, 1974, 13.

_____. "Staubach Keeps Winning." *The Corpus Christi Times*, December 13, 1971, 32.

_____. "Steeler 'Basics' Destroy Vikes." *Star News*, January 13, 1975, 24.

_____. "Steelers Flop in Minnesota." *Indiana Evening Gazette*, October 5, 1976, 14.

_____. "Steelers Succumb to Browns." *The Derrick*, November 26, 1973, 18.

_____. "Steelers Will Avoid Panic." *Indiana Evening Gazette*, October 5, 1976, 14.

_____. "Strife-Torn NFL Arrives at Truce." *The Arizona Republic*, August 4, 1970, 27.

_____. "Surprise Play Reverses Game." *Hutchinson News*, November 29, 1974, 9.

_____. "Tarkenton Breaks Ankle." *Kennebec Journal*, November 14, 1977, 12.

_____. "Tarkenton Sheds Tag with Touch of Bitterness." *The Danville (Virginia) Bee*, December 31, 1973, 8.

_____. "The Trick Is to Roll Sevens and Threes in Playoffs." *Piqua Daily Call*, December 29, 1975, 11.

_____. "Vikes Shave Cowboys." *Abilene Reporter News*, October 7, 1974, 1B.

_____. "Vikes' Tarkenton Has a Field Day." *Montana Standard*, December 2, 1974, 17.

_____. "Vikings Full of Surprises." *The Huron Daily Plainsman*, December 31, 1973, 10.

_____. "Vikings Mad Over Officiating." *The Independent Press-Telegram*, December 26, 1971, S-4.

_____. "Vikings Top Rams 14–10 for NFC Championship." *Emporia Gazette*, December 30, 1974, 10.

_____. "Vikings Use Special Teams to Carry Them to Super Bowl." *The Danville Bee*, December 27, 1976, 8.

_____. "Willie Ellison Breaks Record." *The Hutchinson News*, November 29, 1971, 7.

_____. "Wright Right on the Spot for Victorious Vikings." *Journal News*, December 22, 1974, C3.

_____. "Yepremian, Miami Take Big Step." *The Montana Standard*, December 26, 1971, 9.

Atchison, Lewis F. "Does NFL Playoff Structure Need an Incentive Plan?" *Football Digest*, April 1972, 84–86.

Atkin, Ross. "Sam 'Bam' Cunningham: If He Can't Go Through, He Goes Over the Top." *Football Digest*, August 1975, 38–41.

Attner, Paul. "Washington Running Back Mike Thomas: Determination Makes the Difference." *Football Digest*, June 1977, 69–71.

Baker, Jim. "O.J. Simpson's Six Greatest Performances." *Football Digest*, June 1977, 82–92.

Banaszak, Pete, as told to Payne, Dave. "The Game I'll Never Forget." *Football Digest*, October 1979, 82–87.

Barnidge, Tom. "America's Team at 40." *NFL Insider*, February/March 2001, 122–130.

_____. "Happy Day in St. Louis ... Finally." *The Long Beach (California) Independent Press-Telegram*, December 11, 1972, 34.

_____. "How Bud Wilkinson's Legend Was Reborn in Defeat at St. Louis." *Football Digest*, April 1979, 72–77.

_____. "Ottis Anderson Rookie of the Year." *Football Digest*, March 1980, 72–77.

_____. "Terry Metcalf: Pro Football's Most Exciting Player." *Football Digest*, November 1976, 23–28.

_____. "What Really Happens at Halftime?" *Football Digest*, January 1979, 62–65.

Barreiro, Dan. "Dallas' Randy White: Beware of the Manster." *Football Digest*, March 1983, 24–31.

Bauer, Steve. "Broncos, Steelers Battle to Thrilling 35–35 Tie." *Greeley Daily Tribune*, September 23, 1974, 34.

Bayless, Skip. "Ken Anderson: The Bengals' Unfulfilled Quarterback." *Football Digest*, February 1977, 20–25.

_____. "Silent Running." *Pro!* October 30, 1978, 2B–8B.

Beard, Gordon. "Colts, Cowboys Blank Playoff Foes." *Appleton Post Crescent*, December 27, 1970, 42.

Becker, Bob. "Broncos Lose Heartbreaker in Division Title Encounter." *The Colorado Springs Gazette Telegraph*, December 17, 1973, 3C.

Bennett, Tom. "The Invisible Men in the Striped Shirts." *Pro!* September 8, 1974, 3C–7C.

_____. "O, Sudden Death, Where Is Thy Sting?" PRO! December 22, 1974, 3B–7B.

_____. "The Science of Linebacking." *Pro!* December 8, 1973, 3B–8B.

_____. "What's New in 1976?" *Pro!* August 20, 1976, 2A–5A.

Berger, Dan. "NFC '77." *Pro!* August 13, 1977, 3B–4B.

_____. "Number 16...On the Way to 17–0." *PRO!* January 1, 1978, 3C–8C.

_____. "Pro! Talk. A Conversation with Dave Casper." *Pro!* September 9, 1977, 1D–3D.

Bernstein, Ralph. "Allen's Quick Thinking Helps Him Win 100th." *Fon Du Lac Reporter*, September 28, 1976, 20.

_____. "Eagles Victory Big Enough to Save Manager's Job but Maybe Not Enough for Coach." *The Gettysburg (Pennsylvania) Times*, December 21, 1970, 22.

Bierig, Joel. "Bud Grant: The Vikings' One-Of-A-Kind Coach." *Football Digest*, March 1982, 54–58.

Biletnikoff, Fred, as told to Payne, Dave. "The Game I'll Never Forget." *Football Digest*, January 1979, 48–54.

Billings, Bob. "Are Field Goals Ruining Pro Football?" *Football Digest*, January 1974, 38–42.

_____. "The Best and Worst Trades of 1973." *Football Digest*, February 1974, 32–37.

_____. "The Bomb Is Back." *Football Digest*, September 1974, 44–48.

_____. "Changes to Look for in the '73 Season." *Football Digest*, November 1973, 24–29.

_____. "Cornerback: The Most Demanding Position in Pro Football Today." *Football Digest*, December 1974, 30–35.

_____. "Five Biggest Blunders of '71 Season." *Football Digest*, April 1972, 21–26.

_____. "Have NFL Owners Forgotten the Fan?" *Football Digest*, August 1973, 58–62.

_____. "How the Steelers Became a Contender." *Football Digest*, February 1973, 25–30.

_____. "How the WFL Will Change Pro Football." *Football Digest*, August 1974, 20–25.

_____. "How to Beat the Zone Defense." *Football Digest*, July-August 1972, 55–58.

_____. "Pro Football's Most Dramatic Games Are in the Playoffs." *Football Digest*, January 1975, 22–27.

_____. "Quarterback Report: Leadership Makes the Difference." *Football Digest*, October 1972, 43–46.

_____. "Rookie All-Stars of 1973." *Football Digest*, March 1974, 30–37.

Bisheff, Steve. "As the Press Sees It." *Pro!* August 19, 1973, 19.

_____. "Isaac Curtis: Is He the Next Paul Warfield?" *Football Digest*, January 1975, 38–40.

_____. "The MVPs." *Pro!* October 25, 1975, 3D–11D.

_____. "Paul Warfield Best of the Deep Receivers." *Football Digest*, February 1972, 81–83.

_____. "Trademaking: Dealing in NFL Commodities." *Pro!* October 30, 1978, 8D–13D.

Bledsoe, Terry. "Brock & Mac." *Green Bay Packers 1973 Yearbook*, 1973, 7–9.

_____. "John Brockington: A Peaceable Man." *Green Bay Packers 1972 Yearbook*, 1972, 8–10.

_____. "John Brockington: Green Bay's TD Weapon." *Football Digest*, November 1972, 48–50.

Bluth, Jack. "Brodie Credits Pass Protection." *The San Mateo Times*, December 21, 1970, 38.

_____. "Humidity, Tenacity Spoil Niner Opener." *The San Mateo Times*, September 17, 1973, 15.

_____. "NFC Title Game Next for Niners." *The San Mateo Times*, December 27, 1971, 29.

Boesch, Barry. "NFL Refs Should Use Instant Replay." *Football Digest*, April 1982, 4–5.

Bortstein, Larry. "Alan Page, Key Man in Vikings' Defensive Line." *Football Digest*, January 1972, 22–25.

_____. "The Biggest Surprise of Last Season." *Football Digest*, March 1976, 36–41.

_____. "Can the Vikings Recover from the Disaster That Was 1972?" *Football Digest*, August 1973, 46–54.

_____. "A Dozen Stars Recall Their Super Bowl Memories." *Football Digest*, February 1980, 68–79.

_____. "Expansion Teams: The NFL's Biggest Winners & Losers." *Football Digest*, April 1977, 58–67.

_____. "Five Biggest Surprises of NFL Season." *Football Digest*, March 1972, 18–23.

_____. "5 Veterans Tell How to Watch Football on TV." *Football Digest*, December 1977, 48–56.

_____. "How the Punting Game Has Changed: High and Far Is No Longer Enough." *Football Digest*, January 1978, 62–67.

_____. "Is the Role of the Middle Linebacker Diminishing?" *Football Digest*, April 1978, 56–62.

_____. "Is This the Year of the Punter?" *Football Digest*, November 1974, 36–40.

_____. "John Niland the Cowboys' Unsung Hero." *Football Digest*, May-June 1972, 16–20.

_____. "The Kickholders." *Pro!* November 2, 1975, 3D–7D.

_____. "The Most Unusual Records of 1976." *Football Digest*, August 1977, 78–91.

_____. "Pro Stars Rate the Playing Fields." *Football Digest*, November 1976, 30–36.

_____. "Rick Upchurch: Rocket on Kickoff Returns." *Football Digest*, August 1977, 38–39.

_____. "Seven Biggest Surprises in a Year of Change." *Football Digest*, March 1973, 34–40.

_____. "Super Bowl Memories." *Football Digest*, February 1974, 22–29.

Boss, David. "The Druggist Had the Prescription." *Pro!* August 18, 1973, 31–33.

_____. "Like a Living Thing." *Pro!* December 10, 1972, 3B–12B.

_____. "This Year's Champions." *Pro!* October 1, 1972, 5C–12C.

Bradshaw, Terry, as told to Payne, Dave. "The Game I'll Never Forget." *Football Digest*, January 1978, 46–53.

Brady, Dave. "Kemp Says Players Back Merger." *The Washington Post*, October 23, 1966.

_____. "NFL Issues a 'Yellow Paper' on TV Blackouts." *The Washington Post*, February 17, 1973.

Brauchner, Bill. "Buonticonti, Key to the Dolphins' Defense." *Football Digest*, October 1972, 59–62.

_____. "The Private World of Bob Griese." *Pro!* September 9, 1978, 4C–14C.

_____. "Seven Dolphin Regulars Ignore Pickets, Report." *The Miami Herald*, July 18, 1974.

Brock, Ted. "Girls of the Game." *Pro!* September 9, 1977, 9B–14B.

_____. "A New Cake in the Oven." *Pro!* December 4, 1977, 7B–15B.

Brown, Willie, as told to Payne, Dave. "The Game I'll Never Forget." *Football Digest*, June 1981, 74–77.

Browning, Wilt. "Dave Hampton Finally Crashes 1,000-Yard Club." *Football Digest*, March 1976, 96–97.

Bryant, Bobby, as told to Payne, Dave. "The Game I'll Never Forget." *Football Digest*, June 1978, 38–43.

Buck, Ray. "All-Purpose Running Backs." *Football Digest*, August 1978, 23–26.

_____. "Is This Finally the Year of the Bengals?" *Football Digest*, December 1977, 16–21.

_____. "Pro! Talk. A Conversation with Bum Phillips." *Pro!* September 16, 1979, 9B–10B.

Burnes, Robert L. "Terry Metcalf: Sparkplug of the Big Red." *Football Digest*, March 1975, 69–74.

Bush, Blair, with Brock, Ted. "The View from Center Stage." *Pro!* August 25, 1979, 3C–12C.

Butkus, Dick. "An Inside Look at the Super Bowl." *Football Digest*, April 1974, 28–30.

Callahan, Tom. "The Quiet Noisemaker." *Pro!* October 17, 1976, 15B–18B.

Cameron, Steve. "The Yearlings." *Pro!* August 31, 1974, 104–108.

Campbell, Dave. "The Thrills (And Spills) of a Roller-Coaster Ride." *Dallas Cowboys 1973 Outlook*, 80–88.

Campbell, Jim. "George Blanda: 1970 Miracle Worker." *Football Digest*, March 1976, 74–79.

_____. "Pro! Talk. A Conversation with Harold Carmichael." *Pro!* September 9, 1979, 9B–10B.

Carnicelli, Joe. "Browns Aren't Only Team Fighting to Make Playoffs." *Elyria Chronicle Telegram*, November 27, 1978, 13–16.

_____. "Cards Win Eastern NFL Title for First Time in 26 Years." *The Berkshire Eagle*, December 16, 1974, 35.

_____. "Dallas Opens 'Rebuilding' Year with 18–7 Upset of Los Angeles." *Kingsport Times*, September 22, 1975, 2.

_____. "Dolphins Get Past Steelers." *The (Provo, Utah) Herald Sports*, January 1, 1973, 9.

_____. "Improved Pats Knock Off Miami 34–24." *Berkshire Eagle*, September 16, 1974, 26.

_____. "Vikings' Purple Gang Brings Home the Bacon." *South Mississippi Sun*, December 30, 1974, 11.

Carroll, Jane. "I Was a Raiderette." *Pro!* December 2, 1979, 3D–13DC.

Cassady, Steve. "5 of a Kind Wins." *Pro!* November 27, 1977, 5B–11B.

_____. "IV for XIV." *Super Bowl XV Program*, January 25, 1981, 39–48.

_____. "NFL Playbook: At the Goal Line." *Pro!* December 16, 1979, 9E.

_____. "NFL Playbook: Flex Defense." *Pro!* September 9, 1979, 15B.

_____. "NFL Playbook: Misdirection." *Pro!* September 16, 1979, 9E.

_____. "NFL Playbook: Motion." *Pro!* December 9, 1979, 15B.

_____. "NFL Playbook: Nickel, Dime Defenses." *Pro!* October 14, 1979, 13D.

_____. "NFL Playbook: Pass Blocking." *Pro!* August 16, 1980, 3F.

_____. "NFL Playbook: Two-Minute Offense." *Pro! Magazine*, August 25, 1979, 15D.

_____. "NFL Playbook: Weakside, Strongside." *Pro!* October 21, 1979, 13D.

_____. "Superduper Bowl." *Super Bowl XIV Program*, January 20, 1980, 43–55.

_____. "Three Four, Shut the Door." *Pro!* December 4, 1977, 3C–8C.

Casstevens, David. "Houston's Earl Campbell: The No. 1 Runner in Football." *Football Digest*, March 1980, 32–34.

_____. "Success Hasn't Changed Houston's Bum Phillips." *Football Digest*, December 1979, 66–71.

Caster, Rich, as told to Payne, Dave. "The Game I'll Never Forget." *Football Digest*, February 1978, 36–38.

Chandler, Bob, as told to Payne, Dave. "The Game I'll Never Forget." *Football Digest*, November 1980, 76–78.

Chapin, Dwight. "Dos De La Misma Clase." *PRO!* August 1981, 45–51.

_____. "Lawrence McCutcheon: The Rookie Nobody Wanted." *Football Digest*, March 1974, 85–87.

_____. "O.J. on the Run Again." *Pro!* October 28, 1973, 3B–8B.

Chapin, Dwight, and Smith, Rick. "Not Bad for Openers." *Pro!* September 12, 1976, 2D–6D.

Chapman, Scooter. "Seahawks Sharp in 30–13 Victory." *Port Angeles Daily News*, November 8, 1976, 9.

Chester, Raymond, as told to Payne, Dave. "The Game I'll Never Forget." *Football Digest*, September 1976, 52–56.

Christl, Cliff. "Brockington: Super Bowl ... That's No. 1." *Green Bay Packers 1974 Yearbook*, 1974, 12–15.

_____. "Defense Plays as a Unit." *Green Bay Packers 1975 Yearbook*, 1975, 19–21.

_____. "Linemen Bask in Sunshine of Brockington's Efforts." *The Manitowoc (Wisconsin) Herald Times*, December 14, 1971, 13.

_____. "The Young Nucleus of a Team on the Rise." *Green Bay Packers 1978 Yearbook*, 1978, 4–8.

Clary, Jack. "The Coach Who Plays Football for the Fun of It." *Pro!* October 17, 1976, 17C–21C.

_____. "Dan Pastorini: From Frustration to Fruition." *Pro!* November 30, 1975, 3B–7B.

_____. "No Respect for Their Elders." *Pro!* August 25, 1979, 7D–13D.

_____. "A Passing Grade Is Not Enough." *Pro!* October 7, 1973, 15D–18D.

_____. "Pro! Talk. A Conversation with Art McNally." *Pro!* December 24, 1978, 9A–10A.

_____. "Pro! Talk. A Conversation with John Hentz." *Pro!* November 26, 1978, 9A–10A.

_____. "Pro! Talk. A Conversation with Ted Nathanson." *Pro!* December 9, 1979, 9B–10B.

_____. "The World Football League Had a World of Troubles." *Football Digest*, November 1983, 28–31.

Connor, Dick. "Coffin Corner Alive Again with New Rules Changes." *Pro!* September 15, 1974, 8–9.

_____. "Craig Morton: Still Trying to Prove He's a Winner." *Football Digest*, August 1979, 22–26.

_____. "The Last 2:00 Minutes." *Pro!* August 31, 1974, 2B–7B.

_____. "Painting the Town Orange." *Pro!* September 3, 1978, 3C–11C.

_____. "Pro! Talk. A Conversation with Randy Gradishar." *Pro!* October 14, 1979, 9B–10B.

_____. "Why Otis Armstrong Is a Marked Man." *Football Digest*, August 1975, 16–20.

Cooney, Frank. "NFL Defenses: Recent Adjustments Reduce Offensive Firepower." *Football Digest*, November 1975, 54–58.

Corona, Al. "Skip Vanderbundt: Filling the Shoes of a 49er Great." *Football Digest*, October 1975, 66–67.

Costello, Jack. "Be Mean, Joe Greene. Be Mean." *Lowell Sun*, December 20, 1976, 17.

Coughlin, Dan. "Why Paul Warfield Left Miami." *Football Digest*, September 1975, 60–63.

_____. "Why the Cowboys Keep Winning." *Football Digest*, June 1978, 76–79.

Cour, Jim. "Rams Dump Steelers, 10–7." *Tyrone Daily Herald*, November 13, 1978, 9.

Cushman, Tom. "The Worst Day in Craig Morton's Career." *Football Digest*, April 1978, 32–35.

Daley, Art. "A Championship Identity: Title Defense." *Green Bay Packers 1973 Yearbook*, 1973, 2–3.

_____. "Enter Competition ... Within Family." *Green Bay Packers 1977 Yearbook*, 1977, 2–3.

_____. "A New Identity." *Green Bay Packers 1972 Yearbook*, 1972, 2–3.

_____. "1976 Outlook: Improvement." *Green Bay Packers 1976 Yearbook*, 1976, 2–3.

_____. "Packers Start No. 60." *Green Bay Packers 1978 Yearbook*, 1978, 2–3.

Darden, Burt. "Bum Celebrates Win with Cigar." *Port Arthur News*, September 29, 1975, 9.

Davis, Buddy. "Terry Bradshaw—The Problems of Being No. 1." *Football Digest*, November 1971, 20–24.

Dawson, Len, as told to Billings, Bob. "The Game I'll Never Forget." *Football Digest*, October 1972, 63–66.

Den Herder, Vern, as told to Janoff, Barry. "The Game I'll Never Forget." *Football Digest*, October 1982, 78–83.

Denlinger, Ken. "Another Swann Song by Pittsburgh." *Football Digest*, April 1979, 34–36.

Didinger, Ray. "Actions Speak Louder." *Pro!* September 16, 1979, 2C–11C.

_____. "Any Combination Can Win." *Pro!* August 23, 1975.

_____. "Archie Manning and the Art of Survival." *Football Digest*, November 1972, 41–44.

_____. "Bill Bergey: Pro Football's Best Linebacker." *Football Digest*, October 1979, 23–27.

_____. "Call Him 'Dangerous' ... for Short." *Pro!* October 1, 1978, 2B–8B.

_____. "Drew Pearson: He Answers the Cowboys' Prayers." *Football Digest*, June 1981, 24–27.

_____. "Mean Joe Greene Remembers Goose Bumps of First Super Bowl." *Gameday*, August 7, 1982, 1D–2D.

_____. "The MVPs." *Pro!* October 14, 1973, 3B–8B.

_____. "Ron Jaworski: Can He Inspire the New Eagles?" *Football Digest*, October 1978, 21–24.

_____. "The Saga of Super Bill: 'I'm Just Me—I Do What Comes Naturally.'" *Gridiron Magazine*, December 20, 1971.

_____. "Sensational Is Routine for Fred Biletnikoff." *Football Digest*, April 1977, 26–27.

_____. "Vince Papale Ain't Just Another Bum from the Neighborhood Anymore." *Pro!* October 9, 1977, 3D–12D.

_____. "Why the Dallas Offense Worked So Well in '75." *Football Digest*, February 1976, 40–42.

_____. "Yesterday's Heroes." *Football Digest*, November 1982, 70–77.

Diliberto, Buddy. "Richie Petitbon Analyzes the Redskins." *Football Digest*, July-August 1972, 82–84.

Ditrani, Vinny. "The Bucs Have Finally Found a Quarterback." *Football Digest*, January 1979, 28–30.

_____. "Can Bud Wilkinson Make the Transition to the Pros?" *Football Digest*, October 1978, 30–34.

Dodd, Mike. "Curtis Brown: Buffalo's Quiet MVP." *Football Digest*, December 1979, 26–30.

_____. "John Hannah: Built to Be an All-Pro Guard." *Football Digest*, November 1980, 44–47.

_____. "Pats Coach Chuck Fairbanks Preachers Patience and Organization." *Football Digest*, February 1979, 48–53.

Douglass, Bobby, as told to Payne, Dave. "The Game I'll Never Forget." *Football Digest*, November 1978, 66–71.

DuPree, David. "Redskins Safeties Saw Turning Points Coming." *The Washington Post*, October 9, 1973.

Durkee, Rob. "What'll Browns' Critics Say Now?" *Elyria Chronicle Telegram*, November 27, 1978, 13–16.

Durslag, Melvin. "In 1972 the Running Game Came Alive Again." *Football Digest*, February 1973, 17–19.

Dwyre, Bill. "Former NFL Official Fred Swearingen Speaks Out." *Football Digest*, April 1982, 78–85.

Echternacht, Jon. "The Jim Carter Story." *Green Bay Packers 1977 Yearbook*, 1977, 34–36.

Eidge, Frank. "'Records Is Cool' Says Mack 'But I'd Rather Have a Win.'" *Nashua Telegraph*, December 16, 1974, 24.

Elderkin, Phil. "Clarence Davis: The Raiders' Unsung Hero." *Football Digest*, April 1977, 38–39.

_____. "How the Buccaneers Lured John McKay from USC." *Football Digest*, March 1976, 88–90.

_____. "Why Franco Harris Is Running Better than Ever." *Football Digest*, February 1976, 24–27.

Eldridge, Larry. "The Clock Runs Out on Johnny Unitas." *Football Digest*, November 1974, 22–26.

_____. "Determined Buoniconti Spearheads Miami Defense." *Football Digest*, February 1974, 42–44.

Eldridge, Larry, Jr. "Hidden Heroes: Heralding Some Un-heralded Super Bowl Superstars." *Super Bowl XVII Game Program*, January 30, 1983, 32–49.

_____. "How Bengals' Boobie Clark Bounded Out of Obscurity." *Football Digest*, March 1974, 38–41.

Evans, Luther. "The Day Dick Anderson Destroyed the Colts." *Football Digest*, May-June 1972, 35–39.

Fair, Don. "Year One—An Evaluation: The Seattle Seahawks." *Football Digest*, April 1977, 68–73.

Feaster, Ken. "Vikings Hold Off Detroit 31–23." *Winona Daily News*, November 8, 1976, 10.

Felser, Larry. "Buffalo's Bob Chandler Is Tired of Being 'Under-Rated.'" *Football Digest*, June 1977, 48–51.

_____. "Can O.J. Simpson Bring Champagne to the Buffalo Bills?" *Football Digest*, August 1973, 34–38.

_____. "Curtis and Mad Stork Bulwark Colts Defense." *Buffalo Evening News*, June 26, 1971.

_____. "The Dismantling of a Contender: How and Why the Bills Fell Apart." *Football Digest*, March 1977, 72–75.

_____. "The Electric Company: Buffalo's Big Blockers." *Football Digest*, March 1974, 48–53.

_____. "Football Digest's All-Star Team of the '70s." *Football Digest*, February 1980, 28–33.

_____. "How Chuck Knox Is Rebuilding the Bills." *Football Digest*, January 1980, 22–25.

_____. "Pro! Q and A: A Conversation with Roone Arledge." *Pro!*, September 22, 1974, 15A–17A.

_____. "The Return of the Running Game." *Pro!* October 14, 1973, 5D–12D.

_____. "The Story of Y." *Pro!* December 5, 1976, 3C–11C.

_____. "Who Won the 1974 Player Draft?" *Football Digest*, June 1974, 18–26.

Fimrite, Ron. "Better Let George Do It." *The San Francisco Chronicle*, November 10, 1970.

Fink, David. "Jack Lambert: The Meanest Man in Football." *Football Digest*, September 1976, 46–50.

Finney, Peter. "The Agony of Archie Manning." *Football Digest*, August 1974, 14–19.

_____. "Just Kicking Around." *Pro!* November 5, 1978, 8D–13D.

Florence, Mal. "Cedrick Hardman 'Mr. Nasty.'" *Football Digest*, March 1972, 56–58.

_____. "Cowboys' Cliff Harris: Hitter of the Dallas Defensive Backs." *Football Digest*, November 1976, 38–41.

_____. "Fran Tarkenton Survives His Critics." *Football Digest*, January 1977, 12–19.

_____. "The Los Angeles Rams: A Team on the Run." *Football Digest*, August 1974, 30–33.

Flowers, Charles. "The NFL's Top Tight End: Charlie Sanders." *Football Digest*, November 1973, 46–53.

Flynn, John. "Intercepting Bill Bradley." *Football Digest*, June 1973, 83–91.

Forbes, Gordon. "Cowboys Blast 'Cheap Shot' Steelers." *Football Digest*, April 1976, 34–37.

_____. "I'll Never Forget ... Eagles End a Streak." *Gameday*, October 23, 1983, 1D.

_____. "Player Agreement Likely, with No Strike, NFL Told." *The Philadelphia Inquirer*, February 27, 1974.

_____. "Saints' MLB Joe Federspiel Plays Mean to Gain Respect." *Football Digest*, April 1978, 84–85.

Fouts, Dan, as told to Payne, Dave. "The Game I'll Never Forget." *Football Digest*, October 1978, 56–60.

Fowler, Bob. "Minnesota's Vikings: Best of the Kick Blockers." *Football Digest*, August 1980, 32–35.

Fox, Larry. "Jocks and Jingles: A Marriage Made on Madison Avenue." *Pro!* October 21, 1979, 10E–16E.

_____. "Pickets Fail to Halt 'Fame' Game." July 27, 1974, 83.

_____. "Riding Shotgun." *Pro!* August 1981, 98–106.

Francis, Wallace, as told to Payne, Dave. "The Game I'll Never Forget." *Football Digest*, November 1981, 72–77.

Freeman, Denne H. "Minnesota Super Bowl Bound." *Huron Daily Plainsman*, December 31, 1973, 10.

Freeman, Don. "Monday Night!" *Pro!* December 4, 1978, 37.

Freeman, Mike. "A Trainer Feels the Vikings' Grief." *The New York Times*, August 5, 2001.

Gambini, Bert. "Super Bowl V and the End of the AFL." *Coffin Corner*, November/December 2013, 4–10.

Gordon, Dick. "Chuck Foreman: Key to the Vikes' Comeback." *Football Digest*, January 1974, 13–17.

Gosselin, Rick. "Made to Be Broken." *Super Bowl XIX Program*, January 20, 1985, 92–101.

Graham, Jim. "Charlie Johnson Sheds His Image as a Loser." *Football Digest*, August 1974, 40–43.

Green, Jerry. "One on One." *Pro!* Division Playoff Edition, December 24, 1972, 2D–6D.

_____. "The Unhappy Saga of Donny Anderson." *Football Digest*, July-August 1972, 46–48.

Green, Ted. "Alan Page Proved the Vikings Wrong." *Football Digest*, June 1980, 50–55.

_____. "Lynn Swann's Not Worrying About Headhunters Anymore." *Football Digest*, March 1979, 36–38.

_____. "The Rams Can Be Proud of Their Performance." *Football Digest*, April 1980, 44–50.

_____. "The Rams' Defense Anonymous: 'Better than the Fearsome Foursome.'" *Football Digest*, February 1980, 48–55.

Greenberg, Alan. "Fulton Kuykendall Earns a Reputation as a Hard-Hitting Falcon." *Football Digest*, March 1979, 76–79.

_____. "The Saints Are Marching to Respectability." *Football Digest*, March 1979, 46–50.

Greenberg, Jay. "Inside Pro Football Special Teams." *Football Digest*, June 1977, 62–67.

Greene, Bob. "Ambushing Defense Leads Washington." *The Charleston (South Carolina) Daily Mail*, December 25, 1972, 21.

_____. "Roger Not Satisfied." *The Cumberland Evening Times*, November 22, 1971, 15.

Greer, Thom. "Nobody's Doubting Houston's Mike Reinfeldt Now." *Football Digest*, June 1980, 46–49.

Grey, Dave. "Brockington Gets 1,000." *The Oshkosh (Wisconsin) Daily Northwestern*, December 13, 1971, 29.

Grogan, Steve, as told to Payne, Dave. "The Game I'll Never Forget." *Football Digest*, January 1981, 80–84.

Gross, Joe. "Colts Upset Dolphins 16–3." *The Evening Capital*, December 10, 1973, 25.

_____. "Mistakes Cost Colts Loss to Pats." *Annapolis Capital*, November 15, 1976, 24.

Gross, Milton. "Duane Thomas the Cowboys' Enigma." *Football Digest*, March 1972, 71–72.

_____. "Larry Csonka the Dolphins' Solid Man." *Football Digest*, February 1972, 40–42.

Guback, Steve. "'Air Coryell': Is There a Way to Stop San Diego's Passing Attack?" *Football Digest*, June 1981, 28–33.

_____. "Has Washington Mortgaged the Future?" *Football Digest*, April 1976, 56–60.

_____. "How Oakland Pulverized the Vikings." *Football Digest*, April 1977, 14–17.

_____. "Line Stunts: How Defenders Get to the Quarterback." *Football Digest*, January 1976, 26–29.

_____. "New Blocking Rules Give an Edge to Scrambling QBs." *Football Digest*, October 1978, 38–40.

_____. "O.J.'s Main Man: Reggie McKenzie." *Football Digest*, August 1974, 45–46.

_____. "Petitbon Sees Different View Now." *The Washington Star-News*, June 2, 1974.

_____. "The Pride and Courage of Billy Kilmer." *Football Digest*, December 1976, 17–21.

_____. "Why Instant Replays Won't Solve Controversial Plays." *Football Digest*, June 1976, 90–92.

Hamilton, Ray, as told to Payne, Dave. "The Game I'll Never Forget." *Football Digest*, February 1979, 86–90.

Hand, Jack. "The Hart of the Cardinals." *Pro!* September 9, 1979, 13, 113.

Harris, Cliff. "The Game I'll Never Forget." *Football Digest*, September 1979, 74–78.

Harris, Franco, as told to Janoff, Barry. "The Game I'll Never Forget." *Football Digest*, March 1983, 80–83.

Hartman, Sid. "Paul Krause: Minnesota's Quiet Thief." *Football Digest*, November 1975, 52–53.

Hartnett, Dwayne. "Seattle's Surprising Success." *Football Digest*, June 1978, 18–23.

Harvey, Randy. "Walter Payton: He's His Own Toughest Opponent." *Football Digest*, November 1977, 21–27.

Heaton, Chuck. "Browns Are Tough—Shula." *The Cleveland Plain Dealer*, December 25, 1972.

_____. "The Maturing of Mike Phipps." *Football Digest*, February 1973, 39–41.

_____. "My Best Victory—Paul." *The Cleveland Plain Dealer*, November 16, 1970.

Heller, Dick. "Mark Moseley: The NFL's Best Long-Range Field Goal Kicker." *Football Digest*, October 1978, 80–82.

Hendricks, Ted, as told to Payne, Dave. "The Game I'll Never Forget." *Football Digest*, March 1976, 62–65.

Hendrickson, Joe. "49er Operation Successful." *The Star News*, October 1, 1973, 41.

_____. "Rams Give Vikes Snow-Job." *The Star News*, November 29, 1974, 18.

Herbert, Michael K. "Ken Stabler Player of the Year." *Football Digest*, March 1977, 22–29.

_____. "Did You Know That...." *Football Digest*, September 1978, 10–14.

_____. "O.J. Simpson Player of the Year." *Football Digest*, March 1976, 20–26.

Herman, Brian. "O.J., Bills Buffalo Steelers." *Monessen Valley Independent*, September 29, 1975, 9.

Hersh, Phil. "'I Don't Play Dirty,' Jack Tatum." *Football Digest*, January 1979, 32–37.

Hershey, Steve. "Vince Ferragamo Proved Himself Against the Steelers." *Football Digest*, April 1980, 40–41.

Herskowitz, Mickey. "A Doctor in the House." *Pro!* September 22, 1974, 3B–7B.

_____. "From Dante's Inferno to Heaven on Earth." *Pro!* October 14, 1979, 2D–11D.

_____. "Rebel with Cause." *Pro!* October 9, 1977, 11C–16C.

_____. "Talking a Good Game." *Pro!* December 14, 1975, 5A.

_____. "Three's Company." *NFL Insider Magazine*, February/March 2000, 224.

_____. "The Ubiquitous One." *Pro!* September 21, 1975, 5A.

Hintz, Gene W. "Chester Would Like More Work." *Green Bay Packers 1975 Yearbook*, 1975, 31–33.

_____. "Room for Improvement." *Green Bay Packers 1972 Yearbook*, 1972, 19–20.

_____. "We Love Chester." *Green Bay Packers 1973 Yearbook*, 1973, 30–33.

_____. "Willie Buchanon: A Good Place to Start." *Green Bay Packers 1974 Yearbook*, 1974, 45–46.

Hochman, Stan. "Why Ray Guy's Superb Punting Allows Oakland to Gamble on Offense." *Football Digest*, October 1976, 66–69.

Hofmann, Dale. "Fred Carr: Starts with Optimism." *Green Bay Packers 1976 Yearbook*, 1976, 7–9.

_____. "Gary Weaver: More Sure of Himself." *Green Bay Packers 1977 Yearbook*, 1977, 21–23.

_____. "Rich McGeorge Wants the Ball." *Green Bay Packers 1974 Yearbook*, 1974, 5–7.

_____. "The Running Game." *Green Bay Packers 1975 Yearbook*, 1975, 34–36.

Holbert, Allan. "Do the Fans Help Their Team Win?" *Football Digest*, January 1975, 62–64.

Horgan, John. "Care and Feeding of Quarterbacks." *Pro!* September 9, 1979, 1E–7E.

Houston, Ken, as told to Lundgren, Hal. "The Game I'll Never Forget." *Football Digest*, November 1976, 78–80.

Hudspeth, Ron. "Falcons' November 19, 1973 Classic." *Pro!* October 30, 1978, 6–7.

_____. "New England Tight End Russ Francis Lives the Renaissance Life." *Football Digest*, January 1977, 58–61.

Hutson, Lee. "Some New Rules and a Look at Some Testy Old Ones." *Pro!* October 23, 1971, 6B–11B.

Hyman, Mark. "Hank Stram: A Successful Transition from Coach to Announcer." *Football Digest*, February 1980, 60–66.

Insider's Pro Football Newsletter. *Sport Magazine*, November 14, 1972.

Jackson, Derrick. "Ex-Player Reps Recall the 1974 Player Strike." *Football Digest*, January 1983, 50–61.

Jackson, Harold, as told to Payne, Dave. "The Game I'll Never Forget." *Football Digest*, December 1976, 60–66.

Jackson, Wilbur, as told to Payne, Dave. "The Game I'll Never Forget." *Football Digest*, March 1980, 88–91.

Jankowski, Mike. "Why Kansas City Turned to the 'Unselfish-T.'" *Football Digest*, January 1979, 70–72.

Janofsky, Mike, and Newman, Mark. "The NFL Recognizes Drug Use Is Now a Serious Problem." *Football Digest*, November 1982, 58–63.

Jasner, Phil. "The Eagles' Stan Walters: He Just Blocks, and Blocks, And...." *Football Digest*, December 1977, 63–65.

Jaworski, Ron. "Ron Jaworski Has Ill Memories of Mexico City." *Football Digest*, November 1978, 80–82.

Jeansonne, John. "1978 Wrap-Up: A Wild and Crazy Season." *Football Digest*, April 1979, 78–85.

Jenkins, Chris. "Little Leads Broncos Romp." *Colorado Springs Gazette*, December 15, 1975, 25.

Jennings, Dave, as told to Janoff, Barry. "The Game I'll Never Forget." *Football Digest*, March 1982, 90–93.

Johnson, Charlie, as told to Billings, Bob. "The Game I'll Never Forget." *Football Digest*, June 1974, 42–44.

Johnson, Chuck. "The Black and Blue Division." *Green Bay Packers 1972 Yearbook*, 1972, 32–33.

Kallestad, Brent. "Vikings Overcome 49ers 27–17." *Winona Daily News*, September 22, 1975, 9.

Kane, Randy. "The Flea-Flicker Isn't a New Deception." *Football Digest*, December 1979, 44–47.

Kaufman, Ira. "Eagles Sack Redskins." *The Huntingdon Daily News*, October 16, 1978, 5.

Keating, Tom, as told to Payne, Dave. "The Game I'll Never Forget." *Football Digest*, August 1978, 78–82.

Kelleher, Terry. "Terry Bradshaw: The M-V-P Who Can't Spell C-A-T." *Football Digest*, April 1979, 30–33.

Kelly, Doug. "The Coach at Work." *Pro!* October 1, 1972, 3B–10B.

_____. "Johnny U. and the Wild Bunch." *Pro!* December 2, 1973, 12D–16D.

_____. "Pro! Q&A. A Conversation with John Brodie." *Pro!* December 8, 1974, 15A–17A.

Kilmer, Billy, as told to Payne, Dave. "The Game I'll Never Forget." *Football Digest*, October 1981, 76–79.

Kinzly, H.M. "New Life for an Old Pro." *Football Digest*, February 1974, 15–19.

Kirkland, Cliff. "Rams Upstaged by Brilliant Scott." *South Mississippi Sun*, October 31, 1977, 13.

Klein, Dave. "Larry Csonka: His Return to Miami Is a Smash!" *Football Digest*, January 1980, 17–21.

_____. "NFL's Super Bowl Is Filled with Cash." *Football Digest*, February 1977, 40–41.

_____. "Open Forum: The United Way." *Pro!* September 3, 1978, 5A–6A.

_____. "Realignment Would Improve the NFL." *Football Digest*, October 1979, 6–9.

Klobuchar, Jim. "The Greening of Chuck Foreman." *Football Digest*, March 1977, 40–45.

_____. "Jim Marshall: The Legend Keeps on Rolling." *Football Digest*, October 1978, 48–54.

_____. "The Most Valuable Players: Chuck Foreman." *Pro!* September 25, 1977, 7C–9C.

_____. "Off Their Rockers." *Pro!* September 16, 1979, 10E–16E.

_____. "Paul Krause: The Vikings' Open-Field Burglar." *Football Digest*, March 1977, 64–69.

Koster, Rich. "Pro Football's Meanest Men." *Football Digest*, August 1973, 24–27.

_____. "A Tackle Who Takes the Offensive." *Pro!* November 27, 1977, 3C–8C.

_____. "Why the 3–4 Defense Is So Popular." *Football Digest*, December 1978, 48–53.

Krikorian, Doug. "A Great Game—But Some Questions Remain." *Football Digest*, April 1979, 24–28.

_____. "Pete Rozelle's Pressure Against Oakland Was Hypocritical." *Football Digest*, October 1980, 6–9.

_____. "The Saints' Archie Manning: There's Finally a Team Behind Him." *Football Digest*, June 1979, 22–27.

Kucner, Richard. "Joe Ehrmann: The People's Choice in Baltimore." *Football Digest*, November 1976, 46–47.

_____. "The Most Valuable Players: Bert Jones." *Pro!* September 25, 1977, 3C–5C.

Kuenster, John. "Ken Stabler Player of the Year." *Football Digest*, March 1975, 21–25.

_____. "Oh Johnny, Where Have the Years Gone?" *Football Digest*, August 1973, 4–8.

_____. "O.J. Simpson: Player of the Year." *Football Digest*, March 1974, 18–23.

_____. "Out of the Huddle." *Football Digest*, March 1972, 4–7.

_____. "Shula's Dolphins: In 1974 It Wasn't Meant to Be." *Football Digest*, March 1975, 6–10.

Kupper, Mike. "Dave Roller Plays Football Because He Loves It...." *Green Bay Packers 1978 Yearbook*, 1978, 14–16.

_____. "David Whitehurst: Now the Pack's Confident Leader." *Football Digest*, November 1978, 84–85.

_____. "For John Brockington There's Nothing Like a Run." *Football Digest*, January 1976, 76–78.

_____. "The Offensive Line Can Be a Mighty Force." *Green Bay Packers 1975 Yearbook*, 1975, 22–23.

_____. "Rushing: A Strong Point." *Green Bay Packers 1976 Yearbook*, 1976, 48–49.

Kwalick, Ted, as told to Billings, Bob. "The Game I'll Never Forget." *Football Digest*, June 1975, 71–73.

LaMarre, Tom. "Branch Rewrites Wells' Script." *Oakland Tribune*, November 8, 1976, 31.

_____. "Jack Tatum Leaves Opponents Reeling." *Football Digest*, March 1974, 27–28.

_____. "A Mulligan Saves Raiders." *Oakland Tribune*, November 24, 1975, 109.

_____. "Pass Receiving or Blocking, Dave Casper Overpowers Opponents." *Football Digest*, January 1977, 78–82.

_____. "Raiders, Steelers in New Showdown." *Oakland Tribune*, December 29, 1975, E39.

Lamb, Kevin. "Chicago's Bob Avellini: The Bears Find a QB." *Football Digest*, March 1978, 84–87.

_____. "The Coach Who's Phi Beta Kansas City." *Pro!* February 1982, 57–60.

_____. "Doug Plank: The Bears' Pure Hitter." *Football Digest*, June 1979, 44–51.

_____. "The Most Valuable Player: NFC Walter Payton." *Pro!* August 19, 1978, 4B–8B.

_____. "Super Trends." *Super Bowl XVIII Program*, January 22, 1984, 61–68.

Langford, George. "Mike Reid, No. 74." *Pro!* October 7, 1973, 3C–7C.

Lanier, Willie, as told to Billings, Bob. "The Game I'll Never Forget." *Football Digest*, November 1974, 32–35.

Lauck, Dan. "The Steel Rod and Green Bay's Lynn Dickey." *Pro!* August 16, 1980, 13E–16E.

Lea, Bud. "Linebackers Make Defense." *Green Bay Packers 1974 Yearbook*, 1974, 18–20.

_____. "No Soft Spots." *Green Bay Packers 1972 Yearbook*, 1972, 17–18.

_____. "The Offensive Line ... More Flexibility Gilly's Back." *Green Bay Packers 1973 Yearbook*, 1973, 38–41.

LeBar, Paul. "Cowboys Set for Playoffs." *Appleton Post Crescent*, December 17, 1973, 24.

Lincicome, Bernie. "They've Taken the Artistry Out of Pass Receiving." *Football Digest*, March 1973, 25–29.

_____. "We Should Have Left the Rules Alone." *Football Digest*, October 1978, 41–43.

Lippman, Andy. "Peace Is Questionable, Despite Truce." *The Oil City (Pennsylvania) Derrick*, August 13, 1974, 10.

Little, Larry, as told to Payne, Dave. "The Game I'll Never Forget." *Football Digest*, March 1979, 80–83.

Lockwood, Wayne. "The Complex Quarterback." *Pro!* October 21, 1979, 2C–11C.

Long, Gary. "Butch and Sundance: A Dolphins Sequel." *Pro!* October 21, 1979, 1E–9E.

_____. "Delvin Williams' Dream Is to Play for a Champion." *Football Digest*, October 1978, 26–29.

_____. "Don Shula: Is He the Greatest Pro Coach of All Time?" *Football Digest*, February 1979, 22–27.

Lorge, Barry, and Solomon, George. "George Allen Blames Spoiled Players for His Firing." *Football Digest*, November 1978, 90–92.

Lowitt, Bruce. "Dallas Nabs East Lead, Plays Rams Turkey Day." *The Cumberland Evening Times*, November 22, 1971, 15.

_____. "Jets Stun Patriots, 30–27." *Bridgeport Post*, October 3, 1977, 12.

_____. "Long Day for QBs." *Charleston Daily Mail*, October 27, 1975, 18.

_____. "NFL Surprise Teams: Hosses, of Course." *Hagerstown Daily Mail*, December 22, 1975, 35.

_____. "Over-the-Hill Gang Smothers Dallas Attack." *The Abilene Reporter-News*, January 1, 1973, 46.

_____. "Rams, Vikings, Raiders Capture NFL Divisions." *Lumberton Robesonian*, December 1, 1975, 18.

_____. "Redskins Remain Unbeaten." *The Times Standard*, October 11, 1971, 11.

_____. "Simpson, Bills Rout Steelers." *Valparaiso Vidette Messenger*, September 29, 1975, 16.

_____. "WWIII to Upstage Super Bowl." *Lowell Sun*, December 20, 1976, 17.

Luksa, Frank. "Cliff Harris, One of the NFL's Toughest Hitters, Calls Csonka His Toughest Opponent." *Football Digest*, November 1977, 28–31.

_____. "Drew Pearson: Dallas' Record-Setting Wide Receiver." *Football Digest*, February 1978, 26–29.

_____. "How Dallas Was Rebuilt—From the Front Four Up." *Football Digest*, December 1975, 24–27.

_____. "Is the Dallas Shotgun a Rinky-Dink Offense?" *Football Digest*, October 1976, 20–26.

_____. "Jan Stenerud: He Can't Help but Remember." *Football Digest*, April 1976, 76–78.

_____. "The Landry Mystique." *Pro!* March-April 1982, 83–88.

_____. "Larry Cole: The Quiet Man on Dallas' Front Four." *Football Digest*, January 1981, 58–61.

_____. "The Names Have Changed, but Dallas' Doomsday Defense Lives." *Football Digest*, January 1978, 40–43.

_____. "Pro Football's Hottest Feud—Dallas Cowboys Vs. Washington Redskins." *Football Digest*, November 1973, 30–35.

_____. "Pro! Talk. A Conversation with Preston Pearson." *Pro!* December 23, 1979, 9B–10B.

_____. "Talking Football with ... Tom Landry." *Football Digest*, March 1983, 50–54.

_____. "Tony Dorsett Rookie of the Year." *Football Digest*, March 1978, 28–33.

Lundgren, Hal. "Earl Campbell Player of the Year." *Football Digest*, March 1979, 18–23.

_____. "Elvin Bethea: They're Beginning to Notice Him." *Football Digest*, August 1974, 53–56.

_____. "Gregg Bingham: Houston's Young Hitter." *Football Digest*, October 1975, 76–77.

_____. "Ken Burrough Comes into His Own as a Troublesome Receiver." *Football Digest*, January 1977, 54–57.

_____. "The MVPs." *Pro!* August 25, 1979, 2B–11B.

_____. "Talking Football with ... Terry Bradshaw." *Football Digest*, December 1979, 54–58.

_____. "Talking Football with ... Jack Tatum." *Football Digest*, September 1980, 56–60.

Lustig, Dennis. "Jack Lambert: Rookie Success in a Violent World." *Football Digest*, October 1975, 45–47.

Mack, Tom, as told to Payne, Dave. "The Game I'll Never Forget." *Football Digest*, June 1980, 80–85.

MacLean, Norm. "An Inside Look at Dallas' Famed Flex Defense." *Football Digest*, October 1979, 32–39.

_____. "An Inside Look at NFL Pass Defenses." *Football Digest*, June 1979, 64–71.

_____. "An Inside Look at the 3–4 Defense." *Football Digest*, January 1978, 32–36.

_____. "It's Time to Change the Rules and Protect the Quarterbacks." *Football Digest*, December 1977, 30–36.

_____. "Pete Rozelle's New NFL—Is It Parity or Mediocrity?" *Football Digest*, June 1980, 30–36.

_____. "WFL Flashback." *Football Digest*, June 1978, 60–71.

Madden, John, with Cassady, Steve. "Using the Spread Is a Loaded Expression." *Pro!* November 1981, 25–26.

Madden, Michael. "Al Davis Vs. the NFL: The Problems Are Black & White." *Football Digest*, January 1983, 34–41.

Magee, Jerry. "The Lean Years of Coy Bacon." *Football Digest*, November 1973, 74–75.

_____. "The Measure of a Draft." *Pro!* December 4, 1978, 3C–11C.

_____. "Rickey Young: His First Year as a Viking Was a Record-Setter." *Football Digest*, March 1979, 62–64.

_____. "San Diego's Charlie Joiner: He's Getting Better with Age." *Football Digest*, November 1980, 48–51.

_____. "There's a Catch to Being a Runner These Days." *Pro!* October 5, 1975, 3C–6C.

_____. "What the Pros Say About the Bump and Run." *Football Digest*, April 1974, 68–69.

Maher, Charles. "George Allen—The Redskins' Miracle Man." *Football Digest*, January 1972, 77–83.

_____. "Why Cowboys Traded Away Duane Thomas." *Football Digest*, November 1972, 51–55.

Mann, Jack. "Have the Washington Redskins Peaked Out?" *Football Digest*, August 1973, 28–32.

Manning, Archie, as told to Dave Payne. "The Game I'll Never Forget." *Football Digest*, June 1976, 60–65.

Markus, Robert. "Butch Johnson's Sensational Catch." *Football Digest*, April 1978, 40–42.

_____. "Craig Morton Doesn't Want to Be No. 2." *Football Digest*, October 1972, 47–49.

_____. "Dallas Had Edge in Talent and Team Effort." *Football Digest*, April 1972, 14–16.

_____. "A Last Look at the College All-Star Game." *Football Digest*, August 1977, 26–31.

_____. "Rocky Bleier Knows the Real Fear." *Football Digest*, March 1975, 82–85.

Marshall, Joe. "The MVPs." *Pro!* September 6, 1974, 2B–7B.

Martin, Harvey, as told to Buck, Ray. "...How We Won!" *Football Digest*, April 1978, 12–17.

Matuszak, John, as told to Janoff, Barry. "The Game I'll Never Forget." *Football Digest*, November 1982, 78–81.

Maule, Tex. "A Cowboy Stampede." *Sports Illustrated*, January 24, 1972, 10–15.

_____. "Eleven Big Mistakes." *Sports Illustrated*, January 25, 1971, 12–17.

McDonough, Will. "Leon Gray Proved the Patriots Made a Mistake." *Football Digest*, October 1980, 54–57.

_____. "The NFL's Best Offensive Lineman." *Football Digest*, March 1979, 32–34.

_____. "Steve Grogan: Best of the NFL's Young QBs." *Football Digest*, June 1977, 23–26.

McEwen, Tom. "Big Buc Lee Roy Selmon: Tampa Bay's Tower of Strength." *Football Digest*, June 1980, 22–28.

_____. "An Expansion Year: Tampa." *Pro!* November 30, 1975, 3D–8D.

_____. "No. 1 Pick Ricky Bell: Glad He's a Buccaneer." *Football Digest*, October 1977, 74–77.

_____. "Year One—An Evaluation: The Tampa Bay Buccaneers." *Football Digest*, April 1977, 74–80.

McGinn, Bob. "David Whitehurst: Can He Lead the Pack Back?" *Football Digest*, December 1979, 21–25.

McGrane, Bill. "Pete Rozelle, Architect." *Super Bowl XIV Program*, January 20, 1980, 31–37.

McGuane, George. "Pats' Veteran Sees Dynasty." *Lowell Sun*, December 20, 1976, 17.

McGuff, Joe. "Jim Tyrer: The Chiefs' Unheralded All-Pro Offensive Tackle." *Football Digest*, January 1972, 74–76.

_____. "San Diego's Don Coryell: Football's No. 1 Motivator." *Football Digest*, October 1980, 50–53.

_____. "Willie Lanier: Best Linebacker in NFL?" *Football Digest*, May-June 1972, 25–28.

McKenzie, Reggie, as told to Payne, Dave. "The Game I'll Never Forget." *Football Digest*, March 1978, 42–47.

McQuade, Drew. "Eagles Give Owner Another 'Ticker' Test." *Doylestown Intelligencer*, October 15, 1979, 35.

Meyers, Georg N. "Let's Keep Instant Replay Out of Pro Football." *Football Digest*, June 1980, 6–7.

Meyers, Jeff. "The Big Surprise of 1974." *Football Digest*, February 1975, 18–23.

_____. "Dick Butkus Played One Way—Tough." *Football Digest*, September 1974, 63–65.

_____. "Floyd Little: A Star Without Glory." *Football Digest*, November 1972, 45–47.

_____. "Has Expansion Watered Down the NFL?" *Football Digest*, February 1978, 44–47.

_____. "Pro! Q&A. A Conversation with Don Shula." *Pro!* August 17, 1974, 11A–13A.

_____. "You Can Take the Cowpoke Out of the Country, But...." *Pro!* October 27, 1974, 3C–7C.

Mihoces, Gary. "'Everyone Decided to Play Football.'" *Bradford Era*, November 14, 1977, 11.

_____. "Oilers Add Steelers to List of Upset Victims." *Clearfield Progress*, December 2, 1974, 17.

_____. "Super Bowl Next Step for Steelers." *Hagerstown Daily Mail*, January 5, 1976, 20.

Miller, Ira. "Even Dave Casper Doesn't Like the New 'Dave Casper Rule.'" *Football Digest*, November 1978, 62–63.

Mitchell, Jim, as told to Payne, Dave. "The Game I'll Never Forget." *Football Digest*, April 1980, 76–79.

Montville, Leigh. "The MVP's." *Pro!* September 12, 1976, 15B–19B.

Moore, Bob. "Hoh: Levy Revives the Wing-T." Kcchiefs.com, August 28, 2012.

Mooshil, Joe. "Hadl Directs Rams Over Punchless Bears, 26–0." *Daily Leader*, December 3, 1973, 8.

Morris, M.D. "Miracle at Foxboro." *Pro!* October 3, 1971, 3B–12B.

Morrison, Robert. "Vets Won't Be Hurt." *The St. Louis Post Dispatch*, June 9, 1966.

Mossman, John. "Denver Broncos Will Try to Erase 2-For-27 Embarrassment Sunday." *Greeley Daily Tribune*, November 24, 1973, 15.

_____. "Second Half Packer Spurt Stopped Short by Broncos." *Evening Independent*, September 30, 1975, 18.

Murphy, Jack. "Pro! Talk. A Conversation with Don Coryell." *Pro!* August 9, 1975, 10A–11A.

Musick, Phil. "Are the Steelers Hungry Enough to Win Again." *Football Digest*, November 1976, 60–61.

_____. "The Private Life of Chuck Whatshisname?" *Pro!* September 21, 1975, 2B–7B.

_____. "What Is Chuck Noll Really Like?" *Pro!* August 16, 1980, 3D–7D.

Myslenski, Skip. "Pro! Q&A. a Conversation with Ed and Steve Sabol." *Pro!* September 6, 1974, 11A–13A.

Natal, Jim. "Coming of Age in Pittsburgh." *Pro!* September 9, 1979, 3C–13C.

_____. "NFL Cheerleaders: The Hottest New Teams in Pro Football." *Pro!* September 9, 1978, 3B–9B.

_____. "The Pride of Z-Eattle." *Pro!* November 26, 1978, 3B–8B.

_____. "Prime Time Football." *Pro!* November 26, 1978, 2C–10C.

Nelson, John. "Tampa Bay—Repeat, Tampa Bay—Only Unbeaten Team." *Alton Telegraph*, October 1, 1979, 62.

Newnham, Blaine. "Davidson's Sweet Foul." *The Oakland Tribune*, November 2, 1970, 40.

_____. "Lions Get Last Laugh." *The Oakland Tribune*, November 27, 1970, 51.

Oates, Bob. "The Balance of Power." *Pro!* September 8, 1974, 3B–7B.

_____. "Bert Jones of Baltimore: The NFL's Premier Quarterback." *Football Digest*, February 1978, 18–25.

_____. "How Hashmarks Rule Hurt the Passing Game." *Football Digest*, February 1974, 48–50.

_____. "How Miami Zonked Minnesota." *Football Digest*, April 1974, 18–23.

_____. "How Pittsburgh Won Again." *Football Digest*, April 1980, 18–25.

_____. "How Pittsburgh Won." *Football Digest*, April 1979, 18–22.

_____. "How Tampa Bay Became a Winner." *Football Digest*, January 1980, 32–37.

_____. "Ken Houston the Oilers' 'Master Thief.'" *Football Digest*, May-June 1972, 58–60.

_____. "Lawrence McCutcheon: Key to the Rams' Rushing Game." *Football Digest*, January 1976, 30–35.

_____. "Middle Linebacker: Kingpin of the Defense." *Football Digest*, March 1974, 42–47.

_____. "No Man's Land—Where Receivers Fear to Tread." *Football Digest*, October 1980, 44–49.

_____. "Pro 'Wishbone' Is It Inevitable?" *Football Digest*, March 1972, 76–78.

_____. "The Secondary: L.A.'S Last Line of Defense." *Football Digest*, March 1976, 56–60.

_____. "Sign Language: Pro Football's New Way to Call Offensive Plays." *Football Digest*, January 1977, 66–71.

_____. "Talking Football with ... Al Davis." *Football Digest*, January 1981, 68–71.

_____. "Talking Football with ... Fred Dryer.' *Football Digest*, February 1982, 74–77.

_____. "What's So Special About Special Teams?" *Pro!* October 14, 1973, 2C–7C.

_____. "Where Have All the Punters Gone?" *Football Digest*, June 1976, 42–46.

Oates, Bob, Jr. "For Offensive Linemen, Little Things Mean a Lot." *Pro!* November 27, 1977, 1D–8D.

_____. "Getting a Kick Out of the New Rules." *Pro!* September 22, 1974, 3C–7C.

_____. "Miracle Finishes." *Pro!* December 23, 1979, 3D–15D.

_____. "The MVPs." *Pro!* August 5, 1972, 1B–8B.

_____. "Safeties...First and Last." *Pro!*, September 15, 1974, 3B–7B.

_____. "Super Bowl X." *Super Bowl XI Game Program*, January 9, 1977, 37–44.

_____. "What Is Big and Smothering and a Menace to Men Who Catch Footballs? The Zone Defense." *Pro!* September 24, 1972, 5C–12C.

Oberjuerge, Paul. "Injured Youngblood 'An Inspiration' to Rams." *Santa Fe New Mexican*, January 7, 1980, 50.

O'Brien, Jim. "Chuck Muncie: He's Finally Living Up to His Billing." *Football Digest*, June 1980, 38–41.

_____. "Franco Harris: Redskin Larry Brown Was His Inspiration." *Football Digest*, January 1980, 27–31.

_____. "A Look Inside Jack Lambert's Evil Image." *Football Digest*, August 1982, 38–43.

O'Brien, Mike. "Macarthur Lane: A Love of Hitting." *Green Bay Packers 1972 Yearbook*, 1972, 11–12.

_____. "Marcol, Brock, Opportunism Spell Win." *The Fond Du Lace (Wisconsin) Reporter*, October 2, 1972, 11.

_____. "Pack's Pride Returns in Spectacular Upset." *Madison Capital Times*, October 2, 1979, 17.

O'Hara, Dave. "Steelers Clinch Title." *Uniontown Morning Herald*, December 9, 1974, 27.

Olney, Ross R. "Tom Dempsey Kicks 63-Yard FG." *Football Digest*, October 1976, 76–80.

Ostler, Scott. "The Heave, the Spike, the Dance, and the Prance." *Football Digest*, June 1978, 48–59.

Ostrum, Bob. "Long Run Sets Pace as Cowboys Roll Past N.Y. Jets, 52–10." *San Antonio Light*, December 5, 1971, 38–40.

Owens, Brig, as told to Billings, Bob. "The Game I'll Never Forget." *Football Digest*, April 1974, 58–61.

Pascarelli, Peter. "Jack Lambert: The Darth Vader of the NFL." *Football Digest*, February 1979, 36–40.

_____. "Trading His Shoulder Pads for a Stethoscope." *Pro!* November 5, 1978, 2B–7B.

Paige, Woodrow, Jr. "Denver's Wild Linebackers: 'They Get After People.'" *Football Digest*, January 1978, 78–85.

_____. "How the Cowboys Crushed the Broncos' Dreams." *Football Digest*, April 1978, 18–31.

_____. "The Most Valuable Player: AFC Craig Morton." *Pro!* August 19, 1978, 3B, 7B.

_____. "Talking Football with ... Red Miller." *Football Digest*, June 1981, 44–51.

Paustian, John L. "The Playoffs." *Green Bay Packers 1973 Yearbook*, 1973, 16–19.

Payne, Dave. "AFC vs. NFC: Why AFC Teams Are Dominating the NFL." *Football Digest*, October 1977, 44–55.

_____. "The AFC West: Is It Now Football's Toughest Division?" *Football Digest*, September 1978, 44–53.

_____. "Are Holding Penalties Ruining Pro Football?" *Football Digest*, June 1977, 28–36.

_____. "Dan Fouts Player of the Year." *Football Digest*, March 1980, 22–29.

_____. "The Extra Point Is No Longer Automatic." *Football Digest*, August 1979, 44–50.

_____. "George Allen and Merlin Olsen Analyze Super Bowl XIV." *Football Digest*, April 1980, 26–33.

_____. "The Gold Rushers: San Francisco's Standout Defensive Linemen." *Football Digest*, March 1978, 48–57.

_____. "How Art Shell and Gene Upshaw Whipped the Minnesota Defense." *Football Digest*, April 1977, 18–22.

_____. "How the 16-Game Schedule Will Change Pro Football." *Football Digest*, August 1978, 28–34.

_____. "Inside Free Safety with Oakland's Jack Tatum." *Football Digest*, December 1976, 46–54.

_____. "Jim Plunkett: New England's Young, Strong-Armed Quarterback." *Football Digest*, October 1975, 15–20.

_____. "Linebacker Willie Hall: Key to the '76 Raiders' Success." *Football Digest*, April 1977, 40–45.

_____. "Monday Night Football's 10 Most Memorable Games." *Football Digest*, November 1980, 34–43.

_____. "Overtime Games: Good or Bad for Pro Football?" *Football Digest*, October 1976, 44–53.

_____. "The Raiders Say ... 'We Beat 'Em Last Year, We'll Beat 'Em Again.'" *Football Digest*, October 1977, 24–36.

_____. "The Reasons Behind So Many Coaching Changes." *Football Digest*, August 1978, 36–46.

_____. "The Super Bowl Buildup: Two Zany Weeks of Chaos." *Football Digest*, February 1978, 48–57.

_____. "Talking Football with ... John Madden." *Football Digest*, June 1980, 60–68.

_____. "The 10 Most Memorable Games of the Decade." *Football Digest*, February 1980, 34–42.

_____. "Why Players Excel on Monday Night Football." *Football Digest*, October 1975, 22–28.

_____. "Will Paul Krause Reach the All-Time NFL Interception Record?" *Football Digest*, November 1977, 62–68.

_____. "Will the Jinxed Oakland Raiders Ever Win the Big One?" *Football Digest*, January 1977, 30–38.

Pearson, Drew, as told to Janoff, Barry. "The Game I'll Never Forget." *Football Digest*, January 1983, 76–81.

Peebles, Dick. "Robert Newhouse's Surprise Touchdown Pass." *Football Digest*, April 1978, 43–45.

Penick, Bob. "Is This Character Building?" *Connellsville Daily Courier*, October 6, 1975, 6.

Perkins, Steve. "As Promised, Rams Wait in West." *Dallas Cowboys Weekly*, January 6, 1979, 3–7.

_____. "As the Hawk Flies...." *Dallas Cowboys Weekly*, December 10, 1977, 3–7.

_____. "By George, They Did It!" *Dallas Cowboys Weekly*, December 3, 1977, 3–7.

_____. "Cards Trumped, Big Game Next." *Dallas Cowboys Weekly*, October 15, 1977, 3–7.

_____. "Cowboys Were Heading for a Fall—And Fell." *Dallas Cowboys Weekly*, September 29, 1979, 3–7.

_____. "Defense Carries the Load." *Dallas Cowboys Weekly*, October 28, 1978, 3–7.

_____. "Exploding from the Starting Gate." *Dallas Cowboys Weekly*, September 9, 1978, 3–7.

_____. "Game, Set and Match." *Dallas Cowboys Weekly*, December 9, 1978, 3–7.

_____. "How Sweet an Orange Crushed!" *Dallas Cowboys Weekly*, January 21, 1978, 2–7.

_____. "If the Left One Don't Get You, the Right One Will." *Football Digest*, December 1976, 70–82.

_____. "Offense Soars on Blocked Punt." *Dallas Cowboys Weekly*, October 29, 1977, 3–7.

_____. "On Any Given Monday...." *Dallas Cowboys Weekly*, November 19, 1977, 3–7.

_____. "Rising Expectations." *Dallas Cowboys Weekly*, October 13, 1979, 3–7.

_____. "Rushing Toward a Title." *Dallas Cowboys Weekly*, December 15, 1979, 3–7.

_____. "Scalped by Harvey." *Dallas Cowboys Weekly*, October 22, 1977, 3–7.

_____. "Second Season to Be Jolly." *Dallas Cowboys Weekly*, December 31, 1977, 3–8.

_____. "Winging It Past the Cardinals." *Dallas Cowboys Weekly*, September 8, 1979, 3–7.

_____. "Wrong Way Streak." *Dallas Cowboys Weekly*, November 26, 1977, 3–7.

_____. "Yet Another Trouncing." *Dallas Cowboys Weekly*, September 22, 1979, 3–7.

_____. "You Can't Blame This on Cosell." *Dallas Cowboys Weekly*, November 4, 1978, 3–7.

Perry, Vernon, as told to Lundgren, Hal. "The Game I'll Never Forget." *Football Digest*, December 1981, 72–76.

Piacente, Steve. "Pats Drown in Dolphins Defense." *Naples Daily News*, November 1, 1976, 33.

Pierson, Don. "Minnesota's Jim Marshall: The Lou Gehrig of Pro Football." *Football Digest*, February 1977, 26–31.

_____. "Pro! Q&A. A Conversation with Dan Rooney." *Pro!* September 22, 1974, 15A–17A.

_____. "Wally Chambers: Big Man for the New Chicago Bears." *Football Digest*, November 1975, 21–26.

_____. "Wally Chambers: Only Injury Can Stop Him Now." *Football Digest*, November 1976, 48–54.

_____. "Walter Payton Player of the Year." *Football Digest*, March 1978, 21–25.

_____. "Walter Payton: The Greatest Halfback of All Time." *Football Digest*, November 1980, 16–20.

_____. "What Next for Bobby Douglass?" *Football Digest*, November 1973, 17–22.

Pike, Marvin R. "Bengals Go Wild in Romp Over Buffalo." *The Portsmouth (Ohio) Times*, November 9, 1970, 18.

Podolak, Ed. "I Remember." *Pro! Magazine*, November 30, 1975, 34.

Podolak, Ed, as told to Payne, Dave. "The Game I'll Never Forget." *Football Digest*, April 1976, 70–74.

Pollack, Joe. "Where Watching Football Is the Living End ... Zone." *Pro!* October 17, 1976, 3D–6D.

Pope, Ed. "Two If by Land." *Pro!* October 22, 1972, 5C–10C.

Prewitt, Eric. "Blanda Does It Again as Browns Fall." *The Portsmouth (Ohio) Times*, November 9, 1970, 18.

Pro! Talk. "A Conversation with Garo Yepremian." *Pro!* Divisional Playoff Edition, December 22, 1974, 15A–17A.

Prugh, Jeff. "Merlin Olsen, No. 74." *Pro!* October 7, 1973, 2C–6C.

_____. "Q & A. Pro! Talks with Pete Rozelle." *Pro!* October 4, 1970, 2D–3D.

Queenan, Bob. "How Television Affects Pro Football Spectators." *Football Digest*, November 1977, 36–39.

Ranallo, Phil. "Joe Delamielleure: The Guy Who Wouldn't Quit." *Football Digest*, January 1976, 36–38.

Rand, Jonathan. "Loud Tom Henderson Quiet After the Defeat." *Football Digest*, April 1979, 46–47.

Rappoport, Ken. "NFL Pro Vets Issue Strike Call." *The Steubenville (Ohio) Herald Star*, July 31, 1970, 10.

_____. "Vikings Top Rams, 10–9, for Seventh Straight." *Bridgeport (Connecticut) Post*, October 29, 1973, 16.

Rathet, Mike. "Baltimore Cruises to Easy 20–3 Win Over Cleveland." *The Uniontown (Pennsylvania) Morning Herald*, December 27, 1971, 33.

_____. "I'll Never Forget ... the Perfect Season and a 38-Year Old Quarterback." *Pro!* December 30, 1978, 67.

_____. "Jackie Smith: 480 Catches Quickly Forgotten." *Football Digest*, April 1979, 42–44.

Remmell, Lee. "Bart Starr and the Art of Concentration." *Green Bay Packers 1977 Yearbook*, 1977, 4–6.

_____. "Bart Starr: First...A Positive Attitude." *Green Bay Packers 1976 Yearbook*, 1976, 15–18.

_____. "Bart Starr Takes a Look at the Expanded Schedule." *Green Bay Packers 1978 Yearbook*, 1978, 34–37.

_____. "Bart Starr: The Art of the Unexpected." *Green Bay Packers 1975 Yearbook*, 1975, 4–11, 13.

_____. "Dan Devine 'We Still Have a Long Way to Go ... Talent Wise.'" *Green Bay Packers 1973 Yearbook*, 1973, 4–7.

_____. "Dan Devine: Not Looking Back." *Green Bay Packers 1974 Yearbook*, 1974, 10–11, 42.

_____. "I'm Certainly Not Discouraged." *Green Bay Packers 1972 Yearbook*, 1972, 4–6.

_____. "Packer Foes Held to 16.1 Point Average." *Green Bay Packers 1973 Yearbook*, 1973, 12–14.

_____. "Steal of the Year." *Green Bay Packers 1972 Yearbook*, 1972, 14–16.

Reynolds, Harold. "Cardiac Saints Flog Atlanta's Falcons." *South Mississippi Sun*, November 21, 1977, 13.

Richardson, Bill. "Does 'Wishbone-T' Have a Place in Pro Football's Future?" *Football Digest*, February 1972, 71–72.

_____. "Kearney Interceptions Have Point." *The Kansas City Times*, November 16, 1972.

_____. "The 247-Yard Rushing Day." *Football Digest*, December 1973, 60–61.

Robbins, Danny. "Chicago's Mike Phipps: He's Finally Gaining an Ounce of Respect." *Football Digest*, September 1980, 52–55.

Rockne, Dick. "An Expansion Year: Seattle." *Pro!* December 14, 1975, 3D–8D.

Roesler, Bob. "I'll Never Forget...." *Pro!* October 14, 1979, 2F.

Rollow, Cooper. "Great Games of the 1970s." *Pro!* August 16, 1980, 1E–7E.

_____. "Tarkenton Says '77 May Be His Last Year; Expects Vikes in Super Bowl Again." *Football Digest*, November 1977, 58–61.

Rosenthal, Bert. "Blanda Flashes His Magic Again." *The Salinas (California) Journal*, November 1, 1971, 16.

_____. "The Great Tampa Famine Ends." *Bakersfield Californian*, December 12, 1977, 19.

Ross, Frank. "Herb Adderley Money Ballplayer." *Football Digest*, May-June 1972, 48–56.

_____. "How the Chiefs Lost Longest Game in History." *Football Digest*, April 1972, 27–37.

_____. "Mike Curtis: The Colts' Enforcer." *Football Digest*, October 1971, 16–21.

_____. "The Patriots, Most Improved Team in Pro Football." *Football Digest*, July-August 1972, 31–40.

Ross, George. "Hank Intended to Open It Up." *The Oakland Tribune*, October 1, 1973, 31.

_____. "When 2 Wrongs Right for Raiders." *The Oakland Tribune*, November 2, 1970, 40.

Roswell, Gene. "Fran Tarkenton's Tutelage Was Kay to Sammie White's Success." *Football Digest*, August 1977, 24–25.

_____. "John Fitzgerald: Triggering the Dallas Shotgun." *Football Digest*, August 1977, 74–75.

_____. "Should Dallas Have Run More?" *Football Digest*, April 1976, 28–31.

Rozelle, Pete. "Game Plan '78." *Pro!* December 4, 1977, 3B–4B.

_____. "NFL Television Policy." *Pro!* November 12, 1972, 29, 56, 85, 135.

Rudman, Steve. "Howard Cosell: He's the Best Because He Makes You Think." *Football Digest*, March 1980, 6–8.

_____. "Stanley Morgan: The NFL's No. 1 Deep Threat." *Football Digest*, February 1981, 40–43.

_____. "Steve Largent: He's Quietly Been Sensational." *Football Digest*, June 1980, 42–44.

Russell, Andy, as told to Billings, Bob. "The Game I'll Never Forget." *Football Digest*, January 1974, 29–31.

Russell, Andy, and Musick, Phil. "The Last Season of Andy Russell." *Pro!* August 6, 1977, 1B–16B.

St. John, Bob. "Newhouse Wiped Stickum, Stuck 'Em." *Dallas Cowboys Weekly*, January 21, 1978, 3, 27.

Saladino, Tom. "Rams Find Nick Can Kick!" *The Charleston (South Carolina) Daily Mail*, November 5, 1973, 2B.

Sargis, Joe. "Raiders Only 1 Step Away from Super, Edge Bengals." *Eureka Times Standard*, December 29, 1975, 11.

Scherf, Chris. "Cardinals Pull Out Win Over Rams." *New Castle News*, November 15, 1976, 35.

Schneider, Russell. "Cleveland's Dave Logan: Part of the Browns' Aerial Circus." *Football Digest*, March 1980, 78–80.

Scholl, Bill. "Cleveland's Brian Sipe: He Fights His Critics Every Season." *Football Digest*, August 1979, 29–31.

_____. "Fred Biletnikoff's Fingers Really Are Sticky." *Football Digest*, January 1975, 54–56.

_____. "Zebras: On the Spot Again This Year." *Football Digest*, January 1979, 66–69.

Schwebel, Mike. "Csonka Power ... Griese Power ... and Now Hanky Power!" *Pro Quarterback,* February 1973, 32–34.

Seiden, Henry. "Was the Sack Ruled Out of Football?" *Football Digest,* October 1979, 28–31.

Seppy, Tom. "Eagles Present Coach Early Christmas Gift." *Hagerstown Daily Mail,* December 22, 1975, 35.

_____. "Redskins Hang on for Victory," *Salisbury Daily Times,* November 18, 1974, 13.

_____. "Skins, Talbert Got to Morton." *Danville Bee,* September 29, 1975, 21.

Shapiro, Leonard. "Charley Taylor Keeps Adding to His Records." *Football Digest,* December 1977, 22–27.

_____. "Cowboys Rip Erring Broncos." Washington Post, January 16, 1978.

_____. "Eddie Brown: The Man Who Makes Washington's Nickel Defense Work." *Football Digest,* February 1978, 40–42.

Shapiro, Mark. "Raiders Got Some Help." *Madison Wisconsin State Journal,* September 25, 1972, 31.

Shattuck, Harry. "Pete Rozelle Talks About the Challenges Facing Pro Football Today." *Football Digest,* November 1978, 24–31.

Shearer, Ed. "Viking Passes Rip Falcons, 37–7." *Brainerd Daily Dispatch,* December 21, 1970, 12.

Sheeley, Glenn. "Getting Down to the Nittany Gritty." *Pro!* November 5, 1978, 3C–11C.

_____. "Tim Mazzetti: The Placekicker Who Wouldn't Quit." *Football Digest,* October 1979, 64–69.

_____. "Why Pittsburgh Started So Poorly in '76." *Football Digest,* March 1977, 46–48.

Shefski, Bill. "Charlie Harraway: Advance Man for Larry Brown." *Football Digest,* March 1973, 32–33.

Shook, Richard L. "Lions Win 20–0 to Make Playoffs." *Ludington Daily News,* December 21, 1970, 5.

_____. "Over Hill? Not Yet." *Eureka Times Standard,* November 23, 1973, 15.

Siegel, Eric. "Baltimore's Passing Attack Dazzles Its Opponents." *Football Digest,* February 1977, 32–34.

Siemon, Jeff, as told to Payne, Dave. "The Game I'll Never Forget." *Football Digest,* April 1979, 62–67.

Sillia, George. "Stopping Browns Twice Early Is Key." *The Akron Beacon Journal,* December 27, 1972.

Simpson, O.J., as told to Billings, Bob. "The Game I'll Never Forget." *Football Digest,* September 1974, 32–36.

Skinner, John R. "Camouflaged Defense Gives Phipps Trouble." *The Charleston (South Carolina) Daily Mail,* December 25, 1972, 21.

Slay, Dick. "Premiums Payment Tops List of 57 Demands by NFL Players." *The Washington Star-News,* March 17, 1974, E-4.

Smith, Bubba, as told to Billings, Bob. "The Game I'll Never Forget." *Football Digest,* September 1972, 59–62.

Smith, Gary. "Wilbert Montgomery Can Run, but He Can't Hide from Fame." *Football Digest,* March 1979, 40–44.

Smith, Jim. "Talking Football With ... Pete Rozelle." *Football Digest,* August 1980, 36–45.

Smith, Rick. "The Linebacker Who Can't Win for Losing." *Pro!* December 5, 1976, 3D–6D.

_____. "Pro! Q&A. A Conversation with Bob Lilly." *Pro!* November 3, 1974, 15A–17A.

_____. "Pro! Talk. A Conversation with Art McNally." *Pro!* November 23, 1975, 10A–11A.

_____. "Pro! Talk. A Conversation with Fran Tarkenton." *Pro!* August 15, 1976, 10–11.

_____. "The Raiders' Way." *Pro!* October 12, 1975, 3C–7C.

_____. "Super Bowl XI: Portrait of a Big Game." *Pro!,* January 1, 1978, 3B–11B.

Smith, Walt. "Falcons Kick Rams." *Altoona Mirror,* October 31, 1978, 39.

Snyder, Cameron C. "Curtis Would Ignore Strike." *The Baltimore Sun,* March 30, 1974.

_____. "Joe, Jets Dazzle Colts." *The Baltimore Sun,* September 25, 1972.

Soliday, Bill. "Freak Play Eliminates Raiders." *The Daily Review,* December 24, 1974, 17.

_____. "Stabler-to-Casper Finishes Colts." *Argus,* December 25, 1977, 22.

Solomon, George. "Charley Taylor's Return to Excellence." *Football Digest,* November 1972, 33–35.

Spander, Art. "I'll Never Forget ... Black Saturday in the Bay Area." *Pro!* November 5, 1978, 15D.

_____. "Where There's a Will-Iams, There's a Way." *Pro!* September 9, 1979, 3D–8D.

Stabler, Ken, as told to Payne, Dave. "The Game I'll Never Forget." *Football Digest,* December 1977, 66–73.

Stark, Jayson. "The Eagles' Tony Franklin: Kicking Barefoot Comes Naturally." *Football Digest,* March 1980, 66–70.

Staubach, Roger, as told to Luksa, Frank. "The Game I'll Never Forget." *Football Digest,* November 1975, 40–44.

Steadman, John. "Bert Jones: The Next Great Quarterback." *Football Digest,* August 1976, 12–18.

_____. "Have the Colts Peaked Out?" *Football Digest,* July-August 1972, 20–24.

_____. "Lydell Mitchell: The Colts' Record Slasher." *Football Digest,* March 1976, 66–68.

Stellino, Vito. "Chuck Noll: He's the Big Reason the Steelers Are Winners." *Football Digest,* October 1979, 56–59.

_____. "Doubling Their Pleasure in Pittsburgh." *Pro!* October 14, 1979, 2C–11C.

_____. "Franco Harris: The Heart of the Steelers." *Football Digest,* December 1978, 18–23.

_____. "Frenchy Fuqua Remembers Franco's Miracle Catch." *Football Digest,* January 1975, 28–30.

_____. "Pittsburgh's Steelers: The Decade's Best Team." *Football Digest,* February 1980, 20–26.

_____. "The Steelers Say...'We've Got Some Paying Back to Do.'" *Football Digest,* October 1977, 24–36.

_____. "Steelers Were Super in the Trenches." *Pro!* August 25, 1979, 18–19.

Stillwell, Paul. "Designs on Football's Future." *Pro!* October 9, 1977, 3B–14B.

Stone, Ed. "Walter Payton: 'Give Me Time, I'll Give 'Em a New Sayers.'" *Football Digest,* January 1976, 40–44.

Stowers, Carlton. "Bradshaw Vs. Staubach: A Friendly Rivalry." *Football Digest,* February 1980, 56–58.

_____. "The Pressure Increases at Cornerback." *Football Digest,* November 1978, 64–65.

_____. "Roger Staubach, Dallas' Greatest Quarterback Ever, Retires." *Football Digest,* October 1980, 37–39.

_____. "Roger Staubach: Winning Makes Football Fun in Dallas." *Football Digest,* September 1978, 38–43.

Strother, Shelby. "Remember When...." *Football Digest,* March 1983, 70–79.

Sudyk, Bob. "Greg Pruitt: Cleveland's Under-Rated Star." *Football Digest,* August 1977, 16–23.

_____. "There's No Room for Tatum's Tactics." *Football Digest,* August 1980, 4–6.

Sullivan, Bill. "The Dallas Cowboys' 'Other' Super Team." *Dave Campbell's Dallas Cowboys Magazine,* 1978, 14–16.

Suter-Kegg, J. "A 'Senior Citizen' John Unitas Is Not." *Cumberland Evening Times,* January 4, 1971, 10.

Swann, Lynn, as told to Payne, Dave. "How We Won!" *Football Digest*, April 1976, 14–21.

Swenson, Bob, as told to Payne, Dave. "The Game I'll Never Forget." *Football Digest*, September 1980, 72–77.

Tatum, Jack, as told to Payne, Dave. "The Game I'll Never Forget." *Football Digest*, December 1975, 32–38.

Thalman, L. Budd. "I'll Never Forget ... 2003:O.J.'S Odyssey." *Gameday*, September 5, 1983, 12D.

Thielman, Jim. "Vikings Reached Emotional Peak in Win Over Redskins." *Winona Daily News*, December 20, 1976, 14.

Thompson, Pat. "Vikings 'Listen' to Eller's Pep Talk." *Winona Daily News*, December 23, 1973, 21.

Thomy, Al. "Why the NFL Outlawed the Head Slap." *Football Digest*, December 1977, 80–81.

Todd, Doug. "The Man Beneath the Hat." *Pro!* September 3, 1978, 2B–8B.

Tonelli, Charles. "Staubach Rallies Dallas, 30–28." *The Daily Review*, December 24, 1972, 17.

Tribune Wire Services. "Raiders Cage Bears; Redskins Survive." *Salt Lake Tribune*, November 8, 1976, 21.

Tucker, Bud. "Browns Let Fans Down." *Santa Ana Orange County Register*, November 28, 1977, 15.

Twersky, Marty. "Billy 'White Shoes': Speed Burner." *Football Digest*, January 1976, 80–81.

Twombly, Wells. "Old Quarterbacks Never Die." *Football Digest*, January 1972, 56–64.

_____. "The Shameful Sacking of Johnny Unitas." *Football Digest*, February 1973, 14–16.

_____. "Steve Bartkowski and the All-American Love Story." *Pro!* September 21, 1975, 3C–6C.

_____. "Ted Kwalick Approaches Superstardom." *Football Digest*, November 1973, 60–63.

United Press International. "And Then There Were Two." *Bucks County (Pennsylvania) Courier Times*, December 31, 1973, 12.

_____. "Bengals Found Colts' Backs, Defense Tough." *The Twin Falls (Idaho) Times-News*, December 27, 1970, 20.

_____. "Bengals Mistakes Sparked Browns." *The Times Recorder*, December 10, 1972, 4.

_____. "'Best Comeback We've Ever Made.'" *The (Provo, Utah) Herald*, December 24, 1972, 9.

_____. "Bills' 'Juice' Was on the Loose." *Kingsport Times*, September 21, 1975, 2.

_____. "Calm Grant Glad His Team Got Breaks." *South Mississippi Sun*, December 30, 1974, 11.

_____. "Cardinal Coach Coryell Named NFC's Best." *Playground Daily News*, December 22, 1974, Section C.

_____. "Casper's Few Catches Count Most." *Argus*, December 25, 1977, 22.

_____. "Controversial Call Makes Loss Bitter One." *Clearfield Progress*, January 7, 1980, 14.

_____. "Denver Defensive Avalanche Buries Pats." *Cedar Rapids Gazette*, November 12, 1979, 15.

_____. "Detroiters Down Fired Up Packers." *Holland Evening Sentinel*, December 21, 1970, 7.

_____. "Dolphin Defense Guns Down Jets." *Naples Daily News*, November 7, 1977, 33.

_____. "Dolphins and Raiders Upset." *Doylestown Intelligencer*, November 27, 1978, 17.

_____. "Dolphins Rack Up Fourth Straight at Ram Expense." *The Redlands (California) Daily Facts*, November 1, 1971, 11.

_____. "Dolphins Take Over First Place." *Naples Daily News*, October 27, 1975, 34.

_____. "Donzis' Creations Save Oilers from Collapsing." *New Castle News*, November 17, 1979, 15.

_____. "Doubting Thomas' Silenced." *Sandusky Register*, December 5, 1977, 9.

_____. "Eagles Get Extra Push to Win on Last Play." *Lebanon (Pennsylvania) Daily News*, October 15, 1973, 13.

_____. "49ers Celebrate, Praise Defense." *Argus*, December 28, 1970, 9.

_____. "Franco Harris Sparks Steelers Over Vikings." *Tyrone (Pennsylvania) Daily Herald*, November 27, 1972, 5.

_____. "Haden's Show Paces Ram Rout of Vikings." *Syracuse Post Standard*, October 25, 2977, 15.

_____. "Harris Regrets Ram Mistakes." *South Mississippi Sun*, December 30, 1974, 11.

_____. "Hart Teaches Cowboys Lesson." *Bucks County Courier Times*, October 18, 1976, 17.

_____. "Jets Set Sail Behind Windbreaker Namath." *Bucks County (Pennsylvania) Courier Times*, December 2, 1974, 22.

_____. "Joe Washington First in Hearts of Colt Fans." *Hutchinson News*, September 19, 1978, 49.

_____. "Lane Lauds Packs Great Team Effort." *The Capital Times*, December 11, 1972, 23.

_____. "Lions Say They Beat Themselves." *The Twin Falls (Idaho) Times-News*, December 27, 1970, 18.

_____. "Lions Stadium Debut Ruined, 36–10." *Elyria Chronicle Telegram*, October 7, 1975, 9.

_____. "NFL Owners, Players Reach Accord." *The Bucks County (Pennsylvania) Courier Times*, August 3, 1970, 29.

_____. "NFL Players Strike for Benefits." *The Columbus (Nebraska) Telegram*, July 30, 1970, 10.

_____. "Pack Has Reversed NFL Image." *The Capital Times*, December 11, 1972, 23.

_____. "Packers Whip Vikings, 23–7, to Capture Division Crown." *The Capital Times*, December 11, 1972, 23.

_____. "'Poke Defense' Ends Landry's Worrying." *Denton Record Chronicle*, September 16, 1974, 11.

_____. "QB Kilmer Regains Youth; Passes 'Skins Over Cards." *Kittanning Simpson Leader Times*, October 3, 1977, 12.

_____. "Raiders Finally Win Opener." *Salina Journal*, September 23, 1975, 8.

_____. "Raiders Insist They're Ready." *The Billings Gazette*, December 20, 1976, 40.

_____. "Rams Can't Weather Viking Storm." *The Oakland Tribune*, December 27, 1977, 24.

_____. "Rams Clinch Division with Win Over Bears." *Redlands Daily Facts*, December 3, 1973, 9.

_____. "Redskins Scalped." *The Port Arthur (Texas) News*, December 10, 1973, 9.

_____. "Scott's Catch Spurs Colts 10–3." *Centralia Daily Chronicle*, November 8, 1977, 8.

_____. "Sideline Practice Cures Bakken." *Lebanon Daily News*, November 8, 1976, 36.

_____. "Skins Win with Quarter Football." *El Paso Herald*, December 25, 1972, 68.

_____. "Steelers Get Gift Berth in Playoffs." *Connellsville Daily Courier*, December 19, 1977, 8.

_____. "Steelers Need Help from Hated Rivals—Raiders." *Delta Democrat Times*, November 29, 1976, 10.

_____. "Steelers Open Like Champions." *New Castle News*, September 22, 1975, 22.

_____. "Steelers Rally Rips Colts; Rams Thump Cards." *Cumberland Times*, December 28, 1975, 34.

_____. "Steelers Win on De-E-E-Fense." *Lebanon Daily News*, January 13, 1975, 24.

_____. "Terry Bradshaw Happy." *Lebanon Daily News*, January 13, 1975, 24.

_____. "This Team Hasn't Been Given Credit." *Elyria Chronicle Telegram*, January 1, 1979, 27.

_____. "Vikes Scorch 'Skins in Playoff." *The Times Standard*, Eureka, California, December 23, 1973, 16.

_____. "Vikings' Volley Corrals Cowboys." *Bucks County (Pennsylvania) Courier Times*, December 31, 1973, 12.

_____. "Willie, Rod Were in the Right Place." *Argus*, December 28, 1970, 9.

Usiak, Dick. "Dolphins Breeze Past Bills, 17–0." *The Evening Observer*, November 19, 1973.

_____. "Hill Leads Cowboys by Buffalo, 49–37." *The Brownsville Herald*, September 20, 1971, 8.

Waechter, Rick. "Yesterday's Heroes." *Football Digest*, October 1981, 86–88.

Wagner, Len. "Hunter & Tagge." *Green Bay Packers 1973 Yearbook*, 1973, 20–22.

_____. "Hunter Becomes a Pro." *Green Bay Packers 1972 Yearbook*, 1972, 21–23.

_____. "John Hadl: A Brand New Arm." *Green Bay Packers 1975 Yearbook*, 1975, 26–27.

_____. "Lynn Dickey." *Green Bay Packers 1976 Yearbook*, 1976, 4–6.

_____. "Lynn Dickey: 'He Is Going to Be a Nucleus.'" *Green Bay Packers 1977 Yearbook*, 1977, 25–28.

_____. "McCoy: A Critical Season." *Green Bay Packers 1974 Yearbook*, 1974, 8–9.

_____. "The Offensive Line ... A Team Game." *Green Bay Packers 1976 Yearbook*, 1976, 12–13, 50.

_____. "Tagge: A Winner." *Green Bay Packers 1974 Yearbook*, 1974, 22–24.

_____. "The Three Best." *Green Bay Packers 1972 Yearbook*, 1972, 24–29.

Wald, Mark. "Running (And Passing) to Extremes: The Weather and Pro Football." *Coffin Corner*, July/August 2015, 17–22.

Walter, Tony. "Whitehurst Surprised Himself." *Green Bay Packers 1978 Yearbook*, 1978, 30–33.

Ward, Al. "Perspectives." *Pro!* August 25, 1979, 9A.

Warner, Gary. "Otis Taylor Needs to Win." *Football Digest*, February 1972, 35–39.

_____. "What Happened to the Kansas City Chiefs?" *Football Digest*, March 1973, 57–60.

Washington, Gene, as told to Payne, Dave. "The Game I'll Never Forget." *Football Digest*, January 1977, 84–91.

Watson, Michael. "Brodie 'Runs' 49ers into Playoffs." *The Daily Review*, December 20, 1971, 15.

_____. "Tough Week Ahead for 49ers." *The Daily Review*, October 11, 1971, 15.

Weisberger, Jed. "Colts Show Steelers Heels." *Indiana Evening Gazette*, October 31, 1977, 21.

White, Russ. "Larry Brown: The Redskins' Superstar." *Football Digest*, March 1972, 32–39.

White, Sherman. "The Game I'll Never Forget." *Football Digest*, October 1976, 56–61.

Whiteside, Larry. "Mack Herron: Big Man in the Patriots' Rebirth." *Football Digest*, February 1975, 80–85.

Wiebusch, John. "AFC Previewing & Reviewing." *Pro!* September 8, 1973, 17A–19A.

_____. "AFC: New Directions. Reviewing and Previewing." *Pro!* September 9, 1972, 4A–7A.

_____. "The Game Against the Years, Part III, the 60s and 70s." *Pro!* October 17, 1976, 7B–12B.

_____. "Living the Life of Russ Francis." *Pro!* December 18, 1977, 3B–10B.

_____. "NFC: New Directions. Reviewing and Previewing." *Pro!* September 9, 1972, 3A–7A.

_____. "The Nine Lives of Jim Marshall." *Pro!* November 1, 1971, 7B–12B.

_____. "Pro Bowl Spotlight." *Pro!* December 23, 1972, 22.

_____. "Pro! Talk. A Conversation with Pete Rozelle, Part I." *Pro!* September 21, 1975, 10A–11A.

_____. "The War Hero as a Folk Hero as a Human Being." *Pro!* November 2, 1975, 3C–7C.

Wilbur, R.A. "Card Kicker Jim Bakken: The NFL's Ice Man." *Football Digest*, February 1977, 36–39.

Wilcox, Dave, as told to Billings, Bob. "The Game I'll Never Forget." *Football Digest*, February 1975, 86–90.

Wiley, Ralph. "Los Angeles Ends Years of Frustration." *Santa Fe New Mexican*, January 7, 1980, 50.

Williams, Marty. "Why Isaac Curtis Refuses to Spike After TD Catches." *Football Digest*, January 1976, 82–83.

Wynn, Jerry. "I'll Never Forget...." *Pro!* August 25, 1979, 2D.

Yake, D. Byron. "Lambert Feels Steelers Stronger Club This Year." *Hagerstown Daily Mail*, January 5, 1976, 20.

Young, Dick. "Cowboys' Front Line Made Big Difference." *Football Digest*, April 1972, 17–20.

Youngblood, Jack, as told to Payne, Dave. "The Game I'll Never Forget." *Football Digest*, January 1980, 74–78.

Zagorski, Joe. "Great Games of the 1970s: The Return of Broadway Joe." *The Coffin Corner*, March/April 2011, 10–12.

_____. "Season of Change: The 1972 Packers." *PFRA Annual*, 1988, 83–96.

Zaleski, Robert. "Ken Payne: How Lucky Can a Guy Get." *Green Bay Packers 1976 Yearbook*, 1976, 41–42.

Zampa, Mike. "Shootout on Christmas Eve." *Pro!* Division Playoff Edition, January 7, 1979, 3B–14B.

Zimmerman, Paul. "Jim Zorn: The QB Nobody Wanted." *Football Digest*, September 1979, 60–63.

_____. "This One Was Super." *Football Digest*, April 1976, 22–26.

_____. "Was It Interference or Not?" *Football Digest*, April 1979, 37–41.

_____. "Why Injuries Will Be More Important in 1975." *Football Digest*, November 1975, 28–31.

Editorials

Baker, Jim. *The Buffalo Courier-Express*, February 27, 1974.

Dawson, Len. *The Kansas City Times*, June 9, 1966.

Gibson, Mike. *The Doylestown Intelligencer*, November 5, 1979.

Herbert, Michael, K. *Football Digest*, September 1975.

_____. *Football Digest*, March 1976.

_____. *Football Digest*, November 1976.

_____. *Football Digest*, April 1977.

_____. *Football Digest*, June 1977.

_____. *Football Digest*, August 1979.

Hickey, Lowell. *The Daily Review*, December 12, 1972.

_____. *The Daily Review*, November 14, 1977.

Kegg, J. Suter. *The Cumberland Evening Times*, September 25, 1972.

Kuenster, John. *Football Digest*, April 1972.

_____. *Football Digest*, March 1973.

_____. *Football Digest*, February 1974.

_____. *Football Digest*, April 1974.

_____. *Football Digest*, August 1974.

_____. *Football Digest*, November 1974.

_____. *Football Digest*, December 1974.

_____. *Football Digest*, January 1975.

Levitt, Ed. "Accent on Sports." *Oakland Tribune,* November 8, 1976.

Markus, Robert. *The Chicago Tribune,* October 26, 1972.

Murray, Jim. *The Oakland Tribune,* December 27, 1977.

Schrader, Gus. "Red Peppers," *The Cedar Rapids Gazette,* December 28, 1970.

Twombly, Wells. *The San Francisco Examiner,* November 9, 1970.

Wolf, Bob. *Football Digest,* December 1979.

Yanos, Larry. *Hagerstown Daily Mail,* October 11, 1970.

Zimmerman, Paul. *Football Digest,* February 1979.

Books

Barron, Bill, et al., eds. *The Official NFL Encyclopedia of Pro Football.* New York: NAL Books, 1982.

Bennett, Tom. *The Pro Style: The Complete Guide to Understanding National Football League Strategy.* Englewood Cliffs, NJ: Prentice-Hall, Inc., 1976.

Boss, David. *Prolog: The Official National Football League Annual for 1973.* Los Angeles: Dell, 1973.

_____. *Prolog: The Official National Football League Annual for 1974.* Los Angeles: Dell, 1974.

_____. *Prolog: The Official National Football League Annual for 1975.* Los Angeles: Dell, 1975.

_____. *Prolog: The Official National Football League Annual for 1976.* Los Angeles: Dell, 1976.

_____. *Prolog: The Official National Football League Annual for 1977.* Los Angeles: Dell, 1977.

_____. *Prolog: The Official National Football League Annual for 1978.* Los Angeles: Dell, 1978.

_____. *Prolog: The Official National Football League Annual for 1979.* Los Angeles: Dell, 1979.

_____. *Prolog: The Official National Football League Annual for 1980.* Los Angeles: Dell, 1980.

Carroll, Bob, Gershman, Michael, Neft, David, and Thorn, John. *Total Football: The Official Encyclopedia of the National Football League.* New York: HarperCollins, 1997.

Clary, Jack. *The Gamemakers: Winning Philosophies of Eight NFL Coaches.* Chicago: Follett, 1976.

_____. *Great Teams' Great Years: Washington Redskins.* New York: Macmillan, 1974.

_____. *30 Years of Pro Football's Great Moments.* New York: Rutledge Books, 1976.

Cohen, Richard M., Deutsch, Jordan A., and Neft, David S. *The Scrapbook History of Pro Football (Expanded and Updated).* Indianapolis: Bobbs-Merrill, 1979.

Connor, Dick. *Kansas City Chiefs: Great Teams' Great Years.* New York: Macmillan, 1974.

Crawford, Denis M. *Hugh Culverhouse and the Tampa Bay Buccaneers: How a Skinflint Genius with a Losing Team Made the Modern NFL.* Jefferson, NC: McFarland, 2011.

Croke, Ed, and Poretz, Art, eds. *Illustrated Digest of Pro Football. 1972 Edition.* New York: Stadia Sports Publishing, Inc., 1972.

Didinger, Ray. *Pittsburgh Steelers: Great Teams' Great Years.* New York: Macmillan, 1974.

Evans, Mary Candace. *A Decade of Dreams.* Dallas: Taylor, 1982.

Fleischer, Jack. *Pro Football at Its Best.* Washington, D.C.: Acropolis Books, 1977.

Green, Jerry. *Great Teams' Great Years: Detroit Lions.* New York: Macmillan, 1973.

Gutman, Bill. *Gamebreakers of the NFL.* New York: Random House, 1973.

Henderson, Thomas "Hollywood," and Knobler, Peter. *Out of Control: Confessions of an NFL Casualty.* New York: G.P. Putnam's Sons, 1987.

Holst, Art. *Sunday Zebras.* Forest Lake, IL: Forest Publishing, 1980.

Horrigan, Joe, and Thorn, John. *The Pro Football Hall of Fame 50th Anniversary Book.* New York: Grand Central Publishing, 2012.

Lorimer, Larry, and Devaney, John. *The Football Book.* New York: Random House, 1977.

MacCambridge, Michael. *America's Game.* New York: Random House, 2008.

Maule, Tex, and Didinger, Ray. *The Professionals.* New York: New American Library, 1980.

McGuff, Joe. *Winning It All: The Chiefs of the AFL.* New York: Doubleday, 1970.

Meyers, Jeff. *Great Teams' Great Years: Dallas Cowboys.* New York: Macmillan, 1974.

Namath, Joe, with Oates, Bob, Jr. *A Matter of Style.* Boston: Little, Brown, 1973.

Nash, Bruce, and Zullo, Allan. *The Football Hall of Shame.* New York: Pocket Books, 1986.

Neft, David S., and Cohen, Richard M. *The Sports Encyclopedia Edition 6. Pro Football the Modern Era, 1960–1988.* New York: St. Martin's Press, 1988.

Oates, Bob, Jr. *Prolog: The National Football League Annual.* Chicago: Follett, 1971.

_____. *Prolog: The National Football League Annual.* Chicago: Follett, 1972.

Perkins, Steve. *The Dallas Cowboys: Winning the Big One.* New York: Grosset & Dunlap, 1972.

Radakovich, Dan, and Prato, Lou. *Bad Rad Football Nomad.* Moon Township, PA: Touchdown Books, 2012.

Reidenbaugh, Lowell, and Attner, Paul. *The Sporting News Super Bowl Book.* St. Louis: The Sporting News, 1987.

Riffenburgh, Beau. *The Official NFL Encyclopedia, Fourth Edition: Updated and Revised.* New York: New American Library, 1986.

Rubin, Bob. *Green Bay's Packers: Return to Glory.* Englewood Cliffs, NJ: Prentice-Hall, 1973.

Sahadi, Lou. *Broncos! The Team That Makes Miracles Happen.* New York: Stein And Day, 1978.

St. John, Bob. *The Man Inside ... Landry.* Waco: Word, 1979.

Staubach, Roger, with Luksa, Frank. *Time Enough to Win.* Waco: Word, 1980.

Stowers, Carlton. *Dallas Cowboys: The First 25 Years.* Dallas: Taylor, 1984.

Treat, Roger. *The Official Encyclopedia of Football.* South Brunswick, NJ: A.S. Barnes, 1973.

Tatum, Jack, with Kusher, Bill. *They Call Me Assassin.* New York: Everest House Publishers, 1979.

Weiss, Don, et al., eds. *1972 Official National Football League Record Manual.* New York: New American Library, 1972.

_____. *Official National Football League Record Manual, 1971.* New York: Fawcett World Library, 1971.

_____. *Official 1973 National Football League Record Manual.* New York: NFL Properties, 1973.

Whittingham, Richard. *The Dallas Cowboys: An Illustrated History.* New York: Harper & Row, 1981.

Wiebusch, John, Editor-in-Chief, National Football League Properties. *Great Teams' Great Years: San Francisco 49ers.* New York: Macmillan, 1974.

_____. *The Super Bowl. Celebrating a Quarter-Century of America's Greatest Game.* New York: Simon & Schuster, 1990.

Zimmerman, Paul. *A Thinking Man's Guide to Pro Football (Revised Edition)*. New York: E.P. Dutton, 1971.

Magazines

Dallas Cowboys Cheerleaders "A Touch of Class." Jordan & Company Publishers, Inc., 1979.
Pro! Conference Championship Edition. December 30, 1973, 2B–8B.
Pro! Division Playoff Edition. December 24, 1972, 3B.
Prolog: The Official National Football League Annual for 1971. New York: NFL Properties, 1971.
Prolog: The Official National Football League Annual for 1972. New York: NFL Properties, 1972.
Prolog: The Official National Football League Annual for 1973. New York: NFL Properties, 1973.
Prolog: The Official National Football League Annual for 1974. New York: NFL Properties, 1974.
Prolog: The Official National Football League Annual for 1975. New York: NFL Properties, 1975.
Prolog: The Official National Football League Annual for 1976. New York: NFL Properties, 1976.
Prolog: The Official National Football League Annual for 1977. New York: NFL Properties, 1977.
Prolog: The Official National Football League Annual for 1978. New York: NFL Properties, 1978.
Prolog: The Official National Football League Annual for 1979. New York: NFL Properties, 1979.
Prolog: The Official National Football League Annual for 1980. New York: NFL Properties, 1980.

Press Releases

Cleveland Browns News Release. *NFL Properties*, December 18, 1972.
Game Book. *NFL Properties*, December 14, 1971.
Game Book. *NFL Properties*, December 25, 1971.
Game Book. *NFL Properties*, September 17, 1972.
Game Book. *NFL Properties*, October 17, 1972.
Game Book. *NFL Properties*, November 19, 1972.
Miami Dolphins Fact Sheet. *NFL Properties*, October 2, 1972.
Miami Dolphins Fact Sheet. *NFL Properties*, November 6, 1972.
Miami Dolphins Game Book, 1973.
Minnesota Vikings Game Book, 1973.
Game Book, Baltimore Colts, December 19, 1976.
Game Book, Dallas Cowboys, December 19, 1976.

Films

"The Defenders," *NFL Films*, 1976. Produced by Steve Sabol. Directed by Bob Smith. Executive Producer: Ed Sabol.
"A Glorious Game," *NFL Films*, 1971. Produced by Steve Sabol. Executive Producer: Ed Sabol. Written and directed by Bob Ryan.
"NFL Game of the Week," *NFL Films*, 1970 to 1979. Various producers and directors. Executive Producer: Ed Sabol.
"NFL Team Highlights" for every team from 1970 to 1979.
NFL Films, 1970–1979. Various producers and directors. Executive Producer: Ed Sabol.
"Pro Football Playback," *NFL Films*, 1976. Various producers and directors. Executive Producer: Ed Sabol.
"Rebels in the NFL," *Double J Films*, 2011. Produced by Jay Meyers.
"The Sensational Sixties," NFL Films, 1970. Written and Directed by Buzz Ringe. Executive Producer: Ed Sabol.
"The Super 70's," NFL Films, 1980. Written and Directed by Bob Angelo. Executive Producer: Ed Sabol.
"This Is the NFL," *NFL Films*, 1975, 1977–1979. Various producers and directors. Executive Producer: Ed Sabol.
"This Week in Pro Football," *NFL Films*, 1970–1974. Various producers and directors. Executive Producer: Ed Sabol.

Websites

ColdHardFootballFacts.com. Byrne, Kerry J., editor.
FootballZebras.com. Austro, Ben, editor. December 28, 2010.

Yearbooks

Green Bay Packers 1972 Yearbook. Daley, Art and Yuenger, Jack. Green Bay, Wisconsin.
Green Bay Packers 1973 Yearbook. Daley, Art and Yuenger, Jack. Green Bay, Wisconsin.
Green Bay Packers 1974 Yearbook. Daley, Art and Yuenger, Jack. Green Bay, Wisconsin.
Green Bay Packers 1975 Yearbook. Daley, Art and Yuenger, Jack. Green Bay, Wisconsin.
Green Bay Packers 1976 Yearbook. Daley, Art and Yuenger, Jack. Green Bay, Wisconsin.
Green Bay Packers 1977 Yearbook. Daley, Art and Yuenger, Jack. Green Bay, Wisconsin.
Green Bay Packers 1978 Yearbook. Daley, Art. Green Bay, Wisconsin.

Personal Interviews

Herb Adderley
Rocky Bleier
John Bunting
Jim Carter
Ben Davidson
Joe DeLamielleure
Herman Edwards
Weeb Ewbank
Donnie Green
Jim Houston
Lamar Hunt
Earl Morrall
Brent Musburger
Tom Nowatzke
Dave Robinson
Johnny Robinson
Dick Schafrath
Bart Starr
Dan Sullivan

Index